BRITAIN SINCE 1945

A Political History

Sixth edition

David Childs

Routledge
Taylor & Francis Group

LONDON AND NEW YORK

Fifth edition published 2001
by Routledge
2 Park Square, Milton Park, Abingdon, Oxon OX14 4RN

Simultaneously published in the USA and Canada
by Routledge
270 Madison Ave, New York, NY 10016

Sixth edition published 2006

Reprinted 2007, 2008, 2009

*Routledge is an imprint of the Taylor & Francis Group,
an informa business*

© 2001, 2006 David Childs

Typeset in Times by
BC Typesetting Ltd
Printed and bound in Great Britain by
the MPG Books Group

British Library Cataloguing in Publication Data
A catalogue record for this book is available from the British Library

Library of Congress Cataloging in Publication Data
Childs, David, 1933–
Britain since 1945: a political history/David Childs. – 6th ed.
p. cm.
Includes bibliographical references and index.
ISBN 0–415–39326–4 (hardback) – ISBN 0–415–39327–2 (pbk.)
1. Great Britain–Politics and government–1945– I. Title.
DA588.C54 2006
941.085–dc22   2005034332

ISBN10: 0–415–39326–4 (hbk)
ISBN10: 0–415–39327–2 (pbk)
ISBN10: 0–203–96991–X (ebk)
ISBN13: 978–0–415–39326–3 (hbk)
ISBN13: 978–0–415–39327–0 (pbk)
ISBN13: 978–0–203–96991–5 (ebk)

CONTENTS

CONTENTS

CONTENTS

CONTENTS

LIST OF TABLES

PREFACE

I have attempted a thorough revision of this book taking account of the new material available, the changing perspective and the need to keep it to a reasonable length. I hope supporters of the earlier editions will not be disappointed. I am conscious of its limitations. Later writers will benefit from more archival material and memoirs. Eventually, someone will write the 'real' or 'secret' history of the second half of twentieth-century Britain. They will investigate the activities of lobbyists and foreign business interests in British politics. They will want to uncover the influence of bodies such as the Free Masons,[1] London Clubland and organized crime. They will be able to give more attention to the penetration by Soviet and other foreign intelligence agencies of British institutions,[2] and to the influence of domestic security agencies. I can only mention them to a slight degree. These influences should be neither underestimated nor overestimated. One does not have to be a protagonist of conspiracy theories to recognize that they do form part of the whole story of Britain during this period. It is the story of the decline of a state which, in 1945, was briefly second only to the United States as a world power, and which, by 1995, was hobbling along attempting to keep up with the middle rank of the European Union.

David Childs
Nottingham, February 1997

NOTES

1 Martin Short, *Inside the Brotherhood: Further Secrets of the Free Masons* (1993).
2 Tom Bower, *The Perfect English Spy: Sir Dick White and the Secret War, 1935–90* (1995).

ACKNOWLEDGEMENTS

I want to express my sincere thanks to a number of people who have read and commented on various chapters of this book – Dr David Butler, Nuffield College, Oxford (Chapter 1); Col. R. L. Frazier, Department of History, University of Nottingham (Chapters 2, 7 and 8); Professor F. S. Northedge, Department of International Relations, London School of Economics and Political Science (Chapter 3); the Rt Hon. Lord Boyle, Vice-Chancellor, University of Leeds (Chapters 4, 5 and 6). The writer alone bears responsibility for any errors of fact or judgement contained in the book.

In addition, my thanks are due to many busy people who have either agreed to be interviewed or who have taken the trouble to reply to written questions. Among them are Kingsley Amis, the Lady Attlee, the late Lord Avon, Mr A. A. Best, Lord Boothby, Lord Brockway, Lord Butler, Douglas Dodds-Parker, MP, Bob Edwards, MP, the Rt Hon. Ernest Fernyhough, MP, the late James Griffiths, Arthur Lewis, MP, Marcus Lipton, MP, Christopher Mayhew, the Rt Hon. Philip Noel-Baker, MP, Maurice Orbach, MP, John Parker, MP, Baroness Phillips, the Rt Hon. J. Enoch Powell, MP, J. B. Priestley, Lord Ritchie-Calder, the Rt Hon. William Ross, MP, Alan Sillitoe, Mrs Margaret Simpson, the Rt Hon. Michael Stewart, MP, Lord Taylor of Manfield, Woodrow Wyatt, Lord Wigg.

Finally, I would like to thank Mrs Ann Morris and Miss Elaine Dexter for typing substantial parts of the manuscript.

D.H.C.
Nottingham, April 1979

NOTE AND ACKNOWLEDGEMENTS TO THE SECOND EDITION

I was very pleased to be asked, as a result of readers' requests, to write an extended version of *Britain since 1945*.

I have tried to take the second edition as seriously as the first by attempting to talk to a wide variety of witnesses. It was a pleasant surprise to find so many busy individuals who were prepared to be interviewed or reply to written questions. Unfortunately, one or two MPs felt unable to help. I am therefore all the more grateful to those who did: Joe Ashton, Margaret Beckett, Alan Beith, Mark Carlisle, Kenneth Clarke, Don Concannon, Roy Hattersley, Denis Healey, Jim Lester, Sir Anthony Meyer, Richard Ottaway, David Owen, Cyril Smith and Ray Whitney. I am equally grateful to Beryl Bainbridge, Lynne Reid Banks, Stan Barstow, Melvyn Bragg, Malcolm Bradbury, Maureen Duffy, John H. Gunn, Ken Livingstone, David Lodge, Iris Murdoch, Tom Sharpe, Leslie Thomas, Stuart Thompstone, Fay Weldon and Arnold Wesker. Finally, I want to thank my old friend Karl Sparrow for his continuing interest in my work. With so many different and conflicting points of view represented among those who have helped me I must emphasize very strongly that all the views, ideas, interpretations and descriptions in this book are entirely my own responsibility – as are any errors.

There are obvious pitfalls in writing about events as recent as those between 1979 and 1985 (or even between 1945 and 1979). Some events (the Falklands War?) which seem important at the time will seem less so at greater distance. Other events (like the miners' strike and the changes in South Africa and China) could prove to be of very great significance for the future of Britain. I hope the reader will take this into account and also remember the limitations of time, space and resources open to the writer of a book of this kind, and not judge the result too harshly.

D.H.C.
Nottingham, September 1985

ACKNOWLEDGEMENTS TO THE
THIRD EDITION

Since the second edition, many dramatic changes have occurred in the world, such as the demise of communism and the restoration of German unity, the further development of the 'ever closer union' of the European Community, and the Gulf War. At home, in Britain, we have witnessed the fall of Margaret Thatcher and the victory of the Conservative Party under John Major. Britain has further declined in international importance and most of its politicians and people seem to accept this as they are more and more influenced by American culture, foreign travel, the economies of Japan, the USA and Germany, and by Britain's membership of the EC.

On my many travels since 1986, I have had the opportunity to discuss the changes in Britain and elsewhere with a considerable number of politicians, businessmen, academics and diplomats. I am grateful for these opportunities. I am also grateful to Martin Brandon-Bravo (MP, Nottingham South 1983–92) and to Sir Frank Roberts, GCMG, CGVO, who gave me some of their time to discuss our changing world and their views on it. Professor Vincent Porter gave me the benefit of his experience of the changes in the mass media and I want to take this opportunity to thank him. Finally, I want to thank my old friend Dr Robert L. Frazier for reading the new material and making many useful suggestions.

D.H.C.
Nottingham, April 1992

ACKNOWLEDGEMENTS TO THE FOURTH EDITION

I have attempted to get views from a cross-section of politicians, from all parties, both sexes and from all parts of the UK. Some politicians were clearly too busy to respond. I am therefore more grateful to those who gave me their time and shared with me the benefits of their experience. They include: Donald Anderson, MP, the Rt Hon. Tony Benn, MP, the Rt Hon. Kenneth Clarke, QC, MP, Chancellor of the Exchequer, Cynog Dafis, MP, Mrs W. M. Ewing, MP, the Rt Hon. Lord Roy Jenkins, Mrs Angela Knight, MP, Economic Secretary to the Treasury, Sir Jim Lester, MP, Kevin McNamara, MP, the Rt Hon. Michael Portillo, MP, Secretary of State for Defence, Alan Simpson, MP.

I am also grateful to Mrs Joan Frazier for sharing with me her experiences of going to Japan in 1952.

Finally, I think it is high time that I record my thanks to all my teachers, tutors and others in the education system without whose help I would never have got into any position to write this, or any other, book. Among them are Raymond Gill, Wigan and District Mining and Technical College, the late Professor F. S. Northedge (LSE), the late Professor W. A. E. Manning (LSE), the late Professor Ralph Miliband (LSE and Leeds University), Professor R. H. Pear (LSE and University of Nottingham).

D.H.C.
Nottingham, April 1997

ACKNOWLEDGEMENTS TO THE FIFTH EDITION

I am thankful to the late Lord Rothermere for telling me about his experiences and his conversion to Blair's New Labour. I am grateful to my former students Kelvin Hopkins, MP and John Hayes, MP for giving me their impressions of the Commons as newly elected Members and for their hospitality. I wish to thank Piara Khabra, MP for sharing with me his experiences as an immigrant in politics; Andrew Stunell, MP for giving me a Liberal Democratic view on contemporary affairs; and Martin Bell, MP for an independent perspective. The Rt Hon. Stephen Dorrell, MP gave me a long interview at short notice for which I express my thanks. Gisela Stuart, MP, Parliamentary Under-Secretary of State, Department of Health, took time from her busy schedule to give me an interesting perspective on her life and times. My thanks are due to the Howard League for Penal Reform, the Police Complaints Authority and to the Ministry of Defence for material provided. Once again I must emphasize that I alone am responsible for the views expressed and for any errors of fact or judgement in this fifth edition.

D.H.C.
Nottingham, May 2000

ACKNOWLEDGEMENTS TO THE SIXTH EDITION

For this edition I must offer my thanks to the following parliamentarians who agreed to be interviewed or who answered written requests for information: Henry Bellingham (Con), Harry Cohen (Lab), Brian Cotter (Lib Dem), Ann Cryer (Lab), John Denham (Lab), Mrs Gwyneth Dunwoody (Lab), Don Foster (Lib Dem), Kelvin Hopkins (Lab), John Gummer (Con), Alun Ffred Jones (PC), Alice Mahon (Lab), Austin Mitchell (Lab), Nicholas Palmer (Lab), John Pugh (Lib Dem), Joan Ruddock (Lab), Gillian Shephard (Con), Anthony Steen (Con), Sir Peter Tapsell (Con), Dr Richard Taylor (Independent), Sir Teddy Taylor (Con), Dr Jenny Tonge (Lib Dem), Hywel Williams (PC); Lords Howe (Con), Merlyn-Rees (Lab), Prior (Con). My thanks are also due to the eight anonymous interviewees, in Belfast, 7 October 2003, who told me of their experiences and thoughts for the future. Robin Cook had agreed to be interviewed but, sadly, this was prevented by his tragic and unexpected death.

D.H.C.
Nottingham, November 2005

ABBREVIATIONS

ACAS	Advisory, Conciliation and Arbitration Service
AEU	Amalgamated Engineering Union
AIOC	Anglo-Iranian Oil Company
ANF	Atlantic Nuclear Force
BBC	British Broadcasting Corporation
BMA	British Medical Association
BNOC	British National Oil Corporation
BNP	British National Party
BOAC	British Overseas Airways Corporation
BP	British Petroleum
BSE	bovine spongiform encephalopathy
CAP	Common Agricultural Policy (of EEC/EC)
CBI	Confederation of British Industry
CDS	Campaign for Democratic Socialism
CJD	Creutzfeldt-Jakob Disease
CND	Campaign for Nuclear Disarmament
CPGB	Communist Party of Great Britain
CPS	Centre for Policy Studies
CSE	Certificate of Secondary Education
DEA	Department of Economic Affairs
DfES	Department for Education and Skills
DTI	Department of Trade and Industry
DUP	Democratic Unionist Party (N. Ireland)
EC	European Community
EEC	European Economic Community
EETPU	Electrical, Electronic, Telecommunications and Plumbing Union
EFTA	European Free Trade Association
EMS	European Monetary System
EMU	Economic and Monetary Union
ERM	Exchange Rate Mechanism
EU	European Union
FIS	Family Income Supplement

GATT	General Agreement on Tariffs and Trade
GCE	General Certificate of Education
GCHQ	Government Communications Headquarters
GCSE	General Certificate of Secondary Education
GDP	Gross Domestic Product
GLC	Greater London Council
HDI	Human Development Index
HMC	Headmasters' Conference
IBA	Independent Broadcasting Authority
ICL	International Computers Limited
IEA	Institute of Economic Affairs
ILP	Independent Labour Party
IMF	International Monetary Fund
INA	Indian National Army
IRA	Irish Republican Army
IRC	Industrial Reorganization Corporation
ITA	Independent Television Authority
ITV	Independent Television
JRC	Joint Representation Committee
MAP	Medical Assessment Programme
MEP	Member of the European Parliament
MI5	Military Intelligence 5, the informal name given to the Security Service
MI6	The informal name given to the SIS or Secret Intelligence Service
MLF	Multilateral Nuclear Force
NATO	North Atlantic Treaty Organization
NBPI	National Board for Prices and Incomes
NCIS	National Criminal Intelligence Service
NEB	National Enterprise Board
NEC	National Executive Committee (of the Labour Party)
NEDC	National Economic Development Council
NFFC	National Film Finance Corporation
NGA	National Graphical Association
NHS	National Health Service
NIRC	National Industrial Relations Court
NOP	National Opinion Poll
NUM	National Union of Mineworkers
NUS	National Union of Seamen
OAPEC	Organization of Arab Petroleum Exporting Countries
OECD	Organization for Economic Co-operation and Development
OEEC	Organization for European Economic Co-operation
ONS	Office of National Statistics
OPEC	Organization of Petroleum Exporting Countries
OUP	Official Unionist Party (N. Ireland)

PC	Plaid Cymru
PCA	Police Complaints Authority
PCC	Press Complaints Commission
PLP	Parliamentary Labour Party (the Labour Members of the Commons)
PNC	Police National Computer
PPS	Parliamentary Private Secretary
PSBR	Public Sector Borrowing Requirement
RAF	Royal Air Force
RFMC	Rank and File Mobilizing Committee (Labour)
RP	Referendum Party
RPM	Resale Price Maintenance
SAS	Special Air Service
SDLP	Social Democratic and Labour Party (N. Ireland)
SDP	Social Democratic Party
SET	Selective Employment Tax
SF	Sinn Fein
SIS	Secret Intelligence Service
SNP	Scottish National Party
SSP	Scottish Socialist Party
TGWU	Transport and General Workers' Union
TSR2	Tactical Strike and Reconnaissance Aircraft
TUC	Trades Union Congress
UDA	Ulster Defence Association
UDI	Unilateral Declaration of Independence (Rhodesia)
UFC	University Funding Committee
UGC	University Grants Committee
UKIP	UK Independence Party
UUP	Ulster Unionist Party
UVF	Ulster Volunteer Force
VfS	Victory for Socialism
WMD	Weapons of mass destruction
YC	Young Conservatives
YTS	Youth Training Scheme

1

SUMMER VICTORIES

JAPANESE TO 'FIGHT RESOLUTELY'

On 26 July 1945 the Japanese Prime Minister, Admiral Kantaro Suzuki, called a press conference to announce that his country rejected Allied calls for unconditional surrender. It would fight resolutely for the successful conclusion of the war in which it had been engaged since December 1941 when it attacked the US naval base at Pearl Harbor. He had been warned by the new US President, Harry S. Truman, that failure to surrender would result in the 'complete and utter destruction' of Japan. Outside Japan few people took much notice of the Admiral's defiant words. Benjamin O. Davis, Jr probably did. From the battlefields of Italy he had returned in June 1945 to command the US Air Force 477th Composite Group at Godman Field, Kentucky. He was the second Black general in the history of the US regular armed forces.[1] No doubt he wondered whether his next journey would be to take part in the final assault on Japan. Lieutenant Helmut Schmidt, of the German anti-aircraft artillery, was hoping for an early release from a British prisoner-of-war camp, to return to his devastated home town of Hamburg. He was part of the defeated German armed forces which had surrendered unconditionally on 8 May, thus ending the Second World War in Europe which had started on 1 September 1939. He was released in August.[2] He later became the Chancellor of West Germany. In the stifling heat of a bug-infested Russian prison, Captain Alexander Solzhenitsyn, a Soviet war hero, contemplated his sentence of eight years forced labour for an alleged anti-Stalin remark. He was one of millions of victims of the Stalinist system.[3] Later he received the Nobel prize for literature. Second-Lieutenant Eric Lomax endured another sweltering day of near starvation in the squalor of Changi jail, Singapore. He had been captured by the Japanese in 1942 and had survived working on the notorious Burma–Siam railway. Many thousands of his comrades had already perished.[4] There was a rumour that the Japanese would shoot their prisoners as Allied armies drew near, as they had done on any number of occasions.[5] In Plymouth, England, Michael Foot, a journalist, was not thinking of any of these individuals. He did not know them. He was contemplating his new life as a Labour Member of Parliament. On that date he was unexpectedly the victor in the constituency of Plymouth Devonport, beating the former minister Leslie Hore-Belisha.[6] By the time Foot knew his fate, he realized that he was part of a landslide. Everywhere Labour was winning in the wartime election of 1945. It was a win on the scale of the Liberal victory of 1906 and the 'National' (mainly Conservative) victory of 1931.

Voting day was 5 July – but not for everyone. There had been objections to 5 July as polling day because it clashed with holiday weeks in some northern towns. To cover this, the Postponement of Polling Day Act, 1945 was rushed through Parliament. It delayed voting for a week in 18 constituencies and for a fortnight in one. Once the voting was over, there was the long wait until 26 July before the results were known. This was because of the delayed voting in the nineteen constituencies, and to allow the armed services' vote to be brought back from overseas. The parties got the reports from the constituency organizations and made their predictions. *The Times*, 10 July, reported that the Conservatives felt there was no evidence of a swing either way! The Labour Party expected a 1929-style situation in which they would be the largest party without an overall majority. The Liberals were looking for between 80 and 100 seats, and the Communists thought they had gained 4 or 5.

CHURCHILL'S DEFEAT

All over Britain people listened to the results coming through over the BBC radio (or 'wireless' as people then called it). Among the early results which startled Conservatives were the defeats of two Cabinet members, Brendan Bracken at Paddington in London, and Harold Macmillan, the future Prime Minister, at Stockton-on-Tees. By lunchtime, a Labour victory appeared certain as seats fell to them in London and Birmingham. Churchill handed in his resignation as Prime Minister to King George VI just after 7 p.m. Clement Attlee, the Labour Leader, was asked by the King to form a government. The final figures gave Labour 393 seats. In addition, four other MPs joined Labour after being elected. These were three from the Independent Labour Party (ILP), which had broken with Labour in 1931, and one from the left-wing Common Wealth Party. The two Communists elected, William Gallacher and Phil Piratin, usually voted with Labour, as did the Labour Independent, D. N. Pritt, QC, elected at Hammersmith (London) and the independent Vernon Bartlett. The Conservatives and their allies won 213 seats and the Liberals 12. In addition, the Conservatives could usually count on 12 university members elected by the graduates of the universities. The total Churchill government vote recorded was 9,960,809, over 900,000 of which had gone to candidates describing themselves as National or Liberal National. The total opposition vote was

15,018,140, of which Labour got 11,992,292, the ILP 46,679, and Common Wealth 110,634. The Communists attracted 102,780. Also on the Left, the Scottish and the Welsh nationalists gained 30,595 and 14,751 respectively. The Scottish nationalists lost the only seat they had previously held, Motherwell. Dr R. D. McInyre, their chairman, had won it from Labour at a by-election. He held it for just 32 days! Irish nationalist candidates got 148,078 votes and other independents (Pritt among them) 325,203. Finally, Liberal candidates secured 2,245,319 votes.[7]

Although Labour's victory in votes was exaggerated in terms of seats, the 'Left' had clearly won a great victory. Even the Liberals had campaigned on a platform nearer to that of Labour than that of the Conservatives. Perhaps the results did not fully reveal the swing to the Left. The election had been fought on an old register, which probably helped the Conservatives. Young people, more inclined to vote Labour, had been more mobile during the war and were, therefore, more likely to be on the register where they had grown up rather than where they were living at the time of the election. This must have been true of many women war workers. Moreover, only those over 21 had the vote. Thus, many who had served the country in its hour of need were excluded. Nor must the effect of the service vote be exaggerated.[8] Only 59.4 per cent of the service vote was used. Just over 1 million service men and women voted themselves, and 750,000 votes were cast by their proxies – wives, fathers, mothers, sisters and brothers. In any case, most of servicemen were blue-collar workers in uniform. In peacetime they would have been more likely to vote Labour than Conservative. The Conservatives had the advantage of greater funds at their disposal. The average expenditure by Conservative candidates was £780, for Labour candidates it was £595.[9] They also had the advantage of more cars to take aged voters to the poll, greater office and publicity skills, and so on. The Conservatives also benefited from the business vote, which enabled business owners to vote in their place of business as well as where they lived. It is believed this gave the Conservatives between 3 and 5 seats.[10]

'INCREDULITY' AS CONSERVATIVES LOSE

Winston Churchill, who had been Prime Minister from May 1940, was thought to be the Conservative Party's greatest asset. They put great emphasis on him during the election campaign. They thought they could repeat the performance of David Lloyd George, Prime Minister in the First World War, who won so convincingly in 1918. Yet, although he was not opposed by the other parties in his constituency, an unknown independent candidate gained 10,000 votes against Churchill, who of course retained his seat. Many people, it seems, felt that although he did well during the war he was not the leader Britain needed for the post-war reconstruction. In broad terms, the Conservatives lost because they were seen as the government party which had failed to deal with Britain's interwar social and economic problems, including the misery of great unemployment, and had failed to prepare Britain to stand up to Hitler. They had been in office from 1916–22 (in coalition), 1922–24, 1924–29, 1931–40 and 1940–45 (in coalition). They were seen as the party of privilege, wealth, stuffiness and nostalgia. Labour was seen as the party of the underdog, of ordinary people and of hope. The 'Conservative class' was undoubtedly linked in many people's minds with incompetence. There had been so many disasters in the war which pointed to amateurism and incompetence on the part of the officers, the generals, the strategists, Churchill himself. The defeat at Singapore in 1942, 'the greatest disaster in our history',[11] was one of these, the fiascos in France, Norway and Greece were others. There were the naval tragedies, including the sinking of the *Prince of Wales* and the *Repulse*. Many of the Labour leaders, on the other hand, were tried and trusted politicians, having served in Churchill's coalition but not having been tainted by his policies. This was true of Attlee, Ernest Bevin, Herbert Morrison, Sir Stafford Cripps, Arthur Greenwood, Dr Hugh Dalton, A. V. Alexander and Lord Jowitt. Others had served in more junior roles. It was unconvincing to present these men as a threat to liberty, as Churchill did in his campaign, when he claimed, 'They would have to fall back on some form of Gestapo' to realize their socialist plans.[12] Although too much emphasis should not be placed on the fact, Labour, in its candidates, was an all-class party. It had many aspiring middle-class contenders in addition to its traditional trade union candidates. The Conservatives, on the other hand, stood as a middle-class and upper-class party. The overall impression of 1945 is that many people wanted a Britain in which social origins, family background and place of education would no longer be of great importance. They wanted a Britain in which people were treated with equality and had equal opportunities to make something of their lives; a Britain in which poverty, unemployment, malnutrition, ignorance and fear were banished.

There was surprise around the world as news spread that Churchill had been dismissed by the British electorate. On the London stock market prices fell. The *Financial Times* commented, 'The City, with the nation was shocked by the political landslide revealed yesterday.'[13] Were Labour, Liberal and other opposition voters not part of 'the nation'? Shock? There was jubilation in the copper factory in Widnes where Jack Ashley, himself later a Labour MP, worked.[14] A. A. Best, a 53-year-old insurance agent in 1945, was on holiday in Hove on that dramatic day. A woman school teacher at his hotel table expressed incredulity as Labour gains mounted and wondered 'what would become of us all. I said that this was something I had been working for most of my life and was feeling very excited at the prospects.'[15] He found many other guests shared his feelings in varying degrees. Nor was the Establishment wholly disappointed by Labour's victory. Montagu Norman, Governor of the Bank of England

1920–44, commented in a letter in 1946 that, had Churchill remained Prime Minister, 'I daresay we should have had more disturbances and ill-feeling within this country and possibly elsewhere in Europe'.[16] Sir William Beveridge, author of the famous report on national insurance and himself a defeated Liberal, felt the Conservatives had 'somewhat surprisingly' got what they deserved.[17] Thomas Jones, ex-leading civil servant and intimate of Prime Ministers, wrote on 4 August, that 'Many old people are alarmed at what may happen. I cannot develop the slightest feeling of panic.'[18] The Fellows of the Royal College of Physicians heard the news while taking afternoon tea: 'They were so taken aback they stood there in complete silence.'[19]

ATTLEE'S TEAM: 'THESE FINE MEN'

Attlee's first task was to select his government team. Like all Prime Ministers he had to attempt to find suitable jobs for powerful personalities, reward talent and service, consider public opinion and ensure that the different wings of his party were placated. A surprise appointment was Ernest Bevin, leader of the transport workers' union and former Minister of Labour and National Service, as Foreign Minister. Attlee's rival, Herbert Morrison, former leader of the London County Council and former Home Secretary and Minister for Home Security, was appointed Lord President. Hugh Dalton, an academic economist and Churchill's Minister of Economic Warfare, took over as Chancellor of the Exchequer. James Chuter Ede went to the Home Office. He had served as a junior minister in Churchill's coalition. The Admiralty, then an important post, went to A. V. Alexander, who had held this post under Churchill. The Colonial Office, also important at that time, went to George Hall. The separate, and very important, India and Burma Office was given to Lord Pethick-Lawrence. He had served as a junior Treasury minister in the 1929–31 Labour government. The key post of Minister of Health went to Aneurin Bevan, an ex-miner, who, although relatively unknown to the general public, was well known as a left-winger within the Labour ranks. Another rebel appointed was Sir Stafford Cripps, a science graduate, wealthy lawyer and Christian, as President of the Board of Trade. Emanuel Shinwell was put in charge of Fuel and Power, regarded as vital to post-war recovery. Of Glasgow Jewish background, he was regarded as a former rebel. Sir William Jowitt was appointed Lord Chancellor. He had served as Attorney-General in MacDonald's 1929–31 Labour minority government, briefly in his 'National' government and in the Churchill coalition. Three other veterans of the MacDonald Labour government were Lord Addison, Lord Stansgate (W. Wedgwood Benn) and Arthur Greenwood. Addison was given the Dominions Office, which dealt with relations with the independent Empire states. He held Agriculture and Fisheries under MacDonald

5

and his experience went back to Lloyd George's coalition in which he had served as Minister of Reconstruction. Stansgate got the Air Ministry. He had held the India Office under MacDonald. Greenwood was appointed Lord Privy Seal. He had served as Minister of Health in MacDonald's administration and in Churchill's War Cabinet as Minister Without Portfolio. His career had been marred by alcoholism. The other appointees were George Isaacs at Labour and National Insurance, J. Lawson at the War Office, J. Westwood at the Scottish Office and Tom Williams at Agriculture and Fisheries. Lawson and Westwood had held junior posts under MacDonald. The only woman appointed was Miss Ellen Wilkinson, who had been the Personal Private Secretary to Morrison. She served but briefly as Minister of Education. She was a graduate of Manchester University. Her life ended with an overdose of pills in 1947.

Attlee's first Cabinet with 20 members was a fair mix both in terms of the Left and Right within the Labour Party and social structure of the country. Ramsay MacDonald's first ever Labour government of 1924 included nine former officials of working-class organizations, Attlee's included 10. MacDonald's included more members with aristocratic or upper-class backgrounds than Attlee's. Bevin, Bevan, Morrison, Alexander, Shinwell, Hall, Isaacs, Lawson, Westwood and Williams were all from working-class backgrounds, men whose only universities had been 'Life'. Cripps, Dalton, Jowitt and Pethick-Lawrence were upper class. Attlee's 1945 Cabinet included 10 university-educated MPs, five of them, including Attlee, at Oxbridge. Of the other graduates three were from London University, one from Leeds and one from Manchester. Five were ex-public school boys, two of these from Eton. Only two members of the 1945 Labour Cabinet had not previously held government office. It was certainly a talented and experienced government. Of it, Harold Macmillan said, 'These fine men constituted a body of Ministers as talented as any in the history of Parliament.'[20]

ATTLEE: 'ONE OF THE BEST CHAIRMEN'

What of Attlee himself? At 62 Attlee was younger than his predecessors – Churchill and Chamberlain – when they took over as Prime Minister. He was very experienced in government, being the only member, apart from Churchill, of the wartime coalition who had served from 1940 to the end. Although Churchill's style of government had been autocratic, Attlee was officially Deputy Prime Minister from 1942, and had had a free hand in many domestic areas, if only because Churchill was uninterested. Attlee had served outside the Cabinet as Chancellor of the Duchy of Lancaster and Postmaster-General in MacDonald's 1929–31 administration. Attlee was a 'dark horse' who was in the right place at the right time. The impression is that few expected him to become the Leader of the Labour Party. His physique, bearing, personality and lack of oratorical skills led to this conclusion. He served as MP for Limehouse, Stepney, 1922–50. Thus, when Labour representation was cut from 288 to 52 after the electoral débâcle of 1931, he was one of the few Labour MPs with any experience. He was elected Deputy Leader, with pacifist Christian socialist George Lansbury the Leader. When Lansbury resigned just before the election of 1935 Attlee became acting Leader. Labour increased its Commons strength to 154 and Attlee was elected Leader, beating Greenwood and Morrison. Dalton, who himself would have gladly taken on the leadership, called Attlee at the time 'a little mouse'.[21] Like Churchill, he was more impressed by Mussolini![22] Part of Attlee's success was because he was underestimated by rivals. Macmillan, who had served with him in the wartime government, remembered him as 'one of the best Chairmen I have ever sat under'. Attlee was also a 'good butcher', a quality said to be essential for a good Prime Minister.[23] The son of a wealthy lawyer, he took up law himself after Oxford. Like Dalton, he served in the First World War, rising to the rank of major. The poverty he witnessed doing social work in the East End of London led him to the Labour Party. He was essentially a conservative reformist who, as an admirer of monarchy and of his old public school (Haileybury), sought not to abolish the class system but to end squalor by affirmative action, and give more people the chance to rise up from the ranks into middle-class society.

BRITAIN: 'IT WON'T BE EASY'

On 6 and 9 August 1945 the US dropped atomic bombs on Hiroshima and Nagasaki. The Soviet Union invaded Japanese-controlled territory on 8 August. On 14 August Tokyo was hit again by a total of 1,014 US aircraft. Before the planes returned to their bases without a single loss, President Truman announced the Japanese surrender.[24] The surrender was unconditional, except that the Allies agreed that the Emperor could and should remain as head of state under an Allied occupation. The Japanese surrender, welcome though it was, was something of an anti-climax compared with the surrender of Germany. Most people regarded Germany as the main enemy and the campaign against the Japanese as a sideshow. Yet, had the Allies been forced to invade Japan, the costs in lives and materials would have been enormous.

The war had cost Britain about 264,433 armed forces dead, 60,595 civilian dead and 30,248 merchant navy dead. Thousands of Indians, Australians, New Zealanders, South Africans and others died as members of the British Empire armed forces. By comparison, Germany lost an estimated 3,600,000 civilians and 3,250,000 service casualties. US armed services suffered 362,561 deaths.[25] The Japanese lost 2 million civilians and 1 million military casualties. The Soviet Union lost an estimated 13,300,000 military deaths and 7 million civilian deaths. Although terrible, the British figures were about half those of the 1914–18 war.[26] Relative to population size, they were much lower than some other countries.

About a quarter of Britain's wealth had been used on the war. By 1941 its foreign exchange reserves had vanished. Britain then became dependent on American Lend–Lease. By the autumn of 1945 Britain was only able to pay for about 40 per cent of its overseas expenditure.[27] About two-thirds of its merchant fleet was lost and about one-third of the housing stock had been damaged or destroyed by enemy action. In addition, other buildings – factories, schools and hospitals – had been hit.[28] Germany and Japan were in far worse shape. Yet the expectations of the British people were high. They did not want to return to the conditions of uncertainty and poverty which many of them had endured before the war. After all that effort and all those promises, they expected a better life soon. Remarkably, Attlee's situation was summed up very well by the Countess of Ranfurly, who wrote in her diary that she felt sorry for the new Prime Minister, Clement Attlee: 'it won't be easy to succeed a hero like Churchill; ghastly to be faced with the repair of our country – to help the thousands returning from the war all wanting a job; and frightful having to raise money from a weary, bereaved and poor population.'[29]

NOTES

Unless otherwise indicated, the place of publication is London.

1 Department of Defense, *Black Americans in the Defense of Our Nation* (Washington, DC, 1985), 114–15.
2 Helmut Schmidt *et al.*, *Kindheit und Jugend unter Hitler* (Berlin, 1994), 574.
3 Michael Scammell, *Solzhenitsyn* (1985).
4 Eric Lomax, *The Railway Man* (1996).
5 Martin Gilbert, *Second World War* (1990), 618, 635. See also John Dower, *War Without Mercy* (1986), 300.
6 Mervyn Jones, *Michael Foot* (1994), 134.
7 *The Times Guide to the House of Commons 1950* (1950), 274.
8 Robert J. Wybrow, *Britain Speaks Out, 1937–87: A Social History as Seen through the Gallup Data* (1989), 17–18.
9 R. B. McCallum and Alison Readman, *The British General Election of 1945* (1947), 296–8.
10 D. E. Butler, *The Electoral System in Britain since 1918* (1963), 146–8.
11 Clive Ponting, *Churchill* (1995), 558. This was Churchill's comment to Roosevelt.
12 ibid., 718.
13 HMSO (ed.), *When Peace Broke Out: Britain 1945* (1996), 84.
14 Jack Ashley, *Journey Into Silence* (1973), 61.
15 Letter to the author.
16 Andrew Boyle, *Montagu Norman* (1967), 326.
17 Lord Beveridge, *Power and Influence* (1953), 349.
18 Thomas Jones, *A Diary with Letters 1932–1950* (1954), 536.
19 Lord Moran, *Winston Churchill: The Struggle for Survival, 1940–1965* (1966), 286. He was Churchill's doctor.

20 Harold Macmillan, *Tides of Fortune, 1945–1955* (1969), 64, 67.
21 Ben Pimlott (ed.), *The Political Diary of Hugh Dalton, 1918–40, 1945–60* (1986), 196.
22 ibid., 173. For Churchill see Ponting, op. cit., 350, 374, 377.
23 Macmillan, op. cit., 50.
24 Dower, op. cit., 301.
25 Gilbert, op. cit., 746.
26 John Stevenson, *British Society 1914–45* (1984), 448.
27 Alec Cairncross, *The British Economy since 1945* (1992), 45.
28 Stevenson, op. cit., 448–9.
29 The Countess of Ranfurly, *To War with Whitaker: The Wartime Diaries of the Countess of Ranfurly, 1939–45* (1995), 362.

2

ACHIEVEMENT AND AUSTERITY UNDER ATTLEE, 1945–51

BRITAIN BEING 'FLAYED TO THE BONE'

'We are the masters at the moment, and not only at the moment, but for a very long time to come.' These words were spoken by Sir Hartley Shaw-cross, Attlee's Attorney-General in the House of Commons on 2 April 1946. Probably said in the heat of the moment, it was a foolish comment, and not very accurate. Some Conservatives, up and down the land, are reported to have remarked, 'Yes, but we have the pen nibs'. They were refer-ring to the fact that most of the business elite supported them, as did many in the civil service, local government and the armed services. They implied that a radical government was limited in what it could do, even in a demo-cratic capitalist state. Shawcross's remarks were also untrue in another sense. Britain was increasingly coming under the shadow of the US. All the fine words about British sovereignty spoken since 1940 have been largely rhetorical appeals ignoring the actual situation.

By July 1940 Lord Halifax, the Foreign Secretary, put a paper to the Cabinet which for the first time accepted that Britain's future survival depended upon substantial assistance from the US.[1] Britain was negotiating to obtain 50 First World War destroyers from America in exchange for granting the US bases in seven British colonies. On 22 August, Sir Kingsley Wood, Chancellor of the Exchequer, presented a paper to the Cabinet indi-cating that Britain was virtually bankrupt. It 'marked the effective end of Britain's status as an independent power'.[2] Churchill sent Professor Tizard to the US in August with design details of some of Britain's most secret inventions – microwave radar, the cavity magnetron, chemical warfare formulae, special explosives, jet engine designs, and so on.[3] Before it received aid, Britain was forced to sell all its assets in the US, some below their market value.[4] Churchill felt Britain was being not just skinned, 'but flayed to the bone'.[5] By March 1941 the US Congress approved Lend–Lease, which meant American war materials did not have to be paid for. But Britain had to accept US views on what rules should guide future international trade. At the second Quebec conference in 1944

President Roosevelt committed Lend–Lease funds to restore Britain's industrial capacity after the war.[6] However, his successor, Truman, reneged on this, terminating Lend–Lease immediately after Japan surrendered. Britain was once again in a jam! Dalton and his colleagues had to face this appalling situation, which was 'very grim, grimmer than the worst nightmare of most experts'.[7]

AMERICAN LOAN: 'THIS WAS A DISASTER'

Churchill had been regarded by many in Roosevelt's administration as a reactionary. Some thought it would be easier for Labour to obtain financial help from Washington. Attlee's chief negotiator, Lord Keynes, was optimistic about the chances of getting renewed US help. In fact, only after months of hard negotiations was a loan secured on which interest had to be paid with conditions attached. Britain was offered a credit of up to $3,750 million at 2 per cent interest with repayments starting in 1951. To the US credit was added a Canadian loan of $1,250 million. Britain was required to end British Empire preferences. At the time a 2 per cent rate of interest was not considered low. The system of imperial preference had been built up from the end of the nineteenth century, due to fear of the rising German and US economies. It matured at the Ottawa conference in 1932. Under this system many goods from the independent British Empire states faced lower tariffs than goods from outside the Empire. The US now set the international economic agenda. Britain had to accept policies of increasing multilateral trade by joining the General Agreement on Tariffs and Trade (GATT) agreed in 1947. Britain also had to agree 'in a formidable imposition of orthodoxy on common sense', as Kenneth Galbraith called it, to give up the wartime controls and make sterling fully convertible within one year. 'This was a disaster.'[8] In July 1947 sterling was made convertible and there was heavy selling of it in exchange for dollars. The economy, which had been recovering well, came under great pressure. Within weeks the suspension of convertibility had to be announced by Dalton. A considerable part of Britain's problem was government overseas spending on its massive commitments.

The terms of the American loan provoked widespread dismay. Both Empire loyalists and socialist planning enthusiasts opposed them. The government took the view that it had no alternative but to accept. The Commons accepted the terms by 345 to 98, with many Conservatives abstaining. Among the Labour 'noes' were future Prime Minister James Callaghan, Barbara Castle and future Labour Leader Michael Foot. In all, some 21 Labour MPs voted against the government. The two Communists and the small group of fellow travellers approved the loan. The Cold War had not yet reached the House of Commons.

The British had thought the Americans would be grateful to them for 'standing alone' against Nazi Germany in 1940 and for their subsequent war effort. They did not realize that many Americans felt Britain (or the Jews)[9] had got them into a European war again, as in 1917, against their better judgement. They saw Britain as an old-fashioned imperialist power attempting to exploit American generosity to maintain its decaying empire. Many Irish Americans still regarded Britain as the oppressor of the 'Emerald Isle'. Many Jews regarded Britain as the power preventing the Zionists from attaining nationhood in Palestine. As for the less influential American groups at that time, it is doubtful whether Japanese returning from their internment camps[10] or Black Americans in the ghettos or returning from their segregated army units cared about Britain's fate. For neither the Italian-Americans whose own 'old country' was shattered from north to south, nor the Mexican-Americans, facing an uncertain future, would Britain's economic resurrection have been top of the agenda.[11] Other Americans viewed Attlee's government with suspicion, as it called itself 'Socialist'.

A large body of independent experts believed the conditions of the loan were impossible to fulfil,[12] and their view was proved correct when, in August 1947, the government was forced to suspend the dollar convertibility of sterling. This was after barely one month of convertibility. Though the government was an easy target for right-wing propaganda on the grounds that it was squandering the loan, a similar dollar crisis struck Western Europe in the same year. Marshall Aid was introduced by the Americans in the following year because, by that time, the prosperity of Western Europe was seen as crucial to American defence. Britain took its share of aid, but again faced difficulty in 1949. A recession in the United States had made dollar exports more difficult, while strong demand at home placed a new strain on the precarious balance of payments. Cripps, by that time Chancellor, attempted to solve the crisis with a massive devaluation of sterling, from $4.03 to $2.80.

PUBLIC OWNERSHIP: 'I'VE WAITED ALL MY LIFE FOR THIS MOMENT'

Writing in 1944, John Strachey, the ex-Communist Labour intellectual, told his readers that 'socialism involves the *public* ownership of all the means of production; but that does not mean that they should all be owned by the State'.[13] Industries like the railways would be state-owned; others would be owned by the local authorities or would be co-operatives. And, he conceded, for a long time to come 'there will be a secure place in a socialist society for the small one-man, or two-men, business, which exploits no one'. Strachey's view was in fact close to what Attlee had himself written in the 1930s.[14] Despite the writings of Strachey and Attlee, Labour fought the election on a moderate programme of nationalization.

Socialists advocated public ownership to prevent unemployment, redistribute wealth, rationalise production and create better relations in industry. The war years saw an increase in interest in public ownership because of the successful role played by the government in the economy at the time and, not least, because of the successes of the Red Army, which were thought to be based on a highly successful economic system created by the state from nothing.

Virtually all the industries taken into public ownership had a history of state intervention, and in most cases there were non-socialist arguments for the state taking them over. In many respects, Labour's nationalization programme was a continuation of the policies of earlier governments. Explaining his party's attitude to public ownership in 1947, Conservative Quintin Hogg (Lord Hailsham) reminded his readers, 'Disraeli encouraged the purchase by the Government of a minority shareholding in a private profit-making concern, the Suez Canal Company. The British Government became under Conservative auspices perhaps the principal shareholders in the Anglo-Persian Oil Company.'[15] Rail nationalization had first been advocated in the nineteenth century by non-socialists such as William Galt and Edwin Chadwick, on the grounds that British railways were less efficient than those on the Continent, and though nationalization was resisted, successive governments increasingly regulated the railways.[16] In the interwar period Conservative governments carried out selective nationalization policies. A Conservative government set up the BBC and the Central Electricity Board in 1926. The legislation establishing the London Transport Board, which put public transport in the capital under one authority, was passed by a Conservative-dominated Commons in 1933. The Conservatives were responsible for the nationalization of mining royalties and tithes in 1938 because they had 'become a nuisance in private hands – the former because they interfered with the technical layout of the coal mines, the latter because they no longer formed an equitable or even impost on property'.[17] Finally, the Chamberlain administration brought Imperial Airways Ltd and British Airways Ltd into public ownership in 1939. Churchill admitted in the debate on rail nationalization that he had advocated it after the 1914–18 war.

Despite any continuation of previous policies, the importance of the nationalization measures for many communities should not be underestimated. C. F. Grey, a Methodist lay preacher and a miner until his election to the Commons in 1945, spoke of the conditions the miners had endured.

> Low wages, long hours, miserable compensation, bad conditions, wretched death benefits, and virtual slavery were the lot of the miner. For years, the miner stood this, until it got to breaking point. Now we have a younger miner who is determined that he is not going to be a beast of burden.[18]

Another MP pointed out that mining accidents killed, on average, two men every day. In 1943, 713 men had lost their lives in mining. The work-force was ageing and not enough new miners were being recruited.[19] The government was forced to conscript men into the mines. Many of the mines were in poor shape and massive investments would be needed to modernize them.

On Vesting Day, the day the mines were taken over, 1 January 1947, there were celebrations throughout the mining communities, including dances, marches, socials and bonfires. Typical was Hucknall, Nottinghamshire, where 200 people attended a dance at the Co-op Hall and 600 children celebrated with a visit to the pictures, tea and a huge bonfire at Clipstone, also in Nottinghamshire. In Durham, the Minister of Fuel and Power, Emanuel Shinwell, returned to celebrate with his constituents:

> Orators skilled in their art had sent fiery words over the assembled gathering. The platform sustained the imposing authority of the Cabinet, of big business, of smaller business, of the powerful unions and of civic bodies in the district. The band was smart and vigorous. But without question, the show belonged to one man – an aged miner in a spotted muffler and a cloth cap. They helped him to the platform. 'I'm ninety-one years old and I've waited all my life for this moment', said Jim Hawkins.'There's little time left. Let's cut the cackle and get on with it.' Aided by willing hands, the old man made his way to a flagpole, clutched the cord and ran up a blue flag on which was written in white the letters 'N.C.B.'. By his act, Jim Hawkins had translated nationalization into an accomplished fact.[20]

For the miners and their representatives the Coal Act alone justified the Labour government, it was the acid test of the potentialities of parliamentary politics. The same was true for the steel and rail communities, which had been bedevilled by poor conditions and, not least, by rigid hierarchies.

Table 2.1 Industries taken into public ownership, 1946–51

Industry	Date of takeover	Numbers employed
Bank of England	1 March 1946	6,700
Civil aviation	1 August 1946	23,300
Coal	1 January 1947	765,000
Cable & Wireless	1 January 1947	9,500
Transport	1 January 1948	888,000
Electricity	1 April 1948	176,000
Gas	1 April 1949	143,500
Iron and steel	15 February 1951	292,000

NATIONAL INSURANCE: A 'PALTRY SUM'

Though the implementation of the public-ownership pledges was a crucial test for the miners and the committed socialists in the Labour Party, the 'masses' gained immensely more from the welfare legislation passed in 1946. This legislation included the National Insurance Act, the Industrial Injuries Act and the National Health Act. In 1948 the work was completed with the establishment of the National Assistance Board. Another piece of relevant legislation, that covering family allowances, had been enacted in 1945 by Churchill's caretaker administration.

Under the National Insurance Act the whole population was brought, for the first time, into a comprehensive system covering unemployment, sickness, maternity, guardianship, retirement and death. A Ministry of National Insurance was set up along with a National Insurance Fund with an initial capital of £100 million. Annual grants from the Exchequer were foreseen, but both employers and employees had to make weekly contributions. The latter was something that many in the Labour Party were unhappy about. Some Labour MPs, Sydney Silverman and Barbara Castle among them, rejected the idea that there should be a time limit on the payment of benefits. Under the Act, an unemployed person became eligible, after the first three days of unemployment, to receive a weekly payment for 180 days, an insured person who then got a job and lost it again after not less than 13 weeks qualified for another period of benefit.

Sickness benefit was provided after three days of enforced absence from work. It could be drawn indefinitely up to retirement age, when it was replaced by a pension. The maternity grant consisted of a single payment to the mother on the birth of her baby, and mothers doing paid work received an allowance for 13 weeks to compensate for absence from employment.

The death grant was a lump sum to help cover the cost of the funeral. Widows were taken care of under the Act. For the first 16 weeks, a widow under retirement age was paid an allowance. There were allowances for her children up to the age of 16 (if they remained at school to that age). Widows between 50 and 60 (60 being the retirement age for women) could also be eligible for a continuing allowance. Finally, if a widow reached 40 while her children were still at school, she could also receive an allowance. To be eligible for these benefits, the widow had to have been married for 10 years. One other provision made for death was that an orphaned child's guardian could claim an allowance, provided one of its parents had been insured under the Act.

Retirement pensions were granted under the Act to men at 65 and women at 60. Those eligible could continue working for a further five years with a slight reduction of pension. As with all the benefits listed, pensions did not rise automatically with the rise in the cost of living nor were they related to previous earnings. Over the years their purchasing power declined

15

because successive governments failed to increase them to keep pace with inflation.

Family allowances were given to mothers for second and any subsequent children up to the age of 15, or 16 if they remained in full-time education. The allowance was fixed at 5 shillings (25 p) per week, what Barbara Castle called a 'paltry sum'. In fact it was just about enough to buy 1 lb of Brooke Bond Dividend Tea, a tube of Colgate toothpaste, and a Mars bar.[21]

THE NHS: 'VESTED INTERESTS LINED UP'

Despite the wartime agreement on the need for a National Health Service, it was this part of the post-war welfare legislation that was most actively contested. In theory, the Conservatives agreed with the principle, but they voiced varying degrees of opposition to the Labour government's proposals. Greater than the opposition of the Conservatives was that of the spokesmen of the British Medical Association, the professional body to which the great majority of medical practitioners belonged.

The National Health Service Act nationalized the nation's hospitals, about half of which belonged to the local authorities. They were placed under regional boards. The teaching hospitals obtained a special status giving them a large measure of autonomy. The aim was to provide adequate hospitals throughout the country, replacing a system based on local initiative and charity, which had resulted in widely differing local and regional standards. The local authorities retained important health functions, such as maternity and child welfare, the ambulance service, health visiting, and so on. Aneurin Bevan, the minister responsible, wanted a service which would encompass all the nation's citizens, and provide them all, irrespective of their financial circumstances or where they lived, with completely free and comprehensive medical care. Broadly speaking, he achieved this, but not without considerable compromises. Firstly, although the buying and selling of practices, which was thought to have led to an imbalance in the distribution of general practitioners, ceased. But doctors did not become salaried employees of the state. Secondly, he agreed to having private beds in the hospitals in order to encourage specialists to join the new scheme. The patient remained free to choose his or her own GP. The Act was a personal triumph for Bevan, and was described by Dr H. B. Morgan, MP, medical adviser to the TUC, as 'as fine a piece of compromise health work as is possible in this country at the present time'.[22] There were some in the Cabinet, like Morrison, and in the Labour Party in the country, who had certain reservations about taking the hospitals away from the local (elected) authorities. But these reservations were overcome.

In judging the effectiveness of the Labour government one can ask this question: was it merely extending the work of social welfare inaugurated by previous administrations, or was it introducing something more fundamental? The legislation was based on Sir William Beveridge's report on *Social Insurance and Allied Services* of November 1942 which recommended public protection for all 'from the cradle to the grave'. Churchill, whose coalition had commissioned the report, had not been prepared to implement any legislation incorporating any of the report's proposals during the war.[23] Public opinion polls indicated that the majority of people in the country were disappointed with the government on this issue, feeling that vested interests had won once again. In February 1943, virtually the whole of the Labour back-bench voted against the government, and their own leaders, in demanding the immediate implementation of the Beveridge proposals. Even allowing that, had the Conservatives won in 1945, the Tory reformers would have been better represented in the Commons,[24] it seems likely that a Conservative government would have been less ready to realize Beveridge's proposals than were Labour. As it was, their performance over the National Health Service Bill was not reassuring.

> Poor leadership and the absence of a coherent alternative policy allowed the party to drift into a reactionary posture and become the mouthpiece for the vested interests lined up in opposition to the bill.[25]

If Labour built on the foundations laid by earlier administrations, to many working people the post-war measures appeared revolutionary. Pre-war unemployment relief had excluded significant sections of the employed population. Once benefit ran out, the unemployed faced the hated 'means test', which enquired into the financial situation of his entire household. And even in the 1930s there was the possibility of being committed to the equally hated 'workhouse'.[26] Sickness insurance was far from comprehensive. It did not cover an insured person's dependants and it discriminated against those with a poor health record. Hospitals charged patients according to means. Children's allowances, maternity and death benefits had not existed in pre-war Britain, and many citizens were still not included in the old-age pension scheme. Alan Sillitoe, the writer who, in 1945, was a capstan-lathe operator in Nottingham, has commented:

> the Health Service was a sort of enormous sign of relief – no more Panel – it made the most incredible difference to the mentality of the less well off – probably the greatest single factor in this century in creating a new pride in the English working class.[27]

Attlee told the author in 1962 that he believed it to be his government's biggest single achievement in home affairs.

HOUSING AND EDUCATION: 'HANDS WERE TIED'

If unemployment, public ownership and social security had been key domestic issues for the pre-war Labour movement, housing and education had never been far behind them. Yet in these last two areas Attlee's government had less that was new to offer. In both cases lack of time and resources played their part.

Bevan, who was also responsible for housing, inherited a poor housing situation. During the war perhaps one-third of the housing stock had been damaged or destroyed. Yet he was under constant attack from the Conservatives and the Left over housing. Under Attlee's governments over a million homes were built, which was not bad, considering the shortages of men and materials. The government faced embarrassment over squatters and the wrath of the better-off who had money but still could not easily find a home of their own. One solution that was tried was factory-made 'pre-fabs' of which 124,000 were erected by local councils. These were relatively well designed and comfortable by the standards of the time, yet many thought they were not quite real houses. They proved to be far more durable than anyone expected. Wartime rent controls were extended in an effort to prevent profiteering and to help steady the cost of living. The Town and Country Planning Act, 1947 obliged local authorities to survey their areas and present plans for their development. Previously their powers had been merely discretionary. The planning authorities were given extended powers and grants from central government, but many local Labour politicians were disappointed that their authorities did not get greater powers to deal with the complex problems of urban renewal.

As Professor Marwick reminds us, the Labour administration's 'hands were tied', in education, 'by the fact that a major Education Act had just been put on the statute book, so that it was scarcely feasible to bring in another one'. And he rightly points out:

> Yet if ever there was a good Psychological moment for dealing with the snobbism built into the system, it was in the aftermath of the 1945 election victory. The major public schools were then at a low ebb, and certainly expected little mercy at the hands of a Labour government.[28]

Given Attlee's own view of socialism as a process of levelling-up, and his own pride in his old school, it is surprising that no attempt was made to integrate the public schools into the state system. One would not have expected nationalization, rather, state scholarships for 75 or 80 per cent of the places. This would have been in keeping with wartime discussions and would have won the support of Liberal and Conservative reformers.

Labour did implement the pledge to raise the school-leaving age to 15 in 1947. They also implemented the tripartite system of secondary education embodied in the 1944 Education Act without apparently considering its divisive features.

CONSTITUTIONAL AND TRADE UNION REFORM

Attlee brought in constitutional reform, which many thought was long overdue and some thought did not go far enough. Firstly, the power of the House of Lords to delay legislation was cut from two years to one. Secondly, the Representation of the People Act, 1948 abolished the business premises qualification to vote. This caused bitterness on the Right.[29] Legislation to restrict the use of cars to convey electors to the polling station, passed in 1949, was repealed by the Conservatives in 1958. Thirdly, the Trades Disputes Act, 1927 was repealed in 1946. 'Contracting-in' was, once again, replaced by 'contracting-out' for trade unionists paying the political levy which usually went to the Labour Party. In other words, if a member of a trade union affiliated to the Labour Party did not wish to pay his political levy, he had to seek out his branch secretary and sign the appropriate form. Under the 1927 Act the onus was on the individual to take the initiative to pay the levy. The importance of this move for the Labour Party is shown by reference to the Amalgamated Engineering Union (AEU). During the war the union tried hard to get its members to pay the levy. By 1945, 24.66 per cent did so. In the first full year after the Act had been repealed, 1947, it was 82.21 per cent.[30] The repeal of the 1927 Act also made it possible once again for civil service unions to affiliate to the TUC.

Given the economic situation, the government needed the trade unions more than ever before. In 1945 it knew it could count on the complete support of the union leaders and most of their members. Later, the government became worried, unduly so, as it turned out, about Communist influence.

The war had brought impressive gains for the Communist Party of Great Britain (CPGB) in the unions. They had consolidated their positions in the National Union of Mineworkers (NUM) in Scotland and Wales. They had a strong following in the Amalgamated Engineering Union (AEU) and among the London dockers. They had gained some influence among the Draughtsmen, the Scientific Workers, the Clerical and Administrative Workers, and the lower grades of the non-manual civil service. A Communist had been elected General Secretary of the Fire Brigades Union in 1939, another was elected National Secretary of the Foundry Workers. In the Electrical Trades Union, their men had clawed their way into the posts of President and Secretary. Even in the Transport and General Workers' Union (TGWU), Bert Papworth, the Communist busmen's leader, had been elected in 1944 as one of its two representatives on the Trades Union Congress (TUC) General Council. The Communists had warmly welcomed the Labour government in 1945. And even after a year of Attlee in Downing Street they remained enthusiastic.[31] Yet with the coming of the Cold War the Communist line changed. In August 1947, CPGB Secretary, Harry Pollitt, argued in the *Communist Review*, 'There is nothing in common with socialism in what the Labour Government is doing'. In this situation 'important changes in the policy of the Communist Party . . . should be made'. There could be little room for doubt: the Communists were going over to the offensive against the Labour government.

In its campaign against the Attlee government the CPGB found any amount of combustible material. There were immediate issues which it could take up, not as matters of ideological dispute, but as practical, bread-and-butter issues. The White Paper on Wages and Personal Incomes (February 1948) was the principal one. It was the first of many attempts by post-war governments at an incomes policy. It related personal incomes to increases in the volume of productivity, emphasizing the need to export to allow Britain to pay its way in the world. It was accepted by the General Council of the TUC and by the bulk of the Parliamentary Labour Party (PLP). Phil Piratin, the Communist MP, called it 'an attack on the working class'. Another, literally bread-and-butter, issue was the government's problem in maintaining the rations. At the end of the war the country had expected a steady expansion of the food supply leading to an early ending of rationing. Through no fault of the government, this did not happen. In fact, some rations went down. In November 1948 the bacon ration went down from 2 ozs per week to 2 ozs per fortnight. In 1949 the average consumption of many basic items of food was still lower than it had been in 1939.[32] Both Communists and Conservatives attacked this state of affairs. For the Communists, the most effective vehicle for their attack was the trade union movement.

In the tough economic and international situation, the Labour leaders decided to act to neutralize the Communist influence. Any form of co-operation between individual members of the Labour Party and Communists was prohibited. A purge of the civil service was carried through and the TUC was asked to expose Communists in its member unions. In the Labour Party itself the leadership expelled several Labour MPs who had consistently supported the Communist line. Many other MPs who had opposed government policies, and who continued to do so, were not affected. Further, a whole series of Communist-dominated 'front' organizations were proscribed for Labour Party members.

The move against Communists in the civil service came in March 1948. Attlee announced that it had been decided that no one known to be a member of the Communist Party, or associated with it 'in such a way as to raise legitimate doubts about his or her reliability', would be employed on work 'vital to the security of the State'.[33] To mollify opinion among his own back-benchers, he said the same rule was being applied to fascists. This did not convince the 43 Labour MPs who put down a resolution regretting the statement. But other MPs rallied to the Prime Minister and 31 Labour

MPs put their names to a resolution congratulating him. The Co-operative Party and the TUC approved the government's action.

Distasteful though many in the Labour Party thought the purge was, they also felt it was necessary. It came within a month of the Communist *coup* in Prague which destroyed democracy in Czechoslovakia. Consciences were eased a little in 1950 when it was announced that the atomic scientist Klaus Fuchs had confessed to supplying nuclear secrets to the Soviet Union. The case of the two defecting diplomats, Burgess and Maclean, in 1951, further strengthened the case for the purge.

The trade unions were far more difficult to police than the civil service. Many members who did not agree with communism believed that once a purge started, it would not stop at Communists but would be directed against anyone considered militant or even just a nuisance to the leadership. Communists, they believed, should be dealt with by the normal democratic machinery, defeated at elections and disciplined if they sought to extend their influence by breaking the rules. On the other hand, some officials saw how Communists, usually very small minorities, by concerted and untiring action, got their resolutions passed, their nominees elected and their policies adopted. Such officials, who perhaps had spent all their adult lives building up their unions, felt angry when they observed how the apathy of the majority enabled unrepresentative minorities to push through unrepresentative policies. One such official, Arthur Deakin, General Secretary of the TGWU, in an ill-advised statement urged that Communists be banned.[34] If anything, such statements merely increased sympathy for the Communists as victims of illiberal trade union bosses. But Deakin saw how, occasionally, having got control of a union, the Communists would stop at nothing to keep control. Such was the case in the Electrical Trades Union.

The outbreak of the Korean War in 1950, discussed in the next chapter, increased the fear of Communists in the unions, who, it was thought, might seek to interfere with defence supplies or even resort to sabotage. G. A. Isaacs, himself a former printing union leader, warned the Commons about this possible threat. In fact, the fears were greatly exaggerated. Most of the ordinary Communists were basically law-abiding citizens who would never have got involved in sabotage. In any case, their influence was very limited. At a time when the Communists were either hostile to strike action, during the war, or still officially reluctant to endorse it, up to 1948, there were many more workers on strike than later, when the Communists were dedicated to militancy. The incidence of strikes would seem to have nothing to do with Communist influence.[35]

RAF: 'INCITEMENT TO MUTINY'

Opposition to Attlee's colonial policies within the armed forces gave the Establishment a shock, but it erupted at a time when the Communists still

Table 2.2 Workers directly involved in strikes in all industries and services, 1944–53

Year	Workers	Year	Workers
1944	716,000	1949	313,000
1945	447,000	1950	269,000
1946	405,000	1951	336,000
1947	489,000	1952	303,000
1948	324,000	1953	1,329,000

endorsed his government and it was as much about dissatisfaction with service conditions and the pace of demobilization as it was about political issues. Nevertheless, there was resentment among some servicemen who were compelled to implement Attlee's colonial policies although they felt repelled by them. Veterans of the RAF's largest 'mutiny', which took place in 1946, claim that the men resented being made tools of imperialism. Speaking about their experiences in 1996, they said this was certainly a factor in the strikes which spread across RAF bases in India, Ceylon (Sri Lanka), Singapore and elsewhere in the Far East. Over 50,000 airmen refused to obey orders and were threatened with the firing squad if they did not return to duty. As the firing squad had been widely used in the 1914–18 war, they had to take the threat seriously.[36] The men were also angry about their poor living conditions and the slow pace of demobilization. In contrast, their officers lived in luxurious conditions. Norris Cymbalist, a Jewish Londoner and Communist, who had volunteered for service in the RAF, was sentenced to 10 years' imprisonment. Arthur Attwood, also one of a small number of Communists in the RAF, was accused of being a protest leader. He was found not guilty of 'incitement to mutiny', but the RAF top brass were not satisfied with the verdict and he was re-arrested. There had been strikes in the army at the end of the First World War, and there had been the 'mutiny' of the Fleet at Invergordon in 1931,[37] but these had been about demobilization, in the first case, and about pay cuts in the second. The RAF strikes looked ominously political. On 27 February, the Conservative MP, Wing-Commander N. J. Hulbert, wanted an assurance from the government 'that these Communist agitators who have brought disgrace' to the RAF 'will be severely dealt with'. Although most of the media followed the Air Ministry line of saying nothing about the strikes, in Parliament Tom Driberg, Emrys Hughes and W. Griffiths (Labour), Phil Piratin (Communist) and J. McGovern (ILP) challenged the government over the treatment of Cymbalist and others. Calling the sentence 'savage', McGovern claimed to have received more letters on this case than on any during the war.[38] Outside Parliament a vigorous campaign was waged on behalf of those sentenced. Attwood was released and Cymbalist served 'only' 22 months of his sentence.[39]

The strikes brought attention to the question of civil liberties and the responsibility of ministers. The RAF HQ 232 Group issued an order (Ref. 232G/2929/2/P.1) on 17 December 1945 warning airmen that they were not allowed 'directly or indirectly' to communicate with an MP to obtain redress of grievances. John Strachey, the Under-Secretary of State for Air, repudiated this order, calling it, on 20 February 1946, 'a foolish mistake'. Clearly, in the higher reaches of the RAF there were those who did not believe in civil rights for their subordinates. What about the ministers involved? How much control did they exercise over developments? Strachey, an old Etonian, was a former Communist intellectual, who had served in the information department of the RAF with the rank of wing-commander.[40] Yet he seemed not to be in control of events. His superior minister was Viscount Stansgate; a veteran of the Royal Flying Corps, he too had been in the Second World War RAF and his son had been killed serving in the RAF. Attlee gave him the task of negotiating with the Egyptians, leaving Strachey to carry on in the Commons.[41] Attlee was himself Minister of Defence at the time. Strachey was moved on 27 May 1946 to the Ministry of Food. Stansgate gave up in October 1946.

Other mutinies followed. Perhaps the most serious was one involving 258 men of the 13th Bn, The Parachute Regiment at Muar Camp near Kuala Lumpur in Malaya. They were arrested on 14 May 1946 after expressing dissatisfaction about their living conditions and refusing to return to their lines. Most of them had fought at D-Day, the Ardennes and the Rhine Crossing. Tried for mutiny in September, eight of them were sentenced to five years' imprisonment with hard labour and 247 received two years. The sentences were later quashed on the grounds of technical irregularities.[42]

CONSERVATIVES GET 'BEST SALESMAN'

The Conservative Party reacted to its defeat in 1945 with a mixture of arrogance and courage. The arrogance came naturally to a party which considered only itself to be fit to rule, a party that had suffered its last decisive defeat in 1906. Having been defeated at a time when the Left was surging forward throughout Europe, it needed some courage to believe there was any major role for the party in the future. Not surprisingly, thought was given to the idea of changing the name and broadening it out into an alliance of non-socialists.

The Conservative Party did not succeed in becoming a broad coalition of non-socialists, but it did succeed in attracting some popular figures who had not previously been too closely associated with it. Most important of them was Lord Woolton, who had shown his skills as Minister of Food during the war. Macmillan called him 'the best salesman that I have ever known'.[43] Churchill made him party chairman, with the job of modernizing the organization. Another popular figure was Dr Charles Hill, who had become well known through his broadcasts as the 'radio doctor'. Hill and some of the younger recruits could have been at home in the Labour Party. Iain Macleod and Edward Heath were among them, and even Macmillan had considered joining Labour at an earlier period.

Woolton got the Conservatives to agree to put the constituency agency service on a more professional basis, with great improvements in the standing and remuneration of agents. Certainly, under Woolton's guidance, they were able to build up far better constituency organizations than Labour, an advantage they have retained up to the 1990s. Woolton also played a major role in building up the Young Conservatives. The YCs, as much a social as a political movement, probably did help to orientate young people towards the Conservatives in the 1950s. Another major initiative of Woolton's was his attempt to make Conservative representation in the Commons more 'democratic'. Until the Woolton reform, those able to pay the most towards the upkeep of the constituency they sought to represent were most likely to be selected as candidates, especially in safe seats. This restricted the choice to about 'half a per cent of the population', Woolton claimed. If the Conservatives continued in this way, they deserved to be beaten.[44] The Party therefore agreed that 'In no circumstances shall the question of annual subscription be mentioned by any constituency selection committee to any candidate before he has been selected'. Candidates could, however, contribute up to £25 per annum to their constituency association, MPs up to £50. Though it was certainly a move in the direction of modernization, it is doubtful whether this change has had quite the impact which was expected at the time. It is even more doubtful whether it played any part in the Conservative revival. Few of the Conservative candidates who fought the 1950 election were chosen after the recommendations of the Maxwell-Fyfe Report, of which this was a part, came into effect. The Report admitted, there was a tendency to select 'obscure local citizens with obscure local interests, incapable – and indeed downright reluctant – to think on a national or international scale'.[45]

During this period the Conservative Party refurbished its policies, committing itself formally to the mixed economy and the welfare state. The focal point of this revised policy was the *Industrial Charter* announced by R. A. Butler in May 1947. An *Agricultural Charter* followed, as well as policy documents on Wales and Scotland, Imperial policy, and women. Butler, who had been given the task of recasting policy by Churchill, later wrote that his aim was to give the party 'a painless but permanent facelift'.[46] If he did, it was more an operation to remove a few warts than cranial-facial surgery. Butler himself admitted the Charter was '"broad" rather than detailed, vague where it might have been specific', because Churchill did not want to be bound too much in opposition. It was also, he admitted, written with 'flatness of language' and 'blandness of tone'.[47] It is doubtful whether it took the Conservatives very far along the road to electoral victory.

ELECTION 1950: 'REAL DETESTATION OF . . . LABOUR'

In the election of 1950 Labour seems to have been adversely affected by a number of factors which had nothing to do with changes in the Conservative Party. Boundary revisions probably lost Labour between 25 and 30 seats.[48] The Conservatives were undoubtedly the main beneficiaries of the new postal-vote facility, which probably gained them a further 10 seats.[49] With these 10 seats Labour would have had a viable majority and could have looked forward to a four-year Parliament, at the end of which the world would be far more favourable to the party in government. On the other hand, the Conservatives lost several seats due to the abolition of university seats. On a higher poll than in 1945, Labour gained 13.2 million votes, the Conservatives 12.5 million, and the Liberals 2.6 million. Overall, Labour was reduced to a majority of six seats. Labour had retained, even extended, its working-class support, but there had been a hardening of middle-class opposition to Labour. As one Conservative writer has explained, there was a markedly bigger pro-Tory swing in the suburban areas.

> It is clear that long before 1950 there had grown up in that class a real detestation of . . . Labour . . . these years can be seen in retrospect as a sort of twilight period between the era of cheap servants and the era of cheap washing machines. The effect of the disappearance of servants constituted a revolution in the middle class way of life far more drastic than anything that followed the First World War; the effects were felt more acutely at this time than later when prosperity returned, labour-saving devices became the norm and people had recognized the need to adjust themselves to a change which, they now saw, would never be reversed. However, illogically, this state of affairs greatly conduced to middle class disenchantment with Labour.[50]

NOTES

Unless otherwise indicated, the place of publication is London.

1 Clive Ponting, *Churchill* (1994), 501.
2 ibid., 505.
3 ibid., 501.
4 ibid., 509.
5 ibid., 510.
6 Peter L. Hahn, in F. M. Leventhal (ed.), *Twentieth-century Britain: An Encyclopedia* (New York, 1995), 453.
7 Hugh Dalton, *High Tide and After: Memoirs 1945–1960* (1962), 70.
8 John Kenneth Galbraith, *The World Economy since the Wars* (1994), 157–8.

9 Charles E. Silberman, *A Certain People: American Jews and Their Lives Today* (New York, 1985), 57. Hostility to the Jews, according to opinion polls, actually increased between 1940 and 1944.

10 About 120,000 Japanese, many US citizens, were interned in 1942. Their racial ancestry was the sole reason for their internment. Many young Japanese-Americans fought in the US forces in the war. See Gerald D. Nash, *The Great Depression and World War II: Organising America, 1933–1945* (New York, 1979), 156–7. See also Roger Daniels, *Concentration Camps USA* (New York, 1971).

11 In 1950, 52 per cent of Americans were of British origin, 21 per cent of German origin, 16 per cent African, 14 per cent Irish and 7 per cent Italian. Daniel Snowman, *The USA: The Twenties to Vietnam* (1968), 179.

12 G. D. N. Worswick and P. H. Ady, *The British Economy 1945–1950* (1952), 32.

13 John Strachey, *Why You Should Be a Socialist* (1944), 66.

14 Rt Hon. C.R. Attlee, MP, *The Labour Party in Perspective* (1937).

15 Quintin Hogg, *The Case for Conservatism* (1947), 113.

16 E. Eldon Barry, *Nationalisation in British Politics* (1965), 85.

17 Hogg, op. cit., 112.

18 *Hansard*, vol. 418, col. 752.

19 ibid.

20 *Illustrated*, 25 January 1947.

21 As advertised in *Illustrated*, 23 August 1947.

22 *Hansard*, vol. 422, col. 130.

23 Angus Calder, *The People's War: Britain 1939–45* (1969), 531.

24 J. D. Hoffman, *The Conservative Party in Opposition, 1945–51* (1964), 46.

25 ibid., 235.

26 Arthur Marwick, *Britain in the Century of Total War* (1968), 172.

27 Letter to the author.

28 Marwick, op. cit., 357.

29 The Hansard Society, *Parliamentary Reform 1933–1960* (1961), 5–6.

30 Irving Richter, *Political Purpose in Trade Unions* (1973), 246.

31 See review by William Gallacher in *Labour Monthly*, August 1946.

32 These figures are taken from *All the Answers* (Conservative Research Department, 1949), 39.

33 *Hansard*, vol. 448, col. 1703.

34 *The Economist*, 23 September 1950, 502.

35 Department of Employment and Productivity, *British Labour Statistics: Historical Abstract 1886–1968* (HMSO, 1971), 396, Table 197.

36 Julian Putkowski and Julian Sykes, *Shot at Dawn: Executions in World War I by Authority of the British Army Act* (Barnsley, 1989), discuss this and believe in 312 cases the victims should be exonerated.

37 See Alan Ereira, *The Invergordon Mutiny* (1981).

38 House of Commons, 29 March 1946.

39 *Observer*, 4 August 1996. The strikes were discussed in great detail in Channel 4's *Secret History* programme, 'The strikes in the RAF', on 8 August. In a half-hearted attempt to justify the sentence on Cymbalist, Strachey reported to the Commons (15 May 1946) that he had been convicted in January 1943 of stealing £24 from a fellow airman. In 1944 he had been convicted of 'using insubordinate language to a superior officer'.

40 Strachey had written *The Coming Struggle for Power* (1932), regarded as the definitive Marxist analysis in English at the time.

41 I am grateful to Tony Benn for reminding me of this fact. Stansgate was his father.

42 Trevor Royle, *The Best Years of their Lives: The National Service Experience 1945–63* (1988), 25–6.
43 Harold Macmillan, *Tides of Fortune, 1945–1955* (1969), 292.
44 ibid., 294.
45 ibid., 296.
46 Lord Butler, *The Art of the Possible: The Memoirs of Lord Butler* (1971), 145–6.
47 ibid., 145.
48 H. G. Nicholas, *The British General Election of 1950* (1951), 4.
49 ibid., 9.
50 Robert Blake, *The Conservatives from Peel to Churchill* (1970), 263–4.

3

COLONIAL RETREAT AND COLD WAR

PAUL ROBESON CONGRATULATES

When he heard the results of the British general election Paul Robeson sent Clement Attlee his congratulations. Robeson, a Black American actor and singer, was well known to British cinema and theatre audiences. He saw Labour's victory as a defeat for imperialism. He was soon disappointed.[1]

Robeson was just one of many who felt let down by Attlee's overseas policies, including many in the Labour Party. Some thought Hong Kong should be returned to China, Britain's wartime ally, immediately (and not in 1997). Many were shocked that British troops were being used, in some cases in co-operation with the defeated Japanese, to restore the Dutch and French colonial empires in Java (Indonesia) and Indo-China (Vietnam) respectively.[2] They fought native resistance groups built up with Allied help to fight against the Japanese occupiers.

There was also the problem of what to do with the followers of the Indian nationalist Subhas Chandra Bose. Despairing of British promises about the future of India, he had thrown in his lot with the Japanese and, with their help, formed the Indian National Army (INA). Most of its members were prisoners-of-war, some of whom had been forced to join, others who had volunteered. Bose himself died in an air crash, but many of his soldiers fell into British hands in 1945. In November 1945 three INA officers were sentenced to death in Delhi. Their sentences were subsequently commuted to 'rigorous imprisonment'. Protests against the sentences led to violence in Calcutta, Bombay and Delhi. Within three months 11,000 INA soldiers were released from internment and sent home. They were greeted as heroes.[3]

INDIAN INDEPENDENCE: 'STRUCK ME . . . WITH A RIDING WHIP'

Shortly after the strikes in the RAF (see Chapter 2) there followed similar developments in the Indian air force and navy. In February 1946 a naval mutiny occurred in Bombay and was followed by others in Calcutta,

Madras and Karachi.[4] As soon as one fire was put out another started somewhere else.

It was clear that Britain could not maintain its world-wide Empire, especially if the local population was opposed to it. In the case of India, there was a growing cross-party agreement that Britain would have to relinquish power, it was only a question of how and when. Britain had made vague promises of independence within the Empire in the First World War. These did not satisfy nationalist opinion and, in the interwar period, tension erupted in India on many occasions. India was perhaps the central issue of parliamentary life for six years between 1929 and 1935.[5] Eventually, the Government of India Act, 1935 was passed against the opposition of Churchill and other extreme imperialists. The Act set up a complicated system of federal states dependent on Britain for defence and with emergency powers in the hands of British governors.[6] The Act did not satisfy Indian aspirations and was in any case set in abeyance during the Second World War. Wartime negotiations with India's main political party, Congress, had failed, resulting in the internment of its leaders and much violence and repression. It was obvious that a speedy settlement was needed to avoid civil war conditions.

Labour had stood for Indian independence in opposition and was ready to implement it but the question was 'how?'. Churchill had opposed independence before and during the war, but by 1946 realized it could not be stopped. He and the Conservatives 'stood for a weak and divided India still dependent on Britain'.[7] He had secret lines of communication with the Muslim League leader Mohammed Ali Jinnah, whom he encouraged in his aim of a separate state, Pakistan.[8] He also encouraged the princely states to break free from India. Attlee and his colleagues favoured a united India if possible, but were not prepared to use force in this direction. Attlee dispatched a mission to India to attempt to find a solution. Led by Lord Pethick-Lawrence, it included Cripps and A. V. Alexander, First Lord of the Admiralty. Pethick-Lawrence had first visited India in 1897 and had met the Indian leader Gandhi before 1914. Like Gandhi and other Indian leaders, he had seen the inside of a British prison. He had been jailed in the First World War for being a conscientious objector. Cripps had led a wartime mission to attempt to placate the Indians, but this had been sabotaged by Churchill, who sent him. The mission advocated a united, federal state. In the face of Jinnah's opposition to a united India, Pethick-Lawrence could achieve little. Attlee therefore appointed Admiral Lord Louis Mountbatten, who had served as Supreme Commander of Allied Forces in South East Asia, as the last Viceroy. He was known to sympathize with the aspirations of the Asian peoples for independence. His job was to lead India to independence. Attlee gave him *carte blanche*, including the definite date for British withdrawal, not later than June 1948. It was hoped that, if the Indians were clear that the British were

29

going, they would work harder to achieve a settlement among themselves. This did not happen. India was partitioned into an Indian state and Pakistan. The provincial assemblies were to decide to which state they wished to join. Hyderabad and Junagadh, with Muslim majorities, were invaded and forced to join India.[9] The official transfer of power took place on 15 August 1947 and the last British troops left on 13 February 1948.

Bloodshed erupted as Hindus migrated to India from Pakistan, and Muslims left in the opposite direction. In Kashmir there was fighting before that state decided to opt for India. And in the Punjab there was widespread violence between Muslims, Hindus and Sikhs. Gandhi announced he would fast until the violence ended. It appears that, because of his prestige, his action did cause many to relent.[10]

The British withdrawal from its Indian Empire, which included India, Pakistan, Ceylon (Sri Lanka) and Burma, has been much debated. The fact is Attlee and his colleagues were realists and many of them had long been convinced India should be free to decide its own destiny. Had Churchill been in government, Britain could well have been embroiled in a massive colonial war, as were the French in Indo-China and the Dutch in Indonesia. Churchill's attitude is demonstrated by the fact that he would not shake hands with Mountbatten for years, and said to him, 'What you did in India is as though you had struck me across the face with a riding whip.'[11]

PALESTINE: 'ARABS . . . ENCOURAGED TO MOVE OUT'

Of all the controversies over external affairs Palestine was the one which caused the Attlee government the most bitter recriminations from its own supporters. Alas, it remains of great present-day significance. For this reason a little more space has been allocated to it here.

As part of the doomed Turkish Empire, Palestine fell under British military occupation at the end of the First World War. The bulk of the inhabitants were Arabs. The Jews had lost their pre-eminence there with the final destruction of Jerusalem in AD 135. Britain's official interest in Palestine started with the Balfour Declaration of November 1917. It pledged the British government would use its 'best endeavours' to facilitate the establishment of a 'national home for the Jewish people'. It stressed, however, that 'nothing shall be done which may prejudice the civil and religious rights of existing non-Jewish communities in Palestine'. Finally, it stressed that the existing rights enjoyed by Jews in any other country would not be prejudiced by the establishment of a Jewish home in Palestine.[12] By 1923 the League of Nations had approved both the Declaration and the British occupation. Throughout the interwar period the Zionists[13] sought to realize the promise of the Declaration and eventually create a Jewish state. British policy, between the wars, was never entirely clear. The government knew from the start that the Palestinian Arabs opposed Jewish immigration, and they demonstrated that opposition in civil disorders throughout these years.[14] With a full-scale Arab revolt on its hands, and war approaching, the British government decided to impose a solution. This was set out in the White Paper of May 1939. It called for a two-stage, ten-year, transitional period, leading to independence. Jewish immigration would be allowed until the Jews made up one-third of the population. After that, it could only take place 'if the Arabs are prepared to acquiesce in it'.[15] In short, Palestine was to become a democratic state, with power-sharing between the Arab majority and the Jewish minority, and was to be linked to Britain by treaty. In the Commons the majority of the Labour Party attacked the new policy, Morrison was joined by Churchill, still out of office, in the onslaught on Malcolm MacDonald, Secretary of State for the Colonies. MacDonald, the son of Ramsay, paid tribute to the Jewish settlers, 'they have turned the desert into spacious orange groves', but reminded his critics that the Arabs too had rights, they 'had been in undisturbed occupation of the country for countless generations'.[16]

In 1940 the annual conference of the Labour Party passed a resolution favourable to Zionism, but Labour participation in government circumscribed the debate during the war years to some extent. A Cabinet sub-committee chaired by Morrison decided the partition of Palestine would be the best solution.[17] Meanwhile, Dalton's thoughts, slightly amended, became Labour policy, as agreed at the annual conference in December 1944. Representations by the Palestine Workers' Society appeared to have been completely ignored.[18] The Labour resolution called for allowing Jews into

> this tiny land in such numbers as to become a majority. There was a strong case for this before the war. There is an irresistible case now, after the unspeakable atrocities of the cold and calculated German Nazi plan to kill all the Jews in Europe . . . Let the Arabs be encouraged to move out as the Jews move in. Let them be handsomely compensated for their land and let their settlement elsewhere be carefully organised and generously financed. The Arabs have very wide territories of their own; they must not claim to exclude the Jews from this small part of Palestine, less than the size of Wales. Indeed, we should examine also the possibility of extending the boundaries by agreement with Egypt, Syria and Transjordan. Moreover, we should seek to win the full sympathy and support both of the American and Russian Governments for the execution of this Palestine policy.[19]

Before Attlee had settled properly in Downing Street he felt the pressure from Zionism's most powerful friend. At the end of August 1945 President Truman wrote to him asking that 100,000 Jewish displaced persons be admitted to Palestine immediately. Both because of the practical difficulties involved, and because of the likely reaction of the Arabs, Attlee was not very enthusiastic. Attlee was prepared for Britain to withdraw from the Middle East, but the government's military advisers, led by Lord Tedder, Chief of the Air Staff, believed Britain's vital defence needs dictated that Britain be able to station forces in Palestine. This meant Britain remaining there.[20] After discussions with both Zionist and Arab representatives, Bevin announced on 13 November that an Anglo-American Commission of Inquiry would consider the Palestine question. Meanwhile, in Palestine itself violence had broken out. In November 1944, Lord Moyne, British Minister-Resident in Cairo, was murdered by Zionist extremists, an act condemned by Dr Chaim Weizmann, President of the Zionist Organization, and most other Jewish leaders. By 1945 the main Jewish fighting forces in Palestine were embarking on a campaign of rail sabotage and attacks on military installations. In the Arab states demonstrations turned into riots, as the fury against Zionism mounted on 2–3 November 1945. Nearer home, Bevin faced criticism from the Board of Deputies of British Jews and, remarkably, on 19 November the Jewish Brigade of the British Army of the Rhine went on hunger strike in protest against Bevin's statement.[21]

The Anglo-American Commission published its report in May 1946. Predictably, it satisfied neither side. Basically, it called for a continuation of the mandate regime 'until the hostility between the Jews and the Arabs disappears'. It recommended the admission of 100,000 Jewish victims of persecution, some easing of the restrictions on Jewish land purchase, and the suppression of violence. It did, however, talk about 'ensuring that the rights and position of other sections of the population were not prejudiced'. While the British government was considering the implications of the report, the British forces were subjected to renewed violence from the Zionists. On 1 July, Attlee announced, with regret, the arrest of some leading members of the Jewish Agency, the governing body of the Jewish community in Palestine. Attlee claimed those arrested were connected with Hagana, the Jewish underground army, and that this body had been involved in violence, which it had. The premier stressed that the security operations were not against the Jewish community as a whole. In the Commons Attlee came under fire from his own back-benchers led by Barnet Janner, President of the British Zionists, and Sydney Silverman, and the non-Jews, Richard Crossman, Michael Foot and Konni Zilliacus.

Even in a world used to violence, the blowing-up of the King David Hotel on 22 July 1946 caused genuine shock and anger. The hotel housed the British military HQ, but it still carried on the civilian functions for which it was built as well. The explosion, which was the work of the Jewish group Irgun Zvi Leumi, claimed about 100 deaths. A number of leading British officials were among the dead, and there were also a number of Arab and Jewish victims.[22] The deed was condemned by the Jewish Palestinian press and by Jewish leaders, but it inevitably led to a worsening of relations between the Jews and the security forces. During the next 23 or so months there followed what one Jewish writer called a 'deadly round-dance of terror raids, assassinations and blind reprisals'.[23]

After the Morrison Plan (31 July 1946), which advocated a federal Palestine, failed to take off, the British government started to consider returning its mandate to the United Nations. On 14 February 1947 Bevin announced that Britain would submit the problem to the UN. A special UN committee of small- and medium-sized states then investigated and on 31 August 1947 issued a minority report, which roughly corresponded to the Anglo-US federal plan, and a majority report, which called for partition. The majority report recommended the setting up of separate Jewish and Arab states. But it would have left 500,000 Arabs within the Jewish state, deprived the Arabs of their only port, Jaffa, failed to provide them with compensation, and put the Arab state under the economic domination of its Jewish neighbour. As this plan was not endorsed by the two parties in the dispute, Britain was not prepared to implement it, and announced its intention to withdraw. The General Assembly of the UN endorsed the partition plan by a vote of 33 to 13, with 10 abstentions, on 29 November 1947. The majority included the United States and the Soviet Union. The Islamic states and India, Cuba and Greece voted against. Britain, China, Mexico and Yugoslavia were among those abstaining. The vote was, at least in part, the result of pressure by the United States on its clients.[24]

Throughout this period Palestine suffered from mounting violence, except, that is, for the brief interval of the 22nd World Zionist Congress (December/January 1946/47). There were several angry confrontations between Labour MPs and their leaders. Harold Lever, Jewish MP for Manchester Exchange and future Cabinet member, charged, on 12 August 1947, that government policy represented 'two years of planless, gutless and witless behaviour'. He described British rule as 'this military dictatorship . . . this police State, this State of the flogging block and the gallows'.[25] This view was challenged by, among others, Tufton Beamish (Conservative), who had served as a regular in pre-war Palestine. In 1938 and 1939 a total of 109 Arabs had, after being sentenced by the British, 'paid the extreme penalty'. In 1939, 5,700 Arabs were in detention. Arab casualties had been as 'high as 4,000' in these years.

> But yet the terrorist activities of the Arabs in those years were never on such a large scale as are the Jewish activities today. These figures provide an extraordinary contrast with the total of only seven Jews who have paid the extreme penalty for their terrorist activities during the last 18 months. I feel we are entitled to know the reason for this contrast.[26]

The Labour MP for Wednesbury, Stanley Evans, expressed the fear that the King David Hotel bombing could lead to repercussions at King's Cross.[27] It took another year of terrorist activities before this happened. As a reprisal for the execution of three Jewish terrorists, two British sergeants were kidnapped and then hanged in a eucalyptus grove on 29 July 1947. One of the bodies was booby-trapped. In Britain during the weekend of 1–2 August and on subsequent days, there were outbreaks of unorganized rioting in Liverpool and Manchester. Incidents, mainly the smashing of the windows of shops owned by Jews, occurred in different parts of London and Cardiff, Eccles, Halifax, Glasgow and some other places.[28] Although very worrying at the time, this tide of spontaneous violence disappeared almost as suddenly as it had erupted.

The biggest, and final, revolt of Labour MPs against their government's Palestine policy took place in March 1948. This was over the Palestine Bill which sought to tie up the loose ends of the British withdrawal. The debate on the second reading gave the government's critics a chance to have a final go on the issue. They claimed the government was running away, failing to keep its electoral pledges, frustrating the work of the UN and condoning Arab threats of violence. One Labour loyalist, Tom Reid from Swindon, a member of the earlier Palestine Partition Commission, summed up the situation rather differently. He believed the UN solution would lead to 'war which will last 10, 20 or 50 years. The Arabs will not submit so long as their sovereignty is to be taken away from them.' He wanted a Palestinian state.[29] When the Commons was divided by the Labour rebels, they were defeated by 242 votes to 32 (including the tellers). Among the rebels were Sydney and Julius Silverman, Harold Lever, Barnet Janner, Maurice Edelman, Ian Mikardo, Benn Levy, and some other Jewish MPs, including the Communist, Phil Piratin. Other Jewish MPs backed the government. Among the other rebels were John Platts-Mills, D. N. Pritt, William Warbey and Konni Zilliacus. The vote did not fully reflect the unease on the Labour benches. Among the ministers who had doubts were Bevan, Creech Jones, Dalton, Shinwell, Strachey, George Strauss and Tom Williams.[30] The vote was a miserable end to a sad episode.

The Palestine emergency had cost the lives of 338 British subjects since 1945, and the taxpayer had been forced to find £100 million to finance it. Over 80,000 British troops, one-tenth of the total at that time, had been used to police the territory.

The Labour leaders had found themselves in a dilemma, torn between the need for British friendship with the Arabs and their own friendship with the Jews. Attlee himself probably had strong reservations about Labour's pro-Zionist stance before 1945, but had sought, by silence, to avoid a clash with such powerful pro-Zionist colleagues as Dalton and Morrison. For many non-Jewish Labour intellectuals, the Jews were a special breed who had made a massive contribution to humanity. They were the victims of the hated Tsar and the detested Führer. Moreover, the Jews were often comrades. The Labour government, by 'betraying' the Jews, was betraying itself, probably as a result of 'advice' from reactionary Foreign Office officials.[31] It was a process which had started with Greece in 1944 (see p. 39), about which the leaders had done nothing. As for the Arabs, British socialists of this type regarded them as the hoodwinked dupes of reactionary rulers, and saw them as being in a similar position to British working-class Tories. They were the reserve army of reaction and it was no wonder that they found supporters on the Conservative side. The Jews were the apostles of the new, the modern, of 'progress', and, therefore, as Dalton put it, 'we should lean . . . towards the dynamic Jew, less towards the static Arab'.[32]

The weakness of the pro-Zionist position was precisely that it either treated the Arabs with contempt or simply ignored them. The weakness of the pro-Arabs was that they did not recognize that a new nation had grown up in the womb of the mandate territory. And, because of its pride and its experience, this nation was not prepared to put its security in the hands of its traditionalist neighbours with vastly different standards from its own.

COLONIES: 'UNDER THE GUIDANCE OF THE MOTHER COUNTRY'

During the war Labour had promised the colonies that, should Labour take office, they would experience 'a period of unprecedented development and progress under the guidance of the Mother Country'.[33] Once in office, the ministers were to find the situation far more complicated than they had anticipated. Firstly, the financial resources necessary for this 'unprecedented development' were not available. Secondly, difficult choices had to be made. Should limited funds be channelled into the colonies according to the needs of the inhabitants, or should they go into those colonies where they were most likely to bring a return for Britain in terms of higher living standards and dollar exports? As it was, 'Decision-making on colonial economic policy suffered, as always, from constraints imposed by the Treasury, which had to honour commitments to the USA and to Britain's Commonwealth partners.'[34] This need to stimulate exports from the colonies certainly influenced government thinking on nationalization of Tate and Lyle sugar interests in Jamaica and United Africa Company mining interests in Rhodesia; 'it appeared wiser not to disturb entrepreneurs British or American'.[35] Nevertheless, British money did get to the colonies. The Colonial Development and Welfare Act, 1945 provided some of the means – £125 million to be spent over 10 years. In addition, two new corporations were established to develop agricultural and other projects: the Colonial Development Corporation with borrowing powers of £100 million and the Overseas Food Corporation with initial borrowing powers of £50 million. Further legislation in 1949 and 1950 approved an increase in the funds available. Over £30 million were wasted on the Tanganyika groundnuts scheme. The scheme, which originated with the United Africa Company, a subsidiary of Unilever, was based on inadequate analysis of soil and rainfall. Strachey, Minister of Food, who was ultimately responsible, was mercilessly attacked by the press and the Opposition. But, as his biographer, Hugh Thomas, has reminded us, the loss 'of public money on a scheme which attempted to alleviate the world food shortage is admittedly less of a catastrophe than the loss of many more millions on military projects or upon expensive aircraft such as has occurred since that time'.[36]

Labour's colonial experts put economic development ahead of political progress in their priorities. Economic advance would lead the way to greater political maturity in the future. As it turned out, they underestimated the development of political consciousness among the Africans. Serious disturbances took place in the Gold Coast (Ghana) in 1948. There was discontent among cocoa farmers over the low price they received for their products, and among ex-servicemen over poor pensions. When the police fired on a peaceful ex-servicemen's demonstration, riots broke out. After two commissions of inquiry a new constitution was introduced in 1950, 'a system well on the way to responsible government'.[37] Elections under the new constitution were won by Kwame Nkrumah's Convention People's Party, Nkrumah graduating from jail to become Prime Minister in 1952.

There was also a good deal of political activity in central Africa – Northern Rhodesia (Zambia), Southern Rhodesia and Nyasaland (Malawi). The war had brought about the awakening of African political consciousness in these territories. African National Congresses were formed in Nyasaland in 1943 and in Northern Rhodesia in 1948. With the help of British trade unionists, the Northern Rhodesian African Mineworkers' Union was set up in the same year. These developments were seen as a threat, as indeed they were, to white supremacy in both Northern and Southern Rhodesia. Most of the white political leaders now sought to retain their supremacy by means of a Central African Federation, a project about which many harboured doubts. With the victory of the Afrikaner nationalists in South Africa in 1948, the English-speaking whites felt that federation was the only alternative to either eventual domination by the Blacks or by the South Africans. To the Black Africans, their freedom seemed to depend on maintaining Colonial Office control until they were ready to govern themselves. They saw federation as exchanging control by London for control by the white settlers. If the three territories were united, it would be Southern Rhodesia that would play the most influential role. There were nearly two and a half times as many white settlers in Southern Rhodesia as in the other two areas put together. The Blacks feared that the racial policies pursued in Southern Rhodesia since it attained self-government in 1923 would be extended to the other two territories. Creech Jones believed this too, and during his term of office he played his part in resisting settler pressure.[38]

WAR IN MALAYA

Another area which caused the Labour government a headache was Malaya. It was important as a producer of tin and rubber, an important dollar-earner which had come under British control between 1874 and 1910. Singapore, at its southern tip, was still regarded as a vital naval base. But Malaya had its problems. It was an ethnic melting pot. Less than half its population were Malay. The Chinese, who dominated the commercial life of the country, actually outnumbered the Malays in 1947. In addition, there were considerable numbers from India and Pakistan, as well as Indonesians and Aborigines.[39] Malaya had been ruled by the British indirectly through the native rulers, the sultans, and this arrangement had seemed to work until the Japanese invasion of 1942. The occupation which followed greatly influenced Malaya. The native peoples witnessed the defeat of the British and realized they were not omnipotent. The Japanese encouraged, to a limited extent, Malay nationalism, discriminating against the Chinese. The British promoted resistance and the Malayan People's Anti-Japanese Army was established with their help. It was a mainly Chinese, communist-influenced, force. After the war the British disbanded it, but not before it had settled some old scores against, mainly, Malays accused of collaboration with the Japanese. In general, there was a feeling that there could be no simple going back to the old scheme of things.[40] The new Labour government recognized this and introduced a constitution designed to reduce the sultans to constitutional figureheads, give Malay citizenship to most inhabitants irrespective of racial origin, and prepare the way for eventual self-government. This radical change met with stiff opposition from influential Malays and their allies in London. Malay nationalism was aroused against the Chinese and Indians, and the British were forced to back down. The new Federation of Malaya agreement of 1946 restricted citizenship and restored at least some of the privileges of the sultans. At the head of the government system was a British High Commissioner, Sir Edward Gent, responsible to the Colonial Office in London. The reversal of policy provoked unrest among the Chinese and this, along with the high price of rice, led to civil disturbances. In 1948 armed struggle replaced civil disturbance as the Malayan Communist Party attempted to exploit genuine grievances. As in Burma, the Philippines and Indonesia, it started as part of Moscow's strategy of militancy world-wide,[41] but the guerrilla war which followed tied up considerable numbers of British and native troops and police between 1948 and 1960.[42] The British troops were often national service conscripts. Malaya was, of course, ideal guerrilla country, but the rebels lacked a safe cross-border sanctuary so vital in such campaigns. The British found themselves trapped in an 'anti-insurgency' campaign similar, in some respects, to their earlier campaigns in South Africa, Ireland and Palestine. This involved collective punishments, the forced resettlement of 600,000 Chinese peasants and the abandonment of normal democratic norms. Both Labour and Conservative governments followed a policy of 'ruthlessness where ruthlessness is necessary' coupled with 'equal firmness and vigour in pressing on with economic and political development of the country'.[43] In the end, the defeat of the insurgents was probably due as much to political developments as to military action. Firstly, the rebellion was largely confined to the Chinese community, a fact which set severe limits on its success.[44] Secondly, most of the fighting was over by 1955. This was a period when both the Soviet and Chinese leaders were seeking *détente*, and had therefore ceased supporting armed insurrection. Thirdly, in Malaya itself constitutional advance had led to the election of the Triple Alliance Party of Tunku Abdul Rahman, a party uniting Malays with Chinese and Indians. A Malay of royal descent, Tunku became Chief Minister, and then Prime Minister, of an independent Malaysia in 1957. Tunku pursued a policy of peace by negotiation, amnesty and reconciliation towards the rebels. The emergency was formally ended in 1960.

COLD WAR: 'MAGNATES . . . WHO FINANCED HITLER'

By June 1946, less than a year after Labour's assumption of office, there was open criticism at the annual conference of Bevin's handling of external affairs. There seemed to be a widespread feeling that Bevin was being blinded by reactionary Foreign Office officials. His failure to stem the growing breach with the Soviet Union caused the delegates most concern. The world was far more complex than most of them realized and the developing Cold War was far more the result of great power rivalries than of ideology. In 1945 the world desperately needed statesmen of vision. What it got was Stalin, a little-travelled Georgian dictator whose only foreign language was Russian; Truman, an American President new to the world stage; and Bevin, a trade union boss already suffering from a terminal illness which forced him from office in 1950. All three thought in terms of their respective 'empires' and their needs. Each was influenced by his country's experience of pre-war appeasement, and the determination not to be caught off guard a second time.

In the latter stages of the war the Western powers watched resignedly as Stalin regained most of the outer provinces of the old Tsarist Empire, especially in the Baltic states and Poland. Pressure on neutral Turkey in March 1945 to cede the provinces of Kars and Ardahan, taken by Russia in 1878 and retaken by Turkey in 1918, failed, pushing Turkey into the arms of the United States. Pursuit of old Tsarist aims in northern Iran, taken under Soviet military occupation, also helped lead that country into dependence on the United States. Between the end of 1944 and 1947, Britain and the United States fought a weak, diplomatic rearguard action in Bulgaria, Hungary and Rumania. They protested as these ex-enemy states were reduced, step by step, to the level of Soviet satellites.[45] They were equally helpless when Poland suffered the same fate. Yugoslavia and Albania too appeared to have allowed themselves to be reduced to the level of Soviet dependencies. In this latter case, though, appearances proved to be deceptive.

Apart from certain undercover operations in Albania, only in Greece did Britain, and later America, actively intervene in Eastern Europe. The struggle in Greece appears as a turning-point in the Cold War. Greece was traditionally within the British sphere of influence. Since the end of 1944 Britain had been involved in helping the exiled royalist government of Greece prevent the communist-led, anti-Axis, resistance movement from taking over the country. On 21 February 1947 Britain informed the United States that it was withdrawing financial aid to Greece in five weeks' time. It asked the United States to assume the burden of supporting Greece. Truman responded to the British call, introducing the 'Truman Doctrine', involving, initially, support for Greece and Turkey, and ultimately leading to the Marshall Plan and NATO. If the United States had really been contemplating renewed isolation before February 1947, after that date it became deeply engaged in European affairs once again.[46]

The British withdrawal from Greece was dictated as much by financial as by other considerations, and finance played a major role in shaping British policy in Germany. Before the surrender of Germany the Allies had agreed on the division of the country into four zones of occupation – Soviet (Russian), American, British and French – and on the division of Berlin into four sectors. Germany was to be ruled, for the time being, by a four-power Control Council in Berlin. The Allies were also agreed on the need to eliminate all vestiges of Nazism and militarism, and on the need to give the German people a democratic future. They differed to some extent in their views of Germany's frontiers, in their judgement of what Germany should pay in reparations and, most importantly, in their interpretation of the term 'democracy'. At Potsdam, in July 1945, Britain, the Soviet Union and the United States agreed further on treating Germany as an economic whole, that the Germans should have living standards 'not exceeding the average . . . of Europe' (excluding the Soviet Union and Britain) and that payment of reparations should leave enough resources to enable the Germans to subsist without external assistance. The three powers did not bind themselves to an exact figure on reparations, nor did they reach final agreement on Germany's eastern frontier, which they left for a future peace settlement.

In practice, all pursued policies in their respective zones based on their own economic needs, their experience of the Germans and their own political traditions. The British left many of the old officials, tainted with Nazism, in their posts because, it was thought, their professional experience was vital for the rapid rehabilitation of the administrative machine.[47] At first, the British and Americans, who had co-operated so closely in the war, went their separate ways.[48] Both soon regretted this. Britain 'gained' an area which was largely industrial and needed foodstuffs from elsewhere. These were not forthcoming and the British people had to tighten their belts just a little bit more to feed *their* Germans. Clearly this could not go on for long, and Britain welcomed the American proposal, made in July 1946, to merge the economies of the occupation zones. The French and the Russians rejected this. By September 1946 it was clear that the US was taking a much more positive view of how Germany should be treated than hitherto. Secretary of State James F. Byrnes, in a speech at Frankfurt, recognized that European recovery would be that much slower if Germany were 'turned into a poorhouse'. This mirrored the greater realism which was entering into American thinking and the growing belief that Germany would be needed as an American ally against the Soviet Union.

Welcome though the Anglo-US co-operation was from the standpoint of Britain's precarious finances, it did carry with it one important penalty. In all important respects Britain had to defer to the United States on Germany. One key example of this was the fate of the basic industries in the British zone.

> We have to consider the ownership of the German basic industries. These industries were previously in the hands of magnates who were closely allied to the German military machine, who financed Hitler, and who, in two world wars, were part and parcel of Germany's aggressive policy. We have no desire to see those gentlemen . . . return to a position which they abused with such tragic results . . . Our intention is that these industries should be owned and controlled in future by the public.[49]

Bevin's view coincided with that of the German Social Democrats, the left wing of the Christian Democrats, and the Communists. Even though such socialization measures were approved by democratically elected regional parliaments and by referenda, they were blocked by the United States, because of that country's opposition to socialism.[50]

The Soviets in their zone pursued contradictory policies. The excesses of Soviet troops in the early days of the occupation, and Soviet territorial ambitions, greatly weakened the appeal of communism in Germany. Soviet reparations policy had the same effect. Yet, at the same time, the Russians proclaimed their support for German anti-Nazis, and talked in terms of a united, democratic Germany deciding its own future.[51] On the whole, the Soviet Union's need for massive reparations determined most of its policies most of the time. Thus, it played a decisive part in destroying the communist movement in Germany and making socialism unpopular in that country.

In addition to the reparations they took from their own zone, the Russians demanded more from the Western zones, including a say in the running of the mighty Ruhr industries. This the British and Americans were not prepared to concede. The conference of the four foreign ministers in Moscow in March 1947 ended in failure.

MARSHALL AID AND NATO

The pro-Soviet Communist Parties of Western Europe implemented a new policy of militancy, at a time when the economies of their countries were facing extreme difficulties resulting from a severe winter and a severe shortage of dollars. They were powerful in France and Italy and at least significant forces in several other states. It was in these circumstances that the US Secretary of State, George Marshall, made his offer, in June 1947, that if the countries of Europe could agree on a combined plan for recovery, the American government would finance it. Britain, France and the other states of Western Europe accepted setting up the Organization for European Economic Co-operation (OEEC). On 2 July 1947 the Soviets turned it down. Many regard that date as of crucial significance for East–West relations.[52] It is doubtful whether the Americans expected them to accept, but the Soviet rejection was a blunder. Their cause would have been better served by subjecting the American proposals to closer scrutiny and perhaps forcing the Americans to reject them.

In September 1947 the Soviets set up the Communist Information Bureau (Cominform) consisting of the East European Communist parties together with those of France and Italy. This was probably in part a reaction to growing Western co-operation.[53] A further conference of the British, US, French and Soviet Foreign Ministers held in London in November 1947 ended in deadlock. The French now agreed to their zone being integrated in Bizonia, as the Anglo-US zones were known. The Soviets stepped up their control of Eastern Europe, the most dramatic event of which was the Communist *coup* in Czechoslovakia in February 1948. Czechoslovakia had been seen as a test case for the ability of Communist and non-Communist, East and West, to live and work together.

The West's next move was the signing of the Brussels Pact (17 March 1948). This united Britain, France, Belgium, the Netherlands and Luxembourg for defence purposes. It was designed by Bevin as the forerunner of the North Atlantic Treaty Organization (NATO) at a time when West European morale was low, and some responsible politicians even thought 'the Russians would be in Paris by August, an opinion in which the French Chief of Staff concurred'.[54] The Treaty was meant to convince the reluctant Americans that the nations of Western Europe were prepared to get together to defend themselves. Under the Treaty, the Western Union was established which has continued to exist independently of NATO, although its military organization was merged with NATO in 1950. Allied moves to carry through their West German currency reform in West Berlin led to the Russians withdrawing from the Control Council and blockading the three Western sectors of the city. Cut off from the West by land, West Berlin was, rather miraculously, supplied by air. Bevin played a major role in persuading the Americans to attempt this with RAF support. As part of the Western response to the Berlin crisis, two groups of American B29 bombers, with atomic bombs, were dispatched to Britain in July 1948. Czechoslovakia, Berlin and other Soviet moves made the setting up of NATO in April 1949 a virtual certainty.[55] Early in May 1949 the Russians called off the blockade, having achieved nothing. In the same year the two German states were called into existence.

Britain took a leading part in the creation of a West European defence community, and in the setting up of the OEEC, yet it hung back from a future in a united Europe. Attlee was on record, as Leader of the Opposition in 1939, as saying Europe must federate or perish. Bevin, Bevan and other members of the government had expressed similar sentiments. However, post-war Europe appeared less attractive in reality than it had in wartime dreams. The main European states, Germany, France, Italy and Spain, did not appear to add up to much before the mid-1950s (Spain much later). And Europe's apparent demise enhanced Britain's status and sense of its own importance. The British Empire, being transformed into a Commonwealth and with Britain at its head, appeared poised for a new world-wide role. London was still the centre of the world's second international trading system, and Britain had as many men under arms as the United States.[56] In Labour's ranks, too, there were those who feared that a united Western Europe would be capitalist, clerical and reactionary, especially as Christian Democracy gained the ascendancy in Italy, West Germany, Belgium and even France. Further, British ministers argued that only 25 per cent of Britain's trade was with Europe, the other 75 per cent was extra-European. Britain helped to found the Council of Europe in May 1949, thus paying lip-service to a united Europe. But Bevin made sure it was harmless, with 'splendidly vague' aims 'to achieve a greater unity between its members for the safeguarding and realising the ideals and principles which are their common heritage, and facilitating their economic and social progress'. Nor did Britain join the European Coal and Steel Community, the forerunner of the European Economic Community (EEC), set up on French initiative in 1951. This marked the beginning of the split between Britain and 'the Six' which proved so difficult to heal.

Another reason for Britain's sense of superiority during those years was its application to join the nuclear club. The decision to develop the bomb was taken in 1946 by the Defence Committee of the Cabinet. Attlee had been influenced by the Advisory Committee on Atomic Energy chaired by Sir John Anderson, who had occupied this position under Churchill. Attlee went ahead despite American refusal to provide Britain with the detailed technical know-how. There appears to have been little discussion before the decision was taken, and little questioning of it afterwards. It must be remembered that the US was not yet committed to European defence and, given Britain's experience of the wartime nuclear project, the temptation to develop the bomb must have been strong. Yet, by the time Britain had tested a nuclear device (1952), its defence was based on the nuclear umbrella of the United States. Nor did Britain possess an effective delivery system. Moreover, Britain's bomb was partly devised to wipe out the numerical advantage of Soviet land forces at a time when the Soviet Union did not yet have a nuclear capacity. By 1949, to the surprise of Western experts, the Soviet Union had successfully tested its first bomb. Undoubtedly, the feeling that having the bomb was part and parcel of remaining a great power influenced the decision to go ahead. After all, France did the same. The cost to Britain must have been enormous at a time when the nation faced continuing economic difficulties, although it was hoped the atom bomb would reduce defence costs over all.[57]

KOREA: AS 'DEMOCRATIC . . . AS CALIGULA'S ROME'

With the outbreak of the Korean War, the Cold War looked as if it were turning into the real thing. Briefly, Japan had controlled the destiny of Korea between 1895 and 1945. Soviet and US troops occupied it in 1945. Both powers set up regimes to their own liking in North and South Korea respectively. In June 1950 North Korean units crossed the demarcation line into the South in force. Dismayed by the Communist take-over in China in 1949, the Americans felt they must act. They committed large military forces to the defence of South Korea and got the United Nations to condemn the aggression and authorize counter-action. The war appeared to be almost over as US–UN troops rolled back the Communists virtually to Manchuria. The UN forces were then taken by surprise when Chinese ground forces entered the war on 20 October 1950. After initially driving the UN forces back, they were held on roughly the original demarcation line along the 38th Parallel. Armistice negotiations began on 10 July 1951. An armistice was signed and a cease-fire came into effect on 27 July 1953. The war had not formally ended in the late 1990s. It cost the loss of 687 British lives, with 2,498 British service personnel being wounded. The United States' forces lost 33,629 lives and 105,785 were wounded.[58] In addition to the South Koreans, small numbers of Belgian, Canadian, Dutch, Ethiopian, French, Greek, Filipino, Thai and Turkish troops also participated as part of the UN force.[59]

One disquieting aspect of the war were the atrocities committed by Britain's ally South Korea. Atrocities by North Korea had been expected, but not by the 'democratic South'. War correspondent James Cameron of *Picture Post* regarded the South as 'democratic . . . as Caligula's Rome'. His reports were censored by his paper's owner. The editor, Tom Hopkinson, resigned. Later *The Times* and *Daily Telegraph* had to follow the *Daily Worker* in publishing news of atrocities. In one case, Captain Butler Williams of the 29th British Brigade had to threaten to shoot the local police chief in order to stop a mass execution of civilians at Sinmak.[60]

British support for American action in Korea was speedy. Despite this, there was also anxiety lest General MacArthur, the American Commander-in-Chief, should extend the conflict to China or America should use the atom bomb on China, provoking a third world war – Mao's China and Stalin's Russia had, by that time, concluded a formal alliance. Attlee flew to Washington in December to seek assurances from President Truman. It appears that Truman had not contemplated using the atom bomb.[61] He was able to allay Attlee's fears and later relieved MacArthur of his command.

The Korean War had important effects on the British economy and the British political scene. Increased American purchases of Australian wool and Malayan tin and rubber greatly improved the position of the sterling area, leading to suspension of further Marshall Aid to Britain from the end of 1950. Later in 1950, Britain and other European states experienced severe balance of payments difficulties as the cost of the raw materials they had to import increased more rapidly than the value of their exports. The massive rearmament programme embarked upon under US pressure[62] greatly handicapped British export industries in competition with those of West Germany, which were not engaged in arms production. Britain was spending a higher percentage of its national income on defence than any of its European NATO allies, and as a fraction of national income its defence expenditure was not very much below the US figure.[63] The government openly admitted that the additional rearmament would lead to a reduction in the standard of living.

The increase in the period of conscription from 18 months to two years was also unpopular with many of the government's own supporters. Differences over the pace of rearmament brought about a serious split in the government ranks, which made its downfall more inevitable. On 23 April 1951 it was announced that Bevan and Harold Wilson, President of the Board of Trade, had resigned from the government. The following day, John Freeman, Parliamentary Secretary to the Minister of Supply, joined them. A number of Bevan's colleagues claimed that he resigned because he was disappointed. Hugh Gaitskell had replaced Cripps as Chancellor on 17 January, Bevan became Minister of Labour at the same time. On 9 March, Morrison replaced Bevin at the Foreign Office. Bevan felt he had been unjustly passed over. Be that as it may, the fact is that Bevan, whilst in no way rejecting the need for adequate armaments, took a different view of Britain's ability to cope with the actual scale of rearmament proposed. More fundamentally, he took a different view of the Communist challenge. He saw it more as an ideological challenge born of evil social and economic conditions. He feared 'the western democracies were in grave danger of undermining their economic strength'.[64] He also felt the Soviet Union was too weak economically to be contemplating military aggression. The decision to introduce National Health Service charges to help to pay for rearmament was the last straw for Bevan rather than merely a pretext for resignation. James Callaghan, then a junior minister, found him 'tormented as to whether he was taking the right course'.[65] What Labour's constituency activists thought of Bevan's action was indicated at the Labour Party conference in October. Bevan topped the list in the election for the constituency section of the National Executive Committee (NEC). Emanuel Shinwell, identified as an anti-Bevanite, lost his seat after 15 years, and was replaced by Barbara Castle, one of Bevan's supporters.

IRAN: 'PROUD AND SUBTLE A PEOPLE'

Before it fell from office the Labour government faced new problems in the Middle East, especially in Egypt and Iran. As the problem with Egypt came to a head after the change of government in Britain, it is best left until the next chapter.

Iran decided unilaterally to cancel its 1933 agreement with the Anglo-Iranian Oil Company (AIOC) and to nationalize it. Founded in 1909, the company was British-owned and operated. In 1914 the British government obtained a controlling interest. Up to 1933 Iran had received 33 per cent of the profits; from that date it got a better deal, but Britain still took the lion's share. Moreover, Britain regarded most of Iran as being in its sphere of influence and treated it accordingly. Reza Shah, dictator throughout the interwar period, was initially installed by the British. When he showed signs of independence and wished to keep his country out of the war, he was forced to abdicate after the Anglo-Soviet invasion of 1941. His son succeeded him. In their Tehran Declaration of December 1943, Churchill, Roosevelt and Stalin recognized Iran's help in the war and promised economic aid when it was over.[66] It was partly as a result of not receiving US aid that the demands for nationalization of the AIOC grew. A second factor was the Labour government's policy of dividend limitation, which had the unforeseen effect of reducing the Iranian government's oil revenue from 1948 onwards. Another important factor was the genuine sense of outrage among Iranians that their only asset was in foreign hands. Though the

British argued that they, and not the Iranians, had developed that asset, the Iranians argued that, after more than 40 years of exploitation, they had more than paid for the development costs. Just as important were the colonial-style relations which existed between the Iranians and the British. As Harold Macmillan has commented, the high AIOC officials 'did not seem to know how to handle so proud and subtle a people' as the Iranians.[67] An insider found the British officials 'confused, hidebound, small-minded and blind'.[68] The British Ambassador, Sir Francis Shepherd, was an 'imperialist of the Curzon school'.[69] Few British understood that many Iranians were still angry over the invasion, even though these Iranians were not uncritical of the old Shah. The main weakness of the Iranian position was not the abrogation of the agreement, but the lack of a coherent, stable, national democratic movement. The best-organized component among the anti-British elements was the Moscow-orientated Tudeh Party. This party was built up with Soviet and British help during the war, at a time when both powers sought an anti-Nazi party.[70] It attracted many intelligent and dedicated sons and daughters of Iran,[71] who sought to redress the fearful injustices which existed in that country.[72] Later, its naive pro-Soviet stance represented a danger not only to British interests but to Iranian as well. Most Iranians were immune to Soviet wiles due to the appalling record of the Soviet occupation, 1941–45. Dr Mossadegh, 'an honourable but emotional septuagenarian'[73] and a right-wing patriot, who had become Prime Minister, commanded no well-organized movement of his own. At the official level, Britain 'equivocated between gestures of force to protect its Persian oil interests and compliance with United States "representatives" to find a settlement'.[74] The British Chiefs of Staff argued for military action in July 1951. Lord Fraser, the First Sea Lord, wanted to dispatch the entire home fleet into the Mediterranean as a preliminary to large-scale military invasion of Abadan.[75] While Morrison favoured action, Attlee, Gaitskell, Dalton, Philip Noel-Baker and Griffiths urged caution.[76] Attlee was ready to accept the principle of nationalization and that the British would operate the oil industry on the basis of friendly partnership: 'we must not alienate genuine nationalist feeling in Persia by clinging to the old technique of obtaining concessions and insisting upon exact compliance with their terms'.[77] At another level, the hysteria of the British popular press and the pathetic jingoism of some MPs[78] did nothing to help Anglo-Iranian relations or the British public's understanding of the situation. By the time Britain offered a 50–50 share of the profits and accepted the principle of nationalization – already agreed to by the Americans in Saudi Arabia – it was too late. Britain resorted to blockade, effective because Iran had no tanker fleet, independent outlets or navy. Eventually, Mossadegh was overthrown by an American/British *coup* in 1953.[79] Certainly, in part, Iranian attitudes in the 1990s have their origins in the actions of the West in the 1950s.

ELECTION '51: AFTER 'EXHAUSTING AND UNDIGNIFIED PROCESS'

Having been returned with an overall majority of six in 1950, Attlee and his colleagues were hard pressed to retain control of the Commons. MPs were brought from hospital beds in ambulances to Westminster to vote. It was 'an exhausting and undignified process', wrote George Wigg. The government, tired men, nevertheless held out longer than expected, from 6 March 1950 to 5 October 1951. Perhaps from Labour's point of view Attlee would have done better to have retired from office, he was already 68 and ill, giving a new leader the chance to establish himself and then fight an election. On the other hand, it was a time of crisis in the world and dissension in the party. Perhaps he convinced himself that his own personal standing was a great asset to his party, and that it was right to let the country decide as soon as possible for or against the government.

One last interlude in the Attlee period which deserves a mention was the Festival of Britain, May to September 1951. By 'injecting a note of gaiety and fun at a time of economic crisis and war in Korea, the festival played a vital role in restoring public morale and in demonstrating British resilience to the rest of the world'.[80] The Festival in part marked the centenary of the Great Exhibition of 1851, but its greater purpose was to 'demonstrate to the world the recovery of the United Kingdom from the effects of war in the moral, cultural, spiritual and material fields'.[81] It was about Britain, rather than the British Empire, and covered the arts, sciences, technology and manufacturing. Although the main exhibition was centred on the South Bank in London, there were events in various parts of the country. The Royal Festival Hall remains as a symbol of the hopes of the Festival and the period.

The election was a relatively quiet one. Labour stood by its record and warned of the dangers of a third world war. Perhaps it went too far and, like the Conservatives in 1945, attributed to its opponents extremist tendencies which were not there, implying that Churchill was not to be trusted with issues of peace and war.

When the election results were in, the Conservatives found they had not done as well as expected. They had a majority over Labour of 26 and of 17 over all parties combined. Labour had a net loss of 20 seats. Most of the Conservative gains were probably the result of Liberals turning to the Right, there being only 100 Liberal candidates throughout the country. The Conservatives were better organized and used the postal-vote facilities to greater effect than Labour. Indeed, it has been suggested that the postal vote reduced Labour from a viable to a hairsbreadth majority in 1950 and gave the Conservatives their clear majority in 1951.[82] The slight drop in turn-out, partly the result of bad weather, would also have helped the Conservatives. Yet Labour could feel it had scored a moral victory, for it achieved not only a higher vote than the Conservatives, but the highest vote ever recorded for any political party in Britain. Only the peculiarities of the British electoral system had given the Conservatives a majority.

DECLINE OF SOCIALISM: 'SOME FORM OF GESTAPO'

The election of 1945 finally established the Labour Party as a full-sized alternative to the Conservatives. However imperfectly, the working class was represented for the first time at the centre of the political arena. Labour gave hope to the democratic socialists throughout Europe, socialists who sought fundamental change by civilized means. What exactly had Labour achieved, and where had it failed? Abroad it led the way in decolonization in a manner which compared favourably with the policies of other colonial powers. It failed to appreciate the opportunities that existed for building a new Europe, though it must be admitted that Europe did not seem to add up to much at that time. It committed Britain to defence expenditure far beyond the means of the country, setting the pattern to be followed by other post-war governments. At home, it succeeded in shifting the emphasis in the economy from war to peace production remarkably smoothly. It carried through its domestic reform programme in fulfilment of its election promises. This programme seemed more radical at the time than it actually was. For instance, despite the pleas made by Labour educationalists, Attlee's government did nothing to restructure the country's unfair and divisive education system. Its conception of relations within industry was also very limited. It took up the ideas of the German trade unions and introduced employee participation in industry in the British zone of Germany, but did not attempt to apply this lesson in Britain.

Government is about priorities and power. Politicians in office are harassed individuals with little time to consider anything other than day-to-day issues. When it comes to positive change, they respond only to their perception of the popular mood or to strong, organized opinion both inside and outside Parliament (as with coal). Attlee and his colleagues were cautious men who went just about as far as popular consciousness thrust them.

Looking back at the Attlee government period Britain appears remarkably conservative despite the massive move to the Left in 1945. Britain was conservative in the sense of order, people 'knowing their place', in the sense of the place of women, official attitudes to capital punishment, homosexuality, interracial marriages, sex, unmarried mothers, and so on.[83] In the cinema (so important before the age of television), in the theatre and on the 'wireless', the accents were predominantly southern and middle class (the old order); the working class, the great majority, were still largely figures of fun. Attlee and his colleagues were restricted by their own ideologies (or lack of them). Attlee, and many like him in Labour's ranks, wanted to abolish poverty and give more people the chance to become 'middle class'; they were not seeking to abolish the 'middle class' and its values. Keynesian economics appeared to give them the tools with which to maintain full employment. Redistributive taxation could 'level-up' society, making socialism redundant.

The socialists of the period were also undermined by the nightmare of Stalinism. The reality of Stalinism was so appalling as to lead to doubts about the socialist ideal as such. As more came out about the Soviet forced labour system, the regimentation of artists, the bloody terror as practised from 1948 to 1953, it was easier to believe Churchill's propaganda of 1945, that all socialist measures must lead to some form of Gestapo to enforce them. Although they remained socialists, those towering figures of George Orwell, Bertrand Russell and J. B. Priestley helped to create an atmosphere in which the stuffiness and pomposity of Britain, with all its illusions, eccentricities and complacency, seemed infinitely preferable to great socialist experimentation. The brilliant Marxist intellectuals like J. D. Bernal (X-ray crystallography), Alan Bush (music), Maurice Dobb (economics), R. Palme Dutt (ideology), J. B. S. Haldane (biology), Arnold Kettle (English literature), Ivor Montague (film) and the 'Red Dean' of Canterbury, Dr Hewlett Johnson, were marginalized by their slavish acceptance of Moscow's farcical claims.[84] The same was true of Communist Leader, Harry Pollitt, who could rouse audiences with his attacks on conscription, prescription charges and imperialism, but was less convincing when he defended Eastern European show trials, denounced the Labour leaders and demonized Tito of Yugoslavia.[85] Raymond Williams, whose *Reading and Criticism* was published in 1950, was one of the few who attempted to 'reject Stalinism and to sustain, under heavy attack, an indigenous socialism'.[86] There was 'heavy attack' on anything socialist in the media. The BBC had a monopoly of the radio, and the press was heavily right-wing. Socialism was presented as at best romantic nonsense and at worst evil. Many of the 40,000 or so Communists and their sympathizers remembered how the press had predicted the defeat of the Soviet Union in 1941 and had been proved wrong. The press had then heaped praise on the Soviet Union only to do a somersault again after 1945. To a degree, something of the same happened in its attitude to Germany. Why should anyone believe the press in its new campaign of vilification against the Soviet Union, the left-wingers argued. Nevertheless, public opinion polls showed a growing concern with what was seen as a loss of liberty.[87] All this, too, helps to explain how the Conservatives were able to regain power in 1951 and to hold on to it.

NOTES

Unless otherwise indicated, the place of publication is London.

1 Martin Duberman, *Paul Robeson: A Biography* (New York, 1989), 299.
2 John Saville, *The Politics of Continuity: British Foreign Policy and the Labour Government 1945–46* (1993).
3 Martin Gilbert, *Second World War* (1990), 725.
4 Denis Judd, *Empire: The British Imperial Experience from 1765 to the Present* (1996), 335.
5 Lord Butler, *The Art of the Possible: The Memoirs of Lord Butler* (1971), 38.
6 Lynn Zastoupil, 'Government of India Act (1935)', in F. M. Leventhal (ed.), *Twentieth-century Britain: An Encyclopedia* (New York, 1995), 332–3.
7 Clive Ponting, *Churchill* (1995), 471.
8 ibid., 740.
9 Roger D. Long, 'India, Partition of', in Leventhal, op. cit., 394.
10 General Sir William Jackson, *Withdrawal from Empire: A Military View* (1986), 42.
11 Ponting, op. cit., 742.
12 *The Times*, 9 November 1917.
13 Zionists: the followers of Theodor Herzl, who had revived the idea of a Jewish state as a result of anti-Semitic outbreaks in nineteenth-century Europe. Herzl (1860–1904) lived in Vienna.
14 In 1922, out of a total population of 752,048, there were only 83,177 Jews; in 1941, out of a total population of 1,585,500, there were 474,102 Jews. *Palestine and Transjordan* in the Geographical Handbook Series (BR 514; Naval Intelligence Division, London, December 1943), 172.
15 Walter Laqueur, *The Israel–Arab Reader: A Documentary History of the Middle East Conflict* (1969), 74.
16 *Hansard*, vol. 347, col. 1940.
17 Michael J. Cohen, 'The British White Paper on Palestine, May 1939 Part II: The Testing of a Policy, 1942–45', *Historical Journal* (1976), 727–58.
18 International Department of the Labour Party Box 5 File: Palestine Labour Party Policy 1944–47, letters from Palestine Arab Party (3 May 1944) and Palestine Arab Workers' Society (11 May 1944).
19 Hugh Dalton, *The Fateful Years: Memoirs 1931–45* (1957), 425–6.
20 Ritchie Ovendale, 'Britain and the End of the Palestine Mandate, 1945–48', in Richard J. Aldrich and Michael F. Hopkins (eds), *Intelligence, Defence and Diplomacy: British Policy in the Post-war World* (1994), 139.
21 *Keesing's Contemporary Archives*, A7563, 17–24 November 1945.
22 *Keesing's*, op. cit., A8019, 20–27 July 1946.
23 Maxime Rodinson, *Israel and the Arabs* (1968), 37.
24 Walter Millis (ed.), *The Forrestal Diaries* (New York, 1951). James Forrestal, US Secretary of Defense, commented on 1 December 1947 that Robert A. Lovett, Under-Secretary of State, had said, 'he had never in his life been subject to as much pressure as he had been' at that time by Zionists. He mentions pressure on Liberia (p. 346). See also Margaret Truman, *Harry S. Truman* (New York, 1973); the President was 'deeply disturbed by the pressure which some Zionist leaders put on him to browbeat South American countries and other nations where we might have influence into supporting partition' (p. 384), and (p. 386) Zionist contributions to Democrats' campaign fund.
25 *Hansard*, vol. 441, cols 2340–2.

26 ibid., vol. 441, col. 2354.
27 ibid., vol. 426, col. 1056.
28 *Keesing's* op. cit., A8782, 16–23 August 1947.
29 *Hansard*, vol. 448, cols 1332–3.
30 The deep emotions felt, not recorded in votes, are shown in the case of John Strachey, who was prepared to use his position in the government to advise the Jewish Agency on whether they should sabotage British installations: 'Strachey gave his approval to Crossman. The Haganah went ahead and blew up all the bridges over the Jordan. No one was killed but the British Army in Palestine was cut off from its lines of supply with Jordan.' For this remarkable incident see Hugh Thomas, *John Strachey* (1973), 228–9. As the Cabinet papers indicate, in the Cabinet, Bevan, Dalton and Creech Jones put the Zionist case. See CAB 128/11CM(47)4; CAB 129/16/CP(47)32.
31 See the comments of Lord Wigg, *George Wigg* (1972), 144. See also the same line in R. H. S. Crossman, *A Nation Reborn* (1960), 67–8. For Dalton's view see Hugh Dalton, *High Tide and After: Memoirs 1945–1960* (1962), 147.
32 ibid., 146.
33 Quoted in Partha Sartha Sarathi Gupta, *Imperialism and the British Labour Movement 1914–1964* (1975), 282.
34 ibid., 303.
35 ibid., 319.
36 Thomas, op. cit., 254.
37 Sir Andrew Cohen, *British Policy in Changing Africa* (1959), 43.
38 Colin Leys and Cranford Pratt (eds), *A New Deal for Central Africa* (1960), 29–30; Martyn Dyer, *The Unsolved Problem of Southern Africa* (1968), 105.
39 J. M. Gullick, *Malaya* (1963), 245.
40 ibid., 83.
41 Brian Crozier, *Free Agent: The Unseen War 1941–1991* (1993).
42 Noel Barber, *The War of the Running Dogs* (New York, 1972), 34, believes there were local issues provoking the revolt and (pp. 156–7) puts the number of security forces in action in 1952 at 40,000 regular troops (25,000 from Britain), 60,000 full-time police and 200,000 home guard. For a critical look at British policy see Victor Purcell, *Malaya: Communist or Free?* (1954).
43 According to Thomas (op. cit., 264), this was the essence of the policy advocated by Strachey, then Secretary of State for War, to Attlee in December 1950. For another view of Labour policy see James Griffiths (Colonial Secretary, 1950–51), *Pages from Memory* (1969).
44 Gullick, op. cit., 102.
45 Elizabeth Barker, *Britain in a Divided Europe 1945–1970* (1971), 44–9.
46 Barker (ibid., 68) and others assume Bevin was having to plot to engage US interest in Greece and other areas of Europe, but US influence in Greece was increasing, though somewhat slowly. R. L. Frazier gives us a thorough investigation of the British decision to withdraw in *Anglo-American Relations with Greece: The Coming of the Cold War* (1991).
47 Willy Brandt, *My Road to Berlin* (1960), 154, quotes the example of the police in the British zone. The British liked the old police because they knew their job and obeyed orders promptly. Interestingly, Brandt (p. 152) claims Schumacher, the Social Democratic leader, was 'too socialist' for the Americans, 'too aggressive' for the British and 'too German' for the French. Ivone Kirkpatrick, *The Inner Circle* (1959), 232, says he was never to establish relations 'of confidence and friendship' with Schumacher, though he did with some other Social Democrats. Kirkpatrick was High Commissioner in Germany, 1950–53.

48 Harold Zink, *The United States in Germany 1944–1955* (Princeton, NJ, 1957), 112.
49 B. Ruhm von Oppen, *Documents on Germany under Occupation 1945–54* (1955), 184.
50 John Gimbel, *The American Occupation of Germany* (Stanford, CT, 1968), 117–20, 228–34.
51 The conflicting Soviet attitudes are brought out in Henry Krisch, *German Politics under Soviet Occupation* (New York, 1974).
52 Robin Edmonds, *Setting the Mould: The United States and Britain 1945–1950* (New York, 1986), 168.
53 Barker, op. cit., 77.
54 Kirkpatrick, op. cit., 205.
55 C. J. Bartlett, *The Long Retreat: A Short History of British Defence Policy 1945–1979* (1972), 47.
56 Edmonds, op. cit., 166.
57 For a discussion of this see A. J. R. Groom, *British Thinking about Nuclear Weapons* (1974).
58 Trevor Royle, *War Report* (Edinburgh, 1987), 177. See also David Rees, *Korea: The Limited War* (1964), 460–1.
59 Edwin P. Hoyt, *The Bloody Road to Panmunjom* (New York, 1991), 262.
60 Royle, op. cit., 190–3.
61 See John W. Spanier, *The Truman–MacArthur Controversy and the Korean War* (New York, 1965).
62 Attlee quoted by Michael Foot, *Aneurin Bevan, 1945–1960* (1973), 310, said in 1959: 'Pressure on rearmament was very heavy from the United States. I think they were inclined to press too hard.' James Callaghan, then a junior navy minister, says, 'the Cabinet, under American pressure . . . took a decision to rearm'. See James Callaghan, *Time and Chance* (1987), 107.
63 David Rees, *Korea: The Limited War* (1964), 233. Coral Bell, *Negotiation from Strength* (1962), 56–9, has a good discussion of the economic effects.
64 John Campbell, *Nye Bevan and the Mirage of British Socialism* (1987), 236.
65 Callaghan, op. cit., 110.
66 L. V. Thomas and R. N. Frye, *The United States and Turkey and Iran* (Cambridge, MA, 1952), Appendix III.
67 Harold Macmillan, *Tides of Fortune, 1945–1955* (1969), 343.
68 Kenneth O. Morgan, *Labour in Power 1945–1951* (Oxford, 1994), 466.
69 ibid., 468.
70 I. G. Edmonds, *The Shah of Iran: The Man and his Land* (New York, 1976), 99.
71 Sepher Zabith, *The Communist Movement in Iran* (Berkeley and Los Angeles, CA, 1966), gives a detailed history of the party.
72 George Lenczowski, *Russia and the West in Iran* (New York, 1949), supplementary Chapter 12, 2.
73 George E. Kirk, *A Short History of the Middle East* (1961), 274.
74 ibid., 274. For a study of Iran's foreign policy see R. K. Ramazani, *Iran's Foreign Policy, 1941–1973* (Charlottesville, VA, 1975).
75 Morgan, op. cit., 469.
76 ibid., 469.
77 Wm. Roger Louis, *The British Empire in the Middle East, 1945–1951* (Oxford, 1985), 669.
78 See, for example, Ray Gunter, 21 June 1951, *Hansard*, vol. 489, cols 755–9.
79 Edmonds, op. cit., 135–8; Crozier, op. cit., 19; Robert Graham, *Iran: The Illusion of Power* (1979), 66.

80 F. M. Leventhal, 'Festival of Britain (1951)', in Leventhal, op. cit., 286–7.
81 Quoted in Robert Hewison, *Culture and Consensus: England, Art and Politics since 1940* (1995), 58.
82 David Butler, *British General Elections since 1945* (Oxford, 1995), 63–4.
83 I have written more about British society from 1945 to 1955 in my *Britain since 1939: Progress and Decline* (1995).
84 Henry Pelling, *The British Communist Party: A Historical Profile* (1958) is a good general outline. For an inside view see, Willie Thompson, *The Good Old Cause: British Communism 1920–1991* (1992). For the intellectuals see Neal Wood, *Communism and British Intellectuals* (1969). For the Communist Party in this period see David Childs, 'The Cold War and the "British Road", 1946–53', *Journal of Contemporary History*, vol. 23 (1988), 551–71. For Bernal see Maurice Goldsmith, *Sage: A Life of J. D. Bernal* (1980). For Haldane see Ronald W. Clarke, *J. B. S.: The Life and Work of J. B. S. Haldane* (1968).
85 For Pollitt see Kevin Morgan, *Harry Pollitt* (Manchester, 1993). The most disreputable Communist attack on Tito was made by James Klugmann, *From Trotsky to Tito* (1951). It was made worse because Klugmann knew the wartime Yugoslav partisans.
86 As quoted in Hewison, op. cit., 56.
87 Roger Eatwell, *The 1945–1951 Labour Governments* (1979), 154.

4

CHURCHILL AND EDEN, 1951–57

'OUR FUTURE . . . LITTLE BETTER THAN A GERMAN SATELLITE'

On 5 October 1952 the 16,000-ton Japanese freighter *Heiyo Maru* sailed from Tilbury docks, London, on its way to Kobe. On board, four passengers – an Australian, a British diplomat and his Danish wife, and a British woman joining her husband who was a serving officer in the US Army – shared the boat with a cargo of concrete and Volkswagen cars.[1] The trip, which took 49 days, was significant in that the *Heiyo Maru* was the first Japanese merchant vessel on the high seas after Japan's defeat in 1945. On 23 April Japan had regained its sovereignty. At that time Britain followed the US with the world's second-largest merchant fleet. Japan produced virtually no cars and the German Volkswagen was regarded by the British as a joke! Unobserved by most people in Europe, Japan was already taking the first steps towards world economic superpower status. 'The Korean War proved a salvation for the Japanese economy.'[2] The Americans found they needed vast supplies for their armies in Korea. Japan supplied $3 billion-worth of them. This was a sum nearly double Britain's gold and dollar reserves in 1952. Former members of the Japanese navy manned 46 ships in Korean waters during the conflict.[3] Sony, the Japanese company, developed the first pocket-sized transistor radio in 1952. The transistor had been invented by English-American physicist William Bradford Shockley and others in 1948.

The world was changing in 1952. On 1 November the US exploded its first hydrogen bomb. The Soviet Union had become a nuclear power in 1949 and was also attempting to make an 'H-bomb.' It succeeded in 1953. West Germany, the Federal Republic of Germany, had become an independent state. Like Japan, it had agreed not to develop nuclear weapons. In Korea the war continued. The Anglo-Iranian oil dispute continued. In October diplomatic relations between the UK and Iran were severed. In Egypt, Britain's ally, the corrupt King Farouk, had been overthrown by military reformers. In the US, General Dwight D. Eisenhower defeated his Democrat opponent,

Adlai Stevenson, to be elected President. He was inaugurated in January 1953 as the 34th President and the first Republican since 1933. The CBS television network used a UNIVAC computer, the first to be commercially available, to predict the results. Its first, correct, prediction of a landslide for Eisenhower was not believed and it was quickly reprogrammed and so gave an incorrect forecast. In Moscow Stalin's paranoia increased, as he believed that the leading Soviet doctors were plotting to kill the Soviet leadership. This was the world of Churchill's final ministry. In this changing world Britain experienced difficulty in finding its place, clarifying its position and renewing its identity. Dalton recorded in his diary on 26 June 1952 that Tony Crosland, MP, had just returned from lecturing in West Germany. His view was that West Germany was going ahead very fast. 'Our future, as he sees it, is little better than a German satellite!'

In reality Britain was in decline, but various factors masked that decline. Britain was feeling good; tea rationing ended and identity cards, a wartime measure, were abolished in 1952. In the following year sweet rationing was abolished. Britain became a nuclear power on 3 October 1952, when its first atom bomb was exploded in the Monte Bello Islands just off North West Australia. It still had its ticket to sit at the 'top table'.[4] In the same year the world's first pure jet airliner, the British Comet, went into service with the British Overseas Airways Corporation (BOAC). In May 1953 Edmund Hillary and Sherpa Tenzing Norgay became the first men successfully to climb Mount Everest. Though Hillary was a New Zealander, it was counted as a British success; such was the feeling for the Commonwealth in those days. At Jodrell Bank, the 76.2 m (250 ft) radio 'dish' telescope was completed in 1955. This achievement led to the widespread illusion that Britain was in the forefront of the space race. The 'New Elizabethan Age', as the media called it, was inaugurated after the death of George VI in 1952 and the accession of his daughter Queen Elizabeth II. Her coronation on 2 June 1953, at a magnificent, feudal ceremony, was watched by 25 million people on television. There was honour too for Winston Churchill; in 1953 he was awarded the Nobel Prize for literature. He followed such literary giants as T. S. Eliot (1948), William Faulkner (1949), Bertrand Russell (1950) and François Mauriac (1952). He also got a garter from the Queen! Roger Bannister thrilled the nation by becoming the first man to run a mile under four minutes. It seemed to some, even many, there was still a lot of greatness left in Great Britain.

CHURCHILL'S CABINET: 'REMINISCENT OF BYGONE TIMES'

At 77, Churchill was not expected to remain long at the helm. This dismal election result, remarkable though it was considering the defeat of 1945, gave him no mandate for great changes. In an attempt to broaden his support, the former Liberal Churchill offered a coalition to his old party.[5] This was turned down. The old chieftain argued that the Conservative Party's return to office was due to his charisma and this gave him the right to exercise his own preferences in making Cabinet appointments. It was a 16-member Cabinet of old men, mainly veterans of the wartime government. To a degree, Churchill was curbed by the need to present a broad, moderate image to the electorate. R. A. Butler, who was regarded as a moderate, was appointed Chancellor of the Exchequer. Eden got the Foreign Office, a reward for his ability in foreign affairs, popularity and, not least, his pre-war anti-appeasement role. Lord Woolton's appointment as Lord President was both a tribute to his services in renovating the party machine and an acknowledgement of his presumed appeal to non-committed middle-class voters. Macmillan, like Woolton and Eden, had served Churchill during the war, and was a moderate on home affairs. He became Minister of Housing and Local Government. The appointment of the Marquess of Salisbury as Lord Privy Seal was a sop to the party traditionalists. Walter Monckton was sent to the highly sensitive Ministry of Labour because of his reputation as a conciliator. Sir David Maxwell-Fyfe was invited to turn his tough legal mind to the problems of the Home Office. As during the war, Churchill acted as Minister of Defence. There was only one woman in the government, Florence Horsbrugh, and she served only briefly in the Cabinet from September 1953 to October 1954.

Already deaf, Churchill's age was telling against him and he was less and less effective as Prime Minister. According to Woolton, he ran his Cabinet in a way which was 'often reminiscent of bygone times'.[6] He drank too much, wandered too much and was too erratic. He was a poor chairman of his Cabinet and one who ignored vast areas of government activity.[7] Within three months of taking office he had another mild stroke, which for a while left him unable to speak coherently.[8]

In this situation it must be asked who was running Britain during this period? When Churchill was officially ill Butler held the fort. The only trouble was that the government's main priority in its first year was the economy, and Butler had no experience in this area. Butler relied heavily on the Permanent Secretary to the Treasury, Sir Edward Bridges, who was not himself an economic specialist. He in turn relied on his subordinates, Sir Edwin (later Lord) Plowden and William (later Lord) Armstrong, to brief the Chancellor.[9] In 1952 disagreements about economic policy led to Budget Day being postponed.[10] Britain's difficult economic situation, resulting from the Korean War and rearmament, led Butler to call for massive cuts, but he faced stiff opposition from within the government about where they should fall. Education and the NHS faced cuts, and so did the foreign travel allowance for tourists. Even the meat ration was cut to less than its wartime value. Once peace broke out, in the second half of 1952, the economic situation changed. The terms of trade moved dramatically in favour of Britain and the other industrial nations.

> If Labour had hung on a little longer, they might have been the beneficiaries of the rising tide of affluence which would have been to some extent a feature of the 1950s, whichever party had been in office. The years from 1951 to 1955 can be seen in retrospect as a lull in our turbulent post-war history. Churchill's presence at the top masked the decline of Britain's world power status.[11]

The 'affluent society' was just around the corner and the Conservatives were going to get the credit for it!

THE BEVANITES: 'COMPLACENT ASSUMPTIONS'

The Labour Party had been at war with itself since its defeat in 1951. Attlee, 68 in 1951, did the party no good by remaining Leader. It is not clear whether he did so because of his rivalry with Morrison or Churchill, hoping for one final taste of office before his final farewell. The rivalries among those hoping to replace Attlee – Bevan, Gaitskell and Morrison – increased. Personal rivalries fuelled ideological disagreements and vice versa. Bevan certainly wanted a more 'traditional' socialist policy based on public ownership at home and a quasi-pacifist, anti-imperialist, policy abroad, than did Morrison or Gaitskell. He did not believe that Keynesian economics could solve the problem of unemployment under capitalism. This was clear from his *In Place of Fear* (1952). In personal terms, he probably resented the prominence of the London element in the Labour leadership – Attlee, Bevin, Cripps, Dalton, Morrison – and later Gaitskell and George Brown. It is interesting that his wife, Jenny Lee, was Scots. Ironically, his most devoted followers, Richard Crossman, Tom Driberg and Michael Foot, were from privileged backgrounds. Given his background, it is understandable that he felt that a great, predominantly working-class movement should be led by someone like himself, rather than by someone who had no direct experience of the physical hardship and psychological humiliation of the interwar working class. Though popular with the Left of the party, 'Nye' could not have united Labour or gained enough floating voters to put Labour back in government.

In 1952 Labour's individual membership reached a record high, 1,014,524, as did trade union affiliated membership, 5,071,935; this seemed to favour Bevan. His supporters won six of the seven constituency party seats on the NEC at the annual conference in Morecambe (1952). In a speech at Stalybridge, Gaitskell alleged some Communist infiltration of the delegates.[12] This is likely, though it should not be exaggerated.

The Parliamentary Labour Party had decided by the small margin of 113 to 104 to support the principle of German rearmament.[13] This Bevan opposed. In April 1954 he resigned from the 'shadow cabinet' ostensibly over Labour's Indo-China policy, which was close to the government's.[14] His intention was to lead the campaign against German rearmament at Labour's annual conference. Tempers flared when it endorsed German rearmament by a very small margin with allegations that the small Woodworkers' union delegates had voted against the policy of their union. Bevan also lost to Gaitskell in the contest for the treasurership of the party.

Tony (Anthony Wedgwood) Benn, MP, wrote in his diary (20 November 1952), 'Particularly obnoxious do I find the complacent assumptions by the Bevanites that the ark of the socialist covenant resides with them.' As well as intrigues on the Labour Right, including some organized Catholic activity, this was also a reason for the Bevanite failure.

EDEN: 'HIGH ORDER OF INTELLIGENCE'

Churchill played 'cat and mouse' with his colleagues regarding his retirement. Eden, the 'crown prince', became more and more tense at the delay.[15] Churchill finally went on 6 April 1955. As expected, Eden replaced him.

Educated at Eton and Oxford, Eden (1897–1978) was the personification of the classic English gentleman. After service in the trenches in the Great War he entered the Commons in 1923. He came to prominence as Foreign Secretary, 1935–38. He resigned from Chamberlain's government because he disagreed with appeasement of Nazi Germany. There was disappointment in many quarters that he did not follow up his resignation with a popular crusade against the government. He 'lacked the courage to continue the fight'.[16] On the outbreak of war in 1939 he agreed to rejoin Chamberlain's government as Dominions' Secretary. In 1940 the new Prime Minister, Churchill, put him in charge of the army, but elevated him to Foreign Secretary later in the year. He occupied this post until Churchill's defeat in 1945. He made a good impression on Cordell Hull, Roosevelt's wartime Secretary of State, 'as an agreeable personality and a high order of intelligence',[17] but some of his Cabinet colleagues were less impressed. Reginald Bevins, Macmillan's Postmaster-General, thought he should not have been Prime Minister. He found he 'chopped and changed his mind' and 'was no judge of men'.[18] As Prime Minister he constantly interfered in the work of his colleagues.[19] Eden was a sick man when he took over and continued to be troubled by serious health problems.

1955: 'FIRST OF THE ELECTIONEERING BUDGETS'

On 15 April, nine days after becoming Prime Minister, Eden decided on an election six weeks later, on 26 May. Fear that the economic situation was deteriorating influenced this decision.[20] Lancashire cotton workers, then an important group in the North West, traditionally went on holiday in May, 'which would mean that a considerable number of traditional Labour voters would be unable to vote'.[21] Labour was handicapped by party splits and by the moderation of the Conservatives since 1951. There was no unemployment, incomes were rising ahead of inflation and Butler presented 'the first of the electioneering Budgets which from then on bedevilled the British economy with "stop-go"'.[22] The international climate was mild. During the campaign the Austrian Peace Treaty was signed, with the Americans, Soviets, British and French agreeing to withdraw from a neutral Austria. Macmillan, Eden's Foreign Secretary, was seen with Molotov, his Soviet counterpart, talking peace. The message was that the Conservatives could deliver on peace, though Macmillan had played no part in the deal. One fact which could have given Labour useful ammunition, a Monopolies Commission report on rubber tyres, was suppressed by the Board of Trade after strong representations from Dunlop, strong supporters of the Conservatives. The report concluded that rubber tyre manufacturers operated a massive price ring against the public interest.[23]

For the first time, this 'least memorable of all the post-war contests'[24] gave the leaders the chance to appear on television. Eden, Macmillan, Butler and Iain Macleod (Minister of Health) appeared to answer editors' questions. Attlee did a cosy fireside chat with his wife and one journalist. The honours were about even.[25] Most people still did not have television.

The election on 26 May gave the Conservatives 345 seats (321 in 1951), Labour 277 (295), Liberals 6 (6) and others 2 (3). The turnout this time was down from 82.5 per cent in 1951 to 76.8 per cent. The Conservatives actually lost over 400,000 votes compared with 1951, but Labour had lost over 1.5 million! The Liberal vote declined very slightly. The small Communist vote increased from 21,640 to 33,144 (0.1 per cent). The Conservative gains were mainly in the South, but they also picked up seats in the North, the Midlands and one in Scotland.

Gaitskell, soon to be Labour's Leader, believed strikes were one of the major contributions to Labour's defeat.[26] These included an inter-union dispute in the docks, which was in full swing during the election. Benn saw prosperity as the key.[27]

GAITSKELL'S 'GREAT TALENT AND FIRM LOYALTY'

After the election Labour held its inquest into the results. Investigating for the NEC, Wilson found Labour's organization had been defective. The number of full-time agents in the constituencies had fallen from 296 in 1951 to 227 in 1955.[28] There was pressure on the old leaders to go. Attlee succumbed and retired in December 1955 to become Earl Attlee. Morrison (67) was not prepared to retire and fought hard to succeed Attlee. As expected, Gaitskell won the leadership contest by 157 votes to 70 for

Bevan and 40 for Morrison. With 111 votes Bevan was also defeated in the deputy leadership race by fellow Welshman and fellow ex-miner, James Griffiths (141 votes).

Hugh Gaitskell (1906–63) was only 49 at the time of his election. He had served as Attlee's Chancellor of the Exchequer and, like 'Clem', was from an upper-middle-class background; his father was in the Indian civil service. After education at Winchester and New College, Oxford, he spent some months as Rockefeller Research Fellow in Vienna. There he experienced the brief, bloody, civil war in 1934. Before lecturing in economics at University College, London, he worked as an adult education tutor in Nottingham. During the war Gaitskell worked for Dalton at the Ministry of Economic Warfare, becoming MP for South Leeds in 1945. Gaitskell's public image was that of a sincere man who could readily manipulate facts and figures but who was less clever in human communication. In private life, his friend, John Betjeman, the poet, remembered the young Gaitskell as 'a gentle and kind person who had no objection to a drop of drink and was very easy company and full of jokes'.[29] According to Dalton, he stood, 'high out of the ruck of rivals. During his ministerial apprenticeship he had displayed, both in public and in inner council, great talent and firm loyalty.'[30] In 1953 Benn found Gaitskell, 'intellectually arrogant, obstinate and patronising. I respect – but cannot quite admire – him.'[31]

ITV: 'FOR THE SAKE OF OUR CHILDREN . . . RESIST IT'

The Conservatives had nationalized the British Broadcasting Company in 1926, transforming it into the British Broadcasting Corporation (BBC). It had a monopoly of radio broadcasting and, after television was introduced in 1936, of that too. It was financed by an annual television licence fee which was regulated by Parliament. After being interrupted during the war, television was restarted on the same basis in 1946. The BBC had a reputation for providing reliable news services, a wide variety of programmes, bringing culture to the masses, and for being rather stuffy. The *Report of the Broadcasting Committee 1949* rejected advertising and any breach of the BBC's monopoly. A Conservative member of the Committee, Selwyn Lloyd, favoured the introduction of the American system. Churchill never gave a television interview and seemed not to be interested in the issue.[32] But he did think the BBC was Communist infiltrated.[33] It appears that Lord Woolton sold the idea of commercial television to the Cabinet. Outside Parliament, Norman Collins, a former BBC executive, was the key figure promoting the idea. He was backed financially by Sir Robert (later Lord) Renwick, an old-Etonian stockbroker, who was a large contributor to the Conservative Party. C. O. Stanley, Chairman of Pye Radio, was also important. These, and a small number of determined and powerful business interests, fought the combined opposition of the churches, the universities, the professional educational bodies, most of the press and cinema industries, the Labour Party and the TUC, and a host of other bodies.[34] The Archbishop of York's view that 'For the sake of our children, we should resist it' was ignored. Any number of Conservative MPs favoured breaking the monopoly. Some shared Churchill's view of the BBC; some had financial interests involved; and some opposed public ownership on ideological grounds. After a long debate, the Television Act, 1954 was passed establishing commercial television under an Independent Television Authority. The new service commenced in September 1955. Under the Act, Britain was divided into regions, with regional companies licensed to broadcast commercially supported programming within a single region. These companies each had a monopoly in their individual regions. The coronation and the election of 1955 showed the potential of television. In March 1955 4.5 million television licences had been issued; by March 1958 the number had grown to 8 million.[35]

The growth of television and the competition between the BBC and Independent Television (ITV) both reflected changes in society and helped to produce them. The BBC was forced to become more 'popular' in much of its output, with much more emphasis on light entertainment. It was hard pressed to compete with 'soap operas' like *Coronation Street* and *Crossroads*. Controversy about television continued, and the Pilkington Committee on Broadcasting was appointed to review the position. Its report, published in June 1962, showed that the BBC put out more news and current affairs, serious drama, sport and travelogues. ITV was slightly ahead on light entertainment and religion, but devoted much more of its output to crime, westerns and comedy. There was concern about violence, sex and depravity on television. The Committee reported that there was a belief that 'the way television has portrayed human behaviour and treated moral issues . . . had . . . done something . . . to worsen the moral climate of the country'. It also attacked television for being 'trivial'. Many mass-appeal programmes were 'vapid and puerile, their content often derivative, repetitious and lacking in real substance'.[36] In all this the BBC fared better than ITV. The Committee also felt the regions and Scotland were neglected. Although the government rejected many of Pilkington's recommendations, it did allow only the BBC to go ahead with a second TV channel: BBC2 began transmitting in April 1964.

Pilkington was not entirely fair to ITV, in that Granada Television, one of the main companies, had led the way in providing controversial current affairs programmes of a high standard. It also pioneered the coverage of election news. In 1958 it gave the first extensive coverage to a by-election, in Rochdale.[37] In 1959 it broke new ground with a series of 'election marathons', in which the candidates from 100 seats in 'Granadaland', the North West, debated the issues.

The competition between BBC and ITV broadened and raised the level of debate and discussion about all national and international problems. This is not necessarily an argument in favour of commercial television, but it is certainly an argument against any organization having a monopoly in this vital sector of mass communications. It is convenient to mention here that Edward Heath's Conservative government ended the BBC's monopoly of radio in June 1972 with the passing of the Sound Broadcasting Act. This provided for the setting up of commercial radio stations in October 1973. One innovation they forced on the BBC was the phone-in, which started in 1974 and has since been widely used in elections.

CINEMA AND THE PRESS

The cinema, which had always suffered from American competition, underwent a revival during the war as fewer American films were available and the government showed a greater interest in it. This continued under the Attlee governments. Harold Wilson, as President of the Board of Trade, established the National Film Finance Corporation (NFFC) to help finance British films. These were seen as potential foreign currency earners and propaganda for 'British values' abroad. At that time Britain could use its position in Germany and Austria as well as the Empire to secure the screening of British films. Adaptation of the classics, such as David Lean's filming of Dickens's *Great Expectations* (1946) and *Oliver Twist* (1947) were successful. War films, costume dramas and the Ealing Studios comedies (e.g. *The Lavender Hill Mob*, 1951) were also popular.[38] The film industry did little to enhance the status of women in these years.[39] Two films which will be always recalled when discussing the period are the restraint romance, *Brief Encounter* (David Lean, 1945), and the Cold War drama, *The Third Man* (1949), from the Graham Greene story. In the 1950s, more American competition, the decline of German and Empire markets and, above all, the onslaught from television, led to a crisis in the cinema. Thousands of cinemas were transformed into bingo halls as cinema audiences declined. Most of the cinemas belonged to two chains, Rank and ABC. They determined what the public saw. Rank were also important as film producers. As in the 1930s, American financing and involvement became more important once again. The unanswered question was why could the British not make (cheap) films of the quality of the French *nouvelle vague* or like the Italians, Swedes or, in the 1970s, the West Germans.

Attempts were made in the late 1950s and early 1960s to create a British 'new wave'. This was based on what had proved successful on television and on the adaptation of successful novels about provincial, working-class life. It was also based on money from the US and the NFFC. The decline of the cinema seemed to make it easier for independent producers like Tony Richardson and Bryan Forbes to break in. Films like *Saturday Night and*

Sunday Morning (1960) and *The Loneliness of the Long Distance Runner* (1962), taken from Alan Sillitoe's books, and *Look Back in Anger* (1959) and *The Entertainer* (1960), based on John Osborne's plays, won critical acclaim, but did little to halt the drift from the cinema.[40]

Both the cinema and newspapers were hit by the fall in advertising revenue due to television. According to the Royal (Shawcross) Commission on the Press (1961–62) the advertising revenue going to the press fell from 55 per cent in 1952 to 47.5 per cent in 1960. It then rose over the 1960s, and according to the next (McGregor) Commission on the Press (1974–77), it reached 70.1 per cent in 1975. By contrast, television's share of advertising rose from 3.4 per cent in 1956 to 17.5 per cent in 1960, and 24.4 per cent in 1975. The percentage of revenue going to the cinema went one way all the time – down. The Shawcross Commission expressed concern about the continued growth of concentration in the press. In 1948 the top three newspaper groups were responsible for 43 per cent of total daily and Sunday newspaper circulation. By 1961 the top three controlled 65 per cent of circulation. With costs rising sharply, the weaker papers went to the wall. The Liberal *News Chronicle* was closed in 1960. Later the Conservative *Daily Sketch* and the Labour *Daily Herald* died after years of decline. The *Sun*, owned by the Australian tycoon Rupert Murdoch, replaced it. Shawcross was also concerned about newspaper groups owning substantial shares in television, like the Mirror group, Lord Beaverbrook and Roy (later Lord) Thomson, the two Canadian newspaper wizards. Increasingly, British papers were foreign-owned. McGregor found the trends noted in 1961 had continued. These were concentration of ownership, economic difficulties due in part to the massive price increase in newsprint and overmanning, continued dependence on advertising and a sharp division between the 'quality' papers and the 'popular' press. The two commissions offered no solutions to these problems. By 1977 left-wing opinion was even more poorly represented than in 1961. Down to the 1990s, the Conservatives maintained their press advantage during election campaigns.

EUROPE: 'MUCH ADO ABOUT NOTHING'

In 1956 industrial production in Japan reached its pre-war level.[41] In the same year West Germany overtook British car production.[42] Britain's key industry was already beginning to suffer from a 'sclerosis of technique'.[43] The Cabinet gave itself little time to think about the implications of these facts. It was more concerned about immigration and hanging, at home, and, abroad, by the Common Market and the Suez Canal.

Post-war immigration to Britain from its colonies started to grow in the early 1950s as news of British prosperity spread and the country faced a shortage of labour. Under Churchill, the Cabinet started to discuss the implications and debates continued under Eden without resolving the matter. Under British law any Empire citizen, or citizen of Southern Ireland, could come to Britain and reside there. UK citizens did not enjoy reciprocal privileges. The fear was the rising trend of West Indian immigration. Again and again the matter was raised, but the divided Cabinet could not agree on any action. Most immigrants were in fact from Ireland – an estimated 750,000 since the war.[44]

The government fought hard to defeat a private member's bill introduced by the Labour MP Sydney Silverman to abolish capital punishment. Doubts had grown in the Commons about hanging as a result of the execution, in 1955, of Ruth Ellis and of Timothy Evans in 1950. In the case of Ellis it was felt that a 'crime of passion' committed by a woman did not merit the death penalty. In Evans's case there were serious doubts about his guilt. These doubts were later confirmed and he was pardoned posthumously in 1966. Silverman secured a Commons majority of 19 in favour of abolition, with some Conservatives, led by Peter Kirk, voting with most of the opposition. The unrepresentative and unelected Lords threw out the Bill two weeks later after the government had orchestrated the action. It could have killed the Bill earlier and saved much parliamentary time. Although this controversy generated much anger, it was struck off the agenda by far more dramatic events elsewhere.

The European Economic Community of six states – West Germany, France, Italy, Belgium, the Netherlands and Luxembourg – the so-called Common Market – came into being on 1 January 1958. Questioned in 1957 about the 'Common Market' nearly 50 per cent of those asked were 'don't knows'. But those who did come off the fence were in favour of Britain joining.[45] By then it was almost too late. Attlee, Churchill and Eden had all rejected membership as the negotiations progressed. In 1956 Selwyn Lloyd, the Foreign Secretary, replied to a memo on the subject from his junior minister, Anthony Nutting, with a note saying 'Much ado about nothing'.[46] The feeling was very much that Britain had its special role to play in the Commonwealth and in association with the US and therefore should not get involved in a common market. Britain did, however, attempt to slow down the negotiations by feigning continuing interest.

SUEZ 1956: 'THAT DOES AMOUNT TO A LIE'

Though officially independent, Egypt had been dominated by Britain since 1882, and British troops, mainly conscripts, were stationed there in 'fly-blown, sand-strewn . . . forlorn and disagreeable' camps.[47] The climate was vile and the population hostile. There was constant tension between the 70,000 British and the Egyptians. Between 1950 and 1956, 54 British servicemen were killed.[48] In one retaliatory incident, on 25 January 1952, the British killed 40 Egyptian auxiliaries in a battle in Ismailia.[49] In July

1952 the Egyptian Free Officers movement overthrew King Farouk, and then, in February 1954, its own leader, General Neguib. The new man was Colonel Gamal Nasser. It was not known at the time that Nasser had been sponsored by the CIA.[50] He was seen as a modernizer who could unite the Arab peoples and prevent the Soviet influence spreading in the area. Under the Anglo-Egyptian Agreement of 1954, the British bowed to US pressure to evacuate, within two years, the Suez Canal Zone.[51] The last British troops left in March 1956.

Britain, with the blessing of US Secretary of State John Foster Dulles, set up the Baghdad Pact in 1955 comprising Iran, Iraq, Pakistan, Turkey and Britain. Its aim was to keep the Soviets at bay. Nasser refused to join the Pact, rightly feeling that it would undermine his influence with the Arab masses. Eden at first supported Nasser and met him in Cairo just before taking over from Churchill as Prime Minister.[52]

The other major problem was Nasser's relations with Israel. A precarious peace had existed since the 1949 Arab–Israeli cease-fire. Moshe Sharett, Israeli Prime Minister between December 1953 and February 1955, had established contacts with the Egyptians, but his replacement was the hawkish David Ben Gurion. France supplied the Israelis with the modern weapons, punishing Egypt for its assistance to the Algerian rebels seeking freedom from the French. With his forces in a poor state Nasser sought military aid. Neither the Americans nor the British were prepared to supply heavy weapons to the Egyptian armed forces. Nasser joined the Bandung bloc of neutral states led by Nehru's India and Tito's Yugoslavia and sought military aid from the Soviet bloc. In September 1955, a barter deal of arms-for-cotton was announced with Czechoslovakia. To keep their influence, the Americans, together with Britain and the World Bank, promised aid to Nasser to build the Aswan Dam. This would massively increase Egypt's electricity supply and greatly increase irrigation. Eden and the Americans were also busy designing a package, code-named, 'Alpha', to bring Egypt and Israel together.[53] Dulles fell out with Nasser after he recognized Communist China in May 1956. The Americans withdrew the promise of economic aid in July. In any case, the Senate Appropriations Committee was jibbing at voting the loan; an alliance of Southern Democrats, who feared increased Egyptian cotton exports, the anti-Communist Chinese lobby and the highly influential pro-Israelis, was organized to block the loan in July 1956. According to Anthony Nutting, then junior Foreign Office Minister, Britain had decided against the loan in March after Glubb Pasha, the British officer commanding the Jordanian armed forces, had been replaced. It was in these circumstances that the British-owned Suez Canal Company was nationalized by Egypt on 26 July 1956.

Britain was the biggest single user of the Canal. Two-thirds of Western Europe's oil was imported via the Canal.[54] It could not be denied that its efficient operation was a matter of serious concern to the UK and some other states. Of course, Egypt needed the fees collected and had made it plain the Canal would remain open to all as in the past (except for Israel). Britain, France and the US reacted by freezing Egyptian assets in their countries. Britain called up 20,000 reservists and dispatched reinforcements to the eastern Mediterranean. At home, Labour Leader Gaitskell, on 2 August, compared Nasser to Mussolini and Hitler and even admitted there might be circumstances in which Britain would be compelled to use force. He did, however, link it to reference to the UN.[55] Eden was looking to use force.

The British and French 'cooked up with Israel a secret plan for a joint simultaneous invasion'.[56] The Americans attempted to dissuade them. On 13 September Dulles publicly rejected the use of force. Meeting secretly in Paris in October, British, French and Israeli representatives agreed the Sèvres Protocol. Under it, Israel attacked Egyptian positions near the Canal on 29 October. Britain and France then gave both sides an ultimatum to withdraw, knowing Egypt could not comply. Anglo-French air attacks commenced on 31 October and on 5 November their invasion began. On 7 November Britain and France were forced to agree to a UN demand for a cease-fire.

The Americans had not been informed of the plan and President Eisenhower mobilized diplomatic forces at the UN to condemn the action. Eisenhower declared, 'The US was not consulted in any phase of these actions, which can scarcely be reconciled with the principles and purposes of the United Nations.'[57] Dulles, within days of being operated on for cancer, felt 'just sick about the bombings'.[58] Britain and France were forced to use their vetoes at the UN Security Council. They could not do this when a US motion in the General Assembly was adopted on 2 November. This called for an immediate cease-fire and withdrawal of the attacking forces. The Soviet Union threatened Britain with nuclear attack. Many Commonwealth countries distanced themselves from the British position. Worse still, there was a run on sterling, mainly in the American market.[59] This caused some in the Cabinet to think again. The Chancellor of the Exchequer, Macmillan, 'switched almost overnight from being the foremost protagonist of intervention to being the leading influence for disengagement – as well he might, for the loss of 279 million dollars in that November represented about 15 per cent of our total gold and dollar reserves'.[60] The US Treasury opposed British requests to withdraw capital from the International Monetary Fund (IMF) until it agreed a cease-fire.[61] Britain had little choice. The interruption in British oil supplies and the blocking of the Canal by Egyptian-scuttled ships added to Britain's rapidly worsening economic situation. Moreover, the campaign divided Britain. Most of the Labour and Liberal parties opposed the move. In the Commons, MPs demanded to know whether Eden had known of the Israeli attack. He vehemently denied any collusion. Speaking in 1996, Sir Donald Logan, then Assistant Private Secretary to Selwyn Lloyd, then Foreign Secretary, who had attended the Sèvres talks, admitted he had known of the Anglo-French–Israeli collusion. When he heard Eden in the Commons he noted, 'I thought to myself, "That does amount to a lie"'.[62] He did nothing to expose it. Anthony Nutting, MP, junior Foreign Office Minister, resigned from the government on the issue, as did another junior, Sir Edward Boyle, MP. Eden also lost his press secretary William Clark.

Field Marshal Lord Carver, then a colonel and deputy Commander-in-Chief East Africa, believed Operation Musketeer showed 'complete blindness to the likely after-effects'.[63] The cost to Britain was immense. There was not only the actual cost of the operation, but the cost from lost production and exports. The Suez Canal was only re-opened in March 1957. Nasser was strengthened by the attack. Had the Israelis acted alone they would possibly have toppled him. To a degree, the Anglo-French–Israeli attack helped to divert attention from the Soviet invasion of Hungary which occurred at the same time. British prestige and influence were weakened world-wide.

The best that can be said about Eden, as Lord Carrington found him in October 1956, was that he 'was nervous and his manner neurotic. It was easy to see he was a sick man.'[64] He was haunted by memories of the 1930s' appeasement policy towards Hitler. There is some evidence from opinion polls that Eden's popularity in the country rose during the crisis. A majority of those asked opposed military action, but once it was taken 49 per cent favoured it early in November. On 19 November it was announced that Eden was ill again and when he retired 56 per cent of those asked expressed themselves satisfied with him.[65] He resigned on 9 January 1957. At the final Cabinet meeting he broke down in tears and cried, 'You are all deserting me, deserting me.'[66]

NOTES

Unless otherwise indicated, the place of publication is London.

1 Information from one of the passengers, Mrs Joan Frazier.
2 In the words of Aneurin Bevan.
3 Roger C. Thompson, *The Pacific Basin since 1945* (1994), 60.
4 ibid., 60.
5 Lord Butler, *The Conservatives: A History from their Origins to 1965* (1977), 427.
6 Quoted in ibid., 428.
7 Clive Ponting, *Churchill* (1995), 756–7.
8 ibid., 756.
9 Anthony Howard, *RAB: The Life of R. A. Butler* (1987), 182.
10 ibid., 186.
11 Robert Blake, *The Conservatives from Peel to Churchill* (1970), 269–70.
12 Denis Healey, *The Time of My Life* (1990), 152, called the estimate 'ridiculous'. He felt the speech cast doubt on whether Gaitskell should be leader. Philip M. Williams, *Hugh Gaitskell: A Political Biography* (1979), 308, conceded the speech was 'badly worded and the Communist passage a mistake'.

13 Henry Pelling, *A Short History of the Labour Party* (1961), 111.
14 John Campbell, *Nye Bevan and the Mirage of British Socialism* (1987), 288.
15 Richard Lamb, *The Failure of the Eden Government* (1987), 3.
16 James Margach, *The Abuse of Power* (1978), 102.
17 Cordell Hull, *The Memoirs of Cordell Hull*, vol. II (1948), 1474.
18 Reginald Bevins, *The Greasy Pole* (1965), 37.
19 Lamb, op. cit., 13–14.
20 ibid., 4.
21 ibid., 5.
22 ibid., 8.
23 ibid., 12.
24 David Butler, *British General Elections since 1945* (Oxford, 1995), 14.
25 Lamb, op. cit., 11.
26 ibid., 25.
27 Ruth Winstone (ed.)/Tony Benn, *The Benn Diaries* (introduced by Ruth Winstone) (1995), 37.
28 Pelling, op. cit., 114.
29 John Betjeman, 'School Days and After', in W. T. Rodgers (ed.), *Hugh Gaitskell* (1964), 17. Healey (op. cit., 154) was amazed by Gaitskell's dancing!
30 Hugh Dalton, *High Tide and After* (1962), 352.
31 Winstone/Benn, op. cit., 35.
32 John Whale, *The Politics of the Media* (1977), 22.
33 Ponting, op. cit., 759.
34 H. H. Wilson, *Pressure Group* (1961), gives a good account of the campaign for commercial television. One of the key figures in commercial television tells his story in Lew Grade, *Still Dancing: My Story* (1991).
35 Whale, op. cit., 33.
36 Sir Harry Pilkington, *Report of the Committee on Broadcasting 1960* (HMSO), June 1962, Cmnd 1753, 31, 33. Most of the report was written by Professor Richard Hoggart, well known for his book *The Uses of Literacy* (Harmondsworth, 1959).
37 Jeremy Tunstall, *The Media in Britain* (1983), 9.
38 Robert Murphy, *Realism and Tinsel: Cinema and Society in Britain 1939–49* (1992), contains some very useful material and comments.
39 Murphy, op. cit., 101–9.
40 Alexander Walker, *Hollywood, England: The British Film Industry in the Sixties* (1986), discusses these films.
41 William Horsley and Roger Buckley, *Nippon New Superpower: Japan since 1945* (1990), 53.
42 Roy Church, *The Rise and Decline of the British Motor Industry* (1994), 44.
43 Michael Dintenfass, *The Decline of Industrial Britain 1870–1980* (1992), 25.
44 Lamb, op. cit., 20.
45 Robert J. Wybrow, *Britain Speaks Out, 1937–87: A Social History as Seen through the Gallup Data* (1989), 51.
46 Lamb, op. cit., 91.
47 Trevor Royle, *The Best Years of Their Lives: The National Service Experience 1945–1963* (1988), 179.
48 ibid., 181.
49 ibid., 182.
50 Brian Crozier, *Free Agent: The Unseen War 1941–1991* (1993), 25.
51 General Sir William Jackson, *Withdrawal from Empire: A Military View* (1986), 146.

52 Lamb, op. cit., 159–60.
53 ibid., 161.
54 Robert Blake, *The Decline of Power 1915–1964* (1985), 366.
55 Leon D. Epstein, *British Politics in the Suez Crisis* (1964), 66.
56 John Campbell, *Edward Heath: A Biography* (1993), 92.
57 Russell Braddon, *Suez: Splitting of a Nation* (1973), 94.
58 Braddon, op. cit., 96.
59 Lord Butler, *The Art of the Possible: Memoirs of Lord Butler* (1971), 194.
60 ibid., 194.
61 Hugh Thomas, *The Suez Affair* (1966), 174.
62 *The Times*, 17 October 1996.
63 Michael Carver, *Out of Step: The Memoirs of Field Marshal Lord Carver* (1989), 272.
64 Lord Carrington, *Reflect on Things Past: The Memoirs of Lord Carrington* (1988), 119.
65 Wybrow, op. cit., 48.
66 Margach, op. cit., 113–14.

5

MACMILLAN AND THE AFFLUENT SOCIETY, 1957–64

MACMILLAN: 'MORE COUSINS AND LESS OPPOSITION'

When Eden fell in January 1957, Butler (55) looked a likely candidate to be premier. He had held the fort when Eden was absent with as much efficiency as anyone, and he was well qualified in other respects. He had served under five Prime Ministers, having held office 1932–45 and from 1951 onwards. As Minister of Education he was credited with the Education Act, 1944 and more recently he had served as Chancellor (1951–55), and as Lord Privy Seal and Leader of the House. Within the Conservative Party he was too statesmanlike to arouse the activists. The widely used term 'Butskellism', used to draw attention to the similarities between his economic policies and those of Gaitskell, did him no good with the Right of Centre in his own party, nor did his doubts about Suez. With two Suez hardliners, Salisbury and Kilmuir, organizing the consultations, before Salisbury and Churchill advised the Queen on Eden's successor, Butler's fate was sealed.

The new Prime Minister, Harold Macmillan (1894–1986), did not have as much experience as his rival. In the pre-war period he had an honourable record of dissent over the government's failure to deal with unemployment and over appeasement. He first gained office under Churchill during the war, serving as Resident in North Africa. He was successful as Minister of Housing and Local Government (1951–54), then at Defence (1954–55). After a few months at the Foreign Office, he served at the Exchequer (1955–57). Educated at Eton and Balliol, he joined his father's publishing business. In the First World War he served as a captain in the Grenadier Guards, was wounded three times and ended the war 'badly wounded'.[1] His military experience became very important for him and he developed a 'certain contempt' for those who had not served in the forces.[2] This contempt was to influence his judgement of colleagues and opponents. As MP for Stockton-on-Tees between the wars, he had been shocked by the poverty of his working-class constituents and turned to the Left on economic and social issues. It is believed that, had the war not intervened, he would have joined Labour.[3] Macmillan had another life in the interwar period.

In 1920 he married into the influential Cavendish family and soon was related by marriage to 16 MPs.[4] 'Perhaps most important, the Cavendish connection increased his fascination with the life of the great country houses – a life which cut across his own austere family background, and his intellectual discipline. He loved the aristocratic style of their politics.'[5] Whether the long-standing relationship between his wife, Lady Dorothy, and Robert Boothby, MP influenced his political life is impossible to say.

Macmillan was one of those Conservatives who worked to remove Chamberlain from leadership in 1939, and one of those who voted against him at the end of the decisive debate in 1940. His reward came days later when the new Prime Minister, Churchill, appointed him parliamentary secretary to the Ministry of Supply under Herbert Morrison. In June 1942 he was moved to the Colonial Office with the higher rank of Under-Secretary of State and in November Churchill asked him to go to North Africa as Minister Resident. This involved the difficult task of working in co-operation with the Americans and the French. He had the advantage with the Americans that his mother was American and with the French that he spoke their language. 'He could show his diplomatic skills, Anglo-American relations were crucial and very difficult.'[6] He impressed many of those he met at this time. Lady Diana Duff Cooper, who had met many men of power, saw in him a future Prime Minister.[7] After a number of other moves in the Mediterranean theatre Macmillan ended his first period of office as Secretary for Air, with a seat in the Cabinet, in Churchill's caretaker government of six weeks' duration. Defeated at the election he was returned at the Bromley by-election in November 1945.

Macmillan first earned the approval of his parliamentary colleagues in the dark days of opposition. As a member of the shadow cabinet he was the party's expert on industrial policy. He specialized in studied scorn of Labour's proposals, even though, as in the case of coal nationalization, this sometimes involved him in condemning policies he had advocated before the war. His 'Edwardian' appearance became fixed at this time .

As Minister of Housing, Macmillan talked about a crusade. Yet his success was based on plans inherited from Dalton for a smaller 'People's House'.[8] His brief period at Defence coincided with the announcement of Britain's intention to build the hydrogen bomb. At the Foreign Office he was largely responsible for the ill-fated Baghdad Pact which helped to push Egypt towards Russia.[9] Though invited, he did not go to the Messina conference in 1955, which led to the setting up of the Common Market.[10] As Chancellor, he will be remembered, if at all, for his introduction of Premium Bonds. The Suez affair tipped the balance decisively in his favour. Remarkably, considering he was Chancellor, he was strongly for resolute action against Nasser. He did not appear to consider the possible financial implications. Remarkably, too, as one who had worked so closely with Eisenhower, he was obviously wrong in his estimate of American reactions to British intervention. He did, however, have the good sense to advise Eden to accept a cease-fire when he saw the gold and dollar reserves rapidly disappearing.

MACMILLAN: 'CAPABLE OF BEING RUTHLESS'

Macmillan realized he needed Butler in the Cabinet if further schisms were to be avoided, and he was fortunate that Butler, who wanted the Foreign Office, agreed to take over the Home Office. Selwyn Lloyd was kept on as Foreign Secretary to appease the Suez Group and as an act of defiance to the world. Kilmuir was reappointed Lord Chancellor, and Peter Thorneycroft, another Suez hardliner, became Chancellor of the Exchequer. Alan Lennox-Boyd stayed on at the Colonial Office. Duncan Sandys, a son-in-law of Churchill, was appointed Minister of Defence with increased powers. It was not surprising that, in a Cabinet led by Macmillan, the 'Suez Inner Cabinet', those responsible for the planning of the operation, should be well represented. What is surprising, considering the Conservative Party's attempts to present itself as a broad people's party, was the extent to which it was still a highly exclusive body. Of the 16 members of the Cabinet in January 1957, six had been to Eton and only two had not attended Headmasters' Conference (public) schools. Eden had kept his Cabinet an all-male affair and, at first, Macmillan followed his example. Admittedly, Macmillan's choice was limited. There were only 10 female Tory MPs in the Commons. Labour, even in defeat, had 14 women MPs. One other feature of Macmillan's 1957 government was that the new generation of Conservatives – Heath, Maudling, Powell, Profumo and Soames among them – were starting their rise to prominence. Sir Edward Boyle, who had been with Macmillan at the Treasury, was persuaded to return. He had opposed Suez, but Macmillan 'had a very high regard for his talents as well as for his character'.[11] Boyle served in Education under Lord Hailsham who, like his junior, was an old Etonian. Hailsham was promoted to the Cabinet in June 1957.

There was another astonishing feature of Macmillan's Cabinets. As Christopher Hollis, himself then a Conservative MP, wrote, in 1961:

> What is even more interesting is the lavishness with which Mr Macmillan had filled his offices with relations by marriage. *John Bull* on January 4, 1958, calculated that of the eighty-five members of his government, thirty-five were related to him by marriage, including seven of the nineteen members of his Cabinet . . . There has been nothing like . . . since the days of the eighteenth century . . . What is the reason for this extraordinary reversion – particularly at the hands of a man who is . . . more attuned to 'the wind of change' than to traditional policies? Doubtless it simply is that nepotism is one of the

strongest of human emotions . . . Mr Macmillan has more cousins and less opposition than any Prime Minister in our history.[12]

How did Macmillan run his Cabinet? Dr Charles Hill paid tribute to Macmillan's chairmanship of the Cabinet, which he dominated by sheer superiority of mind and judgement. But he also commented that Macmillan annoyed his ministers because, 'now and again the Cabinet was consulted at too late a stage in the evolution of some important line of policy'.[13] John Wyndham (later Lord Egremont), who was 'rich, high-born and [belonged] far more to the eighteenth century than to the age of the common man', worked for Macmillan as unpaid private secretary. He found his master

> always polite, courteous and outwardly calm, and he was very quick in getting through his work . . . because of his seniority both in years and experience, and because despite that gentleness of manner, he was capable of being ruthless – as were his small staff – managed to interfere time and again with Ministries over the heads of various Ministers. Sometimes this riled other Ministers.[14]

Macmillan's public image was moulded by (Sir) Harold Evans, his press spokesman. As the veteran lobby correspondent James Margach has commented:

> Macmillan's public panache – the more remarkable since he was shy to the point of sickness before big occasions – is testimony to the value of highly professional public relations behind the scenes. In this crucial sector of power Macmillan avoided the errors committed by so many other Prime Ministers . . . Evans . . . proved the most outstanding No. 10 spokesman in my long experience.[15]

CYPRUS: 'NO QUESTION OF ANY CHANGE'

Macmillan's first priority was to rebuild the confidence of his colleagues, of the party at Westminster and in the country at large. Secondly, he had to reassure the world that Britain was not finished, but was still able to play a considerable role in world affairs. Remarkably, he was able to do both. When he took over, the Conservatives appeared to be heading for certain defeat. Yet two years later they were returned with an increased majority.

Macmillan was not at first certain he could achieve these objects, and within weeks of taking over the first crack appeared in his Cabinet. Lord Salisbury resigned on 28 March. The issue was Cyprus. Officially it had been 'leased' from Turkey in 1879 and annexed in 1914. It was seen as a barrier against Russian influence in the Mediterranean. After 1945 the great majority of its people, Greek by language and culture, sought an end to the colonial status and union with Greece. Violence erupted in

1955 after a junior minister at the Colonial Office, Henry Hopkinson, had said on 28 July 1954 that 'there can be no question of any change of sovereignty in Cyprus'. In 1955 Eden had ordered the arrest of Archbishop Makarios, who was the spiritual leader of the Greek Cypriots, and his deportation to the Seychelles in 1956. The violence escalated and the incoming Prime Minister realized that the only possible course was renewed talks with Makarios. To Salisbury and some other Conservatives this appeared to be another retreat in the face of violence. Macmillan put forward a plan which looked like a partition scheme, which was unacceptable to the Greek Cypriots. Hundreds were to die in Cyprus before the Zurich Agreement, worked out by Greece, Turkey and the Cypriots, was concluded in 1959. Under this Cyprus became independent within the Commonwealth in 1960. Special safeguards were included to placate the Turkish minority. Britain was able to retain certain bases there. The Americans had thrown their weight behind the ending of the British colonial regime, fearing a conflict between Greece and Turkey, both members of NATO.[16]

Apart from the blow of Salisbury's resignation Macmillan's position started to improve. Much of the debris of Suez had already been cleared up by Butler, acting for Eden, before January 1957. The Canal itself was cleared by 9 April and opened to shipping. Soon oil supplies to Britain improved so much that petrol rationing, introduced in December, had ended by May 1957. In the same month Britain felt strong enough to ignore protests from Japan and appeals from the Pope and Nehru, and went ahead with exploding its first H-bomb in the Pacific near Christmas Island. Bevan too had made a last-minute appeal against the British H-bomb.[17] For the 'get tough' section of Macmillan's own party, and many of the electorate, the test, and the others which followed, signified Britain's continuing importance. On the other hand, they were worried by the note of 'softness', 'liberalism', or 'realism', depending on one's point of view, which was soon an established theme of Macmillan's ministry. Some regretted the announcement on 4 April that there would be no further call-ups for military service after 1960. In addition to the possible implications of this move for Britain's ability to hold its colonies together, some felt national service had a value as a means of disciplining youth. In March 1957 Ghana gained its independence and Dr Kwame Nkrumah, a man heartily detested by the Right in Britain, became its President. At the end of August the Federation of Malaya became independent. In Britain, the Right could take no comfort from 'Rab' Butler at the Home Office. Yet the Homicide Act, 1957, which further restricted capital punishment to certain specified types of murder, such as killing a police constable or prison officer on duty, was not the work of Butler. He had inherited it from his predecessor.[18] In seeking to modernize the penal system he was to fall foul of the 'hangers and floggers' in his own party in later years, thus weakening his chances of succeeding Macmillan.

74

ECONOMY: 'LIKE BICYCLING ALONG A TIGHTROPE'

Macmillan understood that the electorate was more concerned about economic policy than colonial policy, but economic management was a dilemma. As he put it,

> to maintain the British economy at the right level, between inflation and deflation, balancing correctly between too much and too little growth, was a delicate exercise . . . It was not a subject to be solved by mathematical formulae, or exact calculation. It was like bicycling along a tightrope.[19]

It is doubtful whether there has been a Prime Minister since the war who has not thought like that, despite the confident words they have uttered, from time to time, about Britain's economic prospects. Nevertheless, it would be wrong to suggest, as Macmillan seemed to do, that it was impossible to identify some of the sources of Britain's economic problems during the post-war period, and during his period of office. What experts have differed on is the weighting they attach to particular factors. All agree that Britain was bound to decline relatively as a world economic power. As other states developed, Britain's share of world trade would inevitably decline. In particular, as pre-war competitors recovered from the ravages of war, this was clearly going to happen.[20]

Table 5.1 Share in world trade (per cent), by country, 1938–62

	1938	1950	1951	1959	1962
UK	22	25	22	17	15
USA	20	27	26	21	20
West Germany	23*	7	10	19	20
Japan	7	3	4	7	7

Note: * refers to whole of Germany. The figures are taken from the Board of Trade Journal

What became controversial was the extent of Britain's decline. Why should West Germany, Italy, Japan, and certain other countries perform consistently better than Britain in the 1950s? One answer was that they were starting from such low bases, compared with Britain, that they were likely to find it easier to increase their production in goods and services, at least for a number of years, than the more 'mature' economies.[21] This did not apply to countries such as Sweden and Denmark, which achieved greater increases in their per capita gross national product during the period 1951–62 than did Britain.[22] The movement of relatively cheap labour from agriculture to industry was another factor in some countries – Japan, Italy, France, and later Spain – which made it easier to increase production compared with highly urbanized Britain. Germany was helped by 3 million refugees from the East. This factor should neither be forgotten nor exaggerated. Andrew Shonfield, in a much-praised study, laid bare some of the key causes of Britain's economic weaknesses. One was too much investment abroad and too little at home. 'History', he wrote in 1958,

> once again is the greatest impediment to clear thinking on the subject of British investment overseas. The words themselves have a subtly pleasing and adventurous sound. One way or another it has gone pretty deep into folk myth that British greatness and wealth have depended on pouring out our treasure abroad.[23]

Shonfield found that in most cases, oil being one of the exceptions, it was better to invest in undertakings at home rather than abroad. However, the 1957 Budget encouraged investment abroad at the expense of home investment.[24] A second source of weakness, according to Shonfield and some other observers, was defence expenditure, especially overseas. Aside from the United States, Britain consistently spent more on defence than its NATO allies.[25] With regard to this, Shonfield urged,

> an obvious course for a British government seeking a rapid way of strengthening the country's balance of payments would be to review the whole of this military spending abroad, the subsidies to foreign governments as well as the cost of actual British garrisons, with a determination to make a drastic cut.[26]

He had doubts about Hong Kong, Gibraltar, Malta and the high cost of British forces in Germany. His point seemed to be that Britain would have earned more abroad than Germany, had it not been for its overseas defence expenditure.[27]

The maintenance of the pound as a reserve currency was another factor holding back British industry. As Samuel Brittan put it:

> We are often told that growth has had to be halted 'to protect the pound sterling' . . . Yet in the ten years from 1953 to 1963, British prices rose faster than those of every other major European country except France; and our gold and foreign exchange reserves were, at less than £1,000m., hardly any higher at the end of this period than at the beginning . . . Britain now has to maintain the sterling area on a reserve less than half of Germany's and a good deal smaller than that of France. Yet neither country maintains an international currency, and France has a much smaller foreign trade than Britain. Britain has thus done just as badly in the 'sound finance' league of conservative bankers as in the production league of modern-minded economists. We have too often sacrificed rapid growth for the sake

of a strong pound and as a result of all our pains frequently ended up with neither.[28]

'NONSENSE . . . THAT OUR TRADE UNIONS . . . ARE IRRESPONSIBLE'

The trade unions and industrial management were also often criticized for the poor record of the British economy. Strikes got a great deal of space in the media. The situation was seen as far worse than it actually was. Gradually, a kind of hysteria built up, which, as with the balance of payments, made matters worse. British trade unions certainly had their problems; there were too many of them, with well over 180 unions affiliated to the TUC in the Macmillan era. In some cases, several operated in one industry, leading to inter-union rivalry and demarcation disputes. This contrasted with West Germany's 16 industrial unions affiliated to the DGB. But whereas Britain's unions had grown up over a long period, Germany's trade union structure had been imposed by Hitler. The democratic trade unions decided it was convenient to retain structure after 1945. Britain's trade unionists were criticized for their apathy which led, in some cases, to unrepresentative minorities taking control, a problem common to all voluntary bodies. Usually, the leadership of unions is more moderate than many of the local activists who do most of the unpaid, yet necessary, work. On this point, a Conservative publication of the day commented,

> about 90 per cent of Britain's strikes are 'unofficial', in so far as they are not supported by the executive of a trade union. This may well be evidence of poor communications within some unions, or lack of authority from the top, but it makes nonsense of any implication that our trade unions, as such, are irresponsible or unduly militant.[29]

As mentioned in Chapter 2, the only serious case of Communist abuse of power in a British trade union was in the Electrical Trades Union. In that union the Communists used 'fraudulent and unlawful devices' to keep power. This situation was brought to light by Woodrow Wyatt, then a Labour MP, in collaboration with two leading members of the union, Les Cannon and Frank Chapple. Wyatt published the accusations in the *New Statesman* and they were broadcast on BBC's *Panorama*. The union was eventually expelled from the TUC and the Labour Party, but it was six years between the allegations being made in 1956 and the removal of the offenders.[30] The activities of these Communists was a blow to the whole trade union movement. External supervision of union elections and secret ballots on strike action would have helped to assuage public fears. Unfortunately, these measures were not always in place. On the other hand, the idea that the unions were largely responsible for Britain's economic decline must be resisted. The Conservatives themselves pointed out in 1964 that in the past 10 years, Britain had lost fewer days through strikes than any other major industrial country in the free world except Western Germany. And in the 15 years after the Second World War, we lost only one-ninth of the working days which were lost through industrial disputes in the 15 years after the First World War.[31]

Table 5.2 Average number of days lost per 1,000 employees in mining, manufacturing, construction and transport, 1951-62[32]

Country	Days
USA	1,185
Italy	780
Canada	649
Japan	579
Belgium	501
Australia	462
France	391
UK	**272**
West Germany	72
Sweden	53

Most of the unrest in the 1950s occurred in four industries – shipbuilding, the docks, mining and motor vehicle manufacture – which only employed about 7 per cent of the working population. They were industries with special problems. Certainly, in the case of the docks and motor manufacturing, unrest could unduly upset the export trade. Another point which needs to be made in relation to strikes and the economy is that there is not necessarily any relationship between growth and strikes. In West Germany there was little labour unrest but much growth. Italy, Japan and Canada experienced great increases in economic development and also industrial relations which were much worse than Britain's. Some other countries came in between on both counts. It is also difficult to prove that radical leadership of unions produces more labour unrest. American trade unions were free of Communists, yet they were much more strike-prone than Communist-led French unions. Even in West Germany, the biggest union, IG Metall, was headed in the 1950s by Otto Brenner, a left-wing socialist. If British trade unions were only marginally responsible for the nation's economic problems in the 1950s, what about British management?

Increasingly in the 1950s, a feeling developed that British industry was failing to attract enough young people of high calibre. It was also believed that managers were badly trained compared with their rivals abroad, and that there was too little upward mobility from the shop floor. On the shop floor itself there was not enough technical training, a fact recognized in a White Paper, *Technical Education*, published in 1956. It proposed expansion of technical training opportunities at all levels, including a doubling of the number of workers given 'day-release' by their employers. Higher up the ladder, a committee set up by the Ministry of Labour to investigate the selection and training of supervisors in industry found, in 1962, that 'the provision of systematic training for supervisors is still relatively limited . . . Moreover, some of the training given is inadequate, superficial and sporadic.'[33] Higher up still, in the boardroom, an Institute of Directors' study early in 1969 revealed that only 18 per cent of their sample of managing directors held a university degree. Most of those who did had been to Cambridge. The majority of managing directors surveyed had been to public school. They were mainly from

> what might be called the upper and upper-middle class of business owners, executives, and professionals. Seven out of ten managing directors had fathers in this group, while one out of ten had fathers in the last three categories of skilled and unskilled workers and farmers. Overall we can say that potential success in British industry is quite closely linked to parental occupation and family status.[34]

The American management expert Dr David Granick called Britain 'the home of the amateur'. He stressed that professionalism was a serious charge against an individual in British industry.[35] Apparently, British managing directors did not think there was any special experience which was useful to a future managing director, though marketing was favoured by some. Neither foreign experience, nor legal or technological training, were considered essentials.[36] Much of this contrasted with top management in the United States, Japan and West Germany.

'MOST OF OUR PEOPLE HAVE NEVER HAD IT SO GOOD'

What is remarkable about the second half of the 1950s, given the discussion above, is that this period came to be regarded as idyllic, the era of the affluent society, a society in which, because of unprecedented prosperity and full employment, Britain was changing fundamentally and for the better. Unemployment had disappeared during the war, had remained minimal under Labour, and stayed that way for the remainder of the 1950s. That in itself was a dramatic change for many of the working class. Better still was the fact that earnings had risen faster than prices. Between October 1951 and October 1953, wage rates rose by about 72 per cent and retail prices by nearly 45 per cent. The increase in earnings had been even greater. On average, earnings of men in industry had risen by 95 per cent since 1951.[37] Further, there had been a reduction in the official working week. The new degree of affluence was measured in the acquisition of consumer durables:

according to the *Observer* (2 January 1966), by 1965, 88 per cent of households in Britain had television, 39 per cent were equipped with refrigerators, and 56 per cent with washing machines. Yet this was not so amazing as it appeared at the time. In atom-bombed Japan, by 1964, 90 per cent of homes had TV and over 50 per cent had refrigerators and washing machines.[38] In 1951 there had been 2.25 million cars on the roads; in 1964 the figure had increased to over 8 million. In Britain, this great rise in the ownership of these, and other, consumer goods was the result of the extension of hire purchase and the lowering of purchase tax, as well as the rise in earnings. In 1951 there had been 100 per cent purchase tax on such items as electric fires, cosmetics and cars. In 1963, the rate of tax on these goods was down to 25 per cent. Refrigerators, washing machines, vacuum cleaners, and radio and TV sets had all been taxed at a rate of 66.33 per cent under Labour. Under Macmillan it was down to 25 per cent. Pots and pans, which had not been subject to tax under Labour, were taxed by Eden. Under Macmillan there was still a 10 per cent tax on these items.[39] Home ownership just about doubled under the Conservatives. Britain was being transformed into a nation of home-owners: over 40 per cent of the population owned their own homes. If there were still too many slum-dwellers, the Conservatives could claim that between 1955 and 1964 over half a million slums had been taken out of the housing stock and over 1.5 million people rehoused.[40]

Far more people were taking their holidays away from home than ever before – something like three-fifths in 1964, and a significant minority of them were going abroad. In one other area affecting standard of living, Macmillan and his colleagues felt proud of their achievements, though this was a more ambiguous achievement than the others. Income tax had been reduced five times during the Conservatives' term of office. The standard rate fell from 9s. 6d. (47.5p) to 7s. 9d. (39p) in the pound. Cutting income tax is always popular; people seldom ask themselves whether the cuts in government expenditure which must follow are in their, or the country's, long-term interest. Macmillan commented, rather rashly, some believed, in July 1957, only a few months after becoming Prime Minister:

> let's be frank about it; most of our people have never had it so good. Go round the country, go to the industrial towns, go to the farms, and you will see a state of prosperity such as we have never had in my lifetime – nor indeed ever in the history of this country.

He went on to admit, 'we cannot forget that some sections of our people have not shared in this general prosperity',[41] and promised them help. The Prime Minister could have said again in 1959, with greater conviction, most people 'have never had it so good', and even more so when he retired from office in 1963. Given Macmillan's own view of the fragile nature of the British economy, one can rightly ask how it was all achieved. The answer was rooted in increased production, improved terms of trade and some reduction in the arms burden. The index of industrial production, which excludes agriculture, trade, transport and other services, had risen from 85 in 1951 to 115 in 1962.[42] Moreover, the pattern of industrial production was changing. Electronics, computers, synthetic fibres, agricultural machinery and motor vehicles were making great headway. Britain had developed the largest petro-chemical industry in Europe, and the British automobile industry had doubled production since 1951. Great strides had been made in agriculture too. With fewer holdings, less land and less labour, far more was being produced than before the war.[43] Before the war, Britain had produced, in terms of value, about one-third of its food. By the 1960s it was producing about half. The second source of prosperity was the great improvement in the terms of trade Britain enjoyed in the 1950s. Samuel Brittan estimated that

> After the collapse of the Korean boom, food and raw material prices fell so much that in 1953 we could buy thirteen per cent more imports for the same amount of exports than in 1951. The 1957–8 world recession triggered off another, and a slower slide in commodity prices, which eventually improved our terms of trade by another fourteen per cent, making twenty-nine per cent altogether. These two movements together were worth the best of £1,000m a year to the British public.[44]

This happy state of affairs changed in the 1960s. Under the Conservatives defence expenditure declined as a percentage of the gross national product (though it remained higher than that of the other members of NATO, excepting the United States). This also made it easier for the government in its efforts to create an affluent society.

RUSSIANS IN SPACE: 'FRIVOLITY' OF BRITISH

Although British defence expenditure was seen by Macmillan as too high, it continued to weigh down the economy throughout his period of office. At the beginning of the 1960s, Britain was still spending £51 every second on arms; £3,060 a minute; over £1,608 million a year. By November 1963 there were still approximately 357,000 regular servicemen and boys in the forces. By comparison, in 1960, £894.6 million was spent in Great Britain on education. Few doubted that Britain needed armed forces; but did it need its own nuclear capacity, and did it need so many troops abroad? Those who did believe Britain required its own 'deterrent' argued, in the words of Harold Macmillan, that it 'gives us a better position in the world, it gives us a better position with respect to the United States. It puts us where we ought to be, in the position of a Great Power.'[45]

The arrival of the space age in 1957 indicated, once again, that Britain was no longer in the first division. Contrary to Western expectations, the Russians launched the world's first artificial Earth satellite, Sputnik 1, on 4 October 1957. This successful launch put 83 kg. into space. It remained there until 4 January 1958. On 3 November the Russians followed this up with the equally successful launching of Sputnik 2, containing the dog 'Laika', the first mammal in space. Macmillan records that 'The Americans were not unnaturally alarmed by so striking a proof of Russian scientific and technological progress'. Macmillan received many letters protesting about the cruelty to the dog, which he found to be indicative of the 'characteristic frivolity' of the British.[46]

The first American riposte to the Soviet challenge came only on 31 January 1958, when the United States launched Explorer 1. But the Soviets continued their exploits, being the first to 'hit' the moon with an unmanned craft in 1959. In the same year they produced the first photographs of the hidden side of the moon. Their man, Yuri Gagarin, was the first man in space in 1961, and their woman, Valentina Tereshkova, was the first woman in orbit in June 1963. The Soviet Union had clearly demonstrated its capability of producing intercontinental missiles of the greatest accuracy and of sufficient weight to carry megaton warheads to any town or city of the United States. One would have thought that this would have led to a drastic reappraisal of Britain's independent nuclear deterrent. As Professor Northedge has commented, the Sputniks

> had the effect of carrying the two super-Powers still further away from lesser states like Britain which aspired to remain in the nuclear league. This was a moment, if ever there was one , when Britain without any dishonour might have renounced pretensions to remain in the front-rank class of nations and come to terms with the west European states when the shape of the EEC was still in process of moulding. But that opportunity was not taken.[47]

Instead, the pro-British deterrent lobby argued that, given the progress of Soviet rocketry, the United States could become increasingly inhibited in using its nuclear retaliatory power to defend Western Europe. With the single possible exception of defending West Berlin – and even there the Americans appeared firm when faced with Soviet threats in 1959 – there seemed no likelihood of Eisenhower abandoning his NATO allies. This was equally true of his successors. Nor did there appear to be any conceivable situation in which Britain dare contemplate using its nuclear capacities independently of the US. Britain relied on the American nuclear umbrella in peace and war. Originally envisaged as carriers of Britain's deterrent, the V bombers – Vulcans, Valiants and Victors – were obsolete when they were first introduced in 1956. The installation in Britain of American 'Thor' intermediate range ballistic missiles in 1957–58, with a two-key system – an American key activated the nuclear warheads and a British key launched the missile – served to emphasize British dependence on American technology and leadership. This was not changed by Macmillan's success, as a result of meetings with Eisenhower at Bermuda (March 1957) and Washington (October 1957), in getting the Americans to amend the Atomic Energy Act of 1954. Under the amended legislation of 1958 Britain was able to get American nuclear weapons know-how of the kind it had been deprived of since the passing of the McMahon Act in 1946. Britain was able to buy from the US component parts of nuclear weapons and weapons systems and to make possible the exchange of British plutonium for American enriched uranium. It also made possible the sale to Britain of nuclear propulsion plant for the first British nuclear submarine, the *Dreadnought*.

The other draining and damaging (to Britain's image) aspect of defence was its policeman's role in the Middle East, Africa and Asia.

KENYA: HOLA CAMP 'SUB-HUMAN INDIVIDUALS'

As we have seen, British troops were involved in shooting wars in Malaya and in Cyprus. If Britain's friends had sympathized in the first case, they were more critical in the second. British forces were also used to suppress the elected left-wing government of Dr Cheddi Jagan in British Guiana in 1953, and found themselves 'restoring order' there again in 1962 after Jagan's People's Progressive Party (PPP) had, once again, won the elections. Though there were racial tensions in the country and the PPP was not above reproach, it looked as though British and American interests were changing the rules of the game – the electoral system was altered to ensure that a leader enjoying their confidence emerged. The colony eventually became independent as Guyana in 1966.

The situation in Malta was, to say the least, badly handled. In 1947 Malta had been granted internal self-government and had elected a Labour administration. Britain still regarded the naval and military base there as essential, and in 1956 it was agreed that the island should become part of the UK, sending three MPs to Westminster. Malta had served Britain well for 150 years and had earned itself warm praise for its help during the Second World War. The British government showed itself parsimonious when evaluating Malta's annual grant, and the 1956 talks broke down, therefore, on the question of money. At the beginning of 1959 the constitution was suspended and direct rule reimposed. At the elections which followed, Labour was defeated by the (Conservative) National Party backed by the Catholic Church. The new government was also dissatisfied with the financial arrangements and Maltese political opinion turned to thoughts of complete independence. The island, with a population of just over 300,000 and few resources, achieved this in September 1964.

In Africa, too, hauling down the Union Jack was by no means easy. The difficulty was greater where white-settler interests were involved. This was so in Kenya and Southern Rhodesia. Armed revolt broke out in Kenya in 1952 and continued until 1956, when the Commander-in-Chief of the African 'Mau Mau' insurgents, Dedan Kimathi, was wounded and captured.[48] During the 'emergency' 10,527 Mau Mau were killed, 2,633 captured and 2,714 surrendered. British losses were 12 soldiers and 578 police and King's African Rifles (63 Europeans). Civilians killed included 32 Europeans, 26 Asians and 1,817 loyal Africans.[49] Between 75,000 and 80,000 Kikuyu, nearly 30 per cent of the men of the tribe, were interned[50] in camps which were often 'living hells'.[51] The most notorious of these, Hola Camp, where 11 detainees were murdered, was exposed by Barbara Castle in the Commons on 27 July 1959.[52] John Peel, MP and ex-colonial service officer, called those killed 'sub-human individuals'.[53] Enoch Powell denounced this remark by his fellow Conservative, calling it 'a fearful doctrine which must recoil upon the heads of those who pronounce it'.[54] The nationalist wind which was beginning to sweep across the African continent went unrecognized by this 'privileged, anachronistic society'.[55] Much of the land was in the hands of the 50,000 whites who dominated the 5 million Africans. The situation was further complicated by tribalism, the Kikuyu being the majority, and by the presence of an Asian trading and professional class. Iain Macleod, who became Colonial Secretary in October 1959, recognized the inevitability of majority rule and immediately started to release detained Africans. The London conference of January 1960 recognized eventual majority rule. In August 1961 Jomo Kenyatta, jailed in 1953 for alleged Mau Mau activities, was released because his dominance of Kenya African politics was recognized. Kenyatta had been fighting for African rights since the 1920s.[56] His 1953 conviction was due to the bribing of the presiding judge and the chief prosecution witness.[57] It was to take two more conferences and two more Colonial Secretaries, Maudling and Sandys, to finalize the independence constitution. At midnight on 11 December 1963 Kenya obtained its independence and entered the Commonwealth as the eighteenth sovereign member.

AFRICA: 'THE WIND OF CHANGE IS BLOWING'

The Labour government had resisted the demands of the European settlers for the creation of a Central African Federation. Yet the Federation comprising Southern Rhodesia, Northern Rhodesia (Zambia) and Nyasaland (Malawi) came into being on 1 August 1953. Thus, 300,000 white settlers came to dominate 9 million Africans. The scheme had been opposed by the great majority of Africans and, in Britain, by the Labour and Liberal Parties, the Archbishop of Canterbury, the Moderators of the Church of Scotland and the Free Church Federal Council. The (non-Communist)

International Confederation of Free Trade Unions also opposed it. Opposition from the Africans boiled over in early 1959. African organizations held meetings which were technically illegal. A state of emergency was declared, first in Nyasaland and then in Southern Rhodesia, where deaths occurred when the police attempted to quell protest demonstrations. Many politically organized Africans were arrested, including Dr Hastings Banda, widely recognized as that territory's African leader. A British government-appointed commission under Mr Justice Devlin reported adversely on some aspects of the way the disturbances had been handled. Macmillan himself first became convinced that there could be no progress without the release of Banda a year later on his famous African tour. He also convinced himself of the increasing African opposition to the Federation. It was during this trip in January 1960 that he made his speech in the South African parliament containing the much-quoted passage:

> the most striking of all the impressions I have formed since I left London a month ago is of the strength of this African national consciousness. In different places it takes different forms, but it is happening everywhere. The wind of change is blowing through this continent, and whether we like it or not, this growth of national consciousness is a political fact. We must all accept it as a fact, and our national policies must take account of it.[58]

His hosts refused to bend to this wind and left the Commonwealth in 1961. Macmillan recognized the inevitable in Northern Rhodesia and Nyasaland, allowing the development of internal self-government based on African majority rule, with Kenneth Kaunda and Hastings Banda emerging as leaders in the respective territories. Both territories were allowed to secede from the Federation and become independent in 1964.

As the Central African Federation was dying, the British government was planning other federations. There was the Federation of Nigeria, which gained its independence in 1960, a land with a population much larger than that of Britain. Like the Central African Federation, its basic weakness was that it was an attempt to unite separate regions which were different in economic and political development, and whose peoples had different tribal loyalties, different languages and different religions. In 1966 Nigeria's attempt at a democratic federation ended with a military *coup*. It was then held together by force of arms.

The wind of change also swept through Sierra Leone (1961), Uganda (1962), and Tanganyika and Zanzibar (which joined together to form Tanzania in 1964). All four became independent members of the Commonwealth under the Conservatives.

In 1962 the curtain was finally drawn on the West Indies Federation. This had been weak from the start. Inter-island communications were poor in an organization in which Jamaica and Trinidad, the two main components, were a thousand miles apart. The Federation had been run on a shoestring because the central government had no real power to raise revenue. Jamaica withdrew from the Federation after a referendum, and Trinidad and Tobago after a general election. Both became independent members of the Commonwealth in August 1962. This left the problem of what to do with the smaller islands. However, by 1966 Barbados, with a population of just over 200,000, became independent, Grenada, whose population was 104,000 in 1970, followed in 1974.

The one other attempt to set up a federation during this period was in Malaysia. Characteristically, it too failed. In August 1965 Singapore seceded from Malaysia to become an independent republic. Both states, however, remained members of the Commonwealth.

KUWAIT: 'EXPENSIVE TO STAY; HARD TO GET OUT'

Not deterred by such failures, the British government went ahead with the merging of Aden with the Federation of South Arabia. Since the Suez action Egypt had become more, not less, significant. So had the Soviet Union. Britain and the US grew alarmed at each manifestation of Arab nationalism, wrongly judging it to be a threat to their interests or a device of Soviet imperialism. In July 1958 the pro-British, reactionary regime of Nuri es-Said was overthrown by a military revolt following the Egyptian model, and Iraq withdrew from the Baghdad Pact. Earlier in 1958 Syria and Egypt had proclaimed their union in the United Arab Republic. This experiment was brought to an end by a Syrian military *coup* against Nasserite officials in Damascus in 1961. Alarmed, the pro-Western Lebanese President Chamoun requested US help under the Eisenhower Doctrine. He wrongly supposed that Egypt was interfering in the civil war which was developing in Lebanon. American marines were landed, but did not get involved in any fighting, and a compromise resulted. King Hussein of Jordan made a similar request to Britain and paratroops were duly dispatched. These were withdrawn after an all-Arab resolution was agreed in the UN General Assembly pledging non-interference between Arab states. British troops were also ordered to Kuwait, a British-protected state since 1899. In 1961 Kuwait, by that time an important oil producer, became independent and immediately came under pressure from General Kassim's regime in Iraq. A request for British help followed. Macmillan recorded in his diary (8 July 1961):

> We worked through some long and anxious nights, especially when we thought Kassem would seize Kuwait city and territory virtually unopposed. Now our worry is the opposite. Since the Iraqi attack has *not* in fact developed, all the pressure will be turned on us. It is going to be difficult, and expensive, to stay; hard to get out.[59]

British troops did in fact withdraw in September 1961. Kuwait was admitted to the Arab League and the members of this body sent a mixed force, including Egyptians, to ensure its independence from Iraq. Britain meanwhile had a problem in Yemen.

ADEN: 'TOLPUDDLE MARTYRS OF THE MIDDLE EAST'

The Yemen was a truly medieval kingdom which laid claim to Aden and the British-protected sheikhdoms bordering it. It had been too weak to realize its ambitions, even though from the mid-1950s it had received arms from the Soviet bloc. In 1962 a revolution broke out and the new rulers orientated the country towards Cairo. Most states recognized the new regime. Foolishly, Britain did not. Civil war followed in the Yemen and continued for many years.

Given all this turmoil in the Middle East, Aden did not look like a good prospect as an independent state. It had been seized by the British in 1839 as a vital refuelling port *en route* to India. With a population smaller than Nottingham, and in an area only half the size of the Isle of Wight, its inhabitants were dependent largely on a declining entrepôt trade, an oil refinery and the British base. Most of the population of 220,000 (1963) were Arabs, either born locally or from the British-protected states or Yemen. There was also a minority of Indians and Pakistanis, many of them engaged in trade. The Aden TUC, like the British TUC, affiliated to the International Confederation of Free Trade Unions, had a powerful hold over the Arab workers and was not satisfied with the constitutional progress made in the colony. Even the middle-class moderates in the Aden Association wanted an elected legislature, an elected ministry and Arabic as the official language. It was 1958 before Arabic was recognized, but the fulfilment of the other demands seemed far off.[60] Most of the population were not eligible to vote. The trade unions demanded complete independence from Britain and some form of association with the surrounding states, but not under their prevailing regimes. In 1959 there were widespread strikes. The government's answer was to make strikes virtually illegal. Aden was becoming more prominent in British defence planning by the 1960s. It was a familiar pattern. With the liquidation of the Canal Zone, Cyprus had become more important. When Cyprus became independent, Kenya was upgraded as a military base. As Kenya moved towards its freedom, Aden's future was scrutinized more closely. In August 1962 the British government published a White Paper proposing the merger of Aden with the surrounding Arab Emirates to form the Federation of South Arabia. Politically advanced Aden was to be tied to the feudalistic neighbouring sheikhdoms which were under British protection. Under the proposed constitution, Aden would have been in a minority position. In the Commons, Denis Healey, for Labour, claimed it meant ranging Britain 'with all that is most backward and anachronistic in the Middle East'.[61] George Thomson attacked the flogging and imprisonment of several Aden trade unionists who had gone on strike against the proposed merger. They were, he said, 'the Tolpuddle martyrs of the Middle East'.[62] In December 1962 Abdullah al-Asnag, Aden's trade union leader, and some others, were jailed for 'conspiring to publish a seditious publication'. More repression followed and the merger took place in spite of local protests on 18 January 1963. It was left to the incoming Labour government to deal with the mounting violence and disorder.

The last military excursion under the Conservatives was happier in its results than most of the others. In January 1964 British troops were sent to Kenya, Uganda and Tanganyika at the request of their governments. The British, with speed and efficiency, quelled army mutinies in those countries. The failure of the colonial administrations gradually to lay the foundations of professional officer corps before independence, and the attempt to do so hastily afterwards, together with dissatisfaction over pay, were at the root of the trouble.[63]

'SOCIALISM THAT DARES NOT IS BOUND TO FAIL'

The Suez campaign had given Labour the chance to unite over a great national issue. This mood did not last, and unresolved differences within the party soon came to the fore again. They were divided over their long-term aims and over the more immediate issues of public ownership and defence. Groups and individuals within the party re-examined Labour's experience of office and reasons for its two successive electoral defeats. They looked again at the changes in British society and asked themselves whether their policies needed refurbishing in the light of those changes. By 1954, G. D. H. Cole, who, as a professor of Politics at Oxford, a writer and a Labour activist, had influenced many of those who played significant roles in the Labour movement, asked, 'Is our goal the classless society, or only the so-called "open" society which is in fact still closed to a majority of the people?'[64] Cole was in no doubt himself what he wanted: 'a society of equals, set free from the twin evils of riches and poverty, mastership and subjection'.[65] He felt Attlee had done little to realize this dream, and the post-Attlee leaders were becoming even more timid.

> Democratic Socialism . . . dare not frighten possible marginal supporters; and it dare not flout that so-called 'public opinion' which is really newspaper opinion put about by the reactionary press. It dare not offend the Americans . . . A Socialism that dares not is bound to fail; for the fighting spirit which created the Socialist movement is no less needed to carry it through to its goal. The use of parliamentary and constitutional methods need not destroy this spirit.[66]

Cole was articulating the doubts and fears of thousands of Labour members, and a significant minority in the parliamentary party. For these people, Labour seemed to be dying from the Establishment embrace. Cole had always consciously rejected Marxism, but he believed that, in order to realize Labour's aims, more public ownership, not necessarily state ownership, was imperative. He had always advocated economic democracy, that is, workers' control of industry, the participation by all those employed in a particular industry in making the decisions which affect their lives and livelihoods. He wanted to see many other changes in society as well, but he thought economic democracy was the key to the transformation of society. Crossman wrote in a similar vein in his *Socialism and the New Despotism* (1955):

> We seek to make economic power responsive both to the community as a whole (the consumer) and to the worker in any particular industry (the producer). Plans for nationalization which do not satisfy the aspirations to workers' control are the technocrats' perversion of our Socialist ideal. We must frankly admit that, so far, our nationalized industries have been little better than that.[67]

Crossman, who was already a members of Labour's NEC, recommended his colleagues to study the experiment of *Mitbestimmung* (co-determination) in German industry. This was something Labour had ignored. It was also ignored by more conservative writers who were impressed by West Germany's good industrial relations. Crossman thought Keynesian economics had weakened the economic case for public ownership but not the moral case. He was concerned, however, about all types of irresponsible power – in private industry, in the state, in parties and in trade unions – in the mass society and the threat they presented to personal freedom. Both these writers agreed with Bevan that more common ownership would be necessary to achieve the socialist ideal.

Other, thoughtful members of the Labour Party came to different conclusions on economic policy. In 1956, the Socialist Union, a group based on the monthly journal *Socialist Commentary*, saw a danger in any monopoly in any sector of economic life. They were forcefully impressed by the totalitarian nature of the Soviet economy and the implications of that for the rest of the world. 'Where revolutions have overthrown the regimes of the past . . . public enterprise, a planned economy, even social services – are deliberately employed to reduce every individual to the helpless victim of the state.'[68]

Cole and the Left denied that Soviet-style regimes inevitably followed nationalization where there was a free electoral system, free trade unions, free media and workers' control. But the Socialist Union believed competition was needed for both political and economic reasons:

> The private sector of a socialist economy is not there merely on suffer-
> ance, to be tolerated only on grounds of political expediency . . .
> Within the limits of equality, there must be opportunities for people
> to spend as they wish, to own, to initiate and experiment; they must
> be able to form associations to further their economic interests.[69]

At greater length, Anthony Crosland argued in the same way in his *The
Future of Socialism* (1956). Gaitskell, in his contribution to the debate,
looked for ways Labour's aim of a society in which 'there are no social
classes, equal opportunity . . . a high degree of economic equality, full
employment, rapidly rising productivity, democracy in industry, and a
general spirit of co-operation between its members'[70] could be achieved
without nationalization. These measures included the growth of social services, severe taxation on high incomes, an increase in the share of national
income enjoyed by wage- and salary-earners, and educational reform.

All the writers, on the Left as well as on the Right of Labour, were deeply
influenced by the new, negative image of the Soviet Union, a vision strongly
coloured by (socialist) Orwell's *1984,* which was widely discussed. They were
also influenced by the indifference of the majority of the workers to the issue
of public ownership. Further, they, and much of the public, had suffered disappointment over the nationalized industries in Britain; though it must be
stressed that such disappointment resulted from a naively optimistic view
of what could be achieved in run-down industries over a short period.
Finally, Gaitskell, as party leader, was concerned about the damage to
Labour's image by the close association of the Party with nationalization.
At successive elections pro-'Free Enterprise' bodies had launched massive
publicity campaigns against further nationalization. For all these reasons,
whereas Cole, Bevan and others still placed a great deal of emphasis on
'common ownership', Gaitskell drastically restricted the role of public enterprise. It was his view which prevailed.

At the Labour conference at Brighton in 1957, Wilson, for the NEC,
introduced *Industry and Society*, which set out the party's view on public
ownership. It was basically Gaitskell's conception. It committed Labour
to the renationalization of the steel industry and road haulage, but there
was no 'shopping list' of industries to be taken over. Only those industries
which were – through monopoly power, bad labour relations, failure to
export, and so on – 'failing the nation' were possible candidates for nationalization. This policy was adopted by 5.3 million to 1.4 million, with Bevan's
wife, Jennie Lee, the National Union of Railwaymen and, more strongly,
Morrison and Shinwell against.[71]

H-BOMB: 'NAKED INTO THE CONFERENCE CHAMBER'

The other big issue which caused Labour much heart-searching was the

H-bomb. The Bevanites had opposed Britain's decision to manufacture the H-bomb. In 1957 Bevan changed his position dramatically and thus deprived Labour's Left of its leader, destroying in the process the faith of some of the rank-and-file in all leaders. This shift was announced at Brighton. Britain's bomb, Bevan now argued, could force the other superpowers to take notice of Britain and could give the UK a decisive voice in international affairs. In opposing a unilateralist resolution, he declared: 'if you carry this resolution . . . you will send a Foreign Secretary . . . naked into the conference chamber'. He believed the bomb could give Britain 'the opportunity of interposing' between the US and Russia, 'modifying, moderating, and mitigating influence'.[72] The offending resolution was then thrown out with the help of the block votes of the big trade unions rather than the rhetoric of Bevan. Most delegates from the constituency parties, representing the activists who did most of the menial political work, delegates who had previously supported Bevan, voted the other way.

Some of those dismayed, defeated, and disgusted activists were already working in what was to become a new mass movement to rid Britain of its nuclear weapons – the Campaign for Nuclear Disarmament (CND). CND was announced in February 1958, but for some time before this various groups had been set up to oppose British, and all other, nuclear weapons. In 1954, a small group of MPs under the chairmanship of Fenner Brockway formed the Hydrogen Bomb National Campaign Committee. Among its more prominent members were Tony (Anthony Wedgwood) Benn and Anthony Greenwood. CND itself, a much larger, non-party, non-sectarian movement, resulted from discussions which followed an article by J. B. Priestley in the *New Statesman* (2 November 1957). Priestley wrote:

> The British of these times, so frequently hiding their decent, kind faces behind masks of sullen apathy or sour, cheap cynicism, often seem to be waiting for something better than party squabbles and appeals to their narrowest self interest, something great and noble in its intention that would make them feel good again. And this might well be a declaration to the world that after a certain date one power able to engage in nuclear warfare will reject the evil thing for ever.

It was a patriotic appeal to idealism and it impressed many young people who were searching for something more elevating than mere affluence. The movement was headed by (Earl) Bertrand Russell, the philosopher, its secretary was Canon L. John Collins of St Paul's Cathedral. On the executive committee they were joined by Michael Foot, close friend of Bevan and editor of the Left Labour weekly *Tribune*; Ritchie Calder, noted as a scientific journalist; Priestley; James Cameron, a well-known journalist; Kingsley Martin, editor of the *New Statesman*; Howard Davies of the UN Association; and Lord Simon of Wythenshawe.[73] In April

1958 the movement organized a protest march from London to the Atomic Weapons Research Establishment at Aldermaston. Marchers covered the 50 miles between 4 and 7 April. Frank Allaun, Labour MP for Salford East, Dr Donald Soper, the Methodist leader, and Pastor Martin Niemöller, the German pacifist and First World War U-Boat commander, led 5,000 marchers on the final day. CND was established 'to demand a British initiative to reduce the nuclear peril and to stop the armaments race, if need be by unilateral action by Great Britain'. Despite the support of a number of Labour MPs it remained largely a movement of the intelligentsia, the middle classes and youth. Among the more prominent intellectual supporters were the writers John Braine, John Brunner, Mervyn Jones, Doris Lessing, Sir Compton Mackenzie, Iris Murdoch, Alan Sillitoe and Arnold Wesker. Others prominent included art critic John Berger, sculptor Henry Moore, historian A. J. P. Taylor, actors Spike Milligan, John Neville and Vanessa Redgrave, and film directors Anthony Asquith, Basil Wright and Lindsay Anderson.[74] Such a list by no means exhausts the star-studded lists of sponsors and activists.

NEW LEFT: A 'SENSE OF OUTRAGE'

CND drew strength from the anger of a section of the literary class over what was considered to be the complacency which appeared to be smothering post-war Britain. Their spokesmen were dubbed by the press the 'angry young men'. One of the most significant was John Osborne (1929–94), who became famous overnight with his play *Look Back In Anger*. Put on by the new English Stage Company at the Royal Court Theatre in 1956, it marked a turning-point in the British theatre, with greater interest in social criticism and experimentation. Arnold Wesker (b. 1932) was successful with his portrayals of East-End, Jewish working-class life. Alan Sillitoe described the problems, tensions and hopes of the working class in Nottingham, where he had himself been a factory worker. David Storey (b. 1933), the son of a Yorkshire miner, made his name with *This Sporting Life*, about the tough life of Yorkshire Rugby League players, which he knew first-hand. Of all the characters who emerged from the pages of this new genre, the best known was Joe Lampton, hero of John Braine's (1922–86) *Room at the Top*. Joe 'was brought up on the fringes of poverty and squalor in an ugly North Country town. He had emerged with one overriding aim: to fight his way into the bright world of money and influence.'[75] Joe was not particularly political and he, and his creator, subsequently found much of their anger against the system appeased by fame and fortune. These, and some other similar writers, probably had marginal political influence, but they were much more important for helping to revitalize the British theatre and cinema. Indirectly, they exposed the weakness of the English education system. Only Storey had managed to get to an institution of higher education. Some of them had not even been to a grammar school.

The writers were not the only young critics of society in the late 1950s. The Suez campaign and the Hungarian Revolution produced what became known as the New Left. Roughly speaking, the New Left was a coming together of Communists disillusioned by Soviet actions in Hungary and disillusioned young members of the Establishment who disapproved of the Suez campaign. The core of the New Left was the group of supporters of the *New Left Review*, which was a merger of the *Universities and New Left Review* and the *New Reasoner*. Whether they were ex-Communists or ex-Conservatives, New Lefters were often Oxbridge graduates. Ralph Samuel and the West Indian and later sociology professor, Stuart Hall, were the driving force behind the movement which presided over the establishment of a chain of Left clubs and coffee bars throughout the country. At a time when political parties were complaining about apathy and the difficulty of finding audiences for prominent politicians, considerable numbers of people in London paid to attend New Left meetings. Among their contributors, Ralph Miliband, of the London School of Economics, derided the Attlee governments for their lack of radicalism; Brian Abel-Smith, also LSE, felt the middle classes were benefiting more from the welfare state than the working classes; Hugh Thomas, ex-Foreign Office and future Conservative, denounced the Suez operation. Paul Johnson, journalist and later Thatcherite, suffered from a sense of outrage. He wanted an end to the monarchy, the Lords, the public schools and Oxbridge, the regimental system, the Inns of Court, the honours list and much else. He warned that if Labour 'surrenders its sense of outrage, and allows the power-motive to become its political dynamic, it will cease to be a progressive movement, and something else will take its place'.[76]

With the interest generated by CND and the New Left, with the Labour leadership looking reasonably united, and with by-election swings against the Conservatives, things appeared to be looking up for Labour. However, when the election was called for 8 October 1959, the polls revealed the Conservatives as the favourites. The Conservatives had mounted a successful advertising campaign, aimed at the aspiring housewife, with the slogan, 'Life's better with the Conservatives . . . Don't let Labour ruin it'. They had also played on their credentials as seekers of international accord, with Macmillan flying to Moscow earlier in the year and then to Washington and other capitals. The government also announced the ending of conscription. Labour had some good TV broadcasts, and the Liberals fought well under their new leader, Jo Grimond, but the Conservative bandwagon was rolling. Gaitskell made one campaign blunder. He had advocated an ambitious pensions' scheme. When asked, 'Where's the money coming from?', he gave a doubt-raising pledge: 'There will be no increase in . . . income tax so long as normal peacetime conditions continue.'[77]

The results put the Conservatives back with a net gain of 21 seats. Labour had a net loss of 19 seats. Liberal representation remained at 6 seats. The Liberals took some comfort from the fact that their share of the vote had increased from 2.5 per cent in 1951, and 2.7 per cent in 1955, to 5.9 per cent in 1959. Both major parties had their share of the poll reduced, Labour by 2.6 per cent to 43.8 per cent, the Conservatives by 0.3 to 49.4 per cent.[78] Labour had gained slightly among women and lost among men. It had lost any advantage it had with young voters, but more older people had voted Labour. Labour also suffered from abstentions, though turnout was up from 76.8 to 78.7 per cent. The swing to the Conservatives tended to be smallest in places where turnout increased most. Most of the Conservative gains were in the Midlands and outer London. Clydeside and South Lancashire swung more decisively to Labour. The Conservatives had a 100-seat majority and an unprecedented three electoral victories in a row. Among the new Conservative intake was Margaret Hilda Thatcher, returned for the safe Conservative seat of Finchley.

LABOUR'S 'CLASS IMAGE'

It was inevitable that the third election defeat of Labour would lead to more argument at all levels about its aims and methods. Immediately after the election Labour 'revisionists' began to prescribe medicine to save their party from what they diagnosed to be a slow, lingering, but certain, death. Douglas Jay, who had served as Economic Secretary to the Treasury under Attlee, led the attack in the Labour weekly *Forward* (16 October 1959), claiming Labour was suffering from 'two fatal handicaps – the class image and the myth of nationalization'. Many prosperous workers, especially women, no longer classified themselves as working class. They aspired to something more. They were also hostile to nationalization. Labour should drop nationalization and get away from its cloth cap image. Even the name 'Labour' was a disadvantage, though he did not propose to ditch that. Gaitskell supported Jay's views, but at the annual conference in November he expressed himself more cautiously. He questioned whether Clause IV, adopted in 1918, which called for the common ownership of the means of production, distribution and exchange, and the best obtainable system of popular administration and control of each industry or service, gave the correct impression of Labour's aims. 'It implies that common ownership is an end, whereas in fact, it is a means.'[79] He was right that Labour did not contemplate nationalizing everything, 'the whole of light industry . . . every little pub', but he was not correct that common ownership was seen as an end in itself. According to Clause IV, the end was 'To secure for the producers by hand and by brain the full fruits of their industry'. He was right when he urged that Labour was not just about common ownership, and clearly Labour needed to recast its image. The problem was that the delegates felt bitter and angry about Labour's defeat. They felt it was the victim of the Conservatives' slick public relations campaign which had cost far more than Labour felt it could afford. With talk of changing Labour's constitution and engaging in public relations activities, Gaitskell seemed to be indicating a lack of faith in the tenets of the party at a time when many were looking for a reaffirmation of faith. In other words, his intervention was psychologically ill-timed. It received, therefore, the appropriate rebuff from speaker after speaker.

In an attempt to resolve matters, Gaitskell commissioned a survey of opinion on voters' attitudes. Dr Rita Hinden, for 10 years secretary of the Fabian Colonial Bureau, and editor of the *Socialist Commentary*, believed the survey revealed Labour's weakness as poor class image, nationalization and 'weak, divided leadership'.[80] When one looks at the survey, carried out by two skilled investigators, Mark Abrams and Richard Rose, the evidence is not unequivocal. Labour was identified with the working class rather than with the 'nation as a whole', and this was a problem in attempting to win over non-Labour working-class voters who were less likely to see themselves as working class. Yet Labour did far better than the Conservatives on 'Raise the standard of living of ordinary people'. Far more non-Labour voters believed this of Labour than Labour supporters applied this to the Conservatives. On public ownership, the researchers found there was neither 'blind faith or blind rejection'.[81] Some nationalized industries – electricity, atomic energy, airlines – were regarded as successes. For gas 'the votes for success are about 50 per cent higher than for failure; only when people come to judge coal-mining and the railways were they emphatically convinced that public ownership has been a failure'.[82] Even among Conservative supporters, 'favourable attitudes towards public ownership exceed unfavourable views for four out of six listed industries'.[83] But there was little enthusiasm for additional nationalization. Hinden concluded that Labour could not afford to be doctrinaire on this issue. Other conclusions are of course possible. It could be argued that the survey merely revealed the ignorance of the public at large about the problems of the railways and the mines. It is also plausible to conclude that the airlines, atomic energy and electricity benefited from a more modern and exciting image than coal and railways. Further, a great deal of money had been spent on anti-nationalization campaigns which Labour had done little to counter. The Left had not thought creatively about the alternatives to state corporations and many had still not digested the negative aspects of the Soviet experience. The 'revisionists' made a mistake with their timing, and some were too dogmatic on too little evidence. Probably due to ignorance, few supporters of 'common ownership' used as evidence the successes of such publicly owned firms as Volkswagen, Renault and some of the Italian and Austrian state enterprises.

The surveys did show that Labour suffered from its leadership battles, with Macmillan scoring over Gaitskell as a leader 'Strong enough to make unwelcome decisions'. This was considered the most important quality in a Prime Minister. One surprise in the survey was that Labour was seen as the party which was more likely to work to prevent a nuclear war, and this was put top of the list of priorities by those interviewed.[84] How best to do this was the issue which provoked more controversy than any other in Labour's ranks in the two years which followed.

'PACIFISTS, UNILATERALISTS AND FELLOW-TRAVELLERS'

The two big events in Labour's history in 1960 were the death of Bevan and the defeat of Gaitskell on the nuclear issue. Despite not seeing eye to eye on public ownership, they stood together in public. James Griffiths had decided, in 1959, not to seek re-election as deputy leader, and Bevan was unanimously elected in his place by the parliamentary party. He died of cancer in July.

Opinion seemed to be moving in favour of CND, but a great break-through was made when Frank Cousins, who had led the TGWU since the spring of 1956, brought his union into line with CND. Cousins (1904–86), the son of a railwayman, had worked in the Nottinghamshire pits, and as a truckdriver, before becoming a union organizer.[85] Labour's nuclear defence policy was also under attack from the Victory for Socialism (VfS) group, which included Allaun, Foot, Ian Mikardo, Stephen Swingler and some other Labour MPs. The group had been revitalized in 1958 and pursued a consistently left-wing line on all aspects of party policy. Important at this time were policy differences over defence. With the cancellation of Blue Streak in April 1960, Gaitskell was caught off balance as 'it seemed at first that the defence of British nuclear independence was now academic. Without a delivery system the defence of the British bomb seemed absurd and unrealistic.'[86] When the party conference discussed the issue at Scarborough in October 1960, it was the CND line that carried the day. Cousins, with his union's block vote, tipped the balance. He proposed a resolution on behalf of his union calling for 'A complete rejection of any defence policy based on the threat of the use of strategic or tactical nuclear weapons'.[87] It not only sought the end of the British bomb, it also sought the withdrawal of all American nuclear bases from Britain. It did not, however, call for a withdrawal from NATO and, as Gaitskell was able to point out, left important matters unclear. It was adopted by the slender margin of 3,282,000 to 3,239,000. The leader, despite his passion, oratory and obvious sincerity, did his cause no good by his comment, 'What sort of people do you think we are? . . . Do you think we can become overnight the pacifists, unilateralists and fellow-travellers that other people are?'[88] Cousins was certainly no fellow-traveller and resented the accusation. The Communists had withheld support from CND until mid-1960 because the movement criticized both the US and the Soviet Union. Seeing in CND's growing strength a chance to defeat Gaitskell, they changed their tune. Despite their later high visibility on marches, they did not make serious inroads into the movement.

On 13 August 1961 the East Germans sealed off their part of Berlin and started building the notorious Wall. Macmillan felt, 'The danger is, of course, that with both sides bluffing, disaster may come by mistake.'[89] This is what many in CND were worried about. Even more hair-raising was the Cuban missile crisis of 1962. The Soviets had installed offensive missiles on Cuba, which were withdrawn when Kennedy gave assurances that Cuba would not be invaded.

EEC: 'THE END OF A THOUSAND YEARS OF HISTORY'

Gaitskell's defeat led to the setting up of the Campaign for Democratic Socialism (CDS) in November 1960. It was the brainchild of William Rodgers, General Secretary of the Fabian Society, and Anthony Crosland. Its aim was to support Gaitskell and his policies. Gaitskell as Party Leader was not directly involved. Jay and Jenkins were among the MPs involved. Several members of the shadow cabinet – Brown, Callaghan, Healey among them – supported it. From the Lords, Attlee, Dalton and Pakenham (Lord Longford) were associated with it. The CDS also managed to secure the support of a number of leading trade unionists, such as William Carron, leader of the AEU; Sam Watson of the Miners; Ron Smith, General Secretary of the Post Office Workers' Union; Anne Godwin, General Secretary of the Clerical and Administrative Workers' Union; and W. J. P. Webber, General Secretary of the Transport Salaried Staffs Association. Disagreements within CND and the CDS helped to bring about a partial reversal of the Scarborough policy on nuclear defence at the 1961 conference. The conference supported NATO and US bases in Britain but called for the abandonment of Britain's bomb. The same conference opposed West German troops training in Wales and the establishment of Polaris nuclear submarine bases. The conference also adopted the moderate home policy document *Signposts for the Sixties*.

By 1962 Labour was facing another major issue: Britain's proposed entry into the European Economic Community (EEC). Most of the Left, including the VfS group, opposed this. The Parliamentary Labour Party (31 July 1961) wanted entry dependent on approval by the Commonwealth Prime Ministers and the European Free Trade Association (EFTA).[90] Most of the CDS favoured entry, but Jay and Gaitskell did not. At the Brighton conference in October 1962, Gaitskell announced what amounted to a rejection of entry. Gaitskell spoke of 'the end of a thousand years of history' and the end of the Commonwealth if Britain joined.[91] The conference agreed a resolution. It opened: Labour 'regards the European Community as a great and imaginative conception'. It went on to lay down five tough conditions of entry: strong and binding Commonwealth safeguards; freedom to pursue an independent foreign policy; fulfilment of pledges to Britain's partners in EFTA; 'the right to plan our own economy'; and guarantees to safeguard the position of British agriculture.[92] It was a moment of triumph for Gaitskell. His speech had endeared him to many constituency activists who had previously regarded him with suspicion. But he was robbed of full and final victory by his short illness and strange death on 18 January 1963.

EEC: 'NO THREE CHEERS FOR BRITISH ENTRY'

All Labour's debates about the EEC were purely academic; so were the government's negotiations. Britain had no chance of entry at that time. At the end of the two-day Commons debate in July 1961 announcing Britain's application to join, only one Conservative and four Labour MPs[93] voted against the proposal; 25 Conservatives and the official Opposition abstained. Macmillan had already sounded out opinion among influential groups, and got a favourable response. Important sections of the press were positive and public opinion, to the extent that it existed, did not appear to be hostile. The plan to take Britain into the EEC originated, not in Parliament, but in the Treasury, the Foreign Office and the boardrooms of big business. The EEC, it was argued, would provide British industry with the two things it badly needed: a larger home market and the stiff competition which would force it to improve. There were those who were less certain about the future of the Commonwealth. Would not Commonwealth states look increasingly to other states than Britain for increased trade and aid? The Commonwealth Immigration Act, 1962 represented a turning away from the older intimacy with the Commonwealth. Implicitly, it was part of the reappraisal of Britain's role and direction, but not by the man who carried the responsibility for it, R. A. Butler. He had reservations about the EEC. Macmillan did, however, succeed in convincing his colleagues, and the initiative was endorsed by the Conservative annual conference.

Macmillan got on well with Kennedy, whose sister Kathleen had married Macmillan's wife's nephew. This was in spite of their differences of age, style, background, nationality and the fact that Kennedy claimed to lead the 'party of hope' rather than the 'party of nostalgia'. The two 'found the same things funny and the same things serious'.[94] The EEC was serious. Macmillan got the blessing of President Kennedy in April 1961, and again in April 1962, for Britain's entry. Kennedy did, nevertheless, warn Macmillan, on the second occasion, 'that Britain must not expect to take care of everyone in its economic wake – either in the Commonwealth or the European Free Trade Association – at America's expense'.[95] The United States wanted Britain in for political, rather than economic, reasons. 'Britain, with its world obligations, could keep the EEC from becoming a high-tariff, inward-looking, white man's club. Above all, with British membership, the Market could become the basis for a true political federation of Europe.'[96] Kennedy demonstrated how important he thought Britain's membership to be by mobilizing half his Cabinet to impress this on Gaitskell when he visited Washington in 1962.[97] He raised the matter with President de Gaulle in June 1961. The French President was, however, wary of Britain, regarding it as the Trojan Horse of Washington. Anglo-French co-operation in nuclear defence could have recommended Britain to de Gaulle; Macmillan foolishly did not see this.[98] Anglo-US nuclear co-operation 'became a major element in de Gaulle's determination to keep Britain out of Europe'.[99] The Nassau Agreement (discussed below) 'fully confirmed his basic assessment that British strategy with its dependence upon the United States clashed with a European orientation of Britain's economic policy'.[100]

Another adversary of Britain's admission to the EEC was Konrad Adenauer, who had been West German Chancellor since 1949. Adenauer and Macmillan did not see eye to eye on the Soviet Union. Adenauer believed Macmillan was inclined to make concessions to the Soviets for electoral purposes, and was too ready to suggest German concessions in Britain's interest. He is said to have described Britain as the exploiter of 'us poor dumb Continentals'.[101] Adenauer told de Gaulle that Macmillan had offered economic union to the US – without success. Adenauer was also worried that sterling was weak, that the administrative apparatus of the EEC could not yet integrate Britain and the other applicants, and that Britain was hoping to undermine Franco-German unity. Britain and the Federal Republic were also at odds over the cost of stationing British troops in Germany. De Gaulle fed Adenauer's suspicions. He claimed to the Chancellor that Macmillan had sought to include the Commonwealth in the EEC, and feared the US would be next in line for admission. Adenauer is reported to have concluded his discussion with de Gaulle on the issue by saying, 'No three cheers for a British entry'.[102] The negotiations, led by Edward Heath, started in October 1961, and when they looked close to success, on 14 January 1963, de Gaulle held a press conference in Paris, declaring that his country would veto the UK's entry into the EEC, come what may. The other members of the Community would have, in principle, welcomed Britain's admission. The same was true of many members of the West German Establishment and the opposition Social Democrats.

After the failure of his EEC bid, Macmillan clung even more to the US. At Nassau in December 1962, when the failure in Europe was in sight, he got Kennedy to agree to sell Polaris missiles for launching British nuclear warheads from British-built submarines. Polaris replaced the Skybolt missile which, jointly developed by Britain and the US, had been cancelled because of mounting costs. In some quarters this gave renewed credibility to the government's claim to have a British, independent deterrent, and to the claim to a 'special relationship' with the United States. Macmillan's last major initiative in external affairs was the Nuclear Test Ban Treaty. This was signed in Moscow in August 1963 by Britain, the Soviet Union and the United States. The treaty banned nuclear explosions in the atmosphere, outer space and underwater, but not, alas, underground. Many other states immediately signified their readiness to sign; unfortunately, France and China were not among them. Macmillan could be proud of the outcome, limited though it was, for he had sought it longer, and with greater zeal, than any other statesman.

ECONOMIC TROUBLES: THE 'GUIDING LIGHT'

By early 1961 the economy started to show signs that it was entering the 'stop' part of the 'stop–go' cycle which had become a feature of the post-war economy. At home output was rising slowly, abroad the pound was under pressure and the balance of payments remained in the red. In April, Selwyn Lloyd, who had replaced Amory as Chancellor in July 1960, introduced a politically damaging Budget – a combination of increases in the insurance stamp and health charges, and reductions in surtax. More action followed in July. This included raising the bank rate from 5 per cent to 7 per cent, a surcharge on purchase tax, cuts in public expenditure and the prospect of a pay pause and long-term planning of the economy. Within a month Britain was granted a large credit by the International Monetary Fund (IMF). In February 1962 the Chancellor announced a 2–2.5 per cent 'guiding light' for pay settlements.

A new feature of government policy to counter Britain's economic weakness was the setting up of the National Economic Development Council (NEDC), proposed by the Chancellor in July. Its task was to examine British economic prospects, stretching five or more years into the future. Its membership consisted of appropriate ministers, civil servants, academics, and management and unions in industry. Among the eight industrialists on NEDC were Reay Geddes of Dunlop, F. A. Cockfield of Boots, Lord Robens of the Coal Board, a former leading Labour politician, and Dr Richard Beeching of the British Transport Commission. Beeching became the target of popular wrath for his plans to prune the railways. On the union side were Cousins, Carron, Sid Greene of the rail union, and Ron Smith. George Woodcock, General Secretary of the TUC, 1960–69, was also a member. Remarkably, Woodcock was one of the few professional economists on NEDC. A former Lancashire spinner who had started work at twelve, he gained a first-class honours degree in economics at Oxford. After an interlude in the civil service, he worked as senior economist to the TUC for 10 years.

Macmillan had favoured 'planning' in the 1930s and had published a book, *The Middle Way*, which advocated what became known as indicative planning. But NEDC was not the product of his fertile mind. A group of somewhat unorthodox industrialists, led by Sir Hugh Beaver of Guinness and reinforced by Reay Geddes, had convinced Lloyd of the idea.[103] They, and some others, had been impressed by French experience. Despite wartime devastation, colonial retreat, labour unrest and severe political turmoil, France was achieving higher economic growth than Britain. The French claimed to take economic planning seriously, so it was thought that Britain should follow their example.[104] One idea behind NEDC was the need for an economic forecasting and advisory body independent of the Treasury. There was a good deal of scepticism about the quality of the Treasury's advice, and the crisis of 1961 strengthened that scepticism. The NEDC was also designed as a body through which the two sides of industry could work out a strategy for the future. It was sold to the public as planning by consent. In terms of what the Conservatives had said about planning for over 10 years, it represented a dramatic shift in policy. As the Conservative journalist Henry Fairlie put it in *Encounter* (September 1962), it represented

> almost the exact reverse of the attitude of 'Set the People Free', which was Conservatism in 1951; of 'Conservative Freedom Works', which became Conservatism before and after 1955, and of 'I'm all right, Jack', which was Conservatism in 1959.

There was dismay in certain Conservative circles and a majority of the Cabinet opposed it.[105] Another measure conceived to help the country's limping economy was the National Incomes Commission announced by the Prime Minister in July 1962. This was presented as an impartial review body on pay, but it never got off the ground because the unions did not regard it as such. 'Neddy' and 'Nicky', as the NEDC and the Commission became known, did nothing to help the Conservatives' sagging fortunes.

MAC THE KNIFE'S 'JULY MASSACRE'

From June 1961 Labour led the Conservatives in the polls, and a number of by-elections warned the government of its likely fate at a general election. The most dramatic of them was the loss of the 'safe' Conservative seat at Orpington in March 1962. The interesting aspect of this result was that the Liberals won, not Labour. It marked part of a trend of rising Liberal support. Although Orpington was not Labour-type territory, there was much speculation that this Liberal victory marked a more permanent trend towards the Liberals. This was not the case. The new Liberal voters were, in many cases, part of the suburban revolt against the Conservatives rather than positive conviction that the Liberals had anything to offer. Orpington, however, was no flash in the pan. It highlighted a trend. Dissatisfied or bored with the two main parties, more voters were prepared to experiment with minor parties from the early 1960s on. The major parties' grip was loosening a little. In June 1962 Labour took their first seat from the Conservatives since the general election, at Middlesbrough West. On the same day the Liberals pushed Labour into third place at Derbyshire West, where the Conservatives retained the seat but with a much reduced percentage of the vote. In the following month, Labour retained Leicester North East, and this time the Liberals pushed the Conservatives into third place. The next day occurred what became known as the 'July massacre'.

Macmillan had been ridiculed as 'Macwonder' and 'Super Mac'. Now he was christened 'Mac the knife'. The Opposition scoffed at him, though some admired his audacity in private. Among Conservatives there was shock and anger. He had embarked upon the biggest Cabinet reshuffle of the post-war period. Out went his Lord Chancellor, Chancellor of the Exchequer, Minister of Defence, Ministers of Education, Housing and Local Government, and a number of others of lesser importance. Lord Mills, Minister without Portfolio, also departed. Those so slain had not formed any 'anti-party group' against Macmillan, nor could they be said to represent the Right or the Left of the party. In the main they seemed to be 'fall guys' for policy failures. In two major areas the vacancies gave Macmillan the chance to appoint younger, reform-orientated, ministers. These were Reginald Maudling (Chancellor of the Exchequer) and Sir Edward (later Lord) Boyle (Education). Some of the changes gave hope to Tory reformers, but at the grassroots level confidence was shattered. The electorate was not impressed either. In November 1962, in the first by-elections after the reshuffle, Labour took Dorset South and Glasgow Woodside from the Conservatives, and scored a near miss at Norfolk Central. Nor did the death of Gaitskell in January 1963 seem to alter the trend very much. It was still, however, much more a trend against the government than positively for Labour.

'SPECULATORS . . . HOLDING COMMUNITY TO RANSOM'

In addition to the economic and other problems facing Macmillan, the government was confronted with a series of scandals which, taken together and stretching over a fairly long period, must have harmed the credibility of the Conservatives. First of all there was public anger over the effects of the property boom of the 1950s and early 1960s. Over 100 people became millionaires between 1945 and 1965 as a result of their activities as property developers.[106] Jack Cotton, Charles Clore, Harry Hyams, Jack and Philip Rose, and Sir Harold Samuels became well known for their *coups* and take-overs of property firms, and the controversy much of their redeveloping caused. War damage and economic development naturally led to the redevelopment of towns and cities. But the frenzied redevelopment of the period owed much to the repealing – 1953, 1954 and 1959 – of the Labour government's town and country planning legislation, under which development profits went to the state, and the creation of a free market in development land. The familiar skyline of London was shattered by the high-rise blocks – in part, office blocks no one wanted, luxury flats no one could afford and hotels which were beyond the means of the natives. Most developers kept within the law; some did not. One notorious case, which became a symbol of the time, was that of the landlord Peter Rachman. He bought run-down property for redevelopment. His problem was sitting tenants who would not move. He therefore used any number of brutal and illegal means to get them out. Sir Basil Spence, President of the Royal Institute of British Architects, said:

> The speculators are cornering the limited supply of building land in town and country and holding the community to ransom. The money that should be going into better architecture and higher standards is being taken by people who have contributed nothing to the building process.[107]

PROFUMO: 'TAWDRY CYNICISM'

There were a number of other scandals which cast their shadows over the affluent society and the Conservative Party. The hold-up of the Glasgow–London mail train and robbery of £2.5 million on 8 August 1963 must rank as one of the most spectacular crimes in history. Although the Prime Minister could not be blamed for this, it did appear to be one more indication that Britain was as out of date and Edwardian as Macmillan's image. It came at the tail-end of a number of spy and security affairs. There was the Portland (Underwater Weapons Establishment) spy scandal in March 1961.[108] There was the case of John Vassall, a Foreign Office clerk blackmailed into spying for the Russians and convicted in November 1962. There was the conviction of the double agent George Blake, who had betrayed many British operatives behind the Iron Curtain. In January 1963 Kim Philby, former Middle East correspondent of the *Observer*, and former head of the Soviet section of Britain's Secret Intelligence Service, reached the safety of the Soviet Union, for which he had been working for many years. Worst of all for Macmillan was the Profumo affair. John Profumo, Secretary of State for War, a minister not in the Cabinet, had an affair with Christine Keeler, a 20-year-old model, who was simultaneously involved with Captain Eugene Ivanov, assistant Soviet naval attaché and an intelligence officer. Profumo's mistake was to deny, in the Commons, his sexual relations with the girl. This untruth was exposed by the *Sunday Mirror*. During June–September 1963 Lord Denning investigated the matter. He criticized Macmillan in his report: 'It was the responsibility of the Prime Minister and his colleagues . . . to deal with this situation: and they did not succeed in doing so.'[109] Denning did not believe the case revealed a fall in the integrity of public life in Britain. The difference was that, compared with the past, 'Scandalous information about well-known people has become a marketable commodity'. Doubtless this was so, but many people thought the affair revealed the hypocrisy in high places. An editorial in *The Times* (4 July 1963) summed up what many dis-illusioned Conservative voters thought: 'The tawdry cynicism that the worst Conservatives flaunt needs to be exorcized.' Ronald Butt, in the *Financial Times* (20 September 1963), blamed the 'pay pause' and Profumo for the decline in Conservative support. He believed 'a large section of the middle-class had come to think the government was not "fair"'. Pounded from all sides, and suffering from an illness which was not just diplomatic, Macmillan resigned in October 1963. Maudling reported him as saying that 'he never thought he could be "brought down by two tarts"'.[110]

HOME PREMIER: 'BAD JOKE OF DEMOCRACY'

At the Conservative conference at Blackpool Home read out Macmillan's letter of resignation. It caused 'consternation, confusion and intrigue'.[111] There appeared to be four potential successors: Maudling, Macleod, Heath and Butler. Two others, Home and Hailsham, seemed disqualified by virtue of being in the Lords rather than the Commons. The removal of this disqualification was, however, made possible by the Peerage Act, 1963, which was given all-party support and became law on 31 July. Under the Act, a peer can disclaim his peerage for his lifetime. The cam-paign to change the law was led by Tony Benn, the Labour MP, who suc-ceeded to his father's title in November 1960. Butler was well qualified in terms of experience; Maudling in terms of youth. Maudling (1917–79) was brought up in comfortable circumstances in Bexhill and London. After war-time service in the RAF and Oxford, he qualified as a barrister and worked for the Conservative Research Department. Elected to the Commons in 1950, he served as Minister of Supply (1955–57), Paymaster-General (1957–59), President of the Board of Trade (1959–61) and then as Colonial Secretary before his appointment as Chancellor in 1962. He was promoted to the Cabinet in September 1957. Hailsham won the Oxford by-election in 1938 as a staunch supporter of Chamberlain's appeasement policy. His major appointments were First Lord of the Admiralty, Minister of Educa-tion, Lord President of the Council and Minister of Science. He unexpec-tedly renounced his peerage to make himself a contender. Macleod was joint Chairman of the Conservative Party with Lord Poole. He was thought to be out of the race because he was 'too left-wing, too tired'.[112] Conserva-tive leaders were not elected in those days. As Maudling has recorded, the decision was reached through 'the rather mysterious channels of communication within the Party'.[113] Butler tells us that Macmillan switched his support to Home, ignoring the mounting opposition within the Cabinet to him, and advised the Queen to ask him to form a government.[114] Both Hailsham and Maudling withdrew in favour of Butler, but to no avail. The row over the new Prime Minister led to Macleod and Enoch Powell refusing to serve under Home. Pressure forced the Conservatives to change their method of selecting the Leader from 'mysterious channels' to election.

The Times (19 October 1963) drew attention to the new Prime Minister's weaknesses: 'It is not the earl but the politician over whom the doubt arises. Except for a spell in the junior office of Minister of State for Scotland in 1951–55 Lord Home has no administrative experience of home affairs.' Home (b. 1903) was first elected, as Lord Dunglass, to the Commons in 1931 and worked as Chamberlain's Parliamentary Private Secretary (1937–39). Tuberculosis kept him out of the political arena for some time, and he was defeated in 1945. He was briefly an MP again (1950–51) before succeeding as 14th Earl. He entered the Cabinet as Secretary of State for Commonwealth Relations in 1955, becoming Foreign Secretary in 1960. His promotion to the Foreign Office caused a storm. He fell in with Macmillan's attempts at détente. On the EEC, though not enthusiastic, he went along with official attempts to gain entry. On southern Africa and the Middle East he was more to the Right than Macmillan. The new tenant of 10 Downing Street was estimated by the Observer (20 October 1963) to be owner of 96,000 acres of farmland, forest and grouse moor in Scotland. This empire included 56 large farms and many other properties. Home had married the daughter of his old headmaster at Eton, a lady with a reputation for having a social conscience. He disclaimed his earldom, becoming plain Sir Alec Douglas-Home, and was duly elected MP for Kinross and West Perthshire.

In his conference speech Butler talked about the Conservative society where 'there are a variety of ladders to the top and . . . positions of responsibility are not reserved for one coterie or class or band of education'.[115] He was postulating an ideal, something to be aimed at, but it is not unfair to ask what progress the Conservatives had made towards realizing this society. We need not dwell on the fact that it was not true of the Cabinets of Macmillan or Sir Alec: out of 23 members of Douglas-Home's Cabinet 10 were old Etonians, only three had not been to public schools. It one looks at the background of Conservative candidates in the election that followed, one is forced to the conclusion that Butler was either a voice crying in the wilderness or merely a politician engaging in empty demagoguery, mouthing the rhetoric of the time to win back Mr Orpington. Out of 304 Conservative MPs elected in 1964, 229 were products of public schools, 97 of them from Eton, Harrow and Winchester. More than half had been at Oxbridge. Perhaps more significant still was the fact that the replacements for

Conservative MPs who either had died or had retired during the period 1960–64 were of exactly the same background as the MPs they replaced.[116] Although it was estimated that between 30 and 40 per cent of trade unionists voted Conservative, there was only one bona fide Conservative trade unionist in the Commons: Ray Mawby, a former electrician. What was true of education was also true of occupation. Bank employees, computer operators, local government officers, draughtsmen, works managers, white-collar civil servants, GPs, and all the rest – hardly any one of these occupational groups, 'Orpington man', were likely to be found on the Conservative benches. Did it matter? Reginald Bevins, Macmillan's Postmaster-General, answered the question in 1965:

> A Party that cannot gain power without a big share of the working class and lower middle classes' vote cannot afford to be led predominantly by a group of old Etonians, however gifted they may be. This makes a bad joke of democracy and nowadays it is seen that way, especially by the younger generation. It is also dangerous because when a majority of our leaders come from the same social strata, far removed from ordinary life, they are unlikely to make decisions which are acceptable to ordinary people . . . The notion that some people are born to rule, or even know how to rule, must be destroyed.[117]

BRITAIN: 'RELEGATED TO . . . THIRD-CLASS'?

Sir Alec found his party divided not only over his leadership, but also over legislation, which nearly robbed the government of its majority. This was the abolition of resale price maintenance (RPM). Heath, as Secretary of State for Industry, Trade and Regional Development, was responsible. The Abolition of RPM was designed to increase competition in the retail trade and thus contribute to keeping prices down. The small shopkeepers who were regarded as solidly Tory felt they needed RPM to enable them to compete with the supermarkets. At one stage, the government's majority dropped to one. It was the closest a government had come to defeat on an important measure since 1951.

One important measure which Sir Alec's regime agreed to implement was the expansion set by the Robbins Committee on higher education. This was probably the most important single domestic reform embarked upon by the Macmillan–Home governments. The Committee had been set up by Macmillan in December 1960 under the chairmanship of Lord Robbins, a professor of economics. University places were to double, reaching 218,000 within 10 years, with 390,000 places in higher education as a whole. Robbins had examined higher education in the United States, the Soviet Union, West Germany, France and certain other countries. It was by no means critical of what had been achieved in Britain. Staff/student ratios were better in Britain, few students failed to graduate, and more students were assisted from public funds than in most countries. Yet it was felt that many more could benefit from higher education, and many more graduates would be needed if Britain was to maintain its place in the modern world. It was particularly concerned about technology, applied science and management. The Committee recommended that the existing Colleges of Technology be developed as technological universities. It also recommended five special institutions to promote technology. It was influenced by the lack of any parallel in Britain of the Massachusetts Institute of Technology and the technical universities of Zurich and Delft. Robbins found that education for management was not satisfactory. There had been criticism of this both from the business community and the NEDC. It was recommended, therefore, that at least two major postgraduate schools should be established in key business centres. It also stressed the need for foreign-language courses for those at technological universities. Another innovation Robbins wanted was a National Council for Academic Awards to award degrees to students studying in institutions other than universities. Robbins also called for improvements in the pay and conditions of university staff. Finally, it wanted a separate Minister of Arts and Sciences. This recommendation was not accepted by the government.

Robbins's was the fifth report on education since February 1959. It was a sign of the great public interest and anxiety on the issue. The McMeeking Committee (1959) wanted improvements in technical training and more apprenticeships. The Crowther Report (1959) wanted the school-leaving age raised to 16, and part-time education for those who left school. A government White Paper published in 1961 recommended more and better technical education, with new courses, high entry standards, extension of day-release opportunities and more sandwich courses. Finally, the Newsom Committee (1963) also advocated raising the school-leaving age and offering an alternative to the General Certificate of Education (GCE) ordinary level.

The Conservatives could claim that, since 1951, students in higher education had doubled and seven new universities had been created. The number of teachers in training had risen from 28,000 in 1955 to 55,000 in 1963 and there had been an explosion in the numbers taking GCE 'O' and 'A' levels. Yet this did little to change the impression that Britain was failing in the international league table, and that this failure would have consequences for its future commercial and industrial competitiveness. Dr Jacob Bronowski, Director-General of the National Coal Board's process development department and a popular television figure and writer, wanted more scientists in boardrooms and politics. Unless Britain thoroughly and rapidly upgraded the status of scientists, it would soon be 'relegated to the status of a third-class power'.[118]

CHILDREN: 'IF THEY BELIEVE THEY'RE SECOND CLASS'

There was also much debate about the divisive nature of secondary education. The Education Act, 1944 had established secondary schooling for all, but it was based, in theory, on selection at 11 for one of three types of education: modern, technical or grammar. The technical schools remained few. The great majority of working-class children went to modern schools and the majority of pupils in grammar schools were from the middle class. At first, as the 11-plus was supposed to test intelligence, it was presumed that most working-class children were less intelligent than their middle-class peers. However, after 1951 doubts were raised about the validity of these tests. In that year the GCE replaced the School Certificate as the academic examination which would eventually lead to university. It was presumed that 'modern' pupils would not take it. Later some secondary modern headteachers started to introduce a GCE stream in their schools, with surprising results. The numbers of modern pupils achieving GCE results similar to those of grammar school entrants, though a minority of those taking the exam, were significant enough to lead to serious doubts about the usefulness of the 11-plus.[119] The 11-plus came to be seen as a test which discriminated strongly, if not deliberately, against the working class. With the increasing demand for paper qualifications, middle-class parents whose children were 11-plus failures demanded a chance for their children to take the GCE, so the number of moderns offering GCEs rose. But critics of the system pointed out that these schools suffered from poor staffing ratios, less-qualified teachers and poorer facilities, as compared with grammar and public schools. If selection at 11 was an arbitrary, often unfair, method, with great variation according to which part of the country one lived in,[120] then this unfair distribution of resources in secondary education could not be justified. It discriminated against the great majority of the country's children.

Both the discrediting of the 11-plus and the maldistribution of resources provided powerful arguments in favour of comprehensive schools, which were supposed to provide equal opportunities for all children, allowing individual children to rise as far as their abilities would take them. The comprehensive system was also designed to give the children a greater sense of security and self-esteem than the selective system, which had marked so many children as failures. The government was not prepared to take action to force through comprehensives, and doubtless many Conservative politicians were not convinced of the need for change. Sir Edward Boyle, who became Minister of Education in the summer of 1962, was sympathetic towards reform. He commented that if children are made to feel they are 'second-class children, then they react by behaving as second-class children. You must never make children feel they are being divided into sheep and goats.'[121] He welcomed the London County Council's decision to end the 11-plus.

THE PUBLIC SCHOOLS: 'A DIVISIVE FACTOR'

The other big issue in secondary education was the future of the private sector, both the direct-grant grammar schools, which received some support from local authorities, and the more exclusive public schools. The public schools generated much anger on the Left because their pupils did so well at gaining university places and getting into the civil service and the professions. If socialists and Liberals were angry about the situation, Tory reformers were embarrassed. As Sir Robin Williams of the Conservative Bow Group put it, 'The public schools . . . attract a degree of envy and resentment which is unhealthy in a stable democracy.' He continued:

> since the pupils at these schools come with limited exceptions from well-to-do homes . . . and mix with children of similar backgrounds, they have little chance of learning about the way of life and habits of mind of those different from themselves. The lack of this knowledge means that the understanding which must form the basis of 'the social unity which makes all men brothers' is also absent. Although such is not the intention of those who run the public schools, they are in fact a divisive factor in society.[122]

Sir Robin proposed Queen's Scholarships and other means so that eventually 35 to 50 per cent of admissions at leading public schools would be 'grant-aided pupils'. As a party the Conservatives had no plans to tamper with this area so important to the upper echelons of their clientele. Labour, in its *Signposts for the Sixties*, advocated the setting up of an educational trust which, 'after full consultation', would integrate the public schools into the state system. This was Labour's policy under Winchester-educated Gaitskell and it remained the policy under its new, grammar-school-educated Leader, Wilson.

WILSON: 'LET'S GO WITH LABOUR'

Harold Wilson (1916–95) was elected Leader of the Labour Party in February 1963, when he beat George Brown on the second ballot by 144 votes to 103. In the first round James Callaghan had come bottom of the poll with only 41 votes and had been thus eliminated from the contest.[123] As was customary then, only Labour MPs took part in the vote. Wilson had won with many votes from the Centre and Right of the party as well as from the Left. Yet his election was seen by many as a shift to the Left. A careful study of his record would have led to the conclusion that his stance was slightly Left of Centre. As President of the Board of Trade, he had resigned from Attlee's Cabinet with Bevan, not as an anti-rearmer, but because he believed the degree of rearmament would cripple the economy. When Bevan resigned from the shadow cabinet in 1954, Wilson took his place, and his impressive analytical skill, knowledge of economics, ability to deal with statistics and, not least, the ability to make people laugh, earned him a reputation for professionalism. In November 1960 he stood against Gaitskell in the election for the party leadership, losing by 166 votes to 81. It was not that he was a unilateralist, he claimed, but because he disagreed with Gaitskell's failure to accept the conference decision on nuclear disarmament. On the Clause IV issue he took up a nicely ambiguous position. He wanted to unite on policy, not divide on theology. Basically, he advocated a moderate policy on public ownership. He had got two cheers from the Left for his advocacy of increased trade with the Soviet bloc and for his support for a campaign against world poverty. Like his close political companion Crossman, he was a friend of Israel, which was not without significance in the Parliamentary Labour Party. So much for Wilson the platform figure. What was he off the platform?

Wilson's father was an industrial chemist by profession, a Lib–Lab by political conviction and a Baptist by religion. Wilson was born in Huddersfield, where his family were prosperous enough to own a car and to send Harold and his mother for a visit to his uncle in Australia. In 1932 the family moved to Merseyside and lived in 'pleasant semi-rural surroundings'.[124] Harold's next move was to Jesus College, Oxford, with a scholarship from Wirral Grammar School. He read philosophy, politics and economics. On graduation he was appointed lecturer in economics at New College, where he came into contact with Sir William Beveridge. When war came, he was drafted into the civil service, soon becoming head of the Manpower, Statistics, and Intelligence Branch of the Ministry of Labour. By the end of the war he had had a wide variety of appointments in the service. His contribution was significant enough to be mentioned in the official history.[125] He was in an excellent position to choose the civil service, academic life or politics as a career. He won Ormskirk for Labour in 1945, and by 1947 was the youngest member of the Cabinet and President of the Board of Trade. In 1940 Wilson married Gladys (Mary) Baldwin, daughter of a Congregationalist Minister from Cambridge. They had met in 1934 when she worked as a typist at Port Sunlight.

Like Home, Wilson was limited by what he inherited and by the knowledge that an election was not far off. The party realized that too and responded to the challenge. The ginger groups of Left and Right, VfS and CDS, disbanded and put themselves at the disposal of the new leader. With the possibility of a Labour victory apparently strong, the energies of some CND activists were transferred to Labour, and the movement retired, once again, to the outer fringes of the political scene.

If Wilson believed in anything, he certainly believed in the influence of the media. And he was determined to exploit this to his own advantage. On the basis of research done by Dr Mark Abrams's polling agency, Labour's publicity was aimed at the 'target voters', and especially those in the marginal constituencies. Target voters were thought to be one-sixth of the electorate, who might be expected to change their views and, just as important, actually vote. On nationalization and defence they inclined towards the Conservatives; on housing and education, they were closer to Labour. Luckily for Wilson, they were not too interested in defence or nationalization, but they were interested in Britain's general standing in the world. John Harris, Labour's Director of Publicity, had recruited a small, unpaid team of supporters who worked in public relations and the media. This team worked with Abrams. In May 1963 Labour launched an advertising campaign based on Abrams's findings. This was conducted through a number of national dailies. A portrait of Wilson featured prominently, together with the campaign symbol and slogan – a thumbs-up sign and the invitation, 'Let's GO with Labour and we'll get things done.' This campaign was something entirely new for Labour. Wilson could thank the Gaitskellites for it. Most of the unofficial publicity team had been Gaitskellites. Wilson did not hesitate to employ their skills.

The Conservatives were old hands at public relations and they too started a publicity campaign in May 1963. They did not concentrate on Macmillan, more on what they considered to be their own achievements and the failings of their opponents. Moreover, they had more to spend than Labour. Once the leadership issue was settled, they went over to popularizing the new Prime Minister.

KENNEDY SHOT: 'I DIDN'T BELIEVE IT'.

Tony Benn recorded that when he was told over the phone of Kennedy's assassination on 22 November 1963, 'I didn't believe it'.[126] The President's death could have been bad for Labour. Wilson tried to present himself as a British Kennedy, but had little to go on. His rhetoric contained a certain similarity to that of Kennedy, but there the similarity ended.[127] Their backgrounds had nothing in common. They were born within a year of each other, but there was no physical resemblance between either Wilson and Kennedy or Wilson and the two aspiring ersatz Kennedys – Willy Brandt and Pierre Trudeau. Wilson's rhetoric of science, efficiency, meritocracy, new frontiers, the New Britain, led many of his acolytes to overlook his lack of height, his utterly non-athletic appearance and his lack of any sartorial style. Still, with the hero dead, would voters fall back in shock to a more traditional leader?

Sir Alec too had his problems. The New Year found him facing army mutinies in Africa, rioting in Southern Rhodesia and fighting between

Greeks and Turks in Cyprus. In Vietnam the conflict escalated. At home there were the traditional worries. In February he received a Treasury memorandum warning of a sharp deterioration in the balance of payments' outlook. Unless remedies were applied quickly there would be another serious payments crisis in October.[128] In an interview with the *Financial Times* (7 February 1964) Maudling admitted that Britain was going to have a 'tight situation in the latter half of the year'. Despite the dangers, Home decided to hold on until the autumn. He knew the possible advantages. It gave him more time to project himself, a good summer could have a soothing effect upon the electorate, the Opposition could run out of steam or simply bore the electorate to death by campaigning during the holiday period. This turned out to be a good gamble. Labour wisely abstained from too much campaigning in the summer, but the summer was good and it did seem to help the government.

ELECTION '64: 'THINGS MIGHT START SLIPPING'

As the election campaign opened in September 1964, Labour's hopes were dashed with Gallup and NOP polls putting the Conservatives ahead – for the first time in three years! Labour looked destined for the role of perpetual opposition. How was it possible that the Conservatives had made such a total recovery? Did Sir Alec have a certain charisma after all? Deference, among men as well as women, was not dead by 1964. Some women felt he looked in need of help – he brought out their maternal instinct – and they were prepared to give it. Having been out of office for so long, Labour were open to the charge that they lacked the ability to govern. Wilson was good on television, but the Conservatives claimed that Labour was just a one-man band. They also alleged that Labour's proposals were either impractical or too costly. Brown repeated a similar slip by Gaitskell in 1959. In answer to a question on housing asked at an uneventful meeting in a Derbyshire village, he talked in terms of a possible 3 per cent interest rate for new home loans. At the time the interest was 6 per cent. The *Sunday Express* translated Brown's words into a definite commitment.[129] The 'commitment' made Labour appear at best amateurish, at worst, irresponsible. Yet, as Butler expressed his fear in a *Daily Express* interview, 'things might start slipping in the last few days . . . They won't slip towards us.'[130] He was right. On 30 September there was bad news on the balance of payments front. Home was more confident when dealing with defence than with domestic issues. But most voters were more interested in prices and the balance of payments than in prestige and the balance of terror. Hogg's remark that anyone voting Labour was 'stark staring bonkers' did the Conservatives no good. When the polling-stations closed, it was anyone's guess, and it was still anyone's guess hours later after most of the results were out. Even when Wilson arrived in London at lunchtime the next day, he could only comment, 'It's getting more like the Kennedy story all along. We'll get the result from Cook County soon.'[131] His relentless pursuit of supreme political office ended at 3.50 in the afternoon when he got the call from Buckingham Palace. Labour had a majority of four.

It has been estimated that had 900 voters either not voted for Labour or abstained, Wilson would have lost the election.[132] If there had been no postal vote, Labour's overall majority would have been 20 and possibly 40.[133] Labour's poor organization and Liberal interventions had also cost a few seats. Yet, all in all, it was a disappointing result after such high hopes. Labour had to ask itself why it had lost working-class support. Certainly in a few areas, most notably in Smethwick, it was due to fears of unrestricted Commonwealth immigration which had come to be associated with Labour. But this was not the whole explanation. The parties had to ask themselves what factors lay behind the lower turnout compared with 1959. Did it indicate greater contentment with the state of Britain, or did it mean greater disillusionment with both major parties? No satisfactory answers were found to these questions. The 1964 result was a harbinger of the unsettled state of opinion, the more questioning, more doubting, more cynical attitude of the 1970s, which distinguished that period from the period 1945–59.

NOTES

Unless otherwise indicated, the place of publication is London.

1 James Stuart, *Within the Fringe* (1967), 47.
2 Harold Macmillan, *Winds of Change, 1914–39* (1966), 99.
3 James Margach, *The Abuse of Power* (1978), 116–18.
4 Anthony Sampson, *Macmillan: A Study in Ambiguity* (1967), 25.
5 ibid., 25–6.
6 ibid., 64.
7 Diana Cooper, *Trumpets from the Steep* (1960), 174.
8 Sampson, op. cit., 99.
9 ibid., 107.
10 ibid., 109. Reginald Maudling, *Memoirs* (1978), 231, makes the same comment.
11 Harold Macmillan, *Riding the Storm, 1956–1959* (1971), 191.
12 Christopher Hollis, 'The Conservative Party in History', *Political Quarterly*, 3 (July–September, 1961), 219–20.
13 Lord Hill, *Both Sides of the Hill* (1964), 235.
14 Lord Egremont, *Wyndham and Children First* (1968).
15 Margach, op. cit., 118.
16 F. S. Northedge, *Descent from Power: British Foreign Policy 1945–1973* (1974), 186. Barbara Castle, *Fighting all the Way* (1993), 291–308, gives her personal involvement with the Cyprus problem.
17 Frank Parkin, *Middle Class Radicalism* (Manchester, 1968), 112.
18 Lord Butler, *The Art of the Possible: Memoirs of Lord Butler* (1971), 201.

19 Conservative and Unionist Central Office, *The Campaign Guide 1964* (1964), 42.
20 ibid., 42.
21 ibid., 11
22 ibid.
23 Andrew Shonfield, *British Economic Policy since the War* (1958).
24 ibid.
25 See figures in Michael Balfour, *West Germany* (1968), 317; also those in *Stockholm International Peace Research Yearbook 1978*, 144–5.
26 Shonfield, op. cit., 107.
27 ibid., 153.
28 Samuel Brittan, *The Treasury under the Tories, 1951–1964* (Harmondsworth, 1965), 136.
29 *The Campaign Guide 1964*, op. cit., 153.
30 Henry Pelling, *A History of British Trade Unionism* (1963), 253.
31 *The Campaign Guide 1964*, op. cit., 153.
32 ibid.
33 Ministry of Labour, *Report of the Committee on the Selection and Training of Supervisors* (HMSO, 1962), 12.
34 'Profile of an M.D.', *Financial Times*, 14 February 1969.
35 ibid.
36 ibid.
37 *The Campaign Guide 1964*, op. cit., 174.
38 William Horsley and Roger Buckley, *Nippon New Superpower: Japan since 1945* (1990), 76.
39 *The Campaign Guide 1964*, op. cit., 31.
40 ibid., 190.
41 ibid., 173.
42 ibid., 9.
43 ibid., 115.
44 Brittan, op. cit., 138–9.
45 Andrew J. Pierre, *Nuclear Politics: The British Experience with an Independent Strategic Force* (1972), 178.
46 Macmillan, *Riding the Storm*, op. cit., 314.
47 Northedge, op., cit.
48 General Sir William Jackson, *Withdrawal from Empire: A Military View* (1986), 113.
49 ibid., 114.
50 ibid., 114, 352.
51 ibid., 347.
52 Castle, op. cit., 288.
53 *Hansard (Commons)*, vol. 610, col. 193.
54 *Hansard (Commons)*, vol. 610, col. 235.
55 Nigel Fisher, *Iain Macleod* (1973), 144; Jackson, op. cit., 109.
56 Denis Judd, *Empire: The British Imperial Experience from 1765 to the Present* (1990), 349.
57 ibid., 352.
58 Harold Macmillan, *Pointing the Way, 1959–61* (1972), 156.
59 ibid., 385.
60 Gillian King, *Imperial Outpost: Aden: its Place in British Strategic Policy* (1964),148. See also W. P. Kirkman, *Unscrambling an Empire* (1966).
61 *Hansard (Commons)*, vol. 667, col. 266.
62 *Hansard (Commons)*, vol. 667, cols 309–10.

63 W. F. Gutteridge, *The Military in African Politics* (1969), 37.
64 G. D. H. Cole, *Is This Socialism?* (1954), 16.
65 G. D. H. Cole, *World Socialism Restated* (1956), 5.
66 ibid., 47.
67 R. H. S. Crossman, *Socialism and the New Despotism* (1955), 13
68 Socialist Union, *Twentieth Century Socialism* (1956), 15.
69 ibid., 147.
70 Hugh Gaitskell, *Socialism and Nationalisation* (1957), 5.
71 *Keesing's Contemporary Archives 1956–57*, 15892–3.
72 Michael Foot, *Aneurin Bevan, 1945–60* (1975), 575.
73 *Keesing's Contemporary Archives 1956–57*, 16175A.
74 Parkin, op. cit., 104–5.
75 John Braine, *Room at the Top* (Harmondsworth, 1959), inside cover.
76 Paul Johnson, 'A Sense of Outrage' in Norman Mackenzie (ed.), *Conviction* (1958), 217.
77 David Butler, *British General Elections since 1945* (Oxford, 1995), 19.
78 D. E. Butler and Richard Rose, *The British General Election of 1959* (1960), 204.
79 Vernon Bagdanor, 'The Labour Party in Opposition, 1951–1964', in Vernon Bagdanor and Robert Skidelsky (eds), *The Age of Affluence, 1951–1964* (1970), 98.
80 Mark Abrams, Richard Rose and Rita Hinden, *Must Labour Lose?* (1960), 100.
81 ibid., 31.
82 ibid.
83 ibid.
84 ibid., 13, 16.
85 Margaret Stewart, *Frank Cousins: A Study* (1968).
86 Stephen Haseler, *The Gaitskellites: Revisionism in the Labour Party 1951–64* (1969), 189.
87 Stewart, op. cit., 101.
88 ibid., 102.
89 Macmillan, *Pointing the Way*, op cit., 393.
90 *The Campaign Guide 1964*, 584–5.
91 The Labour Party, *Report of the Sixty-first Annual Conference of the Labour Party* (1962), 159.
92 ibid., 246.
93 The four Labour MPs were technically independent because they had had the Whip withdrawn because of their earlier opposition to the PLP's defence policy. Much of the argument that went on at this time over the EEC in Britain is given in Lord Windlesham, *Communication and Political Power* (1966).
94 Arthur M. Schlesinger Jr., *A Thousand Days: John F. Kennedy in the White House* (New York, 1965), 340–1.
95 Schlesinger, op. cit., 720.
96 ibid.
97 ibid.
98 John Campbell, *Edward Heath: A Biography* (1993), 128.
99 Joseph Frankel, *British Foreign Policy 1945–1973* (1975), 306.
100 ibid.; Campbell, op. cit.,128.
101 Terence Prittie, *Konrad Adenauer 1876–1967* (1972), 268.
102 Prittie, op. cit., 293.
103 Samuel Brittan, *Steering the Economy: The Role of the Treasury* (1969), 150.

104 Thomas Wilson, 'Planning and Growth', *Crossbow*, Supplement No. 3, 1962. This gives some clues about the government's 'rethinking' on economic planning and outlines French experience. Christopher Dow's *The Management of the British Economy 1945–60* (Cambridge, 1964) was also influential, as were the works of Shonfield.
105 Brittan, op. cit., 152.
106 Stephen Aris, *The Jews in Business* (1970), 163.
107 *Financial Times*, 17 June 1960.
108 Gordon Lonsdale, the spy in question, gives his version in *Spy: Twenty Years of Secret Service* (1965). For Philby see Bruce Page, David Leitch and Philip Knightley, *Philby: The Spy who Betrayed a Generation* (1968).
109 *Guardian*, 26 September 1963.
110 Maudling, op. cit., 124. Two young women featured in the affair.
111 Lord Butler, *The Art of the Possible*, op. cit., 242.
112 *Observer*, 13 October 1963.
113 Maudling, op. cit., 128.
114 Lord Butler, *The Art of the Possible*, op. cit., 128.
115 ibid., 244.
116 D. E. Butler and Anthony King, *The British General Election of 1964* (1965), 239.
117 Bevins, op. cit., 156–7.
118 *The Times*, 17 September 1963.
119 Brian Simon, *Intelligence Testing and the Comprehensive School* (1953); David Rubinstein and Brian Simon, *The Evolution of the Comprehensive School 1926– 1972* (1973), 56.
120 J. W. B. Douglas, *The Home and the School* (1964), 24.
121 *Sunday Times*, 9 September 1962.
122 Robin Williams, *Whose Public Schools?* (1957), 21.
123 The votes on the first ballot were Wilson 115, Brown 88, Callaghan, 41.
124 Gerald Eyre Noel, *Harold Wilson and the New Britain* (1964), 27.
125 Noel, op. cit., 48–9.
126 Ruth Winstone (ed.)/Tony Benn (introduced by Ruth Winstone), *The Benn Diaries* (1995), 105.
127 Kennedy's influence on Wilson is discussed in David Nunnerley, *President Kennedy and Britain* (1972), 232–4.
128 See William Rees-Mogg and Anthony Vice, 'Treasury Warns Sir Alec of a Balance of Payments Crisis', *Sunday Times*, 16 February 1964.
129 Anthony Howard and Richard West, *The Making of the Prime Minister* (1965), 163–72.
130 Campbell, op. cit., 164.
131 Howard and West, op. cit., 235. Cook County, in the district of Illinois, whose marginal vote for Kennedy in 1960 swung the state and therefore the United States in his favour.
132 ibid., 225.
133 Butler and King, op. cit., 226.

6

WILSON'S ATTEMPTS AT REFORM, 1964–70

'THE NEWS FROM MOSCOW'

On the day that Sir Alec Douglas-Home was being overthrown by the ballot-box, Soviet leader, Nikita Khrushchev, was overthrown by a Kremlin intrigue. Harold Wilson reflected later, 'It was an open question whether, if the news from Moscow had come an hour or two before the polls closed, there would have been an electoral rush to play safe and to vote the existing Government back into power.'[1] He could also have mentioned that on the same day the Chinese were exploding their first atom bomb. However, millions of people around the world were not watching events in London or Moscow but in Tokyo, where the Olympic Games were in full swing, thus reflecting the economic success and stability of Japan. In South Africa Nelson Mandela was attempting to come to terms with the hard realities of the ruthless prison sentence which had just been imposed upon him. Happy to be Prime Minister but disappointed that his majority was only four, Wilson moved quickly to construct his government.

WILSON: 'A MODERN COUNTERPART OF RICHARD III'

Like his predecessors Wilson had to strike a balance between various sections of his party, disarm potential rebels by including them, and satisfy the aspirations of his rivals. He achieved a fair degree of success in this. He showed commendable loyalty to Patrick Gordon Walker by offering him the Foreign Office. He had lost his seat at Smethwick which he had held since 1945. Gordon Walker (1907–80, educated at Wellington and Oxford), had served Attlee at Commonwealth Relations, 1950–51. He had been a leading Gaitskellite. George Brown (1914–85) was given the new post of Secretary of State at the Department of Economic Affairs (DEA). Brown left school at 15 to become a clerk and then a fur salesman. At 22 he was working for the TGWU. Elected to the Commons in 1945, he served as Minister of Works (1947–51). He was something of an embarrassment for his fits of temper, his drinking and public lapses.[2] Wilson

117

appointed James Callaghan (b. 1912) Chancellor of the Exchequer. He was a Cardiff MP, the son of a chief petty officer, who had served as a wartime naval officer and as junior minister at the Admiralty and at Transport under Attlee. Like Brown, he had come to prominence on the trade union wing of the party. Douglas Jay (1907–95, Winchester and Oxford), an experienced economist and Gaitskellite, got the Board of Trade. Sir Frank Soskice (1902–79 St Paul's and Balliol) had been Attlee's Solicitor-General and, briefly, Attorney-General; Wilson made him Home Secretary. The Earl of Longford (b.1905, Eton and Oxford), a scion of the Anglo-Irish aristocracy, banker, publisher, prominent Catholic, friend of Gaitskell and, as Lord Pakenham, Attlee's Minister of Civil Aviation and later First Lord of the Admiralty, was appointed Lord Privy Seal. The Ministry of Defence went to Denis Healey (b. 1917, Bradford Grammar and Oxford), who was regarded as a distinguished commentator on defence matters. He had served with distinction in the war. A student Communist, the Cold War thrust him to the Right of the Labour Party, as did the experience he gained as head of Labour's International Department, 1945–52. Agriculture went to Fred Peart (b. 1914, secondary and Durham), a former school teacher and wartime captain. Ray Gunter (1909–77), a former official of the Transport Salaried Staffs Association, was given the Ministry of Labour. The new Minister of Education and Science was Michael Stewart (1906–90, Christ's Hospital and Oxford). A wartime captain in intelligence, he served Attlee as Under-Secretary of State for War. Lord Gardiner (1900–90, Harrow and Oxford) served as Lord Chancellor, 1964–70.

What of Wilson's friends, his old Bevanite comrades who had done so much to help him succeed? Barbara Castle (b. 1911, Bradford Girls' Grammar and Oxford), a journalist from an old ILP family, was named Minister of Overseas Development. Charming as well as intelligent, she had been on Labour's NEC since 1950. Richard Crossman (1907–74, Winchester and Oxford) took over Housing and Local Government. Anthony Greenwood (1911–82, Merchant Taylors' and Oxford), the son of Arthur Greenwood, took over the Colonial Office. Arthur Bottomley (1907–) went to the Commonwealth Office. He had served Attlee as a junior minister at the Dominions Office and Overseas Trade and was a former trade union organizer. Another former union organizer, James Griffiths (1890–1975), who had been Deputy Leader of the party, 1955–59, and Attlee's Colonial Secretary, 1950–51, got the Welsh Office. Griffiths was Centre-Right. An unexpected member of the Cabinet was Frank Cousins (1904–86), General Secretary of the TGWU, who was given the new Ministry of Technology (see p. 127).

The architect of Wilson's 1963 victory, George Wigg (1900–83), had to be content with being Paymaster-General, which was a post outside the Cabinet. He had risen through the ranks of the army to become a colonel in the Education Corps. He had done more than anyone to bring down Profumo. In his memoirs he commented about Wilson's appointments:

the more violent and loud-mouthed an opponent had been, the better
his chance of being included in the Wilson administration . . . Many
times I told Wilson he was a modern counterpart of Richard III,
who advanced his enemies, forgot his friends, and 'got done' for his
trouble.[3]

Wilson had a Cabinet of 23 – the same size as that of Douglas-Home. Of
this number, 10 had attended Headmasters' Conference ('public') schools
and Oxford; one, the Prime Minister, a maintained grammar school and
Oxford. Two others had gone from non-public schools to provincial or
Scottish universities, and 10 had not received higher education.

Although Barbara Castle was the only woman in the Cabinet, Miss
Margaret Herbison was appointed Minister of Pensions and National Insurance, outside the Cabinet. A graduate of Glasgow University and a teacher,
Herbison had served as junior minister under Attlee. Four women were
appointed as junior ministers.

CIVIL SERVICE: 'EXCESSIVE POWER'

Marcia Williams described Wilson as a traditionalist who enjoyed much of
the ceremonial.[4] Yet *before* gaining office he had written about sweeping
away the 'Edwardian establishment mentality'.[5] In office, one finds
Wilson going along with archaic rituals. 'I left the Palace boiling with indignation and feeling that this was an attempt to impose tribal magic and personal loyalty on people whose real duty was only to their electors.'[6] Thus
wrote Tony Benn on 21 October 1964 after having been sworn in as a
member of the Privy Council and Postmaster-General in Harold Wilson's
government. The ceremony, at Buckingham Palace, was quite elaborate.
Crossman was equally scathing: 'I don't suppose that anything more dull,
pretentious, or plain silly has ever been invented.' The ministers had to
learn how to kiss the Queen's hand, bow, kneel and walk backwards.[7]
Jenkins remarked on the 'fantastic archaism of the oath'.[8] These were
ministers with crippling official schedules facing a disappearing pound yet
Wilson, the 'moderniser', did nothing to bring this to an end.

Another area which proved resistant to change was the honours system.
Benn records his frustration at how the distribution of honours seemed to
be effectively controlled by a small committee of civil servants rather than
by the ministers supposedly running the departments.[9] Even Wilson had
'a fantastic struggle' to get the footballer Stanley Matthews a knighthood.[10]
Barbara Castle believed Wilson was

instinctively conventional. He had been a backroom boy himself
during the war . . . so he had a natural appreciation of the work
that civil servants do. When he became Prime Minister, flanked by a
charming and co-operative Cabinet Secretary in Sir Burke Trend,

and backed by a Cabinet Office trained to service his every whim, his appreciation turned into something dangerously like an uncritical acceptance of the status quo . . . he never seriously challenged the establishment.[11]

J. R. Colville, formerly Joint Private Secretary to Churchill (1951–55), believed the government had been let down by lack of a proper statistical service.[12] When Crossman took over the Ministry of Housing and Local Government he was amazed that the first statistician had been appointed nine months previously and his department was still not fully manned.[13]

Labour politicians were not alone in being critical of the civil service. Reginald Bevins wrote, in retirement, that the civil service is 'seriously affected by its self-importance and its judgement . . . [is] sometimes corrupted by its excessive power'.[14] Critics, on both Left and Right, alleged three major weaknesses at the top end of the civil service. Firstly, lack of expertise. Secondly, an educational and social exclusiveness which limited the value of their judgements about a complex industrial society which was also a political democracy. Thirdly, a lack of experience of industry, commerce and local government, producing the same effect. All these criticisms were made by the all-party Estimates Committee in its sixth report in 1965. The Committee found that the proportion of Oxbridge entrants to the Administrative Class (the top level) had risen from 78 per cent (1948–56) to 85 per cent (1957–63), and that the proportion from local authority maintained and aided schools went down from 42 to 30 per cent. Those whose fathers were manual workers dropped from 22 per cent to 15 per cent. The proportion who took degrees in classics went up from 21 to 24 per cent, while social sciences fell from 24 per cent to 17, and only 3 per cent recruited were mathematicians, scientists or technologists. Finally, the proportion of successful candidates with first-class honours fell from 40 per cent to 30 per cent. At a time when the fields of university recruitment were widening, the proportion of Administrative Class recruits from these wider fields, instead of rising, was actually falling.

It was concern about the power, technical competence and efficiency of the civil service which led to the setting up of the Fulton Commission on the Civil Service in 1966. When it reported in 1968 the Commission commented, 'The Service is still essentially based on the philosophy of the amateur . . . Today this concept has most damaging consequences . . . The cut is obsolete at all levels and in all parts of the Service.' Fulton wanted more professionally qualified entrants, more training within the service, abolition of the class system with better prospects of promotion from the lower ranks, more entrants with 'relevant' degrees from a wider variety of universities and more secondment from the civil service to other parts of the public service and private sector. In 1978 Lord Crowther-Hunt, who drafted much of the Fulton Report, commented, 'In general, the Civil Service implemented those parts of Fulton that it liked and which added to its power, and failed to implement the ideas that would have made it more professional and more accountable to Parliament and the public.'[15]

LABOUR: 'TREATED AS SHIPS PASSING IN THE NIGHT'

The tiny majority in the Commons was obviously a major headache which no one had contemplated. In theory it would have been possible to come to some kind of arrangement with the Liberals. The difference between them and the Labour Party on many issues was not all that great. The Liberals argued that they had earned the right to recognition and consultation, as their vote had increased from 1.6 million in 1959 to over 3 million in 1964. This represented over 10 per cent of votes. Yet they had only 9 votes to deliver in the Commons. For Wilson this course was, in practice, virtually impossible. Any kind of agreement with the Liberals would have aroused the worst suspicions of most of the rank-and-file of the Labour Party, recalling the times of Ramsay MacDonald. Wilson did not hesitate in deciding to see it through with the meagre forces available to him. That was undoubtedly the right decision. With or without the Liberal votes, ministers and back-benchers alike were going to be under tremendous pressure. The Opposition had the initiative and could pounce at any time.

The slender majority must have caused some difficulties with many of the top civil servants, who, being only human, could not help but view the new administration as less than permanent. No doubt, as Marcia Williams, Wilson's political secretary and confidante, put it, the civil servants at 10 Downing Street gave Labour a cold reception when they arrived there: 'We were treated as ships passing in the night.'[16]

No doubt the civil servants regarded Williams and what came to be known as Wilson's 'kitchen cabinet' as interlopers. This was a small group around Wilson, the key figure of which was Marcia Williams.

> It is impossible to understand the real Wilson and ignore Mrs Marcia Williams, whom he later created Lady Falkender. For more than twenty years she remained the greatest political influence in his life . . . I doubt very much whether Harold Wilson would ever have become Party leader and Prime Minister but for the ambitious thrust provided by Mrs Williams.[17]

So wrote James Margach. In Wilson's own account of the period her name does not appear. His press secretary, Joe Haines, and Wigg, Benn and Crossman came to the same conclusions.[18] The 'kitchen cabinet' included, in addition to Williams, Wigg, Professor (later Lord) Kaldor, Professor (later Lord) Balogh, both academic economists, Peter Shore, MP, Gerald Kaufman, MP, and others at various times.[19] Clearly, any Prime Minister needs aides and advisers, individuals he knew in opposition, whose judgement he trusts. But there are dangers. Firstly, the civil service can start to feel underrated and gradually become demoralized. Secondly, the Prime Minister's colleagues can feel that their legitimate influence and power are being undermined, that their ideas and contributions are not wanted, and that they can either resign or simply become yes-men. Thirdly, the public can feel that the politicians they have elected are being outmanoeuvred by shadowy figures hovering in the background. This can undermine public confidence in the government and the democratic process. In the Wilson case all three happened to some extent. Wilson believed Britain was in fact becoming a more presidential system of government. This did not always work out happily for Britain or the Labour Party. George Brown felt this, and gave it as the reason for his resignation in 1968.

> [It] seemed to me that the Prime Minister was not only introducing a 'presidential' system . . . that is wholly alien to the British constitutional system . . . but was so operating it that decisions were being taken over the heads and without the knowledge of Ministers, and far too often outsiders in his entourage seemed to be almost the only effective 'Cabinet'.[20]

Wilson had come to office carrying on as Prime Minister almost on a day-to-day basis, and had inherited a bad economic situation, which needed immediate attention. These two factors, as much as his distrust – of civil service, of many of his old Gaitskellite rivals, of sections of the mass media – and his Kennedy complex, must have greatly determined his political style. In these circumstances he would have felt it imperative to have a tight grip of hand-picked individuals he could rely on – his 'kitchen cabinet'.

STERLING: 'A SYMBOL OF NATIONAL PRIDE'

The massive and mounting balance of payments deficit, the biggest since the war, was Wilson's first major problem. It was dealt with by Wilson, Brown, Callaghan and Jay. The action taken was not put to the Cabinet for discussion; on the contrary, 'Cabinet as a whole had no advance notice so we simply had to accept the *fait accompli* or resign'.[21] Wilson wrote that this was the central thrust of his administrations during 1964–70.[22] He decided that devaluation of sterling was not going to be part of his plan to deal with the deficit. It was felt that this would be politically damaging for Labour, reviving memories of the earlier devaluation under Attlee. Labour could have devalued and rightly blamed the situation on the outgoing administration. It chose not to do so, clinging to the old dollar–sterling rate 'as a symbol of national pride'.[23]

On 11 November, Callaghan introduced a crisis Budget, a package containing the stick and the carrot. National insurance contributions were raised, up too went the duty on petrol, and income tax would go up in the spring. For Labour supporters the carrot included a capital gains tax and the replacement of the existing income and profits taxes on companies with a corporation tax. The Budget also increased retirement pensions and abolished prescription charges for medicines. Earlier in October the government had placed a surcharge on imports at the rate of 15 per cent. Finally, it promised to examine ways of cutting public expenditure. The temporary surcharge, which attracted criticism abroad, had been planned by the outgoing Conservative government. The measures were not enough to ease the pressure on sterling. On 23 November the bank rate was raised to a record 7 per cent, and Lord Cromer, Governor of the Bank of England, was set to get assistance from foreign central banks. The mission was completed by 25 November, when pledges of massive support stabilized the situation, leaving the country dazed and deeply in debt.

That the country was not exactly enthusiastic over Wilson's policies was indicated by two by-elections on 21 January. Both were in safe Labour seats and both were caused by the need to get Gordon Walker and Cousins into the Commons. Both previous MPs had been hustled off to other pastures to make way for the ministers. Understandably, the voters were not very impressed by this procedure and some protested by not voting. In Leyton, Gordon Walker was defeated and at Nuneaton Cousins was returned with a much-reduced majority. Gordon Walker was replaced by Michael Stewart. If the electorate was less than enthusiastic about the new government, this was not because it favoured the Opposition. The Conservatives too did badly in by-elections. On 24 March, David Steel, an unknown young Liberal, took Roxburgh, Selkirk and Peebles, from the Conservatives.

Callaghan's April, 1965, Budget was more deflationary than the special crisis Budget, but foreign financial centres were not impressed, and by the end of June he sought help from Henry Fowler, the American Secretary of the Treasury. Less than a month later the Chancellor announced the severest package so far introduced by Labour – still more tightening-up on hire purchase, delays in or cancellation of government projects, and restrictions on local authority borrowing.

BROWN AT THE DEA

Despite the difficulties involved in setting up a new ministry, and despite the tug-of-war with the Treasury and the Bank of England, Brown had moved with enthusiasm and resourcefulness in the weeks following his appointment. In December 1964 he produced the *Joint Statement of Intent on Productivity, Prices and Incomes* signed by representatives of the government, the TUC and the employers' side of industry. Trade unions and management agreed to ensure that increases in all incomes would be related to increases in productivity. The government promised to prepare and implement a general plan for economic development, providing for higher investment, improving industrial skills, modernization, balanced regional development, higher exports and for the largest possible sustained expansion of production and real incomes. The NEDC was to be the vehicle through which this was to happen.[24] In February 1965 the National Board for Prices and Incomes (NBPI) was established, headed, perhaps surprisingly, by a former Conservative MP, Aubrey Jones, a director of Guest, Keen & Nettlefolds and chairman of Staveley Industries. He had been a minister in the outgoing government. At this stage the NBPI had very little power. The brave words of the statement of intent were not translated into practice, and incomes went up ahead of productivity in the first half of 1965. The Americans were not impressed. Fowler expressed the view that it would be difficult to give further aid if the voluntary system were maintained. 'It was in these circumstances that we began first to think in terms of statutory powers.'[25] The situation was regarded as critical enough to recall the Cabinet early from holiday.[26] Brown came back from the south of France to go into conclave with the TUC. The result was that the TUC accepted the statutory control of prices and incomes. The NBPI was made a statutory body, with the Secretary of State having the right to refer any price or wage proposal to it. He had the power to enforce decisions by ministerial order and to defer the implementation of any wage or price settlement while the Board's investigations were continuing. The legislation provided for an 'early-warning' system for price increases and wage and salary settlements. Two weeks after his success at the TUC conference, which ratified the agreement between Brown and the TUC leaders, Brown published, on 16 September, his department's National Plan. It set the annual rate of growth at 3.8 per cent. This seemed reasonable to most people, though it was a higher rate than Britain had been achieving. As the summer drew to a close, the Prime Minister and his colleagues felt reasonably happy about progress on the economic front. They were less happy about the developing situation abroad.

DEFENCE: 'THEY WANT US WITH THEM'

Like many in the Labour Party, Wilson had been strongly critical of American policy in the Eisenhower era, especially over foreign policy. He had also been strongly critical of the sale of British companies to American interests and of the evolution in Britain of an 'Americanized society'.[27] The arrival of Kennedy at the White House brought about a change in Wilson's appraisal of the US. He early identified himself with Kennedy and saw little to criticize in the Kennedy administration's policies. By the time Wilson was in Downing Street, Lyndon Baines Johnson had taken over the White House. Within six weeks of assuming office Wilson was off to confer with

President Johnson. It seems clear that Johnson wanted to avoid devaluation of the pound, fearing repercussions on world trade. In return for financial help, the Americans sought support from Britain for Johnson's foreign and defence policies.[28] According to Crossman, Wilson reported to the Cabinet, 'They want us with them.' He seemed to think his government could 'influence events'.[29] This was largely self-delusion, however. According to Wilson, he resisted the call for British involvement in Vietnam apart from a jungle-training team from Malaya and 'our teams for anti-subversive activities'.[30] The Wilson-Healey-Walker team were also urged by Johnson to keep up their commitments east of Suez. Healey is reported to have told the Cabinet that, although the Americans did not want Britain to maintain huge bases, they wanted it 'to keep a foothold in Hong Kong, Malaya, the Persian Gulf, to enable us to do things for the alliance which they can't do'.[31] Drew Middleton, the distinguished American correspondent, writing in 1965, commented that Britain's tremendous defence expenditure 'reduced Britain's competitive commercial position'. He continued, 'Both the Kennedy and Johnson Administrations encouraged the British to maintain these bases. Did this advantage to the United States in terms of world stability outweigh the risk of encouraging a steady decline in the British economy?'[32]

One other major defence problem confronted Wilson – what to do about Britain's nuclear force. The party had been led to believe it would give up a weapon which Wilson had claimed was neither independent nor a deterrent. Wilson thought he could appear to be doing that, without in reality doing so, by participation in an Atlantic Nuclear Force (ANF). Such a force would serve a second purpose. It would serve as a counter-proposal to the American-backed Multilateral Nuclear Force (MLF), which had been talked about for years. When presented to NATO in 1960 by the Americans, it meant 'a force of Polaris missile submarines to be jointly owned and operated . . . and to be manned by crews of mixed nationality'.[33] The MLF would add to NATO strength, help the United States financially by the NATO allies' financial contributions and 'funnel the Federal Republic's supposed nuclear appetite, and . . . court her away from France by forging new German–American links'.[34] Neither the Conservatives nor Labour had been enthusiastic. There were strong doubts about the practicality of mixed manning. There was some fear of a German finger on the nuclear trigger and that this would weaken Britain's 'special relationship' with the United States. The ANF was in fact a modified version of a proposal of the out-going Conservative government. By December 1965 the Americans were losing their enthusiasm for the MLF and gave Wilson the go-ahead to explore his ANF idea, which would have been based on existing US, British and possibly French nuclear forces, with a small 'mixed-manned' element to assuage German feeling. The 1966 Defence White Paper stated that it was the 'aim to internationalize our nuclear strategic forces in order to discourage further proliferation and to strengthen the alliance'.[35] After early 1965 the great debate on the British deterrent 'came to a standstill as the issue faded away'.[36]

It can rightly be asked, after the fierce controversy within the Labour Party in 1960, how Wilson was able to retain the British bomb with so little fuss. A number of factors contributed to this. Firstly, key unilateralists were prisoners in the government – Cousins, Castle and Greenwood. Secondly, Wilson's tiny majority helped to keep the Left in line. Thirdly, most Labour MPs and activists felt Wilson had a steadier trigger-finger than Douglas-Home or any other likely Conservative premier. Fourthly, the government used the argument that the Polaris submarine fleet was already too advanced to turn back and that it was creating jobs in an industry badly needing them. Fifthly, it was hinted that Britain's bomb could be used to protect democratic India against Mao's China, for China had carried out its first nuclear explosion on the day of the British election. Sixthly, it was argued that Britain's abandonment of the bomb would be an empty gesture when it looked likely that any number of states would soon have it. Two other arguments, which did not appease the quasi-pacifists but carried conviction with those worried about the costs and the practical side of Britain's nuclear force, were that the Polaris submarines, unlike the earlier V-bombers, were cheap, and that possible co-operation with France could be used as a ticket of admission to the EEC. Wilson was also helped by the noisy opposition of the Tory Right when it was suggested that Britain internationalize its nuclear force. This helped to make Wilson's proposal appear more radical than it really was. The innovatory appointment by Wilson of a Minister for Disarmament, Lord Chalfont, was also another factor in his favour, though Chalfont's complete lack of any connection with the Labour Party weakened the effect of the move.

One other practical defence problem which the Cabinet had to decide during this period was the future of the Tactical Strike and Reconnaissance Aircraft (TSR2), which is discussed below.

TECHNOLOGY: BRITAIN'S 'INABILITY TO STAY IN THE BIG LEAGUE'

One of the innovations brought in by Wilson was to create a Ministry of Technology. It was not much of a ministry with not much of a minister. The trade union leader Frank Cousins was persuaded to take it on rather than a high-powered scientist or technologist. This made many think Wilson's only motive was to imprison the leader of Britain's biggest trade union. Tony Benn took over from Cousins in July 1966. Benn (b. 1925), a former President of the Oxford Union, had worked for the BBC before his election in 1950. Like his father, Viscount Stansgate, and his brother, he had served as a wartime officer in the RAF. Of the eight junior ministers who served between 1964 and 1970 only two, Lord Snow and Dr Jeremy Bray, had any scientific/technological background. Jenkins at Aviation admitted later he had difficulties with the briefings because of his 'non-technical cast of mind'.[37] Under Wilson the Cabinet did discuss technology. Crossman noted a 'dreary' discussion on computers lasting an hour and a half on 3 June 1965. 'If we are going to force Whitehall to buy British, we are going to subsidize inefficiency in a way which will be difficult to defend.' Cousins apparently favoured buying British computers. Professor Tom Kilburn, Alan Turing and others at Manchester University had led the way in computer technology in the 1940s, and Lyons, the restaurant chain, had developed the first business computer in 1951. However, by the 1960s Britain was outstripped by the United States, whose government had put large sums into defence-related computer technology. Government was divided about just what could now be achieved.

Apart from difficulties because of their lack of scientific/technological training, there were problems because of the overlapping responsibilities of the different government departments. There was Jenkins at Aviation, Healey at Defence, Benn at the Post Office and Cousins at Technology. Jay at the Board of Trade also felt he needed to be consulted and Callaghan as Chancellor held the purse strings. This problem was not, of course, peculiar to Wilson's regime. Jenkins and Benn suffered from not being in the Cabinet.

Did Britain have much technology to oversee? Well, there was the TSR2, there was the Harrier vertical take-off jet, there was the Hovercraft, there was fuel injection for car engines introduced in 1966. The Anglo-French Concorde project was well-advanced. Britain was ahead in the peaceful uses of nuclear energy which was seen in the 1960s as the future. These were all 'firsts' for Britain.

Work had begun on the TSR2 in 1959 and 'it was reputed the most sophisticated aircraft ever built'.[38] Yet within months of Wilson taking office this swing-wing or variable-geometry plane was axed. According to Jenkins, 'The essential trouble was that it showed no sign of achieving any market beyond the Royal Air Force.'[39] Jenkins was instrumental in setting up the Plowden Committee on Aviation. It advised that Britain should buy US planes.[40] In 1962, 35 per cent of the pounds spent by British firms on R&D went to aircraft, while chemicals, vehicles and machinery claimed 12 and 10 per cent, respectively. German firms spent nothing on aircraft, but 33 per cent of R&D on chemicals and 19 per cent on vehicles. For Japan the figures were 28 per cent on chemicals, 13 per cent on vehicles and nothing spent on aviation.[41]

In terms of its Nobel prize winners since 1945, Britain is a rich country. The impressive list of names is given at the end of the book (pp. 315-16). Writing in January 1965, Benn lamented:

Defence, colour television, Concorde, rocket development – these are all issues raising economic considerations that reveal this country's basic inability to stay in the big league. We just can't afford it. The real choice is, do we go into Europe or do we become an American satellite?[42]

RHODESIA: 'HER CONSCIENCE HAS HAUNTED HIM'

On 11 November 1965 Ian Smith, Prime Minister of Southern Rhodesia, proclaimed his country independent of Britain. Southern Rhodesia had enjoyed internal self-government since 1923, but was still technically a British colony. Out of a population of 5.3 million only the 252,000 or so whites had any say in the running of the country. In April 1964 the white electors had voted overwhelmingly for Smith's white supremacist Rhodesia Front Party. Between October 1964 and November 1965 Wilson worked hard to promote a settlement with Rhodesia. He met the Rhodesian leader at the funeral of Sir Winston Churchill in January 1965. Smith visited London again in October 1965, expressly to parley with Wilson. In between, Bottomley and Gardiner visited Rhodesia to study the situation. In the summer another British emissary, Cledwyn Hughes, visited Rhodesia. The Labour government laid down five principles which had to be fulfilled before it could agree to formal independence. The first and most important of these was that the 'principle and intention of unimpeded progress to majority rule, already enshrined in the 1961 constitution, would have to be maintained and guaranteed'.[43] Implementation of these five principles would have required a radical change in the way of life of the whites, which they were not prepared for. Wilson appeared ready to go to any lengths in order to delay the Unilateral Declaration of Independence (UDI).[44] He ran the danger of making himself appear ridiculous. Wilson succeeded in splitting the Conservative Party over Rhodesia. Yet many of his parliamentary colleagues, and some in the Cabinet, remained sceptical. Barbara Castle, in particular, according to Crossman, wanted Wilson to take firm action; 'even if her influence hasn't prevailed, her conscience has haunted him and made him uneasy and unsure of himself'.[45] It was the issue she came nearest to resigning over.[46] The governor was instructed to declare the Rhodesian government dismissed and the regime illegal – without practical effect. A policy of mild sanctions was also adopted: expelling Rhodesia from the sterling area, loss of Commonwealth preference on Rhodesian exports and a ban on the purchase of Rhodesian sugar and tobacco. Wigg thought sanctions were 'a soft option'.[47] Callaghan too thought stronger measures could have been used.[48] But few really wanted to use force. It was certainly a mistake to announce *before* UDI that Britain would not use force. Wilson had to try to satisfy many different constituencies. At the UN the African and other non-aligned states, backed by the

Soviet bloc, pressed for immediate action, including the use of troops and imposition of majority rule. At home many influential groups were against such action. The government also had to consider Rhodesian action against Zambia, on which Britain was dependent for 40 per cent of its copper. Wilson believed that interruption of this supply would cause widespread dislocation in British industry and could render 2 million unemployed.[49] On 20 November the UN Security Council called on all states to sever economic relations with Rhodesia and for an oil embargo. In April 1966 the UK secured authority to prevent, by use of force if necessary, the arrival of tankers bringing oil to Rhodesia at Beira, in Portuguese Mozambique. As with his economic policy, so with Rhodesia – and in his relations with the United States – Wilson was walking the tightrope.

HEATH REPLACES HOME: 'NO GRATITUDE IN POLITICS'

On 22 July 1965 Sir Alec Douglas-Home announced that he was giving up the leadership of the Conservative Party. The Conservatives had never quite got together again after their defeat. Sir Alec's supporters claimed the narrow majority won by Wilson showed he had done a good job. The fact was, however, that he trailed Wilson in the opinion polls after October 1964. The loss of the Roxburgh seat in Douglas-Home territory, in March 1965, gave ammunition to the critics of the 14th Earl. As Maudling put it, 'As usually happens in the Conservative Party the old rules of public life applied, namely that there is no gratitude in politics, and you should never kick a man until he is down.'[50] The Conservatives faced the problem that an election could not be far off and they had to settle the leadership question, one way or the other, as soon as possible. This time they had an election procedure which was similar to that of the Labour Party. There were three candidates: Edward Heath, Reginald Maudling and Enoch Powell who, already something of an *enfant terrible* of the party, did not expect to win. He was merely testing the ground to see how much support there was for his peculiar brand of *laissez-faire*, anti-Establishment Conservatism. Iain Macleod, who reviewed a book of Powell's speeches just before the contest, conceded he 'has the finest mind in the House of Commons. The best trained and the most exciting.'[51] That did not help much. The *Daily Mail* and the *Daily Express* predicted a Maudling victory and the polls too indicated his popularity.[52] Yet when the votes of the 298 Conservative MPs were counted on 26 July, Heath was clearly the victor. He gained 150 votes to 133 for Maudling and only 15 for Powell. Under the rules, Maudling could have forced a second ballot, but he decided not to. In Heath the Conservatives had decided for a Macmillan-type, that is, as far as his policies were concerned; in other respects, he was similar to Wilson. Through his powerful attacks on Labour as shadow Chancellor, Heath had gained the respect of his colleagues and overcome his association with the failed attempt to get into the EEC.[53] Despite this, Heath was the victim of snobbery because of his ordinary, provincial background.[54]

In his background, Heath had much in common with Wilson and with his rival, Enoch Powell, yet he differed from both. It could be said of Powell (1912–96), as of Heath (b. 1916), that his mother made him. Powell's mother was a teacher; Heath's had been in service. Powell's father too was a teacher; Heath's was a carpenter who set up his own business. Powell had the grit of the Black Country in him; Heath grew up in the more placid atmosphere of Broadstairs on the south coast. Powell attended a HMC school; Heath a grammar school. Both gained scholarships to university, Cambridge (Trinity) and Oxford (Balliol), respectively. As young men both were loners. Heath was a highly successful organist and student politician; Powell pursued his scholastic ambitions and became the youngest professor of Greek (Sydney University) in the British Empire. Both were anti-appeasement Tories before the war, and both had had 'good' wars. Powell ended the war as a brigadier in intelligence, Heath as 'only' a lieutenant-colonel of anti-aircraft artillery in the socially prestigious Honourable Artillery Company. Before entering Parliament in 1950 Heath worked as a civil servant, news editor of the *Church Times* and trainee merchant banker. Powell worked for the Conservative Research Department, also gaining election in 1950. Both were known as frugal bachelors who did not smoke and drank little. Powell married his former secretary in 1952, whereas Heath remained unmarried. Politically, from the start, Powell was a doctrinaire right-winger, while Heath was a pragmatist of the Centre-Left. Powell was an imperialist; Heath was pro-Europe. Powell served Macmillan as Financial Secretary to the Treasury and Minister of Health. Heath served under Eden and Macmillan as Chief Whip (1955–59), Minister of Labour (1959–60), Lord Privy Seal attached to the Foreign Office, and Secretary of State for Trade and Industry (1963–4). Both had Cabinet experience.

Benn found Heath in 1957 'a most amiable and friendly soul'.[55] Jenkins wrote of his 'grumpy integrity'.[56] Willy Brandt, German Chancellor, recorded, 'I never felt Edward Heath's reputed lack of personal warmth.'[57] Macleod felt he did not know Heath much better after their 20 years as colleagues than when they had entered the Commons together in 1950. Lord Carrington, who served in Heath's government, believed Heath was 'A somewhat lonely man, he needed friendship, yet found it hard to unbutton himself to the affection of others'. He found that Heath could be 'touchy and autocratic. But in my experience Prime Ministers tend to become autocratic.' He also believed Heath to be 'extremely courageous'.[58]

Under Sir Alec, the Conservatives had started to look at their party structures, policies and appeal. This work continued under Heath. Lord Chelmer recommended improved status, training and remuneration for constituency agents. The (Iain) Macleod Committee recommended more political discussion in the Young Conservatives and the raising of the upper age limit for membership to 35. Not without some pain, the list of approved parliamentary candidates was overhauled. It was hoped there would be a trend against the preference for landowners, retired businessmen and service officers. The results were not impressive. Butler and King in their survey of the 1966 election concluded that the educational pattern remained much as in previous years. There was a slight decline of old Etonians, from 94 candidates in 1964 to 84 in 1966.[59]

WILSON'S 1966 VICTORY: TIMING 'WAS FAULTLESS'

In theory, the British Prime Minister has the initiative in the timing of the election. In practice, his choices are circumscribed by the economic situation, the international climate, public opinion and, not least, his majority. Wilson had a majority of one when he called the election for 31 March 1966. Callaghan believed his timing was 'faultless . . . we owed our victory to his tactical skill, his determination, his orchestration, and the confidence he conveyed to the electorate'.[60] Labour had had a notable by-election success in Hull in January and this helped Wilson make up his mind.[61] The Conservative manifesto, *Action not Words*, moved strongly in favour of EEC entry and trade union reform, and advocated retaining the east of Suez bases. Labour's *Time for Decision* echoed the themes of 1964, calling for steel nationalization, a national transport plan, regional planning, planned growth of incomes and a Ministry of Social Security. Both parties promised 500,000 new homes. Labour blamed the country's woes on the previous administration and many people thought this reasonable. Labour were expected to win and were returned with a 96-seat majority on a 47.9 per cent share of the vote (44.1 in 1964). The Conservatives gained 41.9 per cent (43.4) and the Liberals 8.5 per cent (11.2). Turnout fell from 77.1 to 75.8 per cent, the lowest since 1945. Labour won back both Smethwick and Leyton, and appeared to have increased its support higher up the social scale, especially among the young. It gained even more support among the unskilled and the very poor.[62] The Liberals took comfort from the increase in their parliamentary strength from 9 to 12.

Labour's victory was remarkable for a number of reasons. It was the first time that a twentieth-century Prime Minister had led his party to a second electoral victory with an increased majority. For Labour it was only the second time that it had achieved a comfortable majority since the Labour Representation Committee was established in 1900. It was important too in that it proved 1945 was not a special case caused by the unique conditions of war. It demolished those who thought Labour could not win without a Lib–Lab pact. Some political soothsayers began saying that Labour had become the natural party of government. Heath was held up to ridicule as a loser. Some of Labour's more gullible socialists were in a state of shocked ecstasy over the results. Suddenly their wildest dreams looked like becoming reality. The long, sometimes bitter and often sterile arguments about resolutions on party policy, the hours in dingy, half-empty assembly halls, in shabby, smoke-filled committee rooms, canvassing in wind and rain, had not been in vain. Uncannily, even before all the election posters had been superseded on the hoardings, socialist dreams were turning into nightmares.

'LABOUR GOVERNMENT IS REALLY FINISHED'

On 14 June 1966 Crossman expressed the view that 'the Labour Government is really finished'.[63] This was less than three months after their spectacular win. What had gone wrong?

One factor undermining morale was undoubtedly the seamen's strike which began on 16 May and lasted until 1 July. Only half British shipping was affected by it. The union wanted a pay increase larger than the government's 3–3.5 per cent norm. The seaman's wage was low, his work was hard, his conditions of service were Victorian – or worse! Later Wilson wrote that for years the seamen's union

> had been little more than a companies' union, and the shipowners and union officials had an equal responsibility for the utter frustration of union members . . . Frustrations outside the field of wages and conditions related to such matters as the failure to press for the modernisation of the 1894 Merchant Shipping Act.[64]

The government had allowed handsome salary improvements for judges. In depressed mood Crossman recorded on 19 May, 'The Cabinet is formally committed to breaking the strike in the way we didn't break the doctors', the judges' and the civil servants' strikes . . . We listen to George Brown telling us to resist to the death. We listen to James Callaghan telling us to resist to the death, although it would cost us a small fortune in foreign exchange.'[65] As the strike continued, with all the drama of a national emergency having been declared giving the government sweeping powers, Crossman got more depressed.[66] His mood, as he himself recognized, was shared by very many in the Labour movement, from MPs down to humble party members. By not allowing the employers to settle the dispute, the government were really undermining their own policy on prices and incomes. They seemed to have a double standard, one for the better off and another for the poorer, or less well-organized, section of the working classes. The only chance for such an incomes policy to succeed was to be fair and to be seen to be fair.[67] It could be claimed, as Crossman said so often about the administration of which he was a member, that they never thought ahead, never anticipated difficulties and had simply to react to an immediate situation. If this was so and the government was merely reacting instinctively, then it was an indication of how far apart were the instincts of most of the Cabinet from those of their followers. The strike ended as a technical victory for Wilson. He used the feat of Communist influence in the union to torpedo the strike, a tactic often denounced by Labour in the past. This tactic caused dismay among some members of the Cabinet, including Peter Shore and Benn.[68] The ordinary seamen supported the stoppage, but the leadership advocated a return to work, pressurized by the government and media as being dupes of a Communist plot. It is doubtful whether Wilson convinced any of his own rank-and-file by this tactic that his incomes policy was a just one. More likely, it marked the beginning of real and sustained disenchantment with a hitherto popular leader.

CRISIS, 1966: 'THE FRAILTY OF A CHANCELLOR'S HOPES'

On 1 July, the day the seamen's strike ended, Callaghan met Wilson and Brown to discuss the future. He assured his colleagues they would get through the summer without the need for any further 'economic measures'. 'Such is the frailty of a Chancellor's hopes and forecasts, I had scarcely left the Cabinet Room and returned to the Treasury when I learned that serious selling of sterling had begun that very morning.'[69] Two days later Frank Cousins resigned because of his opposition to the government's prices and incomes policy. In the US, his resignation 'proved particularly disturbing to market confidence'.[70] A further blow was France's terms for Britain's entry into the EEC. Prime Minister Pompidou called on the British to devalue and carry through another dose of deflation.[71] On 14 July the bank rate was raised from 6 to 7 per cent, a harbinger of the gathering economic storm. On the same day Labour lost the Carmarthen by-election to Plaid Cymru (PC). As the situation got more critical, the triumvirate were unable to agree. Brown favoured devaluation; Callaghan and Wilson were against it. 'With a tactically foolish decision',[72] Wilson warned the Commons that deflationary measures would be announced in two weeks' time. He still insisted on playing his world role and flew to Moscow to act as a go-between for President Johnson over the escalating war in Vietnam. Officially, he was promoting British exports! Within hours of his return the Cabinet met to discuss the austerity package on 19 and 20 July. 'Nothing had been adequately prepared. Nothing thought out properly.'[73] The package included 10 measures which together were regarded as the toughest deflation since 1949. Hire purchase, as usual, was hit, with down-payment on cars, motor-cycles and caravans raised to 40 per cent. There were higher down-payments on other items and shorter repayment periods. The 'regulator' was invoked, a device introduced by Selwyn Lloyd in 1961 under which a Chancellor could raise or lower indirect tax rates by 10 per cent. Callaghan used it to increase taxes on drink, oil, petrol and purchase tax. Certain postal charges were increased. There was an increase of 10 per cent on the year's surtax liabilities. More controls on building were introduced, except in the development areas. Big cuts were made in investment programmes in the nationalized industries and local and central government; but housing, schools, hospitals and government-financed factories, including advance factories built in development areas, were excluded from the cuts. There was a tightening-up of foreign-exchange controls. What probably had the greatest psychological sting was the six-month freeze on wages, salaries and 'other types of income', to be followed by a period of severe restraint.

Devaluation was again rejected in Cabinet by 6 in favour to 17 against.[74] One other item was a proposed cut in overseas civil and military expenditure. Of particular concern were the costs of maintaining the British forces in Germany; the Chancellor flew to Germany immediately to emphasize that concern.[75] As Wilson later wrote, he faced 'the roughest House any Prime Minister had faced for a very long time. But it was nothing to the evening that lay ahead.'[76] Brown announced he was going to resign on the devaluation issue. He was, however, persuaded not to do so by a 'round robin of Members'.[77] It was a most unusual situation caused by a most unusual politician. On that day Benn found him 'in many ways an attractive and full-blooded figure'.[78]

Brown had to make his contribution by incorporating proposals for a wage freeze into his prices and incomes legislation. This contained an element, no more than a threat or a hint, of compulsion. In the case of a deliberate breach of the pay standstill, an Order in Council could be laid before Parliament to impose penalties of up to £500.[79] When the Bill came before the Commons on 4 August, 25 Labour MPs abstained. In the circumstances, the government could consider itself very lucky.

On 24 July, in his diary, Crossman assessed Wilson's position, 'I suppose it is the most dramatic decline any modern P.M. has suffered. More sudden than Macmillan's.'[80] Callaghan, writing later, admired Wilson as a fighter who never lacked courage when his back was to the wall.[81] There was truth in both views. Wilson was able to get the TUC General Council to 'acquiesce', by a majority vote of 20 to 12, in the incomes policy, subject to the proviso that 'social equity' was preserved.[82] He was given strong public support when he visited President Johnson on 28 July.[83] He returned to see England beat West Germany in the World Cup at Wembley. This event certainly did a little to restore the nation's confidence.

Having succeeded thus far, Wilson reshaped his Cabinet in August. Brown was relieved of the burdens of the DEA and swapped jobs with Michael Stewart at the Foreign Office. Crossman was promoted to Lord President of the Council and Leader of the House. Greenwood succeeded him at Local Government. Greenwood's place at the Ministry of Overseas Development was taken by Arthur Bottomley, who in turn handed over Commonwealth Relations to Herbert Bowden. The latter's responsibilities went to Crossman. By promoting Crossman, Wilson probably believed he was making the former Housing Minister more dependent on him. He was also giving him the unpleasant task of disciplining the Parliamentary Labour Party, thus forcing the former rebel to become a policeman.[84]

The final hurdle for Wilson was the Labour conference in October, at which the wage freeze was adopted by a substantial majority. The government found it necessary to use its compulsory powers in only a tiny handful of cases. For the six-month period of the freeze, from July to December 1966, there was no increase in weekly wage rates. For the following six months there was a rise of 2 per cent in average earnings. During the same period the retail price index increased by 2 per cent.[85] To a limited extent the policy was successful.

IRC: 'A KIND OF GOVERNMENT-SPONSORED MERCHANT BANK'

Already in April 1966 Richard Marsh was promoted by Wilson to the Cabinet as Minister of Power and given the job of piloting through the Bill to nationalize steel. This went through and the British Steel Corporation was established in 1967. Marsh (b. 1928), MP for Greenwich, had been a CND member. He later served as Minister of Transport (1968–69), resigning his seat in 1971 to become Chairman of the British Railways Board, 1971–76. He was created a life peer in 1981 and left the Labour Party.

In addition to steel nationalization, a number of other measures were introduced designed to regenerate British industry. One was legislation to create the Industrial Reorganization Corporation (IRC). This body had been established in January 1966, but an Act of Parliament was required to provide it with funds. It was 'a kind of government-sponsored merchant bank, to encourage efficient firms to take over the less efficient, to encourage mergers and help finance them, to be, in effect, a stimulator of change by the mere fact of its existence'.[86] Its first chairman was Frank Kearton who, according to Brown, 'did an absolutely fantastic job there while still having his own job as chairman of Courtaulds. How he managed to find the time for both has always puzzled me.'[87] The most notable take-overs helped by the Corporation were GEC's take-over of AEI and English Electric, and the merger of Leyland Motors with the British Motor Corporation. The idea was not just to bail out ailing industries, nor simply to subsidize prestige projects, as the Conservatives had done in the cases of Concorde and the ocean liner *Queen Elizabeth II*. It was to provide Britain with large companies which could compete effectively in international markets. Thus, British Leyland, it was hoped, would be able to take on the state-owned Renault, and Volkswagen, which had been developed from public funds. British Leyland, formed in 1968, continued to have troubles, results of inefficient plant location, overmanning and poor industrial relations, and was only saved from collapse by nationalization in 1975 on the recommendation of the Ryder Report. The ailing computer industry was also helped, and after a series of shake-ups International Computers Limited (ICL) finally emerged as the only British computer firm. The Ministry of Technology had been involved in this task since 1965. Wilson also tried to encourage industry by introducing the Queen's Award to Industry, and more industrialists were given recognition in the honours list than previously. Finally, industrial training boards were established. They were soon in operation for the road transport, hotel and catering, civil air transport and petroleum industries. Others followed.

One other measure of modernization was decimalization. In December 1966 the Decimal Currency Board was created under the chairmanship of Sir William Fiske to prepare the introduction of decimal currency in 1971. Little or no effort was made to line Britain up with Europe in other areas of weights and measures, and even in the 1990s many in Britain still had not got the hang of the metric system, which must be damaging economically.

RHODESIA: 'ROUND AND ROUND IN CIRCLES'

Wilson's final major trial in the eventful summer of 1966 was the meeting of Commonwealth leaders. Inevitably, the main item on the agenda was the situation in Rhodesia. The conference very nearly led to the break-up of the Commonwealth, because the great majority of the African states wanted to commit Britain to NIBMAR – no independence before majority African rule. Wilson was not prepared to agree to this. He stuck to his earlier five principles and added a sixth, 'just as, in the period *before* majority rule, there must be no exploitation of the majority by the minority, in the period *after* majority rule was reached the minority must equally have built-in guarantees against exploitation by the majority'.[88] He succeeded, a remarkable feat, in getting the conference to agree to a communiqué embracing the six principles and calling on Rhodesia to restore the authority of the governor. If the Smith regime did not do so, the British government would not be prepared to submit to the British Parliament any settlement involving independence before majority rule. Backed by the Commonwealth, the communiqué ended, Britain would sponsor in the UN Security Council a resolution providing for effective and selective mandatory sanctions against Rhodesia.[89] The illegal regime had until the end of November to call off the rebellion. On the advice of the governor, Wilson agreed to see Smith again. He feared failure to reach agreement could lead to a confrontation with South Africa, with economic costs to Britain.

The two leaders met between 2 and 5 December. Rather dramatically, this took place on board the cruiser HMS *Tiger*, which went 'round and round in circles' in the Mediterranean.[90] Though Wilson was prepared to agree to

Rhodesian independence on terms which would have meant Black majority rule would have been a very long way off, the talks failed to produce a settlement. The leaders held further fruitless talks, this time on HMS *Fearless*, moored at Gibraltar, in October 1968. Even so, in the spring of 1969 the farce continued, with further 'desultory exchanges'[91] between London and Salisbury, but Rhodesia drifted more and more in the direction of South Africa, acquiring the trappings of an authoritarian racist regime. Undoubtedly some domestic opinion was appeased by all Wilson's efforts to reach an agreement. If the Prime Minister's efforts to come to terms with Smith won him some brief improvement in his image at home, they surely weakened Britain's image abroad. So fond of recalling Dunkirk, Wilson was inviting comparison with Chamberlain rather than with Churchill. In his memoirs Callaghan regretted that his preoccupation with sterling

> prevented me from urging forceful action by Britain . . . A number of the most senior officers of Southern Rhodesia's armed forces were in great mental turmoil . . . and we might have successfully capitalised on these feelings to bring about Smith's quick capitulation. I must accept my full share of collective responsibility . . . more forceful action by us . . . might have saved Britain from many uncomfortable moments in later years.[92]

Tied up with the Rhodesia issue was that of dealing with South Africa. In opposition, Wilson had spoken with some eloquence in condemning the apartheid regime. He promised a Labour government would not sell arms to South Africa. However, he refused to go further, to a general boycott of trade. The argument used was that such a policy would hit the Black South Africans harder than the white minority. The problem of trade in military hardware was never satisfactorily solved by Wilson. On the one hand, he had to square anything his government did with the clear commitments given before October 1964. On the other hand, however, he was under pressure, at a time when the economy was particularly vulnerable, to allow industry to sell as much as possible overseas. He was also under pressure from the Ministry of Defence and, some of the time, the Foreign Office, because of the Simonstown Agreements. These dated from 1955 and provided for co-operation between Britain and South Africa in the defence of the sea routes round the Cape of Good Hope, regarded by defence experts as vital for the West's supplies of strategic raw materials. Primarily, South Africa would need naval equipment, including naval aircraft, to fulfil this commitment. Soon after taking office, Wilson weakened the effect of the arms embargo by agreeing that existing contracts would be honoured; under this loophole, 16 low-flying Buccaneer strike bombers already on order were delivered. Trade seemed to have been as important as defence in this case.[93] In this earlier period Vauxhall Motors was given permission to sell four-wheel-drive chassis for armoured cars or motor lorries for the South African army.[94] Clearly, this was equipment which could be used for internal repression. A crisis blew up over the question of arms sales to the Republic in December 1967. According to Wilson, the strains caused by this issue in the Cabinet were 'strains more serious than any other in our six years of Government'.[95] Remarkably, neither Benn nor Callaghan recall this in their respective books. Wilson was pressed by Brown, Healey, Callaghan and Gordon Walker to lift the ban on the sale of arms to South Africa. Wilson opposed this and was backed by Castle, Greenwood, Shore and some others. After much heat and anger, the Cabinet decided on 18 December against any change of policy.[96] The government did agree a deal between Rio Tinto Zinc and South Africa on uranium mining which virtually gave the Republic a nuclear capacity.[97] This was not, apparently, discussed at Cabinet. Finally, it should be added that Britain was bound, as a member of the UN, to carry out the resolution of 18 June 1963 banning arms supplies. Under Wilson, trade with South Africa grew. Remarkably, the system of imperial preference was still in operation for trade between the two states, even though the Republic had left the Commonwealth in 1961.

WAR IN NIGERIA

Yet another difficult and painful African problem was the civil war in Nigeria. From its independence in 1960, Nigeria had been plagued by tribal rivalries. Never far below the surface, these were a key element in the civil war which erupted in July 1967. Colonel Odumegwu Ojukwu proclaimed the independence of the south eastern (Ibo) region of Nigeria. At first, the new state, Biafra, had considerable success against the military forces of the junta led by General Yakubu Gowon, which ruled Nigeria. In autumn 1967 Gowon requested military supplies from Britain. The British government responded favourably to this request and eventually the 'federal forces' of Gowon prevailed over the Biafrans. The official British position was that it did not want to assist, by neutrality, the Balkanization of Africa. Secondly, Britain was worried that if it failed to assist Federal Nigeria, the Soviet Union would. In fact, some Soviet military supplies were sent to Nigeria. The British government was also worried about British investments and supplies of oil. Ten per cent of Britain's oil came from Nigeria at this time, when Britain's other supplies were less than certain because of the situation in the Middle East. One other factor was that most other African states were against Biafra, which was in strange company, with Zambia, Tanzania, Rhodesia, South Africa and Portugal, for their different reasons, sympathizing with it. Outside financial interests were providing Biafra with arms from France, and the infant state's backers launched a highly successful publicity campaign. Biafra was presented as a long-suffering nation caught between the alternatives of liberation or genocide.[98] In December 1968 Gallup showed that the great majority of British people were emotionally involved with Biafra.[99] In the Labour Party, the respected former Colonial Secretary James Griffiths supported Colonel Ojukwu. There was considerable support for Biafra in the Parliamentary Labour Party and in the Cabinet. Wilson paid a brief visit to Nigeria and certain other African states in March 1969 in an attempt to urge moderation on the Nigerian government and offer his services as a mediator. Little came of the visit. In Britain the government and independent organizations offered relief to both sides. The controversy ended only with the defeat of Biafra in 1970.

ANGUILLA: 'MOCK-GUNBOAT DIPLOMACY'

Britain had failed effectively to promote peace in Nigeria just as it had failed to promote peace in the war between India and Pakistan in 1965. On that occasion the leaders of the two belligerent states went not to London but to Tashkent for the Soviet Union's help in settling the dispute. It was a measure of Britain's decline and the decline of the British government's credibility in the world at large. Potential tragedy turned to farce when Britain sent a detachment of troops and metropolitan police to the rebellious island of Anguilla, in the Caribbean, one of the left-over bits of the ill-fated Caribbean Federation. The occupation of the island of roughly 6,000 inhabitants in 1969 meant that, in Wilson's own words, 'The musical-comedy atmosphere, the mock-gunboat diplomacy, the colourful personalities of some of the leading police, made it the joke of the year. The cartoonists inevitably had the time of their lives, and who could blame them?'[100]

Labour's idealistic hopes of the late 1950s and early 1960s for the Commonwealth were shattered in another way. The party had advocated greater assistance to the developing countries. Wilson had set up a new Ministry of Overseas Development, with Mrs Castle in charge, to emphasize this interest. As we have seen, Bottomley replaced Castle in August 1966. Both were in the Cabinet. When Bottomley left the Cabinet a year later, the new

Table 6.1 Net official overseas assistance from Britain, 1964 and 1970

| Year | Amount | | |
	£ million	% of GNP	£ million (1970 prices)
1964	176	0.53	201
1970	186	0.36	186

minister, Reg Prentice, was not included in the Cabinet. Nor was his successor, Mrs Judith Hart, in 1969. This marked the downgrading of this priority. Net official assistance from Britain to the developing countries fell under the Wilson government.[101] Though the Labour leaders kept up the rhetoric about the Commonwealth, many of them had decided, quite early on in the life of the Wilson administration, that Britain needed a new, European orientation in its relationships.

EEC: 'GET US IN SO WE CAN TAKE THE LEAD'

Labour had said little about Europe in the 1966 election, but the changing trade pattern caused hard thinking on the subject. EFTA was not proving adequate for British purposes, and the EEC seemed unlikely to accept some form of British associate membership. Britain's trade pattern was changing. In the period 1959–66 exports to the EEC states had increased annually by 9.6 per cent, to EFTA countries by 9.5, to the US by 6.4, to Australia, New Zealand and South Africa by 3.8, and to the less-developed countries by 1 per cent. There had been big percentage increases in exports to Japan and Eastern Europe too, though these areas were not very significant as trading partners. In 1966, Britain still sold 24.5 per cent of its exports in the less-developed countries, with the EEC coming second (19.2), EFTA third (14.9), the United States fourth (11.8) and Australia, New Zealand and South Africa taking 12.3 per cent.[102] The decline in the relative importance of trade with the old Commonwealth states and South Africa took place in an environment of preferential tariffs and high national income growth rates. Trade with the EEC had improved in spite of trade barriers, which would get worse if Britain remained outside. Some politicians had thought in terms of a North American Free Trade Area as an alternative route for Britain, but this was a purely academic concept, not even under consideration by the United States. It was with these kinds of figures that the members of the Cabinet, together with a number of officials, went to Chequers in October 1966. Brown, Stewart and Callaghan were fundamentally in favour of joining the EEC; Castle, Jay and Peart were fundamentally against, and most of the others were in between. There was a 'really furious row',[103] but the meeting agreed that Wilson and Brown should go on a grand tour of the EEC to test the ground. This they did, and Britain formally applied to join the Community in May 1967. On 10 May the government managed to get an impressive vote in favour of the application – 488 to 62. Among the 'Noes' were 35 Labour MPs. Another fifty or so abstained. The Wilson–Brown attempt to get into Europe ended on 27 November 1967 when de Gaulle once again vetoed Britain's application. He talked about Britain's economic weaknesses, but his real motive was that he saw Britain as still an American satellite with undue pretensions to grandeur. The fault was not of course all with the President. The British economy *was* weak, the

British government *did* at times sound like the Voice of America on Vietnam and other issues, and British leaders still seemed to be living in a world which was not quite real. Willy Brandt, a friend of British entry, then West German Foreign Minister, recalled how he visited Brown in December 1967: 'I was greeted by the perplexing and disillusioning plea: "Willy, you must get us in so we can take the lead".'[104] Brown himself wrote in 1971, 'Britain's future rests upon her emergence as the leader of a new bloc in the world . . . a new European bloc which would have the same power and influence in the world as the old British Commonwealth had in days gone by.'[105]

Wilson knew that the French President was still the same man who had put paid to Britain's previous application. In such circumstances, they would have done themselves, and the country's prestige, more good by sounding out the possibilities through the normal diplomatic channels, and through George Thomson, who had been given special responsibilities for Europe. As Crossman recorded in his diary on 9 February 1967, 'Here we have Harold and George who should be concentrating on vital domestic problems like prices and incomes gallivanting round Europe and occupying the time of very important officials.'

DEVALUATION: 'THE MONEY IN OUR POCKETS'

Callaghan prepared his 1967 Budget in a mood of optimism. The sterling exchange rate was steady and the currency was under no speculative attacks.[106] In May the pound started to come under pressure again. A set of bad trade figures, tension in the Middle East and Britain's EEC application were key factors. The sterling area and Britain's balance of payments' problems were regarded as obstacles to entry, as was the parity of sterling at $2.80.[107] Unofficially, Callaghan held discussions for a multi-billion-dollar loan in early summer.[108] According to one source,[109] this would have involved Britain maintaining a major military presence in the Far East, turning its back completely on Europe and becoming a virtual US dependency. Wilson rejected this, doubting he could sell it to the party or the British people. Callaghan ended his Budget speech with the words, 'We are back on course. The ship is picking up speed. The economy is moving ahead.'[110] He was hit two months later by the Arab–Israeli Six-Day War which closed the Suez Canal and sunk sterling. Worse was to come. In September an unofficial strike of dockers broke out in Hull, London, Liverpool and Manchester. Cousins's best efforts could not resolve it. This too weakened sterling. What the voters thought about the situation was revealed by Conservative gains from Labour at Cambridge and Walthamstow West by-elections on 21 September. On 2 November Labour lost Hamilton to the Scottish National Party (SNP) and Leicester South West to the Conservatives. It limped home at Manchester Gorton. In October Callaghan bravely faced his many critics at the Labour Party conference at Scarborough. Yet the delegates gave him a standing ovation. He had won a skirmish but, on 18 November 1967, he lost the battle to banish devaluation. The devaluation took the pound down from $2.80 to $2.40. Benn recorded it as a 'great moment of defeat for the Government'.[111] The following day Wilson did his 'absurd broadcast on television' saying, 'Devaluation does *not* mean that the value of the pound in the hands of the British consumer, the British housewife at her shopping, is cut correspondingly. It does not mean that the money in our pockets is worth 14 per cent less.'[112] Heath called it 'the most dishonest statement ever made by a Prime Minister'.[113] This was an exaggeration, but Wilson had been very badly advised. Callaghan resigned. Wilson sent for Jenkins and 'with singular directness' told him he wanted him to be Chancellor. 'I said, "thank you very much," and accepted without question or reservation.'[114] Remarkably, Callaghan did not leave the government, but took over from Jenkins at the Home Office. At this dangerous time, Wilson wanted to keep his two main rivals tied up in the government.[115] The son of Arthur Jenkins, a Welsh miners' MP, Jenkins (b. 1920) took a first in PPE at Balliol and served as a captain in the Royal Artillery. A highly successful author of biographical and historical works, he was director of operations for the John Lewis Partnership.

INDUSTRIAL RELATIONS: 'COMMITTING POLITICAL SUICIDE'?

Barbara Castle served as Minister of Transport, 1965–68. One of her notable achievements was to introduce the breathalyser test, which cut down road accidents but got her much abuse.[116] She was, however, to get far more abuse from within the Labour movement in her next job as Secretary of State for Employment and Productivity, 1968–70. She was under no illusion that 'I may be committing political suicide'.[117] She faced aggressive union leaders such as Jack Jones of the TGWU and Hugh Scanlon of the AEU, the problems of inter-union rivalry[118] which so bedevilled the British trade union scene, unofficial strikes, union opposition to equal pay for women,[119] rivalries within the government itself possibly made worse by the reshuffles which helped to fire the ambitions of her colleagues and, above all, opposition to prices and incomes policy.

As inflation mounted so did strikes. There were 2,116 disputes in 1967 and over 2.7 million working days lost. In 1969 the number of disputes had risen to 3,116 and over 6.8 million working days were lost. Britain's record was still better than those of the United States, Canada, Italy, Ireland and a number of other industrial countries, but much worse than West Germany and Sweden. Japan had improved its position relative to Britain, so had France, except for the year of the massive strikes of 1968. Unofficial strikes, those called by a group of workers without union authority, accounted for

95 per cent of all strikes. As Castle argued, they were often more disruptive than major official ones because of their unpredictability.[120] In 1965, Wilson set up the Royal Commission on Trade Unions and Employers' Associations under the chairmanship of Lord Donovan, a Lord Justice of Appeal and former Labour MP. The Commission reported in June 1968. It drew attention to the problems caused by the large number of trade unions. This meant fragmented bargaining between employers and employees in individual firms, inter-union rivalry, leapfrogging in pay claims, and unofficial strikes. The Commission was reluctant to put much emphasis on legal sanctions as a means of improving industrial relations. The reason for this view was that such sanctions would be difficult to enforce and would make a tense situation worse. The conclusion was based on foreign experience and the reluctance of employers in Britain to go to court. The Commission wanted a special Industrial Law Committee to keep the law under review. Castle consulted with the TUC, the CBI and the Parliamentary Labour Party about Donovan[121] and invited various people for a final go at Sunningdale. Cabinet colleague Peter Shore proposed taking power to impose a conciliation pause during which the two sides to a dispute could be brought together to talk over their differences and try to avoid a strike.[122] Castle took this up.

Meanwhile, the Conservatives had been thinking out their proposals on industrial relations and had published them under the title *Fair Deal At Work*. The government was under considerable pressure to initiate legislation from the public, as well as the Opposition, and, not least, from Britain's creditors abroad.

Castle published her proposals on 17 January 1969 in a White Paper, *In Place of Strife*, the title consciously playing on Bevan's *In Place of Fear*. Despite 'sharp reactions from the Labour movement',[123] at the end of the Commons debate on the White Paper, it was approved by 224 votes to 62, of which 53 were cast by Labour MPs. The Conservatives abstained. The Industrial Relations Bill which followed foresaw the setting up of a permanent Commission on Industrial Relations to carry out a variety of functions in relation to unions and employers. It would have also established an Industrial Board to hear certain types of case against employers, trade unions and individual employees. It was by no means merely designed to restrict the activities of trade unions. It contained many proposals which would have strengthened employees' rights. It sought to establish the principle that no employer had the right to prevent or obstruct an employee from belonging to a trade union. It sought safeguards against unfair dismissal and greater rights for employees under the Contracts of Employment Act, 1963. It proposed giving trade unions the right to have certain sorts of information from employers, subject to safeguards for confidential information. What worried trade union leaders were certain proposals which, in the words of Vic Feather (later Lord Feather), would 'introduce the taint of criminality into industrial relations'.[124] Under the proposed legislation the Secretary of State could, by Order, require those involved to desist for up to 28 days from a strike or lock-out which was unofficial. The Secretary of State would also have had the power to order a ballot where an official strike was threatened. Another clause enabled the proposed Industrial Board to hear complaints by individuals of unfair or arbitrary action by unions. Finally, the Bill would have included the Donovan proposal withdrawing the immunity of unofficial strikers from legal sanctions. This was the proposal which ran into most trouble. It soon became clear that the government had no chance of securing passage of the Bill. Castle was supported by Wilson, Benn, Jenkins and Shore. Against them were Callaghan, Crosland, Marsh, Roy Mason and Fred Lee.[125] After endless 'negotiations of almost Byzantine complications with a variety of trade union leaders',[126] a face-saving formula was worked out on 19 June 1969. The TUC General Council agreed to a solemn and binding undertaking, setting out the lines on which they would intervene in serious unofficial strikes. The government would not continue with the proposed legislation during the current session of Parliament, but would continue its discussions with interested parties about possible future legislation. This situation made it easy for Heath to score points in the Commons. 'What will happen', he asked, 'should unofficial strikers ignore the trade union leaders, and go on striking?' Wilson had no answer.[127]

CUTTING DEFENCE: 'WE WERE ALL DOGS'

After a 'marathon series of Cabinets'[128] on 16 January, other measures were taken to deal with the economic malaise. Labour stalwarts had to swallow many a bitter pill. Most of the soothing words spoken at the previous party conference became just one more catalogue of broken promises. Prescription charges, which had caused so much anger in the Labour Party, out of all proportion to their effect, were reintroduced. The national insurance contribution was increased. The number of houses to be built was cut. Free school milk for secondary school pupils was ended. The raising of the school-leaving age, demanded for so long, was deferred until 1973. This last measure was too much for Lord Longford, who resigned from the government, Wilson's only Cabinet casualty. The Conservatives could gloat, but they too saw some of the things dear to many a Tory heart being destroyed in the financial holocaust. The Territorial Army was virtually to disappear and so was Civil Defence. After two votes, the threat of resignation from Healey[129] and a strong warning from President Johnson,[130] the order for the American F111A aircraft was cancelled. Millions had to be paid in compensation but, nevertheless, hundreds of millions of pounds were saved. Going too were Britain's commitments east of

Suez. 'Harry Lee', Lee Kuan Yew, Socialist Singapore Prime Minister, flew in to lobby against the British withdrawal. He gained a nine-month delay.[131]

Labour MPs had argued for years that Britain should give up its remaining global commitments; now this was happening, but for the wrong reasons – simple financial expediency – the whole business began to look like a series of panicky pullbacks caused by a collapsing currency. In March 1967, 63 Labour MPs had voted against the Defence White Paper, which contained renewed justification for staying east of Suez. Wilson warned that MPs could bite once like a dog, but if they did it again their licence would not be renewed. Benn and many others found it deeply insulting: it implied that 'we were all dogs and he was our trainer'.[132] The Middle East war of June 1967 had revealed Britain's inability to influence events in that area in any way. Yet it took some time for the lesson to sink in. Wilson later admitted, 'I was one of the last to be converted.'[133]

A 'POST-MIDNIGHT' PRIVY COUNCIL

The next financial crisis came a short time after the January 1968 cuts, and could easily have resulted in another devaluation. The dollar was weak because of the United States' deficit on the balance of payments. The underlying cause was 'the beginning of the end of the role of the dollar, battered by the improvident financing of the Vietnam War, as the effortless sun of the Bretton Woods [1944] solar system . . . whatever currency the gale was directed against the side-winds were devastating for sterling.'[134] By March 1968 the situation was desperate. Washington 'requested' Jenkins to close the London gold market, the principal market through which traders were deserting the dollar for gold. The alternative for Britain was 'to be drowned within twenty-four hours'.[135] Jenkins had 15 minutes of advice from the banker, Siegmund Warburg, who told him to use the closing of the gold market, 'as a smokescreen to close the foreign exchange market as well . . . He confirmed the official view that we were on the very brink of another devaluation.'[136] Wilson hurriedly called a 'post-midnight', 10-minute Privy Council at Buckingham Palace to issue an Order in Council proclaiming a bank holiday.

The financial crisis was as notable for its accidental, political consequences as for any economic ones. Somehow, Brown was not informed of the meeting and felt, not for the first time, slighted and dejected. An ugly scene took place at Downing Street and he resigned on 15 March. Crosland and Stewart were 'also very niggled about not having been consulted'[137] but stayed. Stewart replaced Brown at the Foreign Office.

Jenkins faced another nightmare. The Commons, facing an all-night session on the Transport Bill, was in uproar and demanded to hear from the Chancellor. At 3.20 a.m. Jenkins made a statement and answered questions.

Before Labour MPs could recover their composure, they were hit again. When the Budget proposals were announced on 19 March, they must have believed their 1964 programme had been sentenced to death by a thousand cuts. The Budget 'turned out to involve the most swingeing increases in taxation the country had ever faced on one single occasion'.[138] Tax on petrol, cigarettes and whisky, road fund licences, corporation tax, SET, betting tax – all were increased. Income tax allowances were cut so as to neutralize the previous family allowances except for the poorer families. As a sop to the Left there was to be a special surcharge on large investment incomes. The only consolation was that income tax was not going up. Castle thought Jenkins 'won the reluctant admiration of the Tories opposite, and brought our people to their feet waving their order papers at the end'.[139] When the voters were given their chance to show what they felt about the Budget, they threw out Labour from Meriden, Acton and Dudley. All went to the Conservatives on 28 March.

STUDENT PROTESTS: 'NASTY TOUCH OF AUTHORITARIANISM'

The economy apart, 1968 was a sad and frightening year in other respects too. In May 1968 an unexpected crisis blew up in France. Student protests at the University of Nanterre, just outside Paris, over conditions there spread to Paris. Students occupied university buildings and set up 'counter-universities'. Peaceful demonstrations soon became violent confrontations with armed police. The streets of Paris were lit up at night by blazing cars. Students at other universities in France took similar action. Then, to the astonishment of their own leaders, workers started to go militant. Strikes and factory occupations spread like wildfire throughout the country. Suddenly it looked as though de Gaulle, in office since 1958, would fall and France would be plunged into civil war. De Gaulle and his family left for Germany and appeared to give up.[140] It was only after the government had given in to most of the economic demands of the workers, and called new elections, that the Republic returned to some sort of normality. The French students had learnt something about the art of protest, 1960s-style, from the Germans and the Americans. German students were incensed by the successes – 1966–69 – of the extreme right-wing NPD, which appeared an effective political force at that time. They also opposed Chancellor Kiesinger (1966–69) who had been a member of the Nazi Party, and they opposed the Vietnam War. In the US the protests were also about Vietnam, and about racial discrimination.

Britain experienced its own more modest, and more moderate, form of student protests in 1968. There were protests about living conditions at universities, about their hierarchical structures, methods of teaching and sexual segregation. The most extreme protests were at the London School of Economic and Political Science, and Essex University. There were also occupations of libraries and offices, stealing of confidential papers and other actions at many other universities and polytechnics. Some reforms followed these actions. As elsewhere, students also took to the streets protesting against the Vietnam War and racism. Left-wing students were angered by the Labour government's general support for the United States over Vietnam. The horrors of Vietnam were seen nightly on television and many felt sympathy for a small nation which seemed to be the hapless victim of power politics. Michael Stewart, the Foreign Secretary, faced catcalls and jeers at Hertford College, Oxford, when he defended the government's stand on Vietnam to a student audience. He silenced many when he said he enjoyed teach-ins and would rejoice 'when students in China, the Soviet Union and even in North Vietnam would have the same freedom to express their views'.[141] The government discussed the student protests. Wilson could not understand why the universities were not taking a stronger line, and wanted to know whether student grants could be withdrawn. Stewart was attracted to this idea. Crossman saw parallels with the fall of Weimar and wanted no hesitation in dealing with people who destroyed free speech. Benn, recording this, felt 'there was a nasty touch of authoritarianism from other Ministers which I found depressing'.[142]

The Soviet invasion of Czechoslovakia in August 1968 to overthrow the Reform Communist regime briefly united all shades of opinion in Britain, including the Communists, in condemnation of this aggressive act against another small nation.

IMMIGRATION: THIS 'DISTASTEFUL NECESSITY'

In February 1967 the extreme right-wing National Front came into being, gaining limited support largely on the immigration issue. Fear of the extent of 'coloured' Commonwealth immigration led Macmillan to introduce the Commonwealth Immigration Act, 1962. Under this Act, immigrants were admitted as one of three categories. There were those who had been offered definite jobs (Category A), and those who had certain specific skills which were in short supply (Category B). There was also Category C, made up of those who did not qualify under the other two. This third category was dropped in 1964. In July 1965 Wilson placed a ceiling of 8,500 on the total number of vouchers to be issued. Of this total 1,000 were reserved for Maltese. The net total number of non-white Commonwealth immigrants was officially estimated at 42,700 in 1955. It fluctuated downwards to 21,850 in 1959, jumping up to 57,700 in 1960. There was an upsurge in 1961–62 because of the impending legislation. Over 240,000 came in those two years. Though the numbers fell away, the average for the three years 1963–65 was over 53,000. The majority of those entering in these years came in as dependants.[143] Obviously, the Act was not as effective as its authors had expected.

In 1968 a new problem aggravated the situation. Substantial numbers of Asians had gone to East Africa when that area was under British colonial rule. They became of key significance in the commercial life of those territories and in the professions. When the three territories in the area became independent as Tanganyika (1961, later Tanzania), Uganda (1962) and Kenya (1963), special provision was made for these Asians. Those born there would become citizens of the newly independent state, provided at least one parent had been born in that state. Those not so covered remained citizens of the United Kingdom and colonies or British-protected persons. These then had the option of remaining British passport-holders or applying, within two years, for citizenship of the state where they lived.[144] Increasingly, these states put pressure on their Asians. They were pursuing a policy of Africanization and wanted to rid themselves of these foreign communities. In 1967 the pressure was on in Kenya. The numbers of Asians coming to Britain from this source started to increase. Britain sent Malcolm MacDonald, who knew Kenyan leader Kenyatta, to try to persuade the Kenyan government to moderate its policy, but to no avail. The result was that further restrictive legislation was passed after little discussion and much heart-searching. Crossman saw it as another Cabinet 'balls-up': 'Already in 1965 we should have known all about the Kenya Asians because a paper was put up to Cabinet raising all the issues.'[145] He put the blame on the Cabinet Secretariat 'which is supposed to be a kind of super progress-chaser and keep a look-out for all Cabinet decisions and watch that they're adequately carried out'.[146] Even had the Secretariat done so, the dilemma which faced the government and Parliament would not have been solved: should Britain break its pledge to these Asians or run the risk of racial violence in the future? The government decided it could not take the risk and a Bill was rushed through Parliament in seven days to become law on 1 March 1968. It extended the operation of the 1962 Act to those possessing citizenship of the United Kingdom and colonies if they were without substantial personal connection with this country. This was defined in terms of birthplace of parents or grandparents. The Liberals, 15 Conservatives, including Iain Macleod, and 35 Labour MPs voted against the Bill.[147] The official Opposition line was to abstain. Callaghan, who was responsible for this 'distasteful necessity', was 'upset at the harsh tone of some of the personal criticism'.[148]

The government did not deal with the problem of immigration and racism merely by imposing restrictions. It did make a start to providing equality for those already in Britain. Two Race Relations Acts were placed on the statute book. The first, in 1965, made it unlawful for any person to practise discrimination on the grounds of colour, race, or ethnic or national origins against anybody seeking access to facilities or services at restaurants, cafés, pubs, theatres, cinemas, dance halls and all other places of public entertainment or recreation. It also covered public transport and places maintained by local authorities. The Act set up a Race Relations Board, with local committees to hear complaints and attempt conciliation. Where this was not possible, civil proceedings could be instituted by the Attorney-General. The Act of 1968, the result of the investigations of a committee under Professor Harry Street, was much wider in scope and extended the law to employment and housing. The government hoped to appease the anti-restrictions minority in Parliament as well as the immigrants. It realized that legislation would not change attitudes overnight, and put the emphasis on conciliation rather than compulsion. Divided on the issue, the Conservative Party voted against the 1968 Act though about 20 Conservatives, led by Sir Edward Boyle, abstained. Wilson also sought to take the heat out of the immigration issue by providing extra help for those local authorities with high concentrations of immigrants. The immigrants made up, in 1966, about 3.2 per cent of the population of Greater London, about the same in the West Midlands, 1.8 per cent in West Yorkshire and 1 per cent in South East Lancashire. However, within those areas there were particular boroughs – Brent and Hackney, Wolverhampton, Huddersfield, Birmingham and Bradford – and parts of boroughs, where concentrations were higher.[149]

POWELL: 'A NATION . . . HEAPING UP ITS OWN FUNERAL PYRE'

Depending on one's point of view, the government had, by its new restrictionist policies, either taken a realistic stand or appeased the racists and the ignorant. At any rate, it looked as though it had got the problem of the Kenyan Asians under control. At this time television viewers were given nightly a reminder of the horrors of racial tension from the United States. Martin Luther King, Black civil rights leader and Nobel Prize winner, had been assassinated on 4 April 1968. Severe racial tension and violence exploded in the days that followed. In Washington, DC 'entire blocks of buildings were going up in smoke . . . Before the holocaust was over, 40 other cities had experienced similar tragic outbreaks . . . from coast to coast.'[150]

It was in this situation of remorse and fear that Enoch Powell, defence spokesman of the shadow cabinet, made a widely publicized speech on immigration and race relations, on 20 April, before the passage of the second Race Relations Bill. He wanted to stop the inflow of immigrants and promote the maximum outflow, 'with generous grants and assistance'. He opposed the Bill as something which 'is to be enacted to give the stranger, the disgruntled and the *agent provocateur* the power to pillory [Britons] for their private actions'. He also opposed it because, 'Here is

149

the means of showing that the immigrant communities can organize to consolidate their members, to agitate and campaign against their fellow-citizens, and to overawe and dominate the rest with the legal weapons which the ignorant and the ill-informed have provided.' His rhetoric and emotion-laden examples were skilfully deployed to back up his views. 'Those whom the gods wish to destroy, they first make mad. We must be mad, literally mad, as a nation to be permitting the annual inflow of some 50,000 dependants . . . It is like watching a nation busily engaging in heaping up its own funeral pyre.' He spoke of the formerly 'quiet street' which had become 'a place of noise and confusion', where lived a single old white lady, who was abused by her immigrant neighbours and had 'excreta pushed through her letter-box'.[151]

Powell found he had struck a popular chord. Hundreds of letters of support poured in. According to Gallup three in four agreed with what he said.[152] In London a group of 200 dockers and meat porters marched to Westminster to congratulate him, and 'shout obscene things at Labour MPs'. According to Benn, 'there were strikes all over the place in support of Enoch Powell'.[153]

Heath sacked Powell from his team on 14 April 1968, calling his speech racist. Powell denied he was a racist, saying there were many of the peoples of India who were 'in many respects' superior to Europeans.[154] Boyle, Hogg, Macleod and Willie Whitelaw, the Chief Whip, had indicated they would resign if Powell stayed. Most Conservative MPs supported Heath[155] but he was flooded with hostile letters, often obscene.[156] Trouble had been brewing between Heath and Powell for some time. Powell was ambitious. Perhaps his Birmingham speech was part of the provincial revolt against the accepted complacency of Establishment London, or simply a reflection of a fatal maverick streak, a protest against the polite consensus politics aimed at the middle ground where passion is dead and the clash of principles is replaced by the calculations of pollsters, psephologists and speech-writers. Whatever its origin, the speech could not have done race relations, law and order or, in the long run, its tormented author any good. If anything, it strengthened Heath. It certainly strengthened Wilson. On 2 May he gave a forthright and eloquent answer to Powell which did much to restore, temporarily at least, his sagging popularity with his own supporters. Finally, the speech marked the beginning of the widening gulf between Powell and the Conservative Party.

NORTHERN IRELAND: 'BLATANT DISCRIMINATION'

On 17 April 1969 a remarkable young woman was elected to Parliament – Bernadette Devlin, a 21-year-old student, and a left-wing, independent Irish republican. She had beaten the Ulster Unionist candidate at a by-election in the Mid-Ulster constituency. This was the culmination of a struggle which had begun over two years before and, some would say, it was part of a larger struggle which had been going on for centuries.

In 1921 the British government and Irish nationalist representatives signed a treaty under which Ireland was to become a self-governing dominion of the British Empire, similar in status to Canada, and styled the Irish Free State. Northern Ireland, six counties, was to be free to stay out of the new dominion and remain part of the United Kingdom. The two parts of Ireland, the predominantly Catholic South, and the predominantly Protestant North, already had parliaments set up under the Government of Ireland Act, 1920. The treaty of December 1921 brought to an end years of armed conflict between the forces of the British Crown and the Irish Republican Army – a somewhat different body from the ones competing for that title in the 1960s. Total peace did not come to either part for some years, mainly because extreme republicans could not be satisfied with anything less than a republic, free of Britain and incorporating the whole of Ireland. Various forms of discrimination against the Catholics in the North, who make up roughly one-third of the population, meant that no chance was given for the development of non-sectarian politics. In 1935 British troops had to restore order in Ulster. Catholics felt they could never achieve their full rights in the mini-quasi-state of Ulster ruled permanently by the Ulster Unionist Party. For their part, the Northern Protestants felt under siege, as the state based on Dublin did not relinquish its claims to the six counties making up Northern Ireland. The constitution of 1937 claimed to be for the whole of Ireland. In 1949 the Catholic state formally became the Republic of Ireland, thus severing all remaining constitutional ties with Britain.

The Irish Republican Army (IRA), the handful of militant irreconcilables, had been ruthlessly suppressed in North and South during the Second World War and it was some years before the organization was capable of any action again. An armed campaign during the period 1956–62 against partition was a failure. With greater prosperity in both parts of Ireland, and opportunities in Britain and the USA, few young men could be recruited for such romantic gestures. By the 1960s the IRA announced the struggle was political rather than military.[157] It began to look as though sectarian attitudes were breaking down on both sides.[158] The coming to office of Captain Terence O'Neill (1914–1990), as Prime Minister of Northern Ireland in 1963, was a sign of this. He replaced Lord Brookeborough (Basil Brooke, 1888–1974), who had led the Unionists for 20 years, during which time 'Blatant discrimination' was practised in housing and other areas.[159] O'Neill was regarded as a moderate and embarked upon a programme of modest reform. For the first time since the partition, the leaders of the two Irish political entities met, O'Neill having invited the Irish Prime Minister Sean Lemass to Belfast in 1965. There were, however, rumblings of discontent among the more extreme elements in the Protestant community.

Prominent among them was Rev. Ian Paisley. In August 1966 O'Neill warned Wilson of the need 'for a short period for Ulster to assimilate his earlier reforms'.[160] By this time the Catholics too were stirring. In 1967 the Northern Ireland Civil Rights Association was formed through the earlier work of Dr Conn and Mrs Patricia McCluskey, who were keenly interested in securing for Catholics a fair share of new council housing so long denied them. They were influenced by the changing political climate in both Britain and Ireland, and by the example of the successful civil rights campaigns in the United States.

On 5 October 1968 a civil rights march, attended by three Labour MPs from London, went ahead in Londonderry as planned, even though it had been banned by the Northern Ireland Minister of Home Affairs, William Craig. The marchers were attacked along the route, and the police used 'needless violence'[161] against them. Backed by the British government, O'Neill was prepared to step up the implementation of the reform programme, including a development commission to replace the Protestant local authority in Londonderry, and an ombudsman to investigate particular grievances. O'Neill was, however, outflanked by the right wing of his own party. He dismissed Craig, and two other ministers subsequently resigned. He called an election in February 1969, hoping his moderate policies would be endorsed. This tactic was not entirely successful. For the first time in 24 years his own constituency was challenged and O'Neill was returned on a minority vote, with Paisley coming close to beating him. There was no kind of understanding between the Catholic civil rights candidates and moderate Unionists. The victory of Ms Devlin in April was another blow in that it aroused the extreme Protestants even more. More demonstrations and disorder took place, and bombings of public utilities seemed to indicate the inability of O'Neill's Stormont government to maintain order. Accordingly, he announced his resignation on 28 April. Major James Chichester-Clark replaced him. Another factor in O'Neill's downfall was his determination to introduce universal adult suffrage for local elections. Northern Ireland still retained franchise laws restricting voting to persons with statutory qualifications as property owners or tenants. The result was that about one-quarter of persons eligible to vote in Westminster elections were not eligible to vote in local elections, and plural votes could be claimed by people with multiple property qualifications. This hit Catholics harder than Protestants.[162] The new Prime Minister, no doubt with one eye on London, agreed to implement this measure of reform and proclaimed an amnesty for political offenders.

COMMONS 'SPELLBOUND'

Devlin's maiden speech held the Commons 'spellbound', but both Wilson and Crossman recalled they found her negative and uncompromising in her approach.[163] No doubt the new, working-class MP fresh from Queen's University believed the Commons understood little and cared less about Ulster. She knew the reality behind the statistic that there the unemployment rate was always above the UK average, being three times higher for Catholics than for Protestants. She and her lonely Belfast colleague Gerry Fitt knew the reality of the discrimination against educated Catholics which drove them out of the province to find jobs, of the discrimination in the shipyards where the bulk of those employed were Protestants. Crossman remarked on how little the Cabinet knew about the conditions in Ulster and quotes Healey as admitting the same.[164] He called both O'Neill and Chichester-Clark inarticulate, upper-class landowners, and this did seem to be part of the problem. O'Neill, it could be claimed, knew the world, and was refreshingly open to outside influences, but did he know Ulster? Both he and his successor were set apart from the bulk of their own party by education, speech, manners, lifestyle and money. Such men could only maintain their leadership as long as they mouthed the traditional shibboleths of Unionism, but they proved incapable of leading their flock into new, non-sectarian, pastures. As the Ulster crisis deepened, they were put aside. Chichester-Clark went in March 1971. Paisley came more and more to prominence as an authentic leader of a considerable section of Protestant opinion. Unfortunately, his colourful personality and oratory were put to destructive, rather than constructive, purposes.

In August 1969 there was renewed violence. The annual (Protestant) Apprentice Boys of Londonderry March led to Catholic fears of a violent passage through their territory, Bogside. For 48 hours Catholics hurled abuse, stones and petrol bombs at the Royal Ulster Constabulary, who responded with tear gas. The Irish Republic's tricolour flew over Bogside and 'Free Derry' was proclaimed. All this led to tension in Belfast. There too barricades went up and firing broke out (it is not clear who started it)[165] between the police and Catholics. Five Catholics and two Protestants died. Catholics were forced out of their homes which were then burned.[166] Callaghan, as Home Secretary, sent in British troops to restore order and establish truce lines. He visited the devastated areas himself. More promises of reform followed. Official investigations substantiated Catholic complaints. The Cameron Commission of September 1969 concluded that civil rights grievances had a 'substantial foundation in fact and were in a very real sense an immediate and operative cause of . . . disorders'.[167] The Hunt Report in October recommended the disbandment of the B Specials, a Protestant auxiliary police force, and the disarming of the regular police. The British government implemented these recommendations together with the setting up of the Ulster Defence Regiment, which was to be a non-sectarian body to support the civil power. Unfortunately, many Catholics saw it as merely the B Specials in military uniform. The Protestants were angry about the loss of the 'B's and riots took place. On 11 October the British

Army intervened to crush fierce Protestant riots in the Shankhill, Belfast. The Catholics had won a victory but were split among themselves about their objectives and how to achieve them. Not even the IRA agreed on what they wanted; this body split during the 1960s into the official, or 'Red and Green', IRA and the Provisional, or 'Green', IRA. There was a third group, the Saor Eire, or Free Ireland. The differences of doctrine of the three groups need not concern us; what is of interest is that they could, with a minimum number of recruits and a minimum cover, inflict so much damage on life and property in Northern Ireland. It is also possible to pose the question, but not answer it, of whether the British government could have prevented the worst by earlier intervention, including power-sharing in Ulster. Easter 1970 saw vicious rioting between troops and Catholic inhabitants of the Ballymurphy housing estate on the edge of West Belfast. For the first time since the Second World War British troops were again in conflict with Irish republicans.

LORDS 'FRUSTRATE . . . ELECTED GOVERNMENT'

In 1968 Wilson attempted to fulfil Labour's pledge to deal with the House of Lords. The upper chamber had a built-in Conservative majority, because of the hereditary principle, which had been dented, but not destroyed, by the introduction of life peerages in 1958. Since then the Lords had become only slightly little less unpopular in Labour circles. There was renewed anger when, in June, the Lords rejected the Southern Rhodesia (United Nations) Sanctions Order, 1968. Wilson later wrote that 'not since the Parliament Act of 1911 had the Lords deliberately set themselves out to frustrate . . . the executive actions, and in this case actions to fulfil international commitments, of the elected Government'.[168] But he did not seek to abolish the Lords. In November the government published its White Paper on Lords Reform, the result of all-party talks. At that time there were roughly 736 hereditary peers by succession, 122 hereditary peers of first creation, 155 life peers, 23 serving or retired Law Lords and 26 bishops.[169] The main proposals of the White Paper were that the hereditary basis of membership should be eliminated and that no one party should possess a permanent majority in the Lords. Hereditary peers would still have the right to attend and speak, but not vote. The Bill to reform the Lords was defeated by a strange alliance of left-wing and Conservative backbench opposition led, respectively, by Michael Foot and Enoch Powell. The Left feared that a revived, but still grossly undemocratic, second chamber would exercise more power and authority. Some Conservatives were worried about the increase in the power of patronage which would go to the Prime Minister. Powell himself remained an unashamed believer in the principle of primogeniture in the Lords.

Under Wilson MPs were invited to put their own House in order. New and younger Labour MPs felt that the Commons' hours and methods were inefficient and downright inconvenient. An experiment, introduced in the session 1966–67, of holding sittings of the Commons in the mornings proved a failure because most Conservatives, having outside professions, were against it.

More successful was the experiment with specialist committees. These had been advocated by those who believed the back-bencher had little chance to examine the work of government. Experiments were started with the Select Committee on Estimates by dividing it into six subcommittees covering various aspects of public policy from Defence and Overseas Affairs to Technological and Scientific Affairs. These committees met in private. Interestingly, in view of the problems with this area in the 1990s, a Select Committee on Agriculture was set up at the end of 1966 and wound up again a year later due to lack of interest. More permanent were the Committees on Education and Science, Race Relations and Immigration, and the Select Committee on Scottish Affairs. These produced some useful reports, but it is doubtful whether they increased the back-benchers' power *vis-à-vis* the executive.[170]

The Parliament of 1966–70 also attempted to make the administration more responsible to the public through the Commissioner for Administration Act, 1967. The Commissioner, or Ombudsman, was given the task of investigating written complaints made to MPs by members of the public who claim to have sustained injustice in consequence of maladministration. The Commissioner had only limited impact compared with similar offices in other countries. His jurisdiction was severely limited. He was not empowered to deal with complaints about local government, National Heath Service hospitals, personnel matters in the civil service or armed services, the nationalized industries or the police. In addition, the Commissioner's work attracted little attention, and many MPs preferred to investigate complaints themselves rather than use the Ombudsman. However, by the late 1970s, there was a big increase in the number of complaints lodged, which seemed to indicate the office served a genuine need.

The 1966–70 Parliament also changed the suffrage. Under the Representation of the People Act, 1969 the voting age was lowered to 18. The majority of Conservatives voted against this on a free vote.

DAVID STEEL: EXCEPTIONAL COURAGE

The Parliaments of 1964–70 passed six other Bills which were in keeping with trends in other advanced societies. They were not party political measures, but it is unlikely that a Conservative-dominated Commons would have approved them. The first was the abolition of capital punishment, due to the untiring efforts of Sydney Silverman, who introduced his

Murder (Abolition of the Death Penalty) Bill in 1964. It was passed in July 1965. The Lords then carried a Conservative amendment that the measure should lapse automatically after five years unless both Houses passed motions for permanent abolition. Such motions were approved in December 1969. MPs decided to risk running counter to public opinion on this issue.

In July 1967 the Sexual Offences Act legalized homosexual practices, in private, between consenting adults in England and Wales. This was a private member's bill introduced by Leo Abse, a Welsh Labour MP. In October of the same year the Abortion Act became law. This had been introduced by Liberal MP David Steel. Jenkins, then Home Secretary, commented, 'I think that as a young member . . . with a marginal constituency and without a great party machine . . . he has shown exceptional courage'.[171] The Act made abortion much easier on the grounds of physical or mental risk to the pregnant woman or any existing children of her family, or when there was a substantial risk that if the child were born, it would suffer physical or mental abnormalities. The number of abortions greatly increased after the passing of the Act, which continued to be opposed by a strong pressure group based on the Catholic community. Parliament also modernized the law on divorce in 1969. The irretrievable breakdown of the marriage became the sole reason for granting divorce. In line with other countries where divorce was available Britain was experiencing an explosion of divorce before the Act. Between 1959 and 1969 the annual number of petitions for divorce and annulment in England and Wales had increased by something like 133 per cent. This trend continued. The secularization of society, the improving education of women and the increase in the number of married women at work were probably the main causes for this development. The term 'women's liberation' erupted into the mass media around 1968. Also in keeping with this trend was the National Health Service (Family Planning) Act, 1967, which enabled local authorities to provide a family planning service for all who sought it, either directly or by way of a voluntary body. The advice was free, the contraceptive devices were to be charged for according to the means of the recipient. The Theatre Act, 1968, introduced by Labour MP George Strauss, ended censorship of plays in London, about which there had been controversy for many years. No doubt this move made it easier for provincial theatres to be more controversial with their productions. The legislators resisted change in one area – drugs. Drug-taking, trafficking and other related offences continued to cause mounting concern. Dangerous-drug offences doubled between 1969 and 1972. The causes remained uncertain and somewhat obscure, but this was the start of a long-term trend. All these measures, which recognized the changes in society and attitudes, and in turn helped to produce them, were seen by some as a dangerous lurch in the direction of the permissive society, by others as moves towards a more honest and more humane Britain.

ELECTION '70: 'EXQUISITE JUNE MORNING'

When Wilson appeared on a TV sports programme as a football fan, there were those who thought the election could not be far away. Polling day was on 18 June and everything pointed to another Labour win. The local election results in May had gone Labour's way. The opinion polls gave Labour a good lead. Top people – Cecil King the newspaper magnate, Lord Renwick and Norman Collins of ATV, Lord Crowther of Forte, Lord Shawcross, former Attlee minister turned TV tycoon, Paul Chambers of ICI, Lockwood of EMI, and McFadzean of Shell, and others too – met together and wondered how they could use their mouths and their money to scotch Wilson. King commented gloomily, 'On television Wilson lacks all authority but looks genial and confident; Heath looks a nice man but is just not convincing – it is hard to say why.'[172] Money wages were up and the balance of payments looked healthy. In spite of all the setbacks, ownership of consumer durables and home ownership had continued to rise. Two days before the vote, adverse balance of payments figures for May were announced. England was knocked out of the World Cup and, despite his differences with Heath, Powell urged his supporters to vote Conservative. Within the Labour Party all was not well. In May, Labour MPs had once again demonstrated their disagreements over the government's support for the US on Vietnam. Individual membership of the party had fallen every year since Labour was in office. For those who had to man the creaking, run-down Labour constituency machines, these were years of frustration and failure. In some respects Britain was a franker, freer place to live than it had been even in the early 1960s, but the great plans for reform had not come off.

On 19 June at 4 a.m. Crossman and his wife motored home. It was the 'cool, delicious dawn of an exquisite June morning'.[173] Politically, it was the delicious dawn of the man with the boat rather than the man with the pipe. To everyone's amazement, Heath, the most despised politician in post-war Britain, had won. The Conservatives had fewer votes than in 1951, 1955 or 1959, but they had gained a majority of 43 over Labour. The quiet election with the lowest turnout since 1935 had proved to be Wilson's undoing. It was also Brown's. He lost his seat and therefore his position as deputy leader.

NOTES

Unless otherwise indicated, the place of publication is London.

1 Harold Wilson, *The Labour Government 1964–70: A Personal Record* (1971), 2.
2 Peter Paterson, *Tired and Emotional: The Life of Lord George-Brown* (1993).
3 Lord Wigg, *George Wigg* (1972), 259.
4 Marcia Williams, *Inside Number 10* (1975), 102.

5 Harold Wilson, *The New Britain: Labour Plan Outlined* (1964), 9. This volume includes all the radical, Kennedy-style rhetoric. There was no plan as such.
6 Ruth Winstone (ed.)/Tony Benn, *The Benn Diaries* (introduced by Ruth Winstone) (1995), 117–18. See also comments of Williams, op. cit., 17.
7 Richard Crossman, *The Diaries of a Cabinet Minister, vol. 1: Minister of Housing 1964–66* (1975), 29. Remarkably, Barbara Castle 'enjoyed the novelty of going to Buckingham Palace for the swearing in'. See Barbara Castle, *Fighting all the Way* (1993), 340.
8 Roy Jenkins, *A Life at the Centre* (1991), 160.
9 Winstone/Benn, op. cit., 180.
10 ibid., 124; Joe Haines, *The Power of Politics* (1977), 147.
11 Castle, op. cit., 341–2, 367.
12 *Sunday Times*, 12 September 1965.
13 Crossman, op. cit., 31.
14 *Guardian*, 21 June 1965.
15 *Sunday Times*, 19 March 1978.
16 Williams, op. cit., 27.
17 James Margach, *The Abuse of Power* (1978), 177.
18 Haines, op. cit., 157–75; Winstone/Benn, op. cit., 124; Crossman, op. cit., 582; Wigg, op. cit., 316.
19 Wigg, op. cit., 316.
20 Lord George-Brown, *In My Way* (1971), 161.
21 Jenkins, op. cit., 159.
22 Wilson, *The Labour Government*, op. cit., 5.
23 Jenkins, op., cit., 190.
24 Samuel Brittan, *Steering the Economy: The Role of the Treasury* (1969), 204.
25 Wilson, *The Labour Government*, op. cit., 131.
26 Crossman, op. cit., 315.
27 Paul Foot, *The Politics of Harold Wilson* (1968), 207. He used this term in a speech in 1960.
28 Joseph Frankel, *British Foreign Policy 1945–1973* (1975), 205.
29 Crossman, op. cit., 95.
30 ibid., 94.
31 ibid., 95.
32 Drew Middleton, *Crisis in the West* (1965), 91.
33 Andrew J. Pierre, *Nuclear Politics: The British Experience with an Independent Strategic Force* (1972), 244.
34 Pierre, op. cit., 245.
35 ibid., 290.
36 ibid., 291.
37 Jenkins, op. cit., 159.
38 Roy Sherwood, *Superpower Britain* (Cambridge, 1989), 17.
39 Jenkins, op. cit., 171.
40 Sherwood, op. cit., 23.
41 Michael Dintenfass, *The Decline of Industrial Britain 1870–1980* (1992), 47.
42 Winstone/Benn, op. cit., 121.
43 Wilson, *The Labour Government*, op. cit., 143.
44 Crossman, op. cit., 378.
45 ibid., 378.
46 Castle, op. cit., 384.
47 Wigg, op. cit., 326.
48 Crossman, op. cit., 382

49 Wilson, *The Labour Government*, op. cit., 183.
50 Reginald Maudling, *Memoirs* (1978), 134.
51 Andrew Roth, *Enoch Powell, Tory Tribune* (1970), 328.
52 John Campbell, *Edward Heath: A Biography* (1993), 182.
53 ibid., 168–70.
54 ibid., 199.
55 Winstone/Benn, op. cit., 49.
56 Jenkins, op. cit., 204.
57 Willy Brandt, *People and Politics* (1978), 249.
58 Lord Carrington, *Reflect on Things Past: The Memoirs of Lord Carrington* (1988), 252–3.
59 D. E. Butler and Anthony King, *The British General Election of 1966* (1966), 207–8.
60 James Callaghan, *Time and Chance* (1978), 192.
61 David Butler, *British General Elections since 1945* (Oxford, 1995), 24.
62 Butler and King, op. cit., 265.
63 Winstone/Benn, op. cit., 156.
64 Wilson, *The Labour Government*, op. cit., 237.
65 Crossman, op. cit., 524.
66 ibid., 533–4.
67 ibid., 547.
68 Winstone/Benn, op. cit., 157.
69 Callaghan, op. cit., 196.
70 ibid., 196.
71 ibid.
72 Jenkins, op. cit., 191.
73 Crossman, op. cit., 578.
74 Callaghan, op. cit., 199; Jenkins, op. cit., 195.
75 Wilson, *The Labour Government*, op. cit., 259.
76 ibid., 260.
77 Winstone/Benn, op. cit., 161.
78 ibid.
79 Crossman, op. cit., 577.
80 ibid., 581.
81 Calllaghan, op. cit., 200.
82 Wilson, *The Labour Government*, op. cit., 262.
83 ibid., 265.
84 Richard Crossman, *The Diaries of a Cabinet Minister, vol. 2, 1966–68* (1976), 17.
85 Callaghan, op. cit., 206–7.
86 Brian Lapping, *The Labour Government, 1964–70* (1970), 43.
87 Brown, op. cit., 95.
88 Wilson, *The Labour Government*, op. cit., 278.
89 ibid., 286–7, 138.
90 Williams, op. cit., 170.
91 Wilson, *The Labour Government*, op. cit., 577.
92 Callaghan, op. cit., 145.
93 Crossman, *1964–66*, op. cit., 54.
94 Foot, op. cit., 275.
95 Wilson, *The Labour Government*, op. cit., 470.
96 ibid., 474.
97 Frankel, op. cit., 141.

98 Wilson, *The Labour Government*, op. cit., 556–7; Trevor Royle, *War Report* (Edinburgh, 1987), 212–15.
99 Lapping, op. cit., 67.
100 Wilson, *The Labour Government*, op. cit., 626.
101 *Pears Cyclopaedia 1976–77* (1977), G33.
102 D. G. M. Dosser, 'Britain and the International Economy', *Westminster Bank Review*, May 1968.
103 Crossman, *1964–66*, op. cit., 83.
104 Willy Brandt, *People and Politics*, 161.
105 Lord George-Brown, op. cit., 209.
106 Callaghan, op. cit., 213.
107 Brittan, op. cit., 226.
108 Callaghan, op. cit., 212.
109 Paterson, op. cit., 225.
110 Callaghan, op. cit., 214.
111 Winstone/Benn, op. cit., 174.
112 Wilson, *The Labour Government*, op. cit., 464.
113 Campbell, op. cit., 225.
114 Jenkins, op. cit., 215–16.
115 ibid., 215–16.
116 Castle, op. cit., 375.
117 ibid., 339.
118 ibid., 414–15.
119 ibid., 412.
120 Callaghan, op. cit., 416.
121 ibid., 414.
122 ibid., 415.
123 Wilson, *The Labour Government*, op. cit., 626.
124 Peter Kellner and Christopher Hitchens, *Callaghan: The Road to Number Ten* (1976), 96.
125 Callaghan, op. cit., 276.
126 Jenkins, op. cit., 289.
127 Campbell, op. cit., 229.
128 Jenkins, op. cit., 227.
129 ibid., 227.
130 Winstone/Benn, op. cit., 179.
131 Jenkins, op. cit., 228.
132 Winstone/Benn, op. cit., 168.
133 Wilson, *The Labour Government*, op. cit., 243.
134 Jenkins, op. cit., 234.
135 ibid., 238.
136 ibid., 236.
137 Winstone/Benn, op. cit., 184; Jenkins, op. cit., 238.
138 Andrew Alexander and Alan Watkins, *The Making of the Prime Minister 1970* (1970), 36.
139 Jenkins, op. cit., 245–6.
140 Willy Brandt, *My Life in Politics* (1992), 241.
141 John Dickie, *Inside the Foreign Office* (1992), 94.
142 Winstone/Benn, 220.
143 Frank Field and Patricia Haikin, *Black Britons* (1971), 12.
144 Humphrey Berkeley, *The Odyssey of Enoch: A Political Memoir* (1977), 77–8.
145 Crossman, *1966–68*, 733.

146 ibid., 734.
147 Campbell, op. cit., 242.
148 Callaghan, op. cit., 266.
149 Field and Haikin, op. cit., 15–16.
150 Lyndon Baines Johnson, *The Vantage Point: Perspectives of the Presidency 1963–69* (New York, 1971), 175.
151 Berkeley, op. cit., contains the speech in full.
152 Robert J. Wybrow, *Britain Speaks Out, 1937–87: A Social History as Seen Through the Gallup Data* (1989), 51.
153 Winstone/Benn, op. cit., 187.
154 Robert Shepherd, *The Power Brokers: The Tory Party and its Leaders* (1981), 364.
155 Campbell, op. cit., 245.
156 ibid., 244.
157 Martin Dillon and Denis Lehane, *Political Murder in Northern Ireland* (1973), 35.
158 This is the impression gained by the writer on a visit to Northern Ireland in 1963 when he interviewed Captain O'Neill, Gerry Fitt and others.
159 Callaghan, op. cit., 271.
160 Wilson, *The Labour Government*, op. cit., 670.
161 Lord Cameron, *Disturbances in Northern Ireland* (Belfast, 1969), Cmd 532, para. 51.
162 Richard Rose, *Governing without Consensus* (1971), 441.
163 Richard Crossman, *The Diaries of a Cabinet Minister, vol. 3: 1968–70* (1977), 451; Wilson, *The Labour Government*, op. cit., 674. For Devlin's own views see Bernadette Devlin, *The Price of My Soul* (1969).
164 Crossman, *1968–70*, op. cit., 478–9.
165 Rose, op. cit., 106.
166 James Callaghan, *A House Divided: The Dilemma of Northern Ireland* (1973), 74.
167 Rose, op. cit., 107.
168 Wilson, *The Labour Government*, op. cit., 537.
169 Frank Stacey, *British Government 1966–1975: Years of Reform* (1975), 73.
170 Stacey, op. cit., 21–37.
171 Jenkins, op. cit., 209.
172 Cecil King, *The Cecil King Diary, 1965–1970* (1972), 327, 330–1.
173 Crossman, *1968–70*, op. cit., 949.

7

THE UNEXPECTED PRIME MINISTER: EDWARD HEATH, 1970–74

DOWNING STREET: 'THE SHUTTERS WERE FASTENED'

On 19 June at 2.15 p.m. the 316th Conservative victory was announced, but Wilson could not resign until the Queen had driven back to Buckingham Palace from the race meeting at Ascot.[1] There was 'a shell-shocked feeling' at the last Labour Cabinet meeting in Downing Street.[2] A woman threw paint over Heath as he later went into No. 10. He spent less than an hour there before driving off to Windsor for the Queen Mother's 70th birthday party.[3]

Heath's Cabinet was not one of new faces. Unusually, Sir Alec returned to the Cabinet as Foreign and Commonwealth Secretary. Another aristocrat, Lord Carrington, was given Defence. Maudling got the Home Office and Macleod the Treasury. Hogg became Hailsham once again, returning to the upper house as Lord Chancellor. Not quite so well known to the public was Robert Carr, the Cambridge-educated metallurgist and industrialist as Minister of Labour. Another key appointment was that of Anthony Barber as Chancellor of the Duchy of Lancaster with special responsibility for negotiating Britain's third EEC attempt. Farmer and landowner William Whitelaw became Leader of the House, and Peter Walker, the self-made millionaire and chairman of Lloyd's insurance brokers, took over the Ministry of the Environment. Among the other significant appointments were Sir Keith Joseph, deputy chairman of Bovis Holdings Ltd, as Secretary of State for Social Services, and James Prior, a Cambridge-educated farmer and land agent, as Minister of Agriculture, Fisheries and Food. One other appointment of great significance, though it was not really seen as such at the time, was Margaret Thatcher at Education and Science. Essentially, it was a fairly moderate and meritocratic 18-strong team. If it did not represent, in social terms, the mass of ordinary party members, it did represent a shift from the upper-class emphasis of previous post-war Tory Cabinets to the more middle-class elements of the party. One rough indicator was the fall in the number of old Etonians from eleven to three.[4] One Kennedy-style innovation was the setting up of a 'think-tank' under Lord Rothschild, known as a Labour supporter, to advise the government on possible policy initiatives.

Heath suffered his first 'devastating blow'[5] weeks after taking over. On 20 July his neighbour at 11 Downing Street suffered a heart attack and died. He was the 'one charismatic personality the Government possessed'.[6] Macleod was replaced by Barber, who had served four years in the Treasury followed by a year in the Cabinet as Minister of Health. Geoffrey Rippon took over as 'Mr Europe'. John Davies, former Director-General of the CBI, with only a few weeks of Commons experience behind him, became Minister of Technology.

Heath came across as a civilized and decent man. His facial characteristics made him an ideal target for the cartoonists. His accent, it was said, owed more to the elocution master than to any natural evolution. The fact that he was not married caused rumours about his sexual preference.[7] Before 1970 he got a rough deal from most of the media – whatever their politics. Perhaps the fact that he appeared to have confounded their predictions, by winning the 1970 election, had given him a certain defensive arrogance, behind which the 'real' Ted Heath was condemned to remain hidden. At any rate, according to James Margach, 'When Prime Minister he became authoritarian and intolerant.' At 10 Downing Street 'The shutters were fastened and the door opened only to a select few by a Government which was the most secrecy-conscious since the war. Downing Street became the most closed society in all my experience.'[8]

'RESTRICT PROVISION TO . . . WHERE IT IS MORE EFFICIENT'

When he was elected Heath seemed to represent a break with the post-war consensus. Meeting at Selsdon Park, Croydon in January 1970, his shadow cabinet appeared to have lurched to the Right.[9] This was the image conveyed at the election. 'Selsdon man' appeared to want to break with the state-interventionist and welfare policies of previous administrations, and set compass to sail towards a neo-capitalist El Dorado. In some respects he was influenced by the Republican Right in the United States and by a somewhat false impression of the West German Christian Democrats. The state would interfere less in the economy, but would also give fewer handouts to industry. Firms would have to become more efficient or perish. As Davies told the Conservative Party conference in October 1970, 'I will not bolster up or bail out companies where I can see no end to the process of propping them up.'[10] Public expenditure would be cut, individuals would pay less income tax, but they would have to do more for themselves.

The object . . . is not to destroy the social services but to restrict provision to . . . where it is more efficient. The aim is to free as many people as possible from the need to rely . . . on public authorities, to restore a greater degree of family responsibility expanding the amount of private provision.

In his speech Heath made similar promises. The delegates 'went wild'.[11]

Doctrinaire Conservatives could chuckle with delight at the announcement that Thomas Cook & Son, the successful state-owned travel agency, was to be sold, that the National Coal Board was to be encouraged to sell its brickworks, British Rail its hotels, and the nationalized gas industry was to be prevented from pursuing its exploration of the North Sea gas and oil fields. Given this approach, it was only to be expected that the Industrial Reorganization Corporation should be closed down. Smiles of Job disappeared when the government was faced with the alternative of breaking its pledge on 'lame ducks' or letting Rolls-Royce, a symbol of British engineering skill, go to the wall. Heavily committed to a costly programme of development on the RB 211 engine for the Lockheed TriStar, the company needed immediate financial help to avoid bankruptcy. The government argued it had no choice but to step in with a loan. When the company collapsed three months later, the government nationalized it.

Like the previous government, Heath's administration was worried about inflation. Barber introduced a mini-Budget in October 1970 which cut government expenditure on school milk, council house subsidies, prescription costs and dental treatment. Income tax cuts were promised in six months' time. There was some restriction on credit. These measures could be attacked as socially divisive, and even inflationary. They would fall on the working classes, thus giving rise to increased wage claims. The same was said about the Housing Finance Act of 1972.

The aim of this legislation was to cut subsidies to council house tenants by introducing a 'fair rent' policy. It meant considerable rent increases for very many tenants and a consequent rise in their cost of living. Those who could not afford the increases could get rebates. Over 30 per cent of families lived in council properties at that time. The experiment was started of encouraging local councils to give their tenants the opportunity to buy the homes in which they lived. Apart from being considered as a step along the road to the old Conservative goal of a 'property-owning democracy', it was thought this policy would generate more funds for new council house building. Critics claimed it merely reduced the stock of cheaper housing for the less well-off. House prices did leap up between 1970 and 1972 by about 30 per cent per annum. This also increased inflation.

In opposition the Conservatives were against Wilson's prices and incomes policy. When they returned to office, they abandoned it. The National Board for Prices and Incomes was abolished, only to re-emerge later. Heath sought some kind of voluntary agreement with the unions and the Confederation of British Industry (CBI). This did not work to the government's satisfaction and in November 1972 a 90-day standstill was imposed upon wages and salaries, dividends, rates and rents, and on all prices other than imports and fresh foods. Offenders were liable to be fined. In April 1973 this was replaced by a more flexible form of restraint known as Stage Two. Under new legislation two bodies were established: a Price Commission and a Pay Board. Though there were to be exceptions, the total annual increase for any group of employees should not exceed £1 a week, plus 4 per cent of the current pay-bill excluding overtime. The Pay Board gave its prior approval for settlements involving more than 1,000 employees, but in other cases it had to be notified. It became an offence to strike or threaten to strike in order to force an employer to contravene an order of the Board. Price increases were limited under Stage Two, but there were a fair number of exceptions. Large firms had to give prior notice to the Price Commission, medium firms had to report regularly and small firms had to keep price records. Imports were one of the exceptions and the price of goods from abroad went up rapidly in 1973. Stage Three of the pay policy was introduced in October 1973. Under it there were only modest increases allowed, with a limit of £350 a year on the amount to be received by an individual. Again there were important exceptions for such things as 'unsociable hours', and there was some progress towards equal pay for women. Threshold payments were also introduced, allowing modest, automatic increases in pay each jump in the cost of living index.[12] These measures did not keep down the rate of inflation, the biggest single factor being the soaring cost of imported raw materials, oil and food.

INDUSTRIAL RELATIONS: 'ALL HELL WILL BE LET LOOSE'

The government hoped that legislation relating to trade unions would play an important part in helping the economy. Accordingly, it introduced the Industrial Relations Act, 1971. It was passed in spite of strong TUC opposition. The Act had many similarities with *In Place of Strife*. Under the Act unions were forced to register or forfeit the legal immunities available to registered unions. Registration did, however, bring with it obligations. Union rules had to set out clearly which officers had authority to instigate or direct industrial action; they had to deal with ballots and elections, dues and discipline, and members' complaints against the union. As one authority put it at the time, 'Almost every union . . . will be compelled to redraw its rules in accordance with these guiding principles and they will have to do it quickly because a timetable is laid down and it is a pretty brisk one.'[13] The 'guiding principles' would be those of the registrar. The law introduced the concept of unfair industrial action, under which the threat of a sympathetic strike or other industrial action was included.[14] Also included was industrial action by an unregistered union, a strike to bring about a closed shop, or action designed to induce changes in collective agreements. The legislation established a system of industrial tribunals and a National Industrial Relations Court (NIRC). The Act included a number of items which every trade unionist would favour, such as the statutory right to belong to a union and protection against unfair dismissal. One of the main arguments against the Act was that Britain's industrial relations were much better than those of the United States, with its wealth of labour legislation, from which the framers of the Act borrowed much. Even more important, it embittered relations between government and the unions at a time when the maximum co-operation was needed. Heath simply ignored the experience of his predecessor and crashed on. Industrial relations deteriorated throughout the Heath period and this was partly due to the Act. In February 1971 there was an impressive display of trade union opposition to the Act when over 100,000 members demonstrated in London. In the following month 1.5 million engineering workers staged a one-day strike against it. Other similar strikes followed. After the Act came into force in August, the TUC continued to oppose compulsory registration and subsequently 32 unions were suspended from registering. The TGWU was fined for contempt by the NIRC twice in 1972. On 21 May 1972 five dockers were committed to prison for contempt by the NIRC. Vic Feather, Secretary of the TUC, had warned: 'As soon as the first trade unionist goes to prison, all hell will be let loose.'[15] This did not happen, but opposition continued. The Act probably made unionists more determined to oppose the government's pay policy. Certainly, in this period there was increasing use of industrial action in support of pay claims. Gas and power workers, engine drivers, miners, ambulance drivers, hospital ancillary staff, firemen and civil servants, all contributed to the increase in days lost through industrial action.

LOCAL GOVERNMENT REFORM: 'EXPENSE . . . NOT ADEQUATELY FACED'

Another major piece of legislation was the Local Government Act of 1972. It stemmed from the proposals of the Redcliff-Maud Committee, which was set up under Wilson. Local government in London had been reformed in 1963 and no changes were made there. The system in the rest of the country had remained virtually unchanged since the 1880s. There was widespread feeling that it no longer corresponded to the realities of Britain in the 1970s. There was an artificial distinction between town and country, there was fragmentation of services, and councillors were highly unrepresentative of the communities they served. The Act set up 46 counties in England, with a two-tier system. In six predominantly urban areas new authorities, metropolitan counties, were established. Within them were a number of metropolitan district authorities forming a second tier. In the rest of England existing county boundaries were retained as far as possible, with the new counties having authority over the formerly independent county boroughs. The former county boroughs and district councils then became the second tier. Wales was divided into eight counties with a similar, but not identical, structure to that in England. In Scotland the structure was modified under legislation passed in 1973. Another feature of the Act, designed to make it easier for a wider range of individuals to serve on local councils, was the introduction of a flat-rate attendance allowance. Under the Local Government Act, 1948 a financial allowance had been introduced, but it covered only loss of earnings. The new allowance was a step nearer to actually paying councillors a salary. The aldermanic system, under which a proportion of council members were indirectly elected by fellow councillors, was abolished. This had been introduced in 1835 as a sop to the Lords, and had led to a situation where, occasionally, parties defeated at the polls were able to hang on to power with the help of their aldermen who were not yet up for re-election. These measures failed to produce more representative councils or raise the low level of participation in local council elections. In 1964 over half the county council seats had not been contested; many remained uncontested after the Act came in. The Act did not solve the problem of the relations between local and central government nor the problem of finance. No change was made in the rating system. Massive increases in rates took place in 1974. Some of these had nothing to do with the Act, some were indirectly caused by it, some were directly the result of it. 'The expense of the new system and how to meet it were questions not adequately faced.'[16]

CORRUPTION: 'NO OPTION BUT TO RESIGN'

The lack of competition in local elections, with small groups from one party exercising unchallenged power on councils for many years, was undoubtedly an important cause of corruption which came to light during this period. The key figure was John Poulson, an unqualified architect. In the 1960s he was said to be earning £1 million per annum in fees. He controlled four companies, one with his wife, and was declared bankrupt in 1971. Local authorities claimed negligence over his work. And when his bankruptcy was being investigated, it was discovered he had paid £334,000 to MPs, local councillors and civil servants. Superficially, Poulson was a highly respectable man. He was a Commissioner of Taxes. He was also Chairman of the Executive Committee of the (Conservative satellite) National Liberal Party. His wife was a JP and Chairman of the Yorkshire Women Conservatives. However, he showed no political prejudice when seeking business favours from local politicians and others in official positions. His two best-known associates were Alderman Andrew Cunningham and T. Dan Smith. Cunningham was Chairman of Durham County Council,

Felling Urban District Council, Durham Police Authority, Northumbria River Authority, Tyneside Passenger Transport Authority and the North-Eastern Regional Airport Committee. He worked as regional organizer of the General and Municipal Workers' Union. For a time he represented that union on the NEC of the Labour Party. Smith was, among other things, leader of the controlling Labour group of Newcastle upon Tyne City Council and a member of the Redcliffe-Maud Committee. Poulson, Cunningham, Smith and some others were jailed for their activities. Other trials followed, which were connected with Poulson's affairs, involving officials of British Rail, the National Coal Board, South-Western Metropolitan Hospital Board, and other councils.[17] In London, Glasgow, Yorkshire and Wales there were convictions for corruption in local government unconnected with Poulson. In South Wales alone, there were 19 corruption trials connected with local government in 18 months during 1976–77. Altogether, 30 people, including 20 businessmen, were found guilty in the Welsh cases. Of the 30, 12 were sent to prison.[18]

Heath had one casualty in the Poulson affair. Maudling had been a business associate of Poulson. As Home Secretary he was in charge of the Metropolitan Police, who were investigating the architect's activities in London. As Maudling later wrote, he felt he 'had no option but to resign'.[19] He was replaced by Carr.

NHS: JOSEPH'S 'ADMINISTRATIVE LABYRINTH'

In another 'modernizing' move, the Water Act, 1973 deprived local authorities of their functions as suppliers of water and sewerage services. These became the responsibility of ten regional water authorities and a National Water Board.

In July 1973 the National Heath Service Reorganization Act became law. The intention was to replace the tripartite service of hospital, GP and local authority created in 1948 with a single integrated service, more efficient and more equitable between regions. Designed with the assistance of management consultants McKinsey, the new structure comprised district management teams at the base, 90 area heath authorities on top of them, with these in turn responsible to 14 regional heath authorities, with the Secretary of State at the very top with responsibility for overall planning and resource allocation. It was

> an administrative labyrinth more complex and less efficient than before . . . It created a new army of managers – between 1973 and 1977 the number of administrative and clerical staff rose by 28 per cent: by 1980 . . . Joseph's reorganisation was an undoubted cause of poor performance, low morale and industrial disruption in the NHS.[20]

The long-term problem of underfunding continued, as did the disquiet about the treatment of long-stay patients, the elderly and patients in mental hospitals. Though some progress was made, Britain's infant mortality rates remained higher than in many other modern countries. Proportionate to population Britain had fewer medical practitioners than many other European states, and fewer hospital beds. The NHS remained highly dependent on Asian immigrant doctors to keep the hospitals manned.[21]

NORTHERN IRELAND: 'SEVERE DISCRIMINATION'

Heath certainly did not inherit a happy situation in Northern Ireland. On 3 July 1970, 2,000 British troops were sent into the Lower Falls area of Belfast to search for arms. The troops found 50 pistols, 26 rifles, 5 sub-machine-guns, and a great deal of ammunition in the 3,000 homes they searched.[22] The Catholics retaliated to the raid by stone-throwing, which was answered in turn with tear-gas. A curfew was introduced in a attempt to get the situation under control, but the violence escalated. In the five years of O'Neill's government only three persons had died in disorders.[23] In 1973 alone 250 were killed (171 civilians, 66 army or Ulster Defence Regiment, 13 police). From the beginning of the troubles, in 1968, to the end of 1973, 927 had died, 207 of them British soldiers.[24] Maudling came to the conclusion: 'There was no doubt in my mind that the Catholic community had had less than their fair share in governing their own country, and that there was severe discrimination against them.' But the more the IRA used violence, the greater the reaction among the Protestants against concessions. 'We were really trying to walk up an escalator that was moving down.'[25] Heath accepted the package of reforms announced by Wilson, but it would take time and patience to implement them. The reforms had to be implemented through the Ulster Unionist Stormont regime. On the advice of Brian Faulkner, who had replaced Chichester-Clark as Prime Minister in March 1971, London accepted, in August, the introduction of internment without trial in Northern Ireland. At the same time it attempted to explore a settlement. In September 1971 Heath had talks with Faulkner and Jack Lynch, the Prime Minister of the Irish Republic. These talks led nowhere and the bombings and assassinations continued. One particularly bad incident occurred in Bogside, Londonderry, on 30 January 1972, when a banned civil rights march ended with 13 Catholics dead and 16 wounded, killed by British troops. No British fatalities occurred. On 30 March 1972 the Northern Ireland constitution was set aside and all legislative and executive functions were transferred to London. William Whitelaw was appointed Secretary of State for Northern Ireland with special authority. Exactly one year, and many bombs, later the government published a White Paper, *Northern Ireland: Constitutional Proposals*. This involved a new system of devolution based on elections by proportional representation and an executive equipped with powers similar to the old Stormont regime. Only responsibility for law and order would be retained by the Secretary of State. A referendum, boycotted by all the Catholic-supported parties, produced a 57.4 per cent vote of the total electorate in favour of retaining the union with Great Britain. Elections for the new assembly were held in June 1973. Negotiations were then carried on with the Official Unionists, the moderate Alliance Party, and the (largely Catholic) Social Democratic and Labour Party to set up an Executive. When Whitelaw was replaced by Francis Pym in November 1973, the situation was looking hopeful. One matter remained outstanding, the proposal in the White Paper to establish a Council of Ireland. A conference was held at Sunningdale, Berkshire, in December attended by representatives of the British government, the Northern Ireland Executive-designate, and the government of the Irish Republic. It was agreed to create a Council of Ireland which, though it would have a mainly consultative role, would have certain functions to do with tourism, agriculture and the environment. Direct rule ended on 1 January 1974. During 1973 the death toll was 250 as against 468 in 1972.[26] This was the situation when the Conservatives left office. Britain had committed about 20,000 troops, about the number used in 1921 to dealing with the 'troubles'.[27]

One other aspect of the situation in Northern Ireland was the damage to Britain's image abroad. Internment brought with it accusations of torture by the British forces. By 10 November 1971, 980 men had been detained without trial. Some of them alleged ill-treatment or torture. The government asked the Parliamentary Commissioner, Sir Edmund Compton, to investigate. He dismissed the charge of torture, but he concluded, referring to 11 cases of 'interrogation in depth', 'We consider that the following actions constitute physical ill-treatment: posture on the wall, hooding, noise, deprivation of sleep, diet of bread and water.'[28]

What was perhaps even more disturbing for the government than bombs in Belfast was bombs in London. On 12 January 1971, bombs shattered the peace at Robert Carr's home in Hertfordshire. No one was injured but the police believed those responsible aimed to kill the Carrs.[29] The bombs were the work of a new group calling themselves the Angry Brigade, who claimed to be against the capitalistic, mass-communications society, whether hidden behind the Western democratic or Soviet façade. Its members were mainly the products of Cambridge and Essex universities. They planted other bombs before being detected. They were caught and sentenced to 10 years' imprisonment.

Even with the Angry Brigade out of the way after August 1971, other bombs disturbed the peace of England. In February 1972 seven people were killed by an IRA bomb in Aldershot. Bombs exploded in central London in March 1973, killing one and injuring 238. In August 1973 letter-bombs were received in London and two people were injured at the

Stock Exchange. In the following month there were 13 injured by bombs in London underground stations. A bomb also exploded at Chelsea barracks. On 18 December 60 were injured by further bomb explosions in London. The bombings continued in January 1974.

IMMIGRATION: 'ONLY IN . . . SPECIAL CASES'

At the election the Conservatives had promised that 'work permits will not carry the right of permanent settlement' and that 'immigration will be allowed only in strictly defined special cases'. The Immigration Act, 1971 was designed to redeem these pledges. Under it, permits replaced the former employment vouchers and enabled the holder to remain in Britain initially for one year only, with no automatic right to bring their dependants. The Act created a new category of immigrant – 'Patrials' – individuals having close ties with Britain, by birth for instance, who can come without restrictions. The Act strengthened the law to prevent illegal immigration and introduced a scheme of financial assistance for immigrants seeking voluntary repatriation.

In another area of Commonwealth policy the government was unable to redeem its election pledge – Rhodesia. In 1970 Rhodesia declared itself a republic and introduced a constitution which permanently denied Africans a majority in its parliament. Home nevertheless went to Salisbury and signed an agreement with the rebel regime. He obtained certain limited concessions. Britain even offered aid. The settlement would only come into effect when the British government was convinced that the majority of Africans supported it. Heath accordingly sent Lord Pearce on a mission to assess the state of Black opinion. In May 1972 he reported that Black Rhodesians were generally not favourable to the terms of the settlement, which therefore lapsed.

If the Black Commonwealth states were not too happy about Britain's handling of the Rhodesian situation, they were even less understanding about Britain's relations with South Africa. Once again, the issue of arms sales became a controversial issue. It dominated the Commonwealth conference held in Singapore in February 1971. The British government accepted an obligation under the Simonstown Agreement (1955), signed by Britain and South Africa, to supply the Republic with naval equipment, for it believed that Anglo-South African naval co-operation was necessary to keep open the sea lanes to the Persian Gulf and the Indian Ocean. In effect, Heath was merely continuing the policy of previous governments. Heated words were exchanged in Singapore, with Heath denying that such sales gave a certificate of respectability to South Africa. Britain saw no contradiction between supplying naval equipment and condemning apartheid. There were many examples of a democratic country allying itself with another whose system and whose treatment of its people it disliked. For example, opposition to the Russian system had not prevented Britain and America allying themselves to the Soviet Union in the Second World War. A split was narrowly averted by agreement over a declaration of principles which included the passage: 'We recognize racial prejudice as a dangerous sickness threatening the healthy development of the human race and racial discrimination as an unmitigated evil of society. Each of us will vigorously combat this evil in our own nation.'[30]

EEC: 'SOMETHING TO GET US GOING AGAIN'

In 1969 de Gaulle resigned as French President and was replaced by Georges Pompidou. Wilson decided to have a second attempt to get into the EEC. Labour was defeated at the polls before negotiations were completed. In opposition Labour became divided on the issue. In May 1971 100 Labour MPs, including Healey and Crosland, signed a pro-EEC advertisement in the *Guardian*. Others, including Benn, Castle, Foot and Shore, led the opposition to entry. Wilson wobbled somewhere in between. Meanwhile, Heath had taken up the challenge and started negotiations with Brussels. Heath had told the voters EEC entry was 'something to get us going again'. Yet by mid-year a majority still disapproved of the British application to join the EEC.[31]

On 28 October 1971 the House of Commons voted on the principle of British entry into the EEC. The motion in favour of entry was carried by 356 to 244, with 22 abstentions. The Conservatives had a free vote; Labour a whipped vote to oppose the government. Supporting the government on entry were 69 Labour MPs, led by Roy Jenkins, deputy leader. Another 20 Labour MPs abstained. Heath watched 39 of his own party voting with the Opposition, two other Conservatives abstained. Emlyn Hooson parted company with his fellow Liberals and voted against. It was 'Heath's finest hour'.[32] He had worked very hard for that moment, helped by Francis Pym. His party conference at Llandudno had already endorsed entry, by 2,474 votes to 324, as had the Lords, by 451 to 58.[33] On the Labour side, the TUC opposed entry. Many on the Labour side, and some Conservatives like Powell, called for a referendum. Heath and Wilson rejected the idea as against British traditions and claiming it was a device favoured by continental dictators.

Britain signed for entry on 22 January 1972. Also signing the treaty of accession were Ireland, Denmark and Norway. To pro-Marketeers it lightened the gloom of a bleak month with the start of a miners' strike, unemployment breaking through the, psychologically damaging, 1 million barrier, and the tragedy of Londonderry on 30 January.

OIL CRISIS: 'DANEGELD IS DANEGELD'

On 6 October 1973 Egyptian forces successfully crossed the Suez Canal and stormed the heavily fortified defences of Israel's Bar Lev line, determined to retake territory lost in the 1967 war. The Syrians also attacked Israel, hoping to avenge 1967. With the Americans pouring arms and prestige into Israel, and Soviet weapons and prestige at stake in Egypt, anything could happen. Once again the forces driving the world towards Armageddon were brought to a halt. Before the end of the month this fourth Arab–Israeli war was over. By the time the UN cease-fire came into effect, the Israelis held 1,500 square kilometres of Egyptian soil beyond the Canal, compared with only 500 square kilometres retaken by the Egyptians in Sinai.[34] Perhaps as many as 20,000 Arabs had given their lives in this latest round. Some 2,500 Israelis were killed.[35] As during the previous Middle East war, the pro-Israeli organizations in Britain got into top gear to raise money, gain friends and influence politicians. Traditionally, the Jewish community is better represented among Labour's ranks than among the Conservatives. Many on the Labour side still regarded Israel as an embattled socialist state. The government could, therefore, expect much Opposition criticism of its Middle East policy. Heath's difficulty stemmed from the fact that for many years Britain had supplied arms to Israel and Jordan. He wanted to supply ammunition and spares to neither of these states during the war, claiming this would help to minimize the conflict. This would be changed, however, if Israel's existence were in danger. Home told the Commons on 18 October that Britain would not allow any risk to the security of Israel.[36] But he realized that, with the risk of US–Soviet confrontation and the danger to oil supplies, Britain and the West could face the worst problem since 1945.[37] Wilson admitted that the Palestinians and the Egyptians had a case, but he put his weight behind Israel – 'a democratic socialist country'. He reached his old form when dealing with the oil threat:

> We must not be blackmailed by oil sanctions . . . We had to face the same situation in 1967 . . . that was a most important factor leading to the devaluation of 1967 . . . We must decide what is right as a nation, as a Government, as a Parliament, and abide by it. Danegeld is Danegeld, whether exacted by pillagers from the Kattegat or by the oil-rich monarchs and presidents.[38]

The government also came in for much criticism from Liberal leader, Jeremy Thorpe, and from some of its own back-benchers, like Hugh Fraser, John Gorst, Tom Iremonger, Philip Goodhart and Sir Henry d'Avigdor-Goldsmid, who spoke 'as a supporter of the State of Israel'.[39] The Arabs had few friends in the Commons on that October day. Andrew Faulds, who had won back Smethwick for Labour in 1966, braved the indignation of many of his colleagues to say, 'It is Israel's intransigence which has made the fourth round of the Arab-Israeli conflict inevitable.' The Arabs were only reoccupying their own territory. Would anyone have called the D-Day landings to liberate Europe aggression, he thundered.[40] He voted with the government at the end of the debate, as did a few other Labour MPs. In addition to those named above, some other Conservatives voted with the Opposition. The revolt failed, however; the government carried the House by 251 votes to 175. The vote did nothing to alter events beyond Britain's shores, which were to have a dramatic impact upon the economy and the government.

On 17 October the Organization of Arab Petroleum Exporting Countries (OAPEC) decided to cut back oil production by an immediate 5 per cent, with a further 5 per cent reduction to be imposed each month until a settlement was reached with Israel on the lines of UN Resolution 242 which, in part, called for an Israeli withdrawal from the occupied Arab lands, but also called for the Arabs to make peace with Israel. Coincidentally with this, and of much greater importance, a meeting of the Gulf states of the Organization of Petroleum Exporting Countries (OPEC), including Iran, also decided to denounce earlier price agreements and impose new, much higher, price levels – a measure that had been coming for some time. It was partly the result of the realization by the exporting countries that oil was virtually the only asset they had, and that Western inflation meant they were getting less and less for it. New militant nationalist regimes had gained power in Algeria, Libya and Iraq, and it was only a matter of time before they changed their relations with the companies exploiting the oil. Libya shook the oil world in 1971 with a sudden decision to nationalize BP's Sarir concession. Market conditions had given the governments of the exporting countries a better chance to impose their will on the importing states. The Yom Kippur War speeded up the process. Continued American support for Israel led even the conservative, Western-orientated King Feisal of Saudi Arabia to favour the use of oil as a weapon. The Shah of Iran, not involved in the Arab–Israeli quarrel, saw that his country's oil could be used to help him achieve his grandiose ambitions for Iran's economic development, and for his own role as a world statesman. Suddenly, the industrial nations seemed sentenced to a slow death, for increasingly their prosperity had been based on cheap oil from the Middle East. Attempts at intervention would have been met by Arab sabotage of the pipelines – with disastrous consequences. The Arabs pursued a policy of differentiating between states according to their attitude to the Arab cause. The British policy of neutrality helped the UK compared with some other European states. But oil prices soared and Britain was in a weaker position than many other industrial states to pay the extra cost.[41] Two-thirds of its oil came from the Middle East.

MINERS' STRIKE: 'IT LOOKED AS IF WE WERE NOT INTERESTED'

Even without the oil crisis, Britain's economic situation was not good. The balance of payments was in deficit, inflation was worse than under Wilson and unemployment was higher. The pay policy had somehow staggered on to Stage Three. On 10 October the National Coal Board offered the miners 13 per cent. This was rejected and an overtime ban followed. The government had last faced confrontation with the miners in 1972 and had lost. The industry had been declining for years. Its work-force had fallen from 593,000 in 1960 to 269,000 in 1973. By that time mining looked import-ant again. The miners felt they could enforce higher rewards for the tough and still dangerous work they performed. In March 1973 seven miners were killed by floodwater at Lofthouse colliery, Kirkcaldy. On 30 July 18 lost their lives in a pit-cage accident at Markham colliery in Derbyshire. In 1973, 40,000 miners were suffering from 'The Dust' – pneumoconiosis,[42] accepted as incurable. Most miners did not want to strike if they could avoid it. Strikes cost strikers money; strikes cost unions money; and strikes mean extra work for union officials. Joe Gormley (1917–93), Irish-Lancastrian, President of the National Union of Mineworkers (NUM) (1963–73), and a Catholic, was not looking for trouble.

Mick McGahey, Vice-Chairman of the NUM, had got near the top with-out giving up his genuine anger and determination to change the system. The son of a Scots miner, he was, like his father, a Communist. Gormley had beaten him for the chairmanship of the NUM, so he had to be content with the chairmanship of the Communist Party (1974–78). He became a bogeyman for the Conservatives, who greatly overestimated his influence.[43] The constant obsession with the Communists was probably an important factor in clouding the government's judgement and leading to its downfall. From the Conservatives up and down the country Heath got the message to smash the miners![44] Heath apart, the government was not in good shape. Whitelaw, tired from his ordeal in Northern Ireland, took over the equally vulnerable post of Employment in December 1973. He did not know much about the trade unions. Barber was suffering 'acute fatigue and Carr was close to collapse'.[45] Sir William Armstrong, head of the civil service and close aide to Heath, who was dubbed 'Deputy Prime Minister' by the union leaders,[46] suffered a nervous breakdown during the crisis.[47]

On 2 January 1974 the three-day working-week was introduced. Certain cuts had already been made in November in streetlighting, floodlighting, and television. A State of Emergency was declared. Britain seemed to be sinking day by day. It was in this situation that the TUC offered a possible way out: the government to treat the miners as a special case; other unions not to use the miners' settlement as an argument to better settlements for their own members. For the TUC this represented a big concession, one which could involve union leaders themselves in difficulties later. Chancellor Barber turned it down. Talks went on but, as Margaret Thatcher later wrote, 'the damage had been done: it looked as if we were not interested'.[48] On 24 January the NUM executive asked for a strike ballot of their members. On the same day the Pay Board published its report on relativities. This suggested a long-term arrangement for considering special cases left behind in the pay race. Neither the Board nor Whitelaw felt the miners' case should be investigated, as this would put too much pressure on the Board. Whitelaw later admitted he believed this was a mistake.[49] By 30 January Heath indicated that, if the miners resumed normal working, their case could go to the Board. It was too late. The mood of the miners was revealed on 4 February when it was announced that almost 81 per cent of them had voted to strike. Further talks and manoeuvres failed and on 7 February Heath called a general election for 28 February. Heath had been swayed by Carrington, Chairman of the Conservative Party, by the new Energy Minister, Prior, and by Davies and Thatcher.[50]

ELECTION '74: POWELL – 'VOTE LABOUR'

No one could complain that there was no choice in the election of February 1974. There were 2,135 candidates compared with 1,837 in 1970 and 1,868 in 1950, the previous record.[51] In addition to the three main parties, there were 54 National Front candidates, 44 Communists, Welsh Nationalists contesting all Welsh seats, a confusing array of candidates in Northern Ireland, and the Scottish National Party fielded 70 candidates. Labour was challenged by independents from its own ranks. On the Right, Dick Taverne stood as a Social Democrat in his old constituency of Lincoln, and four others who agreed with his views stood elsewhere. On the Left, Eddie Milne stood for the Blyth constituency he had long represented. Labour feared union unpopularity would drag it down. This could easily have happened, given the long-standing media campaign against the unions. On the other hand, Heath appeared stubborn and bloody-minded. As the campaign developed, a number of developments strengthened this view. On 17 February Wilson appeared to play a trump card by announcing he had concluded a 'social contract' with the unions. This turned out to lack much substance but was good propaganda none the less. Bank profits announced during the month led to the feeling that Heath's society was unfair. On 19 February the National Westminster Bank revealed a 50 per cent increase in its profits. On 25 February Powell, who was not standing, advised Conservatives opposed to the EEC to vote Labour, revealing the following day on television that he had used his postal vote in this way.[52] Worse was to come for Heath. Campbell Adamson, Director-General of the CBI, told a conference of managers that he would like to see the next government repeal the Industrial Relations Act. (He had not realized his speech was being recorded!) Three days before polling news of the largest monthly trade deficit the country had known was published.[53]

Many still thought the Conservatives would win. Yet after much waiting Labour emerged with 301 seats to 297 for the Conservatives. The Liberals were up from 6 to 14. The SNP gained 7, the Welsh PC 2 and the Ulster loyalists 11 of the 12 Northern Ireland seats. Gerry Fitt of the Northern Ireland Social Democratic and Labour Party (SDLP) was also returned. The first inconclusive election since 1929 gave something to all. The Liberal vote went up from 7.5 per cent to 19.3 per cent. The Conservatives remained slightly ahead of Labour in actual votes, but received their lowest share for 50 years. The nationalists had done well. Labour had improved its position but its percentage vote was the lowest since 1931. After some manoeuvring with Thorpe, Heath was forced to concede that the man with the boat had been thwarted by the man with the pipe. The incumbents in Downing Street changed: the problems remained the same.

NOTES

Unless otherwise indicated, the place of publication is London.

1 David Butler, *British General Elections since 1945* (Oxford, 1995), 100.
2 Ruth Winstone (ed.)/Tony Benn, *The Benn Diaries* (introduced by Ruth Winstone) (1995), 234.
3 John Campbell, *Edward Heath: A Biography* (1993), 291.
4 Howard R. Penniman (ed.), *Britain at the Polls: The Parliamentary Elections of 1974* (Washington, DC, 1975), 5.
5 Campbell, op. cit., 302.
6 ibid., 302.
7 ibid., 257.
8 James Margach, *The Abuse of Power* (1978), 160–1.
9 Campbell, op., cit., 264–7.
10 Penniman, op. cit., 11.
11 Campbell, op. cit., 312.
12 *Pears Cyclopaedia 1976–77* (1977), G4.
13 A. H. Thornton, *The Industrial Relations Bill: For and Against* (Nottingham, 1971), 9.
14 ibid., 10.
15 ibid., 30.
16 Peter G. Richards, *The Local Government Act 1972: Problems of Implementation* (1975), 156.
17 *Keesing's Contemporary Archives*, 24 June–30 June 1974, 26583A; Reginald Maudling, *Memoirs* (1978); Edward Milne, *No Shining Armour* (1976), an MP's account of his fight against corruption in the North East.
18 *Sunday Times*, 4 December 1977.
19 Maudling, op. cit., 193.
20 Campbell, op. cit., 384–5.
21 Frank Stacey, *British Government 1966–1975: Years of Reform* (1975), 157–75, gives an account of the various proposals for NHS reform.

22 Richard Rose, *Governing without Consensus* (1971), 111.
23 ibid., 112.
24 David McKie, Chris Cook and Melanie Phillips, *The Guardian/Quartet Election Guide* (1978), 159.
25 Maudling, op. cit., 183.
26 McKie, Cook and Phillips, ibid.
27 Charles Townsend, *The British Campaign in Ireland 1919–1921* (1975), 212.
28 Sir Edmund Compton, *Report of the Inquiry into Allegations against the Security Forces of Physical Brutality in Northern Ireland Arising out of Events on 9th August 1971* (Cmnd 4823, HMSO, 1971), 71.
29 Gordon Carr, *The Angry Brigade: The Cause and the Case* (1975), 15.
30 *Keesing's Contemporary Archives*, 13–20 February 1971, 24441.
31 Robert J. Wybrow, *Britain Speaks Out, 1937–87: History as Seen Through the Gallup Data* (1989), 98.
32 Campbell, op. cit., 405.
33 ibid., 403.
34 Henry Stanhope, *The Times*, 26 October 1973.
35 David Downing and Gary Herman, *War Without End, Peace Without Hope* (no date), 245.
36 *Hansard (Commons)*, vol. 861, col. 424, 18 October 1973.
37 ibid., col. 426.
38 ibid., col. 441.
39 ibid., col. 479.
40 ibid., cols 498–9.
41 This is covered in Christopher Tugendhat and Adrian Hamilton, *Oil: The Biggest Business* (1975).
42 *Sunday Times*, 29 April 1973.
43 Campbell, op. cit., 567.
44 ibid., 569; Lord Carrington, *Reflect on Things Past: The Memoirs of Lord Carrington* (1988), 263.
45 ibid., 570.
46 Peter Hennessy, *Whitehall* (1990), 238.
47 *Sunday Times*, 7 March 1976.
48 Margaret Thatcher, *The Path to Power* (1995), 232.
49 *Sunday Times*, 29 February 1976; 7 March 1976.
50 Thatcher, op. cit., 233; Campbell, op. cit., 571.
51 David Butler and Dennis Kavanagh, *The British General Election of February 1974* (1974), 89.
52 Butler and Kavanagh, op. cit., 105.
53 Barbara Castle, *Fighting all the Way* (1993), 451.

8

LABOUR'S MINORITY GOVERNMENTS, 1974–79

WILSON'S CABINET: 'BUOYANT ATMOSPHERE'

Wilson took over again on 4 March 1974, heading Britain's first minority government since the Labour government of 1929–31. According to Barbara Castle, 'Despite the precariousness of our situation there was a buoyant atmosphere as we met for our first Cabinet.'[1] Wilson's 1964 experience stood him in good stead and he resolved, once again, to act as if he had a working majority. He knew the other parties would think twice before forcing another election. He constructed his Cabinet around well-known figures the country was used to: Healey at the Exchequer, Callaghan at the Foreign Office and Jenkins at the Home Office. Edward Short, the former Durham headmaster and wartime captain in the Durham Light Infantry, became Lord President of the Council and Leader of the Commons. Deputy leader of Labour, 1972–76, he had served at Education and Science, 1968–70. Anthony Crosland (1918–77) went to Environment. A wartime parachute captain, whose father was a senior civil servant and one of the Plymouth Brethren, Crosland gained a first in PPE at Oxford and was a wartime captain in the Parachute Regiment. He had previously served at Education and Science, the Board of Trade and Local Government.

One small advance for women was that for the first time two women were included in the Cabinet: Barbara Castle and Shirley Williams. Castle took over Social Services and Williams was appointed to the new post of Secretary of State for Prices and Consumer Protection. The daughter of well-known academic, Sir George Catlin, she was the first female President of Oxford University Labour Club. Elected to the Commons in 1964, she did postgraduate studies at Columbia University and worked in Ghana and for the *Financial Times*. She had served in the Ministries of Labour and Education, and at the Home Office. Unlike Castle, she was strongly for Britain in the EEC.

Castle found it 'remarkable'[2] that Michael Foot (b. 1913) had been appointed Secretary of State for Employment. Like fellow leftist Benn, his father had been a Liberal MP. He was President of the Oxford Union in

1933 and worked as a journalist for Lord Beaverbrook before becoming editor of the left-wing weekly the *Tribune*. He lost his seat in 1955, but was subsequently elected at Ebbw Vale, Bevan's old seat, in 1960. Anti-Marketeers Benn, Castle and Foot were joined by Peter Shore as Secretary of State for Trade. After King's College, Cambridge, Shore served as head of Labour's Research Department. He was Deputy Leader of the House, 1969-70. Down to the 1990s all four remained opponents of the EEC/EC/EU.

To the uninitiated, Wilson seemed like a miracle-worker. Within a few days of his Cabinet meeting the miners' strike was over, the nation was put back to working full time and the State of Emergency was ended. The balance of payments deficit was larger than any before, though a considerable part of this was due to the increase in the price of oil and therefore beyond Heath's or Wilson's control. Healey presented his first Budget on 26 March, increasing corporation tax, bringing more people into the higher tax bracket and increasing the highest rate of all from 75 per cent to 83 per cent. The standard rate of income tax was also raised. A ceiling on mortgage relief was introduced, with VAT on petrol, ice-cream, soft drinks and sweets. The duty on cigarettes, beer, wine and spirits went up. Healey's Budget was not all punishment, however. The old-age pensioners were promised the biggest increase ever and social security benefits were increased. Considerable food subsidies were introduced and stricter price control was promised by Williams. The government also looked hard at prestige projects, dropping the Channel Tunnel and a third London airport but allowing Concorde to struggle on to the runway. Crosland discouraged the sale of council houses, introduced a rent freeze, and subsidized mortgages for owner-occupiers because of the threat of increased interest charges. The government appeared to be acting decisively to end irrelevant, divisive and inflationary policies, and giving some help to the great mass of the people. Reg Prentice, at Education, attempted to speed up the development of comprehensives. Some opposed this, but many average parents saw it as offering their children a better chance in life.

The miners' strike was over, yet the government still had to prove it could successfully operate its Social Contract with the unions. It abolished the Pay Board, but allowed Stage Three to run its course. Foot managed to steer clear of trouble with the engineering workers and, on the whole, there was relative peace for the next few months. Not so in the NHS. In May nurses turned to striking against low pay. They were given a substantial award of up to 30 per cent. In July hospital workers also turned to industrial action to reinforce their claim against poor pay. The government managed to get the Industrial Relations Act abolished and set up the Advisory, Conciliation and Arbitration Service (ACAS) headed by Jim Mortimer, a socialist, former draughtsman and trade union official with an economics degree from London University. Except for the troubled motor-car industry, there appeared to be a reasonable chance that government and unions could co-operate. This was especially so after the September conference of the TUC, at which Wilson and the unions agreed on moderate wage settlements for the coming year. Healey introduced a second Budget on 22 July, cutting VAT and announcing help for ratepayers. It was a good Budget for an approaching election without being an obvious bribe.

NORTHERN IRELAND: 'CONSIDERING . . . TOTAL WITHDRAWAL'

Merlyn Rees, Secretary of State for Northern Ireland, 1974-76, reported to the Cabinet on 10 April that the situation was getting extremely serious. It was agreed to 'begin considering the implications of a total withdrawal'.[3] Electoral success encouraged the extreme Protestants to greater militancy. On 15 May the authorities were taken by surprise by a massive strike of Protestant workers against the proposed Council of Ireland. The Northern Ireland Executive collapsed and direct rule was reintroduced. The bombings continued, provoking fear and anger. In May a bomb exploded in a car park at Heathrow Airport. On 17 June another went off beside Westminster Hall, injuring 11 people. In the following month there were explosions in Birmingham and Manchester and again at Heathrow. The bomb which went off at the Tower of London on 17 July killed one person and injured 41. In October two bombs in crowded pubs at Guildford killed five and injured 70. There were other explosions later in the year. All these outrages were attributed to, or claimed by, the Provisional IRA. The Prevention of Terrorism Act, 1974, given the Royal Assent in November, was the frightening response to a frightening situation.

One other terrorist attack which did not succeed was the attempt to kidnap Princess Anne in London on 20 March. Only the quick reaction and bravery of her personal bodyguard, James Beaton, foiled the plot. Four people were injured and Beaton himself was severely wounded.

Abroad the situation looked as tense, changeable and dramatic as at home. In Israel, Golda Meir's Cabinet resigned in April. This marked a weakening of the hold of the Labour Party on the government of the state which they had ruled since 1948. In May, Willy Brandt, the Social Democratic Chancellor of West Germany, resigned because one of his aides was exposed as an East German agent. Fellow Social Democrat, Helmut Schmidt, replaced him. In France, President Pompidou died suddenly and Valéry Giscard d'Estaing was elected in May, an event of some significance in the growing closeness of Franco-German relations; Schmidt and Giscard were reputed to be close friends. More dramatic still was the resignation in August of President Nixon after a long campaign against him because of the Watergate scandal. His successor as 38th US President was Gerald Ford. Also of importance was the *coup* which led to the over-throw of the Portuguese dictatorship, which had managed to hold power since 1926. The new government brought to a close the disastrous colonial war and dismantled the Portuguese colonial empire with grave consequences for the Smith regime in neighbouring Rhodesia. In Ethiopia, Haile Selassie was turned out by his armed forces. This too had consequences for the Soviets and the Americans in Africa. Of direct importance for Britain was the overthrow of Makarios in Cyprus in July. Later in the same month the island was invaded by Turkish troops. Britain attempted to mediate with only little success. Wilson cancelled Royal Navy visits to Greece and Chile, states where the democratic governments had been overthrown by the military. This helped raise Britain's prestige abroad, especially as the Greek military dictatorship collapsed. It certainly helped the government with its own back-benchers, who were offended by a Royal Navy visit to South Africa and by the government's readiness to honour a contract for a destroyer for Chile. Undoubtedly, the government's main initiative abroad was its renegotiation of Britain's terms of entry into the EEC, started by Callaghan in April.

ELECTION OCTOBER '74: 'FIGHTING LIKE HELL'

Heath faced a dilemma after February 1974. He risked public indignation if he appeared too partisan, if he appeared to be trying to bring down the government merely for narrow party reasons. Yet not to fight the govern-ment was to demoralize Conservative activists still further. His precarious position was not helped by the loss of some prominent members of his team. Sir Alec Douglas-Home, Barber and Christopher Chataway, the former athlete and TV journalist who had reached Cabinet rank under Heath, all announced their retirement from politics. They gave personal reasons, but their departure cast doubt on their belief in an early Conserva-tive return to office.

The inevitable election came in October. Both major parties were on the defensive. The Conservatives, it could be claimed, had run away from office in the first place and thus brought the country to its present pass. Labour was suffering from defections and splits, especially over the EEC. Christopher Mayhew gave up a safe seat to fight Bath for the Liberals. Lord Chalfont defected in September, claiming the Left had taken over Labour. There was a whiff of scandal close to Wilson whose one-time office manager, Anthony Field, brother of Marcia Williams, was involved in a 'land reclamation' scheme in the North West. It was the kind of deal Labour had long denounced. Mrs Williams was rewarded for her hard work on behalf of Wilson by a peerage, which was announced in May. Benn found it amusing;[4] Castle saw it as a gesture of defiance.[5] Others were just annoyed. The exposure of forged documents foiled attempts to smear Wilson and Short. Nevertheless, the scandal surrounding Cunningham and T. Dan Smith was real enough (see p. 167).

The smaller parties were not all that happy about the election; for them it meant substantial expenditure they could not afford. As usual, the Conservatives spent most. Their national campaign cost £950,000 against Labour's £524,000.[6] The Liberals were afraid that, as in the past, a Labour government would provoke Liberal-waverers to vote Conservative. Only the anti-power-sharing Ulster Unionists could go into the campaign sure of their supporters. This time they had the added attraction of Enoch Powell, who was the candidate in the safe Unionist seat of South Down. This did not stop him from once again letting it be known that he would vote Labour because Labour stood for a referendum on the EEC.

On 10 October, 72.8 per cent of the electorate, 5.3 per cent fewer than in February, braved the showers, the grey and the gloom to record their votes. They gave the Conservatives 35.8 per cent – their lowest percentage vote since 1935 – and put Labour back with a majority over all other parties of just three. This majority was based on winning back three seats from rebel ex-Labour MPs in Lincoln, Sheffield Brightside and Blyth. The polls had predicted a good win for Labour.[7] The campaign was relatively quiet though Benn observed the Conservatives 'fighting like hell' in their marginals. Labour's vote was up by 2.1 per cent, giving them 39.2 per cent. Neither the Liberals' greatest hopes nor their worst fears were realized. They lost 1 per cent of their vote and (net) one seat. Surveys had shown there was some confusion about what they stood for. Many Liberal activists saw themselves on the Left. Liberal MPs regarded their party as a Centre party. The party's vote was drawn more from the Right-of-Centre and Liberal policies were closer to the Conservatives than to Labour.[8]

What of the other parties? The anti-immigrant National Front fielded 90 candidates, without success. It appeared to take votes from all parties equally and gained most support in the East End of London. The only parties which could count the election as a real victory were the anti-power-sharing Ulster Unionists – though they lost one seat on a recount – and the SNP. Both increased their support, the SNP dramatically so. Eleven SNP candidates were elected, four more than in February; their gains were at Conservative expense. In Wales the nationalists, PC, increased their representation from two to three. They took one seat from Labour, but were Labour-orientated on most issues.

Sociologically speaking, British politics had not changed much since 1945. The Conservatives still had a majority among women, but only just. Women, 52 per cent of the electorate, had consistently saved the Conservatives from defeat in 1951, 1955, 1959 and 1970. In terms of social class, the Conservatives still commanded the support of 63 per cent of the middle class (to Labour's 12 per cent) and 51 per cent of the lower-middle class (to Labour's 24 per cent). Labour's greatest support was still among the unskilled and 'very poor', 33 per cent of the voters, 57 per cent of whom declared for Labour as against only 22 per cent for the Conservatives. In terms of age, the Conservatives had a majority of 49 per cent to 37 per cent for Labour among the over 65s, 20 per cent of the electorate. Labour enjoyed its greatest advantage among the 18–24 age-group, who formed only 11 per cent of the electorate. Labour also enjoyed a massive majority among the 2 per cent of 'coloured' voters, a category which did not exist in any significant numbers before 1964.[9]

In terms of their backgrounds, the new MPs were very much like the old. 'Mr Industrial Charter', the much-acclaimed Conservative trade unionist, was nowhere to be seen among their 277 MPs. The Conservatives remained largely the party of the middle and upper-middle classes, particularly from the southern half of England. Labour was becoming a party drawn from the provincial lower-middle class, drawn especially from the teaching and, to a lesser extent, the legal profession. Its 319 MPs increasingly spoke with Scots' or Welsh accents. Women remained very underrepresented in the Parliament which was to take Britain through to the 1980s. Only about 4 per cent of MPs were women, and most of them were Labour. This compared with around 22 per cent in Sweden and Finland, and about 2 per cent in France, Canada and the US.[10] In West Germany 7.3 per cent of the MPs elected in 1976 were women.[11]

THATCHER: 'SHATTERING BLOW . . . TO . . . CONSERVATIVE ESTABLISHMENT'

Having lost three elections out of four it was inevitable that Heath should have been under great pressure to vacate the Conservative leadership. Sir Geoffrey Howe believed ordinary voters hated Heath, regarding him as 'stubborn and insensitive'.[12] Under pressure, Heath accepted the recommendations of a party committee chaired by Lord Home that, when the Conservatives were in opposition, there should be an annual leadership election. This was put into effect on 4 February 1975. Heath was opposed by Margaret Thatcher and Hugh Fraser, MP. Thatcher says she stood because Keith Joseph felt disqualified. He had made a controversial speech at Edgbaston (19 October 1974) in which he lamented the high and rising proportion of children being born to mothers least fitted to have them.[13] Thatcher then stepped forward as standard-bearer of free market economics. There was some surprise that Heath was only able to muster 119 votes to Thatcher's 130, and Fraser's 16.[14] Heath decided to throw in the towel and retire to the back-benches. In the second round Thatcher was elected by 146 votes to 79 for Whitelaw, 19 each for Prior and Howe, and 11 for John Peyton.[15] She regarded her victory as a 'shattering blow . . . to the

Conservative establishment. I had no sympathy for them. They had fought me unscrupulously all the way.'[16] Benn recorded at the time, 'I think we would be foolish to suppose that Mrs Thatcher won't be a formidable leader.'[17] As she met the Conservative MPs after her victory, Howe thought she looked 'very beautiful' at this, 'almost feudal, occasion. Tears came to my eyes . . . her almost reckless courage . . . had won their support, if not yet their hearts.'[18]

When she was elected at Finchley in 1959, Thatcher had far more achievements behind her than most women of her age and social class. Her father was a grocer who became the Mayor of Grantham. She made her way on scholarships from Kesteven and Grantham Girls' School to Somerville College, Oxford, where she read chemistry and gained a B.Sc. and M.A. Not content with this, she qualified as a barrister in 1954. Married to a wealthy businessman since 1951, she was able to get her childbearing over quickly by having twins, a boy and a girl, in 1953. Obviously she had tremendous dedication, drive and determination, as well as intelligence, to go on climbing up and up the ladder. Having a constituency in London helped, given even the minimum of domestic responsibility. Her husband, Dennis, was indispensable, he 'was always *there* – anything I wanted he could provide, and he was always *there*. His being older may have had a lot to do with this.'[19] Although a seasoned MP, Thatcher had less experience than Heath, Home or Macmillan when they took over. Like Heath, she had a manner which excited ridicule in many circles. Benn was *not* ridiculing her when he recorded in his diary: 'She's like the Queen really; she looks like her, talks like her and is of the same age.'[20] Shirley Williams, from a more privileged background and also a product of Somerville College, had, in the 1970s, a younger, more classless, contemporary, and friendlier aura about her.

In addition to her father, Thatcher had two political mentors, Sir Keith Joseph and Alfred Sherman. 'Apart from the fact of their being Jewish, Alfred and Keith had little in common.'[21] Sherman was a London ex-Communist who had fought in the International Brigade in Spain. He became a fervent supporter of capitalism and a *Daily Telegraph* journalist. With Joseph he set up the Centre for Policy Studies (CPS). The CPS wanted to break with what it regarded the post-war Lab./Con. 'socialist' consensus, and introduce thorough-going free market policies. It set the agenda for Thatcher in government. The intellectual framework for the CPS was the book by the Austrian economist, Friedrich von Hayek, *The Road to Serfdom* (1944).

Thatcher had no choice but to retain the members of Heath's shadow cabinet. Hailsham soldiered on in her cause, as did Davies. Carrington led the party in the Lords. Prior, formerly Lord President and Leader of the House, came into prominence as shadow employment minister. Sir Geoffrey Howe, who had served as Solicitor-General, and then as Minister for Trade and Consumer Affairs (1970–72), also played a prominent part, as shadow chancellor. A QC and solicitor's son, he was educated at Winchester and Trinity Hall, Cambridge. He shared Thatcher's views on economics. Among the right-wingers appointed was Airey Neave (1916–79), an old Etonian company director and Second World War Colditz hero, who covered Northern Ireland. Norman St John-Stevas, a barrister and prominent Catholic, who had openly declared for Thatcher during the election, got Education. The other woman in the team was Sally Oppenheim, daughter of a diamond-cutter and Sheffield tycoon. Educated at RADA, she became spokesperson on consumer affairs. Thatcher believed Whitelaw and Joseph were 'the two key figures, one providing the political brawn and the other the policy-making brains of the team'.[22] Between February 1975 and November 1978 Thatcher had four major reshuffles designed to neutralize the Heathites. Heath supporter Sir Ian Gilmour, originally at Home Affairs, was moved to Defence. Maudling brought into the team as shadow foreign secretary was sacked in January 1976. Likewise, Michael Heseltine was moved (November 1976) from Trade and Industry to Environment because he was not enough of a free marketeer for Thatcher.[23]

A DECADE OF WOMEN'S LIBERATION

If the rise of Thatcher was a symbol of the progress made towards equality of the sexes, this progress should not be exaggerated. Labour-saving devices in the home, family planning, higher expectations and economic necessity meant that over 50 per cent of married women were employed. However, at the end of the 1970s women could still complain about their low pay as compared with men. Women's gross hourly earnings as a percentage of men's in 1970 were 63.1 per cent. In 1977 they had advanced to 75.5 per cent. This was partly because Barbara Castle's Equal Pay Act, 1970 covered only women doing 'the same or broadly similar' work as men. And in the decade of 'women's lib', roughly since 1968, the advance of women into the key professions had not been so dramatic.[24]

Table 8.1 Women as total membership of certain professions (per cent), 1968 and 1977

Profession	1968	1977
barristers	5.8	8.2
GPs	9.7	13.5
accountants	1.5	3.1
school teachers	57.3	59.5
electrical engineers	0.2	0.5

There were still few women university lecturers, but more women bus-drivers than before, and women were becoming even more numerous in retailing, banking and the welfare services. The number of women in the police and the armed forces had not changed greatly, but they were playing a more active role. The decade saw, for the first time, women becoming jockeys, Lloyds underwriters and RSPCA inspectors. Dame Rosemary Murray became the first woman Vice-Chancellor of Cambridge University and Dame Josephine Barnes the first woman President of the British Medical Association. The number of women filing divorce petitions rose dramatically, indicating greater independence on the part of women. In 1968 husbands filed 20,600 petitions and wives 34,400. In 1976 the figures were 42,866 and 100,832, respectively.[25] Perhaps the decline in religious wedding ceremonies in the 1970s was due more to the change in women's attitudes than men's. In 1971, 41 per cent of marriage ceremonies in England were held in register offices; in 1976 this figure had risen to 50 per cent.[26] In formal legal terms women's rights were advanced during the 1970s. The Guardianship of Children Act, 1973 gave mothers equal rights to fathers when making decisions about a child's upbringing, whereas previously the father's rights had been paramount. The Domicile and Matrimonial Proceedings Act, 1973 enabled a married woman living apart from her husband to have a legal domicile of her own. The Criminal Justice Act, 1972 ended the property qualification for jury service, thus enabling more women to serve on juries – significant, because even in 1977 only 6.5 per cent of home loans were granted to women, and only 39.5 per cent of home loans were based on two incomes.[27] The Sex Discrimination Act, 1975 made it unlawful to discriminate on grounds of sex in employment and in the provision of educational facilities, housing, goods, services and opportunities. It is also unlawful to discriminate in advertisements in these areas. The Act also created the Equal Opportunities Commission to investigate discriminatory practices. The battering of women by their male partners also became an issue in the 1970s. The result was the Domestic Violence and Matrimonial Proceedings Act, sponsored by Jo Richardson, Labour MP, which gave women who were not in the process of separating from their husbands the power to get injunctions against their spouses or co-habitees to prevent them entering the house. National conferences of the women's liberation movement were held from 1970 to 1978. But in 1978 the conference broke up over the question of whether a single resolution against violence against women should replace all other demands.[28]

Racial discrimination and immigration continued to be an issue throughout the 1970s. Jenkins, when Home Secretary, pursued a liberal course, granting an amnesty to illegal immigrants who had entered the country before 1 January 1973. This measure, designed to remove the threat of blackmail and exploitation from this group, was attacked by the Opposition. Jenkins also gave Commonwealth or foreign husbands of British women the same right of entry as wives of British men. This too was attacked by the Conservatives. Matters were made worse by confusion, which led to controversy, about the reliability of Home Office statistics on the number of immigrants entering the country. Under Merlyn Rees as Home Secretary, there was some tightening up of entry rules. Meanwhile, Parliament also had to decide what to do about ensuring equal treatment for those already in Britain, especially the generation which had been brought up or even born in the country. There were fears that Black youths, living in the decaying ghettos of the inner cities, undereducated, unemployed and dispirited, could become a permanent pool from which the criminals and subversives would be recruited. This was one of the main reasons for the Race Relations Act, 1976, which attempted to deal with discrimination over a broad field, and established the Commission for Racial Equality. For one thing, the Act extended previous legislation to cover most clubs, which was opposed by the Conservatives as an infringement of the rights of the citizen in the private sphere.

One other issue which continued to cause bitter strife was education. As with race, so with education, the parties proclaimed their abhorrence of discrimination and their desire to achieve high standards for all. They differed on their means to these ends. The Labour Party was for the comprehensive system and opposed to fee-paying schools. The Conservatives claimed they favoured improving all schools and that the retention of the independent sector gave freedom of choice to parents. They found it difficult to deny, however, that in practice few parents had any choice. Labour's Public Schools Commission, 1968 had recommended integration of the independent schools, but nothing had come of this. The second 1974 government did abolish grants to the direct-grant grammar schools, schools with high academic standards, many of whose pupils were holders of scholarships awarded by local authorities. These schools had to choose between joining the 'state' sector or going completely private. Most chose to do the latter. Many of the Catholic schools among them joined the 'state' system, retaining their denominational character.

Controversy also continued in educational politics about standards, which some alleged were falling and others alleged were not keeping pace with the needs of the times and the needs of industry. Some of those leading the assault believed that 'informal' teaching methods were to blame. Speaking at Ruskin College, Oxford, Callaghan paid lip-service to this widespread concern. He cautiously criticized 'informal' methods and regretted that many of the more able students preferred to stay in academic life or to find their way into the civil service, rather than into industry There was some truth in this, though it was really playing to the gallery, a gallery where prejudice was strong. Callaghan underestimated the connection existing by then between the universities and industry. As for the civil service, its importance had grown rather than lessened. Obviously, first-class brains were needed there too. The 'informal' methods certainly needed better-trained and more resourceful teachers, with smaller classes. The assault was renewed in the 1970s on mixed-ability groups, a feature of comprehensive schools. It had been argued that by not segregating children according to ability the better pupils stimulated the less able ones. The critics of this system maintained that it held back brighter children, led the poor pupils into frustration because they could not keep up, and was particularly damaging in maths and languages. Sir Alan Bullock's committee, set up to look at the teaching of English in schools, did criticize some of the students in training and called for more stringent entry requirements. The committee, which reported in February 1975, also called for a more professional approach to the teaching of English. Lord James of Rusholme had already led a committee of investigation into teacher training, which recommended an all-graduate profession and more in-service training of teachers. Women's rights activists were disappointed by the lack of progress in providing nursery education. On the positive side, the school-leaving age was raised to 16 in 1972. It is doubtful whether the great majority of schools were really equipped to meet the challenge this extra year represented.

The exam system was hotly debated again in the 1970s. The General Certificate of Education (GCE), introduced in 1951, and the Certificate of Secondary Education (CSE), in existence since 1965, had proved their worth. Both catered for a wide range of abilities and interest. Both offered a wide variety of subjects outside the original hard-core academic ones. Even their overlapping at the bottom end of the GCE and the top end of the CSE was useful. More and more young people were leaving school armed with these qualifications, thus justifying the view of Robbins about the wasted talent in society. In some circles there was a strong view that these exams should be replaced by a single one, which would be administratively tidy and would apparently give all pupils some sort of certificate; but the arguments in its favour did not seem all that compelling. There was the fear, expressed by Conservative spokesmen, that such an exam, virtually under the control of the schools themselves, would substitute subjective judgements for objective assessments. In Britain fewer young people stayed on beyond 16, compared with countries like West Germany, Sweden and Japan.[29] Of those who went on to higher education, many obtained degrees which did not give them easily marketable skills. This was true in many other countries. In Britain, there were unemployed graduate teachers who could not find jobs because local authorities had not the funds to employ them. By the end of the decade teachers, especially in schools and universities, felt less happy than in the days of hope in the early 1960s. The pay of university staff, even more than school-teachers, lagged behind that of comparable professions. In this respect the polytechnics were better off. They were, to a considerable extent, trying to abandon their distinctive role of putting on more practical, more vocational, more 'relevant' courses, and attempting to match the universities. Some departments of some polytechnics, though, were certainly exploring their disciplines in novel and interesting ways. One great success in higher education was the Open University, an achievement of the first Wilson administration. It offered admission to students without formal GCE qualifications. It failed to attract the large working-class clientele originally hoped for, but it gave a second chance to thousands who had either failed to get into a university, chosen not to go to one or had chosen non-university professional qualifications. It pioneered new teaching methods and, for the most part, achieved entirely respectable standards. It led some academics to conclude that in the 1980s the universities should be exploring, together with the government and other interested bodies, ways of encouraging older people to aim for a university education. This was important when one considers the difficulties of finding a place in higher education, especially for the working class and for women, who remained grossly underrepresented in universities, polytechnics and teacher training establishments.

EEC REFERENDUM: WILSON FOUGHT 'LIKE A TIGER'

One of the first problems facing Wilson was how to resolve the explosive issue of Britain's EEC membership. Tough 'renegotiations' went on with Wilson fighting 'like a tiger'.[30] According to Callaghan, who did most of the negotiating, the change in leadership in West Germany (Schmidt) and France (Giscard) in 1974 greatly helped matters.[31] The negotiations were concluded in Dublin on 10 March 1975. A White Paper on the renegotiations was published on 27 March 1975. The four main areas of negotiation were the Common Agricultural Policy; the level of contributions to the EEC budget; relations with the Commonwealth and developing states; and Britain's ability to pursue its own regional and industrial policies. Some concessions were granted. A plan was agreed under which member states would be eligible for reimbursements on their contributions on the basis of their gross national product and economic growth. Britain also managed to negotiate concessions on sugar, beef and New Zealand dairy products. The renegotiated package was presented to Parliament in April. The Commons then voted by 396 to 170 in favour. The government relied on the Conservatives and Liberals to get the legislation through. Only 137 Labour MPs voted in favour; 145 voted against and 33 did not vote.[32] The pro- and anti-Marketeers in the Cabinet agreed to differ, but only after Wilson had threatened to resign.[33] Wilson, influenced by German Chancellor Helmut Schmidt,[34] Callaghan, Healey, Jenkins and Short, headed the 16 supporters. Seven Cabinet ministers rejected the new terms – Benn, Castle, Foot, Ross, Shore, John Silkin and Varley – because they thought EEC membership would be 'markedly unfavourable' from the economic point of view. 'But the gravest disadvantages are political.' They saw these as the inevitable shift of power from the elected Commons to the non-elected Commission and Council of Ministers in Brussels. And they claimed:

> Timid voices and vested interests will now combine in seeking to persuade us we have no choice; that Britain outside the Common Market would suffer great disadvantage. Do not believe them. On the contrary, a far greater danger to our legitimate economic interest, to the continued unity of the UK, and to the practice of democracy in this country arises from our continued membership of the EEC.[35]

On the Right, Powell and his friends put similar arguments. Labour's promised referendum, an idea of Benn's four years earlier,[36] took place on 5 June 1975. Among the campaigners in the cross-party Britain In Europe were Labour's Jenkins, Gledwyn Hughes (Chairman of the Parliamentary Labour Party), Shirley Williams and Vic Feather, the Conservatives' Heath, Maudling and Whitelaw, and the Liberals' Grimond and Steel. Wilson and Callaghan campaigned separately for 'yes' votes, as did Thatcher, who was criticized for her low profile.[37] Only 64.5 per cent of the electorate bothered to vote. They gave the pro-EEC forces a two-to-one majority in favour of the renegotiated terms: 17.3 million voted 'yes', 8.4 million 'no'. The 'yes' vote represented 43 per cent of the total eligible to vote. The Labour special conference had voted overwhelmingly on 26 April against EEC membership. Delegates were not convinced by the argument that the socialists were the biggest group in the European Parliament and that, together with the Communists and Left Christian Democrats, there was likely to be a majority in favour of the working classes in that Parliament. It was argued that the European Parliament was without effective powers. During the referendum Benn and Foot joined Powell to oppose the EEC. The Communists, PC and the SNP also joined the anti-EEC camp. They were opposed, however, by a powerful alliance of the Establishment, most of the press, and big business. Both sides were given equal time on television and literature from both sides was sent at government expense to every household. However, as Thatcher was later to write:

> The 'Yes' campaign was very well organized and very well funded – not least as a result of the efforts of Alistair McAlpine, whom I would shortly recruit to be Conservative Party Treasurer. For all the talk of a 'great debate' it was really a contest between David and Goliath, which Goliath won.[38]

Most of the ordinary voters appeared baffled by the arguments about wine lakes and butter mountains, about sugar and sovereignty, beef and bureaucrats, New Zealand cheese and Italian Communists. Economic arguments were the main ones deployed; the idea of 'an ever closer union of European people' ensuring that war would not take place again between members was hardly touched on. Some voters were persuaded that without an empire Britain needed new friends; others that, having joined, Britain would have to pay a heavy penalty for leaving; more by the possibility of emulating the 'economic miracles' of Western Europe; and still more by the smiles or frowns of their favourite politicians when the EEC was mentioned. Many members of the 'silent majority' felt that if Benn, Powell and the Communists were against the EEC, it must be a good thing. Many trade unionists, despite Feather's argument to the contrary, believed that if British Petroleum (BP), ICI, the big banks and Uncle Sam thought Britain should join, then it could only be bad for Britain. The more thoughtful reflected on what would happen to a lonely Britain nearing the year 2000 faced with high trade barriers, built by mighty new states armed with cheap labour and modern technology, capable of waging fierce trade wars for political as well as economic reasons. They believed it would be better to co-operate with states with similar values, similar standards and similar problems than to be forced to rely on the good-will of totalitarian or unstable regimes, of Japanese corporations, Arab oil potentates or even their American cousins.[39]

The cross-party unity in Britain In Europe gave false hopes to some, and fears to others, that a moderate national government would emerge to run the country in a period of severe strains caused by the oil crisis and a period when consensus would have been very useful to promote badly needed reforms in British society. Wilson[40] and Thatcher[41] did not want this, nor did Benn and others on the Left.

INDUSTRY: 'THE GAP GETS WIDER EACH YEAR'

One of the key items in the Queen's Speech on 29 October 1974 was the proposal for a National Enterprise Board, subsequently set up under the Industry Act of 1975. The NEB became a state holding company to administer government holdings of shares in companies, acquire additional ones and give financial assistance to businesses in trouble. It removed restrictions on the Secretary of State for Industry, included in the Conservatives' Industry Act, 1972, which prevented him acquiring more than 50 per cent of the equity share capital, and required him to dispose of any share acquired as soon as it was practical to do so. Under the British Leyland Act, 1975 the NEB acquired 95 per cent of the equity of that ailing motor company. Ferranti, the electronics and defence company, followed, with the NEB taking 50 per cent of the ordinary voting shares. Rolls-Royce (1971) Ltd, already publicly owned, became part of the NEB empire. Other firms were subsequently assisted. Among these was the American-owned Chrysler company, which needed a massive cash injection to avoid a total shut-down with the loss of about 27,000 jobs. Chrysler was not taken over. The government did take over the ailing aerospace and shipbuilding industries after being forced to drop nationalization of ship-repair companies to get its legislation through. Though the Conservatives tried to denounce much that the government did in this direction, it is doubtful whether they would have done much differently, judged by Heath's record. Had the government not intervened, unemployment would have gone much higher and so would the cost of unemployment. The idea was to rationalize these troubled industries as well as nationalize them. In the other direction, the government sold off a profitable block of shares acquired by BP, itself partly owned by the state, during the earlier rescue operation for Burmah Oil; this was to placate Britain's foreign creditors and allowed some reduction in borrowing. In November 1975 the government held a meeting at Chequers of union chiefs and industrialists to look at the problems of industry and government policy towards them. This led to an agreement which identified 30 sectors of industry deserving of government attention and help, either because they were intrinsically likely to succeed, or because assistance could make the difference between success or failure, or because they were thought vital to the success of others. It looked sensible enough, concentrating the limited resources where they could do the most good. Ferranti was turned round to produce a profit, but went out of business as a private business in the 1990s.

Britain's difficulty as a manufacturing nation was highlighted by a calculation of Dr Frank Jones, industrialist and inventor. According to Jones, in 1976 total assets per employee in manufacturing industry stood at £7,500. In Japan this figure was just over £30,000 and in West Germany about £23,000 per employee. 'The discrepancy in assets per employee . . . has been crucial in enabling the Japanese and German employee to manufacture at two or three times our productivity . . . The gap gets wider each year.'[42] Jones thought the government was taking too much in tax from industry. Others claimed too much capital had been exported over a long period. The banking system also came in for criticism. Some commentators thought British banks could learn from Japanese banks and from British building societies on improving methods to ensure the financing of long-term loans to industry. British building societies operated in ways similar to foreign banks by 'lending long from short-term deposits . . . If such a mechanism were adopted by the banks in Britain for their industrial customers . . . Britain would stand to reap considerable growth benefits similar to those experienced by both Japan and West Germany.'[43]

Controversy about British management and its contribution to the so-called 'British sickness', economic malaise, continued from at least the early 1950s, and was even seriously discussed in the late nineteenth century. There was a feeling that British employers were less qualified than their German, American or Japanese rivals, and that they understood their employees less. There was also the feeling that foremen, technicians and professional engineers were less well qualified and were undervalued. Three writers who had studied German firms put this point about foremen in *Management Today* (March 1978), emphasizing that compared with his British colleague, the German *Meister* was better qualified and enjoyed higher status. The relatively poor prestige of professional engineers in Britain was also thought to be a cause for the failure to attract more, and more talented, applicants to university engineering courses.[44] Many British managers, top executives and businessmen were less well educated than many of their rivals abroad. Unlike Britain, in Japan and Germany an appropriate university qualification was the single most important prerequisite to qualify for managerial rank.[45]

A Brookings Institution team headed by Professor Richard E. Caves of Harvard came to the conclusion, in 1974, that Britain's secondary school system was a key factor in poor management and bad industrial relations.

> Nowhere else does the middle class make such extensive use of private schools and bear such financial burdens to avoid sending children to state-supported schools. Whatever may be said in favour of Britain's private schools, one result . . . is to create two distinct social groups that share no common educational experience. The economic life of the nation cannot be separated from the social context, and lack of common schooling inevitably hampers the kind of communication needed to improve industrial relations.
>
> The prevalence of private schools undoubtedly reinforces the prejudice against being 'in trade'. Although Britain is an urban industrial society, the social ideal of many Britons is still the country squire living on his lands.
>
> The middle-class and upper-class disdain for industry is matched by a curious reluctance among lower-class people to take advantage of what opportunities exist to rise through the management hierarchy, normally an important channel of social mobility in advanced countries.

The team gave British management low marks for professional quality. For instance, the study concluded that overmanning was mainly the fault of management, not the unions, and that financial controls were often deficient. The investigation did, however, point out that Britain's poor growth went back 100 years. 'Industry's chronic reluctance to invest is not due to lack of savings or company liquidity, and has not responded much to tax incentives.'[46]

WILSON GOES: 'ASTONISHED CABINET'

According to Castle, when Wilson announced his resignation on 16 March 1976 it was to an 'astonished Cabinet'.[47] He had warned her that he was going, but gave the impression it would be later. Callaghan had been warned, weeks before, at Wilson's request, via Harold Lever.[48] Wilson told Healey only minutes before in the lavatory at 10 Downing Street.[49] Thus, Callaghan had the opportunity to 'prepare himself to take over'.[50] Callaghan duly stood in the election to replace Wilson. On the first ballot he gained 80 votes to 90 for Foot, 56 for Jenkins, 37 for Benn, 30 for Healey and 17 for Crosland. On the second ballot Callaghan attracted 141 votes, Foot 133 and Healey 38. In the final ballot on 5 April, the 'conservative' Callaghan was elected with 176 votes to 133 for Foot the 'radical'.[51]

There was much speculation as to why Wilson had resigned. He claimed it was because he was 60 and it had long been his intention to do so. Dining with Foot on 7 March Benn had heard 'a very strong rumour' that Wilson was about to go. 'There is a possibility that some papers which were stolen from Harold's desk may envelop him in some way in a scandal.'[52] In 1987, Peter Wright, a senior member of MI 5, the security service, wrote that there had been two plots against Wilson, one in 1968 and another in 1974–5. These involved many members of the service who thought Wilson was 'wrecking the country'.[53] Many thought Wilson was 'soft' on the Soviet Union and its spying activities in Britain.[54]

Sensibly, the new Prime Minister recognized Foot's standing among Labour's left-wingers and those opposed to the EEC, and appointed him Lord President and Leader of the House. Foot's nominee, Albert Booth, replaced him at Employment. Healey remained at the Treasury and Jenkins at the Home Office. Mrs Castle had to make way for David Ennals, and felt she was being discarded 'like so much old junk'.[55] Crosland became the new Foreign Secretary but died suddenly in 1977 to be replaced by the almost unknown medical practitioner David Owen. He was the youngest Foreign Secretary since Eden. He had served as a junior minister at the Department of Health and Social Security, and then at the Foreign and Commonwealth Office. His was a controversial appointment, as there were others better qualified. The controversy increased when, in almost his first act, Owen announced the appointment of Callaghan's son-in-law, Peter Jay, with his 'machine-gun mind',[56] as Ambassador to Washington. Owen also came in for criticism over Rhodesia and his expressions of support for the despotic Shah of Iran.

Callaghan was regarded as a safe bet for Labour. He had been Chancellor, Home Secretary and at the Foreign Office and was, therefore, the most experienced. He was slightly Right of Centre politically, but his strength was thought to be his strong links with the unions. Of Irish descent, due to the early death of his father, he had to leave grammar school at 16. He found a safe berth in the junior ranks of the Inland Revenue. He made his way through the union movement, becoming a full-time official of the Association of Officers of Taxes in 1936. When war broke out he volunteered for the navy, giving up his reserved occupation. He had a quiet war in naval intelligence. A protégé of Dalton and Laski, he was elected MP in 1945 for Cardiff South East.

STEEL: 'QUIET EXTERIOR . . . DETERMINED MAN'

The Liberals were also forced to change their leader. In May 1976 Jeremy Thorpe, who had been leader since 1967, resigned. Under his leadership the Liberals had achieved their best post-war electoral result in 1974, but this was due more to the electorate's boredom, frustration and disgust with the other parties than to identification with Liberal policies. The Liberals enjoyed the advantage of not being in office. They were not more united than the other two parties. The radicalism of Peter Hain's Young Liberals – Hain later defected to Labour – Cyril Smith's Northern populism, Trevor Jones's community politics, Lord Gladwyn's right-wing Liberalism, were all different from each other. As for Thorpe, he thought of the Commons 'as if it were the Oxford Union Debating Society'.[57] His social style and dress – expensive, flamboyant and rather deliberately out-of-date clothes – caused much adverse comment.[58] The son of a Conservative MP and King's Counsel and himself a barrister and television journalist, he was elected to the Commons on the second attempt in 1959. As the Liberal leader, he never managed to escape from the shadow of the previous leader, old Etonian Jo Grimond, who remained in the House. Thorpe was forced to go after allegations made by former male model, Norman Scott,[59] that Thorpe was trying to get him murdered. They had had a homosexual relationship. Scott had received payments from Thorpe for some years. Thorpe was subsequently tried on a conspiracy charge but acquitted. He lost his seat in 1979. This kind of blow to the Liberals made it easier for the Conservatives, especially in the South West.

The new Liberal leader David Steel seemed refreshingly different from Thorpe. Educated in Nairobi and at Edinburgh University, he was the son of a clergyman. Like Thorpe he had been a television journalist, and was the youngest member of the 1964–66 Parliament (see p. 123). He was a supporter of liberal causes such as Shelter and the Anti-Apartheid Movement. He led the Liberals into the 'Lib–Lab' pact of March 1977. Under this arrangement, the Liberals promised to sustain the government, which was by then in a minority, in return for consultations on government legislation. The pact brought the Liberals nearer to office than they had been at any time in the post-war period. Callaghan recorded, 'Beneath his quiet exterior, David Steel is a determined man, but one whom I found scrupulous and always considerate.'[60] Steel could do nothing to stop the loss of support for the Liberals. As usual when Labour was in office, floating Right-of-Centre voters returned to the Conservatives. After arguments and recriminations, with Smith leading the assault, the pact with Labour was terminated in the summer of 1978.

CRIME: 'VIOLENCE . . . A NATURAL ASPECT OF SOCIETY'

In common with other industrial societies, Britain suffered from increasing crime during the 1960s and 1970s. There were the crimes which resulted from increased temptation and opportunity, like shoplifting, and crimes the causes of which baffled the experts, such as vandalism and football hooliganism. And there were more serious crimes, such as assault, muggings and the use of firearms. To meet this challenge, more police were recruited. The police became better trained, more professional, organized in larger units and, perhaps, more discontented. In 1949 there were 58,990 policemen in England and Wales and 1,176 policewomen. The totals for 1959 were 70,156 and 2,338, respectively. They increased to 87,342 men and 3,492 women in 1969. By 1976 there were 101,042 men and 6,997 women serving in the police in England and Wales. The authorized strength was 116,880, so that the police were over 8,000 below strength.[61] Throughout the post-war period, police forces had been under strength. Compared with the early post-war period, the police service had become a centralized force. In 1949 there were 127 police forces in England and Wales. By 1979 there were only 43. Officially, they were still run by committees of local government representatives and magistrates. Although great strides had been made in training, the police still did not have enough specialists to deal with particular types of crime which were becoming more prevalent. These included fraud, corruption and drugs-related offences. Race relations presented the police with a special problem, as surveys indicated that young immigrants felt they were likely to be unfairly dealt with by the police.[62] Undoubtedly the greatest challenge to police ingenuity was the appearance of urban terrorism. This was virtually unknown in Britain during the 1950s. Britain's 'political police', Special Branch, was established during the 1880s to deal with Irish Republican terrorism, but the interwar period was relatively quiet. The IRA engaged in a bombing campaign in England at the start of the Second World War, and there were minor attacks after that. Urban terrorism and the increasing use of firearms by criminals forced the police to give greater attention to training in the use of firearms and to the development of special units to deal with these crimes. Public attention in the 1970s focused a great deal on violence connected with political demonstrations and trade disputes. The Red Lion Square riot between Left and Right extremists in 1974, and the demonstrations and picketing connected with the Grunwick industrial dispute in 1977, attracted a great deal of attention. Too much was made of these by the media but, as Sir Robert Mark, Commissioner of the Metropolitan Police, pointed out one had to consider:

> Whether social violence has increased in this country or whether that is an illusion created, even if unintentionally, by newspapers and television. Violence has always been a natural aspect of society and,

indeed, many social changes now regarded as wholly acceptable have been achieved by it. Local self-government, social legislation and parliamentary reform all owe something to social violence. The trade unions did not emerge without it. The Chartist movement between 1837 and 1848 laid the foundation of what we now regard as constitutional democracy. The suffragette movement between 1905 and 1914 resorted to violence to a degree now largely forgotten or unremarked. There was violence during the General Strike and during the hunger marches of the thirties: but violence had tended to diminish as the claims which inspired it have been conceded.

Sir Robert went on to emphasize that there was nothing new in squatting, sit-ins, demos or even home-made bombs. He was warning against over-reaction to the activities of violent minorities, and recommended the minimum use of force to contain them.

In a free society such as ours, government must be by consent. The forcible suppression of a minority . . . is the negation of freedom and can only be achieved by overwhelming resources of manpower willing to enforce undemocratic laws.[63]

Two aspects of the development of the police since the mid-1960s worried some observers. One was the apparent increase in corruption, the other was the 'Big Brother' aspect of policing. In the 1960s there were a number of cases of police misusing their powers. One led to the conviction of two Sheffield policemen for severely beating up suspects, another involved Detective Sergeant Challenor of the Metropolitan Police, who had acted illegally in 24 cases. Among other things, he planted evidence on left-wing political demonstrators. At his trial he was found unfit to plead through insanity. In the same case, three others were sentenced on charges of perverting the course of justice.[64] There were also a number of cases where immigrants were the victims. The spectacular case of corruption in the 1970s was that involving members of Scotland Yard's Obscene Publications Squad, who had taken large bribes from proprietors of pornographic bookshops. They were jailed in 1977 for offences that had been committed over a considerable period. In 1976 Sir Robert Mark revealed that in the four years he had been Commissioner, 82 officers had been required to leave the Metropolitan Police after formal proceedings. Another 301 left voluntarily amid criminal or disciplinary inquiries. Of 72 officers tried by jury, 36 were acquitted.[65] In the decade before Mark, an average of 16 officers were eased out of the service. Was there more corruption about? Or was it that Mark set higher standards than his predecessors? Or was it that a greater press and public awareness of corruption and malpractice was forcing matters into the open? It is difficult to be sure. But Mark had taken over with the brief to clean up Scotland Yard's CID, and there had been corruption cases at the Yard in the 1930s. Part of the trouble was that laws on gambling, prostitution, licensing, pornography and drugs, which were difficult to enforce, put police officers into temptation's way.[66] Another reason why some officers broke the rules was the pressure to get results. The Police Act, 1976 was an attempt to help restore public confidence in the police by setting up a Police Complaints Board with functions relating to complaints from the public. The chairman and his deputy (or deputies) were to be appointed by the Prime Minister. 'The members of the Board shall not include any person who is or has been a constable in any part of the United Kingdom.'[67] The Minister for the Civil Service was given oversight of the Board's activities. The Board replaced the much-criticized system under which the police dealt with complaints themselves.

Another aspect of police work which worried some was the development of the Police National Computer (PNC). This was just part of the computerization of information by banks, credit firms, insurance companies, employers, local authorities, voluntary bodies and the NHS. The White Paper *Computer and Privacy 1975* recognized the possible dangers from the storage of information in this way: inaccurate, incomplete or irrelevant information being stored; the possibility of access to information by people who should not need to have it; the use of information in a context or for a purpose other than that for which it was collected.[68] By the end of the 1970s Britain was behind some other countries – Canada, Norway, Denmark, France, Sweden, the USA and West Germany – in providing a legal framework to protect its citizens from malpractice.[69] A committee chaired by Sir Norman Lindop reported on the whole issue in December 1978. It dealt with the PNC, which holds five major files: the index to criminal records in the Criminal Records Office; a file of vehicle-owners; a file of stolen and suspect vehicles; an index to the national fingerprint collection; and a file of wanted or missing persons. The advantages of this to the police are too obvious to need further comment. Lindop, while supporting the police in their use of the PNC, urged 'that the best way to avert any fears and suspicions of such systems would be for them to be subject to the data protection legislation which we propose'.[70] The storage of data on patients by the NHS was another sphere which caused concern.

The other 'Big Brother' aspects of police and security work which many found disquieting were the ease with which the Home Secretary could deport 'undesirable aliens', the apparently increasing use of phone-tapping, the vetting of juries and the complete secrecy surrounding these and certain other operations of government and police activities.

NORTHERN IRELAND: 'HOPE TO A TRAGIC COMMUNITY'

Northern Ireland continued to be the most intractable and urgent political problem for Callaghan as for Wilson. Under the Northern Ireland Act,

1974, a 78-member Convention was established to initiate power-sharing. Elections to the Convention, held in May 1975, gave the anti-power-sharing Unionists nearly 55 per cent of the votes and 46 seats. The SDLP and other Catholic groups got 26.2 per cent, and the moderate unionists, Northern Ireland Labour Party, and Alliance Party – all power-sharing parties – nearly 19 per cent. As agreement could not be reached, Merlyn Rees, Secretary of State for Northern Ireland, dissolved the Convention in March 1976. Hopes were raised that at least the violence would end after talks between British officials and Provisional Sinn Fein, the political wing of the Provisional IRA, led to a cease-fire in February 1975. Rees ordered the British forces to keep a low profile. Certainly there was much less IRA activity against the security forces, but there was no end to the sectarian killings. In summer 1975 the cease-fire broke down completely. In January 1976 elements of the Special Air Service (SAS), tough troops trained in irregular warfare, were sent to reinforce the army. This represented a hardening of the government's policy. On the other hand, Rees began to release the detainees held without trial. By Christmas 1975 all had been released.

There was renewed hope again in August 1976 when there were spontaneous mass demonstrations for peace. These had been sparked by the killing of three children by a terrorist car which was out of control. A Peace Movement came into existence headed by Mrs Betty Williams, Miss Mairead Corrigan and Mr Ciaran McKeown. They took part in similar demonstrations up and down the United Kingdom and Ireland. They braved denunciations by the IRA and, as Airey Neave put it, 'The Women's Peace Movement, courageous and sincere, certainly brings hope to a tragic community.'[71] The Movement was awarded the Nobel Prize for Peace. Peace, however, did not break out. In 1976 a total of 296 individuals were killed in Northern Ireland; the total for 1977 was 112. Between 1968 and 1978 about 2,000 civilians and soldiers had died as a result of the disorders. Just about the worst of vicious crimes were the activities of the 'Shankhill butchers', a group of Belfast Protestants who, after heavy drinking, seized individual Catholics off the street at random and tortured their victims before cutting their throats with butchers' knives. The ringleader, William Moore, admitted to 11 murders. In February 1979 11 Protestants were given a total of 42 life sentences for 19 murders and other serious charges. All were judged sane by medical experts.[72]

England too continued to be plagued by the senseless violence of Northern Ireland. As mentioned on p. 181, the Wilson government had to deal with escalating terrorism in 1974, culminating in 20 deaths when bombs went off in Birmingham pubs on the night of 21 November. Under the Prevention of Terrorism Act, passed one week later, the IRA became an illegal organization in Great Britain; the Home Secretary was given power to 'exclude' suspected individuals from Great Britain; and the police got power to detain suspects for up to seven days without charging them.

Necessary though this was, it looked like a step towards *1984*. The Commons refused to be panicked into introducing the death penalty for terrorism when the issue was raised in 1974 and 1975. On both occasions a majority of Conservatives voted in favour. One crucial argument against capital punishment for this crime was that it could easily lead to an escalation of violence, including kidnappings and reprisals.

BULLOCK: 'MORE THOUGHTFUL . . . MANAGEMENT'

The government was forced to put a brave face on one by-election reverse after another. In June 1975 it lost Woolwich West to the Conservatives. In November 1976 Walsall North fell. There a special factor helped the Conservatives. The former Labour MP and former Cabinet Minister John Stonehouse was convicted of corruption and fraud and sentenced to seven years' imprisonment. In March 1977, Birmingham Stechford, Roy Jenkins's old seat, was won by the Conservatives. A similar blow was the fall of Ashfield, a mining constituency, in April. The Conservatives also took Ilford North in March 1978. The government was in the doghouse because, like its predecessor, it could not control the economy. And again, like its predecessor, it had made promises in opposition it could not fulfil in office. Britain had reached a state of 'stagflation' – a stagnating economy with high unemployment which was nevertheless hit by high inflation. Britain's inflation rate in the 1970s was higher than all other EEC states, except for Ireland and Italy; higher than Austria, Sweden, Switzerland, the United States and Japan. Unemployment reached new post-war peaks, nearing 1.5 million. In 1977 it was higher than in other leading Western industrial nations, except for Canada. This unenviable record was due to a considerable extent to Healey's deflationary measures of the previous year, which in turn were the result of the sterling crisis of that year. At the beginning of the year the pound had stood at $2.024; by the last days of September it was down to $1.637. The pound appeared to be dying. Only massive borrowing abroad prevented it from doing so. Then, suddenly, the pound was climbing up once again, towards $2. The heavy dose of public-spending cuts, the greater stability afforded the government by the Lib.–Lab. pact, the expectation of oil revenues from the North Sea fields, all helped to reverse the trend. The freeing of the pound from its previous linkage with the dollar also helped, especially as the dollar crisis deepened, caused by America's large deficit on its overseas trade.

It was all too easy to blame the government or 'socialism' for this state of affairs, but this explanation was hardly convincing. The Social Democrats had been in government in West Germany, the most successful European industrial state, since 1966, and had led that country since 1969. They had led the equally successful Austria since 1970, and had been in government there throughout the post-war period except for 1966–70. France apart, Labour's European sister parties had been in government in most of the other West European states for most of the previous 10 years. Another easy target was the trade unions. In the first two years of the Labour government there was a great improvement in industrial relations; after that there was a turn for the worse. In the period 1973–77 Britain's record was better than Australia, Canada, Ireland, Italy, Spain and the United States. It was true of course, in the 1970s as in the 1960s, that Britain suffered from archaic trade union structures. At the end of 1977 there were still something like 485 trade unions in Britain.[73] In 1977 there were still 74 unions with memberships of under 100, compared with 126 in 1967. Those with memberships between 100 and 499 had actually increased from 136 in 1967 to 144 in 1977, but made up only 0.3 per cent of total union membership. Nearly 63 per cent of British trade unionists were organized in the 11 biggest unions. But the situation was far from satisfactory. The unions did themselves no good, as far as popular esteem was concerned, by failure to have postal voting for important union elections and secret ballots for strikes. In the 1970s unions seemed to enjoy less public approval than at any time since 1945. This is remarkable considering the growth of unions and the fact that they were more representative than ever of the 'workers by hand and by brain'. Indeed, the growth areas had been among the white-collar supervisory and technical employees. In 1977 there were 12.6 million union members in Britain, which probably meant they and their family members made up half the population.

Britain's industrial relations continued to look very bad compared with those of West Germany. For many of the politically interested West Germany remained the state to study and to emulate. The TUC belatedly came round to the view that perhaps there was something in West Germany's system of co-determination, employee participation in management. Under pressure from his own back-benchers Wilson set up the Bullock Committee, under Lord (Alan) Bullock, to investigate the possibilities. In its report published in January 1977, it commented that in West Germany

> many of those we met saw a strong and direct connection between the success of the West German economy since World War II and the presence of employee representatives on supervisory boards. West German industrialists, though opposed to parity representation, were largely in agreement that board level representation provided a system of legally enforced communication between managers and employees which led to an earlier identification of problems involving changes for employees and to a more thoughtful and farsighted style of management.[74]

The Committee also reported favourably on similar developments in Sweden. It might also have considered the position of trade unions in Austria, where they have the right, among other things, to pass judgement on every important draft bill before it is presented to Parliament.[75]

The main proposals of Bullock were that, in an enterprise employing more than 2,000 people, the unions would have the right to call for a ballot of the work-force on proposals for trade union directors. If the ballot were favourable, with a minimum of 50 per cent of employees voting, the unions involved would form a Joint Representation Committee (JRC). The company board would then be reconstructed, comprising two equal groups appointed, respectively, by the shareholders and the JRC, and a third smaller group co-opted in agreement with the other two. There would also be an Industrial Democracy Commission which would give advice and decide the composition of boards in the case of deadlock. A minority of Bullock rejected these proposals in favour of more modest representation at below board level. Bullock's proposals came to nothing. It is doubtful whether the government was ever very serious about them. The Committee was originally conceived to stop a Private Member's Bill, proposed by Labour MP Giles Radice, on industrial democracy. The Conservatives opposed Bullock, so did the employers' organizations and so did some trade union leaders. Certainly, there would have been difficulties in trying to establish a framework for industrial democracy, but it appeared that the leaders of British politics and industry were not ready to break new ground away from old-fashioned, authoritarian structures towards co-operation through participation. Only in the nationalized industries was a limited experiment embarked upon.

One ray of hope in the otherwise gloomy 1970s was the emergence of Britain as an oil power. The first discovery of oil in the British sector of the North Sea was made in 1969 and the first oil was landed in 1975. By mid-1978 nine fields in the British sector were producing oil. Under the Petroleum and Submarine Pipe-lines Act, 1975 a public corporation, the British National Oil Corporation (BNOC), was established. BNOC took over the British offshore interests previously held by the National Coal Board, and those of the Burmah Oil Company. Majority participation agreements were signed between BNOC and all the companies operating North Sea fields. There was controversy about the state's involvement in the oil industry, with the Conservatives preferring to leave things largely to private companies. However, the government's schemes for a public sector plus participation agreements were modest compared with those of many oil-producing states, from Austria and Norway to Mexico. Britain was set to be self-sufficient by 1980. North Sea gas expanded rapidly in the late 1960s and early 1970s and was also making a major contribution to Britain's energy requirements.

PAY POLICY: 'ANKLE-DEEP IN MUCK AND SLIME'

Callaghan announced in July 1978 a continuation of incomes policy with a 5 per cent maximum rise compared with the previous year. There were exceptions for self-financing productivity deals, for low pay and for the fire service, armed forces and police. The TUC were aggrieved that they had not been consulted. The policy was rejected by the annual TUC conference, at Brighton in September, and by the Labour conference in October. On the eve of the TUC conference at Brighton, Callaghan invited the six top trade union leaders to dinner at his Sussex farmhouse to get from them their view of the forthcoming pay round and on the timing of the election. Apart from Scanlon, the others urged him to go to the country swiftly.[76] In fact, he had already decided weeks before not to hold an early election.[77] Some believe, had he been more open with the TUC leaders about his intentions, they would have made greater efforts to keep their members in line.[78] As it was, there followed the 'Winter of Discontent'. Disputes which involved car workers, BBC technicians, oil-tanker drivers and public sector workers ranging from grave-diggers to hospital porters gave the Conservative 'media a field day'.[79] Among the strikers were fitters, 'ankle-deep in muck and slime', processing the excrement of a million Mancunians at Chadderton sewage-works, who felt, after nearly four years of pay policy, that enough was enough. Some strikers would have been better off on social security than working. Some, indeed, were receiving Family Income Supplement (FIS). As one angry tractor-driver is reported to have said, 'But why should I go crawling for FIS when I work a 40-hour week?'[80] He summed up the anger of many of his colleagues who believed Labour had done little for them and that Britain was an unfair society. The incomes policy was not fair between high-paid and low-paid manual workers, nor was it fair between different sections of society. As Katharine Whitehorn explained, at the top end there were ample ways round it:

> Company car, of course – three out of five on our roads are so owned. Big meals, that's old hat. Live in the Tied Penthouse at company's expense, get medical insurance on the firm; school fees are coming into it . . . Go to the races in the company box, get your golf club subscription paid – good for the firm's publicity. Help with moving costs and low-interest mortgages – well, that's still money of a sort.[81]

Then there were the credit cards, free petrol, and free travel. And if you were made redundant, a golden handshake. And there was still old wealth, like that of 26-year-old Gerald Grosvenor, son and heir of the Duke of Westminster who, because of the accident of birth, owns all the lands of Belgravia and one-third of Mayfair – including the south side of Oxford Street and land of 33 embassies. But also has a shopping centre in Wales; shooting in Scotland; trout in Shropshire; family seats in Cheshire and Fermanagh (NI); office blocks in Melbourne; a palm-fringed hotel in Hawaii; and an Island in Vancouver.[82]

Yet the government could claim that they had achieved much *in the circumstances*. By the end of 1978, except for unemployment, the economic indicators were good. Inflation was down, the growth rate had risen to 3.5 per cent, the balance of payments had moved into surplus and the public sector borrowing requirement (PSBR) was under control.[83] In fact, the situation was not as bad as was believed. Up to late in 1976, the way the Treasury measured public expenditure was misleading. As Healey wrote later, 'it was unforgivably misleading'.[84] When they defined public spending in the same way as did other countries, British spending was significantly reduced. And when they costed Gross Domestic Product (GDP) like other countries, 'the ratio of public spending to GDP fell from sixty per cent to forty-six per cent. By 1978/9 my successive cuts had brought it down to about forty-two per cent – about the same as West Germany.' For years the public and the world had been given a false picture about British public spending. Had Prime Minister, the Chancellor and his team taken a more relaxed view of incomes policy, not been so blind to the warnings from the union leaders,[85] or decided to go to the country earlier, history would have been different. It is worth recalling that Healey was surrounded by individuals who were anything but amateurs, with Edmund Dell, former ICI executive, Paymaster-General, 1974–76, Secretary of State for Trade, 1976–78; Joel Barnett, certified accountant and Chief Secretary to the Treasury, 1974–79; the wealthy businessman Harold Lever, Chancellor of the Duchy of Lancaster, 1974–79; Douglas Wass, Permanent Secretary to the Treasury, 'as able an economist as any';[86] and Gordon Richardson, lawyer and former Chairman of Schroders, Governor of the Bank of England, 1973–83. It was left to Leo Pliatzky, who served at the Treasury, 1950–77, to bring Britain in line with the Organization for Economic Co-operation and Development (OECD) definition of public spending.[87] Given this wealth of talent the mystery is how the government got into so many difficulties.

What kind of society was Britain at the end of the 1970s? After the Heath, Wilson and Callaghan governments it remained a divided society with great differences of wealth and status. On an international standardized scale of poverty it had more poor than West Germany or Sweden but fewer than France, the United States or Canada.[88] According to the official statistics, in the mid-1970s, the richest 1 per cent owned one-fifth to one-quarter of all personal wealth. In income terms the richest 1 per cent took home about the same as the poorest 20 per cent.[89] However, although there was argument about the extent, most agreed that Britain was a more equal society in 1979 than it had been in either 1939 or 1959. Wigan had changed for the better from what it was when George Orwell visited it in the 1930s, and nearby Bolton, 'Worktown', was quite different from how Tom Harrison found it in 1936 and 1959.[90] The same was true of the other 'Worktowns'. The great expansion in the ownership of consumer durables, the expansion of home ownership, the development of council housing, social welfare and close to full employment for all but the last few years had raised the level of the majority of the working class. For those who remembered life before the war or even in the 1940s, it was like a revolution. In terms of income, working-class wages had gone up more between 1938 and 1976 than those of many professional people.[91] As in other industrial societies, economic changes produced social class changes. The class structure was no longer a pyramid, it was more like a light bulb, reducing the numbers at the bottom of the pile. Even for the 1.4 million unemployed in 1979, life on the dole was infinitely better than it was for their fathers in 1939, though who can say that the psychological effects were not as devastating?

In other respects too life in Britain was not so bad. The percentage of people who owned their homes was higher than in West Germany, though lower than in France, and 'housing standards in the United Kingdom compare well with those in other developed countries. Densities of occupation are generally lower than in other major EEC countries, for example, and the proportion of dwellings lacking amenities are substantially lower.'[92] Suicide rates had been falling in Britain during the 1960s and 1970s, and Britons were less inclined to kill themselves than were some other Europeans. They were also less inclined to kill each other on the roads.

DEVOLUTION REFERENDA: 'THE VALLEYS WERE DEAF'

As we saw in Chapter 1, the Scottish nationalists briefly held Motherwell in 1945 after a by-election win, losing the seat to Labour in the general election. It was 22 years before their next success, this time in the Hamilton by-election in 1967. Once again, the seat was lost in the subsequent general election, but they got a consolation prize – the Western Isles. A second seat was won in the by-election at Glasgow Govan in November 1973 when Margo Macdonald defeated the Labour candidate. The breakthrough came for the SNP in the 1974 elections. In October of that year the SNP gained 11 seats and 30 per cent of the vote in Scotland. In any European country that would entitle it to be called a major party. In Wales, Plaid Cymru won 3 seats and 10.8 per cent of the vote. Its breakthrough had come when Gwynfor Evans won Carmarthen from Labour in a by-election on 14 July 1967. It came as a shock to many English people that so many voters in Scotland and Wales were so dissatisfied as to vote for parties which sought to establish separate states. In both cases a powerful ingredient of this vote was the failure of the two main parties to deal with the economic and social difficulties of the two countries. In both Scotland and Wales unemployment rates remained higher than the average for Great Britain. Migration had long been the only alternative to the dole queue for many. Housing too remained a problem in the 1970s. In 1976 the stock of housing in Wales was older than that of England. A Department of Environment report showed that Clydeside had 90 per cent of the most concentrated areas of urban deprivation in the United Kingdom.[93] The situation of the rural communities and small farmers was another cause of discontent in both countries. There was a feeling of being forgotten and neglected. With Britain in a state of economic crisis under both Labour and Conservative governments, it was easy for the nationalists to preach political and economic sovereignty as the solution. They could claim their countries were being exploited by England and offer themselves as something new, yet traditional, parties of hope and nostalgia, radical but also respectable.

The two nationalist parties had been fighting since before the Second World War to achieve separation from England. In neither case could it be argued that this was not feasible on the grounds of either size or the state of their economies. Wales had a population of 2.7 million in 1976 and Scotland 5.2 million. Thus, Scotland was bigger in population than Denmark, Finland, Ireland, Israel and New Zealand (among many others), and Wales was bigger than Iceland, Jamaica, Malta or Singapore (among others). Economically, most of the growing oil industry was off the coast of Scotland. Wales 'exported' drinking-water on a massive scale to England. Scotland had a fair degree of autonomy through the Scottish Office which, set up in 1885, took over most Home Office functions and education. Since 1892 the Secretary for Scotland has had a seat in the Cabinet. In 1939 the Scottish Office was opened in Edinburgh, and had come to cover most aspects of government. Scotland had always maintained its own legal system. Under Wilson the Cabinet post of Secretary of State for Wales was created, with wide powers. In the case of both Scotland and Wales, there was more public expenditure per head than in England throughout the 1970s. More than in Scotland, language was an issue in Wales. A radio talk by Saunders Lewis, calling for a new public campaign on behalf of the Welsh language, was taken up in the early 1960s.[94] This led to the Welsh Language Act, 1967, steered by Cledwyn Hughes at the Welsh Office. After ignoring Welsh for years, BBC Wales devoted much of its output to programmes in the Welsh language. According to the census of 1971, only 1.3 per cent of the inhabitants of Wales spoke only Welsh, a further 20.8 per cent spoke Welsh and English.

What kind of policies were the nationalists advocating for their respective countries? Plaid Cymru wanted to set up a co-operative economy of 'living associations of free people' in contrast to Labour's state capitalism and Conservatism's private capitalism.[95] The SNP wanted an Industrial

Development Corporation to stimulate industry and Scottish participation in the oil companies rather than nationalization.[96] In foreign policy both parties opposed the EEC and took up a quasi-pacifist line on defence problems.

The Kilbrandon Commission on the Constitution which reported in 1973 advocated devolution in Scotland and Wales, but only devolution consistent with the preservation of the essential political and economic unity of the United Kingdom. Back in office, Labour, who had originally set up Kilbrandon, gave the people of Wales and Scotland the chance to vote on proposals to establish assemblies in the two countries. These referenda on 1 March 1979 produced an anti-devolution majority in Wales of four to one. As Callaghan put it, 'the valleys were deaf to the sound of our music'.[97] In Scotland there was only a narrow victory for devolution on a low poll. This was to have dramatic consequences. Under the legislation already passed, due to 34 Labour critics of devolution who voted against their own government,[98] devolution could only be implemented if 40 per cent of the total electorate voted in favour. As they had not done so, it was set aside. This eventually led to a vote of censure being tabled by the SNP. The government lost because one Labour MP was dying, and Gerry Fitt (SDLP), who usually supported the government, voted against, angry because he believed the proposed increase in the number of Northern Ireland constituencies would benefit the Ulster Unionists. The government was defeated by 311 votes to 310 – an election was inevitable.

ELECTION '79: CRADLED 'A CALF IN MY ARMS'

Despite their splits and divisions, the Conservatives had been preparing for the election for some time. Thatcher had put herself in the capable hands of Gordon Reece, a successful TV producer. He persuaded her to change her hair, clothes and voice, and taught her how to be more effective on TV. Saatchi & Saatchi were given the Conservatives' public relations account. The election was fought with sound-bites and photo opportunities rather than set political speeches. Reece planned the campaign 'down to the last and most trivial detail . . . most of her supposedly informal meetings with the voters were minutely stage-managed'.[99] The secret was to get television and press photographers to pseudo-events put on to produce nice images. One of these was Thatcher visiting a farm where, as she later admitted, she cradled 'a calf in my arms for the benefit of the cameras and, I hoped, the wider public'.[100] These techniques had been deployed in the US by the Republicans. Harvey Thomas, who had worked for the American evangelist Billy Graham, organized ticket-only rallies. All this cost a great deal of money, and the Conservatives spent £2.3 million compared with Labour's £1.6 million.[101] As for politics, the Conservative manifesto was a moderate document. Little was said, for instance, about denationalization. Thatcher turned down the chance to debate on television with Callaghan, who was regarded as being too experienced to make it worth the risk. Callaghan remained well ahead of Thatcher in the personal ratings of the two contenders. Labour stuck to more traditional styles of broadcasting. All three party leaders featured strongly in the party political broadcasts and were given presidential treatment by the media. Callaghan was given 60 per cent of the time devoted to Labour in BBC1 news bulletins. The percentages of their parties' viewing time for Thatcher and Steel were 63 and 69, respectively.[102] As usual, Labour suffered from press hostility, with only the *Daily Mirror* unequivocally for Labour. The *Sun* waged the most unbridled campaign against Labour, claiming, on 24 April, 'How Many Reds In Labour's Bed? – Power Of The Wild Men Will Grow If Uncle Jim Is Elected Again'. The same paper also featured articles by Labour defectors – Lord George-Brown, Sir Richard Marsh, Lord Chalfont and Reg Prentice – on why they supported the Conservatives.

The 1979 election was more free from extraneous events and sensations than any other contest since the war. It was the first to be fought in April for more than a century and was unusual in that election day was also the day (3 May) on which most of the local councils in England and Wales were elected. None of these factors appears to have had any bearing on the outcome – an effective majority for the Conservatives, and a very bruising defeat for Labour. Britain's first woman Prime Minister was elected with 339 seats (up 62 compared with October 1974). Labour won 269 (down 50) and the Liberals 11 (down 2). Of the small parties, the SNP lost 9 of its 11 seats and the Welsh Nationalists were left with 2 out of 3. Neither the National Front nor the Ecology Party (whose candidates stood mainly in southern Conservative-held constituencies) achieved even any near-misses.[103] With their 43.9 per cent vote, the Conservatives had a smaller percentage than their earlier post-war victories of 1951, 1955, 1959 and 1970. With 37 per cent Labour had taken a lower percentage than at any election since 1931. In crude terms, ignoring the difference in the numbers of candidates, the Liberal percentage (13.8) was their highest post-war total, except for the peaks of 1974. In Scotland, the SNP's 1974 high of 30.4 per cent fell to 17.3 per cent. It lost 7 seats to the Conservatives. In Wales, Plaid Cymru's percentage fell from 10.8 to 8.1 – its lowest share since 1966 – and its leader, Gwynfor Evans, lost his seat at Carmarthen.

Who had deserted Labour? Ivor Crewe was later to write:

> Labour lost through the desertion of its working-class supporters . . .
> as high as 16 per cent among younger working-class men . . . The main
> components of the anti-Labour swing were . . . straight conversion
> from Labour to Conservative, and movement to and from the Liberals
> (especially October 1974 Liberals reverting to their original Conservative loyalties).[104]

Professor Crewe believed that the divorce between Labour principles and working-class opinion had caused this situation. Some, especially the better paid, warmed to Conservative calls for tax cuts and action against welfare 'scroungers'. Some felt the Conservatives were right in calling for tougher action on law enforcement. Some saw Labour as being about working-class solidarity, drinking with your mates at the miners' welfare, shopping at the Co-op, being like everyone else and staying the same. Better education, the media, the exciting, if mythical, world of the advertisers and American soap opera, were all disturbing the old values and causing more and more working-class people to aspire to something else. By 1979 some felt that the Conservatives were more likely to offer chances to improve their lives.

NOTES

Unless otherwise indicated, the place of publication is London.

1 Barbara Castle, *Fighting all the Way* (1993), 453.
2 ibid.
3 Ruth Winstone (ed.)/Tony Benn, *The Benn Diaries* (introduced by Ruth Winstone) (1995), 287.
4 ibid., 289.
5 Castle, op. cit., 487.
6 David Butler, *British General Elections since 1945* (Oxford, 1995), 100.
7 ibid., 32.
8 David Butler and Dennis Kavanagh, *The British General Election of October 1974* (1975), 285.
9 Butler and Kavanagh, *October 1974*, op. cit., 278.
10 Collin Mellors, *The British MP* (Farnborough, 1978), 107.
11 Tina Hoffhaus, 'Wahlsysteme und Frauen Representation', in *Aus Politik und Zeitgeschichte* (3 November 1993).
12 Geoffrey Howe, *Conflict of Loyalty* (1994), 89.
13 Margaret Thatcher, *The Path to Power* (1995), 262.
14 Thatcher, op. cit., 277.
15 ibid., 280.
16 ibid., 277.
17 Winstone/Benn, op. cit., 309.
18 Howe, op. cit., 94.
19 *Observer*, 18 February 1979.
20 Winstone/Benn, op. cit., 309.
21 Thatcher, op. cit., 251.
22 ibid., 286.
23 ibid., 318–19.
24 *Sunday Times Magazine*, 1 October 1978, special feature on the women's movement.
25 Central Statistical Office, *Annual Abstract of Statistics 1977*.
26 Central Statistical Office, *Social Trends 9, 1979* (HMSO, 1978).
27 *Sunday Times Magazine*, 1 October 1978.

28 Susan Pedersen, 'Feminism', in F. M. Leventhal (ed.), *Twentieth-century Britain: An Encyclopedia* (New York, 1995), 285.
29 W. Kenneth Richmond, *Education in Britain since 1944* (1978), 110.
30 James Callaghan, *Time and Chance* (1987), 315.
31 ibid., 316.
32 Harold Wilson, *Final Term: The Labour Government 1974–1976* (1979), 105.
33 ibid., 106.
34 Roy Jenkins, *A Life at the Centre* (1991), 399.
35 *Keesing's Contemporary Archives, 1975*, 27137.
36 Callaghan, op. cit., 309.
37 Thatcher, op. cit., 335.
38 ibid., 334.
39 The referendum campaign is covered fully in David Butler and Uwe Kitzinger, *The 1975 Referendum* (1976).
40 Winstone/Benn, op. cit., 314.
41 Thatcher, op. cit., 331.
42 F. E. Jones, 'Our Manufacturing Industry – The Missing 100,000 million', *National Westminster Bank Quarterly Review* (May 1978).
43 *Management Today*, December 1978.
44 Conservative Political Centre, *The Engineering Profession: A National Investment* (July 1978), 7.
45 M. Yoshino, *Japan's Managerial System* (Cambridge, MA, 1968), 277; Graham Turner, *Business in Britain* (1969), 431.
46 'The English Sickness', *Fortune* (Chicago), May 1974.
47 Castle, op. cit., 487.
48 Callaghan, op. cit., 386.
49 Denis Healey, *The Time of My Life* (1990), 446.
50 ibid., 446.
51 Callaghan, op. cit., 394.
52 Winstone/Benn, op. cit., 347.
53 Peter Wright, *Spycatcher* (New York, 1987), tells of the campaign against Wilson, especially pp. 368–72.
54 Chapman Pincher, *Their Trade is Treachery* (1981), 209.
55 Callaghan, op. cit., 489.
56 David Owen, *Time to Declare* (1992), 299.
57 Winstone/Benn, op. cit., 240.
58 Susan Barnes, 'The Life and Soul of the Party', *Sunday Times Magazine*, 3 March 1974.
59 Winstone/Benn, op. cit., 347.
60 Callaghan, op. cit., 465–6.
61 Central Statistical Office, *Annual Abstract of Statistics, 1957* and *1976*.
62 Peter Evans, *The Police Revolution* (1974), 53.
63 Sir Robert Mark, *Policing a Perplexed Society* (1977), 80.
64 Barry Cox, *Civil Liberties in Britain* (1975), 185–6; he fully documents several important cases.
65 *Guardian*, 26 February 1976.
66 Cox, op. cit., 192.
67 *Police Act 1976*, Chapter 46, Part I, para 1 (2). For the police see also Roy Lewis, *A Force for the Future* (1976).
68 *Report of the Committee on Data Protection*, Cmnd 7341, December 1978, 451–2.
69 *Data Protection*, op. cit., see Chapter 4.

70 ibid., 220.
71 Quoted in *The Campaign Guide 1977*, 584.
72 *Guardian*, 21 February 1979.
73 *Department of Employment Gazette*, January 1979, 26.
74 *Report of the Committee of Inquiry on Industrial Democracy*, Cmnd 6706, January 1977, 57.
75 *Financial Times*, 28 October 1977.
76 John Grant, *Blood Brothers: The Division and Decline of Britain's Trade Unions* (1992), 89.
77 Winstone/Benn, op. cit., 447.
78 Healey, op. cit., 462.
79 Ian Gilmour, *Dancing with Dogma: Britain Under Thatcherism* (1993), 95.
80 Tom Forrester, 'The Bottom of the Heap', *New Society*, 18 January 1979.
81 Katharine Whitehorn, 'The Unfair Exchanges', *Observer*, 10 December 1978. See also Joe Irving, 'A Perk is as Good as a Pay Rise', *Sunday Times*, 5 March 1978.
82 Peter Lennon, 'The World's Richest Wedding Cake', *Sunday Times*, 8 October 1978.
83 Castle, op. cit., 506.
84 Healey, op. cit., 401.
85 ibid., 398.
86 ibid., 391.
87 ibid., 402.
88 *The Economist*, 3 February 1979.
89 A. H. Halsey, *Change in British Society* (Oxford, 1978), 30–1; Anthony Giddens, 'The Rich', *New Society*, 14 October 1975, using Inland Revenue statistics, thought the top 1 per cent owned nearer 30 per cent.
90 Tom Harrison, *Britain Revisted* (1961).
91 *Association of University Teachers Bulletin*, January 1977, 13. The material was from the Economist Intelligence Unit.
92 *Social Trends 9, 1979*, op. cit., 152.
93 Quoted in *The Campaign Guide 1977*, 550.
94 Kenneth O. Morgan, *The People's Peace: British History 1945–1990* (Oxford, 1992), 205.
95 Plaid Cymru, *Towards an Economic Democracy* (Cardiff, 1949).
96 James G. Kellas, *The Scottish Political System* (Cambridge, 1975), 132.
97 Callaghan, op. cit., 558.
98 ibid., 508.
99 Patrick Cosgrave, *Thatcher: The First Term* (1985), 63.
100 Thatcher, op. cit., 450.
101 Butler, *British Elections*, op. cit., 86.
102 David Butler and Dennis Kavanagh, *The British General Election of 1979* (1980), 209.
103 ibid., 419.
104 Ivor Crewe, 'The Labour Party and the Electorate', in Dennis Kavanagh (ed.), *The Politics of the Labour Party* (1982), 11.

9

THATCHER'S 'REVOLUTION', 1979–83

THATCHER'S CABINET: NO 'EXPERIENCE OF RUNNING A WHELK-STALL'

Thatcher's first Cabinet had 22 members, compared with 24 in the outgoing Labour Cabinet. She re-organized some of the ministries. Prices and Consumer Protection (set up in 1974) was merged with Trade. The minister in charge of transport lost Cabinet status and Social Security was to be represented by one Cabinet minister instead of two. Finally, the separate post of Paymaster-General was re-established and went to Angus Maude, a kind of pre-Thatcher Thatcherite. The key appointments were: Whitelaw (Home Secretary), Hailsham (Lord Chancellor), Carrington (Foreign and Commonwealth), Howe (Exchequer), Joseph (Industry), Pym (Defence), Prior (Employment), Gilmour (Lord Privy Seal with special responsibility for foreign affairs), Walker (Agriculture, Fisheries and Food), Heseltine (Environment), Patrick Jenkin (Social Services), Norman St John-Stevas (Leader of the Commons and Minister for the Arts), John Nott (Trade), Humphrey Atkins (Northern Ireland) and Mark Carlisle (Education).

Only three Cabinet members had not served under Heath, most had more experience of the corridors of power than Thatcher. She had inclined towards competitors and Heathites, making them prisoners of collective Cabinet responsibility, but she ensured that such individuals were kept away from financial and economic affairs. Howe was regarded as the 'chief mechanic' of monetarism.[1] John Biffen, Chief Secretary at the Treasury, a friend and disciple of Powell, was regarded by Thatcher as a guru.[2] Nott was a monetarist and David Howell (Energy) a convert.[3] Prior thought they were all theorists: none 'had any experience of running a whelk-stall, let alone a decent-sized company'.[4]

Paul Foot, the left-wing journalist, claimed Thatcher's Cabinet was the 'richest' since 1822.[5] Whatever the truth, they were a wealthy, well-heeled lot. Whitelaw, Carrington, Soames (Leader of the Lords), Prior, Pym and George Younger (Scottish Secretary) represented the traditional Tory gentry. Heseltine and Walker were the whiz-kids of business. Joseph had inherited his father's business, Bovis, while his colleague Atkins had married into wealth. Nicholas Edwards (Wales) and Nott had made their way as merchant bankers, while Howe and Jenkin were successful company lawyers. There were five old Etonians in the Cabinet compared with three in Heath's smaller Cabinet. In the 1924 Conservative Cabinet there were seven out of a total of 21.[6] The great majority in 1979 were Oxbridge educated, none had studied at a provincial university or London. The Conservative victory resulted in a reduction in the number of women MPs from 27 to 19 (11 Labour and 8 Conservative). This was the lowest number elected since 1951. Two women, Sally Oppenheim (Consumer Affairs) and Lady Young (Education and Science), joined the Thatcher government outside the Cabinet. One junior appointment with curiosity value was that of Reg Prentice as Minister of State for Social Security (Disabled). Prentice was the first politician since 1945 to have served in both Labour and Conservative governments.

THATCHERISM: 'MONEY . . . OPENS . . . ASTONISHING RANGE OF CHOICE'

The term 'Thatcherism', was probably invented by Professor Stuart Hall who referred to it in an article in *Marxism Today* (January 1979). Thatcher was not yet in office, but he took her ideas seriously. The term gained popular currency. No one had ever talked of Wilsonism, or Macmillanism. There had been Butskellism (see p. 70) denoting dedication to the mixed economy, indicative planning, the welfare state and consultation with the unions. It is true that in the late 1940s and 1950s the Conservatives had used the rhetoric of free enterprise, setting the people free and freedom of choice, but they had kept to Macmillan's 'middle way' until 1965. Heath had used this rhetoric more sharply, reinforced by the Selsdon Park conference on Conservative principles in 1970. But Conservatives argued that the U-turns of 1972-73 had led Heath away from New Conservatism and back to the old Keynesian consensus. In practice, Healey, who later claimed he was an 'eclectic pragmatist' more influenced by Karl Popper than by Keynes or Milton Friedman, introduced Britain to 'monetarism'.[7] Under pressure from the IMF in late 1976, he engaged in major public spending cuts in conformity with the monetarist analysis.[8] In other words, Keynesianism was already being overtaken before Thatcher took over.

It became fashionable in New Right circles in Britain to claim that Keynesianism was at the root of Britain's problems. Those countries such as West Germany and Japan, which had made a point of emphasizing free enterprise or capitalism, had done far better than Britain. Those states which had claimed to be socialist, the Soviet Union and its satellites, had done worse. The United States still proclaimed itself as the bastion of free enterprise, and although it had economic difficulties, it remained the world's leading economy. To many, all over the world, it still appeared as the land of unparalleled opportunity. However, this view ignored the massive, and growing, social problems in the USA. It also ignored the part played by the state in West Germany, Japan, France, Italy, Spain, the Republic of China (Taiwan) and South Korea – all 'economic miracles', all states with massive welfare programmes. The Thatcherites were simply following the American New Right as well as their own gut feelings. Since the 1960s the Republican Right in America had been on the offensive against what Richard Nixon (President, 1969–74) called, 'the professional welfarists, the urban planners, the day-carers, the social workers, the public housers'.[9]

In theory, by drastic pruning of the welfare programme taxes could be cut. This would in turn give people greater choice of how to use their own money and generate more prosperity because, it was assumed, individuals could spend more money more effectively than public agencies. The freed money in private hands could be used to support a variety of private welfare schemes and privatized services and still leave more money available to spend on consumer goods and services, thereby creating more jobs and less need for state 'handouts'. These ideas appealed especially to those who had started life in humble circumstances but who had subsequently found a place in the American Dream: individuals like Ronald Reagan, Nixon and Milton Friedman. Nixon and Reagan (US President, 1981–89) were practitioners; Friedman the guru. The son of Austro-Hungarian immigrants who became shopkeepers, Friedman 'weathered poverty, anti-Semitism, academic isolation and plain abuse *en route* to an extremely comfortable retirement'.[10] He won the Nobel Prize in 1976 for his work as an academic economist. He became popular with the economists who advised the military regimes in Chile and Argentina, with right-wing Israeli Prime Minister Menachem Begin and with Margaret Thatcher. With him is associated the term 'monetarism': the theory that it is the money supply alone which should determine the amount of spending in the economy. As already mentioned, Hayek was another important influence. He too received the Nobel Prize (1974) for Economics. Hayek preached that, 'It is money which in existing society opens an astonishing range of choice to the poor man, a range greater than that which not many generations ago was open to the wealthy.'[11] Among Hayek's followers in Britain was Anthony Fisher, who founded the Institute of Economic Affairs in 1956. The IEA gradually grew in importance as a think tank. It competed for influence with the Adam Smith Institute and Joseph's CPS (see p. 185).

BUDGET '79: 'AN ENORMOUS SHOCK'

Howe's first Budget in June 1979 pointed to the priorities of the new government with the shift from direct to indirect taxation and top priority given to reducing inflation rather than maintaining employment. Accordingly, the standard rate of income tax was reduced with greater relief at the top end of the scale. VAT went up from 8 or 12.5 per cent to a uniform 15 per cent. Up too went interest rates. A programme of cuts in public expenditure was announced. By November interest rates reached record levels and further spending cuts were announced, affecting all departments except the armed forces and the police. Incomes policy was dropped and, after initially allowing pay increases already in the pipeline, public sector pay was subjected to even more rigorous scrutiny than under Healey. According to Howe,[12] even Thatcher had been worried about the increase on VAT and had assented only when assured there would be no increase in excise duties on tobacco and alcohol. The Budget was bad news for pensioners. In future, state pension increases would be based not on 'the movement in prices and earnings, whichever is the greater', but solely on prices.[13] Pensioners were set to get poorer relative to those in work. Those in work became less numerous. The pound rose in the wake of North Sea oil revenue and the rise in interest rates which attracted foreigners to invest in sterling. This in turn made British goods more expensive to foreigners and led to declining export orders and rising unemployment. The high interest rates led to the same result. In 1978 unemployment had stood at 1.25 million or 5.4 per cent of the work-force. By October 1980 it had reached over 2 million, and in January 1982, 2.67 million. The Cabinet was not at one with this policy. Prior later claimed the first Budget was 'an enormous shock'.[14] He, and some others, felt they were being excluded from the 'Thatcher revolution'. The volatility of public opinion was soon revealed. In the election to the European Parliament in June, the Conservatives repeated their success on a very low poll. But Callaghan remained popular and the mood was already going against the government. The Gallup poll at the beginning of 1980 put Labour 9 points ahead of the Conservatives. This was confirmed at the Southend East by-election on 13 March 1980. A Conservative majority of 10,691 was reduced to 430. This represented a fall in the Conservative share from 56.1 per cent to 36.8 per cent, and a rise in the Labour vote from 29.1 to 35.6. Had the Conservative candidate not been the maverick, anti-EEC Teddy Taylor, the seat would have fallen.

THATCHER: 'JE NE L'AIME'

Although she had undertaken study visits abroad and had a certain reputation in right-wing circles, Thatcher was in no sense an expert on foreign affairs. As she looked around the world she could not have expected a warm welcome on the international stage. In Washington, Jimmy Carter, a Democrat, remained in office until the inauguration of Ronald Reagan, a Republican and Thatcher soulmate, in January 1981, There were lessons for Thatcher in Carter's fate. He had failed to get re-elected for a second term because of mismanagement of the economy and of the crisis of the US hostages in Iran. In Bonn the Social Democrat Helmut Schmidt, a formidable figure, held office until 1982, when he was replaced by the moderate, conservative, Christian Democrat, Helmut Kohl. France was presided over by Valéry Giscard d'Estaing who, though right-wing, was a friend of Schmidt. Giscard is reported to have said of Thatcher, *Je ne l'aime, ni comme homme, ni comme femme.*[15] He fell victim to his country's economic problems and was defeated at the polls in 1981 by Socialist François Mitterrand. In Canada, the Progressive Conservative Joe Clark took office in the same month as Thatcher. Only seven months later he was forced to resign after failing to get Parliament to agree to his austerity budget. Defeat at the subsequent election led to the formation of another Liberal government, once again headed by the sophisticated veteran, Pierre Trudeau. In Moscow another political long-distance runner was still at the helm. Leonid Brezhnev had seen Western leaders come and go since 1964; he had no intention of going and held on until his death in 1983. He was followed in quick succession by Yuri Andropov (who died in 1984) and Konstantin Chernenko (who died in March 1985). In 1985 the new man in the Kremlin was Mikhail Gorbachev, who appeared to get on well with Thatcher when he visited Britain just before becoming the Soviet Union's top politician.

The background against which these actors performed was a dangerous one. The Iranian Revolution of 1979, which eventually brought the Islamic fundamentalist Ayatollah Khomeini to power, brought greater instability in the Middle East. War broke out between Iran and neighbouring Iraq, and in December 1979 the Soviet Union invaded Afghanistan. The following year brought unrest in Poland leading to the setting up of the Solidarity (trade union) movement there, its subsequent banning and the imposition of military rule. In Communist China the elite fought for power and tried to rid themselves of the legacy of Mao. The USA wrestled with its conscience about what to do about revolution and counter-revolution in its client states, El Salvador and Nicaragua. The stage on which Thatcher made her debut was one on which the performers could receive bullets or bombs as well as bouquets. In March 1979 the IRA struck down one of Thatcher's closest associates, Airey Neave, in London. In August they killed Earl Mountbatten during a fishing trip off the coast of County Sligo (Ireland).They also assassinated Britain's Ambassador in The Hague, Sir Richard Sykes. In 1981 there were unsuccessful attempts on the lives of Reagan and Pope John Paul II. President Sadat of Egypt was less lucky. Bombs killed the Iranian head of state and the head of government in 1981 and the much-respected Indian Prime Minister, Indira Gandhi, fell victim to an assassin's bullet in 1984. Most of these outrages were committed in countries with a tradition of political violence, but the world did seem to be becoming a more violent place, with both government agencies – especially in Latin American countries and Libya – and rebel groups using murder, extortion and terror to achieve their political ends.

RHODESIA TO ZIMBABWE: 'THE LARGE GAMBLE'

The fall of the dictatorship in Portugal in 1974 was followed by the rapid decolonization of its empire in southern Africa This sudden change in the political geography of Africa greatly increased the pressures on the white settler regime in Rhodesia. A guerrilla war was fought with 'plenty of tragedy and sickening atrocity',[16] between the white Rhodesia Front and the Black rebels backed directly by Zambia, Tanzania, Mozambique and Cuba and, indirectly, by the other Black African states. The United States wanted a settlement because of the fear of Soviet influence growing in the region. By 1976 Smith had seen the writing on the wall and knew his only option was to negotiate the best surrender terms possible. He sought an 'internal settlement', enabling the whites to retain decisive influence long after formal power had been transferred to the Black majority. As part of this attempt, Bishop Abel Muzorewa was installed as Prime Minister in April 1979, 'with Smith firmly behind his right shoulder',[17] after one-man/one-vote elections. The attempt failed because of lack of recognition by the outside world. Hopes that Britain's new Conservative government would come to the rescue of Smith and his bishop proved unfounded. A significant minority of Conservatives would have recognized the Bishop. Thatcher, not at home with foreign affairs, though lacking sympathy with the leaders of Black Africa,[18] followed the lead of Carrington. She was forced to join most of the Commonwealth, including the Conservative government of Malcolm Fraser in Australia, Washington and the UN in giving Muzorewa the thumbs down. A conference was called at Lancaster House (London) where the Bishop and Smith faced Mugabe and Nkomo, the leaders of the Black parties Zanu and Zapu, united in the Patriotic Front. The conference, which nearly broke down several times, produced an agreement which temporarily returned Zimbabwe-Rhodesia (as it was now called) to the status of a British colony. Thatcher even took 'the large gamble'[19] of sending Lord Soames as governor, even though the war continued and no settlement was near. After tough negotiations a cease-fire was agreed and the guerrilla forces legalized. A Commonwealth peace-keeping force took over the policing of the cease-fire. Economic sanctions against the colony were dropped. A democratic constitution was accepted which gave the whites, who represented 3 per cent of the population, 20 per cent of the seats in parliament. After two months of electioneering Mugabe's Zanu won 57 seats in the 100-seat parliament. Mugabe formed a government which included Nkomo, whose party held 20 seats. On 17 April 1980 Rhodesia became the independent state of Zimbabwe.

In most quarters the settlement was given a euphoric reception. It brought to an end a war which had claimed over 20,000 lives, bringing together implacable enemies pledged to co-operation. It seemed to offer a model of sorts for South Africa. It gave the whites a chance to either learn to live with the Black majority or gradually withdraw, saving at least some of their assets. It boosted Britain's image in the Third World and, indeed, in the wider world. Finally, it restricted the growing Soviet influence in the area. Thatcher's prestige rose, though she later 'tended to sound displeased with her handiwork'.[20] Mugabe managed to stay in power later going against both his former white enemies and his former comrades-in-arms in Zapu. Muzorewa was jailed in 1982 and Nkomo sought refuge abroad in fear of his life. In its reports Amnesty International has criticized widespread detentions and use of torture as well as 'extrajudicial executions' (1984 Report). This does not mean that the Lancaster House settlement was worthless. In 1980 the British government had little room for manoeuvre. Britain was in no position to enforce a solution: it could only work with the parties concerned towards one.

THATCHER: 'LOATHED THE TRADE UNIONS'

Prior, Employment Secretary until September 1981, said Thatcher 'loathed the trade unions' (*Guardian,* 20 May 1985). Had she had a free hand, their activities would have been severely curtailed. There was widespread agreement among Conservatives (and beyond their ranks) that trade union reforms were necessary. Under the Employment Act, 1980 employers were given the right to take legal action against secondary picketing and most kinds of secondary action ('blacking, etc'.). All new closed shops had to be approved by four-fifths of those affected and public funds were made available to encourage unions to hold postal ballots. Tebbit's Employment Act, 1982 laid down that no closed shop should be enforceable unless it had been agreed by an overwhelming majority of the employees concerned in a secret ballot. It provided compensation from public funds to people dismissed from closed shops. It also made 'union labour only' requirements in contracts illegal. Trade unions became liable for damages if they were the cause of unlawful industrial actions. Finally, it gave employers legal redress against industrial action where the action was not wholly or mainly about employment matters (i.e., strikes which could be considered political). Tom King's Trade Union Act, 1984 aimed to give more power to what its authors thought were the moderate majority of trade union members. It required a secret ballot of members before strike action if a union wished to retain its immunity from civil action for damages. It also required secret ballots every 10 years by unions which maintained a political fund (part of which usually goes to the Labour Party). From 1 October 1985 all elections for union officials were to be 'fair, free, secret and direct'.

Naturally enough, many trade union activists saw the legislation as 'union bashing' and advocated ignoring it. They wanted to commit a future Labour government to its repeal. The trouble was that the majority of rank-and-file unionists (as polls indicated) favoured the legislation. And in a number of ballots between 1980 and 1983 trade unionists rejected strike calls by their leaders. The movement was split over the issue of taking government money to fund secret ballots. The electricians (EETPU) and the engineers (AUEW) supported the acceptance of such funding; the majority of the TUC did not. Political fund ballots which were held proved to be victories for the Labour Party. As in the United States and West Germany, union membership fell during this period. According to the *Employment Gazette* (January 1985), it had peaked at the end of 1979 to 13.3 million, but then dropped steadily, and by the end of 1983 had fallen by nearly 15 per cent, even though employment had fallen by only 8 per cent.

LABOUR: 'AN ANGRY CONFERENCE'

As was only to be expected, tension continued to build up in the Labour Party after its defeat in 1979. Callaghan's kindest critics thought he was guilty of bad judgement over the pay policy and the timing of the election; the harshest believed he had betrayed the movement. The truth was that no Labour government, from MacDonald's first minority government in 1924 onwards, had ever satisfied the socialist aspirations of many of its followers. In addition, every Labour administration had made errors of judgement over particular policies which further fuelled dissatisfaction in their own ranks. In the 1970s, Labour's zig-zag course on the EEC had been one of these; pay policy had been another. The myth that the annual conference decided issues made matters worse. Delegates passed resolutions only to find that their leaders in government ignored them. Wilson had been guilty of this over the EEC and defence after 1964. Labour conference in October 1979 was 'an angry conference', according to Benn,[21] tempered only by the need to show unity in face of the Conservative victory. Callaghan was given a standing ovation but the Left scored a number of significant victories. The conference had voted for the mandatory reselection of MPs by their constituency parties. It had vested control of the election manifesto in the National Executive Committee (elected by the conference). It had voted for a commission of inquiry into the party's finances and membership which would also make recommendations about a new way of electing the leader. The Left were well represented on this commission.

At its annual conference at Blackpool in 1980 Labour confirmed mandatory reselection, election of the leader by an electoral college drawn from all parts of the movement, opposition to nuclear arms and to the EEC. It refused the call to leave NATO and the demand that the NEC should have control over the manifesto. Callaghan then decided to bow out, to be replaced by Foot, who defeated Healey by 139 votes to 129 on the second ballot. The polls showed that the public had favoured Healey or Williams as Labour's leader.[22] Never a Marxist, Foot (67) appeared to have moved little intellectually since the 1950s. He remained committed to unilateral nuclear disarmament, withdrawal from the EEC and extensive development of public ownership. Healey was just the opposite. Foot was the last leader to be elected solely by the members of the PLP. A special conference at Wembley in January 1981 decided that the leader would be elected by a process in which the unions had 40 per cent of the votes, the PLP and the constituency parties 30 per cent each. This was a victory for Benn and the Rank and File Mobilizing Committee (RFMC). The RFMC was an umbrella organization uniting the Labour Co-ordinating Committee, the Militant Tendency, Institute for Workers' Control, and other groups. Despite the public's continued antipathy to Foot, Labour ended 1980 12.5 per cent ahead of the Conservatives.[23]

SDP: 'THE CHOICE . . . WILL BE DEEPLY PAINFUL'

All of these developments were just too much for leading ex-Cabinet ministers David Owen, William Rodgers and Shirley Williams. They decided they could no longer fight for their ideals within the Labour Party and that secession was their duty. The break came in stages. On 7 June 1980 they announced they would leave the party if it committed itself to withdrawal from the EEC. At the annual conference in the same year Williams and Tom Bradley refused to speak in favour of the NEC of which they were members. In November Owen announced he would not seek re-election to the shadow cabinet and Williams (who had lost her seat in the 1979 election) said she would not seek a Labour candidature unless party policies were changed. On 1 December Labour announced that the Social Democratic Alliance was a proscribed organization, membership of which was incompatible with that of the Labour Party. The three discussed future co-operation with the Liberals. At the Liberal Assembly in September 1980 David Steel urged them to leave Labour. Another factor in the situation was the return to Britain in January 1981 of Roy Jenkins, who had served since 1976 as President of the EEC in Brussels. It is true, as one of his political followers wrote, 'his image of grand statesmanship, high living and foreign friends threw doubt on his political future', but he was probably the most experienced British politician in 1981.[24] As President of the EEC he had been in a position of responsibility roughly equal to that of head of government and he had been Deputy Leader of Labour, Home Secretary, Chancellor and Minister of Aviation. In his Dimbleby Lecture on BBC TV in November 1979 he had questioned Britain's existing political arrangements and proposed a much stronger 'radical centre' which, he believed, would bring into politics 'many people of talent and good-will' who were alienated by the 'sterility and formalism of much of the political game'.[25] He was in touch with the Liberals and Labour Euro-dissidents and his associate, David Marquand, former Labour MP for Ashfield who worked with Jenkins in Brussels, made suitable noises at the Liberal Assembly in September 1980. Thus it was that the 'gang of three' became the 'gang of four', when Jenkins joined his former colleagues to issue the Limehouse Declaration on 25 January 1981, the day after Labour's Wembley conference. The Declaration claimed that 'A handful of trade union leaders can now dictate the choice of a future Prime Minister' and that Labour had moved 'steadily away from its roots in the people of this country and its commitment to parliamentary government'. Its authors wanted 'to create an open, classless and more equal society, one which rejects ugly prejudices based on sex, race or religion'. To this end they would set up a Council for Social Democracy to rally support. They wanted Britain to play a full part in the EEC, NATO, the UN and the Commonwealth. On the vital question of the economy they said:

> Our economy needs a healthy public sector and a healthy private sector without frequent frontier changes. We want to eliminate poverty and promote greater equality without stifling enterprise or imposing bureaucracy . . . We need the innovating strength of a competitive economy with a fair distribution of rewards. We favour competitive public enterprise, co-operative ventures and profit sharing.

They went on:

> We recognize that for those people who have given much of their lives to the Labour Party, the choice that lies ahead will be deeply painful. But we believe that the need for a re-alignment of British politics must now be faced.[26]

Interestingly, Owen, in his book *Face the Future*, published in 1981, had denounced Fabian paternalism and state socialism in favour of Robert Owen, William Morris and G. D. H. Cole (see p. 88 for Cole).[27]

It was a statement which could have been supported by the great majority in the previous Labour government and many Labour activists, and the majority of Labour voters. On 5 February the Council published an appeal for support in the *Guardian*. It carried 100 names in addition to the four. It included 13 former Labour MPs, among them Lord George-Brown, Kenneth Robinson, Edmund Dell and Lord Diamond, who had all served in recent Labour Cabinets. Several distinguished academics were listed headed by (Lord) Alan Bullock and Sir Fred Dainton (Chancellor of Sheffield University). The business world was represented by Lord Sainsbury and his son David. A touch of 'glamour' was added by Steve Race, the broadcaster, Sir Geraint Evans, the opera singer and Janet Suzman, the actress. Although Frank (later Lord) Chapple, leader of the electricians union (EEPTU), lent his support, he did not join the SDP.[28] In fact, a major weakness of the new party was its lack of major trade union figures. The advertisement produced nearly 8,000 replies,[29] two-thirds of them contained money.[30] On 26 March 1981 the Social Democratic Party (SDP) was launched in the Connaught Rooms, London, in the presence of 500 journalists.[31] Within days it had 14 MPs – 13 Labour and one Conservative, Christopher Brocklebank-Fowler. Within a matter of weeks it was claiming a membership of over 50,000.[32] As was only to be expected, the SDP was attacked from both Right and Left. Mrs Thatcher saw them as socialists. Their erstwhile comrades in the Labour Solidarity Campaign, the group of MPs set up by Roy Hattersley to fight the Left in the party, believed, 'Their lack of firm policies and their determination to be all things to all people ensures them the backing not only of misguided but genuine protesters, but also a ragbag of political misfits and outcasts.'[33] The SDP seemed to be taking off so successfully that even some Liberals were worried and resentful. This was understandable as opinion polls, even before the SDP was formally launched, gave it 23 and then 31 per cent support as against 13 and 13.5 for the Liberals. (In the second poll the Conservatives had 25.5 per cent and Labour 28.)[34]

The leaders of the SDP and the Liberals realized that they needed to co-operate if they were to succeed, and by the autumn of 1981 the conferences of the two parties agreed on an alliance. They then fought a serious of remarkable by-elections at which they grabbed three seats from the Conservatives. At Croydon (22 October 1981) the little-known Liberal, William Pitt, won. At Crosby (26 November 1981) Shirley Williams overturned a Conservative majority of 19,272, and at Hillhead, Glasgow (23 March 1982) Roy Jenkins won against the odds. However one views the SDP, it cannot be said that its founders chose an easy road or that their motives were crudely ambitious. Most of the MPs who joined the SDP had safe seats; had they kept quiet they could have held on. Had Owen, Rodgers and Williams remained with Labour, it is likely they would have been at least tolerated. Williams appeared likely to get another Labour seat. Only Jenkins appeared to be debarred from possible re-election as a Labour candidate. As rational, experienced politicians, they must have known that they were likely to fail. As David Marquand, the biographer of Ramsay MacDonald, could remind his colleagues, those who joined MacDonald's National Labour Party in 1931 became clients of the Conservatives before being eliminated from politics. And Sir Oswald Mosley's attempt to launch the New Party failed totally in the same period. The British two-party system punished severely those brave enough to challenge it. In Italy moderate socialists had broken with the Socialist Party in 1948 because of its pact with the Communists. They succeeded in establishing themselves as Social Democrats and gained a minor, but not insignificant, place in politics. They could only do so because the Italian system was based on proportional representation. The Alliance badly needed to change the British electoral system.

THATCHER: 'I TOO BECAME EXTREMELY ANGRY'

Howe's 1981 Budget was, according to the polls, the most unpopular since the war. Opposition to it mounted in the Cabinet as the fears grew that Thatcher and Howe were digging the party's grave. Matters came to a head at the Cabinet meeting on 23 July. The 'wets' wanted extra public spending rather than tax cuts. Tempers rose. As Thatcher later put it, 'I too became extremely angry.'[35] There was also strong disagreement on trade union reform, with Thatcher wanting tougher legislation than Prior. On 14 September Thatcher re-shuffled her Cabinet. Out went 'huffy' Gilmour and Carlisle 'who leaned to the left'. Joseph replaced Carlisle. A 'shocked' Prior was moved from Employment and exiled to Northern Ireland.[36] Norman Tebbit, a former official of the British Airline Pilots' Association and a 'true believer' of Thatcherism,[37] replaced him. Howell was moved from Energy to Transport and replaced by Nigel Lawson. One curiosity was that Janet Young, who had been leader of Oxford City Council, replaced 'angry' Soames as Leader of the Lords, the first woman to hold the post. Finally, out too went Peter Thorneycroft as Conservative Party Chairman. Cecil Parkinson, a dynamic accountant and excellent presenter, replaced him. The son of a railwayman, Parkinson, who went from local grammar school to Cambridge, had been a Labour Party member. Thatcher now had control of the Cabinet. 'The whole nature of the Cabinet changed as a result of these changes.'[38]

'WHY BRITAIN BURNS'

The cover story of the American magazine *Time* on 20 July 1981 was entitled 'Why Britain Burns'. From Liverpool it reported 'a convulsive release of pent-up hatred in a wild surge of rioting, burning and looting'. Manchester, it continued,

> sank into almost nightly rioting. In London, where the incendiary madness started the previous weekend with a race riot in . . . Southall, the sparks returned to alight in at least a dozen other neighbourhoods . . . The battles pitted racist 'skinheads' against ethnic Asians, have-nots against haves, and just about everybody against the police.

Similar events occurred in Birmingham, Ellesmere Port, Hull, Nottingham, Newcastle upon Tyne, Preston and other towns. The apparently spontaneous riots were a mighty follow-up to what had already taken place in Brixton and Bristol. They shocked foreign observers of Britain. The influential West German magazine, *Der Spiegel* (20 July 1981), thought, 'At the time of the marriage of Prince Charles and Lady Diana England is on the verge of civil war.' The riots highlighted the plight of youth, the inadequacies of the police, the problems of London and other inner city areas, and the difficulties of the immigrant communities.

The riots of 1981 were an important factor in the introduction of the Youth Training Scheme (YTS) in 1983, which replaced the old Youth Opportunities Programme. As a Conservative publication freely admitted in 1983, 'Only half Britain's school-leavers are trained compared with nine-tenths in Germany and four-fifths in France. Over a third of school-leavers entering jobs receive no training at all, and another fifth scarcely any at all.'[39] There was much criticism of the training given and the low pay, but it was better than nothing. In apparent contradiction to this policy, the government, in 1981, 'saved' money by abolishing 16 of the Industrial Training Boards, retaining only seven. Young people were also discouraged from staying at school after 16 by the fact that if they did this they could not claim social security payments, unlike those who stayed at home and did nothing. As the universities and polytechnics were suffering severe cuts under Joseph at Education, some young people felt it was pointless to try for public exams. By the 1980s the government had another major worry about young people – drugs.

After the Brixton riots Lord Scarman was appointed to inquire into the disturbances there. His report (25 November 1981) called for the recruitment of more police from the ethnic minorities, longer training for recruits with more emphasis on policing in a multiracial society and dismissal as the normal penalty for racially prejudiced behaviour (this last was rejected by Home Secretary Whitelaw). Scarman also recommended more foot patrols and an 'independent element in the investigation of complaints' against the police.

Since the early 1950s Brixton was regarded as an area of Black settlement and there were by then other parts of London associated with particular ethnic groups like the Jews and the Irish. By 1982 London was in danger of becoming a series of ghettos for Asians, Australasians, Blacks, Chinese, Cypriots, Irish, Jews, white British working class, middle class and, most recently, those from the Middle East or Hong Kong. The Japanese were starting to move into Finchley. Immigration from 'the New Commonwealth and Pakistan', which numbered 32,200 in 1973 and 37,000 in 1979, fell to 30,300 in 1982. Whether this was because Britain was not as attractive as it had been or because of the tightening up of immigration rules (announced on 14 November 1979) is not clear. The harder look at applicants was designed to reduce the numbers of those who married existing residents of the UK primarily to secure entry. The British Nationality Act, 1981 was also meant to clarify and restrict citizenship to those with close ties with the UK. Those seeking naturalization would have to meet a language standard, and foreigners marrying British citizens would have to wait three years before they could gain naturalization. The minorities felt the new restrictions discriminated against them. The Swann report, *Education For All* (1985), made a strong plea for reforms in the education system to encourage the Black community and concluded that 'ethnic minority teachers have been and are still subject to racial prejudice and discrimination, both in gaining employment and in advancing their careers'. It rejected the separate schools favoured by some Asian groups. Although worried about immigration, the government allowed entry to 10,000 Vietnamese refugees.

Horrific rioting broke out again in the Handsworth district of Birmingham and, a few weeks later, in Brixton in the summer of 1985. In the first case (mainly) Black rioters smashed, looted and destroyed Asian shops, killing two traders. In the second, (mainly) Black rioters took to the streets after the police had shot a Black mother by accident during a house raid. Similar incidents sparked off rioting in Peckham and Tottenham a few days later. Had the rioters been influenced by the scenes of violence from South Africa? By 1985 there were just over 1 million people of Asian origin in Britain, just under 1 million of West Indian origin and 53 million whites.

THE FALKLANDS: 'PICKING UP THE REMAINS . . . IN PLASTIC BAGS'

It is safe to say that many Britons had no idea where the Falklands were when they heard, on 2 April 1982, that Argentina was invading them. Nor did they know that the islands had long been the object of nationalistic fervour in Argentina, where they were known as the 'Malvinas'. Argentina claimed the islands on the ground that it had succeeded to rights claimed by Spain in the eighteenth century. The British title to the islands 'is derived from early settlement reinforced by formal claims . . . in the eighteenth century and completed by effective possession, occupation and administration for nearly 150 years'.[40] In 1982 virtually all the 1,800 inhabitants were of British ancestry and wanted to remain British. But, as Britain's power declined and its purse got smaller, it was prepared to consider 'decolonization'. From 1965 onwards it negotiated with Argentina over the dispute. There is no doubt that the long dispute was intensified by the military regime which had overthrown Argentina's elected President in 1976. In Britain the small, but very noisy, Falklands lobby, headed by Sir Bernard Braine, MP, worked hard to prevent any solution which diminished British sovereignty. It appears that in 1980 Nicholas Ridley, the minister dealing with the dispute, came near to finding a solution. This would have involved recognizing Argentine sovereignty but Argentina agreeing to continued British administration for a limited period. Strong vocal opposition in the Commons (2 December 1980) led to the Cabinet abandoning this idea.[41] This should have indicated to the Argentine rulers that any attempt to seize the islands would be risky. Perhaps other facts helped to mislead them. The British Antarctic Survey announced it was closing its research station on South Georgia. The Ministry of Defence made public its decision to withdraw the armed (Falklands patrol) ship *Endurance*, a move defended by Thatcher when questioned by Callaghan in the Commons.[42] The decision, under the 1981 Nationality Act, not to grant a right of abode in Britain to about 800 Falklanders who did not have a grandparent born in the UK could have led the Argentine government to believe Britain was not really serious about the fate of the islanders. The failure to implement the Shackleton Report (1977), which made proposals for the development of the islands' economy, seemed to indicate London's lack of commitment. Finally, perhaps Argentina misinterpreted Britain's action in giving up its last colony on the American mainland. Belize (formerly British Honduras), with its population of 147,000, became independent in September 1981. British troops did, however, remain because of fear of attack from neighbouring Guatemala which claimed the territory.

Relations between Britain and Argentina deteriorated as talks continued. Facing rapidly growing opposition at home (due to deflationist economic policies and repression), the military leaders led by President, General Leopoldo Galtieri, decided to seize the islands to unite their nation. On 1 April 1982 their Foreign Minister, Nicanor Costra Mendez, informed the British Ambassador that diplomatic channels were closed. The invasion took place the following day. Several Argentine soldiers were killed when the small detachments of British marines resisted. One British serviceman was severely wounded before the final, inevitable, surrender. The British troops, the governor, Rex Hunt, and any islanders who wished to go with them, were evacuated by the invaders.

What could Britain do in these circumstances? The Cabinet heard, from the Chiefs of Staff, that a military operation to retake the islands was 'more likely to fail than succeed'.[43] Thatcher had already appealed to President Reagan, who phoned the Argentine President to no avail. According to Thatcher, the US did not want to see the Galtieri regime fall.[44] Britain got the UN Security Council to adopt a resolution calling for the withdrawal of Argentine forces – even the Soviet Union did not vote against this! It received the support of the EEC, including an embargo on arms and military equipment to Argentina and a ban on imports from Argentina, and the backing too of the Commonwealth and NATO. And even though most Latin American states supported Argentina's claim on sovereignty, few supported its use of force. The Bank of England took action to freeze Argentine assets in Britain. The Argentine regime, which already had a bad image because of its abuse of human rights, faced diplomatic isolation and possibly crippling sanctions.

Had the Argentine junta not been so desperate and waited a few months longer, these measures might have been the limit of British retaliatory actions. Britain was planning, as the *Daily Telegraph* (18 May 1981) put it, 'To Gut The Navy'. Much of the surface fleet was to go, including the aircraft carriers *Invincible* and *Hermes*. The cuts were designed to save money and recognize that in future the Royal Navy's role was mainly the defence of the British Isles and its communications with Western Europe. It could do this, so argued Sir Ronald Mason, Chief Scientific Adviser to the Ministry, by abandoning surface vessels in favour of submarines. Opposition came from Navy Minister, Keith Speed, and senior naval staff. Speed was forced out of office; the sailors remained to fight from within. Unfortunately for Galtieri, these cuts had not been implemented by April 1982 and the First Sea Lord, Sir Henry Leach, saw the Falklands crisis as an opportunity to get the government to think again. In the absence of the Chief of Defence Staff, Sir Terence Lewin, Leach persuaded Thatcher (she needed little persuasion!), and through her the Cabinet, to send a task force to the South Atlantic. 'Certainly without his personal dynamism it is unlikely that the fleet would have sailed so soon, and as a result more cautious counsels might have gained wider currency.'[45]

On 5 April bands played, flags were waved, women wept and men tried to look cheerful at Portsmouth as the task force glided out to sea. On the same day, under the onslaught of the Conservative Right, Carrington and his junior ministers resigned.[46] Carrington had in fact tried to keep *Endurance* in the South Atlantic,[47] but was under attack for the apparent failure of his officials to spot the danger. He was replaced by Francis Pym (60), 'the quintessential old style Tory',[48] an old Etonian 'wet', who had the advantage, like Whitelaw, of having seen action in the Second World War. A former Chief Whip, he had served at Defence, 1979–81, and then as Leader of the House. He had the thankless task of seeking a peaceful settlement without appearing to be an appeaser. Thatcher set up, the Overseas and Defence Committee South Atlantic, known as the War Cabinet, a small committee of Thatcher, Pym, Nott (Defence), Whitelaw (Home Secretary), Parkinson (Duchy of Lancaster/Conservative Party Chairman). Sir Terence Lewin, Chief of Defence Staff, always attended. So did Michael Havers, the Attorney-General, as did senior Defence and Foreign Office staff.[49] The negotiations continued, with Pym more ready to compromise than his colleagues. Even President Reagan put pressure on Thatcher to compromise.[50] And the US Ambassador to the UN, Mrs Kirkpatrick, tilted in the Argentine direction.

The task force eventually comprised over 100 ships and 27,000 personnel. It included aircraft-carriers, destroyers, submarines, auxiliaries, landing craft and merchant vessels, including the luxury liner *Queen Elizabeth II*, used as a troop carrier. The mission would have been impossible had not the armada been able to use US-leased facilities on the British-owned Ascension Island, about mid-way across the South Atlantic. There the troops trained, the supplies were re-checked and re-loaded for combat, and the ancient Vulcan bombers and Nimrod reconnaissance planes found a base.

Meanwhile, the Argentine troops waited on the cold, bleak Falklands. As the diplomats went on talking, the military acted. On 25 April came the news that South Georgia had been recaptured. Remarkably, there were no British casualties. One Argentine sailor was wounded and one was killed by accident the following day. However, Admiral 'Sandy' Woodward, commander of the task force, knew the retaking of South Georgia was a near miracle. To take the main islands would need complete air and sea mastery. The British were operating 8,000 miles from home, the Argentines only 300 miles. For the first time since 1945, the Royal Navy was facing a modern fleet. Woodward knew the weather would take its toll of ships if they remained in those waters for long. The British needed swift action. These kinds of considerations led to the order to sink the cruiser *General Belgrano* on 2 May. The cruiser went down after being hit by torpedoes from the submarine *Conqueror*. Critics argued that it was wrong to attack it as the cruiser was 35 miles outside the Total Exclusion Zone around the Falklands which the British had announced. It was also argued that it escalated the conflict and lost Britain international support. Finally, it was claimed that the *Belgrano* was heading for its home base at the time. Such reasoning ignores the fact that the vessel provided aircraft direction for the Argentine air force and that it was equipped with modern missiles. Further, its removal was a major psychological blow to the Argentine navy, which then kept out of the conflict. Two days later a Type 42 destroyer, *Sheffield*, sank after being hit by an Exocet missile. Of the *Belgrano*'s crew 368 died; 21 men from the *Sheffield* met the same fate. Later the Type 42 *Coventry*, the Type 21s *Antelope* and *Ardent*, the landing ship *Sir Galahad* and the container ship *Atlantic Conveyor* joined the *Sheffield* at the bottom of the South Atlantic.

Operation Sutton, as the landings on the main islands were code-named, began on 21 May as Royal Marines and SAS troops stormed ashore and established a beachhead at San Carlos on the western end of East Falkland island. The mini-war effectively ended with the surrender of Port Stanley on 14 June to the British. In between these dates an assortment of crack British troops – Paratroopers, Marines, Royal Artillery, Scots and Welsh Guards – covered rough terrain in bad weather and forced the surrender of the numerically vastly superior Argentine forces. They had surprised the world, and the government which sent them. They could not know that their courage and daring would play its part in the re-election of the Prime Minister. Nor had they time to think that their actions speeded the fall of the Argentine junta, the members of which were subsequently put on trial. The recovery of the Falklands cost Britain 255 killed and 777 wounded, 'three times the British casualties during the EOKA campaign in Cyprus, one-third the number of British killed in Korea, and a hundred fewer than those killed in Ulster since 1969'.[51] Argentine casualties were far heavier. It is almost a miracle that British losses were so low: the dangers were enormous. This raises the whole question of whether the campaign was an appropriate response to the illegal Argentine occupation. Millions of people in Britain thought it was not; the great majority thought it was. Many people, including Thatcher,[52] felt a sense of excitement, pride and satisfaction at the exploits of 'our boys' on television every night in the carefully censored reports. It was like old movies about the Second World War – only better! Such people forgot, as one MP, a former soldier, put it, that war is 'about picking up the remains of comrades in plastic bags'.[53] It was a change from hearing about national decline, unemployment, cuts, the falling pound and more cuts. Some politicians, like Michael Foot and the Conservative MPs Sir Anthony Meyer and David Crouch, welcomed the sending of the task force, and then were appalled when the shooting started. Yet, once the task force was under way, it would have been irresponsible to leave it treading water in such an hostile environment. The Labour MP Andrew Faulds called the expedition 'absolute lunacy', and his opinion was not without foundation.[54] Benn and about 30 other Labour MPs agreed.[55] Firstly, there was the likelihood of appalling casualties, both military and civilian. No one could have known they would be so light. Without vital US intelligence, satellite communications and other help it could easily have gone the other way. There was a fear that Britain would lose its trade and influence in Latin America, and a fear too that the conflict could lead to increased Soviet/Cuban influence in the area. The expedition provided the Warsaw Pact with valuable information on how Western weaponry stood the test of actual combat. Some were afraid Britain's image among her friends would be dented, but any loss at the time of the *Belgrano* was probably made up later by the swift victory. Finally, there was, and remains, the massive financial cost of the undertaking, and the subsequent attempt to construct a 'Fortress Falklands'. Britain could have resettled the islanders on a lavish scale at a fraction of the cost. There was much talk of honour and dignity during the crisis, but the same politicians who used such terms had no problem in handing over millions of Hong Kong Chinese to Communist China.

ELECTION '83: 'LONGEST SUICIDE NOTE IN HISTORY'

In January 1982 the polls showed the Liberal/SDP Alliance ahead of the other two parties, with Labour second. By March Labour had a six-point lead. A month later the Conservatives had gained a three-point lead, which increased to 12.5 in May. With the defeat of Argentina in July the Conservatives stood at 46.5 per cent, 19 points ahead of Labour and 22.5 points ahead of the Alliance.[56] Clearly, the Falklands campaign had worked wonders for Thatcher.[57] Yet the Conservatives had their difficulties. Unemployment had reached 3 million in May 1983 as against 1.2 million when they took over. If the basis of calculation had remained the same, there would have been another 300,000 in the total.[58] For voters, unemployment remained the most important concern. Public spending was higher than under Labour.[59] The good news was that inflation had fallen dramatically.

When Britain went to the polls on 9 June 1983 the question was not who would win, but merely how big the Conservative majority would be. A secondary question was whether the Alliance would replace Labour as the main opposition. Cecil Parkinson took charge of the Conservative campaign, spending £3.8 million as against the £2.56 million spent by Labour.[60] Thatcher's itinerary was planned down to the last detail. In the middle of the campaign she attended a Western leaders summit in the US. No less than five industrial psychiatrists and behavioural psychologists were consulted about two sets of curtains – dark blue and light blue – for the newly decorated press conference room at (Conservative) Central Office. Once again[61] Parkinson modernized the computer system at Central Office with money from the Dunbar Club, a group of Asian businessmen who supported the Conservatives.[62] With this he developed direct mailing in a number of constituencies which needed strengthening.[63] Once again Saatchi & Saatchi went to work for the Conservatives. Labour helped greatly by presenting themselves as a party at war with themselves, led by an unworldly, ageing idealist. Its programme was called by Gerald Kaufman, 'the longest suicide note in history'.[64] It was too detailed in places, too woolly in others and threatened to disband Britain's nuclear forces unilaterally and take Britain out of the EEC. The Conservatives bought 1,000 copies to be sent to their major supporters lest they forgot what they faced if Labour won![65] According to Healey, 'our electoral campaign was worse organised than any I have known'.[66] The deputy leader also admitted making a bad slip in an attack on Thatcher, for which he later apologized.[67]

The electorate gave the Conservatives 1 per cent fewer votes than in 1979 on a lower turnout of 72.7 per cent (76 in 1979). Yet their majority increased from 43 to 144. The 42.4 per cent (43.9) gained by the Conservatives was lower than their percentage in 1970 (46.4) or in 1950, 1951, 1955, 1959 or 1964. Nevertheless, Labour had been savagely mauled. With 28 per cent, its share was the lowest since 1918. The Alliance felt cheated because, with only 2 per cent fewer votes than Labour, it had won just 23 seats compared with Labour's 209. Among the defeated candidates were Tony Benn, William Rodgers and Shirley Williams. Labour had lost support right across the board, but its losses were heaviest among the skilled working class, trade unionists and owner-occupiers. It was estimated that only 39 per cent of trade unionists voted Labour. Labour also failed to capture young voters; only 33 per cent voted Labour, compared with 42 per cent who voted Conservative. In geographical terms, the North–South divide had been strengthened, with Labour gaining only two seats in the South of England outside London. It looked like becoming a ghetto party of the inner cities and areas of high, long-term unemployment; a party of unskilled council-house tenants. Facing its first major test, the Alliance gained 26 per cent compared with the Liberals' 14 per cent in 1979. This was a great achievement. In southern England it had replaced Labour as the opposition to the Conservatives. It had taken two votes from Labour for every one it took from the Conservatives. But although the Alliance had picked up votes everywhere, it had failed in the old Labour strongholds and it had not done so well in North West Wales and parts of Scotland where the nationalist vote held. Having failed to make a major breakthrough, its problem was to consolidate the votes it had.

NOTES

Unless otherwise indicated, the place of publication is London.

1 Hugo Young, *One of Us: A Biography of Margaret Thatcher* (1991), 142.
2 Young, op. cit., 142.
3 ibid., 145.
4 ibid., 152.
5 *Daily Mirror*, 7 May 1980.
6 Zig Layton-Henry (ed.), *Conservative Party Politics* (1980), 191.
7 Denis Healey, *The Time of My Life* (1990), 383.
8 Young, op. cit., 154.
9 Richard Nixon, *The Memoirs of Richard Nixon* (1979), 424–5.
10 *Observer*, 17 February 1980.
11 Friedrich August von Hayek, *The Road to Serfdom* (1944), 67.
12 Geoffrey Howe, *Conflict of Loyalty* (1994), 130.
13 ibid., 135.
14 ibid., 136.
15 Anthony Sampson, *The Changing Anatomy of Britain* (1982), 52.
16 Lord Carrington, *Reflect on Things Past* (1988), 288.
17 Carrington, op. cit., 289.
18 Patrick Cosgrave, *Thatcher: The First Term* (1985), 76.
19 Young, op. cit., 181.
20 ibid.
21 Ruth Winstone (ed.)/Tony Benn, *The Benn Diaries* (introduced by Ruth Winstone) (1995), 482.
22 Robert J. Wybrow, *Britain Speaks Out, 1937–87: History as Seen through the Gallup Data* (1989), 123.
23 ibid., 123.
24 Sampson, op. cit., 102.
25 *Listener*, 29 November 1979.
26 David Owen, *Time to Declare* (1992), 481.
27 ibid., 483
28 ibid., 494.
29 ibid., 488.
30 ibid., 494.
31 *Daily Telegraph*, 27 March 1981.
32 *Guardian*, 22 May 1981.

33 *Daily Telegraph*, 27 March 1981.
34 Ian Bradley, *Breaking the Mould?* (1981), 95. See also Ivor Crewe and Anthony King, *SDP: The Birth, Life and Death of the Social Democratic Party* (1995).
35 Margaret Thatcher, *The Downing Street Years* (1993), 149.
36 Thatcher, op. cit., 151.
37 ibid., 152.
38 ibid.
39 *The Campaign Guide 1983*, 89.
40 Central Office of Information, *Britain and the Falklands Crisis: A Documentary Record* (1982), 2.
41 Max Hastings and Simon Jenkins, *The Battle for the Falklands* (1983), 56–7. See also comments of Howe, op. cit., 245. Also, Nigel West, *The Secret War for the Falklands: The SAS, MI6, and the War Whitehall Nearly Lost* (1997).
42 Young, op. cit.
43 Howe, op. cit., 245.
44 Thatcher, op. cit., 188.
45 Hastings and Jenkins, op. cit., 87.
46 Thatcher, op. cit., 185.
47 Young, op. cit., 265.
48 ibid., 187.
49 ibid., 188–9.
50 ibid., 220–1.
51 Hastings and Jenkins, op. cit., 357–8.
52 Thatcher, op. cit., 205, 212; Young, op. cit., 273.
53 Ex-Guardsman and MP Don Concannon in conversation with the author.
54 *Hansard* (*Commons*), vol. 24, col. 497, 24 May 1982.
55 Winstone/Benn, op. cit., 536.
56 Wybrow, op. cit., 127.
57 Young, op. cit., 297.
58 ibid., 316.
59 ibid., 318.
60 David Butler, *British General Elections since 1945* (Oxford, 1995), 86.
61 'The Medici of Madison Avenue', *Observer*, 24 March 1985.
62 Cecil Parkinson, *Right at the Centre* (1992), 215.
63 Parkinson, op. cit., 215.
64 Healey, op. cit., 500.
65 Parkinson, op. cit., 229.
66 Healey, op. cit., 501.
67 ibid., 502.

10

THATCHER: TRIUMPH AND FALL, 1983–90

GRENADA: GOVERNMENT 'HUMILIATED'

Having won her second term Thatcher lost no time in reshuffling her government. Howe moved to the Foreign Office and his place was taken by Nigel Lawson (51), who had served as Financial Secretary to the Treasury, 1979–81, and at Energy, 1981–3. Born in Hampstead into a family 'complete with nanny, cook and parlour maid',[1] he was the son of a tea merchant. He was educated, like his father, at Westminster School and Oxford. After national service in the navy he worked for the *Financial Times* and *Sunday Telegraph* before editing the weekly *Spectator*. Leon Brittan (44) got the Home Office, having served as Chief Secretary of the Treasury from 1981. Educated at Haberdashers' Aske's, Cambridge and Yale he had built up a lucrative libel practice. Like Lawson he was Jewish and like him was elected to the Commons in February 1974. Both were regarded as Thatcher's protégés. Michael Heseltine (50) moved from Environment to Defence. Educated at Shrewsbury and Oxford and elected in 1966, he had been the darling of many a Conservative conference. A successful, wealthy, businessman, he was regarded as a Thatcher rival. Of her critics, Pym was demoted to the back-benches and Prior was left brooding in Northern Ireland.

In the Labour camp a dismayed Foot took the responsibility for his party's defeat and resigned. The Cabinet had been told that 'if Healey had been the leader or if he were to replace Foot before a 1984 election it would be touch and go'.[2] But he too decided to step down as deputy leader, remaining only shadow foreign secretary. Although four candidates stood in the leadership contest, it soon became clear that the race was between Neil Kinnock on the Left and Roy Hattersley on the Right. A group of union leaders declared their support for Kinnock, who swept to victory on a majority of nearly 3–1 in Labour's newly established electoral college. This climaxed at the party's annual conference at Brighton, in October, where Roy Hattersley was elected deputy leader on the first ballot against a weak challenge from left-winger Eric Heffer, MP. Thrown out by the electors, Benn wrote in his diary, 'I understand how unemployed people lose their sense of self-worth.'[3] He had some consolation, however, since the conference elected him top of the executive constituency section. In other words, the activists still loved him!

Most ordinary voters knew little about Kinnock, and this was hardly surprising considering that he had not held office and had only been on the executive committee of Labour since 1978. From a Welsh mining family, he had studied at the University of Wales (Cardiff) and had been elected to the Commons in 1970. He had climbed a long way as a 'soft', non-Marxist Leftist supporting CND, opposing the EEC and calling for more public ownership. His personal charm and the backing of Foot had taken him the rest of the way to the top. He had the advantage of youth (41). In certain respects he resembled David Steel rather than David Owen, who was now elected (unopposed) to the leadership of the SDP in place of Roy Jenkins. The two new leaders were soon having an impact. By November, although Kinnock was still behind Thatcher, Steel and Owen, he was thought to be more in touch with the electorate than all his rivals, to be less extreme than Thatcher, to be behind only Steel on sincerity and to be behind only Thatcher on toughness.[4] Tebbit was not alone in thinking he was 'a windbag . . . [who] would pose the Prime Minister few problems'.[5]

Margaret Thatcher was robbed of some of the rejoicing at the Conservative Party conference at Blackpool in October 1983 by one of those silly little scandals which were increasingly afflicting British Conservative politics. As the *Daily Telegraph* (15 October) put it, 'Mr Cecil Parkinson resigned in disgrace from the Cabinet yesterday after his fight to remain Trade and Industry Secretary was undermined overnight when his jilted mistress issued an unexpected statement to "put the record straight" about their affair.' She revealed she was expecting his child. He had been on the verge of being appointed Foreign Secretary after the election.[6] Howe regarded him simply as a consummate executor of Thatcher's commands.[7] But even Thatcher could not save him. Parkinson's replacement at Trade and Industry was Norman Tebbit. The new Chairman was John Selwyn Gummer (43), a parson's son and Cambridge graduate who some thought offered 'presentational skills' and 'youthfulness'.[8]

Thatcher was soon brought down to size, not by the Opposition at home but by friends abroad. On 24 October massive US forces invaded the small Caribbean island republic, and British Commonwealth member, Grenada. The Marxist leader Maurice Bishop had been overthrown and killed by another self-styled Marxist faction. Reagan ordered in the US marines to restore order. Thatcher and Howe were 'dumbfounded . . . What . . . were we to make of a relationship, special or otherwise, in which a message requesting the benefit of our advice was so quickly succeeded by another which made it brutally clear that advice was being treated as of no consequence whatsoever?'[9] The key decision had been taken two and a half days before Reagan had contacted Thatcher.[10] Britain had argued against the operation. The government 'had been humiliated'.[11]

The second direct elections to the European Parliament, which took place in June 1984, indicated that Labour had made considerable headway under its new leader. A miserable turnout (32 per cent compared with 57 per cent in France and West Germany and 84 per cent in Italy) and the old, first-past-the-post system (Britain was the only country in the EEC using it) gave the Conservatives 46 seats (61 in 1979), Labour 33 (17) and the SNP (1). The percentage votes were: Conservatives 40.8, Labour 36.5 and Alliance 19.5. Conservative and Alliance support had weakened since the general election, but the Alliance rightly felt it was the victim of a system which penalized third parties. On the same day as the Euro-elections, Mike Hancock, a well-known local Social Democrat, took Portsmouth South from the Conservatives on a 14 per cent by-election swing. Although the Euro-elections did represent a setback, Thatcher need not have mourned too much, because she was already getting help from unexpected quarters.

SCARGILL: 'NORTHERN CLUBLAND HUMOUR AND POPULARIST SOCIALISM'

In 1981 the government had 'executed a smart U-turn and surrendered to the miners' over the projected closure of uneconomic pits.[12] The reason was that coal stocks were low and the miners were seen to back their moderate leader Joe Gormley.[13] After that 'humiliation'[14] the government built up coal stocks at vital power stations, converted power stations to dual oil/coal firing and built up police mobile units.[15] These measures were based on a 'plan' Nicholas Ridley had conceived in Opposition.[16] Nigel Lawson, as Energy Secretary to June 1983, developed a new mine in the Vale of Belvoir, for political reasons. It would help to persuade the moderate Nottinghamshire miners to go on working if a strike came. He also developed landing sites for helicopters at power stations so that vital chemicals could be flown in during a strike.[17] Ian MacGregor (70) was appointed in September 1983 to head the coal industry. A metallurgy graduate of Glasgow University who emigrated to America, he was 'widely seen as an overpaid, over-aged, ruthless American'[18] who had slashed jobs as chairman of British Steel. Behind MacGregor stood Peter Walker, the new Energy Secretary, and behind him stood Thatcher. She was in no mood to compromise, having just been confirmed in office by the electorate in June 1983. She faced not Gormley, but Arthur Scargill (45), who took over the National Union of Mineworkers (NUM) presidency on Gormley's retirement in April 1982. His Marxist militancy and oratory, which the *Observer* (6 December 1981) called a 'clever blend of northern clubland humour and populist Socialism', led to his election, in 1973, as Yorkshire area president of the NUM.

The massive increase in oil prices had helped coal in the 1970s, but the recession of the early 1980s had changed that. In any case, the old 'smoke-stack' industries were in decline. Less coal was needed. For example, steel, which in 1980 had consumed 7 million tons of coal, used only 4 million in 1983. The coal industry continued to shed labour. Since 1974 its manpower had fallen from 250,000 and 259 pits to 181,000 and 174 pits in March 1984.[19] MacGregor wanted a speeding up of the closure of uneconomic pits and major redundancies. Yet many miners were not looking for a strike. They had rejected strike action in three previous ballots.[20] In response to news of pit closures, the NUM imposed an overtime ban on 31 October 1983. The troubles in the coal fields were temporarily over-shadowed by a printers' strike between the National Graphical Association (NGA) and newspaper proprietor Eddy Shah. Shah won. The NGA paid heavily for breaking the new law restricting picketing.[21] This should have warned the NUM leadership of the changed climate.

The flashpoint for Britain's longest and bitterest major strike since 1926 was Cortonwood pit, Yorkshire. There the moderate NUM was told with-out warning the pit was to close within a month, on 6 April. The NUM had been assured the pit was good for five years. Only months before £1 million had been spent there and miners had been transferred from nearby Elsecar.[22] A similar fate awaited Polmaise pit in Scotland. The Yorkshire and Scots area committees approved strike action. This was then approved by the national executive of the NUM by 21 votes to 3. Strike action in other areas was given prior approval and 'flying pickets' were sent from militant areas to persuade workers not yet on strike to join in. These tactics were designed to bring off a national strike without a ballot. By 14 March 1984, 133 pits were idle.[23] When the national executive met on 12 April the Leicester area called for a national ballot to decide the issue. Scargill ruled this out of order. His colleagues agreed by 13 to 8 with 3 abstentions.[24] It was difficult to understand why Scargill had decided on a strike when winter was over and less coal would be required; coal stocks were high and cheap coal could easily be imported. By May, Benn, himself MP for the mining constituency of Chesterfield and an associate of Scargill, recorded, 'It looks as though the miners cannot beat the Government.'[25]

The strike then intensified, becoming more bitter. Violence crept in between strikers and working miners, and between strikers and the police, especially over a three-week period at Orgreave coking plant near Sheffield. Scargill was among the 273 arrested.[26] On 31 May Benn recorded, 'It looks like civil war.' The two sides came close to a settlement on 9 July, but in the end Scargill refused to compromise.[27] Even Mick McGathy, Communist and veteran Scottish NUM leader, would have regarded acceptance of Mac-Gregor's terms as a victory.[28] On 14 August the *Financial Times* reported that 73 per cent of the miners were still out. Of 181,000 only 48,000 were at work, compared with 40,000 at the start of the strike. Over half those working were in Nottinghamshire. The strike then dragged on led by the 'troika' – Scargill, McGahey and Peter Heathfield, new general secretary of the union.[29] It finally ended in March 1985 when the strikers marched to work with banners held high and bands playing, but without a settlement. Despite the bands there was the bitterness, neighbour against neighbour, brother against brother. Benn watched the return to work in Chesterfield: 'the level of hatred is frightening.' But he also had feelings of 'hope and dignity'.[30] Within a short time 20,000 men had decided to leave the pits.

Sir Ian Gilmour summed up the strike as follows:

> But for Scargill's Leninism and the violence, the NUM would have had a fully arguable case. The NCB clearly did have plans for massive closures, and not surprisingly many miners felt that they were struggling to defend a way of life. The strictly economic arguments were also mixed . . . the miners' strike was enormously costly to the country. And the long-term benefits of running down the coal industry are doubtful . . . in the not-so-distant future the policy of closing most of the country's mines may well seem shortsighted.[31]

For Lawson, 'The miners' strike was the central political event of the second Thatcher Administration.'[32] However, the strike 'reduced output, worsened the balance of payments, exacerbated unemployment, increased public expenditure and borrowing, and undermined the pound . . . the pound fell sharply on the foreign exchanges.'[33]

Richard Bailey, writing in the *National Westminster Bank Review* (August 1985), commented:

> The cost to the public in postponed tax cuts, and the loss of jobs in businesses dependent on the coal industry are impossible to quantify. The 115,000 miners who stayed out for the whole period each lost between £7,000 and £8,000 in wages, and their families piled up a grievous load of debt. The National Coal Board . . . lost between 40 to 50 valuable coal faces, as well as over £50 million worth of machinery and equipment. The miners' union ended the strike with their funds run down.

Benn felt the TUC had been 'pathetic', and the Labour hierarchy had been 'quite inadequate'.[34] But, as Healey pointed out, it was very difficult for Kinnock, himself a miner's son.[35] How could he support Scargill's use of undemocratic means, condoning violence and his 'tactical and strategic errors'? The polls showed that, unlike 1974, the public did not take the miners' side. Nevertheless, unemployment remained the main public concern. And eight out of ten felt the rich were getting richer and the poor were getting poorer. In October they felt Britain was divided into the 'haves' and the 'have-nots', with government policies favouring the 'haves'.[36] The strike led to the break-up of the NUM with the Union of Democratic Miners being set up in Nottinghamshire. No wonder Healey felt Scargill's strike was a 'Godsend' for Thatcher.[37]

MI5 'CONTROLS THE HIRING AND FIRING OF BBC STAFF'

As Britain moved towards 1984 it was only natural that people should measure the reality of society against the nightmare world of Orwell's Airstrip One. Had we escaped Big Brother or had he grown smarter, making his surveillance and control less obvious? Few really believed our world was that of Winston Smith, yet most would admit we had been naive in not realizing the extent of the state's control mechanisms.

In 1980 the Post Office Engineering Union claimed that the practice of phone-tapping went well beyond the categories of terrorism and crime detection, embracing political organizations and trade unions. The *New Statesman* (4 March 1982) claimed that MI5, which is responsible for intelligence and security within Britain, had linked its Mayfair-based computer with a growing number of other government computer data banks, giving it access to information on 20 million people. Its own files had details of 500,000 'subversives'. It seemed unlikely that the Data Protection Act, 1984 would give the individual greater privacy from public data users. Under the Act, data users have to register with an official registrar and individuals have access to information held on them. However, the exceptions, including data involving national security and certain aspects of criminal investigation, reduce the Act's impact. Cathy Massiter, who worked in MI5 for 14 years, claimed that during her years of service (1970–84), its emphasis shifted from being essentially a counter-espionage service aimed at hostile foreign powers to being a domestic surveillance body. It infiltrated agents into organizations such as CND and broke the law to gain information. This happened, she said, under both Labour and Conservative governments. One prominent person who claimed to be a victim of MI5 was Lord Bethell, the writer and Conservative MEP. He was smeared by MI5 and forced to resign as a junior minister. MI5, he claimed, had not checked information given about him. Many people were shocked when the *Observer* (18 August 1985) published a report saying that MI5 'secretly controls the hiring and firing of BBC staff'. The paper published a list of eight individuals whom it said had been blacklisted. The system had been in existence since 1937.

Some people believed the security service wasted so much time hunting the unorthodox that it missed the real targets. In 1979 Britain was shocked to hear that Sir Anthony Blunt, a former intelligence officer and more recently the Queen's art adviser, had been a Soviet agent. Worse still, it was alleged that the former head of MI5 between 1956 and 1965, the late

Sir Roger Hollis, also worked for the Soviet Union. In 1985 the service was criticized for failing to detect the problems of one of its members, Michael Bettaney, who was convicted of attempting to pass information to the Russians. Rumours persisted that over the years several MPs had worked for the Soviets, including double-agent Tom Driberg.[38]

In 1987 the government attempted to stop publication of Peter Wright's book *Spycatcher*. As we saw in Chapter 8 Wright, formerly a senior MI5 official, claimed there had been a plot to bring down Wilson. He also claimed he and his colleagues had 'bugged and burgled our way across London at the State's behest'.[39] In a judgement pronounced on 26 November 1991, the government was condemned by the European Court for breaching Article 10 of the European Convention on Human Rights. The Court did not condemn the government's original attempt to prevent potentially sensitive material from being published, but it did condemn its continued efforts after the book had become widely available abroad. This and similar cases led to the Security Service Act, 1989, an attempt by the government to allay fears about the activities of MI5. The Act established the post of Commissioner (an Appeal Court judge) to oversee the issue of warrants for telephone tapping and other forms of surveillance and a tribunal to investigate complaints. It did not cover MI6 or the Government Communications Headquarters (GCHQ). The government also introduced a new Official Secrets Act which became law in 1990. This reinforced the secrecy rule on civil servants. In future they would not be able to claim that they were leaking information in the public interest, as Clive Ponting had done during the Falklands campaign. At his trial the jury believed him. Heath was one of a number of Conservatives who joined Labour and the Liberals in attacking the new legislation. Heath pointed out that, when a backbencher, Churchill had received leaked information about the inadequacy of Britain's defences. He had used this to warn the country.[40]

In another move, trade unions were banned in 1984 at GCHQ in Cheltenham, which employed some 7,000 people. GCHQ intercepts diplomatic, military, commercial and private communications obtained by spy satellites and listening posts around the world. Those who refused to give up their trade union membership were sacked. This move was opposed by Labour and the Liberal Democrats and 'the case continued to reverberate for years before the European Court of Human Rights and with the International Labour Organization'.[41] According to Howe, but for Thatcher's 'absolutist instinct', a compromise could have been found. She could not 'appreciate, still less accommodate, somebody else's patriotism'.[42] The Conservative Foreign Minister, Sir Austen Chamberlain, in 1927 (only months after the general strike!) did not deny union membership to the recruits of the infant organization.[43] In 1996 under Major there was an attempt to introduce a new tame union to avoid censure by the International Labour Organization.

The police were becoming more the focus of complaints: that they suffered from corruption, harboured racial prejudice and sexism, bent the rules and used, on occasions, excessive force. Such accusations were made about the metropolitan police in a 1983 report drawn up for Sir David McNee, the head of the London police (1977–83), by the influential Policy Studies Institute. There were similar accusations about the Merseyside and Birmingham forces. The debate continued about whether crime was, with few exceptions, really more prevalent than in the past, since crime statistics depend so much on how much crime the public reports and whether police chiefs are interested in particular types of crime such as traffic offences, drugs or pornography at particular times. There was a strong campaign after the Conservative victory of 1983 to reintroduce capital punishment. The Commons rejected this, as it had in 1979 and 1982. As part of its contribution to the debate, the *Guardian* (4 July 1983) published the stories of six men, wrongly convicted of murder, who would have hanged had the death penalty been in force.

1985: 'GOVERNMENT BY SLOGAN'

With rising unemployment and plunging support in the polls, it was to be expected that there would be rumblings of discontent among the Conservatives. In this situation Thatcher decided on cosmetic surgery. In September 1985 the eighth reshuffle since 1979 was announced. Lord Young of Graffham was appointed to Employment. Former Health Minister, Kenneth Clarke, was appointed his deputy and spokesman in the Commons. Both had Cabinet rank. There was criticism that the head of such an important ministry as Employment was not in the Commons. Brittan was demoted and moved from the Home Office to Trade and Industry. Tebbit became Chancellor of the Duchy of Lancaster and Conservative Party Chairman. His predecessor, Gummer, was demoted to Agriculture, Fisheries and Food. Douglas Hurd moved from Northern Ireland to the Home Office with King replacing him. Finally, among the major changes, Kenneth Baker took over from Jenkin at Environment. Howe commented later, he saw Jenkin 'as one of a number of colleagues whose ability to shape the collective wisdom of the government had been diminished, and finally lost, by too frequent job changes and premature disposal'.[44] By this time Thatcher faced more opposition from within her own party than any other Conservative Prime Minister since Chamberlain in 1940. If she glanced behind her towards the back-benches she saw virtually a government in exile: Carlisle, Gilmour, Heath, Jenkin, Prentice, Prior, Pym, Rippon, St John-Stevas. They had all criticized certain aspects of government policy; some, like Heath, criticized almost everything. There was a great comment on Thatcher's alleged authoritarian style of government, the proposal to abolish the state earnings-related pension scheme (serps), the generous pay awards for top public servants in 1985, the privatization of the royal ordnance factories and naval dockyards, cuts in the diplomatic service and BBC external services, effective cuts in student grants and, above all, the failure to cut unemployment and 'rate capping', that is, penalizing local authorities which did not fall in with the government's line on expenditure cuts. Pym denounced what he called 'government by slogan' and in May 1985 set up his Centre Forward ginger group.[45] There were rumours of a 'Walker faction', and Walker was seen by many as a potential successor to Thatcher.[46] In fact, Walker, despite the 'futile bravado of his open disagreements' over policy,[47] remained in the Cabinet until 1990. From the Lords, 23 January 1985, Harold Macmillan (Earl of Stockton) attacked 'the monetarists . . . who have done infinite harm'. He also called for a national government.

On 9 January 1986 Heseltine picked up his papers and walked out of a meeting of the Cabinet. On 24 January Leon Brittan resigned from the Department of Trade and Industry (DTI). Heseltine wanted a European rescue for the British helicopter firm, Westland, which was in difficulties. Thatcher and Brittan favoured a link-up with the US company Sikorsky.[48] Thatcher prevented Heseltine bringing the matter to full Cabinet. He used the media to help his case for a European solution to Westland's problems. Thatcher retaliated. A letter from the Solicitor-General, Patrick Mayhew, to Heseltine, and damaging to him, was leaked to the Press Association by an official at the DTI.[49] Thatcher then attempted to gag Heseltine by insisting that in future all his statements on Westland be cleared by the Cabinet Office. This brought matters to a head and Heseltine made what was 'probably the most spectacular' resignation of the century.[50] Pressure from Conservative back-benchers forced Brittan to go.[51] Howe believed Brittan faced 'jealous critics, some with malodorous streaks of anti-Semitism, [who] were never too far away'.[52] The affair raised the issue of just how far civil servants should be forced to do the dirty work of their ministers, and just how far ministers were responsible for the actions of their civil servants. The Westland affair 'threatened the Government itself' and fuelled 'the flames of anti-Americanism'.[53] The company was sold to Sikorsky.

The largest proportion of parliamentary time between 1983 and 1987 was devoted to abolition of the Greater London Council (GLC) and other metropolitan authorities.[54] This was largely an attempt to undermine the power of Labour in local government rather than for any sensible or rational reasons. The Conservatives believed the only way to wrest London from Labour control was by abolishing the GLC altogether. They later sold the home of London democracy, County Hall, not to the London School of Economics, but to a Japanese business. Ken Livingstone, Labour leader of the GLC, was targeted as a hate figure.[55] Kenneth Baker performed this task.[56]

THE ANGLO-IRISH AGREEMENT: 'TREACHERY'

Just before 3 a.m. on Friday 12 October 1984 a bomb went off in the Grand Hotel, Brighton. The Cabinet narrowly escaped being wiped out by the IRA. There were five fatalities and dozens grievously injured.[57] TV viewers were shocked to see Norman Tebbit being carried strapped to a stretcher from the wrecked hotel. By then they had seen similar scenes before. At Christmas 1983 an IRA bomb killed six people and injured 100 others outside Harrods department store in London. There were other less dramatic incidents. The bombs underlined the need for Britain and Ireland to break the circle of violence. In yet another attempt to do so, Thatcher and the Irish Prime Minister, Dr Garret Fitzgerald, signed the Anglo-Irish Agreement in November 1985. Both governments recognized Ulster as part of the UK, so long as this was supported by the majority of those in the North. Under the Agreement an intergovernmental conference was established which would give the Irish government the right to comment on certain aspects of Northern Irish affairs. It also sought to improve cross-border co-operation, especially on security matters.

What most people saw as a positive move was strongly contested by Ulster Unionist MPs and certain Conservatives. Ian Gow, a Treasury minister, and Thatcher's 'most intimate and devoted supporter',[58] resigned over the issue after only weeks in office. In Ulster all the Unionist MPs resigned their seats because they saw the Agreement as the first step towards Irish unity. All but one of them were re-elected at by-elections on 23 January 1986. A one-day strike in Northern Ireland was organized as a show of force. Powell denounced the Agreement as 'treachery'. Howe argued that 'Two civilized peoples must be able to find ways of living peacefully together. If France and Germany can do it, then why not us?'[59]

PRIVATIZATION: 'SELLING OFF THE FAMILY SILVER'

Lord Diamond, the former Labour minister, speaking in the Lords (23 January 1985) attacked what he called 'using the proceeds of a most valuable national asset (oil), to meet current expenditure'. He then asked rhetorically, 'When will the Government cease . . . selling off the family silver to pay for the groceries?' This turn of phrase came to be associated not with Diamond, but with Lord Stockton, when he criticized the privatization programme on 9 November 1985.[60] By this he meant privatization of public assets by the Thatcher government. Originally, in the 1979 election, the Conservatives said little about this, and the main thrust on this front came after the 1983 victory. Earlier the government's holding in BP was sold, some British Rail assets were put on the market, as were British Aerospace, the National Freight Corporation, Cable & Wireless, Britoil and the radio-chemical centre, Amersham International. The first sales were seen as means of raising revenue and thus keeping down the PSBR.[61] These brought in £1.76 billion in Thatcher's first term.[62] This was a useful but not massive addition to the government's coffers. After the relative caution of the early years, privatization became a crusade and, as Gilmour put it, 'a diversion',[63] a diversion from the other economic failures. The various reasons behind privatization were, so Gilmour thought, improvement of the performances of the industries concerned; sorting out effective management structures caused by the difficult relations between government and nationalized industries; the destruction of the power of the unions; the raising of revenue through the sales; and the popularization of capitalism through wider share ownership.[64] The programme gained coherence and momentum (see table below) when Lawson became Chancellor. John Moore, Financial Secretary under Lawson, had 'day-to-day supervision'. He went about his task 'with missionary zeal'.[65]

The Conservatives argued that they were freeing the taxpayer from the burden of subsidizing the nationalized industries. Most of them were of course profitable businesses, otherwise there would have been far greater reluctance on the part of the public to invest. Gas and electricity competed against each other, and British Airways competed with other airlines. They suffered from having their initiative and commercial development held back by the Treasury. Some of their problems were due to being industries with long traditions (as with the railways, and the Post Office). This applied to

Table 10.1 Privatization in Britain, 1981–91

Date	Company	% of equity initially sold	Proceeds (£m)
Oct. 1981	Cable & Wireless	50	224
Feb. 1982	Amersham International	100	71
Nov. 1982	Britoil	51	549
Feb. 1983	Associated British Ports	51.5	22
June 1984	Enterprise Oil	100	392
July 1984	Jaguar	99	294
Nov. 1984	British Telecom	50.2	3,916
Dec. 1986	British Gas	97	5,434
Feb. 1987	British Airways	100	900
May 1987	Rolls-Royce	100	1,363
July 1987	British Airports Authority	100	1,281
Dec. 1988	British Steel	100	1,281
Dec. 1989	Regional Water Companies	100	5,110
Dec. 1990	Electricity Companies	100	5,092
Mar. 1991	National Power and PowerGen	60	2,230
May 1991	Scottish Power and Scottish Hydro Electric	100	2,880

other parts of British industry and not just the public sector. There is some limited evidence that, in the 1980s, productivity rose faster in the state-owned industries, such as British Rail, than in the privatized ones.[66] Although the privatized shares found a ready market, sold as they often were at great discounts, the public were by no means all convinced that privatization was a good thing. In late October 1983 a Gallup poll showed that 39 per cent favoured selling off British Telecom and 46 per cent were against it. Those in favour believed it would increase competition, lead to a better service and stabilize or reduce prices. The top four reasons given by opponents were that BT was a profit-making concern, that the service would deteriorate, that the profits should go to the public and that prices would rise.[67] In Scotland, in so many respects treated traditionally as a separate entity, where the bulk of the people had voted for parties opposing the privatization, they went ahead anyway.

Although not opposed to privatization as such, Gilmour summed up the actual development as follows:

> Nearly all the industries were sold off for much less than they were worth . . . The City of London . . . through various kinds of fees anyway made a killing . . . Thus the government was negligent guardian of public assets, failing to look after the interests of the collective public. Yet individual members of the public profited mightily from the government's lax generosity. The cut-price sales provided a considerable boost to the private wealth of those who subscribed to them. This was as good a way of bribing voters with their own money (and other people's) as has ever been invented.[68]

By 1992 the proportion of the population owning stocks and shares had risen from about 7 per cent in 1979 to 22 per cent.[69] The number of home-owners rose from 57.2 per cent in 1979 to 71 per cent.[70] These dramatic increases were due largely to privatization. Most shareholders had a few shares in privatized companies or in former building societies, like Abbey National, which had been converted to banks. The government also introduced tax-free savings schemes such as Tessas (Tax-exempt special savings accounts) and Peps (Personal equity plans) which appealed to the moderately prosperous. However, after 10 years of Peps only 1.8 million out of 45 million eligible adults were investors.[71] The likelihood was that the number of shareholders would decline, but that the number of home-owners would continue to increase. Moreover, the number of individuals as a percentage of all shareholders had dropped dramatically since the 1960s. As reported in *Social Trends 25* (1995), an analysis of the share registers of UK listed companies found that the proportion of total equity held by individuals at end-1993 was 18 per cent; this compares with 54 per cent in 1963. Privatization had not halted with this long-term trend.

Why should the number of shareholders decline? Most had been attracted by the massive advertising campaigns for the privatized utilities which were unlikely to be repeated by normal companies. Many sold their shares immediately and took their windfall profits. Many of those who held on hoping for long-term gains or out of loyalty to a regional firm or, in a very small number of cases, because they thought they would go along to the annual general meeting and voice their concerns, came to realize that they were regarded as a nuisance by the directors. Many were shocked to find they were forced to sell their shares when companies were taken over. When East Midlands Electricity PLC was sold to DR Investments (UK) PLC, an American group, in 1997, the small investor was forced to sell his shares. If he did not accept the offer from DR Investments, his shares could be compulsorily acquired under the Companies Act, 1985. The number of shareholders would inevitably fall as most would not invest in the new owner, DR Investments. Those who bought the maximum 100 shares in East Midlands Electricity when the company was privatized in 1990 received cheques for £650 for their shares in 1997, just about enough to buy two cheap out-of-season holidays. Of course they had made a small, temporary gain. But an asset, built up by themselves and previous generations, a part of which they as citizens had owned until privatization, had been alienated from them for a second time. Henceforth, a few foreign investors made the decisions about their electricity. 'We were conned into buying them, now we're bullied into selling them', remarked one West Bridgford (Nottingham) small shareholder, a voter in Kenneth Clarke's constituency. Mysteriously, on the very day the cheque arrived so did a letter from John Major warning of the dangers to the small investor from Labour! It was the same with the utilities up and down the land, which were being taken over by foreign companies. This was the reality of the Thatcher/Major share-owning democracy.

How would the new patterns of ownership influence the voters? Perhaps the council house tenants who bought their homes were, in many cases, drawn from the ranks of the pro-Conservatives. However, these new home-owners would be even less likely to vote Labour than before.[72] And Labour would have to be very careful how it dealt with this sensitive issue.

CONFUSION ON DEFENCE

As the 1987 election approached Labour was still not clear about its defence policy. Since 1979 there had been a resurgence of CND. This was partly because it was easier to support such a movement when Labour was in opposition than when it was in government. There had also been the example of a similar powerful movement in West Germany, and the intensification of the arms race after 1979 gave a boost to a movement which, although of the Left, united people from a wide variety of political backgrounds. CND wanted Britain to give up its own nuclear deterrent unilaterally and it opposed Cruise and Trident missiles. Basically, this was Labour's position too, as revealed in its policy document *Defence and Security of Britain* (August 1984). Labour would work within NATO to get it to agree on a policy of 'No first use' of nuclear weapons. It would also work to reduce defence spending towards the average level of our major European allies. At the 1987 election Labour promised to use money saved from abandoning nuclear weapons on modernizing the conventional armed forces, including the Royal Navy. Where did the Liberal–SDP Alliance stand on defence? Generally, the SDP supported NATO policies, including the aim of multilateral disarmament on the one hand and the deployment of Cruise missiles on the other. It wanted to retain Britain's nuclear force but rejected Trident, which represented a new step in the arms race. The Liberal leader, David Steel, found no difficulty with this approach, but the Liberal Assembly had adopted a more unilateralist stance on 20 September 1984.

Most polls showed that the majority of British people accepted that Britain needed to be in NATO. In a dangerous world it was too weak to defend itself alone. All the parties accepted this. Again the majority of the electorate believed some element of nuclear defence was necessary. Only CND wanted NATO to abandon its nuclear weapons unilaterally. There were great divisions over Britain's own nuclear weapons. Most Labour and Liberal Party members were prepared to abandon the British bomb. The Conservatives and most of the SDP wanted to retain it. The question was, in what form. The last Labour government had started the Chevaline modernization programme which was designed to keep Britain's Polaris fleet effective until the mid-1990s. But what then? Thatcher had decided to acquire the Trident II submarine-launched missile system from the United States to replace Polaris. The government argued that the cost would be only 3 per cent of the total defence budget and 6 per cent of the equipment budget. The four submarines and their nuclear warheads would be designed and built in Britain, bringing employment to British workers. Trident would be a powerful weapon which would give Britain some say in the nuclear future. Its critics said it tied Britain even more to American nuclear strategy, especially since the Trident missiles would be serviced not in Britain but in the USA. The government was on strong ground when it said that NATO's nuclear weapons had helped to prevent war – the invasion of Afghanistan and the Iran–Iraq war had happened because one side thought the other had no deterrent – but it was on much weaker ground in relation to Britain's own nuclear forces. Those who argued that Britain should have an independent nuclear capacity would have been more convincing had they looked to nuclear co-operation with France rather than the United States. France had built up and was maintaining an independent nuclear force. Perhaps this would become of critical importance for an independent European

Community defence strategy in the twenty-first century. This was something totally rejected by Thatcher. There was confusion about Cruise missiles. CND saw them as an intensification of the arms race, but if it was accepted that nuclear weapons were an essential part of defence, then they could be seen merely as a modernization of NATO's defence armoury. Defence policy had never been decided on purely rational grounds but was a product of historical fears, electoral strategies, vested interests and the shape of the economy. No British party before or after 1945 had conceived a well-thought-out strategy based on a ruthlessly realistic appraisal of Britain's future. Relative to what it earned, Britain continued to spend more than its allies (except the United States) and trade rivals on defence. This was one factor in its decline.

THATCHER'S HAT-TRICK

On 11 June 1987 Thatcher scored a historic victory by winning her third successive election. No other Prime Minister since Lord Liverpool in 1826 could claim such success.[73] After 1945 the Conservatives had won in 1951, 1955 and 1959, but under different leaders each time. Thatcher had carefully set the scene by a successful visit to Moscow, to show she was serious about peace, and a tax-cutting budget, which came in the week before polling. Labour had fought a good fight with a 'brilliant broadcast boosting Neil Kinnock'.[74] Labour scored on the NHS, but Conservatives had done well on taxation and defence. The Alliance had suffered marginally from having two equal leaders – Steel and Owen.

On closer inspection the Conservative victory was not as impressive as it seemed. On a turnout of 75.5 per cent, the Conservatives gained 42.2 per cent of the UK vote, Labour 30.8 per cent and the Alliance 22.6 per cent. Labour's result was its worst since 1923, in terms of percentage poll. Yet everywhere there was a swing to Labour, reaching a mere 1.1 per cent in London and the South and a maximum of 7.5 per cent in Wales. Everywhere there was a swing against the Alliance, held at 2 per cent in London and the South, but reaching a maximum of 5.3 in both Wales and Scotland. There was a swing to the Conservatives in London and the South (1.2) and the Midlands (0.9), and swings against them in the North (−1.8), Wales (−1.5) and Scotland (−4.4). The Conservatives suffered a net loss of 21 seats and Labour a net gain of 20, but the Conservatives actually gained seats from Labour in London and the Midlands. Their strength concentrated more and more in the South. The Alliance had a net loss of five seats (a net loss of 1 compared with 1983). Among their casualties was Roy Jenkins, who lost Hillhead (Glasgow) to Labour. Its vote fell by 3 per cent, the Conservative vote declined slightly from 42.4 to 42.2, while Labour's rose by 3.2 per cent.

Only 10 of the 72 MPs elected in Scotland were Conservatives, and only 8 of the 38 in Wales. The SNP and PC each made a net gain of one seat, giving them three seats each. The Afro-Caribbean and Asian communities saw four of their number elected, all as Labour MPs. Among them was Diane Abbott (Hackney North), the first ever Black woman to be elected. The highest ever number of women were elected to the Commons: 21 Labour, 18 Conservative and 2 Alliance.

Northern Ireland produced a slight shift to moderation. The two rival Protestant-based parties, Official Unionist Party (OUP) and Democratic Unionist Party (DUP) of Ian Paisley entered an electoral pact which secured for them 12 of the 17 seats. They lost one to the moderate, Catholic-based Social Democratic and Labour Party (SDLP), which won three seats in all (one in 1983, one by-election win in 1986). The SDLP ended Enoch Powell's 37 years in Parliament by taking Down South from him. The pro-IRA candidate retained for Sinn Fein the seat he won in 1983 in Catholic West Belfast. One independent Unionist retained his seat in Down North. Both the Unionist (54 to 49.5) and Sinn Fein's (13.4 to 11.4) percentage of the vote fell, while those of the SDLP (17.9 to 21.1) and the non-sectarian Alliance Party (8 to 10) increased. Turnout was down from 72.8 to 67 per cent.

David Butler summed up the results as revealing a divide between 'haves and have-nots, the rich and the poor. It was an election of social and political bifurcation, and the most polarized election in living memory.'[75] Many sections of society felt they had never had it so good and were prepared to thank Thatcher for that.

BBC: 'LACK OF BALANCE'?

Roy Jenkins, then Home Secretary under Labour, appointed the Annan Committee on broadcasting in 1974 and it reported in 1977. Unlike Pilkington, it was strong in its criticism of the BBC and was also concerned about the 'diminishing number of independent sources of news, comment and opinion'. Annan led to the launch of Channel 4 in 1982. Responsible to the IBA and financed by the ITV companies through advertising revenue, it tries to give attention to minority interests – ethnic, social, political and intellectual. By 1985 it had broken new ground with programmes of special interest to ethnic minorities, the gay community and other minorities. *Right to Reply* aimed to give viewers the opportunity to make their criticisms of programme-makers face-to-face on television. Channel 4 news was designed to provide in-depth news coverage.

Another development was the extension of the number of hours of broadcasting, with both BBC and ITV offering mainly news and chat from 6.50 a.m. and 6.15 a.m., respectively. In its first year 'Breakfast Television' had only limited impact. All channels started to broadcast until long after midnight.

The Independent Broadcasting Authority (IBA, to 1972 ITA) continued to appoint the programme companies, to supervise their programme arrangements, to control the advertising and to build, own and operate the transmitting stations for both ITV and independent local radio. From 1981 it was chaired by the ex-Labour politician Lord (George) Thomson. The IBA used its powers on occasion to promote regional and local interests by redividing the boundaries of the programme companies. These numbered 15 for television and 42 for local radio in 1985.

The BBC continued to invite criticism of its handling of controversial subjects. In 1981 the then Director-General, Sir Ian Trethowan, ordered severe cuts of a *Panorama* programme on the security services. In 1985 his successor, Alasdair Milne, agreed to withdraw a programme on Northern Ireland at the request of the Home Secretary. The BBC also aroused controversy over the security vetting of job applicants (see p. 239).

The BBC continued to be hated by a section of the Conservative Party who thought it was arrogant and biased.[76] Tebbit claimed, 'The BBC had a well-known record in committing libel and then trying to brazen it out.'[77] As a result of allegations in a *Panorama* programme it was forced to pay substantial damages to Conservative MPs Gerald Howarth and Neil Hamilton.[78] Tebbit accused it of 'failing standards' and 'lack of balance in the drama department and parts of current affairs'.[79] Howe and other members of the government were angered when, on 28 April 1988, Thames Television broadcast *Death on the Rock*, about the shooting of three IRA members in Gibraltar (see p. 262). The programme was broadcast *before* the inquest into their deaths, and suggested they were killed 'unlawfully'. The inquest in Gilbraltar decided otherwise.[80] These Conservatives intended to reduce the power of the BBC and break the power of the unions in independent television. Their weapons were changes in the leadership of the BBC, a financial squeeze and deregulation of TV and radio. Dependent on Parliament for the level of its licence fees, the BBC is more directly open to political pressure than are its rivals. Its board, like that of the IBA, is appointed by the Home Secretary. The Chairman from 1980 to 1983 was a Conservative landowner, Lord Howard. He was replaced by Stuart Young, also Conservative, an accountant whose brother, Lord Young, was in the Cabinet. The appointment of James Marmaduke Hussey as Chairman of the Board of Governors of the BBC in 1986 was seen as a step in the right direction. Other Board and personnel changes followed. Hussey demanded the resignation of Alasdair Milne, and an accountant, Michael Checkland, was appointed Director-General to steer the BBC in the direction of an even greater market orientation. The government restricted its revenue by not allowing its licence fee to keep pace with the rise in inflation. This was one of the policies spelt out in its White Paper, *Broadcasting in the '90s: Competition, Choice and Quality*. Other recommendations included in the new Broadcasting Act were the setting up of a new independent national TV service (Channel 5), three national commercial radio stations, and new local radio and TV channels. The IBA was abolished and it was required to auction its broadcasting licences to the highest commercial bidders. It was replaced by two new bodies, the Independent Television Commission and the Radio Authority, both of which had fewer regulatory powers and whose decisions could be challenged in the courts. Under earlier legislation, the Broadcasting Complaints Commission and the Broadcasting Standards Council were established. The first examines complaints of unjust or unfair treatment on TV or radio, the second sets and monitors standards of taste and decency. The existing TV networks were faced with increasing competition from satellite television, though this had progressed less than expected by the early 1990s. The two satellite companies – Sky and British Satellite Broadcasting – set up in 1986, were forced to merge after sustaining massive losses. Employment for television technicians was deliberately casualized by requiring both BBC and the ITV companies to commission a quarter of their programmes from independent programme-making companies.

Both the BBC and ITV claimed to have financial worries and made staff redundant. Commercial television suffered from increasing competition for advertising revenue from commercial radio and the growing number of free papers funded entirely by advertising. However, television claimed 30.7 per cent of all advertising revenue in 1984, compared with 22.6 per cent in 1970.[81]

Viewers' tastes were undoubtedly changing, but old favourites could not be dislodged. In the 1990s Granada's working-class soap opera, *Coronation Street*, still attracted a great number of viewers. The BBC's Cockney rival, *EastEnders*, was also high in the ratings. One new domestic product was *Brookside*, from Liverpool. Phil Redmond, who devised the Liverpool soap, explained in *Brookside: The Official Companion*: 'I wanted to tackle the relevant social issues. Things like long-term unemployment, women's position in society, the black economy, the micro-electronic technological revolution and its impact on both management and union structures within industry.' Later his programme explored many other issues which *Coronation Street* found too disturbing. These included lesbianism, drugs and incest.

The press remained dominated by four or five key proprietors – Rupert Murdoch, Robert Maxwell, 'Tiny' Rowland, Conrad Black and Lord Stevens. Four out of five of them were not natives of the British Isles. The Murdoch and Maxwell empires were in deep financial trouble by the 1990s, with Maxwell's finally collapsing. Most of the press remained firmly anti-Labour. An attempt to establish a new left-wing Sunday, the *Sunday Correspondent*, failed, though the more centrist new daily the *Independent*, founded in 1986, rapidly established itself as a quality paper with a circulation of 400,000 by 1989, roughly equivalent to those of the

Guardian and *The Times*. On its tenth birthday the *Independent* was in some difficulties. Concerned mounted in the 1980s and 1990s about intrusive, investigative journalism as the tabloids vied with each to expose the sexual lives of prominent people. The result was the Calcutt inquiry into Privacy and Related Matters. It resisted the calls to curb the press through legislation. Instead, it recommended the replacement of the Press Council by the Press Complaints Commission (PCC). Unlike its predecessor, the PCC is simply a complaints body and not a defender of the press. It commenced work on 1 January 1991.

Americanization of British TV continued with countless crime series such as *Starsky and Hutch, Cagney and Lacey*, and *Miami Vice*, and soap operas like *Dallas* and *Dynasty*. Soon there were new challengers from Australia such as *Neighbours* and *Home and Away*. It is remarkable how quickly the Australian products became popular.

'GREED IS GOOD'

The cinema continued its decline over the 1970s and the early 1980s despite the great success of particular films. According to *Social Trends 15* (1985) cinema admissions fell from 176 million in 1971 to 63.1 million in 1983. Between 1984 and 1989 cinema admissions rose annually. *Social Trends 25* (1995) found that in 1993 admissions climbed to 113 million. As always, most of the films shown were American, as were the two most popular films. In 1985 the Government withdrew all support for the film industry, including the Eady levy which had attracted inward investment for film production from Hollywood since 1951. Not surprisingly, by 1990 the production of feature films had fallen to its lowest level since the 1920s. It was only the puny privatized National Film Finance Corporation, renamed the British Screen Corporation, and the larger television companies, which financed new British productions. Support from Channel Four was crucial for the making of many British films. Film-makers had to consider the potential for exhibiting their products on television and as videos – an expanding market – as well as their traditional concern for the American market. Among the British films which made a great impact were a number which to a degree helped their audiences to understand Britain's colonial past and recent British society: Richard Attenborough's *Gandhi* (1982), Wilfrid Shingleton's *Heat and Dust* (1983) and David Lean's *A Passage to India* (1985) examined the Anglo-Indian relationship. Attenborough also scored with *Cry Freedom* (1987) about the anti-apartheid struggle in South Africa, which was highly relevant to black/white relations in Britain. Bernardo Bertolucci's UK/Italian *The Last Emperor* (1987) was a lavish look at twentieth-century Chinese history with Peter O'Toole and was noted for its visual splendour. *Dance With A Stranger* (1985), *Wish You Were Here* (1987) and *Scandal* (1989) took irreverent looks at the 'never had it so good' period. They all centred on women's experiences. In *The Krays* (1990) Peter Medak dealt with organized crime in London in that era. Perhaps film-makers felt unable to cope with contemporary themes and believed audiences preferred to escape into the past. A few did take up the challenge. *My Beautiful Laundrette* (1985), written by Hanif Kureshi and directed by Stephen Frears, said much about the experiences of the Asian immigrant community and about being gay in contemporary Britain. Richard Eyre's *Ploughman's Lunch* (1983) was a sceptical look at Thatcher's Britain during the Falklands conflict, while Ken Loach's *Hidden Agenda* was set in contemporary Ireland. His *Riff-Raff* (1991), a film about building workers, was voted the European film of the year in 1991. The films of David Puttnam achieved international recognition, and at least three of them – *Chariots of Fire* (1980), *Local Hero* (1982) and *Defence of the Realm* (1986) – were very relevant to the British experience. Class differences and the harmful effects of repressed feelings were the subject of the adaptations of E. M. Forster's *Room with a View* (1986) and *Howards End* (1992). Directed by James Ivory, they were set in Edwardian England. The same themes came into *Shadowlands* and *Remains of the Day*, both of which featured stunning performances by Anthony Hopkins, perhaps the most successful British screen actor of the decade. In 1996 *Trainspotting*, set in Edinburgh, touched a raw nerve with the very contemporary theme of the misery caused by drugs, while Kenneth Branagh's *Peter's Friends* focused on reactions to AIDS. Branagh was better known for his Shakespearean adaptations. Sanitized, storybook England proved popular in the form of adaptations of Jane Austen's *Pride and Prejudice* and *Persuasion*.

In post-Thatcher Britain film-makers fought on in their attempt to keep the industry alive with plenty of talent but little cash. Hollywood films accounted for 85 per cent of box office takings in the UK in the first half of the 1990s. Yet British film-makers won a third of all Oscars over the period 1976–96.[82]

The film which best summed up the age of Reagan and Thatcher came from Hollywood: Oliver Stone's *Wall Street*. Loosely based on happenings in the United States – corporate raiding, insider trading and the troubles of the airline business – it was a cautionary tale of a would-be yuppie. The handsome, ruthless, entrepreneur (Michael Douglas) sums up the enterprise culture of the 1980s when he tells a shareholders' meeting:

> Greed, for want of a better word, is good. Greed is right. Greed works. Greed clarifies, cuts through the essence of the evolutionary spirit, greed in all its form. Greed for life, for money, for love, knowledge has marked the upward surge of mankind.

It would not only save their company but 'that other malfunctioning corporation called the USA'. The film delivers the answer from the lips of the trade union leader (Martin Sheen) who tells his yuppie son (Charlie

Sheen), 'Stop going for the easy buck and produce something with your life. Create instead of living off the buying and selling of others.'

'BLACK MONDAY' 1987

How different the elections results would have been had Thatcher waited until Thursday 22 October! The Conservatives enjoyed a great deal of good luck after 1979. The Thatcher era coincided with the exploitation of North Sea oil and with low commodity prices which brought in turn low inflation. Technical innovations such as the auto-bank and credit cards gave many a feeling of being better off, even though many got deeper into debt. The period must also have seen the transfer of modest wealth, by inheritance from the first generation, who had experienced full employment for most of their working lives, to their children. Videos, microwave ovens, computers, radio-cassette-recorders and, to a lesser extent, mobile phones and satellite television all helped to create demand and give an air of excitement. Eight years of strongly rising share prices also helped. Without that rise very many would have been put off buying shares in the privatized undertakings. On 'Black Monday', 19 October 1987, things started to go wrong. Over £50 billion were wiped off the value of shares in London. By the end of the week values had fallen by nearly £102 billion.

The slump in share prices was world-wide and was prompted largely by the lack of confidence in the US economy with its large balance of trade and budget deficits. Prices had, in any case, risen unduly on a speculative wave based on the Reaganite mood of the 1980s. In the City of London sackings became common. In December 1988 Morgan Grenfell announced 450 redundancies in the City. In January 1989 the Chase Manhattan Bank announced that 135 of its staff were to go. The financial services sector entered a lean period which lasted beyond the Thatcher era. Big names got into trouble because of the slump and major scandals helped to make small investors wary about investing their savings in stocks, shares and unit trusts.

RUSHDIE: 'PRISONER IN HIS OWN COUNTRY'

In 1989 the publishing world was involved in a bitter dispute about the novel *The Satanic Verses* by Salman Rushdie. Published in 1988 it was acclaimed by critics and won the Whitbread Prize for fiction. Some Muslims, however, thought it blasphemous, and the Iranian leader Ayatollah Khomeini sentenced Rushdie to death. At issue was a small part of the book which treated the Qur'an and Islam in a satirical way. Rushdie later apologized to Muslims for causing offence but it did him little good and he became 'a prisoner in his own country'.[83] Muslims in Britain called upon the government to ban the book or change the law to make possible its banning. Many writers and intellectuals rallied to Rushdie's support. The issue brought to the surface the sense of injustice felt by many, often younger Muslims, in Britain. The affair caused Britain to delay the restoration of diplomatic relations with Iran. All the EC countries withdrew their ambassadors from Teheran. They were restored in 1990 after the death of Khomeini. In 1997 an Iranian foundation was offering £1.5 million to anyone who killed Rushdie.[84]

Although Britain avoided the open racial confrontation which defaced the streets of France, Germany, Switzerland and other states in the late 1980s, many immigrant groups felt threatened. Reports indicated that ethnic minorities were disadvantaged in many areas of national life. Although the Conservative Party, like the Labour Party and the Liberal Democrats, was adopting more parliamentary candidates from the immigrant communities, some Conservatives made remarks which did not endear them to British Blacks and Asians. This was certainly true of Tebbit, who, in his memoirs, wrote of illegal immigrants attracted by the prospects of easy living without work.[85] Britain, like the other Western European states, was faced with many applicants for political asylum. It was also faced with the new menace of gang warfare in south London, Manchester and elsewhere among the 'crack' dealers. There were signs too that the Chinese community was in danger of being infiltrated by the Mafia-like Triad gangs.

FOOTBALL HOOLIGANISM

Football as an entertainment activity provoked much discussion in the 1980s. Tragedy and violence marred the game. A fire at Bradford City Football Club on 11 May 1985 resulted in 55 deaths and many more seriously injured. Serious criticisms were made of the state of the stadium. On the same day violence stopped the game in Birmingham. Later in the same month (on 29 May) 38 Italian spectators were killed after a wall collapsed during violence at Heysel Stadium, Brussels, before the European Cup Final between Liverpool and Juventus. Subsequently, several British fans were convicted of manslaughter. The violence of English fans led to English teams being banned indefinitely from European competition. Shortly afterwards FIFA imposed a world-wide ban on English football teams. Thus was Britain's image as the home of gentlemanly sport badly shattered. On 12 June British fans were involved in a weekend of violence during the European soccer championships. Tragedy struck Liverpool again when on 15 April 1989 95 Liverpool fans were crushed to death at Hillsborough football ground in Sheffield. Later, North Yorkshire police were blamed for the disaster due to lack of proper crowd control. Questions were again raised about conditions at football stadia. In November 1989 North Yorkshire police agreed to pay over £50 million to relatives of the victims. There was a partial lifting of the ban in 1990/1 when two English clubs – Manchester United and Aston Villa – were re-admitted to Europe. Remarkably, Manchester United won the European Cup-winners' Cup. The ban was finally lifted in the 1991/2 season. It is only fair to mention that Germany, among other states, also had problems with football hooligans.

PRISON RIOTS/CONVICTIONS 'FLAWED'

In 1992 Britain had a higher proportion of its population in prison than any other of the 12 EU states except Portugal.[86] This was partly due to sentencing policy in Britain rather than higher crime rates. This was not new. Who were the prisoners? What had they done? Males were more than 20 times as likely to go to prison under sentence than females. Amongst males the highest rate was the 17–20-year-olds. In England and Wales, 22 per cent of male prisoners in 1993 had been convicted of violence against the person, 14 per cent of robbery, 14 per cent burglary, followed by 11 per cent for drug offences and 8 per cent for theft and handling. Those convicted of rape made up 5 per cent and other sexual offences another 5 per cent. This pattern varies according to ethnic origin with over a fifth of non-white sentenced offenders having been convicted of drug offences.[87]

It was well known that British prison conditions were below par for decades. Many of the inmates held in 160 prisons lived in appalling conditions. Sooner or later serious trouble was expected. In one of a series of incidents, on 5 January 1987, prisoners took over Barlinnie Gaol, taking three prison officers hostage. Then, on 1 June, 26 prisoners staged a mass breakout from Haverigg Prison. All but three were soon recaptured. In Scotland at Longriggend Prison 56 prisoners staged a rooftop protest on 19 July 1988. Early in May 1989 there were three days of rioting at Risley Remand Centre. Its closure was announced in July after an inquiry. On 1 April 1990 prisoners took over part of Strangeways Prison, Manchester, and held it for three and a half weeks. This was the longest siege in British prison history. In August 1991 there were riots at the newly opened showpiece Moorland Gaol near Doncaster, and at Lindholme Prison in South Yorkshire. After the Strangeways siege Lord Justice Woolf was asked by Home Secretary Kenneth Baker to investigate conditions. Baker promised better sanitary conditions and less overcrowding. He also introduced a new (serious) offence of prison mutiny and new security measures. There was also an unacceptably large number of suicides in Britain's prisons, mainly among young male inmates.

Even though Britain had more policemen and women than ever before it faced a tide of rising crime. Perhaps due to media reporting of more spectacular or outrageous crimes, there was widespread misapprehension about crime. While young men had a 1 in 83 risk of being assaulted in a year, only 1 in 50 felt very unsafe. Yet 1 in 3 older women felt very unsafe, with an annual risk of assault of only 1 in 4,000. According to police figures, in 1997, nearly 94 per cent of crime was non-violent. The police claimed that, since 1981, 999 calls were up 136 per cent, reported crime was up 73 per cent, detections had risen by 20 per cent but staffing levels by only 11 per cent.[88] However, crime had certainly broken out of the ghettos and had spread to the leafy suburbs. Firearms were being used more frequently, often in gang wars connected with drug dealing. Britain was horrified by the killing of 16 primary school children and their teacher at Dunblane, Scotland, on 13 March 1997. A deranged gunman entered their school and fired indiscriminately before killing himself. A similar incident had occurred in Hungerford in August 1987. Firearms regulations were strengthened as a result. By 1997, the police were concerned that heroin, once the scourge of inner-city council estates, was being used increasingly by middle-class children as well. According to the Standing Conference on Drug Abuse, there were reports of London, Merseyside, the South West and the North East being flooded with heroin, most of it coming from Afghanistan, Turkey and Iran.[89]

The public were alarmed by rising crime, and politicians took up tough postures to reassure them. However, there was also unease about the number of wrong or unsafe convictions. On 23 June 1988 the Commons again rejected capital punishment. On the same day the West Midlands Serious Crimes Squad was to be disbanded after allegations of fabricated confessions. On 19 October 1989 the 'Guildford Four' were released from jail after their sentences for their alleged part in the Guildford pub bombings of 1974 were quashed. The 'Birmingham Six' had their convictions set aside after they had been in prison over 16 years for their alleged part in the Birmingham pub bombing of 21 November 1974. The IRA had claimed responsibility for this crime which caused the death of 21 people. The Home Secretary, Kenneth Baker, immediately announced a Royal Commission to investigate the entire criminal justice system in England and Wales. The Birmingham Six had been convicted after investigations carried out by detectives of the West Midlands Serious Crimes Squad. In December 1991 the 'Broadwater Farm Three' had their convictions for the killing of a policeman in 1986 quashed. It is convenient to mention here three other cases. On 9 October 1996, Colin Wallace was cleared of manslaughter after a 16-year struggle and more than six years in prison. In 1990 he had received compensation after an inquiry into his dismissal by the Ministry of Defence. He claimed he had been a victim of persecution because of his threat to expose British intelligence tactics in Northern Ireland, including blackmail of prominent Ulster homosexuals.[90] The 'Bridgwater Three', who had been convicted of murder, were released on 22 February 1997 after 18 years in prison, after the Crown admitted their original conviction was 'flawed'. Knitwear entrepreneur, Shafqat Rasool, was jailed for 10 years in March 1996 for plotting to supply heroin, but his conviction was quashed in February 1997. In prison he was refused permission to visit his son, who was dying of leukaemia in a local hospital.[91] These are some of the many cases, most of which did not receive the same publicity. The importance given to confessions as evidence and the pressure on the police to get results were thought to be key elements in these and similar cases.

EDUCATIONAL REFORM: 'LECTURERS' PAY . . . BUYS LESS'

The government pushed ahead with reforms in education and health. They were presented as extending the enterprise culture, giving more choice to consumers, making these services more attuned to modern needs, promoting excellence and, above all, making them more cost-effective. In fact, they were largely a strategy for reducing the cost of increasingly expensive services in a society with an ageing population and a declining economy.

Under the Education Reform Act, 1988 schools were forced to introduce a National Curriculum which included certain core subjects such as maths and English. Few objected to this as it was normal in other European countries and had been under discussion when Callaghan was Prime Minister. Thatcher fell out with her Education Minister, Kenneth Baker, over history. She thought there 'was insufficient weight given to British history'. She also wanted facts taught in a chronological way.[92] Far more testing of children was also on the agenda to ensure that acceptable standards were attained. The two separate exams, GCE 'O' level and CSE, were merged into the new General Certificate of Secondary Education (GCSE), which covered a much wider range of achievement and was less narrowly academic. More controversial was legislation which allowed schools to opt out of local authority control after a vote by parents. There was fear that some of the best schools would do this, leaving only poorer schools in poorer areas under local authority control. The opt-out schools were maintained by a direct grant from the ministry. On 2 November 1988 Skegness Grammar School became the first school to vote to opt out. Local authorities were also required to produce 'league tables' of school exam results. Critics felt this was unfair to schools, especially in inner-city areas, which had special problems in employing and retaining good teachers, and where many children were not academically motivated. In a move which its supporters claimed was trying to help just such children, the creation of 20 city technology colleges was announced in October 1986. These were to be mixed-ability colleges with an emphasis on modern technological skills. They were to be a partnership between local industry and the government, taking pupils exclusively from the inner-city area within which each was located. Critics thought they would be merely taking resources away from existing schools. The government also put money into providing funds for pupils to transfer from local authority schools to the private sector. On 22 July 1986 the

Commons voted by a majority of one to ban corporal punishment in schools. This brought Britain into line with other EC states.

The same trend towards introducing 'market principles' was present in the government's policy towards higher education, which saw a massive increase in student numbers in the late 1980s and early 1990s. The government wanted universities to compete against each other to 'bid' for public money. Within universities, departments and even courses would compete with other for resources. In future their budgets would be determined partly by the amount of research they conducted. They would be expected to get more money from student fees and the research councils, and less from the University Funding Committee (UFC), which replaced the University Grants Committee (UGC) in 1989. Universities had always welcomed overseas students, but now it became imperative to recruit from outside the EU as these visiting students had to pay full fees. Sponsorship by private business and wealthy individuals became more important. The emphasis was on educating more students more cheaply, and preferably in 'relevant' subjects like business studies. Because there was a belief that the polytechnics did this, more importance was given to them. Under the Further and Higher Education Act, 1992 they were released from local authority control and became free to call themselves universities – which they all decided to do. The UFC and the Polytechnics and Colleges Funding Council were merged in 1993 into a single body, the Higher Education Funding Council for England. A mixture of sensible and dubious reforms were being introduced and, as usual, without proper regard to finance. Over 10 years' funding per student was cut by 30 per cent and student–staff ratios declined. In 1987 there were 10 students to every staff member, by 1996 there were 16.5.[93]

The government gave university staff little encouragement. As the *Financial Times* (25 January 1990) commented, 'Since 1979, lecturers' pay has fallen more than 20 per cent relative to average earnings . . . Indeed, lecturers are one of the few groups whose pay actually buys less in terms of goods and services than it did in 1979.' Other changes which were the product of government policies were the abolition of tenure for the new generation of lecturers (or those existing lecturers who were promoted or moved to other universities), the growing number of those on temporary contracts, and the introduction of early retirement and redundancy schemes.

The Education (Student Loans) Act, 1990 provided for 'top-up' loans for students in higher education as an alternative to raising the grants of students in line with inflation. The grant element was to be frozen, with students becoming increasingly dependent on loans, casual work, sponsorship and, perhaps above all, their parents. ('Casual work' did, in a few cases, include striptease and prostitution.) Most of those in higher education, including the students, opposed this development, as did Labour. The greatest fear was that loans would put off potential students from poorer backgrounds.

In the past Britain had prided itself on having a *relatively* large number of students from working-class and other non-academic families.

Great concern continued to be voiced about the relative ignorance of British youth compared with the youth of neighbouring countries. Too few young people in Britain had adequate education in maths, science or a foreign language. Too few continued their education after 16. Too few received training once they entered employment. A report published by the Council for Industry and Higher Education (November 1991) revealed that the British work-force was significantly underqualified compared with those of Germany and France. In a 'league table' of 15 Western industrial states, ranked in order of number of 18-year-olds in full-time education, Britain came fourteenth. In terms of graduates per 1,000 in any one age group, Britain was behind France, West Germany, Japan and the USA in the number of engineering and technology graduates it produced, but ahead of both Germany and Japan in science, maths and computer graduates. Overall, Britain produced fewer graduates than each of these four states.[94] In the winter of 1991/2 there were a number of student sit-ins at universities and polytechnics to protest against the underfunding of higher education. In 1996, for the first time, university staff staged a one-day strike. Meanwhile, Sir Ron Dearing, former head of the Post Office and Chancellor of Nottingham University, was charged with inquiring into the future of higher education.

NHS: 'TERMINALLY ILL'?

Putting money into the National Health Service (NHS) was more important to most people than anything else. Politicians had to promise to protect it. 'Full-scale privatization was electorally impracticable; a sort of ersatz privatization was not.'[95] Nevertheless, Thatcher was determined to introduce market principles into the NHS.[96] Ancillary services were opened up to competitive tendering. These changes produced some savings – 'usually gained by paying the already low-paid even less – though weighed against them should be the hidden administrative costs of contracting out (such as increased monitoring) as well as the disruption and loss of morale in NHS staff and, sometimes, lower standards of cleanliness'.[97] Prescription charges were greatly increased, as were dental charges, and, a new departure, charges were introduced for eye tests. More fundamentally, general practitioners were encouraged to become 'fund holders'. They were allocated budgets to buy health care for patients, including non-emergency operations. Large hospitals, roughly 300 of them, were encouraged to opt out of regional health authority control, becoming self-governing trusts within the NHS. They would sell their services to the NHS health authorities and to private hospitals and patients, and would be responsible for their own budgets.

The regional health authorities would be free to buy the cheapest treatment for their patients wherever it was available, and wherever waiting lists were shortest. Attempts were made to cut down on the 'hotel side' of health care by sending patients home earlier. This was justified on the grounds of improvements in medical techniques and in housing. The government constantly reiterated the point that it was not planning to privatize the NHS, that it was wedded to a universal service, financed by taxation and free at the point of use. Yet the public was bombarded with advertisements for private health care. This was beyond the pockets of most people and, in most cases, could only deal with getting routine operations for subscribers without the waiting they would experience as NHS patients. More complex conditions could only be treated by the NHS. The changes in the NHS threw up costly management teams and led to patients being shunted around the country, either because facilities were no longer available locally or because a service was being provided more cheaply elsewhere. In 1997 the government could cite statistics to show that more doctors were treating more patients than ever before, and that 'over the last 20 years, expenditure has risen faster than total national income. Over the same period the share of NHS expenditure in GDP has risen from 4.8% to 5.8%.' Even so, not enough money was being allocated to maintain the NHS.[98] The government was unable to deny that hospitals were being forced to close wards in order to balance their books. John Chawner, Chairman of the Central Consultants Committee of the British Medical Association, believed in 1990, 'the NHS is chronically underfunded [and] is terminally ill from lack of cash'.[99] By 1997 the situation had not improved. The BMA warned that hospitals were facing the worst cash crisis in 10 years.[100] A survey of nurses in January 1997 revealed that 56 per cent felt the NHS changes made matters worse; only 12 per cent noted any improvement.[101]

The threat of AIDS, first identified in the early 1980s, still seemed very limited in Britain by the mid-1990s. It appeared to be worst in central London and Edinburgh. The death of a few prominent figures – film actor Rock Hudson, rock singer Freddie Mercury and film director Tony Richardson among them – helped to increase public awareness of AIDS, as did a government-sponsored publicity campaign in favour of 'safe sex'.

Table 10.2 Male and female smokers in Britain (per cent), 1972, 1982 and 1992

	1972	*1982*	*1992*
men	52	38	29
women	42	33	28

The threat from cigarettes had not diminished. In its report, *The Smoking Epidemic – Counting the Cost* (November 1991), the Heath Education Council estimated that smoking was killing 110,000 people a year and costing the NHS £437 million. Figures in *Social Trends* (1995) indicated that fewer people admitted that they were smokers of cigarettes. Despite these figures many young people were taking up smoking in the 1990s.

IRA: 'THOSE KILLED . . . NOT . . . CARRYING ARMS'

Twenty years after the arrival of British troops in Northern Ireland to defend the Catholics, the IRA stepped up its campaign against the British Army. It carried the war to Gibraltar and Germany as well as England. Since 1986 the terrorists had a new weapon, Semtex explosive, which was powerful, light and relatively safe to use. It was manufactured in Czechoslovakia.[102] On 6 March 1988 three members of an IRA unit were shot dead in Gibraltar by the SAS. Much controversy followed because, as Howe admitted in the Commons, 7 March, 'Those killed were subsequently found not to have been carrying arms.' And the car they left parked 'did not contain an explosive device'. However, they left 64 kilograms of Semtex high explosive in a Ford Fiesta over the Spanish border in Marbella.[103] Two of the three had convictions for terrorist offences and it seems certain they intended to attack a British military parade in Gibraltar. At their funeral in Milltown cemetery, Belfast, a gunman attacked the mourners, killing 3 and wounding 68. 'It was at the funeral of two of these mourners', Thatcher later recalled,[104] 'that what was to remain in my mind as the single most horrifying event in Northern Ireland during my term of office occurred.' Two British corporals on observation duties were dragged from their car and lynched by IRA sympathizers. The first bomb to be detonated by the IRA in England since 1984 went off at an Army Communications Centre in North London in August 1988 killing one soldier.[105] On 20 August, 7 soldiers were killed and 28 injured when their bus was blown up in County Tyrone.[106] The worst IRA attack was at Deal, in Kent, on 22 September 1989, when 40 musicians were killed at the Royal Marines School of Music. Terrorists had killed the 'witty, clever, industrious, affectionate'[107] Ian Gow, MP, with a car bomb at his home on 30 July 1990. Between 1969 and 1989 deaths due to civil disturbance in Northern Ireland reached a total of 2,772. In July 1989 Thatcher replaced Tom King with Peter Brooke as Northern Ireland Secretary. Brooke had Ulster connections which were not likely to impress the Catholics! Anglo-Irish relations came under strain during this period. Thatcher felt Irish Prime Minister Charles Haughey (1979–81, 1982–83, 1987–92) was not giving whole-hearted co-operation in beating the IRA. 'The border was virtually open so far as terrorists were concerned.'[108]

GOODBYE SDP

Immediately after the 1987 election, Liberal leader David Steel called for the merger of the two Alliance parties. Months of, at times, bitter negotiations followed. Most Liberals favoured the move, a small group who did not, split off to form their own Liberal Party. More in the SDP had doubts about the move. Nevertheless, in January 1988, the two parties voted to merge. Their new party was named the Social and Liberal Democratic Party (SLD). David Owen refused to go along with the majority of his colleagues into the new party and attempted to keep alive the old SDP. He was joined by two MPs, Rosie Barnes and John Cartwright. The other two SDP MPs, Charles Kennedy and Robert Maclennan, together with ex-MPs Shirley Williams and Roy Jenkins, did join. Bill Rodgers, the fourth member of the 'gang of four' also joined. Personal rivalries played an important part in Owen's decision. But Owen claimed he differed strongly from the Liberals over Europe. They wanted a Federal Europe, he wanted to retain the essentials of nationhood within the EC. He resumed the leadership of the rump SDP from March 1988 to June 1990. After bad by-election results, the national committee of the SDP voted, on 3 June 1990, by 17 to 5 to suspend the party constitution, thus terminating the SDP's activities. The decision followed the Bootle by-election (17 May) in which the SDP got fewer votes than the other losers – the Conservatives, Liberal Democrats, Greens, Liberals and Raving Looney Party. The SDP also did badly in local elections. Many Owenites later sought sanctuary with the Conservatives. Though he admired Major, Owen resisted calls to join the Conservatives. As Lord Owen (from 1992) he became the EU mediator in Bosnia.

The SLD, popularly known as the Liberal Democrats, was launched in March 1988 with Steel and Robert Maclennan as joint leaders. On 28 July 1988 Paddy Ashdown was elected leader of the Liberal Democrats with 71.9 per cent of the vote, and Ian Wrigglesworth, formerly of the SDP, was elected President.

The new leader of the Liberal Democrats, Paddy Ashdown, was elected to Parliament in 1983. Born (1941) in India to Irish parents, he was educated at Bedford School and Hong Kong University, where he qualified as a Chinese interpreter. He had served as a captain in the Royal Marines, 1959–71, and then as a diplomat, 1971–76. Later he worked in management, including some time with Westland Helicopters. His last job before his election to the Commons was as a youth worker, 1981–83.

'DISASTER OF THE POLL-TAX'

Anxious to curb the powers of local authorities, which were increasingly non-Conservative, no less than 141 Bills affecting local government were introduced between 1979 and 1989. No less than 17 affected local government finance.[109] The most controversial of them was what Howe in his memoirs called the 'disaster of the poll-tax'.[110] This was pushed through as the community charge in April 1988. It originated in the mind of Lord (Victor) Rothschild,[111] Waldegrave (Local Government)[112] helped to frame it and Kenneth Baker (Environment) convinced the Cabinet.[113] Thatcher had a 'profound personal commitment' to it.[114] Two-thirds of the Cabinet sat through 'innumerable meetings' chaired by Thatcher.[115] Heseltine and Lawson argued against it.[116] In a memo of 15 May 1985, Lawson pointed out: 'The biggest gainers would be better off households in high rateable value properties; the losers would be poorer households, particularly larger ones.'[117] The aim was to make everyone pay towards the costs of local government and not just, as under the rating system, householders. Under the old system, the amount paid was fixed according to the size of dwelling. Under the community charge everyone in a given district would pay the same tax set by their local authority. The unemployed, students and certain other categories could claim exemption from most of the tax. Labour, the Liberal Democrats and the nationalist parties opposed the new system, as did some Conservatives, including Heath. Fearing defeat in the Lords the government called in its 'backwoodsmen' and, on 23 May, secured the second-largest attendance in the twentieth century.

Many people in Scotland and a significant minority in England and Wales refused to pay the new tax. The Labour leaders condemned this type of opposition and disowned those who promoted it. In most cases such non-payment hit Labour-run councils, often already in bad shape financially, more than Conservative councils, which were usually in more prosperous areas. Moreover, those seeking to avoid payment by not registering lost their right to vote, thus depriving the opposition parties of at least some votes.

On Saturday 30 March 1990 rioting broke out in London following a peaceful demonstration against the poll-tax by around 40,000 people. A few hundred protesters went on the rampage in the Whitehall–Trafalgar Square–Leicester Square area of Central London. The Times (2 April 1990) reported, 'London's image as a safe and pleasant city was damaged by the riots which caught thousands of innocent tourists unawares.' Lawson later wrote, 'What was insupportable was the anguish caused to millions of ordinary people, with no political axe to grind, up and down the land.'[118] He considered the poll-tax Thatcher's 'greatest political blunder . . . as Prime Minister'.[119] In April 1991, under Major, the poll-tax was replaced with the Council Tax, based largely on banded property values.

'SOME . . . IDENTIKIT EUROPEAN PERSONALITY'

In October 1972 the original EEC had agreed to move towards Economic and Monetary Union (EMU) and Britain had gone along with that. There was later heated discussion about what the term meant, with Thatcher arguing it meant merely co-operation rather than a move towards a single currency.[120] The European Monetary System (EMS) had been agreed in March 1979 as a mechanism linking the exchange rates of the EC currencies. Its operating arm was the Exchange Rate Mechanism (ERM). The Labour government did not take Britain in. The Conservatives argued at that time in favour.[121] Yet, once in government, they did not set about joining. The truth is: 'Thatcher was against it. The Treasury was sceptical.'[122] By 1985 Lawson and Howe were advocating entry, backed by the Governor of the Bank of England, Robin Leigh-Pemberton. At a crucial meeting of Cabinet and officials on 1 November, only Biffen expressed opposition, that is, until Thatcher spoke. She simply refused to accept entry, leaving her colleagues wondering 'where on earth we went next'.[123] Despite Thatcher's opposition, there was reference to the EMU in the Single European Act, 1986. This removed internal barriers within the EC and sought to reduce the gap between the rich regions and the poorer ones.

In April 1988 came the draft report of Jacques Delors, the President of the European Commission. The report called for a three-stage development to full monetary union. Howe, Lawson and Thatcher objected to the automatic link between stage one ERM and stage three EMU. Later, after being re-appointed as President, Delors made a speech which was decidedly pro-federalist. At the TUC he was given a standing ovation for a speech on the Social Charter. Thatcher's riposte to Delors was given on 20 September 1988 at the College of Europe in Bruges. There she set out her position on Europe. She said,'Willing and active co-operation between independent sovereign states is the best way to build a successful European Community . . . It would be folly to try to fit them into some sort of identikit European personality.'[124] She wanted a 'Europe of Enterprise' not a protectionist Europe. She rejected also defence co-operation which would weaken NATO. Thatcher felt she was blackmailed by Howe and Lawson to announce Britain's readiness to join the ERM.[125] When sterling did finally join the ERM (5 October 1990), she claims she only agreed under pressure from all sides, with only Ridley as her ally.[126] Lawson argued the ERM 'would reduce exchange rate fluctuations and we would be able to use it to assist us in our anti-inflationary policy'. He believed Britain forfeited influence by not joining earlier.[127] Howe concluded, had Britain joined in 1985, 'the United Kingdom would have helped to build a secure bulwark against the excesses of the boom-bust cycle of the late 1980s'.[128]

The third direct elections to the European Parliament in June 1989 were held under the shadow of Thatcher's Bruges speech. According to

Lawson,[129] 'the Conservative campaign . . . was characterized by a crude and embarrassing anti-Europeanism'.[128] Labour, on the other hand, had become the party of Europe. Many Conservative MEPs and MPs started to feel that under Thatcher's leadership Britain was becoming dangerously isolated within the EC. Labour were the clear winners, gaining 45 seats (33 in 1984) as opposed to the Conservatives' 32 (46) and the SNP's 1 (1). In Northern Ireland, where the proportional representation system was in operation, the two Unionist parties – OUP and DUP – gained, as before, one seat each, and the SDLP held its one seat. In the rest of the UK the old first-past-the-post system kept out the Liberal Democrats and the Greens who, to great surprise, won 14.9 per cent of the vote. At 35.9 per cent, the turnout was the lowest in the EU. This compared with 68.3 per cent in the Republic of Ireland, 48.7 per cent in France and 62.4 per cent in West Germany.

THATCHER'S LAST CABINET

In his book *Kill the Messenger*, Bernard Ingham, Thatcher's Press Secretary, wrote, 'I was beginning to dread trips abroad with the Prime Minister. I could never be sure who would resign next on our return.'[130] He was writing about the period 1989–90. After the 1987 election Tebbit had retired, remaining Chairman until the autumn. Nicholas Edwards (Wales) also resigned. Biffen, who had criticized Thatcher's style, was sacked from his post of Leader of the Commons. He was replaced by John Wakeham. Also sacked were Lord Hailsham, Lord Chancellor since 1979, and Michael Jopling (Agriculture). Parkinson was brought back into the Cabinet as Energy Secretary. Two newcomers were John Major as Chief Secretary to the Treasury and John Moore at Social Services. In October 1987 Lord Havers (Lord Chancellor) resigned and Whitelaw, who had served since 1979, went in December 1988. In July 1989 Moore, who had been talked of as a possible future leader, was sacked. Paul Channon was removed at the same time and George Younger (Defence) and Lord Young (Trade and Industry) both resigned.

After the strong showing of the Greens in the 1989 Euro-elections, Nicholas Ridley was moved from Environment, where he had been since 1986, to Trade and Industry. His replacement was the 'wet' Chris Patten. Norman Fowler (Employment) and Walker (Wales) left to 'spend more time with their families' in January and March 1990, respectively. After a row with Thatcher at the EC summit in Madrid (July 1989), Howe was moved from the Foreign Office to become Leader of the House; he came close to resigning. His 'whole family was shell-shocked'.[131] His replacement was Major. After Thatcher's return from the Commonwealth conference in October 1989 she was faced with the resignation of Lawson. He had asked her to choose between himself and her personal economic adviser, Professor

Alan Walters, who frequently disagreed in public with Lawson.[132] She chose Walters. Thus, Lawson gave up his ambition to be the longest-serving Chancellor in the twentieth century. He had served six years and four months. David Lloyd George (1908–15) served seven years and one month. Major replaced Lawson. Hurd replaced Major as Foreign Secretary. On her return from the Houston economic summit in July 1990, Thatcher had to find a replacement for her friend Ridley. He had provoked a storm when he described the EC as 'a German racket'. Ridley (1929–96), educated at Eton and Balliol, was a civil engineer by training and a Thatcherite by conviction.

During her period in office Thatcher sacked 14 Cabinet ministers and 21 resigned. The first Cabinet had 22 members, those of 1983 and 1987 21 each. Between June 1987 and November 1990 all but one of the Cabinet was either sacked or shuffled around. Kenneth Clarke, QC went from Trade and Industry to Health and then to Education. His moves followed strong criticism of his policies at each ministry. Clarke (b. 1940) had joined the Cabinet in 1985 as Postmaster-General and Minister for Employment. He was regarded as a 'wet'. Educated at Nottingham High School and Cambridge, he had been tipped as a potential leader of the Conservatives. Major held the Foreign Office for a few weeks in the summer of 1990. It was difficult to believe that any of the ministers had a firm grip on their departments. By the summer of 1990 there had been 15 major Cabinet reshuffles. This contrasted with the way things were run in Germany by Chancellor Kohl (and his predecessors). There, nine of Kohl's original 17 ministers from 1983 were still serving in the same offices. By contrast, Thatcher had only three left of her 1983 Cabinet.

THATCHER'S FALL: 'FEW . . . SPARED A MOMENT TO REGRET'

On 3 December 1989 an almost unknown Conservative MP, Sir Anthony Meyer, decided to stand against Thatcher for the party leadership. Thatcher was the first Conservative leader to be subject to annual re-election under rules established at the time of Heath. This was the first time she had been challenged. Neither Meyer nor anyone else expected him to win. He merely wished to test the unease in the party over various aspects of domestic policy and, above all, over Europe. Remarkably, since he did not even campaign, he attracted 33 votes to his leader's 314. There were 24 spoilt papers and three did not vote. It was a decent vote for the 'gentle', 69-year-old, old Etonian, former diplomat Member for Clwyd North West.[133] Thatcher did not read the signs and went on as before in her opposition to the EC and in her style of leadership. When Howe resigned on 1 November 1990, after almost 16 years in her service, she was robbed of what was left of her credibility. He gave Britain's role in Europe as his reason.[134] On 14 November Heseltine announced he would challenge her for the leadership. Among his supporters were former junior health minister Edwina Currie and Emma Nicholson, a former vice-chairman, which shocked the Thatcher camp.[135] For many MPs the poll-tax, Thatcher's mounting unpopularity on the doorstep and personal dismay at her style of government came ahead of fears about her attitude to Europe.[136] In the first round Thatcher polled 204 votes to 152 for Heseltine. There were 16 spoilt papers. She was only four votes short, under Conservative Party rules, of victory. She was backed by Tebbit and Parkinson and by those she had appointed to office. She immediately announced that she would stand again. But less than 24 hours later she gave up. Tim Renton, Chief Whip, had told her support was crumbling.[137] The Westminster rumour machine went into 'overdrive'.[138] Gossip 'ran like wildfire'.[139] Parkinson urged her to stand again, as did Portillo, 'a passionate supporter',[140] but a 'deeply hurt'[141] Thatcher resigned. She had made many enemies. Less than half her 1987 Cabinet was still in government and only three had survived since 1983.[142] Yet Parkinson believed that, had she kept her nerve for a few more hours, she could have won.[143] The battle was now on to block Heseltine. In the second round on 27 November, John Major gained 185 votes, Heseltine 131, and Hurd 56. Although just short of the 197 needed for victory, Major was declared elected when the other two candidates withdrew. Nicholas Ridley later wrote of the Conservative Party, 'It is a very cruel animal . . . It is ruthless and cruel. Few that evening spared a moment to regret both the fact and the manner of her going, let alone permit themselves a tear. There was much unconcealed pleasure at the clever way they had got her out.'[144]

Thatcher permitted herself a tear.[145] Abroad, Kohl was about to secure another four years in office in the first election since German reunification. In Moscow, Gorbachev regretted Thatcher's fall,[146] not realizing he would fall himself a year later. In the Middle East the dogs of war continued to gather.

NOTES

Unless otherwise indicated, the place of publication is London.

1 Nigel Lawson, *The View from No. 11: Memoirs of a Tory Radical* (1993), 3.
2 Norman Tebbit, *Upwardly Mobile* (1988), 203.
3 Ruth Winstone (ed.)/Tony Benn, *The Benn Diaries* (1995), 556.
4 *Guardian*, 21 November 1983 for Marplan; Robert J. Wybrow, *Britain Speaks Out, 1937-87: History as Seen Through the Gallup Data* (1989), 132 for Gallup.
5 Tebbit, op. cit., 209; Cecil Parkinson, *Right at the Centre* (1992), 42-3.
6 Geoffrey Howe, *Conflict of Loyalty* (1994), 296; Hugo Young, *One of Us: A Biography of Margaret Thatcher* (1991), 343.
7 Howe, op. cit., 295; Parkinson, op. cit., 234-6, 248-54.
8 Tebbit, op. cit., 209.

9 Howe, op. cit., 329.
10 ibid., 330.
11 ibid., 331.
12 Ian Gilmour, *Dancing with Dogma: Britain under Thatcherism* (1993), 102.
13 ibid., 103.
14 Lawson, op. cit., 148.
15 Gilmour, op. cit., 104; Paul Routledge, *Scargill: The Unauthorized Biography* (1994), 129.
16 Routledge, op. cit., 129.
17 ibid., 131; Lawson, op. cit., 159.
18 Lawson, op. cit., 157.
19 *Observer*, 18 March 1984.
20 Gilmour, op. cit., 106. Peter Kellner, *New Statesman*, 22 March 1985, revealed that private polls indicated that a majority of miners would not have supported strike action in a national ballot in spring 1984.
21 Routledge, op. cit., 135.
22 ibid., 138.
23 ibid., 146.
24 *Keesing's Contemporary Archives*, November 1984, 33230.
25 Winstone/Benn, op. cit., 564.
26 Routledge, op. cit., 154.
27 ibid., 161.
28 Denis Healey, *The Time of My Life* (1990), 504.
29 Routledge, op. cit., 159.
30 Winstone/Benn, op. cit., 575.
31 Gilmour, op. cit., 111
32 Lawson, op. cit., 161. For MacGregor's view see his *The Enemies Within* (1986).
33 Lawson, op. cit., 160.
34 Winstone/Benn, op. cit., 575.
35 Healey, op. cit., 504. See also Mervyn Jones, *Michael Foot* (1994), 523.
36 Wybrow, op. cit., 135.
37 Healey, op. cit., 504.
38 Chapman Pincher, *Their Trade is Treachery* (1986), 237.
39 Peter Wright, *Spycatcher* (New York, 1987), 54.
40 *Financial Times*, 22 December 1988.
41 Howe, op. cit., 346.
42 ibid., 347–8.
43 ibid., 339.
44 ibid., 445.
45 *Guardian*, 15 May 1985, 20 May 1985. Francis Pym's ideas are developed in his *The Politics of Consent* (1984).
46 *The Times*, 3 May 1985. Walker was profiled in the *Observer*, 26 November 1985.
47 Young, op. cit., 267.
48 Howe, op. cit., 464.
49 ibid., 446.
50 Gilmour, op. cit., 226.
51 Peter Hennessy, *Whitehall* (1990), 307; Margaret Thatcher, *The Downing Street Years* (1993), 435.
52 Howe, op. cit., 469.
53 Thatcher, op. cit., 436.
54 Young, op. cit., 449.

55 Howe, op. cit., 287.
56 Young, op. cit., 523.
57 Howe, op. cit., 419; Tebbit, op. cit., 229.
58 Howe, op. cit., 425.
59 ibid., 427.
60 Gilmour, op. cit., 116. Lord Stockton seemed to retract his statement on 14 November 1985 when he said, 'As a Conservative, I am naturally in favour of returning into private ownership and private management all those means of production and distribution which are now controlled by state capitalism . . . What I ventured to question was using these huge sums as if they were income.' *Hansard (Lords)*, vol. 468, col. 391.
61 Peter Riddell, *The Thatcher Era and its Legacy* (Oxford, 1991), 91.
62 ibid., 91.
63 Gilmour, op. cit., 117.
64 ibid., 119.
65 Lawson, op. cit., 226.
66 Riddell, op. cit., 93.
67 Wybrow, op. cit., 132.
68 Gilmour, op. cit., 126.
69 *Social Trends 1993*.
70 Charles Pattie and Ron Johnston, 'The Conservative Party and the Electorate', in Steve Ludlam and Martin J. Smith (eds), *Contemporary British Conservatism* (1996), 46.
71 *Guardian*, 8 February 1997.
72 Pattie and Johnston, op. cit., 53.
73 David Butler, *British General Elections since 1945* (Oxford, 1995), 41.
74 ibid., 40.
75 David Butler, *The Times Guide to the House of Commons, June 1987*, 256, in a chapter with R. Waller 'Election of Haves and Have Nots'.
76 Tebbit, op. cit., 255.
77 ibid., 255.
78 ibid.
79 ibid., 257
80 Howe, op. cit., 533–5.
81 *Advertising Statistics Yearbook*, 1985, 50.
82 *Guardian*, 19 October 1996.
83 Howe, op. cit., 512.
84 *Daily Telegraph*, 15 February 1997.
85 Tebbit, op. cit., 129.
86 *Social Trends 25* (1995), 167.
87 ibid., 166.
88 Association of Chief Police Officers, *Your Police are Making a Difference* (fourth police factsheet, n.d.).
89 *The Times*, 18 November 1996.
90 *The Times*, 10 October 1996.
91 *Manchester Evening News*, 7 February 1997.
92 Thatcher, op. cit., 596.
93 *The Times*, 17 February 1997.
94 Alan Smithers and Pamela Robinson, *Beyond Compulsory Schooling: A Numerical Picture* (1991).
95 Gilmour, op. cit., 191.
96 ibid., 190.

97 ibid., 190.
98 ibid., 187.
99 *Independent*, 9 November 1990, see his letter.
100 *Guardian*, 11 January 1997.
101 *Guardian*, 29 January 1997.
102 Thatcher, op. cit., 411.
103 Howe, op. cit., 551.
104 Thatcher, op. cit., 407.
105 ibid., 410.
106 ibid., 411
107 Alan Clark, *Diaries* (1993), 319.
108 Thatcher, op. cit., 410.
109 Howe, op. cit., 623.
110 ibid., 569.
111 Lawson, op. cit., 570.
112 Howe, op. cit., 520.
113 Parkinson, op. cit., 27.
114 Lawson, op. cit., 561.
115 ibid., 561.
116 Parkinson, op. cit., 27.
117 Lawson, op. cit., 574.
118 ibid., 583.
119 ibid., 584.
120 Thatcher, op. cit., 741.
121 Howe, op. cit., 111.
122 ibid., 112.
123 ibid., 450.
124 Thatcher, op. cit., 745.
125 ibid., 712.
126 ibid., 722.
127 Lawson, op. cit., 925.
128 Howe, op. cit., 689.
129 Lawson, op. cit., 922.
130 Bernard Ingham, *Kill the Messenger* (1991), 386.
131 Howe, op. cit., 590–1.
132 Lawson, op. cit., 960–5.
133 Howe, op. cit., 609.
134 ibid., 649.
135 Parkinson, op. cit., 29.
136 Howe, op. cit., 670.
137 Parkinson, op. cit., 36.
138 ibid., 36.
139 Howe, op. cit., 672.
140 Thatcher, op. cit., 855.
141 Parkinson, op. cit., 38.
142 Howe, op. cit., 446.
143 Parkinson, op. cit., 37.
144 Nicholas Ridley, *My Style of Government* (1991), 252. For an account of the fall of Thatcher see Alan Watkins, *A Conservative Coup: The Fall of Margaret Thatcher* (1991).
145 Thatcher, op. cit., 857, 861.
146 Mikhail Gorbachev, *Memoirs* (1996), 545.

11

IN MAJOR'S 'CLASSLESS SOCIETY', 1990–96

JOHN MAJOR: 'CABINET NO LONGER . . . CONFRONTATION'

When the victory of John Major (b. 1943) for the leadership of the Conservative Party was announced, Margaret Thatcher said she was 'thrilled'. Alan Clark, reflected the view of many Conservative MPs when he wrote, John Major 'being calm and sensible, is infinitely preferable to that dreadful charlatan, H. But John is virtually unknown. He's not at all *flash*, and a lot of colleagues think it's flash that we need at the moment. And he's not classy, which doesn't worry me in the slightest, but worse, he doesn't (like Mrs T.) even *aspire* to be classy.'[1]

Major had reached the top job in British politics after just eleven years in Parliament and three years in the Cabinet. He was the youngest Prime Minister for nearly a century. Born in Merton, Surrey, the son of a circus performer, he was educated at Rutlish Grammar School in Wimbledon. He left school at 16, taking employment as a labourer and as a clerk before joining the Standard Chartered Bank in 1965. He worked for the bank in Nigeria and, later, as personal assistant to the former Chancellor, Anthony Barber. In 1970 he married Norma Johnson and they had a son and a daughter. After joining the Young Conservatives at 16 Major served on the Lambeth Borough Council. He was elected to the safe seat of Huntingdon in 1979. Major's first ministerial experience was at the Department of Social Security (1985–87). He served as Chief Secretary to the Treasury, 1987–89. After a brief spell as Foreign Secretary he was appointed Chancellor in 1989. In ideological terms he was broadly acceptable to all sections of his party. He was liberal on such issues as immigration and in his opposition to capital punishment. He was reckoned to be for 'sound money' in the Conservative tradition but he called for a 'classless society'. Finally, he was much more positive about the European Community than Thatcher had been.

'To many senior ministers, Cabinet government was no longer by confrontation but rather by discussion.'[2] Major retained the services of Douglas

Hurd at the Foreign Office, moved Kenneth Baker to the Home Office, gave Environment to Michael Heseltine, and gave the Chancellorship to Norman Lamont. Tom King stayed at Defence. Kenneth Clarke and William Waldegrave retained Education and the NHS respectively. Hurd (b. 1930) was a product of Eton and Cambridge. A former diplomat and author of political thrillers, he had been associated with Edward Heath. Baker (b. 1934), St Paul's and Oxford, had served at Education since 1986 and before that at Environment (1985–86). Lamont (b. 1942) had been a merchant banker after graduating from Cambridge. He had worked as Financial Secretary to the Treasury from 1986. Christopher Patten (b. 1944) was appointed Chairman of the Conservative Party with a seat in the Cabinet as Chancellor of the Duchy of Lancaster. He had been educated at St Benedict's School, Ealing, and Balliol, Oxford. He was regarded as a 'Wet' and had served at Overseas Development. Major's government was one of Oxbridge lawyers and bankers. Its members lacked experience of manufacturing industry, science, and the educational background of most of the electorate. It was drawn from the south rather than the north of the kingdom. This was not new.

WAR IN THE GULF

One of the first things Major had to deal with was the continuing crisis in the Persian Gulf. On 2 August 1990 Iraq invaded Kuwait, the small Arab Kingdom. Having 13 per cent of the world's known oil supply and a population of only 1.8 million (1986), it was rich, though most of its people were poor. The UN condemned the invasion, as did the Arab League, the United States and the Soviet Union. The Iraqi dictator, Saddam Hussein, declared Kuwait annexed on 8 August, by which time a powerful coalition was building up against him. Months of diplomatic moves followed, until on 16 January 1991 Operation Desert Storm got under way. This was an offensive of air and land forces of (mainly) the USA, Saudi Arabia, the UK, France, Egypt, Syria and Italy. Britain had 45,000 men and women involved, which was less than one-tenth of the US force.[3] Iraq was subjected to heavy aerial bombardment until on 24 February the land forces moved forward. By 27 February, Kuwait was in allied hands and Iraq had announced its readiness to accept unconditionally all UN resolutions. Military action by the US-led coalition ceased the following day.

Mrs Thatcher had announced her support for the US moves immediately after the invasion. She was backed up by the leaders of the opposition parties. This national unity continued under Major until the mini-war was over. The action cost the British forces 24 killed in action. In addition, 23 died on active service, 43 were wounded and 1,688 suffered from other injuries and illness needing hospitalization.[4] The Americans lost something like 79 dead, 213 wounded and 50 missing. Iraq suffered heavy military and civilian casualties. It was estimated in 1997 that the additional military cost of the war to Britain was around £2,494 million. The Export Credits Guarantee Department estimated that total claims arising from the conflict would amount to £637 million. The bulk of these costs were met by Germany (£274m), Japan (£192m), Kuwait (£660m), Saudi Arabia (£582m) and United Arab Emirates (£278m) and other states.[5] British firms got between 8 and 10 per cent of the contracts offered for the restoration of Kuwait.[6]

Despite the national unity over the Gulf War, it raised many questions about the policy of Britain and the other Western powers. They had aided Saddam in his eight-year war against Iran. Iraq had received sophisticated military and scientific equipment from the West as well as from the Soviet bloc. Some asked why the coalition had allowed the Hussein regime to survive, especially when he started attacking, once again, the Kurdish minority in Iraq. The war allied the West with their former enemy Syria, a regime mixed up in international terrorism. The fall of Communism in the old Soviet Union meant that Syria had lost its chief backer and had to repair its bridges to the West. Iran came in from the cold, Britain restored relations with Tehran, and the Iranians remained neutral in the war. The war caused the spotlight to be turned on the Kuwait regime. It was revealed as an absolute monarchy with a poor record on human rights. Kuwait had been under British tutelage until 1961. Questions were also asked about the bombing of civilians by the United States and its allies. This contravened the 1949 Geneva Convention. Saddam was also guilty of this by firing rockets indiscriminately at Israel and Saudi Arabia. In London on 2 February, 30,000 demonstrators gathered to oppose the war. Similar protests were held in Bonn and Los Angeles. Labour MPs Clare Short and Tony Banks were among those opposing military action. Edward Heath had his doubts and tried hard, in his personal capacity, to reason with Saddam.

Saddam attempted to link his occupation of Kuwait with the Israeli occupation of the West Bank and Gaza Strip. Although the USA, Britain and other Western states claimed this was a separate issue, it became clear that it was an issue which would not go away. All the British parties supported the Madrid peace conference at which, in October 1991, for the first time, the Israelis and the Palestinians sat down together to discuss a settlement of their differences.

One unexpected outcome of the Gulf fighting were claims made by about 750 ex-service men and women, that they had been exposed to dangerous chemicals which resulted in permanent disablement. A Medical Assessment Programme (MAP) was established to enable veterans to be assessed by a military medical consultant. By December 1996 around 950 veterans had been examined and a further 217 were on the waiting list.[7] Although the Ministry of Defence helped those concerned it refused to admit there was a 'Gulf syndrome', unlike its counterpart in the USA. In 1996, however, the Ministry was forced to admit that pesticides were used 'which may possibly be a clue to some of the conditions that some Gulf War veterans have suffered from'.[8]

One happy side of the changing situation in the Middle East was the release of Western hostages by Islamic fundamentalist groups allied to Iran. On 18 November 1991, Terry Waite, the Archbishop of Canterbury's special envoy, was released after 1,763 days in chains. He had been attempting to secure the release of others when he was abducted in Beirut. He was the last Briton to be set free in Lebanon.

The Gulf War helped Major's image for a short while, but the halo effect did not last long as the recession hit Conservative voters. Major also had to unite his party, which was divided on Europe.

MAASTRICHT: BRITAIN 'AT THE HEART OF EUROPE'?

In 1991 Major built 'day by day . . . his personal relationship' to Chancellor Kohl.[9] Major held his first speech outside Britain in Bonn, then still the seat of the German government. In this he said, 'I want us to be where we belong. At the very heart of Europe. Working with our partners in building the future.'[10] Although Major also said that 'Europe is made up of nation states: their vitality and diversity are sources of strength', most observers believed the speech represented a shift of emphasis from Thatcher's view.

Major went with his team – Hurd, Lamont and Tristan Garel-Jones (Foreign Office minister responsible for Europe) – to Maastricht in December 1991. There was much to discuss, much to argue about, but a great deal of preliminary work had been done in previous, lengthy negotiations. In one key area, Sir Nigel Wicks, the Treasury's chief negotiator, had demanded tough preconditions to be met before any European countries tried to form a monetary union – the famous 'convergence criteria'.[11] Major's position was: 'He would accept no commitment to a "federal" union; no compulsion to join a monetary union; no subjection of foreign or interior policy to Brussels control.' NATO and British competitiveness must be protected.[12] The Social Chapter was considered by Major as something which would undermine British competitiveness. In the 1980s Britain had committed itself to a 'social dimension' to the EC.[13]

At Maastricht, the tough, tiring negotiations went on; at one point Major lost his notes revealing his negotiating positions.[14] The two heads of government closest to him were Kohl and the Dutch Prime Minister, Ruud Lubbers.[15] Kohl wanted the negotiations to succeed[16] to help Major in the coming British elections. In the end the heads of government of the twelve EC members agreed a draft treaty. The opening words stated that it was designed as a 'new stage in the process of creating an ever closer union among the peoples of Europe, in which decisions are taken as closely as possible to the citizen'.[17] It established a European Union based on the EC, which would, in addition to economic competence, have 'a common foreign and security policy and a common interior and justice policy'. In the economic sphere, economic and monetary union was the aim, and 'Ultimately this will include a single currency'. Another future possibility was a 'common defence'. Owing to British opposition 'federalism' was not included in the Treaty. It was agreed Britain could opt out of the Social Chapter of the Treaty, which was based on the 1989 Social Charter of the EC. Britain, and Denmark, also had the right to remain outside the single currency.

On his return Major got a majority with only seven Conservative rebels, led by Tebbit, in the initial Commons debate on the Treaty negotiations. Thatcher abstained as did most Labour MPs.[18] The full, final English versions of the European Treaties on Political and Monetary Union were signed by Hurd and Francis Maude – on behalf of the Chancellor – on 7 February 1992.[19] In 1993, when the Maastricht Bill was put to Parliament, the opposition was greater and Europe came to plague Major right up to the election in 1997.

Labour was, on the whole, more enthusiastic about the EU than the Conservatives. It criticized the opt-out from the Social Chapter, claiming Major could only offer the British jobs on the basis of poorer wages and conditions than those enjoyed in other EU states. Many European businessmen agreed, feeling that Britain was being given an unfair trading advantage.

ELECTION 1992: MAJOR DEFIES THE ODDS

Major was often accused of lacking a 'big idea'. *The Citizen's Charter*, published on 22 July 1991, was, to a degree, his answer to this.[20] In an address on the Charter (27 January 1992) he set out six principles for the public services: clear published standards; consultation of users and customers; increased information to enable citizens to find out what services are available; more and better choice; greater accessibility; greater responsiveness when things go wrong. There followed charters for patients, parents, tenants, passengers, job seekers, taxpayers and travellers.[21] Although Kinnock called the Charter a 'mixture of the belated, the ineffective, the banal, the vague and the damaging' (22 July 1991), it was good propaganda for the coming electoral struggle. Moreover, the public service had a case to answer, and it is amazing that Labour had not thought of something of the kind themselves!

Labour went into the election with high hopes. In the seven by-elections of 1991 the Conservatives had lost all their four seats where by-elections had been held, two to Labour and two to the Liberal Democrats. Secondly, the economy remained in recession, the worst since the 1930s. The recession was hitting many who would normally vote Conservative – owner-occupiers who could not sell their homes, small businessmen suffering from high interest rates, some in the financial sector suffering redundancy. The polls also put Labour ahead. However, on a higher turnout of 78.1 per cent (75.4 in 1987), Major led his party, on 9 April 1992, to an unexpected victory with an overall majority of 21.

Labour seemed to suffer from the fact that it had not been in office since 1979; some voters feared this: to them, Labour was an unknown party. The Conservatives scored by frightening off potential Labour voters with fears about higher taxes if Labour won. Whether higher Conservative expenditure on its campaign than Labour or the Liberal Democrats could afford, paid dividends, is not certain.[22] All three parties could claim some comfort from the results. For the Conservatives it was their fourth win in a row, something virtually unknown in British politics. They had gained the highest vote ever of any party: 14,092,891 (13,736,405 in 1987). In Scotland, probably due to fears about the break-up of the UK, they had reversed their decline. For Major it was a personal triumph. Kinnock could claim Labour had greatly improved its position on 1983 and 1987 with 11,559,735 (10,029,797 in 1987). In Wales Labour had almost as many votes as the other three parties combined. Labour had also improved its position in the North of England, the Midlands and the South. It had fought off the Liberal Democratic challenge to be the main alternative to the Conservatives. The Liberal Democrats with 20 seats were two down on the 22 won by the Alliance in 1987. They gained four West Country seats from the Conservatives. The last four SDP seats returned to Labour. Owen's SDP remnants had sought, but failed, to get an accommodation with the Conservatives. The Liberal Democrats could claim that, although the election result was fairer than usual between the two main parties, the first-past-the-post electoral system once again produced a distribution of seats that was unrepresentative of the distribution of votes. According to Ivor Crewe's calculations, the Conservatives won 52 per cent of the seats on 42 per cent of the vote, Labour won 42 per cent of the seats on 34 per cent of the vote, but the Liberal Democrats won only 3 per cent of the seats on 18 per cent of the vote. Under proportional representation (assuming a 2 per cent threshold of representation) the result would have been Conservative 274, Labour 225, Liberal Democrats 117, SNP 15, PC 3, others 17.[23] Clearly a coalition government would have been necessary.

In 1992, 22 seats were held by majorities of under 1,000 votes. Labour held 11 such seats and Liberal Democrats 3. Major's overall majority of 21 rested on his 11 most marginal seats won by under 600 votes. Thus the election was decided on a handful of votes. The traditionally superior organization of the Conservatives must be included as a factor. Their better use of the expatriate vote could have swung the election. Perhaps commentators have underestimated the role of the tabloid press in this situation. The *Sun* claimed it had won the election for the Conservatives. Newspapers accounting for 67 per cent of sales backed Major. A general reason for the Conservative win was the person of John Major. The Conservatives' replacement of Thatcher by Major 'was a brilliant act of self-renewal'.[24] Remarkably, voters tended to absolve his government of responsibility for Thatcher's follies even though his Cabinet had served under the Iron Lady.

For Labour the result was a bitter blow. Their 34 per cent vote was lower than at any election since 1931 (32 per cent) except for 1983 and 1987. Kinnock and Hattersley took responsibility for the defeat and resigned.

In 1987 the far Right had fielded no candidates. With Thatcher still at the helm they knew their appeal would not be great even among their usual sympathizers. In 1992, the National Front and the British National Party put up 27 candidates. All of them lost their deposits, gaining only 12,000 votes altogether.[25] Kenneth Baker, the Home Secretary, had warned against Labour and Liberal Democrat policies in this area, which gave the *Daily Express* (7 April), just two days before the election, the chance to proclaim, 'Baker's Migrant Flood Warning – Labour Set To Open Doors'.

EURO '94: LABOUR'S NEW HOPES

John Smith, QC, was elected to succeed Neil Kinnock as Labour Leader and Margaret Beckett as Deputy Leader. Smith (b. 1938) had the advantage of ministerial office between 1974 and 1979, and in the shadow cabinet since then. A lawyer educated at Glasgow University, he was a good speaker and an imposing figure. Beckett (b. 1943) had served as Education and Science Secretary 1976–79. Educated at Manchester College of Science and Technology, she had worked for Granada Television before winning Lincoln in October 1974. Smith attempted to steer a path between the modernizers and the traditionalists in the Labour Party. Smith was a formidable parliamentary debater and was making headway among the public but suffered from ill health. He died from a second heart attack on 12 May 1994. Beckett took over as caretaker Leader to see Labour through the Euro-elections.

Labour had scored a victory in the local elections of 5 May with John Smith as their leader. It was feared his death would do them harm in the fourth direct elections to the European Parliament on 9 June 1994. As it turned out, they went well for Labour. On a turnout of 36.1 per cent (35.9 in 1989), Labour took 44.24 per cent (40.1) to the Conservatives 27.83 per cent (34.7). This gave Labour 62 (45) of Britain's 84 seats and the Conservatives 18 (32). With 16.72 per cent (6.2 plus 0.5 for the SDP) the Liberal Democrats gained two seats. Previously they had none. The SNP increased its representation from one to two, attracting over 32 per cent of the vote in Scotland and 3.19 per cent overall (2.7). In Wales PC gained 17 per cent. The Green Party vote collapsed, falling from 14.9 per cent to 3.24. Labour and the Liberal Democrats had concentrated heavily on domestic issues. The Conservatives had played the Euro-sceptic card and, unlike Thatcher in 1989, Major had been heavily involved in the election. To the applause of the Euro-sceptics Major called for a 'multi-track, multi-speed, multi-layered' Europe. Labour was more positive but promised to offer the electors a referendum before ever agreeing to a single European currency. The Liberal Democrats remained the most pro-Europe. Of the twelve member states only Portugal and the Netherlands had (slightly) lower poll participation than Britain. On the day of the Euro-elections, five by-elections were held. Labour held all of its four seats with hugely increased majorities. The Liberal Democrats took Eastleigh from the Conservatives.

Once the Euro-elections were over, the Labour leadership contest got into full swing on 10 June. The contenders were Margaret Beckett, John Prescott and Tony Blair. The first two also announced they were standing for the deputy leadership as well. Gordon Brown (b. 1951), shadow chancellor, who was widely expected to stand, announced his support for Blair. Beckett and Prescott had traditional 'old Labour' images. Blair was the front runner from the start. When the party voted on 21 July 1994 he was the clear winner. He took 57 per cent of the votes, to Prescott's 24.1 per cent and Beckett's 18.9 per cent.[26] Among Labour MPs and MEPs he took 60.5 per cent. Even among trade unionists, he had 52.3 per cent. In the deputy leadership elections Prescott won by 56.5 per cent to 43.5 per cent. Prescott (b. 1938) had been an MP since 1970 and was the shadow spokesman on transport. He had been a member of the shadow cabinet since 1983. He had worked as a merchant seaman, 1955–63, and then as a union official. He was educated at Ruskin College, Oxford, and Hull University. He was leader of the Labour delegation to the European Parliament, 1976–79.

Blair (b. 1953) was completely different from his deputy. He was a product of public schools and St John's College, Oxford. The son of a Durham University Conservative law lecturer and barrister, Blair also worked as a barrister before entering the Commons in 1983 sponsored by the TGWU. In 1980 he married Cherie Booth, a successful barrister, and the daughter of actor Tony Booth. Like Smith, Blair declared himself a Christian Socialist. He had supported CND, accepted the party's anti-EEC policy, but was roughly left of centre of the Labour Party. He opposed Tony Benn's Leftism, supporting the party leaders Foot, Kinnock and Smith.[27]

Blair appeared to do wonders for Labour. In October 1994, at Labour's annual conference held at Blackpool, he launched the slogan 'New Labour, New Britain'. By the end of the year, opinion polls put Labour at 61 per cent![28]

A Labour special conference, held at the Methodist Central Hall, London, voted on 29 April 1995 to drop Clause IV of the party's constitution which advocated 'common ownership'. It was replaced by a desire to create a community 'in which power, wealth and opportunity are in the hands of the many, not the few, where the rights we enjoy reflect the duties we owe, and where we live together, freely, in a spirit of solidarity, tolerance and respect'. It called for 'A dynamic economy serving the public interest' in which 'the enterprise of the market and the vigour of competition are joined with the forces of partnership and co-operation'.[29]

LITERATURE: 'OVER 8,000 NOVELS'

Salman Rushdie, the controversial British-Asian novelist, wrote in *The Observer* (18 August 1996), that, 'Over 8,000 novels were published in Britain last year. It would be a miracle if 80 of them were good. It would be cause for universal celebration if even one were great.' This was a rather harsh judgement on his fellow fiction writers. There were numerous good storytellers. More often than not they had to provide us with hilarity, comedy, adultery, sex and gloomy muddling through. Increasingly politicians were attempting to entertain us in this way. Edwina Curry published a best seller, *A Parliamentary Affair*, which did, however, come in for much criticism. Like any number of books published in the 1990s, it would have been regarded as pornographic in the 1970s. She followed, among others, fellow Conservatives Lord Archer and Douglas Hurd. They tended to dwell on scandals and 'sleaze' in politics. Despite the need to entertain, much social observation on the state of Britain crept into the literature of the 1990s. In Madeleine Wickham's *A Desirable Residence* (1996), the school-teacher couple, 'go for it', in Thatcherite-style, and buy their own business, a near-derelict tutorial college. Like millions of others in Major's Britain they become the victims of 'negative equity' as housing prices fell well below what many had paid for their homes in the 1980s. The characters in John Irvin's *Trainspotting*, although equally contemporary, inhabited a different world from those of Wickham's. They existed in the very real drugs underworld of one of Europe's most deprived, depressed and dangerous cities – Glasgow. Among the more established 'literary' writers, David Lodge produced the very popular *Therapy* (1995). He satirized the increasing tendency of modern Western man and woman to seek therapy for the unhappy state of their minds and bodies. The book catches the mood of Major's Britain. In his imaginary city of Rummidge, the 1960s centre has been converted into 'The Rialto':

> It was a typical project of the later Thatcher years, that brief flare of prosperity and optimism between the recession of the early eighties and the recession of the early nineties. Now the new buildings, with their stainless steel escalators and glass lifts and piped music, stand expectant and almost empty, like a theme park before opening day,

or like some utopian capital cities of a third-world country . . . The principal patrons of the Rialto in the daytime are unemployed youths, truanting schoolkids, and mothers with infant children . . .[30]

He could have added, 'and old-age pensioners'. There were many 'Rialtos' throughout Britain. Would there be the wealth to sustain them? Robert Harris cashed in on the mood of Britain with its continuing obsession with the Second World War, its anger and dismay that its old enemy, Germany, was doing so well, and the renewed fears of German hegemony in Europe. His book, *Fatherland* (1992), sold very many more copies than *Therapy*. It was a thriller set in Germany in 1964 after Nazi Germany had won the war and ruled Europe! In some ways more compelling than either, Eric Lomax's award-winning *The Railway Man* (1995), told the story of the author's experiences as a prisoner of the Japanese, 1942–45. One cannot help admiring Lomax's determination to survive, his attempts to understand and be reconciled with his former enemies. But the book's popularity was in part due to the continued fascination with the war. It cannot have done anything to allay suspicions of Japan, where, up to 1996, the atrocities of the Imperial Japanese Army had still not been fully acknowledged. Simon Weston drew on his own experience to write *Phoenix* (1996), a disturbing novel about the rise of neo-Nazism among British soldiers. Andrew Roberts with his *The Aachen Referendum* (1995) and Graham Ison with *Division* exploited the fears of some about 'the United States of Europe, the corrupt, bureaucratic, xenophobic, Euro-superstate which . . . almost snuffed out the British national identity' (Roberts).

'IT'S ALL OVER NOW FOR ENGLAND'

The above was the headline in the Conservative *Daily Telegraph* (27 June 1996). It was those beastly Germans again who had defeated England in the Euro '96 football semi-final. The *Daily Telegraph* wrote about 'the hopes and prayers of a nation' being 'shattered'. It was a sad reflection on Britain that such an event was taken so seriously and that it brought out jingoism and xenophobia. The same paper on the same day admitted the British, 'in comparison to their wealthier, better-educated European partners . . . have little to be smug about'. Quoting the 31st annual edition of *Regional Trends*, published by the Office of National Statistics, it pointed out that eight of the fifteen member states of the European Union were wealthier than Britain as measured by gross domestic product per head of population. Britain had a poor record of educating its 16- to 18-year-olds. Of the fifteen EU states only Greece and Portugal had fewer in education or training than Britain. In yet another *Telegraph* article on that same day the news was that 'British companies are continuing to slide down the world's research and development league table, despite rising profits and growth in the economy'. After nearly twenty years of Conservative govern-ment Britain had grown poorer by international standards. And its record on education and training, and research and development, vital for indus-trial and commercial progress, revealed that the downward trend was going to continue into the twenty-first century.

The Conservatives persisted in claiming that Britain was doing well yet so many companies, well-known symbols of British achievement, were foreign-owned. Among them were Champneys, the top people's health farm; Hamleys, the world-famous toy store; Cadbury, the chocolate manufac-turer; Thomas Cook, the travel company; Harrods, the London store; ICL computers; Rover, the car company; Wedgwood, the Staffordshire pottery firm; Rolls-Royce, Britain's most prestigious engine manufacturer. The bulk of British Airway's fleet was American-built. Whatever happened to the great British aviation industry? What was left of British Aerospace was attempting to merge with the Taiwan state-owned aviation company. Boots had sold its pharmaceutical research division to concentrate on retail-ing. Raleigh had given up designing bikes in favour of assembling cycles from overseas. The older industries of coal, steel and shipbuilding almost disappeared in the way the cotton industry had at a slightly earlier period. By 1997 the majority of the original eleven privatized electricity companies were American-owned.[31]

The Conservatives told the electorate this did not really matter so much because the salvation of the country lay in other directions, in the service industries and in its great financial institutions. Up to a point, and as a general principle, this sounded sensible, yet even here the picture was very patchy. According to the UK's National Criminal Intelligence Service (NCIS), in 1996, new fraud trends were reaching beyond conventional finan-cial services.[32] These threatened to overwhelm the limited resources of the NCIS. There were any number of cases of mismanagement or fraud which cost billions to the British economy. They were hardly a good adver-tisement for the much-vaunted 'entrepreneurial culture'. In many cases those responsible walked away from the debris with few consequences to themselves. When British & Commonwealth went down in what the *Daily Telegraph* (5 June 1990) called 'The biggest financial collapse the City has known', many thousands of investors lost most of their money. Thousands of small businesses went under with the collapse of the Bank of Credit and Commerce International in 1991. In the same year thousands of Mirror Group pensioners found their incomes under threat after the strange death at sea of Robert Maxwell,[33] the international businessman. Maxwell, it later transpired, as head of the Mirror Group, had stolen from the pension funds on a massive scale. With losses of £750 million, the 233-year-old Barings Bank had to be rescued from gross mismanagement and near collapse by a Dutch company in 1995.[34] Worse still were the mounting debts at Lloyd's of London, the traditional insurance giant. Morgan Grenfell, on the other hand, found help from Deutsche Bank after its three top-performing European funds collapsed. There were allegations of irregular investments in unquoted securities. Over 90,000 investors took considerable losses.[35] These and other City crashes called into question the City of London's way of doing business and the skills, abilities and integrity of many of its leaders. By the 1990s, many of the City's banks were, in any case, foreign-owned. The fact was ignored by the protagonists of foreign investors that these 'benefactors' could pull out at any time, that any innovation depends on the parent company overseas, and that they reduce the room for manoeuvre of any government as Third World governments had found out in the past. Here the argument is not that there should not be foreign investors; it is that it cannot be healthy when so many key firms are foreign-owned. This is not the case in those economic giants Japan and Germany.

The 'haemorrhage of enterprise' is how Alan Milburn, Labour MP, described the collapse of many small firms in the 1990s. The Conservatives had seen the small firm as an integral part of the enterprise culture, and their owners as a reservoir of Conservative voters. Yet under Major more than a million of them went to the wall. Only 171,175 new businesses were registered for VAT in the year before April 1996, compared with almost 270,000 six years earlier. The number of new businesses registering fell every year from 1989/90 onwards. The total number that had deregistered over the first five years of Major's administration was almost 1.08 million. Only 912,000 new businesses had registered.[36]

CLINTON IN IRELAND: 'MAKING A MIRACLE'

The arrival of Major at 10 Downing Street did nothing to dampen the enthusiasm of the IRA for violence. In 1990 there were seventy-six deaths in Northern Ireland and six outside it.[37] Of the many attacks in the early 1990s the most daring was the mortar attack on 10 Downing Street on 7 February 1991. Shortly before 10 a.m., when fifteen ministers and officials were on the ground floor discussing the Gulf War, a mortar bomb exploded in the garden. Windows were shattered but no one was hurt. The bomb, one of three, was fired from a disguised van 200 metres away. The assailants escaped on a motorbike. On 18 February one man was killed and more than forty were injured when a bomb exploded at Victoria Station in London. Paddington Station was also hit on the same day without casualties. London Bridge Station was hit on 28 February with no casualties. A bomb killed three at the Baltic Exchange in the City on 10 April. One person died from a bomb attack at the Sussex Arms pub in London on 12 October. No details were available on another explosion in Downing Street on 30 October.[38] In March 1993 a bomb killed two small boys in a busy shopping centre in Warrington. A bomb went off in the City of

London on 23 April 1993, killing a photographer and causing £1 billion of damage. On 18 June 1994 six Catholics were slain by the Ulster Volunteer Force as they watched television. The UVF claimed it was a retaliatory attack.

In December 1993 Major and Albert Reynolds signed a joint peace initiative – the Downing Street Declaration – which included the offer to include terrorist groups in political and constitutional negotiations within three months of a permanent end to violence. After months of pressure, including that from the SDLP and the US, the IRA announced a cease-fire on 1 September 1994. Major then lifted the broadcasting ban on the armed groups and their supporters. As a concession to the unionists, he promised the results of negotiations on the future of Northern Ireland would be subject to a referendum. This helped to entice the 'loyalist' armed groups to announce their cease-fire on 14 October. Other concessions followed and British civil servants started exploratory talks with Sinn Fein, the political wing of the IRA. Major insisted, however, that before full-scale talks could begin the IRA would have to surrender its weapons. This the IRA was reluctant to do. During the twenty-five years of violence 3,169 people had been killed, 2,224 of them civilians.[39]

In 1995, with little violence, Northern Ireland enjoyed the 'peace dividend' – an increase in investment and tourism, and the reduction of British troop levels. Yet the promised talks did not get under way. Sinn Fein remained barred from talks until they gave assurances about the decommissioning of the arsenal. The unionists would not attend because they believed a 'framework document', presented by the British and Irish governments on 22 February, was the beginning of moves towards a united Ireland. The document recommended the setting up of a new cross-border body to deal with issues of shared concern. Partly in disgust, James Molyneaux, leader of the main Ulster Unionist Party for sixteen years, announced his resignation on 28 August. London and Dublin were not too happy with his successor, law lecturer David Trimble. He had the reputation for being a hardliner, but proved to be more flexible than his reputation. Despite the difficulties, a wave of hope swept through Ireland when US President Bill Clinton visited both Northern Ireland and the Republic in November 1995. In Belfast he received an unprecedented welcome from both Protestants and Catholics. Given the influence of the powerful Irish-American lobby in Washington, DC, many thought the war was really coming to an end. It was agreed to establish an international body chaired by former US Senator George Mitchell to deal with the decommissioning of weapons and initiating all-party talks. This move, though welcome, revealed the weakness of the British government in a matter regarded as Britain's internal affairs. Various conciliatory gestures had been made by London and Dublin to keep the peace initiative on track. Clinton had told the people of Northern Ireland they were 'making a miracle', but it looked like just another dream (or public relations stunt), for the IRA resumed violence causing massive damage with bombs in London and Manchester in 1996. There were 220 casualties when the commercial heart of Manchester was destroyed by a 3,300-lb bomb on Saturday, 15 June 1996. Over 80,000 shoppers had to be evacuated. Manchester was more surprising as a target when one considers that so many people of Irish background live there. Miraculously, no one died but the damage was estimated at £500 million.[40] Two large car bombs were detonated by the IRA inside the compound of the British Army headquarters (Northern Ireland) at Lisburn in County Antrim on 7 October 1996. These caused one death and over thirty were injured.

MAD COWS AND ENGLISHMEN

The government was 'bombed' from an unexpected quarter when near panic broke out in March 1996 over the safety of British beef. Beef sales had been under pressure for some time due to growing interest into healthy eating, vegetarianism and rising beef prices. It emerged that the country could be facing a major public health crisis because of a possible link between a disease found in cattle, bovine spongiform encephalopathy (BSE) known colloquially as 'mad cow disease', and the fatal disease found in humans known as Creutzfeldt-Jakob Disease (CJD). The story broke as a 'leak'. On 20 March, Health Secretary Stephen Dorrell was forced to admit in the Commons that 'the most likely explanation at present' for the ten most recent CJD cases among young people was 'that these cases are linked to exposure to BSE' prior to the introduction of a November 1989 ban on the use of offal in human food products. Agriculture, Fisheries and Food Minister Douglas Hogg, introduced new measures to deal with the crisis later in March. Beef sales plummeted in Britain and across Europe. The veterinary committee of the European Union voted on 25 March, with only the British dissenting, to ban the export of British beef and beef products. The crisis rumbled on throughout 1996 and into 1997. Farmers had been grappling with BSE since the 1980s. Many people believed the government had been at least incompetent in its handling of the affair, some thought its close links with the farming community had led it to resist the drastic measures necessary to stamp out the disease. The crisis gave the Euro-sceptics more ammunition because of the attitude of the EU.

CONSERVATIVES' WAR: 'PUT UP OR SHUT UP'

After the 1992 election Major revamped his Cabinet. Two women joined the Cabinet: Virginia Bottomley at Health, and Gillian Shephard as Employment Secretary. Hurd remained at the Foreign and Commonwealth

Office. The big change, however, was Heseltine's appointment as Secretary of State for Trade and Industry, and Clarke became the new Home Secretary. This appeared to be a shift to the 'left' and away from Thatcherism. With Lamont still at the Treasury the main priority in economic policy remained low inflation rather than growth. Lamont resigned in 1993 in the wake of the fiasco over the ERM. Britain had only joined in October 1990 but abandoned membership in September 1992. The continued recession and worries about the future of the currencies in the ERM put pressure on the lira and the pound in favour of the German mark. The pound looked sick despite massive support and effective devaluation followed on 16 September 'Black Wednesday'. Britain left the ERM and the pound floated downwards outside it. Major came close to resignation. Lamont soldiered on until 1993 when Clarke took over the Treasury.

The 1980s haunted Major and his colleagues from time to time. Waldegrave, Alan Clark and Lord Trefgarne, when junior ministers under Thatcher, relaxed government guidelines, originally drawn up in 1985, over exports of 'non-lethal military goods' to Iraq. In order to avoid public debate on the issue they declined to draw attention to the changes. The trouble was that three executives of Matrix Churchill, an engineering firm based in Coventry, were put on trial for allegedly breaching export regulations. They were eventually acquitted in November 1992, but only after much controversy. They claimed they had been encouraged by government departments, including MI6 (the SIS) only to be later thrown to the wolves. The controversy led to the appointment of Sir Richard Scott's committee of inquiry. Many prominent politicians, including Thatcher, gave evidence, but when the report came in February 1996, it was soon buried. It threw up questions of the morality of arms exports to dictatorships, government secrecy and ministerial responsibility. The politicians concerned rode out the storm.

Major continued to face criticism from his own side in 1994–95. Increasingly dismayed by these attacks he took the unprecedented step of resigning the leadership of the Conservative Party in order to force his critics into silence. He told them bluntly to 'put up or shut up'.[41] On 4 July 1995 he sought re-election and defeated his opponent John Redwood, who had resigned from the government, by 218 votes to 89 with 20 abstentions. In the reshuffle that followed, Heseltine became Deputy Prime Minister, Malcolm Rifkind went to the Foreign Office (replacing Hurd who had resigned on 23 June) and Michael Portillo took over at Defence. Jonathan Aitken, who had joined the Cabinet as Chief Secretary to the Treasury in 1994, resigned following allegations that a company of which he had been director, had, in the 1980s, circumvented the embargo on the sale of arms to Iran. Major's brave move changed little. The election had shown both his strength and his weakness. It had given Redwood much publicity. The Euro-sceptics continued with their sniping and the government's majority sank lower and lower. It lost the Perth and Kinross by-election to the SNP in May and Littleborough and Saddleworth to the Liberal Democrats on 27 July. When former minister Alan Howarth joined Labour on 7 October, its majority fell to five. Peter Thurnham joined the Liberal Democrats on 13 October and Emma Nicholson MP crossed the floor to join the Liberal Democrats on 29 December 1995, reducing the government's majority to three. The government moved into a minority after the sudden death of Iain Mills, MP for Meriden, on 17 January 1997. Major became dependent on the goodwill of the Ulster Unionists and the Euro-sceptics in his own party. It seemed to get more anti-EU day by day. By 19 February, Chancellor Clarke, appeared isolated after his colleague, Foreign Secretary Rifkind, told the Germans the British government was hostile to a single currency.[42] Former Prime Minister Heath cut little ice when he attacked Rifkind. He lined up with Labour on devolution, the minimum wage and the Social Chapter and, as the *Guardian* reported on 24 February 1997, he was advised by Euro-sceptic Teresa Gorman MP and others to leave their party and join New Labour. The Conservatives faced another threat over their attitude to the EU. The wealthy Sir James Goldsmith set up the Referendum Party and threatened to put up candidates against pro-EU MPs. Beyond adding a little more colour to the political scene, it did not seem likely to have much impact.

It seemed symbolic of the collapse of the enthusiasm for Europe that Eurotunnel, the company owning the cross-Channel tunnel, teetered on the verge of bankruptcy and had to keep being rescued.[43] On 18 November 1996 the 'inevitable' happened. A fire broke out on a freight train going through the tunnel and several people were injured. Services were suspended for a few days.

BOSNIA: 'HELL'S KITCHEN WAS COOKING'

The fracturing of Yugoslavia in 1991 with Slovenia, Croatia and then Bosnia-Hercegovina declaring themselves independent led to the worst conflicts in Europe since 1945. All three states were recognized by the EC/EU and the USA and admitted to the UNO. After brief wars Yugoslavia recognized the independence of Slovenia and Croatia. In Bosnia-Hercegovina a bitter ethnic civil war broke out. The Bosnian Muslims (44 per cent) and the Bosnian Croats (17 per cent) struggled to an agreement with each other against their stronger Serb adversary. The Serbs (31 per cent of the population) were backed by Yugoslavia (by that time reduced to Serbia and Montenegro) and its powerful army. The NATO states were reluctant to get involved but, 'Hell's kitchen was cooking'.[44] The term 'ethnic cleansing' entered the vocabulary as the Serbs forcibly expelled Muslims and Croats from their homes in Bosnia. A turning point occurred on 5 February 1994 when sixty-eight civilians were killed by a mortar attack in Sarajevo, the Bosnian capital. Television pictures of this and other massacres led to increasing calls for NATO action. President Clinton, in office since January 1993, recommended NATO launch air strikes against Serb positions to protect Bosnian Muslim 'safe havens'. When some of these havens fell, in July 1995, the Serbs killed thousands of Muslims as at Srebrenica. The Serbs also detained UN peacekeepers as hostages in retaliation for NATO air strikes. NATO then stepped up its air strikes and on 5 October a cease-fire was announced. The parties signed an agreement at Dayton, Ohio, which was followed up by the Paris Peace Accord of 14 December. The Serbs recognized Bosnian independence and 20,000 US troops joined 40,000 other soldiers from NATO, Russia and other states to monitor the peace agreement. Throughout the conflict, Clinton feared that the use of allied ground troops could lead to high casualties and that the conflict could spread with Russia backing its traditional ally Serbia. NATO's credibility was also at stake. Clinton was not alone in these fears. In Britain, Major found:

> No party was more split than the Conservatives, which was divided into four camps. Some argued that there was no British interest involved, and that we should have nothing to do with the war. Others thought we should try to deliver humanitarian aid, but not if our troops met opposition on the ground. Others urged us to bomb the Serb forces, and others still wanted both bombing and the deployment of ground troops. Overall, there was strong unease about growing British involvement in what were seen as treacherous conditions, with the risk of a military disaster.[45]

In Cabinet, Clarke, Portillo and Defence Secretary Rifkind were uneasy about British involvement; Major, Heseltine and Hurd, in favour. From the back benches, Heath joined forces with Benn to oppose such action. As the Bosnian crisis subsided another Yugoslav crisis worsened in the province of Kosovo.

CHANGING BRITAIN

Britain was continuing its rapid change in the 1990s as it had done in the 1980s. On 26 August 1994 the Sunday Trading Act came into force. This permitted small shops in England and Wales to open at any time on Sundays and large shops to open for six hours between 10 a.m. and 6 p.m. This completed the transformation of the English Sunday which had started in the 1940s when local authorities were given the right to hold referenda on the opening of cinemas on Sundays. The move was part of the continuing secularization of Britain. Figures published in 1997 revealed further loss of support for all the major Christian churches, including the Catholics. Less than a quarter of all English babies were baptized into the Church of England in 1996 compared with more than two-thirds in 1950.[46] In a move to modernize, the General Synod of the Church of England voted on 22 February 1994 to allow women to be ordained as priests. A highly vocal minority refused to accept the change and sought admission to the Catholic Church. Other Christian denominations already had women clergy. The Church of England controversy over women clergy highlighted again the role of women in society.

Women were breaking through on all sectors of the economy. It was particularly noticeable in the media. Kate Adie became well known as a war correspondent in the Gulf War and in Bosnia, but she was just one of a number of women foreign correspondents, behind whom stood an army of women in other areas of the media. Major promoted a number of women into prominence in the public service including the head of MI5, Customs & Excise, and the Crown Prosecution Service. Britain's first astronaut was Helen Sharman, who joined a Soviet space mission. The number of women solicitors rose from 5,175 in 1983/84 to 12,683 in 1989/90. Similar trends were apparent in the other professions. In the Foreign and Commonwealth Office women represented 46 per cent of the mainstream recruitment in 1981, but 77 per cent of those entering in 1991. In the navy women were allowed to put to sea in 1990. By 1997 almost half the navy's ninety ships had a total of 700 women on board.[47] The RAF trained women to fly combat planes, but the army did not send its women to the front.[48] Women still suffered sexual harassment in the forces, but were successfully challenging this. In the 1990s Britain had a larger female proportion of the work-force than any other EU state. Yet women in Britain were worse off in terms of maternity benefits. The lack of nursery places also hampered women in their careers. The government attempted to counter criticism of their record on this with a nursery voucher scheme. Men were losing their dominant role in the economy partly because of the decline of the old heavy industries such as coal, iron and steel and ship-building. Many of the new jobs were part-time in retailing and the service sector which were more likely to suit women than men. There was speculation about what these economic changes would do for the wider relations between the sexes and their roles in the home and in society. The changing position of women appeared to be one of the most fundamental changes gathering speed in society, which would eventually have a fundamental impact on Britain's political life.

Homosexuality became far more acceptable in the 1980s and 1990s. In 1996 the age of homosexual consent was reduced from 21 to 18. There was controversy in the Church of England on the matter with the 'Gays' winning the day. Channel 4 did much to champion the Gay cause. The armed forces continued to fight a rearguard action against homosexuals in its ranks. Any Rip Van Winkle who had gone to sleep in 1979 and woke up in 1989 would have been astonished by the high visibility of homosexuals. The serious press took advertisements for Gays and Lesbians seeking partners. Actors such as (Sir) Ian McKellen and Stephen Fry did much to enhance the prestige of Gays.

Rip Van Winkle would be shocked by the homeless 'sleeping rough' in doorways in the towns and cities of Britain and above all in London. Once again, as they had done in the 1930s, beggars abounded in London and other large towns.

Another noticeable change was the growth of sponsorship. In addition to the normal advertising on television, many other programmes were sponsored by commercial companies – even the weather reports! There was even consideration of allowing sponsorship of the police in certain areas. Police would wear the logos of sponsoring firms on their uniforms.

Britain was getting wired up in the 1990s. It had a higher level of personal computers in use than many other countries. Although still a minority, more and more people were spending more and more time 'surfing' the internet. You could read the newspapers on the internet, form friendships worldwide, exchange ideas, play games, indulge sexual fantasies, and so on. On the one hand, for those who could afford the relatively small investment, this opportunity represented more freedom. On the negative side, it could represent a new age of even less real, face-to-face contact, and less involvement in trying to make society a better place.

After bitter arguments and various promises by Heseltine, most of the coal mines were either closed or sold off. By 1992, Britain had only about fifty pits, not all producing coal, employing 44,000 compared with 211 employing 294,000 in 1981.[49] By 1994 privatization and closure had reduced the number to twelve with 10,000 miners. Major attempted to privatize one of Britain oldest Crown establishments, the Post Office. There was so much opposition, the plan was withdrawn. Yet despite its tiny majority and known public opposition, Major pressed on with privatization of the nuclear industry and the railways. British Rail passed into history.

The year 1997 saw Britain giving up its last major colony. Hong Kong, with a population of around 6 million, reverted to Chinese sovereignty in that year. The Chinese promised to retain the capitalist economy of the former colony. They were not prepared to accept democratic reforms Britain had belatedly introduced under its last governor, Chris Patten. Under the British Nationality (Hong Kong) Act 1990, an estimated 180,000 individuals had the right of abode in the United Kingdom. Not all of them would necessarily come. An unknown number of illegal Chinese immigrants were entering Britain. What impact this new community would have on Britain could only be guessed at.

LOTTERY FEVER

When the National Lottery was launched on 14 November 1994 Britain was the last country in Europe to have one. Britain was the only country in which the Lottery had private enterprise involvement. By 1996 it was estimated that 90 per cent of adults had played the Lottery and 30 million played regularly thus making Britain's lottery 'the biggest in the world'. Of every pound staked, 5p went to the trader selling the ticket; 50p went in prizes; 28p was placed at the disposal of the National Lottery Distribution Fund; 12p was taken in Customs & Excise; and 5p went to Camelot, the company running the operation.[50] Expenditure on the Lottery meant that consumers diverted an estimated £450 million from food, confectioneries and tobacco, and £450 million from entertainment. Remarkably, up to October 1996, there were £58.9m unclaimed prizes.[51] There was fear of lottery addiction, especially among young people, and that the young would get the wrong message. Forget training and qualifications and attempt to strike it rich through the Lottery. The Lottery was creating some new jobs, but others were being lost in other sectors of the gambling industry such as the football pools.[52] London was benefiting most from Lottery projects.[53] The government seemed determined to introduce more and more gambling opportunities into Britain. On 5 February 1997 the first mid-week lottery draw was held. The Home Office announced in November 1996 that, after representation from the gambling and tourist industries, a large London casino would be able to install Vegas-style slot machines, with unlimited stakes and payouts in designated towns. A number of conference towns were designated as suitable. One of them, Croydon, after a free vote of its elected councillors, rejected the idea because of the harmful social impact. But the Home Office wanted to press ahead despite local objections.[54] Three years after it started, the National Lottery had created 320 millionaires.[55] It is appropriate to mention that there were 81,000 millionaires in Britain in 1996. Of individuals with more than £5 million, nearly 60 per cent had inherited their wealth. The *Sunday Times* index of wealth 'still reads like a roll call of the establishment, with the Sainsbury family, Viscount Rothermere and Duke of Westminster at the top'.[56] By the turn of the century, Sir Richard Branson and George Soros were among the top ten. A new generation of internet and mobile-phone millionaires had joined the rich.

THE 'SLEAZE FACTOR'

In the 1990s the seventeenth-century word of unknown origin, 'sleaze', meaning squalid, dirty, filthy, seedy, sordid, disreputable, became increasingly associated with Conservative politics, the Establishment and the monarchy. At one level it was about government ministers privatizing great national assets and later getting well-paid jobs on their boards. It was about MPs taking money from private interests which could clash with their public duties. At another level it was about preaching 'back to basics', returning to the alleged high moral standards of the past and then being engaged in adultery or perverse sexual practices. Cecil Parkinson and David Mellor were notable cases of ministers forced to resign because of extra-marital relationships. Steve Norris, Minister of Transport, actually wrote a book about his exploits![57] In 1993 Asil Nadir, a Turkish Cypriot businessman, facing fraud charges in London, fled to Northern Cyprus. It was later revealed he had been a generous contributor to Conservative funds. Industrialist and Conservative treasurer, Lord McAlpine, admitted that his party had received donations from Hong Kong and from US business interests. Two junior ministers, Tim Smith and Neil Hamilton, were forced to resign after the *Guardian* (20 October 1994) accused them of accepting 'cash for questions' in the Commons in the interest of Mohamed al-Fayed. This was before they became ministers. All this led to the setting up, in October 1994, of the committee, chaired by Lord Nolan, on standards of conduct in public life. Nolan, reporting in May 1995, recommended that MPs continue to be allowed to have outside earnings, but that details of these earnings be published. It also made recommendations about the rules governing civil servants joining the private sector on leaving the public service. The government resisted disclosure but was defeated when twenty-three Conservatives joined the opposition in voting for full disclosure. In 1996 the register of MPs' interests was published for the first time. It related solely to outside earnings connected to their parliamentary work. A total or £3.2 million was disclosed. According to the *Daily Telegraph* (8 May 1996) more than three-quarters of this money went to Conservative MPs for consultancies related to their parliamentary activities. MPs were not required to disclose earnings from directorships and other work not linked to parliamentary work. The total figure earned is, therefore, likely to be far higher. Some MPs, Sir Edward Heath and six former Cabinet ministers among them, refused to reveal their earnings.[58] In the case of Labour MPs, most outside financial support came from trade unions.

On 2 October 1996 the *Guardian* published the names of twenty-one Conservative MPs who, in 1987, had received payments towards their election expenses from Harrods owner Mohamed al-Fayed. More than half of them were, had been, or became, government ministers including Michael Portillo, the Defence Secretary, and Norman Lamont, Chancellor of the Exchequer (until May 1993). The payments were made through an intermediary, Ian Greer. At the same time, two Labour MPs and Alan Beith, Liberal Democrats' deputy leader, received payments. They were not illegal. On 3 October a Labour front-bench member in the Lords, Baroness Turner, resigned when it was revealed she was a business associate of Greer. It is disturbing to consider that a foreign businessman had given money to a group of MPs which together was larger than the government's majority at the 1992 election. The electorate had the right to be concerned that increasingly MPs and parties were being financed by private, even foreign, business interests. Would politicians be able to maintain their independence in these circumstances? Conservatives had often attacked Labour politicians for representing trade unions, but these were democratic bodies whose members were ordinary British voters, and MPs' links with unions were completely visible. The Conservatives had claimed the high moral ground and lost nineteen ministers in almost as many months.[59] David Willetts, the Paymaster-General, was the last to go before the election. He resigned because of his actions as a government whip before joining the government. The last pre-election blow to the government was the loss of the Wirral (Cheshire) by-election to Labour on 27 February.

MONARCHY IN CRISIS

On 29 August 1996 the heir to the British throne, Prince Charles, got confirmation of his divorce from Princess Diana after fifteen years of marriage, many of which were subject to scandal and conflict. More than a little energy was spent on the future title of Diana. On the day of the divorce the Queen decreed that in future divorced wives of male descendants to the Sovereign would not be entitled to use the style Royal Highness.[60] The whole story was significant only as part of the collapse of the myth of the British monarchy. This myth had held up fairly well with the support of all Britain's post-war prime ministers. It started to crack with the ever-increasing exposure of the members of the Royal Family to media attention in the 1980s. Britain's increasing economic difficulties also turned the spotlight on the financing of the monarchy. The mistake of the monarchists was to claim so much for the Royal Family in terms of what it gave Britain in terms of continuity, stability, service and success.

Part of the justification for retaining a monarchy based solely on the accident of birth, which gave the incumbent enormous wealth, massive status and great influence, was that the Royal Family gave the nation an example of traditional values. In fact, by 1996, the Queen's only sister, Margaret, was divorced, as was the Queen's only daughter, Princess Anne, and Anne's brother Andrew was divorced from his wife Sarah. One other prince remained unmarried. There were rumours about Prince Philip, the Queen's husband. Anne made history when she remarried in 1992. This was the first royal remarriage after a divorce since Henry VIII. Far from being positive role models, the Royals appeared to be less stable, less able to cope with life than average Britons.

The life-style of the Royals led questions to be asked about various aspects of the monarch's role. Was it right that the monarch should be head of the Church of England? The various heirs to the throne appeared to be entirely unsuitable as potential inheritors of that title. In any case, in a Britain in which most people led a secular life-style, and considerable minorities followed other faiths, was it healthy to have the state linked so closely to one denomination? Was it right that heirs to the throne should be prevented from marrying adherents of other religions?

Most people acknowledged that the Queen had worked hard in what she considered the national interest. When she reached 70 in 1996 some believed she ought to consider announcing her retirement. Inevitably, the question was raised whether it is sensible to have the position of head of state held at the whim of the existing incumbent with absolutely no rules or even conventions about retirement.

The massive expenditure of time and space by the media on the Royal Family diverted attention from the many other more pressing issues. And all the pomp and circumstance surrounding them led many abroad to doubt the seriousness of the British, particularly in view of the unreal arguments about British sovereignty and membership of the European Union.

Serious doubts were also being entertained about whether Britain could continue to pay the enormous sums involved upholding the monarchy. The monarch had paid tax until George V in the 1930s. The Queen only agreed to pay income tax in 1996. It remained unclear just how rich she was partly because of various attempts by her admirers in the Establishment to obscure the sums involved. Various costs of the monarchy had been farmed out to appropriate ministries. Thus the royal yacht and the Queen's flight were paid for by the Ministry of Defence, the royal train by the Ministry of Transport and so on. Few people realized that even the clothes worn by the members of the Royal Family on their official engagements abroad were paid for out of taxation. According to the *Independent* (27 August 1996), Princess Margaret's week in San Francisco in 1995 cost the taxpayer £7,200 for her clothes. Prince Edward's tailor presented a bill for £2,200 for his four-day trip to Swaziland in 1993. In the same year, the Duchess of Kent's four days in the Seychelles required £4,300-worth of tailoring.

Supporters of the monarchy argued that it helped to bring in tourists. Yet were the French less able to attract tourists to Paris because they had no monarchy? Was it not true that the White House in Washington, DC, attracted great crowds of tourists? Was republican Rome unable to keep its hotels full and its museums overflowing with foreign tourists? The same argument was used that the Royals helped the export drive. Amazingly, those highly successful economies Germany, South Korea and

Taiwan managed without such help, and the Japanese royals have been used little as commercial ambassadors.

By 1996 the popularity of the Royal Family had fallen dramatically as compared with earlier periods and most people felt the monarchy should at least be scaled down, reformed to be more like the less ostentatious monarchies of northern Europe.

FAREWELL TO CASTLEMARTIN

On 13 October 1996 the German Army withdrew from Castlemartin, Pembroke, in Wales. The Bundeswehr had conducted tank training there since 1961. Over 84,000 German soldiers had trained there during this period. Without doubt most people in Britain knew nothing about this, although it was in no way secret. The Germans had attempted to remain unobtrusive, but had tried to maintain good relations with the local community through regular football and darts fixtures, contributions to local charities and so on. German reunification and the end of the Cold War eliminated the need for such training facilities in Britain. The farewell came at a time when Anglo-German relations were in relatively poor shape compared to the 1970s and 1980s. In the 1970s a survey showed that the majority of British people saw (West) Germany as Britain's best friend in Europe. A survey of MPs in 1986 revealed that, although a few MPs could not distinguish between the two German states, West Germany was admired by a majority of Members of all three parties.[61] Margaret Thatcher had opposed Germany reunification in 1989,[62] and Nicholas Ridley had called the European Community a 'German racket'. He had been forced to resign for this remark. But anti-German feeling surfaced over fears of German hegemony in Europe. Most Britons probably did not know that Britain was Germany's fourth largest trading partner[63] and top destination for German foreign investment.[64] Nearly a quarter of German investment abroad in 1995 – DM 10,644 billion – went to Britain. Britain was also the biggest single investor in Germany, with a total of DM 2.7 billion. Switzerland followed with DM 2.036 billion.[65] The average Briton's vision of Germany was the constant stream of films on television about the Second World War and the Holocaust. Crimes committed by other states in that war were virtually ignored. In 1995, a survey of school children revealed that when it came to desirable foreign destinations, Germany was bottom of the list. They would rather go to Bosnia.[66] The mood was, to a large degree, the product of ignorance and the efforts of the Euro-sceptic wing of the Conservative Party. Other factors were the publicity given to the activities of tiny groups of racists in Germany against foreign guest workers and asylum seekers, and the argument about the safety of British beef.

FORMER MINISTERS: 'SHAMELESSNESS OF THIS MOVE . . . '

Another controversy which Lord Nolan sought to mediate was the movement of civil servants and former ministers from ministries to jobs in the private sector. In any number of cases they went to work for firms with which they had negotiated as public servants. Tim Eggar gave up his job as Energy Minister to be a part-time executive chairman of the UK subsidiary of an American engineering firm supplying oil companies. His appointment was announced three months and nine days after his resignation, just within the minimum guidelines laid down by Nolan. Among earlier cases was Tebbit who became a director of British Telecom, the company he privatized in 1984. Lord Young was at the DTI when Cable & Wireless was privatized; later he joined the company as executive chairman. 'From the first day in his new job, he would be negotiating with the government department he had left the previous summer.'[67] Peter Walker, as Energy Secretary, was responsible for the British Gas privatization. Later he joined the board of the privatized British Gas as well as Rothschild, the company that handled the flotation.[68] Steve Norris, former transport minister, who had privatized London's buses, joined Capital City Bus as non-executive chairman. Labour MP Brian Wilson, called it 'This shameless move', which would 'heighten the public impression that Tory ministers legislate for their own futures rather than the national interest.'[69] Norris accepted a £150,000-a-year job as head of the Road Haulage Association, a trade body, four months after leaving office.[70] There was also disapproval when Lord Wakeham joined NM Rothschild, the merchant bank, just six months after leaving the Cabinet. As Energy Minister from 1989 to 1992, he paved the way for the privatization of British Coal. Rothschild handled the privatization and payments to them were later attacked by the all-party Commons Public Accounts Committee.[71]

Another case of massive financial gain was the £6 million in secret loans granted to Roy Thomason, MP for Bromsgrove, by Lloyds, Barclays, Midland, NatWest and TSB, so that he would not go bankrupt. His bankruptcy would have involved his resignation from Parliament and the probable loss of his seat to Labour. The House of Commons committee on standards and privileges ruled that Thomason should have declared the loans.[72] To April 1996, over a million small businesses had gone to the wall since Major became Prime Minister.[73] At least several thousand of them could have been saved by the above-mentioned banks with £6 million. In some cases the business owners lost their homes when their businesses went under.

NEW LABOUR: 'PLEDGE TO RICH'

In terms of its members the Labour Party that Tony Blair took charge of was not so different from that which Foot led or even that of Callaghan and Wilson.[74] It consisted of local parties, which were a mixture of ideologues, trade union activists, ethnic minorities and a few middle-class reformers. The mixture varied enormously. Some parties were virtually just one or other of the first three. In some areas where coal had been king, the NUM still dominated. In areas where there was a strong Irish, Asian or Jewish minority, the particular minority tended to dominate. Sometimes it was a coalition of ethnic minorities. The problem was that the dominance of such groups put off outsiders. Alternatively, local parties dominated in these ways did not welcome new members who did not belong to their particular ideological, ethnic or trade union group. Such was the experience of some who responded to Blair's press advertising campaign in 1995. Yet it was precisely such people Blair said he wanted to recruit, reform-minded individuals who rejected Conservatism, who felt they ought to be more active as citizens, but who did not have a narrow, fixed perspective on politics. If they successfully fought their way into the Labour camp what did Blair offer them in terms of policy?

The *Daily Express* (28 September 1996) headline proclaimed, 'Blair's Pledge To Rich'. The leader of 'New Labour' had apparently pledged, 'I won't hit big earners'. As the election approached there appeared to be no pledge that Labour leader Tony Blair would not break, no policy he would not change in order to win the extra votes to secure his tenancy at 10 Downing Street. As we have seen, Labour had cast off many of its old policies under Kinnock and Smith, but somehow it had remained recognizable as the Labour Party. No one could quarrel with the argument that Labour must change with the times. It is also true that a party in opposition can never be sure just what it will face when taking office, it must therefore not promise too much. On the other hand, if it goes too far down this road it runs the risk of making its own supporters apathetic. Labour normally had greater difficulty in mobilizing its vote than did the Conservatives. New Labour went all out in its drive to prove its adherence to the capitalist system. In 1996 Blair visited a number of Pacific rim 'tiger' economies and pronounced himself impressed. Their growth rates and the increasing skills of their peoples *were* impressive, but success had been achieved by authoritarian regimes, without trade unions and with an unenviable record on human rights. The capitalist system in 1996 had no answer to the problem of growing unemployment. Blair appeared to agree with Major that we would have to learn to live with it. In the twentieth century, Britain only had full employment once the Second World War was in full swing (1940), to around the end of the 1950s. Unemployment had grown with each successive government. Employment had been helped by compulsory national service to 1963 and massive expenditure on armaments. In the days just before he went to meet his maker even Lord Stockton (Macmillan) told the Lords, 'The problem was never solved – let us be frank about it' (23 January 1985).

By January 1997, 31 per cent of voters saw Blair as being in the centre politically, where 44 per cent placed themselves. Only 27 per cent put Major there, but 55 per cent thought Ashdown was also in the centre.[75] However, despite their efforts, the Blair team failed to convince the electorate that taxes would not go up under Labour. A *Guardian/ICM* (4 February 1997) telephone poll revealed that most electors, whether Labour, Liberal Democrat or Conservative, were prepared to pay more in tax for better public service. The trouble for Labour was that Conservative defectors were least ready to do this. Another possible problem for Labour was that those interviewed do not always tell the truth, or are influenced by a number of factors. Some interviewees feel embarrassed to admit to views, which are not entirely 'respectable'. Some of the support for monarchy and religion in the past was probably due to this, and racism is likely to be understated in polls. In 1992 the Conservatives appeared to be so unpopular that their support was understated in the polls. Would this happen again in the run up to the 1997 election?

'FROM INEQUITABLE TO INHUMAN'

The *1996 Human Development Report* prepared by the UN revealed what a sorry state the world was in. The wealthier were getting wealthier, while the poor were getting poorer. The world's 358 billionaires, including such notables as the Sultan of Brunei and Bill Gates, the founder of Microsoft, the computer giant, had more assets than the combined incomes of countries representing nearly half – 45 per cent – of the earth's population. The UN administrator of the report, James Speth, said if the current trends continued, 'economic disparities between industrial and developing nations will move from inequitable to inhuman'. Within the developed nations the report singled out Britain and Australia for displaying growing economic injustice between the haves and have-nots. In both countries, the richest 20 per cent of their populations earned ten times more money than the poorest 20 per cent. Britain came sixteenth on the human development index (HDI) below many of its EU partners including France and Spain. The HDI ranks countries according to access to health care, educational standards and basic purchasing power.

The Cohesion Report, published by the European Commission in Brussels in 1996, showed that on poverty – defined as households having less than 50 per cent of the national average income – Britain fared among the worst of the EU states. It had about 17 per cent of all households on or below the poverty line – the same as Spain and only a little ahead of

Greece and Italy – way behind Germany (11 per cent) or the Benelux countries (5 per cent).[76]

As Britain approached the election of 1997, Major struggled to keep his fragmented party together on a mounting tide of hostility to the European Union and 'German hegemony'.[77] The Conservatives had held office for all but twenty years since 1918. It was a period of almost uninterrupted decline. New Labour attempted to show itself as a safe capitalist-supporting alternative. It seemed that Britain had suffered from the death of a sense of outrage, which had sustained the great reformers of the past. But impoverished, divided, Britain was more dependent than ever on its neighbours in the EU and on the world economy, and Major and Blair knew this. The British Prime Minister had never had so little influence and authority, power and respect in the world. Britons could take little comfort from abroad. Virtually all of the world's most important states faced crises of one kind or another. In the United States the great majority of voters did not even bother to vote in the 1996 Presidential election thus depriving not only President Clinton, but also the system of much of its democratic credibility. In Russia, Boris Yeltsin, notorious for his drinking, clung to office, after major heart surgery, as President of a decaying, near bankrupt empire. In China a clique ruthlessly enforced their dictatorship, which was anything but 'the dictatorship of the proletariat', over one quarter of the world's population. There were fears that the death of leader Deng Xiaoping in February 1997 would bring instability. The ruling family of the rich Indonesian Republic ran it as a family business. Prosperous and democratic Canada crept steadily closer to splitting into two separate states. Germany alone still appeared to be reasonably democratic, well run, prosperous and coping with the problems of post-unification.

ELECTION '97: 'DEEP NATIONAL IMPATIENCE'

As the longest election campaign in modern times got under way, Major sensed that there was

> deep national impatience with our party . . . The feeling was amplified many times by the bickering, squabbling and backstabbing that now afflicted Conservatism almost like a death-wish, and which did more damage to our prospects than Tony Blair could have dreamed of doing.[78]

He believed the electorate were bored with his party after so long in office. There was sleaze – 'the exotic follies of a handful of MPs' – but it was exaggerated.[79] As for Labour, it 'managed not to seem frightening any more'. He was 'bewildered' by New Labour, 'old Labour's devious offspring'.[80] He still hoped that Labour would make 'an unlucky stumble' during the campaign.[81] Luck nearly came to Major's aid when a senior adviser to Blair left 'Labour's entire election campaign' plan at Burger King in Euston Station.[82] The gods were not with Major, Labour's documents were recovered safely. Labour was better prepared than ever before with all the paraphernalia of modern electioneering. Blair seemed to improve as the campaign went on. His wife, Cherie, 'a top lawyer, a have-it-all superwoman, Catholic, a high achiever'[83] and mother of three, was an asset. Behind Blair stood Peter Mandelson (b. 1953), an Oxford-educated MP, former TV producer and grandson of Herbert Morrison, Philip Gould, Alastair Campbell and several other media and public relations professionals. At the heart of their campaign were focus groups of electors who articulated their hopes and fears.

Sleaze dominated the early stages of the campaign. At Tatton, BBC foreign correspondent, Martin Bell, stood as an independent against Neil Hamilton. The opposition candidates withdrew in his favour. As the electors were getting bored the Conservatives turned their attention to the economy, taxation, the unions and, not least, Labour's inexperience. Throughout the campaign posters were displayed on key sites proclaiming 'Britain is Booming, Don't Let Labour Blow It'. In private, Labour strategists admitted these were their weaknesses.[84] Labour hit trouble on 4 April when Blair made a comparison between the tax-raising powers of the proposed Scottish Parliament and a parish council. He appeared to be insulting the Scots with a sham parliament. 'A press conference the following day was like slow torture for Blair as journalists harried him relentlessly.'[85] Labour also got into difficulties over privatization, something the public was not keen on. Gordon Brown announced that, in government, Labour would compile a list of public assets with a view to disposing of the 'inessential' elements.[86] Drama hit the campaign on 23 April, eight days before polling, when a *Guardian* headline announced, 'Bombshell for Labour, Lead Shrinks to 5 Points as Tories catch Euro Mood'. It looked like the Conservatives still had a chance of winning. Also, Labour's *War Book* giving details of confidential polls highlighting Labour's weaknesses as well as its strengths and its campaign strategy, fell into the Conservatives' hands.[87] They held press conferences claiming it revealed Labour was going to attempt to misrepresent the Conservatives' pensions plans.[88] The Conservatives strongly denied they would abolish the state pension. Labour pressed them hard on the issue. Major believed the pensions' issue cost them votes.[89] The Liberal Democrats focused on education, claiming it was 'national suicide' not to raise taxes to improve the system.

All the main parties did reasonably well with their broadcasts. In addition they had ample opportunity to get themselves across in BBC's *Question Time* and *Newsnight*, and other news programmes including those of the new Channel 5. The internet, still a novelty for most people, was also used by the parties. Additional controversy was provided by the screening, by BBC1 and BBC2, of a broadcast by the British National Party (BNP), which was openly nationalistic, calling for repatriation of all immigrants, withdrawal from the EU, and the re-introduction of the death penalty. Channel 4 refused to broadcast it. Also banned, by all channels, on the grounds of taste and decency, was a programme by an anti-abortion group, which was fielding over fifty candidates, the minimum required for a five-minute broadcast. Scargill's Socialist Labour Party, the Natural Law Party, the Referendum Party, the UK Independence Party (UKIP) and the Liberal Party (a splinter group), all got television slots. *The Times* advised its readers which candidates were Euro-sceptic and indicated a preference for them.

Polling day, 1 May, was warm and sunny. This should have helped Labour in that it traditionally found it harder to persuade its supporters to vote. Would people feel happier and therefore less likely to vote for change?

RESULTS: 'A TIDAL WAVE . . . ' OVER THE CONSERVATIVES

The first seat to declare was the safe Labour seat of Sunderland South with a low turnout of 58.77 per cent. 'Old Labour' MP Chris Mullin was re-elected. Although it showed a decisive 10.31 per cent swing to Labour, all sides were cautious about its significance. It soon became clear, however, that a historic political landslide was under way. The first big shock for the Conservatives was the loss of Birmingham Edgbaston at 21 minutes past midnight. It had been in their hands since 1922. To make matters worse for some Euro-sceptics, it was won for Labour by German-born law lecturer Gisela Stuart. By 3.12 a.m. Labour had its majority. The electorate had rejected Euro-scepticism, xenophobia, racism and sleaze. Down went Euro-sceptics Nick Budgen, Norman Lamont, Michael Portillo and Angela Rumbold. But out too were pro-European Conservatives Hugh Dykes and Edwina Currie. Pro-Europe Kenneth Clarke survived at Rushcliffe. Seven of his Cabinet colleagues, including the Foreign Secretary, Malcolm Rifkind, did not. Many junior ministers and former Cabinet members were also defeated, Martin Bell triumphed at Tatton against Neil Hamilton. Wales and Scotland were declared 'Tory-free zones'. Although Labour was the main victor in these two countries, the SNP increased its seats to six and PC retained its four seats. The Liberal Democrats had their best results since the 1920s, a personal triumph for Ashdown. Clearly, tactical voting had helped to bring about this political revolution, which overturned Conservative majorities of over 15,000.

'A tidal wave has burst over the Conservative Party tonight . . . The sea wall is collapsing all around us.' So commented defeated former minister David Mellor. It swept the kingdom from north to south and east to west, giving Labour 45 per cent of the vote. This was their second best ever. Ironically, in 1951 they won 49 per cent and lost! The Conservatives had their lowest percentage (31) vote in any democratic election! The Liberal Democrats declined slightly with 17 per cent. Sadly, at 71 per cent, turnout was the lowest since 1935. It was the highest in Brecon and Radnorshire (82.24 per cent) and Stirling (81.84) and lowest in the inner city constituencies such as Liverpool Riverside (51.93). Where Labour was safe turnout was often lower. It was also on the low side in some Conservative seats, perhaps reflecting a tendency of disillusioned Conservatives to stay at home. In terms of seats, this was Labour's best ever result. For the first time since 1979 Labour voters were evenly distributed between men and women.[90] Traditionally, women were more likely to vote Conservative. Labour had succeeded in attracting more middle-class voters and had spread its representation to all parts of Great Britain. The Conservatives had been pushed back into the rural and semi-rural areas of England and a few outposts in London.

In Northern Ireland Sinn Fein achieved its best result in forty years gaining 16.1 per cent. Gerry Adams seized West Belfast from the SDLP and Martin McGuiness defeated the DUP in Mid-Ulster. This result would put pressure on Blair to grant concessions.

In terms of parties, the electorate had been presented with a wide choice, but all the small parties were defeated. The Referendum Party (RP) attracted 2.7 per cent of the poll. It did better in England than in Scotland or Wales. Its best result was at Harwich, where Jeffrey Titford won 4,923 (9.20 per cent). Many of the RP candidates got higher votes than their leader, Sir James Goldsmith, who attracted only 1,518 (3.45 per cent) and lost his deposit at Putney. There were few places where the RP could have influenced the result. If, as seems likely, it attracted more Conservative votes than Labour votes, it *possibly* influenced the outcome at Harwich, where Labour's majority was only 1,216 and in six other constituencies won by Labour. It possibly helped the Liberal Democrats win Eastleigh, Lewes and Winchester. That Goldsmith's cash had some impact is shown by the fate of the UKIP. Its candidates usually trailed behind those of the RP. It probably attracted the same sort of voters, though its stand on Europe was clearer than that of the RP. Nigel Farage gave it its best result at Salisbury, 3,302 votes (5.72 per cent). The RP did not field a candidate there. Only at Torbay did it possibly affect the outcome. Without competition from the RP, it took 1,962 votes (3.68 per cent). The Liberal Democratic victor's majority was just twelve. The Greens did poorly, their best vote being 2,415 (5.48 per cent) at Stroud, and the Liberals at Liverpool West Derby (4,037 or 9.58 per cent). The BNP made little impact, its best results being in the 1930s hunting grounds of the British Union of Fascists. In Bethnal Green, David King won 3,350 votes or 7.50 per cent. On a 61.20 per cent turnout, he beat the RP and four others with serious programmes. On the Left, the most important challenge came from the Socialist Labour Party, nine of whose fifty-seven candidates got into four figures. The best result was Imran Khan in East Ham. He beat the Liberal Democrat, BNP, RP and National Democrat, gaining 2,697 votes (6.78 per cent). In Scotland the Scottish Socialist Alliance (SSA) gained 3,639 votes (11.09 per cent) in Glasgow, by far its best vote.

The number of women MPs doubled from sixty to 120, 101 of them Labour. Among the Labour MPs were the twin sisters Maria and Angela Eagle. The Commons had become much younger. Labour's Clair Ward (Watford) was only 24. Perhaps this massive increase of women would prove to be a kind of revolution of great significance for the future. The ethnic minorities secured increased representation. All outgoing Labour MPs from ethnic minorities were re-elected. They were joined by Marsah Singh (Bradford West), Dr Ashok Kumar and the first Muslim, millionaire businessman Mohammed Sarwar (Glasgow Gowan). The only Asian Con- servative MP, Nirj Deva, was defeated at Brentford & Isleworth. Labour's Oona King (Bethnal Green & Bow) became the second black woman MP. As ever, the Jewish community was well represented in the new Parliament. A *Jewish Chronicle* (9 May 1997) survey of 'the 20 known Jewish MPs' revealed thirteen Labour (eight in 1992), six Conservative (eleven) and one Liberal Democrat (one). In Thatcher's old seat, Finchley & Golders Green (with redrawn boundaries) her pro-Israel, but non-Jewish, successor, John Marshall, lost to Labour's Dutch-born Dr Rudi Vis.

On 2 May the pictures of the Blair family standing on the steps of 10 Downing Street flashed around the world, offering a refreshingly modern, youthful, democratic image of Britain. 'The world warms to Blair's victory', commented the press. The Stock Exchange responded by climbing

Table 11.1 Election results in seats 1997 and 1992

	1997	1992
Labour	418	270
Conservative	165	336
Liberal Democrats	46	20
Ulster Unionists	10	9
Scottish Nationals (SNP)	6	3
Plaid Cymru	4	4
SDLP	3	4
Democratic Unionist	2	3
Sinn Fein	2	0
Independent (Martin Bell)	1	0
Other Unionist	1	1
Speaker	1	1
Total	659	651

higher than ever. Major responded by resigning as Leader of the Conservatives. Since his party had taken over in 1979 Britain had fallen from the thirteenth richest country in terms of GDP per person, to eighteenth. Despite this, with its youngest Prime Minister since 1812 Britain looked to the millennium with cautious optimism.

NOTES

Unless otherwise indicated, the place of publication is London.

1 Clark, op. cit., 349–50.
2 Peter Riddell, *The Thatcher Era and its Legacy* (1991), 235.
3 General Sir Peter De La Billière, *Storm Command: A Personal Account of the Gulf War* (1992), 4. See also [Major-General] Patrick Cordingley, *In the Eye of the Storm* (1996).
4 Information provided to the author by Michael Portillo, Secretary of State for Defence.
5 Information provided by Michael Portillo.
6 De La Billière, op. cit., 328.
7 Information provided by Michael Portillo.
8 *Independent*, 6 October 1996.
9 Sarah Hogg and Jonathan Hill, *Too Close to Call: Power and Politics – John Major in No. 10* (1995), 76.
10 Hogg and Hill, op. cit., 79.
11 ibid., 140.
12 ibid., 142.
13 ibid., 143
14 ibid., 153.
15 ibid., 147.
16 ibid., 148.
17 The quotes are taken from the full text given in the *Independent on Sunday*, Supplement, 1 October 1992.
18 Hogg and Hill, op. cit., 161.
19 ibid., 162.
20 Keith Dowding, 'Government at the Centre', in Patrick Dunleavy *et al.* (eds), *Developments in British Politics* (1993), 177.
21 Conservative Central Office, *The Campaign Guide 1992,* 229–31.
22 Butler, *British Elections*, op. cit., 88.
23 Ivor Crewe in *The Times Guide to the House of Commons April 1992*, 254.
24 Ivor Crewe, 'Voting and the Electorate', in Dunleavy, op. cit., 114.
25 John Solomos and Les Back, 'Migration and the Politics of Race', in Dunleavy, op. cit., 324.
26 John Rentoul, *Tony Blair* (1995), 399. Blair presented himself in Tony Blair, *New Britain: My Vision of a Young Country* (1996).
27 Rentoul, op. cit., 85.
28 ibid., 403.
29 ibid., 488–9 for full text.
30 David Logue, 85.
31 *Guardian*, 24 February 1997
32 *The Times*, 10 October 1996.

33 Tom Bower, *Maxwell. The Final Verdict* (1995). An interesting account of Maxwell's life.
34 Nick Leeson, *Rogue Trader* (1996). The man at the centre of the storm tells his side of the story.
35 *Sunday Times*, 8 December 1996.
36 *Observer*, 8 September 1996.
37 Hogg and Hill, op. cit., 47.
38 *Keesing's Contemporary Archives*, News Digest for February 1996, 40968 quoting *Hansard*, 4 March 1996.
39 *Britannica Year Book 1995*, 492.
40 Information provided by Manchester City Council.
41 Hogg and Hill, op. cit., 270. A very useful study of the Conservatives is Steve Ludlam and Martin J. Smith (eds), *Contemporary British Conservativism* (1996).
42 *The Times*, 20 February 1997.
43 *The Times*, 3 October 1996.
44 Major, op. cit., 535.
45 ibid., 536.
46 *Guardian*, 7 February 1997.
47 *Guardian*, 7 February 1997.
48 *Guardian*, 7 February 1997.
49 Barry Supple, 'Coal Mining in Leventhal, op. cit., 169.
50 HM Treasury, *Economic Briefing*, April 1996.
51 *Independent*, 20 November 1996.
52 *Independent*, 30 September 1996.
53 *Independent*, 30 September 1996.
54 *Daily Telegraph*, 13 November 1996.
55 *Daily Telegraph*, 15 February 1997.
56 *Daily Telegraph*, 15 February 1997.
57 *Independent*, 24 September 1996.
58 *The Times*, 8 May 1996.
59 *Sunday Times*, 15 September 1996.
60 *The Times*, 29 August 1996. The most serious of the many books on the Queen is Ben Pimlott, *The Queen: A Biography of Elizabeth II* (1996).
61 David Childs/Axel Noack, 'Commons/Bundestag survey revealed', in *Politics & Society in Germany, Austria and Switzerland*, Vol. 1, No. 1, Summer 1988.
62 Thatcher, op. cit., 792–6.
63 German Embassy, 14 November 1995.
64 German Embassy, 3 June 1996.
65 German Embassy, *Economic Report*, 3 June 1996.
66 *Guardian*, 27 September 1996.
67 Mark Hollingsworth, *MPs for Hire: The Secret World of Political Lobbying* (1991). This book gives many cases.
68 Hollingsworth, op. cit., 153.
69 *Guardian*, 7 November 1996.
70 *The Times*, 18 November 1996.
71 *The Times*, 22 November 1996.
72 *Sunday Times*, 28 July 1996.
73 *Observer*, 8 May 1996.
74 Among the many books on Labour are: Andrew Thorpe, *A History of the Labour Party* (1997); Geoffrey Foote, *The Labour Party's Political Thought: A History* (1997).
75 *Observer*, 12 January 1997.

76 *Guardian*, 7 November 1997.
77 David Baker, Imogen Fountain, Andrew Gamble, Steve Ludlam, 'Backbench Conservative Attitudes to European Integration', *The Political Science Quarterly*, April–June 1995. The authors concluded that their 1994 survey revealed the hostility of the parliamentary Conservatives to the EU, 56 per cent of whom wanted 'in effect' to tear up the Treaty of Rome.
78 Major, op. cit., 692.
79 ibid., 693.
80 ibid., 694.
81 ibid., 690.
82 Gould, op. cit., 344.
83 *Independent*, 3 May 1997.
84 Gould, op. cit., 351, 353.
85 ibid., 361.
86 ibid., 362.
87 ibid., 377.
88 Major, op. cit., 716.
89 ibid., 717.
90 Coxall and Robins, op. cit., 206.

12

BLAIR'S FIRST TERM, 1997–2001

BLAIR'S CABINET

In forming his 22-strong Cabinet, Blair kept to his shadow cabinet team. As expected, John Prescott was appointed Deputy Prime Minister and Secretary of State for the Environment, Transport and the Regions. Gordon Brown was made Chancellor of the Exchequer. Robin Cook went to the Foreign and Commonwealth Office. Lord Irvine was appointed Lord Chancellor. Jack Straw went to the Home Office and David Blunkett to Education. Margaret Beckett, the top woman member, was given the Board of Trade and Trade and Industry. Dr Jack Cunningham was handed the relatively lowly Ministry of Agriculture, Food and Fisheries. Donald Dewar got Scotland and his fellow Scot, George Robertson, Defence. The sensitive job of dealing with the NHS was given to Frank Dobson. Ann Taylor was appointed President of the Council and Leader of the House of Commons. Apart from Irvine, all these were well-known public figures.

Cook (1946–2005), son of a school teacher, graduated from Edinburgh University and went on to work for the WEA as a tutor-organizer before his election to the Commons in 1974. Elevated to a life peerage in 1992, Irvine (1940–) had progressed via Glasgow and Cambridge universities to the Bar in 1967. Both Tony and Cherie Blair were among his pupil barristers. A QC, he had worked for the Labour cause in the Lords whilst maintaining his legal practice. Born in Essex, and brought up by a single mother on a council estate, Straw (1946–) was a graduate of Leeds University, a barrister and former President of the National Union of Students. He worked for Barbara Castle before taking over her seat in Blackburn in 1979. Blunkett (1947–) graduated from Sheffield University and was a professional politician in local government before he entered Parliament in 1987. He was the first sight-impaired Cabinet minister. The son of a railwayman, Dobson (1940–) entered the Commons in 1979. A graduate of the LSE from York, he had a career in the electricity industry and was Chair of Camden Council. Cunningham (1939–), son of a well-known Labour local politician, gained a Ph.D. in chemistry from Durham University, where he worked as a research fellow before being elected to Parliament in 1970. The son of a GP, Dewar (1937–2000), a graduate of Glasgow University, first entered Parliament in 1970. Robertson (1946–) graduated in economics from Dundee University and worked for the Boilermakers' Union before his election to the Commons in 1978. Married with two children, Taylor (1947–) was elected to the Commons in 1987, before which she worked as a part-time Open University tutor and Monitoring Officer for the Housing Corporation. She was a graduate of Bradford University. Blair's Cabinet had no experience of government and little experience outside politics.

Ten out of the 21 members of the Cabinet who gave information had attended HMC 'public schools'. At least another six were the products of grammar schools. Five were Oxbridge graduates, two were Durham graduates and two were Edinburgh graduates. All had a higher education behind them. Compared with the previous administration there had been a shift from south to north. No fewer than eight were Scots and two were Welsh; most of the others either represented or came from the Midlands or the North.

More women were in the Cabinet than ever before. Five were members of Blair's original government formed in May 1997. The total was still five after the reshuffle of October 1999, when they were Margaret Beckett, President of the Council and Leader of the House of Commons, the most senior; Ann Taylor, Parliamentary Secretary, Treasury and Chief Whip; Clare Short, Secretary of State for International Development; Baroness Jay, Lord Privy Seal, Leader of the House of Lords and Minister for Women. Jay was the daughter of former Prime Minister James Callaghan. Finally, Dr Mo Mowlam was appointed Minister for the Cabinet Office and Chancellor of the Duchy of Lancaster after serving as Northern Ireland Secretary. Her successor was Peter Mandelson who was brought back into government after 10 months on the back benches. He had been forced to resign after it was revealed that he had omitted details of a massive home loan from a fellow Labour MP, Geoffrey Robinson, on his mortgage application.

No members of the new immigrant communities were included in Blair's first Cabinet, but two were included in the wider government. Paul Boateng served in the Home Office, and Keith Vaz, who came from Aden, served as Minister of State at the Foreign Office from October 1999. Boateng, whose father was from Ghana, had been a junior minister from the start of the Blair administration. Outside the government, Blair nominated the first Sikh, Tarsem King, managing director of Sandwell Polybags and leader of Sandwell Borough Council, to be elevated to the Lords in 1999. Also on the Labour benches in the Lords were Lord Nazir Ahmed (1998) of Rotherham, a well-known member of the Muslim community, Lord Paul (1996), Indian-born standard bearer for British-Asian businessmen, Lord Alli (1998), Lord Bagri (1997), Lord Desai (1990), professor of economics at the LSE, Lord Patel of Blackburn (2000) and Professor Bhikhu Parekh of Hull University.

What was New Labour's parliamentary party in sociological terms? Never before had so few manual workers – 13 per cent – been elected on the Labour side. When Labour last won an election, in 1974, 28 per cent came from manual occupations. A few more ex-manual workers were among the former union officials elected. Of course, many Labour MPs were from working-class homes. Trade union sponsorship of MPs was discontinued in 1995 and replaced by 'constituency plan agreements' between unions and selected local Labour Parties.[1] This was likely to further reduce the manual working class in the Commons. More Labour MPs (66 per cent) than ever before were graduates. Labour was heavily weighted to public sector professions especially teaching and local government. In absolute terms Labour's top professions were school teachers 54, politicians or political organizers 40, polytechnic or college lecturers 35, civil servants/ local government 30, publishers or journalists 29, barristers or solicitors 29, and university lecturers 22. Out of 418 Labour MPs, 111 were in education. Altogether 37 (9 per cent) of Labour MPs claimed business or managerial experience.[2]

HAGUE: CONSERVATIVE LEADER

With the resignation of John Major as Conservative leader after the election defeat of 1997, the Conservatives had to choose a leader from their depleted ranks. Under the rules, the leader, elected exclusively by MPs, had to get a majority of the votes and a margin of 15 per cent of those entitled to vote over his or her nearest challenger. William Hague came second of the five candidates in the first ballot with 41 votes out of 164. Kenneth Clarke led with 49. The bottom two candidates then dropped out. In the second ballot, the winner would be any candidate gaining an overall majority. This time, Clarke scored 64 to Hague's 62. John Redwood was then eliminated. In the third round, Hague beat Clarke by 92 votes to 70. Certainly before the contest, Hague was hardly known to the public. He was born in 1961, the son of a Yorkshire businessman. From Wath-on-Deane Comprehensive School he went to Magdalen College, Oxford, where he was President of the Oxford Union in 1981. After further studies at INSEAD Business School in France, Hague joined Shell UK. He worked for McKinsey and Company, 1983–88, entering Parliament in a by-election in 1989. He thrived under Major ending up as Welsh Secretary, 1995–97, not a job which had got him many headlines. However, he had served under Howe, Leon Brittan and Lamont and thus had covered a broad spectrum of Conservative politics. It was no easy task for him to put together a shadow cabinet to strike the public imagination and he was dogged, like his predecessor, by internal party strife. He had to decide what to keep and what to ditch of the inheritance of Major and Thatcher. Hague lost no time in getting married after becoming Conservative leader.

LIBERAL DEMOCRATS: ASHDOWN GOES

To considerable surprise, Paddy Ashdown, leader of the Liberal Democrats since July 1988, announced he would retire in mid-1999. He was still only 58. In 1997 he had led his party to its greatest success since 1929. It had over-taken the Conservatives at the local government level and had moved back near the centre of the political stage after being so long a party of the Celtic fringe, which occasionally pulled off a spectacular by-election success. Ashdown and other Liberal Democrats had served on a special Cabinet committee under Blair to discuss constitutional and electoral reform. They could claim some success in this direction. Former Social Democrat Charles Kennedy succeeded Ashdown. On 9 August, he was declared the winner in the leadership contest. Over four ballots he defeated four of his colleagues, gaining 56.6 per cent of the vote to 43.4 per cent for Simon Hughes, MP. One disappointing aspect of the election was that only 62 per cent of those eligible voted by returning their postal votes. The Liberal Democrats prided themselves as a party of grassroots activists, unlike the other two parties. The other aspect of the contest was that Kennedy achieved victory with a much lower margin than Ashdown in 1988. A Catholic, Kennedy (1959–) was the son of a Scottish crofter who, after graduating from Glasgow University, studied at Indiana University on a Fulbright Scholarship. He was elected to the Commons in 1983, after working as a journalist. At the Liberal Democrat conference at Harrogate in September 1999, he rejected calls to position the party to the left of Labour. Instead, he called for a strong, inde-pendent, progressive party. He wanted a more powerful European Union and an early referendum on British entry to the euro, which he supported. His difficulty was how to reconcile the desire of many members that the party was a distinctive force in British politics, yet to continue to benefit from association with a popular prime minister.

DECLINE OF POLITICAL INTEREST?

Under Blair, interest in politics seemed to be waning. Turnout at the Euro-pean elections, local elections and by-elections was low. The worst case was the Leeds Central by-election on 10 June 1999, when Labour held the seat on a 19.6 per cent turnout, the lowest at any parliamentary election since 1945. Labour held Wigan on 23 September on a turnout of 25 per cent. In both cases, there was a swing to the Conservatives. Because the SNP was the challenger, there was greater interest in the Hamilton South contest on the same day. There 41 per cent voted and Labour held on in spite of a 22.6 per cent swing to the SNP. Political interest was undermined to a degree by the disarray in the Conservative ranks, discipline in Labour's ranks, the relative closeness of the Liberal Democrats to Labour, the apparent success of the economy promoting optimism, and the growth of other diversions – sport, celebrities and dominance of US stories in the British media. British domestic politics appeared dull and of little relevance. After their massive defeat the Conservatives found it difficult to chart out an area on the political map. There was less to argue about as New Labour had taken over some policies and values associated with their old opponents and the Conservatives wanted to distance themselves from much of their recent past. New Labour did its best to promote these trends by pushing its new ideology of enterprise, achievement and merit which somehow seemed to come across better from 'classless' Labour politicians and 'spin doctors' than they did from the Conservatives most of whom were from more old-style privileged backgrounds. The Prime Minister and his wife, Cherie Booth, were themselves far more of celebrities than their predecessors, the Majors. Football and pop culture celebrities such as Paul Gascoigne, David Beckham, Gary Lineker and Alan Shearer, the Spice Girls and Chris Evans, radio and TV presenter who went on to be a media tycoon himself, came even more to the fore. Blair got his share of positive publicity but he was often seen deferring to his political soul mate, the handsome President Bill Clinton. For most of 1998, the media intrigued television viewers with astonishing, salacious and sordid revelations about the President's intimacies with Monica Lewinsky. The official *Starr Report* did not spare the President and was available as a reasonably priced paperback. Meanwhile, another celebrity vanished suddenly from our screens.

In the early hours of 30 August 1997, the news media stunned many by announcing that Diana, Princess of Wales, had been killed in Paris in a car crash. The death of the former wife of Prince Charles, although of no political significance, hit Britain in the same way as the assassination of President Kennedy had hit the US in 1963. A leggy blonde, Diana had gained millions of fans by constant media attention. She had admitted adultery on television in 1995 and struck a cord with perhaps half her audience who were themselves either divorced or who had divorced parents. She told her audience that the 'biggest disease' was people being unloved. Like millions she used the anti-depressant Prozac.[3] As she got older, Diana got involved with good causes, children's charities, Aids and the anti-land-mines campaign. This endeared her to a more serious audience. The circumstances of her death, with Dodi Fayed, added even greater interest. Fayed senior, Mohamed al-Fayed, claimed the two were victims of a conspiracy by the 'British Establishment'. He claimed they had marriage plans. The days up to and beyond her funeral gave the media thousands of stories. It appeared that every politician and every celebrity had to say something. Typical comments were those of old Conservative Kenneth Clarke, MP: 'She was treated disgracefully by sections of the press.' New Labour MP, Vernon Coaker, called for a national day of mourning. He said the 'nation as a whole needs to grieve properly. This is a devastating day'.[4] Abroad, Michael Jackson cancelled a concert in Belgium on hearing the news of Diana's death. The funeral service in Westminster Abbey presented Blair with an excellent media event. The Royals underestimated the effect of Diana's death and appeared to react slowly, if not coldly. They lost ground rapidly after the death of Diana, who had given them a glamorous, larger than life image. They were ill-suited to the age of informality, instant intimacy, intrusive journalism and total exposure. The death of Diana led to calls for greater protection of privacy.

COMING OUT

Investigative journalism had played a considerable part in the downfall of the Conservatives under John Major. Blair decided that all skeletons should be brought out of the cupboard from the start rather than by journalists at a later stage. One significant change in this respect was the openness about MPs' sexual orientation. Until the advent of Blair's premiership this had been very much a taboo subject. In the Cabinet, Chris Smith, the Culture Secretary, announced that he was gay. Nick Brown, Minister for Agriculture, Food and Fisheries, followed him. Peter Mandelson refused at first to comment on his sexual orientation, but later admitted that he too was gay, without damage to his career. In fact, by the reshuffle of October 1999 he ranked fifth or sixth in a Cabinet of 22. Michael Portillo, Defence Secretary under Major, kept his gay student days out of the media whilst he was in office. It only came to the public attention, in 1999, during the by-election for Kensington and Chelsea, which he won. His Labour successor as MP for Enfield Southgate, Stephen Twigg, had made no secret of his gay orientation during the election campaign of 1997. In the Lords, Lord Alli was the only openly homosexual peer. He had been ennobled, aged 34, by Blair in 1998. He was consulted by Blair on youth and other matters. Outside politics, Michael Barrymore, one of Britain's leading television entertainers, got a divorce from his wife, Cheryl, and announced he was gay. *OK! First for Celebrity News* (29 December 1999) magazine thought its readers would want 15 pages of him with his new, young boy friend, Shaun. The couple told the readers, 'We want to adopt a child one day.' Another sign of the times was the availability of the magazine *Diva Lesbian Life and Style* in WH Smith, a store not renowned for being unorthodox. Following a ruling of the European Court of Human Rights, in September 1999, the armed services were forced to give up their opposition to having open homosexuals in their ranks. Three men and one woman who had been dismissed in 1993–94 because of their sexual orientation were offered reinstatement.

Another aspect of the changed climate was the 'discovery' by politicians of family members who were the product of pre-marital or extra-marital relationships. Clare Short was reunited with her grown-up son, the product of a teenage liaison, whom she had given for adoption. In 1999, former Prime Minister John Major revealed that he had a half-sister, his father's 'love-child', who had been adopted by a cowhand. 'I'm so pleased to have found her', he was reported as saying.[5]

Blair's colleagues also took divorce in their stride. Three had experience of divorce before joining the Cabinet. Robin Cook and his wife of 30 years announced their divorce shortly after he took office. In a classic case, he married his much younger secretary. In 2000, Peter Hain, Cook's junior in the Foreign Office, and his wife announced their separation after nearly 25 years of marriage.

TASKFORCES: 'A MUCH WIDER SOURCE OF ADVICE'?

New Labour seemed to bring with it a new political vocabulary. One solution to any problem seemed to be to set up a 'taskforce' to investigate it. Government figures showed 40 had been set up between 1997 and January 2000. Among them were taskforces on urban renewal, pensions, football and even 'near earth objects'. The first was headed by Lord Falconer who claimed, that

> before they make decisions, Ministers can receive advice from beyond only the traditional advice available either within Whitehall or beyond Whitehall in relation to special interest groups . . . It makes for more transparent government and provides a much wider source of advice.

Unlike 'quangos' (NDPB), part and parcel of the previous government's arrangements, they were not permanent and members were not paid. Some thought they should be subject to parliamentary scrutiny and that they downgraded Parliament.[6] Another way of 'tackling' a problem was to appoint a 'tsar' to sort it out. Most notably Keith Hallawell, a senior police officer, was appointed 'drugs' tsar'. In March 2000 it was announced that heart patients would go on a 'fast track' which was to be overseen by a 'heart tsar'. This was part of a 'national crusade'. Thus heart patients joined young offenders, asylum seekers and others on fast tracks. Hopefully, they would reach a more pleasant terminus. There were education 'hit squads' to take over failing schools. Such terminology was designed by 'spin doctors' to make the public feel that this was a tough 'no nonsense' government, which would take drastic action to solve problems. The term 'spin doctor' was not new nor was the deployment of such publicity experts. In fact, successive governments and institutions had turned increasingly to public relations to make themselves popular. In 1979, Buckingham Palace employed only three information officers, by 1995 it employed twelve. The Inland Revenue employed five and eighteen in those years respectively. In the same period, the Metropolitan Police's public information officers increased from six to sixty-one! In the private sector, the employers' body, the Confederation of British Industry, increased the number of its information officers from eight to eighteen.[7] Betty Boothroyd, Labour MP and Speaker of the Commons, launched what *The Times* (6 April 2000) called 'an astonishing attack on the Government for making major policy announcements in the media before informing Parliament'.

The accusation that Blair and his colleagues were 'downgrading Parliament' was a perception, which was fairly widespread. Labour MPs were less likely to dissent than of old. This was partly the result of the tougher discipline introduced before the 1997 election. There were tighter standing orders and Labour MPs were equipped with electronic message pagers to keep them informed of the party line. The fact that 192 Labour MPs out of 418 had no previous parliamentary experience must have made it easier to keep them in line. Some in Labour's ranks thought their leaders were 'control freaks'. Most of those who did rebel were old hands like Jeremy Corbyn, Tony Benn, Dennis Skinner, Audrey Wise, Tam Dalyell, Alan Simpson, Diane Abbott, Ken Livingstone and Ann Clwyd. These were joined by two of the new intake John McDonnell and Kelvin Hopkins. Even among the top rebels there were wide differences in their propensity to dissent. In the first two sessions of Parliament, Corbyn voted against the government 24 times but Livingstone did so on only 13 occasions. Women MPs seemed less inclined to rebel than men and none of the newly elected ones did so.[8] Women MPs did complain about the unsociable hours they were forced to work and the lack of crèche facilities but this was a matter for Parliament rather than strictly a government matter. What were the issues on which MPs rejected their government's measures? There were rebellions on eight Bills the most important being the Social Security Bill over which 27 MPs dissented, the Teaching and Higher Education Bill (34 MPs), Criminal Justice [Terrorism and Conspiracy] Bill (16 to 29 MPs) and the House of Lords Bill (35 MPs). Briefly, some MPs opposed tuition fees in higher education, some thought the Criminal Justice Bill erred too much on the side of the state rather than the accused and some thought the Lords Bill did not go far enough in favouring its replacement by a democratically elected body. In foreign affairs, 47 Labour MPs disagreed with their government over Iraq mainly on the grounds that continued sanctions harmed innocent people rather than dictator Saddam Hussein. The NATO action in Kosovo also brought opposition from 13 MPs, which is discussed below.[9] One other issue which angered some Labour MPs was the Freedom of Information Bill. On 5 April 2000, 36 Labour MPs voted against the government, believing the Bill gave ministers too much freedom to keep items out of the public domain. Earlier in the week, 41 Labour MPs supported restoring the link, cut by the Thatcher government, between pensions and average earnings.

DEVOLUTION AND CONSTITUTIONAL CHANGE

Blair redeemed his pledge to establish a Scottish Parliament and a Welsh Assembly and to reform the House of Lords. He also brought the voting system for the European Parliament into line with that of the other EU countries. He stopped short of making changes to the voting system for the House of Commons. The Scottish Parliament and the Welsh Assembly came into existence after referenda in both countries. In the Welsh case, the pro-devolution campaigners won by the narrowest of margins. In May 1999, elections to both bodies took place. Voting was by a modified PR system similar to that used in Germany. Each elector had two votes, one to cast for the 'first-past-the-post' constituency, and the second for the party list. The idea is that the elector is empowered to vote for an outstanding candidate of his/her choice, irrespective of party, with his/her first vote. The second vote goes to the party he or she prefers. The overall effect of the 'topping up' system is to produce a parliament that is broadly proportionate to the number of votes each party attracts. Under the old system, the Conservatives would have got no seats in spite of their relatively high poll.

In Scotland, the main protagonists were Labour, traditionally strong there, and the pro-independence Scottish National Party (SNP). In Wales, Labour's main challenger was PC, which captured a number of Labour strongholds. In both cases Labour was hit by the relative apathy of its supporters. There had been dissension about the selection process for Labour candidates, which many thought was rigged in favour of Blair's men. (See Tables 12.1 and 12.2.)

Table 12.1 Elections to Scottish Parliament, 1998

Party	First (% vote)	Second (% vote)	Seats		
			Constituency	Top-up	Total
Labour	38.8	33.8	53	3	56
SNP	28.7	27.0	7	28	35
Conservatives	15.6	15.4	0	18	18
Liberal Democrats	14.2	12.5	12	5	17
Others	2.7	11.4	1	2	3

Note: Turnout: 59 per cent

Table 12.2 Election to Welsh Assembly, 1998

Party	First (% vote)	Second (% vote)	Seats Constituency	Top-up	Total
Labour	37.6	35.4	27	1	28
Plaid Cymru	28.4	30.5	9	8	17
Conservatives	15.9	16.5	1	8	9
Liberal Democrats	13.4	12.6	3	3	6
Others	4.7	5.1	0	0	0

Note: Turnout: 46 per cent

Despite the criticism of Hague, the Conservative Party did improve its standing in the local government elections of May 1999. Although the Conservatives recovered only about half the representation lost to them in the previous elections for the same seats in 1995, the results were seen as strengthening Hague's hand against his critics. The Conservatives also won an unexpected victory in the European Parliament elections of June 1999, gaining 37.77 per cent of the vote in mainland Britain compared with 28.03 per cent for Labour, 12.66 for the Liberal Democrats, 6.96 per cent for the UKIP and 6.25 for the Greens. Labour's poor showing was partly due to the introduction of proportional representation, which gave voters greater choice, and Blair's low-key approach to the elections, which caused apathy among Labour supporters. A third factor, which told against Labour, was the perception among the better informed that Jack Straw was reducing choice by decreeing that the lists would be 'closed'. A closed list means that the voter may only cast a ballot for a party rather than an individual candidate. This was regarded by some in Labour ranks as an attempt to ditch left-wing candidates, and two Labour MEPs, Hugh Kerr and Ken Coates, left the party in protest. Labour's only consolation was that turnout had been abysmally low, 32 per cent for the local government elections in England and 24 per cent for the Europe elections in mainland Britain. Another part explanation was that British voters seemed increasingly likely to offer their support to different parties depending on the type of election. There was a hierarchy of elections.[10] Despite these successes Hague got little respite.

THE LORDS REFORMED

Since it came into existence in 1900 Labour had campaigned against the House of Lords. The Liberal government had in 1911 passed the Parliament Act because the Lords had thrown out its 'People's Budget'. Under that Act the Lords lost their veto over money Bills and could only delay nonmonetary legislation for two years. In 1949, under Attlee, the delaying power was cut to one year. Macmillan's government introduced life peers in 1958. Wilson attempted further reform in 1968 but failed. The main case against the House of Lords was that it was based on the hereditary principle. Secondly, its reform had left it unelected. Even the life peers were appointed for their own lifetime by the Queen on the advice of the Prime Minister. In October 1998, there were 507 life peers, 633 hereditary peers, 26 Lords Spiritual (the two archbishops and bishops of the Church of England) and a similar number of Law Lords. Of the life peers, 172 were Conservatives, 148 Labour, 44 Liberal Democrats, 120 Cross-Benchers and 24 others. Of the hereditary peers 300 took the Conservative whip, only 18 were Labour, 24 were Liberal Democrats, 202 Cross-Benchers and 89 others.[11] After hard negotiations, it was agreed that the hereditaries would lose their sitting and voting rights, except for 92 of their number whom they would elect. Blair announced this as stage one of a more radical reform. His critics alleged that the new, transitionary, system gave him even greater patronage. The defenders of the upper chamber claimed that it did useful work scrutinizing and amending non-financial Bills. Despite the reform it still had a non-Labour majority.

NOT IN EUROLAND

The Labour government's record on the EU bore similarities to that of Major in that Blair, Brown and Cook reached office wanting a 'Britain at the heart of Europe'. Like Major's administration, they seemed to cool in office. Cook put out more pro-EU signals than Brown. Was this just a case of the Foreign Office versus the Treasury rather than the convictions of the ministers? Lord Roy Jenkins, Blair's friend and mentor, confided his disappointment to *Independent* readers on 9 February 2000.

The Amsterdam Treaty was signed on 2 October 1997 after two years of discussion and negotiation. For Britain, it was the culmination of a process which started when Major was in office and was completed when Blair was in Downing Street. Basically, it committed member states to giving their citizens greater rights as citizens and consumers, involving national parliaments more closely in the affairs of the EU, and to closer collaboration and joint action on foreign affairs. The Treaty also broke new ground on public health, giving the Council power to adopt wide-ranging measures.

Smarting under the attacks on British beef, the government was relieved when in 1999 the agricultural committee of the EU decided there was no longer any danger from British beef and the ban on it should be lifted. Dissent came from France and its government refused to lift the ban on the basis of scientific advice taken. This helped to fuel anti-EU feeling in Britain. Later, one of France's leading scientific advisers on BSE admitted that her country had thousands of undiagnosed cases, and infected animals could have entered the food chain. Professor Jeanne Brugère-Picoux said that although France had officially registered 75 cases of BSE in the previous 10 years, she believed the real figure to be 'far higher than that'. Infected French beef could have entered Britain. France's third case of variant CJD – the type linked to eating BSE-infected beef, which killed 48 people in Britain – was confirmed at the end of 1999.[12]

When the ministers of 12 countries met to formally celebrate the introduction of the single currency of the EU, the euro, on 1 January 1999, neither Blair nor Brown was among them. Britain's official policy was 'wait and see'. Blair promised the voters a referendum on the issue if the government recommended joining. Sensing growing hostility to the euro, fanned by sections of the press, the Conservatives declared they would not want Britain to join within the lifetime of the existing Parliament or the next. Hague faced opposition from former Chancellor Kenneth Clarke and Michael Heseltine, both of whom joined Blair's pro-EU Britain In Europe group. The Liberal Democratic Leader, Charles Kennedy, also joined this platform. Pro-entry supporters claimed the artificially strong pound, which everyone agreed was damaging British exports by making them expensive, would fall in value if the government announced it was applying to join.

CONFLICT IN KOSOVO

Up to the millennium, the most important foreign affairs' initiative that Blair got involved in was the war in Kosovo in 1999. Kosovo was part of Serb-dominated Yugoslavia. It was their 'holy land'. They had taken it by conquest in 1912 and in the interwar period had expelled Muslims, Albanians and Turks. It was held after the Second World War by Tito's Yugoslavia but the Albanians in Kosovo, who formed the majority of the population, never gave up their desire for autonomy, independence or union with neighbouring Albania. In 1974, Kosovo was granted autonomy. This was reversed in 1989 and once again Albanians were terrorized by the Serbian police. A secret ethnic Albanian guerrilla army (KLA) was established to fight the Belgrade authorities but most Albanians wanted non-violent resistance. The crisis worsened in 1998–99 when up to 800,000 people fled from Kosovo with accounts of massacres, atrocities and forced expulsions by Serb forces.[13] Long negotiations in Rambouillet, France, failed to produce a diplomatic solution, which would have left Yugoslavia with sovereignty over the province but would have led to the re-establishment of Kosovo's autonomy. Under pressure from TV pictures covering the story, NATO was forced to act. On 24 March 1999, NATO launched air attacks on Yugoslavia's air defences and military installations. This was the beginning of a 78-day air offensive by mainly US and British air forces. Yugoslav President Slobodan Milosevic then agreed to withdraw Yugoslav forces to allow a UN (but largely NATO) international peacekeeping force to move in on 9 June.

A UN administrator was sent in to set up a local administration and co-ordinate efforts to rehabilitate the economy. Most of the refugees returned to their shattered homes. Blair gave complete support to the Americans and NATO throughout the crisis. Some, like Liberal Democratic Leader, Paddy Ashdown, a former soldier, thought NATO should have acted much earlier and on the ground. Blair urged ground involvement after the bombing campaign appeared to be causing 'collateral damage', but Clinton held back fearing heavy US casualties. In Blair's view, this would have reduced the damage and civilian casualties, which despite NATO's sophisti-cated rockets, resulted from the onslaught. Sadly, after their liberation by NATO some Albanians took part in revenge killings in Kosovo of Serbs who had not taken part in the 'ethnic cleansing'. Most of the public supported the government over Kosovo. A small number of Labour MPs did not. Tony Benn put their case. He said they were not apologists for the Yugoslav President Milosevic. Benn and his colleagues were worried about all the refugees, Serbs *and* Albanians. Force should only be used with UN approval not by NATO alone.

> I think it is an insult to our intelligence to personalise all conflicts as if, somehow, shooting Saddam Hussein and Milosevic would return peace to the Middle East and the Balkans. What folly to engage in such schoolboy politics. There are complex historical conditions. If Milosevic were shot, somebody else would come along who is just the same, because the Serbs are united.

Many more Labour MPs had reservations on Bosnia, Kosovo and other issues but believed that public dissension and division had called into ques-tion Labour's credibility in the past.

NAVY: 'OVERCOMMITTED'

By 1999, Britannia no longer ruled the waves. Only three warships could patrol the high seas at Christmas 1999. Unprecedented cost-cutting had brought almost every ship in the fleet into dock to save money. Apparently the Navy was facing a £500m budget deficit which had crippled the fleet's operational capacities. Mike Critchley, author of *British Warships and Auxiliaries*, commented, 'The Navy is overcommitted, undermanned and underfunded.'[14] The drugs patrol in the West Indies had to be scaled down. At the same time an expensive TV advertisement claimed the RN was winning the battle against drugs in foreign parts. A similar situation pre-vailed in the RAF and the Army. The majority of Britain's frontline planes were grounded and there was a severe shortage of pilots. At the end of the century, a third of the Army's newest tanks and more than half of its older models were not fully operational.[15] Britain's ability to mount even Kosovo-type operations was limited.

Defence expenditure started to fall in real terms in the late 1980s as the Cold War thawed. According to the Ministry of Defence *Annual Report 1998/99*, in real terms, it was £29.8 billion in 1986/87 and fell to £26.8 billion in 1991/92, roughly that is, at the end of the Cold War. It continued to fall to £21.6 billion in 1997/98 after which it rose to £22 billion in 1998/99. In 1998, only France and the US of the NATO states spent more than Britain. Yet defence experts believed Britain was not spending enough to fulfil the tasks it had set itself.

'SAS TRAIN ANTI-FRAUD OFFICERS'

According to a government-funded report published in 1999, three-quarters of the 1.7 million people on incapacity benefit were capable of work. Professor Stephen Fothergill of Sheffield Hallam University, who compiled the report, stressed that he was not accusing claimants of fraud, but insisted that most could work. 'We believe that there are 1.25 million of "hidden unemployed" people on incapacity benefit, who are capable of work.' The research revealed that Britain, where 2.5 million people, or 7 per cent of the working-age population, were on incapacity or other sickness benefits, had a worse record than virtually all of Europe. The comparable figure for Germany was 4 per cent, Spain was less than 3 per cent and France was less than 2 per cent. Only Italy among the large European states had an inferior record, with 11 per cent. In 1999, incapacity benefit was being paid to three times more people than the number 20 years ago. The figures were highest in areas of high unemployment. No doubt previous governments had taken a relaxed attitude to the problem in order to reduce the numbers of officially registered unemployed.

According to Conservative MP David Davis, Public Accounts Committee Chairman, social security fraud cost taxpayers £1.53bn in 1997–98.[16] In February 2000, Alistair Darling, Social Security Secretary, claimed that welfare fraud was running at more than £3 billion a year. In one of the worst cases exposed, Awan, a Pakistani, who came to Britain as an illegal immigrant, netted £400,000 over 14 years. He had claimed benefit for 43 children and housing benefit for 11 homes. He admitted 15 charges of forgery and was sentenced to three-and-a-half years in jail.[17] Benefits experts have calculated that money lost to benefit cheats in one year could have paid for 100,000 new nurses, 56 new hospitals or 21,000 new homes. Piara Khabra, MP for Ealing/Southall, commenting on the Awan case, said, 'Cases like this give the whole Asian community a bad name. However, we must not forget that people from all races are capable of defrauding the system and it does not mean that everyone from that race is bad.'[18] As part of its 'get tough' policy the government set up a 'hotline' giving anonymous callers the chance to denounce alleged fraudsters. SAS soldiers were also brought in to train Benefits Agency anti-fraud officers in surveillance methods.[19] The other side of the benefits' coin was that an estimated 900,000 pensioners were not claiming benefits they were entitled to. Thousands of pensioners were also on reduced pensions because of the failure of the new computer system installed at the Benefits Agency.

LONG NEGOTIATIONS IN NORTHERN IRELAND

Blair tried to keep up the peace momentum in Northern Ireland initiated under Major. Dr Mo Molam was appointed as Secretary of State for Northern Ireland, the first woman to occupy the post. Her friendly informal style helped a little and she gained sympathy for carrying on despite a brain tumour. In 1999, she was replaced by Peter Mandelson. On 10 April 1998, Good Friday, all the parties on both sides of the border signed a multiparty peace agreement. This was approved in simultaneous referenda on 22 May by voters of Northern Ireland and the Republic. In the North, 80.95 per cent of those eligible voted and 71.2 voted in favour. In the Republic, on a turnout of 55.59 per cent, 94.39 per cent were in favour.[20] The relatively low vote in the South is partly explained by the fact that a significant number of Irish voters worked abroad. Blair and Irish Prime Minister Bertie Aherne, assisted by Major and Clinton, had worked hard for the 'Yes' campaign. However, six of the ten Ulster Unionist MPs opposed this deal backed by their leader, David Trimble. The deal led to the setting up of the Northern Ireland Assembly elected on the basis of proportional representation. The main Ulster Unionist Party gained 28 seats, the SDLP 24, the Democratic Unionist Party 20, Sinn Fein 18 and the non-sectarian Alliance Party 6. Another 10 Unionists, including independents, were also elected. Finally, 2 members of the Northern Ireland Women's Coalition gained seats. In all, 14 women won seats in the 108-member Assembly. The Assembly in turn elected a power-sharing Executive with ministers from all parties represented in the Assembly. Sinn Fein had reversed its long-standing policy of boycotting elected institutions in the North as 'partitionist'. Long negotiations were needed to thrash out the details of the agreement. Throughout 1998–99, there were minor incidents such as revenge beatings and killings. Drumcree remained a flashpoint. The Protestant Orange Order insisted on its right to parade along the Garvaghy Road, a largely Catholic area, as it had done since 1807.[21] Violence occurred when the march was banned in 1996 and in 1997. In 1998 the new Parades Commission banned the march, and more violence erupted. The march passed off peacefully in 1999.

Overall, optimism prevailed and economic aid poured into the province. Northern Ireland looked set to have its own parliament and government as it had from 1921 to 1972 when Heath suspended them. The difference was that these would be inclusive not sectarian. On 30 November 1999 the new 12-member Executive took office headed by David Trimble (UUP) with Seamus Mallon (SDLP) as his deputy. Sinn Fein was represented by two ministers: Martin McGuinness, Sinn Fein's chief negotiator, was appointed Minister of Education, and Ms Bairbre de Brun got Health, Social Security and Public Safety. Gerry Adams, SF's President since 1983, did not join the government.

On 9 January 2000, Mandelson announced his programme of reform for law enforcement in NI. Over five years the police force was to become evenly divided between Catholics and Protestants instead of being 90 per cent Protestant. The most controversial measure was the proposal to change the name of the police from the Royal Ulster Constabulary to the Police Service.

General John de Chastelain, Canadian head of the disarmament commission set up under the Good Friday Agreement, was increasingly frustrated as no weapons were being handed over. Blair had given assurances that politicians linked to paramilitaries who refused to hand over weapons would not hold office. Trimble had promised his party that he would resign from the Assembly if there were no IRA decommissioning by 31 January. The Unionists had been persuaded to co-operate in the new assembly on the basis that the IRA and other paramilitary groups would 'decommission' their weapons. This did not happen and it led ultimately to the collapse of the Good Friday Agreement. After only nine weeks, on 11 February 2000, Mandelson suspended the Northern Ireland Assembly because of the lack of progress on 'decommissioning'. Here was largely meant the IRA, which was supported by Sinn Fein. SF would not give any unequivocal assurances that the IRA would ever hand over its weapons to the international commission and refused to say 'the war is over'. There were some who agreed with the Sinn Fein view that as the devolved assembly had been working 'why collapse it?' However, Des O'Malley, Chairman of the Foreign Affairs Committee of the Irish Parliament, felt that the Republican movement had to make up its mind, 'either it was going to be a political party or remain an illegal army'.[22] The SDLP disagreed with the suspension decision.

That violence was still viewed as an option by a small minority was evident when a car bomb went off in Omagh only four months after the Good Friday Agreement was signed. It killed 29 people and was the worst atrocity in the history of the postwar 'Troubles'. The bombing was the work of a Republican splinter group calling itself the Real IRA. It was condemned by both sides. According to official figures, a total of 49 people were killed in NI after the Good Friday Agreement. A total of 2,422 were injured as a result of terrorist attacks between April 1998 and 10 February 2000.[23]

An extra complication for Blair and his colleagues was that, according to the 1991 census, there were 582,020 people born in the Republic living in Britain. Countless others were from Northern Ireland. Many more were members of families that originated in Ireland.[24] All were potential voters whose views had to be taken into account.

UNIVERSITIES: 'INCREASINGLY . . . GLOBAL'

In the 1990s, universities around the country were looking increasingly to non-EU students to boost their incomes as they were expected to find ever more funds from non-governmental sources. The government set great store by this. Blair believed, 'The institutions, their students and our economy will reap considerable rewards.' A high-level advertising campaign was mounted to attract overseas students who paid high fees at British universities. In 1999, there were 198,000 higher-education students in the UK. This represented 17 per cent of the market compared with the US, which attracted 68 per cent of international students in the main English-speaking countries. Australia attracted 10 per cent and Canada 5 per cent. Malaysia, Singapore and Hong Kong were Britain's 'traditional strongholds' for recruitment of students. Yet there was an 11 per cent slump in overseas recruitment. This was the first drop in 20 years. The collapse of Asian financial markets and the strong pound were thought to be causes.[25] University admissions tutors were under pressure to admit foreign students even when, in some cases, their qualifications were below those required of British students. Yet there was pressure on academic staff to ensure they passed their exams. Another variation of securing income from overseas was to set up satellite campuses abroad. This did not always work satisfactorily. In 1999, Manchester University stopped selling degree courses to Israel after criticism from an education watchdog, the Quality Assurance Agency (QAA). The same criticism was made of Derby University by NATFHE, the lecturers' union.[26]

In January 2000, it was announced that MIT and Cambridge University were to link up. It was the idea of Gordon Brown, Chancellor of the Exchequer and dedicated America fan. Brown wanted to bring MIT's techniques for encouraging entrepreneurial activity and innovating speedily from the laboratory into industry to Cambridge and to higher education generally. To this end he was handing over £45 million to MIT and another £23 million to Cambridge. They were expected to raise a further £16 million from private industry. The head of MIT, Lawrence Bacow, explained, 'This is an enormous opportunity to build strength upon strength in a number of fields. Increasingly, universities of the calibre of Cambridge and MIT are global.'[27] The arrangement had its critics from those who believed other British universities, which were 'made to dance endlessly to win a small amount of money', had been insulted. Firstly, the deal by-passed the normal competitive bidding procedures. Secondly, a number of universities, like Nottingham and Warwick, had shown themselves proficient at spinning off private sector work from know-how and brains. That universities were under enormous pressure is shown by the fact that nearly a third were running 'continuing deficits'.[28] The financial difficulties of students appeared to be increasing. The numbers taking up loans had increased from 28 per cent in 1990–91 when the scheme began, to 64 per cent in 1997–98.[29]

The Higher Education Funding Council, in a report published in December 1999, found that the growth of the new universities (former poly-technics) had not resulted in any weakening of privilege. The majority of universities have a long way to go to broaden access to all able students. Even those taking a higher proportion from state schools tended to select students from higher social classes. British universities seemed to be set to become divided into an unofficial class system with two, three or four strata. The Russell Group saw themselves as actual or potential world-level institutions. They wanted to charge top-up fees, which would make it near impossible for many potential students to study there. There were reports that, what the National Union of Students told the *Nottingham Topper* (15 March 2000) was 'a tiny minority' of students were turning to prostitution to pay their way. Universities were pleased to be able to report that drop out rates were still lower in Britain than in many other countries. In Britain, they were 18 per cent, Germany 28 per cent, US 37 per cent and France 45 per cent.[30]

PRIMARY EDUCATION: 'IMPROVING'

> Primary schools are improving dramatically after the Government's insistence that standards will rise only if schools get the basics right in the early years. Test results for 11-year-olds show a leap of 10 per cent in the proportion of pupils reaching the expected standards in maths (up to 69 per cent) and a rise of 5 per cent in English (to 70 per cent) . . . Ministers explain the big improvement by pointing to the new literacy hour, the daily period of reading and writing based on what the Government calls 'tried and tested methods', which was introduced just over a year ago [by David Blunkett].[31]

Blunkett believed that the numeracy hour had done wonders for children's mental arithmetic. Some were less sure about the claims because science results went up by 9 per cent even though there was no dedicated hour and no target. By the end of the twentieth century, the British government seemed to be more test orientated than ever before. Blunkett could not be accused of having no ideas. His 'big idea' for 2001 was free summer camps for all 16-year-olds who wanted them. He was impressed by American camps for middle-class children. His camps were to combine outdoor activities with helping out in old people's homes or renovating old buildings in the countryside.[32] In January 1998, Blunkett broke new ground by agreeing to give public funds to two Muslim schools. The previous government had refused this. They joined the state sector in September 1998 to be funded at the same level as other primaries, including those run by Anglicans, Catholic and Jews. Blunkett told *Sunday Telegraph* (12 March 2000) readers that Labour's 'war' with the grammar schools was over. Ballots of parents would decide whether they remained selective or not.

Blair's government was criticized for not reversing the trend of selling off school land and playing fields to make up the shortfall of funds as parents were expected more and more to raise money for their children's schools. However, unlike previous governments, Labour stipulated that money so raised had to be ploughed back into sport or education.[33]

NHS: 'STEADILY . . . TO DETERIORATE'?

In January 2000, in France, an international team succeeded, for the first time, in transplanting arms from a dead donor to a man who had lost his arms. Medical scientists were talking about the prospects, within a decade, of many individuals living 300 years. Yet the NHS remained beset by problems and controversy just as it had done under Major and earlier administrations. A conference of top specialists, in 1999, claimed that Britain's cancer treatment programme was a poor relative to other advanced countries.[34] Government ministers, first Frank Dobson and then Alan Milburn, did their best in the battle of statistics to convince the public that they were solving the problems left behind by the Conservatives. But the voters remained sceptical. The Office of National Statistics reported that in 1998–99, winter deaths of the elderly were the highest for 10 years.[35] A real test of the situation came in the winter of 1999–2000 with the outbreak of a flu epidemic. The NHS could not cope. Scotland seemed to be hit harder than England and Wales but everywhere there were reports of operations being cancelled so that beds could be reallocated for incoming flu patients. A *Times* (11 January 2000) correspondent claimed that France was coping better than Britain. There new cases were being reported at a rate of up to 300,000 a week, compared with about 100,000 in Britain. It was the worst outbreak in both countries in recent years. Yet, in contrast to Britain, the French did not see it as a crisis. About 70 per cent of those most at risk, the over-70s, had been vaccinated in France. In Britain, the figure was much lower. Secondly, there were far more beds available in France. Thirdly, almost all of the flu sufferers in France were treated by GPs, unlike in Britain. The outbreak led to renewed argument about the inadequate funding of Britain's much vaunted NHS. Lord Winston, the fertility pioneer and Labour peer, was severely critical of the way the health service was going. 'Do we want a health service that is steadily going to deteriorate and be more and more rationed and will be inferior on vital areas such as heart disease and cancer compared to our less well-off neighbours?' A poll published in the *Observer* (16 January 2000) claimed, 'Blair in the doghouse on waiting lists'. Only 47 per cent of those polled trusted the government to develop the right policies for the NHS while 49 per cent did not trust the government. This did not help the Conservatives very much as only 25 per cent trusted them and 69 per cent did not trust them. As the paper pointed out the NHS compared badly with those in other developed countries. Britain had one doctor for every 625 people. In France it was one for every 344. In 1997, Britain spent £869 per head on health, compared with £1,245 in the Netherlands, £1,490 in Germany and £2,559 in the US. Women with breast cancer had a 67 per cent chance of living more than five years, compared with 80 per cent in France, Sweden or Switzerland. Blair told viewers on 16 January that his aim was to increase British spending on health to reach *the EU average* within six years. This was not a firm commitment but was based on the assumption that the economy would remain buoyant and would continue to grow. If realized it would still leave Britain behind France, Germany and other more affluent European states. In another blow to the credibility of the NHS figures showed that over 5,000 patients died each year from infections they picked up in hospital.[36] The National Audit Office, the official watchdog, added more fuel to the fire when it reported, in February 2000, that the number of operations cancelled on the day they were due to take place had risen to an all-time high. Between 1998 and 1999 cancellations increased by 12 per cent to a total of 56,000 at hospitals in England. Unnecessary deaths in hospitals were exposed by Sir Brian Jarman of the Imperial College School of Medicine, in February 2000. He estimated that at least 30,000 people might be dying in hospital every year as a result of medical accidents that could have been prevented.[37] Labour had campaigned on the NHS at successive elections as a key issue. Would this become its Achilles' heel?

WEALTH AND SOCIAL JUSTICE

The gap between the richest and the poorest in Britain widened in the first year of the Labour government, with a million more people earning less than two-fifths of the national average income. This was the finding of a report commissioned by the Joseph Rowntree Foundation and conducted by the New Policy Institute. The government's reaction was to blame it on the developments under the Conservatives over the previous 18 years.[38] At the same time, according to the *Independent on Sunday* (12 December 1999), 'The rich got richer last week. City bonuses went through the roof, with 2,500 staff at investment bankers Goldman Sachs sharing £100m in salary top-ups. The extraordinary wealth of celebrities was also highlighted when Manchester United's captain, Roy Keane, broke his team's pay ceiling with a salary of £50,000 a week. Elsewhere in Britain, 2 million children are living in homes where no one has a job . . . There are 14 million people living below the poverty line.' In 1986, according to Inland Revenue figures, 1 per cent of the adult population owned 18 per cent of 'marketable wealth', 10 per cent owned 49 per cent, and 25 per cent owned 71 per cent of the wealth. In 1996, the last published figures revealed that 1 per cent owned 19 per cent, 10 per cent owned 52 per cent, and 25 per cent owned 74 per cent.[39] When measured against such figures, Blair's achievements trumpeted in October 1999 seemed extremely modest, 'We've put in the biggest-ever increase in Child Benefit. The first-ever national minimum wage. The biggest-ever investment in health and education. One and half million families helped by the Working Families Tax Credit.'[40] There was also the £100 winter fuel allowance to pensioners in 1999 but there were no plans to link pension increases to the rise in average earnings, which many in Labour's ranks like Barbara Castle had long called for.

Was the 'Carnival Against Capitalism', in June 1999, a sign that growing numbers were getting frustrated with the way things were going? The Carnival was very modern in that it was organized on the Internet to attract environmental protesters and opponents of capitalism to the City of London. The *Daily Telegraph* (19 June 1999) reported that the Carnival 'deteriorated into violence yesterday as protesters pelted police with bricks and bottles and attacked financial institutions, causing widespread damage. After more than six hours of rioting and vandalism by up to 4,000 protesters, one woman was known to be in hospital after falling under the wheels of a police van'. In May 2000, a riot occurred in London during an anti-capitalist demonstration.

PRIVATIZATION AND SAFETY

Bob Ayling, BA's chief executive and a supporter of Blair, said in a speech that Deputy Prime Minister John Prescott's policy of partly privatizing the National Air Traffic Service meant that commercial returns would be paramount. 'The flying public . . . should be deeply concerned if any future strategic partners did not have as their objectives safety of flight, security of investment and sensible growth in the future.' He added: 'The strategic partner should not have profit as a primary objective.'[41] Fifty Labour MPs, led by Gavin Strang, the former Labour Transport Minister, opposed plans to part-privatize Britain's air traffic control on the grounds of safety. Among them were Tony Benn, Ken Livingstone and Diane Abbott. Michael Moore for the Liberal Democrats said the privatization plans were seriously misguided and his party would vote against the Transport Bill, which contained this proposal.[42] In the week of the debate, on Wednesday, 22 December 1999, a Korean Boeing 747 cargo jet exploded just after taking off from Stansted, near London. All four crew were killed. Korean air, which owned the plane, had rapidly developed into the world's second biggest cargo carrier, but it had a poor safety record.[43] Despite opposition from the Labour majority of the Commons Transport Committee, the government decided to press ahead with part-privatization. The preferred option of Labour MPs was a non-profit-making trust similar to the one set up in Canada. The Conservatives wanted total privatization.[44] Blair also prepared the Post Office for privatization, which made Labour traditionalists see red and made many more fear that local and rural post offices would disappear. Plans to privatize the nuclear industry suffered a setback after it lost orders in Japan and Germany following the falsification of safety records. The Irish and Danish governments called on Britain to stop nuclear reprocessing at the key Sellafield plant. The policy, initiated by Thatcher, of selling off or transferring council housing from local authority ownership to housing associations continued under Blair. Council housing was rapidly becoming history.

Concern about safety on Britain's privatized railways continued to grow as the century drew to a close. This was fuelled by the Paddington rail crash in October 1999, caused by a train going through a red light, and before that the Southall crash in 1997 in which seven people died and 150 were injured.[45] In the Paddington disaster 31 people died. It was revealed that trains frequently went through red lights. The tracks were often in need of attention; the signalling equipment was no longer modern. In addition, trains on some lines were often delayed or cancelled, coaches were old and fares were high relative to standards on western European railways. No wonder that the number of passenger complaints of poor service and delays passed the one million mark in 1998. This was an 8 per cent rise on the previous year, Tom Winsor, the Rail Regulator, reported.[46] The enquiry into the Southall crash concluded that the driver and privatization were responsible for the crash. Despite privatization the railways continued to cost the public billions in subsidies, which were paid to the rail companies. It is only fair to record that even countries like Norway and Germany suffered rail crashes. In February 2000 the German Amsterdam–Basel express crashed in Brühl with the loss of 8 lives and 149 injured. Damaged track was thought to be one possible cause. Like British rail operators, German railways had been cutting back on staff over several years.[47] Earlier in Eschede, Lower Saxony, the worst accident in German rail history had occurred with the loss of 101 lives. On 10 March 2000, another accident occurred in London injuring 30 passengers; luckily no one was killed.

IN FOREIGN HANDS

The sale of British assets to foreign companies continued under Blair as under Major. The Rover motor company was bought by Germany's BMW. Asda, the retail chain, was sold to America's Wal-Mart. EMI, the flagship of the British music and entertainment industry, merged with the much larger US Time-Warner conglomerate. BTP, one of Britain's remaining chemical companies, was bought by a Swiss rival. Schroder, the last major merchant bank quoted on the London stock exchange, sold most of its operations to Citigroup. Glaxo Smithkline Beecham, set to become the world's biggest pharmaceuticals company, announced it was moving its headquarters from London to New York. Four of the six top fund managers that control 70 per cent of British pension assets were foreign owned in 1999. Did it matter? The optimists could say that it brought in foreign capital, better management and in many cases created jobs. The pessimists could argue that jobs disappeared too, other jobs had to be heavily subsidized by the taxpayer and vital decisions about technology, output and products were made elsewhere. One other problem was that foreign penetration of the City attracted more crime. City police were said to be convinced that the Colombian drugs cartels, the Italian Mafia and criminal gangs in Britain and Eastern Europe used the City to launder their money.[48] The dangers of foreign ownership exploded in the face of Stephen Byers, Trade and Industry Secretary, when BMW announced in March 2000 that it was selling Rover with heavy job losses. After weeks of nail-biting tension it was sold for £10 to the Phoenix Group who promised job losses would be kept to a minimum. Meanwhile, Ford announced, on 12 May 2000, car production at Dagenham would cease. In April 2005, MG Rover went into administration with 5,000 redundancies. It was bought by a Chinese motor company.

POLICE: 'INSTITUTIONAL RACISM'?

Two murder cases in London brought into question the attitude of the Metropolitan Police to racism. One was the murder of Stephen Lawrence in April 1993, in south-east London. The other was the killing of Michael Menson in north London in 1997. Lawrence was a teenager, Menson was 30, both were black. In the first case the police were forced to admit they had bungled the investigation. In the second case, they refused at first to regard it as anything other than suicide. The Metropolitan Police's investigation of the Lawrence case was strongly criticized by Sir William Macpherson, who concluded in a report published in February 1999 that, 'The investigation was marred by a combination of professional incompetence, institutional racism and a failure of leadership by senior officers.' Menson's three attackers were eventually tracked down, tried and convicted. One of them, Ozguy Cevat, of dual British/Turkish nationality, fled to Turkish-occupied Northern Cyprus. There he was charged with manslaughter in the Menson case and convicted. Lawrence's attackers evaded justice. In both cases, the families of the victims were responsible for them gaining wide public attention.[49] Despite big gains in status, wealth and jobs by the ethnic communities over the last thirty years of the century, few doubted that racism still existed. Few British whites, racists included, realized that many of them were likely to have black genes. Dr Steve Jones, Britain's leading geneticist, of University College, London University, calculated that one in five white British, had a direct black ancestor. This was the result of his research on census data from the sixteenth century. More black people had come to Britain as slaves or as traders than was generally known. 'Even the Queen has discovered she has black and mixed-race royal ancestors who have never been publicly acknowledged.' Queen Charlotte, the wife of George III, was one of them.[50]

BRITAIN'S ETHNIC COMMUNITIES AT THE END OF THE CENTURY

By the end of the century it was estimated that there were 157,000 people of Chinese origin in Britain, that is 0.3 per cent. According to Professor Tariq Modood (University of Bristol), 41 per cent of Chinese workers were in professional or managerial positions. This compared with 30 per cent of whites, 15 per cent of Asians and 11 per cent of Caribbeans. The Chinese had overtaken whites to emerge as the group most likely to earn salaries in excess of £25,000.[51] Who were the new Britons? The numbers who gained UK citizenship were 40,500 in 1995, 43,100 in 1996 and 37,000 in 1997. Most of them were from the Commonwealth. In 1997, 2,800 were from the 'Old Commonwealth' – Australia, Canada, New Zealand and South Africa – and 16,300 were from the 'New Commonwealth' – mainly Bangladesh, India, Sri Lanka, Pakistan, Caribbean and other African states. In addition there were 4,200 from British dependencies including Hong Kong.[52]

Jack Straw was troubled by figures revealing that in 1999 the number of people seeking political asylum in Britain topped 71,000, a record and over 50 per cent up on 1998. The backlog of applications awaiting a decision reached 100,000 for the first time. In an effort to dissuade asylum seekers and show the electorate he was 'getting tough', Straw ensured that many passengers on a hijacked Afghan airliner, which arrived at Stansted in February 2000, were 'persuaded' to return. The hijackers were arrested and others on the plane were allowed to stay pending the outcome of their asylum applications. People from the former Yugoslavia topped the nationalities seeking asylum.[53] There was also concern about the continued illegal immigrants gaining entry into Britain. Since the fall of Communism in 1989, there had been increasing numbers from Eastern Europe. Often these were Romany from the Czech Republic, Slovakia or Romania, where, they claimed, they faced persecution. Their presence in the coastal towns of southern England caused friction. Often they arrived hidden on freight trains or in trucks. In the summer of 1999, in one incident, immigration officials spotted a group of 50 refugees trying to escape from Willesden freight terminal in north London.[54] In April 2000, under the Immigration and Asylum Act (1999) asylum seekers would be forcibly dispersed from southern England and given vouchers for food and clothing rather than cash. It was hoped this would help to stem the tide. Straw and his Conservative 'shadow', Ann Widdecombe, faced criticism for their advocacy of tough measures on asylum seekers. Bill Morris, the General Secretary of the Transport and General Workers' Union, rattled ministers when he claimed in the *Independent* that Straw and his colleagues had 'given life to the racists'. Morris, himself of immigrant background, was joined by Diane Abbott, the Liberal Democrats, ethnic and refugee bodies and the Catholic bishops.

FIREARMS: 'ENOUGH IS ENOUGH'

Illegal immigration was usually the result of organized crime and brought crime with it. 'Yardie' gangs, dealing in crack and cocaine, brought violence to the streets of London, Birmingham, Bristol and Manchester. Their leaders were often Jamaican-born and in 1999 they were responsible for the deaths of 13 people with many others injured.[55] According to the *Guardian* (14 January 2000), shootings in Cheetham Hill, an area of social deprivation in Manchester, totalled 41 in 1999. The paper reported how Simon Brown was blasted with a shotgun in front of relatives and in the Manchester Black Community Trust centre. The new millennium opened with the shooting of Roger Ormsby on 5 January. In Nottingham, between 1 January and 10 March 2000, there were nine shooting incidents.[56] In Birmingham, where there had been more than 30 shootings within a year, police ran a poster campaign using the words of Martin Luther King, 'Enough is Enough.' This campaign was backed by the black newspaper, *The Voice*, and other bodies. These incidents were part of the growing trend of offences in which firearms were used. In 1983 there were 7,962 such incidents. The figure increased to 10,373 in 1990 and 13,951 in 1993. The police used firearms three times in 1983, three times in 1990 and six times in 1993.[57]

At a time when there was growing alarm about the drugs scene in Straw's own constituency of Blackburn, 'Drugs king' Perwaiz Hassan, a Pakistani national, was jailed for 11 years, for masterminding a shipment of cannabis resin worth £44 million. Hassan, who lived in London, had wealth estimated at £6 million.[58] In 1999, the Home Office was concerned that up to 50 firms of solicitors were raking in millions of pounds of taxpayers' money from legal aid immigration rackets. Four firms were closed after the Legal Aid Board and the Law Society launched a crackdown.[59] Another area of growing crime was credit card fraud, which soared by 40 per cent in 1999. One credit card transaction per 1,000 was said to be fraudulent. The National Criminal Intelligence Service believed that Chinese Triads were mainly responsible for trebling credit fraud between 1994 and 1998.[60] When Jack Straw reported on the crime situation in January 2000, he was forced to admit that violent crimes, including mugging, had increased for the first time for some years. Straw said the Metropolitan Police were afraid to use their right to stop and search suspects for fear of being branded racist since the Lawrence Inquiry.[61] The Police Federation Chairman, Fred Broughton, agreed. He commented 'stops and searches are down, street crimes are up. Cause and effect.'[62] Straw took comfort from figures showing a reduction in car theft and burglary. The Home Secretary was accused of not fulfilling his election pledge to put more 'bobbies on the beat'. In England and Wales there were a total of 124,808 police officers employed in 1998; in March 1999 the number had fallen by 0.8 per cent to 123,845.[63] According to figures given by Lord Bassam in the Lords (17 January 2000) expenditure on England's 39 police forces was to be increased from £6,852,800,000 in 1999/2000 to £7,045,100,000 in 2000/2001. These were hefty sums, but many experts believed they were still inadequate.

Since it took up its work in 1985 the number of complaints against the police referred to the Police Complaints Authority (PCA) had mounted. This could in part be due to the growing awareness of the work of the PCA and to a greater readiness among the public to complain. This appeared to be the trend in every sphere of national life. Certainly before the 1970s the British tended to be passive and accept what they were given. This gradually changed in the remaining years of the century. Once again American influences were important in promoting the idea of rights and litigation. A second factor was the influence of Western Europe's culture of rights as Britain moved closer to its neighbours. Political and commercial competition was a third factor. Privatization had led to the call for safeguards for consumers and this resulted in the setting up of various watchdogs. This is in no way to suggest that complaints were not justified in many cases. Advertising offered so much yet in many cases people were disappointed when products fell below expectations. Protection of minorities also enhanced the call for greater transparency, the setting up of a proper system of redress and recruitment of more police officers from the ethnic communities. In 2000, Tarique Ghaffur was appointed to one of the most senior posts in the Metropolitan Police, Deputy Assistant Commissioner, after a 'meteoric rise' through the ranks of the police service in Leicestershire and Lancashire. From a Punjabi family, Ghaffur came to Britain as a 15-year-old from Uganda.[64]

Another problem that confronted Straw was what to do about British citizens who had spied for Soviet bloc intelligence agencies. As Eastern bloc archives were opened more former spies were being exposed. In the BBC documentary *The Spying Game* (September 1999), Dr Robin Pearson of Hull University was accused of working over many years for the East German secret police. He was suspended from his teaching duties for two years. Jenny Willmott, President of Hull's student union, said, 'Students of Dr Pearson felt they had been betrayed by him.'[65] Pearson was one of a number of spies who had worked for the East Germans or Soviets. The most significant revealed was Melita Norwood, a life-long communist, who had given early nuclear secrets to Moscow. The Solicitor-General decided not to prosecute them because of the cost, and the difficulty of securing convictions.

CELEBRATING THE MILLENNIUM

The previous Conservative government had decided Britain should have a special dome for the end of the millennium to celebrate Britain's achievements. This was taken up by Tony Blair who decided to build a Millennium Dome on derelict land in south London. Peter Mandelson was put in charge as minister for the project. Jennie Page, a former civil servant, was the hands-on boss of the project with a budget of £758 million and a staff of 20,000. Her job was to stage 'the most spectacular millennium event anywhere in the world'.[66] The Dome was attacked as a London-based project, which would be expensive for non-Londoners to visit. It also came under fire for ignoring British history and lacking a 'spiritual dimension'. The spectacular opening on New Year's Eve ran in to problems. Many of the VIPs, notables, celebrities and sponsors invited found they had to queue and wait on a chilly night to get in because of a fault in the initial organization. In the aftermath, the Dome was criticized because it looked like 'an upturned porridge bowl, joyless, ugly, confusing'.[67] Later it was said that 7–8 out of 10 ordinary members of the public admitted in the first weeks found it an enjoyable and worthwhile experience. However, not enough people paid to visit the Dome in January and Ms Page was forced to resign. Her replacement was Philippe Bourguignon from Disneyland Paris.

As the new century approached, Britain decided to take an early and extended break. It was said to be the longest festive shutdown on record. Many were on holiday for 11 days from Christmas Eve until 4 January.[68] Christmas was also cheaper in 1999 for the third year in succession.[69] Unemployment was lower than it had been for twenty years and mortgage interest rates were relatively low. Perhaps these were the reasons why, on Tuesday, 28 December, the *Daily Mail* reported that the British had gone 'sales crazy'. On the day before, there had been a massive surge towards the shops in the hunt for bargains. Savings accounts were raided and credit cards were used generously to finance the spree. Mobile phones were high on the list of purchases as were computers. Although more people attended Christian services over the holiday period, the number of churches open continued to decline. In 1989, there were 38,607 churches of all denominations in England. In 1999, the number had fallen to 37,717.[70] Over the 1990s, Britons had been mesmerized by the desire to get rich quick. The lottery and the high earnings and wealth of a few had focused attention even more than in the past on this. The television quiz programme *Who Wants To Be A Millionaire?*, started in 1999, revealed this and fuelled it. The festivities were clouded slightly by fears that among the Christmas parcels there would be bombs sent by Islamic terrorist groups linked to the

Saudi-born millionaire, Osama Bin Laden.[71] The breakaway 'Continuity IRA' faction threatened to bomb Kempton Park race course. There were also fears worldwide among the interested and informed few that the 'millennium bug' would cause computers to fail. Argentina grounded all its planes. The Russians and the Americans got together to ensure that failing computers in defence systems would not cause a world war. In Britain, 20,000 credit card swipe machines were hit as a system collapsed on 28 December.[72] By mid-January, however, the 'Bug' did not seem to have done much damage in Britain or elsewhere. Shock waves hit the City of London on 5 April 2000, when its computer system crashed. As *The Times* (6 April 2000) reported, 'Where screaming hordes of anarchists, the Blitz and the IRA failed, a computer breakdown succeeded yesterday. The City ground to a halt.' The paralysis lasted seven hours. Because it was the end of the British tax year huge business had been expected. *The Times* believed, 'London's reputation as a world financial centre was seriously damaged.' Businesses suffered again in May, when a 'virus' from the Philippines infected computers worldwide and increased fears of 'cyber terrorists'. Others infections followed.

Despite the official optimism Britain was entering the twenty-first century with a transport system which was poor by the standards of Western European states, and a faltering health service. The term 'rip-off Britain' had come into use, summing up the widespread feeling that British consumers were being forced to pay higher prices than their continental neighbours for cars, food, many consumer goods and banking. Although successive governments had stressed the importance of education and training from 1945 onwards, Britain's school system was below the standards of the majority of European states, all of which were state-run. The great majority of British people could not speak or write grammatical English and had shaky maths. Television and radio still made many documentaries about history and current affairs, yet most people had no knowledge even of twentieth-century history. Industrial and professional training left very many Britons unskilled. According to Unicef, British children were among the least healthy in Europe, affected by poor diet even before they were born.[73] Teenage pregnancies were higher in Britain than in any other EU state. Britain had one of the highest prevalences of drug use in Europe and the government was said to be losing the fight against serious drug abuse.[74] Britain had a growing alcohol abuse problem Britain with more women turning to excessive drinking. It had a record of sending proportionally more of its population to prison than any other EU state except Portugal.[75] No one could explain why the UK had the highest incidence of asthma in Western Europe.[76] Its electoral system was unfair by the standards of Western Europe and it was alone in having an undemocratic second chamber. Yet British people were freer than they had been at any other time and they were certainly enjoying unprecedented prosperity. Real disposable incomes had roughly doubled since 1970. The arts flourished as much as at any time in the past. Gordon Brown was optimistic. He told an American audience, in February 2000, that the government was on a mission to make Britain the world's best place for business, a global leader in e-commerce and the education capital of the world.[77]

WOMEN 2000

Women gained voting rights on the same basis as men in 1928 but in the Parliament elected in 1997 they were still greatly outnumbered by men. They were also, in this respect, well behind most of their sisters in the European Union. (See Table 12.3.) Remarkably, the situation was even worse in France. In most cases there was a rough correlation between their representation in Parliament and their pay as a percentage of men's pay. As we saw above (p. 229), women had made enormous progress since 1945 in moving towards equality with men. Clearly, they still had a good way to go. This is illustrated by the position in higher education. According to figures given in a written reply by George Mudie to Joan Ruddock in the Commons (26 July 1999), 264 men had been appointed professor in 1997–98 but only 41 women. In 1996–97, the figures were 209 and 43 respectively. These figures excluded those promoted within their own institutions. In the armed forces, only 7.7 per cent of total strength in 1999 were women. From April 1998, the number of posts in the Army open to women increased from 47 to 70 per cent.[78] In April 2000 Baroness Prashar (1948–), of Kenyan

Table 12.3 Women in European parliaments

Female members of parliament of the EU states 1998 (percentage)		*Women's pay as percentage of men's pay*	
Sweden	43	Sweden	87
Denmark	35	Denmark	88
Finland	34	Finland	82
Netherlands	31	Netherlands	71
Germany	30	Germany	77 (West)
European Parliament	30 (1999)		90 (East)
Austria	24	Austria	74
Spain	20	Spain	74
Luxembourg	18	Luxembourg	84
Britain	18	Britain	74
Belgium	17	Belgium	83
Portugal	13	Portugal	72
Ireland	11	Ireland	73
France	8	France	77
Greece	6	Greece	68

Source: Das Parlament, 21 January 2000

Asian background, was appointed First Civil Service Commissioner. She was Chairman of the Parole Board in England and Wales. She was made a life peer in 1999. The CSC is responsible for the top appointments in the civil service.

LONELY BRITAIN?

On Friday 10 December 1999, the author had to wait from 23.00 to 23.15 to get through to a Barclaycard customer adviser. What does that say about telephone banking, Barclaycard and Britain? Certainly there were not enough 'advisers' to handle the demand, but why were so many people ringing so late on a Friday night anyway? What did this say about the quality of life in Britain at the end of the twentieth century? On 13 January 2000, the Samaritans disclosed that they were deluged by lonely and depressed callers during the Christmas and New Year. Some 246,000 callers rang the helpline over the period starting 25 December and ending 7 January, 18 per cent more calls than the previous year. The charity believed that high expectations and 'millennium hype' could have contributed to a sense of anti-climax and depression.[79] In the highly successful film, *Four Weddings And A Funeral* (1994), Hugh Grant portrayed the uncertain, lonely Englishman. Earlier, Steve Martin played his American equivalent, in Arthur Hiller's *The Lonely Guy* (1984). Helen Fielding's *Bridget Jones's Diary* (1996) gave expression to the many thirty-something single women who were not happy being alone. It sold over a million copies. Clearly, it was perceived as a growing problem. In 1961, in Britain, the proportion of households occupied by just one person was 10 per cent. In 1999 it was 30 per cent. The Department of the Environment estimated that by 2010 it would be 40 per cent.[80] Divorce was a factor in this; putting off marriage was another. Some believed that many successful young women, and men, were consciously deciding to remain single. They did not want to make the compromises necessary for a long-term commitment or/and bringing up a family. Was Britain gradually dying like Italy and Germany? Writing in 1999, Tom Nairn was pessimistic about the future of British society and the Blair agenda, feeling the 'trouble may be terminal. Even as a trademark "British" has passed from being one of the soundest properties on the international ideas-mart (liberal, trust-worthy, decent, first among equals . . . to being a down-market leftover – not quite a slum but heading in that direction.'[81] These were the challenges facing Blair as, full of confidence, he prepared his party for the next election and the next term.

CONSERVATIVE PARTY'S PROBLEMS CONTINUE

Past scandals continued to haunt the Conservative Party. Jonathan Aitken, the former Cabinet Minister, was sent to prison for perjury and perverting the course of justice. Lord Archer had to withdraw from the race to become the Conservative candidate in the London mayoral elections after being exposed as a liar. Former minister and MP Neil Hamilton (see p. 292) lost his law suit against Harrod's owner Mohamed al-Fayed and was left with over £1 million to pay in costs. Al-Fayed had alleged that Hamilton had corruptly taken money from him to put questions in Parliament and the jury believed him. The *Independent* (22 December 1999) called Hamilton 'a fatally flawed politician on the make who grabbed, gambled, lied and lost'. The Parliamentary Commissioner for Standards, Sir Gordon Downey, concluded in July 1997 that evidence that Hamilton had accepted payments was 'compelling'. Former Conservative Party Treasurer Michael Ashcroft came under attack for being a tax exile.[82]

Although in media time, it seemed already in another age long ago, past Conservative leadership battles were fought again in 1999. John Major's memoirs revealed the animosities between him and Thatcher, and him and many of his other colleagues, 'the bastards'. Judith Chaplin (1939–93), his closest political adviser at the Treasury and at No. 10, 1989–92, kept a secret diary. She felt that as Chancellor, 'he has little economic knowledge he deals mostly in economic platitudes with ill-thought-out ideas'. Major is quoted as saying of his former leader Thatcher, 'I want her isolated, I want her destroyed.' He felt 'she's bonkers'.[83] In February 2000, Teresa Gorman, maverick Conservative right-winger, faced the longest suspension of an MP from the Commons for failing to declare interests, for misleading a disciplinary committee, for making false accusations against her accusers and for interfering with witnesses. The Standards and Privileges Committee concluded she had failed to declare an interest when she promoted two Bills supporting small landlords in 1990 and 1991.[84]

Hague continued to be dogged by problems with his team and his associates into the new century. In the week before Christmas 1999, it was announced that a former Conservative front-bench spokesman for London had defected to Labour. This was Shaun Woodward, MP for Witney, a former BBC producer who had master-minded Major's 1992 electoral victory. Woodward claimed that Hague had thrown away John Major's 'sensible' wait-and-see policy on the euro and described the party's guarantee to cut the tax burden as 'reckless'. He was also critical of the party's stance on gays.[85] Hague came under fire from ex-Chancellor Kenneth Clarke. He told BBC listeners that he feared the Conservative Party had moved 'very strongly to the Right'.[86] Hague's last setback in 1999 was an attack, on 29 December, from his predecessor John Major the day after Clarke's salvo. Writing in the *Spectator*, and referring to Thatcherism, Major argued, 'There are no votes in yesterday and many will be lost if the ghost of government past appears to lead the party by the nose.'[87]

Like Blair, Hague also suffered embarrassment when his party attempted to choose a mayoral candidate for London. The popular Lord Archer was forced to resign after admitting asking a friend to lie for him in an earlier court case. Later, he was suspended for five years from the Conservative Party. The Conservatives eventually settled on Steven Norris, a former Transport Minister with a 'colourful lifestyle'.

In preparation for the May 2000 elections and the final phase of the 1997 Parliament, Hague revamped his team combining former ministers and bringing in younger members. Michael Portillo (1953–), former Defence Secretary and Chief Secretary to the Treasury, was appointed Shadow Chancellor. He was a Cambridge graduate and the son of a Spanish refugee. Michael Ancram (1945–) remained Conservative Party Chairman. The son of the 12th Marquess of Lothian, he was an Oxford graduate and lawyer who had served at the Scottish Office and the Northern Ireland Office. Shadow Home Secretary was Ann Widdecombe (1947–). She remained the most senior woman in Hague's team. A graduate of Birmingham and Oxford in Latin and PPE respectively she was a university administrator before her election in 1987. She had the advantage of considerable ministerial experience including Minister of State, Home Office, 1995–97. Francis Maude (1953–), shadowed on Foreign and Commonwealth affairs. He was the scion of a Conservative parliamentary family. A lawyer, he was a Cambridge graduate and had served at the DTI, the Foreign Office and as Financial Secretary to the Treasury, 1990–92. Also from a well-known Conservative family was David Heathcoat-Amory (1949–), the Shadow Chief Secretary to the Treasury. A graduate of Oxford, he was one of three old Etonians in the 22-member team. Also an old Etonian, Sir George Young (1941–) was Shadow Leader of the House. As Secretary of State for Transport, 1995–97, he had become unpopular as the minister responsible for rail privatization. Archie Norman (1954–), the successful chairman and former chief executive of Asda, was elected to the Commons in 1997. He was a graduate of Cambridge and Minnesota universities in economics and business. His brief was environment, transport and the regions. Former Guards officer Iain Duncan Smith (1954–) was appointed Shadow Defence Secretary. He was first elected to the Commons in 1992. Parson's daughter Theresa May (1956–) was also elected in 1997. An Oxford graduate, her rise was seen in part due to Hague's desire to offer high-profile roles to his few women MPs. She was given the education brief. Angela Browning (1946–) returned to the shadow cabinet as Shadow Trade Secretary. She had served in Major's government as parliamentary secretary for the Ministry of Agriculture, Fisheries and Food. Dr Liam Fox (1961–), a Scottish GP, was elected in 1992 and served his leader well on health matters. Andrew Lansley (1956–) was appointed shadow minister for the Cabinet Office and policy renewal. A politics graduate from Exeter University he was a former civil servant and Director of the Conservative Research Department. He arrived at the Commons in 1997. Bernard Jenkin (1959–), shadow transport spokesperson, a Cambridge graduate in English literature, was elected to the Commons in 1992. Before that he had worked for Ford and Legal & General.

BLAIR CULT

On 19 November 1999, it was announced that Mrs Blair, at 45, was expecting her fourth child. Thus Blair became the first Prime Minister to be fathering an offspring whilst in office. The following day the *Daily Mail*, the *Mirror* and the *Sun* devoted their entire front pages to this. In the *Daily Telegraph*, Cherie Blair competed with the long saga of Ken Livingstone's fight to become Labour's candidate for Mayor of London. The other papers thought the legal battle between former MP Neil Hamilton and Harrod's owner, al-Fayed, was more newsworthy. In Nottingham ten women from 17 to over 60 picked at random on the street gave their views.[88] Eight said they had no interest. Only one was enthusiastic, wishing Mrs Blair well. Two said they thought there were more important things to put in the papers, and one wondered whether it had been planned as a diversion from other issues. The pundits thought it could only help the Prime Minister. After 1,000 days in office, in January 2000, Blair was in a much stronger position than his three predecessors as Prime Minister at a similar stage in the political cycle. Abroad, Social Democratic leaders like German Chancellor Gerhard Schröder sought to improve their public image by identifying with him. He was becoming a cult figure. Yet within the Labour Party there had been rumblings of discontent especially in 1999 and into 2000. Many felt that Blair had unfairly supported Frank Dobson, the former Health Secretary, to be Labour's candidate for the new post of Mayor of London and had been unduly hostile to Ken Livingstone, MP and former GLC leader. Junior Defence Minister Peter Kilfoyle, regarded as a Blair loyalist, resigned in January 2000. The resignation was seen as a warning to the government that it was losing its traditional working-class voters.[89] There was also trouble for the Prime Minister in Wales. There too he had pushed his man, Alun Michael, to take over as the Welsh Assembly's First Secretary. Michael was voted down in February 2000 and replaced by Rhodri Morgan, a more traditional Labour figure. One of the issues in Wales and the north-west was that these and other regions were struggling to get EU funds because the Chancellor Gordon Brown refused to confirm the matching funds that would trigger payments from Brussels.[90] In Wales, Scotland and London, Labour was accused of unfairness in its internal election procedures. The electoral college method was used rather than one member, one vote. Trade union leaders were allowed to cast thousands of members' votes without consulting them. Livingstone received far more votes from individual party members than Dobson who won by a narrow margin based on union votes and MPs. On the 100th anniversary of the establishment of the

Labour Representation Committee, which became the Labour Party in 1906, New Labour faced criticism from its old supporters like Will Hutton who thought the party was moving to the right. Shirley Williams, now representing the Liberal Democratic cause in the Lords, formerly a minister in Callaghan's government, gave a measured judgement.

> What worries me about New Labour, which in many ways is an interesting and impressive party, is its dedication to the concept of the redistribution of income and wealth is much less clear than it used to be. What was once the bedrock was the concept there should be not complete equality, but not huge extremes in inequality. As a country we are very unequal; not as bad as the United States, but much worse than the rest of Europe. So it's not as clear as it was, what the basic philosophy of the Labour Party is.[91]

Livingstone seemed to agree with a lot of this and after testing the waters declared he would stand as an independent in the London mayoral election on 6 March. He was immediately suspended from the Labour Party and subjected to a vicious campaign of abuse by his erstwhile 'comrades' many of whom had been glad to be seen in his company in his GLC days. Would he score a remarkable victory or be swept into the dustbin of history? The first poll, published in the *Guardian* (7 March) gave him a massive lead. The campaign looked like becoming a battle to mobilize the ethnic vote. Bids were made for the substantial Irish, Scottish, Jewish, Turkish, Greek, Asian and black votes.

LONDON: LIVINGSTONE BEATS PARTY MACHINES

On Thursday 4 May 2000, millions of voters had the opportunity to cast their ballots in local elections in England. There was also a parliamentary by-election in the safe Conservative seat of Romsey. The greatest interest was of course in the first election for the London Mayor and for the 25-member London Assembly. In the run-up to the local and London elections Hague launched his 'Common Sense Revolution'. He attempted to raise the temperature by promising to keep the pound and calling for 'bogus asylum seekers' to be detained. This message seemed to go down best in the Euro-sceptic west country and in the south-east, where coastal towns faced growing numbers of would-be refugees. In the west Midlands the problems of Rover hit Labour. Elsewhere, women's job losses in the textile industry could also have lessened enthusiasm for Labour.[92] Throughout the country the Conservatives won about 600 seats mainly at Labour's expense. The poll, under 30 per cent, was even lower than usual and it was reckoned Labour suffered from massive abstentions. There was some evidence of voters switching from Labour to the Liberal Democrats who snatched control of the Labour stronghold of Oldham and took Cambridge from Labour. Labour also lost control of Bradford, where the party had its beginnings in the 1890s. Hague's night of joy was spoiled by the loss of Romsey to the Liberal Democrats on a 12.56 per cent swing. The turnout was a respectable 55.41 per cent. The only consolation for the Conservatives was that the Labour candidate lost his deposit. Labour voters had seen as their priority the defeat of the Conservatives and some Conservatives appear to have abstained. The result was an excellent one for Kennedy, strengthening his position as Liberal Democratic leader. In London, Livingstone won as predicted gaining 58 per cent to Conservative Steve Norris's 42 per cent. Labour's Frank Dobson just managed to come in third ahead of the Liberal Democrat Susan Kramer. Only about 35 per cent of Londoners took the opportunity to vote. The victory was a great personal achievement for Livingstone who defeated three candidates with party machines behind them and seven other candidates. Livingstone had faced a spiteful campaign against him with the traditional Labour daily, the *Mirror* (3 May), urging its readers to vote for Norris and calling Livingstone 'This dangerous buffoon'. The paper attacked Blair's handling of Labour's selection procedure and 'selfish' Dobson. No papers endorsed Livingstone. Despite such attacks Livingstone's win was due to his media exposure over a long period. Although some voters were kicking the government by voting for him, and although his personality and London background helped, he did offer the electorate an alternative agenda. A key issue was the partial privatization of the underground, which he strongly opposed. Having arrived much later on the scene Kramer followed his lead on this issue. The election to the London Assembly was by proportional representation and resulted in Labour and Conservatives gaining nine seats each, the Liberal Democrats four seats and the Greens three. This was based on a vote of 30.30 per cent for Labour, 28.99 for the Conservatives, 14.80 for the Liberal Democrats and 11.08 for the Greens. The Christian People's Alliance attracted 3.33 per cent, the British National Party 2.87, the UKIP 2.05 and the London Socialist Alliance 1.63. Although leading Green Darren Johnson, had stood against Livingstone for Mayor, Livingstone had advised his supporters to give their first vote for Labour candidates and their 'top-up' vote for the Greens in the Assembly elections. Given the fragmented nature of the Assembly the Greens had greater potential significance than their numbers suggested.

Livingstone's life had been inseparably bound up with London since his birth in Streatham in 1945. After leaving comprehensive school in 1962, he worked as a lab technician. He went on to do teacher training but became a professional politician in the early 1970s. His rise started when he was elected to Lambeth Borough Council in 1971. This led to his leadership of the Greater London Council (GLC) in 1981. After the abolition of the

GLC in 1986 he was elected as Labour MP for Brent East in 1987, being re-elected in 1992 and 1997. He served on the NEC of the Labour Party, 1987–89 and 1997–98.

ELECTION 2001: 'IT'S IN THE BAG, TONY'

In March 2001, the *Sun* proclaimed, 'It's in the bag, Tony'. It was referring to the forthcoming general election and the fact that it was backing Blair for the second time. Because of the foot-and-mouth crisis, the election was postponed from 7 May to 7 June. Labour was backed by the majority of newspapers, which was a first. Another first was the widespread use of the Internet and emailing by all three parties. This probably had very little impact. The polls got it right in the 2001 election by predicting a Labour victory from the start of the campaign. Remarkably, only once in four years had Labour fallen behind the Conservatives. This was in autumn 2000, when there was a fuel crisis with protests by road hauliers. Labour's campaign strategy was to focus on the economy, the NHS and education. The Conservatives' main thrusts were on asylum seekers, the single currency, Labour's alleged mishandling of rural affairs, and, towards the end, fears of a Labour landslide. The Liberal Democrats fought on honesty in politics and their leader. Charles Kennedy emerged as the most popular of the three leaders during the campaign. They also focused on the NHS and education. Blair could be proud that Labour's victory was historic. It was the first time that Labour had gained enough seats for a second full term and no party had previously won such a large majority for its second term. The catch was that the victory was achieved on a low turnout across the country. On the lowest turnout since 1918, only 59 per cent of eligible voters cast their votes.

Labour gained 41 per cent of the vote, the Conservatives 31.9 and the Liberal Democrats 18.4. This result gave Labour 413 seats (419 in 1997), with 166 for the Conservatives (165) and 52 (46) for the Liberal Democrats. The SNP held on to five seats (six) and PC four (four). There were a few crumbs of comfort for the Conservatives with gains, mainly at the expense of the Liberal Democrats, in the local elections held on the same day. They regained a foothold in Scotland by capturing a seat in Scotland from the SNP. They also regained Newark and Romford from Labour, and Tatton, the seat Martin Bell had vacated. Apart from Northern Ireland, fewer seats changed hands than at any time since 1910.

The Conservatives failed to retake Ludlow, captured by the Liberal Democrats from the Conservatives, Torbay, where the Liberal Democrats increased their previous majority of 12 to 6,708, and Edgbaston, held by Labour. These were traditionally Conservative constituencies and were typical of other former Conservative seats. The Liberal Democrats also took Chesterfield, which had been held by Labour since 1935. Tony Benn had retired there in 2001. Among the other interesting results were those in the traditional working-class constituencies of Hartlepool, Leicester East and St Helens South, where a wide variety of candidates, including socialists, sought to replace Labour candidates Peter Mandelson, Keith Vaz and former Conservative Shaun Woodward; all had been subjected to strong critical reporting by the media. All three won with ease. Arthur Scargill (Socialist Labour) attracted only 912 votes in Hartlepool. According to the *Morning Star* (9 June 2001), of 113 Socialist Labour candidates, only one kept his deposit. The rival Socialist Alliance saved two deposits, one at St Helens South. The Scottish Socialist Party gained 3 per cent of the vote, but in Glasgow Pollok, its vote reached 9.98 per cent. The Green Party saved 10 deposits in the 145 constituencies it contested. Its best results were in Brighton Pavilion, where it secured 9.3 per cent, and Leeds West, with 8 per cent. Politicians in all three major parties were shocked by the results in Oldham East & Saddleworth and Oldham West & Royton. Labour retained these seats but the anti-immigrant British National Party attracted 11.2 and 16 per cent respectively. Oldham, a town with a considerable Asian population, suffered several nights of violence between Asian and white youths in the period leading up to polling day. Rioting by Asian youths also occurred in Leeds on 5 June. Elsewhere the BNP made little impact. The UKIP also failed to make any impact. The anti-euro stance of the Conservatives and fear of a Labour landslide helped to dissuade Conservative Eurosceptics from voting UKIP. The most unexpected victory was that of Dr Richard Taylor at Wyre Forest. Standing as an independent, he gained a 17,630 majority, defeating the Labour junior minister David Lock, who had previously held the seat, as well as Conservative and UKIP candidates. Taylor, 66, who had received little media publicity, benefited from the anger over the closure of Kidderminster hospital, where he had worked as a consultant, and discontent over the state of the NHS.

In Northern Ireland, the UUP retained only six of its ten seats. David Trimble only narrowly avoided defeat. Paisley's DUP, noted for its opposition to the Good Friday Agreement, increased its seats from two to five. Sinn Fein gained four seats, overtaking its rival in the Catholic camp, the SDLP, which once again secured three. In terms of votes, both DUP and Sinn Fein gained 21 per cent, the UUP fell back to 22 per cent and the SDLP to 19 per cent.

How did the minorities do in the election? The *Irish Post* (16 June 2001) was pleased that 'a host of Irish MPs' (not including Northern Ireland), 25 Labour and three Conservative, were elected. All five Asian MPs were re-elected and they were joined by two others. Five other 'ethnic minority' candidates were also elected. All of them were Labour. The *Jewish Chronicle* (15 June 2001) recorded that 21 Jewish MPs had been elected: 13 Labour, seven Conservative and one Liberal Democrat. These figures represent an inadequate measure of the influence of these and (other groups) on New Labour. The *Guardian* (9 June 2001) reported that eight 'openly gay or lesbian' candidates were returned to the Commons. The total number of female MPs declined slightly from 120 to 118 but, surprisingly, three from Northern Ireland were elected – one each from the UUP, DUP and SF.

The decline of female membership of the Commons was to some degree offset by the increase of women in the new Cabinet. Blair's new government included seven women, which was a record. Nine members of the Cabinet, including Gordon Brown, held on to their posts. Blair's most important change was to move Cook from the Foreign and Commonwealth Office to become Leader of the House. His successor was Straw, who was notable for his earlier anti-EU views. According to the *Jewish Chronicle*, Straw's appointment was 'heralded as good news . . . by Jewish leaders'. Blunkett moved from Education to the Home Office. Estelle Morris, a former school-teacher, took over at Education.

Being the first Conservative leader since Austin Chamberlain (1921–22) not to become Prime Minister, William Hague announced his resignation as Conservative leader. Before the election, as speculation about an election mounted, the Political Parties Elections and Referendums Bill received Royal Assent on 30 November 2000. The Act gave effect to the recommendations of the Committee on Standards in Public Life, published in October 1998, on the funding of political parties. It was rushed through Parliament in an endeavour to frustrate Conservative fund-raising efforts in the run-up to the forthcoming general election. The Act clarified contributions to election campaigns and the policy on donations. Politicians, parties and their local branches must now declare contributions from anyone – corporations, individuals or trade unions – above £200. Individual contributors can hide from publicity by making a number of small donations, but only up to the value of £5,000. There is also now a total cap on party spending in election campaigns. However, political parties can still receive uncapped donations, provided they register them with the Electoral Commission. Would the Act prove to be a fig leaf which changed nothing fundamentally as parties became more and more dependent on rich individuals and corporations? Much controversy had preceded the Act. 'Why is party funding in the news,' asked the *Guardian* (29 January 2002), 'that is, *after* the election?' Its answer?

> Because of the scandal surrounding the collapse of the giant American energy company Enron. The business lavishly funded the election campaigns of many American politicians. Now it has become clear that Enron paid money to both the Labour party and the Conservative party too. Between 1998 and 2000 the Conservatives took £25,000 while the Labour party received a series of donations totalling £38,000. In return Enron executives were able to meet ministers, civil servants and MPs and press their case for the overturning of the government's block on building new gas-

fuelled power stations. The block was subsequently removed – although the government stresses that this was for economic and environmental reasons, rather than because of pressure from Enron.

It is only fair to mention that the businessman who bankrolled the Liberal Democrats' election campaign is wanted in the US, where he could face up to five years in jail for fraud. *The Times* (26 October 2005) revealed that the businessman who donated a record £2.4 million to the Liberal Democrats was arrested three times and has been accused of bouncing 12 cheques. According to the paper, the source of his wealth 'remains a mystery'.

NOTES

1 Butler and Kavanagh (1997), 206.
2 Butler and Kavanagh (1997), 205.
3 Oliver James, *Sunday Times*, 31 August 1997.
4 *Nottingham Evening Post*, 1 September 1997.
5 *Daily Telegraph*, 13 October 1999.
6 *Hansard, House of Lords Weekly*, No. 1790, 10–13 January, Columns 524–26.
7 Davis (2000).
8 Cowley (2000).
9 *Hansard, Parliamentary Debates*, Volume 329, House of Commons, 19 April 1999.
10 Rallings and Thrasher (2000).
11 http://news.bbc.co.uk, 'UK Politics: A–Z of Parliament', 24 February 2000.
12 *Sunday Times*, 2 January 2000.
13 http://news.bbc.co.uk, 29 February 2000.
14 *Independent on Sunday*, 8 December 1999.
15 *Observer*, 23 January 2000.
16 *Independent*, 13 January 2000.
17 *The Asian*, 3–9 February 2000.
18 *The Asian*, 3–9 February 2000.
19 *Independent*, 18 February 2000.
20 http://news.bbc.co.uk, 'Good Friday Agreement', 24 February 2000.
21 http://news.bbc.co.uk, 'Siege of Drumcree', 24 February 2000.
22 BBC2 *Newsnight*, 16 February 2000.
23 *Independent*, 18 February 2000.
24 1991 Census, Volume 1, 24, Table 1.
25 *Daily Telegraph*, 19 June 1999; *The Times Higher Education Supplement*, 11 February 2000 and 7 April 2000.
26 *Manchester Evening News*, 12 November 1999. For Derby, see *Independent*, 4 April 2000.
27 *Independent*, 6 January 2000.
28 *The Times Higher Education Supplement*, 14 January 1999.
29 *The Times Higher Education Supplement*, 14 January 1999.
30 *The Times Higher Education Supplement*, 3 December 1999.
31 *Independent*, 8 December 1999.
32 *Sunday Times*, 2 January 2000.
33 *Daily Mail*, 6 January 2000; *Observer*, 13 February 2000.
34 *Daily Mail*, 9 November 1999.
35 *Independent*, 30 December 1999.

36 *Daily Telegraph*, 16 February 2000.
37 *Independent*, 1 March 2000.
38 *Independent*, 8 December 1999; *Independent on Sunday*, 12 December 1999.
39 Inland Revenue, 1999, 137, Table 13.5.
40 *Inside Labour*, October 1999.
41 *Independent*, 8 December 1999.
42 *The Times*, 21 December 1999.
43 *The Times*, 23 December 1999.
44 *Independent*, 18 February 2000.
45 *Daily Telegraph*, 6 October 1999.
46 *Daily Telegraph*, 26 August 1999.
47 *Der Spiegel*, 14 February 2000.
48 *Independent*, 25 November 1998.
49 *Independent*, 22 December 1999.
50 *Sunday Telegraph*, 3 October 1999.
51 *Independent*, 6 February 2000.
52 Office of National Statistics, Table 4.2.
53 *The Times*, 26 January 2000.
54 *Sunday Telegraph*, 3 October 1999.
55 *Sunday Telegraph*, 25 July 1999; *Voice*, 5 June 2000.
56 *Nottingham Evening Post*, 10 March 2000.
57 Figures supplied by Police Complaints Authority.
58 *The Asian*, 2–9 February 2000.
59 *Independent*, 13 January 2000.
60 *Observer*, 23 January 2000.
61 *The Asian*, 2–9 February 2000.
62 *Police Review*, 4 February 2000.
63 Chartered Institute, 4, Table 2.
64 *The Asian*, 2–9 February 2000.
65 *The Times Higher Educational Supplement*, 11 February 2000.
66 *The Times*, 9 December 1999.
67 *Independent on Sunday*, 9 January 2000.
68 *The Times*, 23 December 1999.
69 *The Times*, 23 December 1999.
70 *Guardian*, 24 December 1999.
71 *Guardian*, 24 December 1999.
72 *Daily Mail*, 29 December 1999.
73 *Daily Telegraph*, 1 July 1999.
74 *Observer*, 23 January 2000.
75 The Howard League for Penal Reform, Fact Sheet 32.
76 National Asthma Campaign, February 2000.
77 *Sunday Times*, 20 February 2000.
78 Ministry of Defence, *What do you know about . . . Equal Opportunities in the Armed Forces*, no. 8, 1999.
79 *Guardian*, 14 January 2000.
80 *Observer*, 16 January 2000.
81 Nairn (2000), 297.
82 *The Times*, 9 December 1999.
83 *Sunday Telegraph*, 19 September 1999.
84 *Independent*, 18 February 2000.
85 *Independent on Sunday*, 19 December 1999.
86 *Daily Telegraph*, 29 December 1999.

87 *Independent*, 30 December 1999.
88 Interviewed by the author, 19 November 1999.
89 *The Times*, 31 January 2000.
90 *Observer*, 13 February 2000.
91 http://news.bbc.co.uk, 'Labour's centenary', 29 February 2000.
92 *Guardian*, 16 May 2000, see Mel Steel, 'Material witness'.

13

BLAIR'S GOVERNMENTS, 2001–05

THE CONSERVATIVES: 'ASSASSINS' AT WORK

After the resignation of William Hague, five MPs put themselves forward to replace him. They were: Michael Ancram, Party Chairman under Hague; Kenneth Clarke, former Chancellor, who was popular with the public but whose pro-euro views worked against him; David Davis, former Chairman of the Public Accounts Committee; Michael Portillo, former Defence Secretary, the favourite with large support amongst the Shadow Cabinet, and Iain Duncan Smith, the candidate of the right-wing Euro-sceptics, backed by (Lord) Norman Tebbit and Margaret Thatcher. Under the new rules, the Conservative MPs chose two by a series of knock-out votes. The candidate receiving the lowest vote in each round withdrew until just two remained. The first ballot, on 10 July, put Portillo ahead. He attracted 49 votes. Next came Smith with 39, followed by Clarke (36 votes). Davis and Ancram received 21 votes each. Two days later, Portillo came first again with 50 votes, followed by Smith (42), Clarke (39), Davis (18) and Ancram (17). Davis and Ancram then withdrew. In the final vote among MPs, Clarke came first with 59 votes (up 20). Iain Duncan Smith came a surprise second with 54 votes (up 12). Portillo got one vote less (53 votes) and was thus eliminated. The remaining two candidates then went forward to a vote amongst Conservative Party members. The result was announced on 13 September – one day later than planned due to the terrorist attacks in the United States. Iain Duncan Smith won, receiving 61 per cent of the vote amongst constituency Conservative Party members. Kenneth Clarke gained 39 per cent.

Smith, or IDS as he became known, born 1954, a Catholic and the son of a Second World War RAF ace, was elected to the Commons in 1992, and educated at Sandhurst. He had served as an officer in the Scots Guards and carried that image with him into Parliament. He had no experience of office. He inherited a demoralized party, split over its future direction. Moreover, the horrific drama of 11 September and its aftermath had swept the Conservatives from the media headlines. The campaigns in Afghanistan and Iraq left him looking like the leader of a Blairist 'front' party as he backed the government on these and other issues. In July 2002, Smith sacked David Davis as Party Chairman but retained him in the shadow cabinet. Teresa May replaced Davis and made a speech, on 7 October, in which she said that some voters saw the Conservatives as 'the nasty party'. Despite Conservative successes in local council elections, in May 2003, Crispin Blunt, MP, called for a new leadership election. In October of that year, IDS was challenged over the employment of his wife as his paid secretary with claims that her job was just a sinecure. In polls carried out for the *Daily Telegraph* and the *Mail on Sunday*, 53 per cent thought it had been a mistake to elect IDS as leader. A mere 10 per cent said IDS was providing the party with 'strong and effective leadership'. Party members were evenly divided between the 49 per cent who wanted IDS to lead them into the next general election and the 45 per cent who thought the party should pick a new leader. After another week of feverish newspaper speculation and a bad opinion poll, Sir Michael Spicer, MP, Chairman of the back-bench 1922 Committee, announced, on 28 October, that he had received 25 signatures calling for a vote of confidence in the Conservative leader. A shocked Westminster saw IDS resign later that day, but he vowed to fight on saying he was not a 'quitter'. The Conservatives faced the fourth leader-ship election in eight years. On 29 October, IDS lost the vote of confidence by 90 votes against him to 75 for him. Michael Howard was then elected to the post of leader (as the only candidate) on 6 November 2003. Michael Howard, born 1941, the son of Romanian Jewish refugees who ran a cloth-ing shop, was brought up in Wales where he attended Llanelli grammar school. From there he went to Peterhouse College, Cambridge, taking up law on graduation. Married with two children, he was elected to Parliament in 1983. In his early days a strong supporter of British membership of the EEC, he moved to the Euro-sceptic position. From being Chairman of the 'left' Bow Group, he moved more and more to the Right. As Local Govern-ment Minister he oversaw the passage of the highly controversial 'poll tax'. After a period as Minister for Water and Planning in 1988–89, in which time he was responsible for implementing water privatization in England and Wales, Howard was promoted to the Cabinet as Secretary of State for Employment, in January 1990, abolishing the closed shop and playing a crucial role in negotiating the UK's opt-out from the Social Chapter at Maastricht. He was remembered as a robust Home Secretary, 1993–97. His image was undoubtedly damaged by the comments of his former Home Office junior, Ann Widdecombe, that there was 'something of the night about him'. A comment never explained.

Howard's election did not stop the bickering and in-fighting in the party. On 12 November, 10 right-wing Tory MPs addressed 1,000 activists at Westminster Hall. They condemned the 25 colleagues who called the no-confidence vote as 'assassins, not just of IDS, but the whole party'. An opinion poll in *The Times* put the Conservatives at 28 per cent, only on level pegging with the Liberal Democrats and five points behind Labour. As the party was strapped for cash, its campaigns had to be cut, and many full-time party workers lost their jobs. In Howard's first major test – the June 2004 elections to the European Parliament – the Conservatives performed badly, partly due to the rise of the Euro-sceptic UK Independence Party (UKIP), and saw their share of the national vote drop from 35.7 per cent in the 1999 election to 26.7 per cent, and their representation fall from 35 to 27 MEPs. Howard suffered from the Conservative support of the government's position on the Iraq War and its pro-American stance. Nevertheless, in February 2004, he called on Tony Blair to resign over the Iraq War, because he had failed to ask 'basic questions' regarding WMD claims and misled Parliament. In July, Howard stated that he would not have voted for the resolution that authorized the Iraq War had he known the quality of intelligence information on which the WMD claims were based. At the same time, he said he still believed the Iraq invasion was right. His criticism of Blair did not earn sympathies among anti-war voters in Britain, nor did it win him friends in Washington, where President Bush refused to see him.

11 SEPTEMBER 2001: 'IMMEASURABLE PAIN'

At 8.45 a.m., 11 September 2001, a hijacked passenger jet, American Airlines Flight 11 from Boston, Massachusetts, with 81 passengers and 11 crew, crashed into the north tower of the World Trade Center, tearing a gaping hole in the building and setting it on fire. A few minutes later, 9.03 a.m., a second hijacked airliner, United Airlines Flight 175 from Boston, with 56 passengers and nine crew, crashed into the south tower of the World Trade Center and exploded. Both buildings were set alight. For the first time in US history, air traffic nationwide was halted at 9.40 a.m. Worse was to come. At 9.43 a.m. American Airlines Flight 77, with 58 passengers and 6 crew, crashed into the Pentagon, sending up a huge plume of smoke. Evacuation began immediately and two minutes later the White House was evacuated. President Bush, who was out of Washington, was taken to an undisclosed place of safety. Just after 10.05 a.m., the south tower collapsed, plummeting into the streets below. At 10.10 a.m., United Airlines Flight 93, also hijacked, crashed in Somerset County, Pennsylvania, south-east of Pittsburgh. The UNO in New York and government buildings in Washington were ordered to evacuate. Around the world millions were spell-bound as TV transmissions reported the unfolding drama. According to the official *9/11 Commission Report*, over 2,000 people were killed in the twin towers, 125 in the Pentagon, and 256 in the four planes. 'The death toll surpassed that of Pearl Habor, in December 1941.' The perpetrators of this 'immeasurable pain' were, '19 young Arabs acting at the behest of Islamist extremists headquartered in distant Afghanistan'. They were armed with only small knives, box cutters and cans of mace or pepper spray. This devastating attack was not the first suffered by the US from this quarter. In February 1993, a group led by Ramzi Yousef tried to bring down the World Trade Center with a truck bomb. They killed six and wounded a thousand. In June 1996, a truck bomb demolished the Khobar Towers apartment complex in Dhahran, Saudi Arabia, killing 19 US servicemen and wounding hundreds. In February 1998, Osama Bin Laden, the Saudi-born millionaire, and four others issued a self-styled fatwa, publicly declaring that it was God's decree that every Muslim should try his utmost to kill any American, military or civilian, anywhere in the world, because of alleged US occupation of Islamic holy places and aggression against Muslims. In August 1998, Bin Laden's group, al-Qaeda, carried out almost-simultaneous truck bomb attacks on the US embassies in Nairobi, Kenya and Dar es Salaam, Tanzania. The attacks killed 224 people, including 12 Americans, and wounded thousands more. Other plots were foiled by US agencies. Various counter measures were taken by President Clinton including diplomatic efforts to get Bin Laden and his al-Qaeda group expelled from Afghanistan, where he had gone originally as part of the US-backed guerrilla struggle against the Soviet occupation. These efforts failed as did those of his successor George W. Bush. Even after 9/11, Bush felt compelled to offer the Afghan Taliban regime a way out. He gave them an ultimatum demanding that they hand over Bin Laden and close down his terrorist training camps. The UN Security Council also issued a resolution on 18 September 2001 directed towards the Taliban, demanding that they hand over the terrorist Osama Bin Laden and close all terrorist training camps immediately and uncondi- tionally. The Council also referred to a resolution it adopted in December 2000, demanding that the Taliban turn over Bin Laden to the US or a third country for trial in connection with the attacks on the US embassies in Africa in 1998.

As these efforts failed Bush went for the military option. The US, with support from the UK, Australia, Canada, Germany, New Zealand and other states, and, importantly, the Afghan Northern Alliance, invaded Afghanistan, on 7 October 2001, as part of its 'War on Terror'. The military campaign was code-named Operation Enduring Freedom and was led by US General Tommy Franks. Its purpose was to target Osama Bin Laden, and his terrorist network al-Qaeda as well as the Taliban government in Afghanistan which provided support to al-Qaeda and gave it safe haven. The war started with air strikes against Taliban positions and drops of food and medical supplies to the Afghan people. Most of the ground fighting was carried out by the Northern Alliance with small numbers of US and British special forces. With the fall of Mazar-e-Sharif, on 12 November, the Taliban regime started to crumble. Many local commanders switched sides rather than fight. The capital, Kabul, fell the following day with virtually no resis- tance. When Kandahar, the last Taliban-controlled city, was captured on 8 December, the regime had ceased to exist. Some foreign al-Qaeda fighters continued to resist in the Tora Bora Mountains. By 17 December, the last cave complex had been taken and its defenders overrun. A search of the area by US forces continued into January, but no sign of Bin Laden or the al-Qaeda leadership emerged. It was believed that they had already slipped away into the tribal areas of Pakistan to the south and east. Meanwhile, an interim Afghan government was established in Kabul under Hamid Karzai, a Westernized supporter of Zahir, the former King, who was over-thrown in 1973. Some criticism was made of civilian deaths caused by US and British bombing and of the treatment of prisoners by the Northern Alliance. Among the critics were members of Blair's own party. However, the war was one of the least bloody of the many recent conflicts. The US-led invasion brought an end of major fighting for the first time since the Soviet invasion of 1978. It also gave the people of Afghanistan more aid and more personal freedom, especially in the urban areas. Karzai was con-firmed as President in democratic elections in 2004. Parliamentary elections were held in 2005. Karzai continued to face assassination attempts and rebels continued to operate from the mountains. The growth of the poppy crop which provides the raw material for heroin continued, despite Karzai's efforts and those of British and American advisers.

SADDAM: 'NOT . . . A CLEAR AND PRESENT DANGER TO BRITAIN'

Since the Gulf War of 1991, Iraq's relations with the UN, the US and the UK remained tense. In the absence of a Security Council consensus that Iraq had fully complied with the terms of the Gulf War ceasefire, both the UN and the US enforced economic sanctions against Iraq throughout the Clinton administration, and US, RAF and, until 1996, French planes patrolled Iraqi airspace to enforce no-fly zones over northern and southern Iraq. The original intent of these zones was to protect the Iraqi Kurds, in the north, and Shiite Muslims, in southern Iraq, who together formed the majority of the Iraq population, from Saddam's air force. But these zones were never specifically mandated by the UN Security Council, and were rejected by Iraq, supported by Russia, China and Malaysia, as a violation of its sovereignty. The US Congress also passed the Iraq Liberation Act in October 1998, which provided $97 million for Iraqi 'democratic opposition organizations' in order to 'establish a program to support a transition to democracy in Iraq'. This contrasted with the terms set out in UN Resolution 687, which was concerned with weapons and weapons programmes, not with Saddam's regime. Following Kuwait's liberation, the UN Security Council required Iraq to scrap all weapons of mass destruction and long-range mis-siles and to allow UN verification inspections. Continued Iraqi non-compli-ance with UN resolutions over a period of 12 years resulted in the US-led invasion of Iraq in March 2003. On 24 September 2002, Blair told the Commons that the Intelligence Service

> concludes that Iraq has chemical and biological weapons, that Saddam has continued to produce them, that he has active military plans for the use of chemical and biological weapons, which could be activated within 45 minutes, including against his own Shia population; and that he is actively trying to acquire nuclear weapons capability. On chemical weapons, the dossier shows that Iraq continues to produce chemical agent for chemical weapons; at previously destroyed production plants across Iraq; has bought dual-use chemical facilities; has retained the key personnel formerly engaged in the chemical weapons programme; and has a serious ongoing research programme into weapons production, all of it well funded.[1]

This statement, and the dossier on which it was based, was to cause possibly more controversy than any other document in British history since 1945.

In the months of tension before the war, there were protests against an invasion of Iraq across the globe, including the US and Britain. The BBC News, on 16 February 2003, reported that hundreds of thousands of people took to the streets of London to voice their opposition to military action against Iraq. Police said it was the UK's biggest ever demonstration with at least 750,000 taking part. There were also anti-war gatherings in Glasgow and Belfast – all part of a worldwide weekend of protest with hundreds of rallies and marches in up to 60 countries. On 26 February, Blair faced the prospect of taking the nation to war with the most divided Parliament since Suez. A cross-party amendment declaring the case for military action against Saddam 'as yet unproven' was supported by 199 votes – almost a third of the total strength of the Commons. The 121 Labour rebels were joined by 13 Tories, 52 Liberal Democrats and the SNP and PC. Senior Tories, including Kenneth Clarke and John Gummer, broke ranks with their leadership to go into the division lobby alongside former Labour Cabinet ministers Chris Smith and Frank Dobson, and Charles Kennedy, Liberal Democrat leader. However, the Government's motion, emphasizing that Iraq had a final opportunity to disarm peacefully, and stressing that Britain was working through the UN, was approved by 434 votes to 124. The rebellion on the anti-war amendment was the biggest Blair had faced, easily outstripping the previous total of 67 Labour MPs who opposed disability benefit cuts in May 1999. Most Conservatives came to Blair's aid and backed the Government. Blair and Straw highlighted an admission by Hans Blix, the UN chief weapons inspector, that he was still uncertain whether Iraq really wanted to co-operate. Kenneth Clarke, the former Conservative Chancellor, said,

There is no evidence of links with al-Qaeda and I do not believe that Iraq poses a threat to New York or London. To claim that is to insult our intelligence. However, I wish to know whether demonstrable evidence exists of sufficient quantities of weapons to pose a threat. I doubt that . . . The next time a large bomb explodes in a western city, or an Arab or Muslim regime topples and is replaced by extremists, the Government must consider the extent to which the policy contributed to it.[2]

On 17 March 2003, Robin Cook, Leader of the Commons, resigned from the Cabinet. He said he could not support a war 'without international agreement or domestic support'. He did not think Saddam was 'a clear and present danger to Britain'. He also praised Blair's 'heroic efforts' in pushing for the so-called second UN resolution regarding the Iraq disarmament crisis. Cook's resignation in the Commons received an unprecedented standing ovation by fellow MPs. Despite his opposition, and others in the Labour Party, Blair's government held together and the majority of his parliamentary party supported the war, as did the great majority of Conservatives and, David Trimble's UUP. Only the Liberal Democrats, the SNP and PC officially opposed it. Clare Short, who after opposing the 1991 war, had backed the second Gulf War, resigned on 12 May, saying that Blair had broken promises to her about the involvement of the UN in the postwar reconstruction of Iraq. On 26 February she had, in effect, made the humanitarian case for the invasion. 'The people of Iraq are already suffering a humanitarian catastrophe. Some 60 per cent of the people in this naturally wealthy and highly educated country are dependent on handouts from the oil for food programme. One third of children in Baghdad-controlled Iraq are chronically malnourished.' She then asserted that planning was on hand to keep order, distribute food and rehabilitate the public utilities. Nevertheless, 'My greatest worry is that there is not yet agreement that the UN should have the lead role in a post-conflict Iraq. Without that, there would be significant legal and other difficulties.' What Short did not know was that Blair had decided, in April 2002, on military action leading to 'regime change' when he met President Bush in Crawford, Texas. At a Downing Street meeting on 23 July 2002, the details of which were made public by the *Sunday Times* (1 May 2005), attended by Straw, the Foreign Secretary, Geoff Hoon, the Defence Secretary, Lord Goldsmith, the Attorney-General, military and intelligence chiefs, Alastair Campbell, then Blair's Director of Strategy, Jonathan Powell, his Chief of Staff, and Sally Morgan, Director of Government Relations, military action was seen as inevitable. The primary impetus to action over Iraq was not the threat posed by weapons of mass destruction (WMD) – as Blair later told Parliament again and again – but the desire to overthrow Saddam. There was little talk of WMD at the meeting. When he addressed the Commons on

18 March 2003, Blair again made much of WMD but he also alluded to the plight of the Iraqi people under Saddam. In the debate that followed, the government faced much criticism from all parts of the Commons. Lembit Öpik (Liberal Democrat) asked Straw, 'How will he and the Government respond if over time it can be shown that an attack on Iraq has prompted or caused sustained international terrorism in the United Kingdom and abroad rather than preventing it?' John Denham, who had resigned from the government that morning, said,

> The action against Iraq is, I believe, pre-emptive, and therefore demands even greater international support and consensus than other sorts of intervention. We do not have it. Such isolation entails a genuine cost and danger. It undermines the legitimacy that we must maintain to tackle the many threats to global security. It fuels the movements that are antipathetic to our values and way of life.[3]

Alex Salmond (SNP) argued, 'one thing is certain: when the Secretary-General of the United Nations doubts the authorization of military action without a second resolution, people can say many things about that action, but they cannot say that it is being taken in the name of the United Nations'.[4] Neither Blair nor Straw could convince the anti-war MPs and 139 Labour MPs, 18 more than in February, backed a rebel amendment. In the end, the amendment opposing military action was lost by 'Ayes 217, Noes 396'. The Government's motion backing military action by reference to upholding the authority of the UN 'as set out in Resolution 1441 and many Resolutions preceding it' was passed by 'Ayes 412, Noes 149'. It has been said that there was unusually heavy drinking and the shedding of tears as MPs wrestled with their consciences before the votes were taken. Britain was going to war without the backing of the UN, the EU or NATO.

On 19 March 2003, approximately 260,000 US troops, with support from 45,000 British, and smaller forces from other nations, collectively called the 'Coalition of the Willing', crossed into Iraq primarily through Kuwait. Plans for opening a second front in the north were abandoned when Turkey refused the use of its territory for such purposes. Iraqi Kurdish militia troops, with US special advisers, moved forward against Iraqi troops in the north. Although Iraqi forces were numerically superior to those of the coalition, they were less well organized and poorly equipped. The invasion was swift, with the collapse of the Iraq government and the military in about three weeks. The British Royal Marines 3 Commando Brigade launched an air and amphibious assault on the Al-Faw peninsula on 20 March to secure the oil fields; the amphibious assault was supported by frigates of the Royal Navy and Royal Australian Navy. The 15th Marine Expeditionary Unit, attached to 3 Commando Brigade, attacked the port of Umm Qasr. The British 16 Air Assault Brigade also secured the oilfields in southern Iraq. In keeping with the rapid advance plan, the US 3rd Infantry Division moved westward and then northward through the desert towards Baghdad, while the 1st Marine Expeditionary Force and 1 British Armoured Division moved northward through marshland. The British 7 Armoured Brigade ('The Desert Rats') fought their way into Iraq's second-largest city, Basra, on 6 April, coming under constant attack by regulars and Fedayeen, while the 3rd Parachute Regiment cleared the 'old quarter' of the city that was inaccessible to vehicles. The entry into Basra had been achieved after only two weeks of conflict, which included the biggest tank battle by British forces since the Second World War, when the Royal Scots Dragoon Guards destroyed 14 Iraqi tanks on 27 March. Three weeks into the invasion, US forces moved into Baghdad where they met fierce resistance. But, once they had captured Saddam's palaces and television coverage of this spread through Iraq, resistance crumbled around the city. On 9 April 2003, Baghdad was formally secured and the power of Saddam Hussein was declared ended. The dictator had vanished. He was, however, captured on 12 December by the US Army's 4th Infantry Division and members of Task Force 121. The military victory of the US-led coalition resulted in the shutdown of much of the central economic administrative structure. Although a comparatively small amount of capital plant was damaged during the hostilities, looting, insurgent attacks and sabotage undermined efforts to rebuild the economy. Meanwhile the anti-war demonstrations continued. Among the most impressive were those of 50,000 people in Leipzig following traditional prayers for peace in the city's Nikolai Church on 24 March 2003; the demonstration of 50,000 people in Boston, Massachusetts, on 29 March, which constituted the biggest rally in that city since the end of the Vietnam War; and those in Rome and other Italian cities on 4 June 2004, when Bush visited Pope John Paul II, a strong opponent of the war. In 2004, the 9/11 Commission concluded that there was no credible evidence that Saddam had assisted al-Qaeda in preparing for or carrying out the 9/11 attacks. Aside from the contentious allegations of Iraq's relationship with al-Qaeda, the former government did have relationships with other militant organizations in the Middle East including Hamas and the Palestinian Islamic Jihad. It is known that some $10–15 million was paid to the families of suicide bombers, presented as compensation for the demolition of their homes in Israeli collective punishment operations.

Dr David Kelly was found dead on 17 July 2003, days after appearing before a Parliamentary committee. He was an employee of the British Ministry of Defence, an expert in biological warfare, and a former United Nations weapons inspector in Iraq. His conversation with a journalist about the British Government's dossier on WMD in Iraq caused a major political scandal, and he was being investigated. The Hutton Inquiry, a public inquiry into his death, which reported in January 2004, found that he had committed suicide. It did not satisfy those who thought that dark actors had been at work in bringing about his death and the war. Several medical professionals voiced their doubts about the evidence.[5] The UN Secretary-General, Kofi Annan, told the BBC, on 16 January 2004, that the US-led invasion of Iraq was an illegal act that contravened the UN Charter. The Hutton Inquiry was regarded as a whitewash by many inside and outside Parliament and continued pressure ensured it was followed by the Butler Inquiry presided over by Lord Butler, a distinguished former Cabinet Secretary who had served five prime ministers. Its remit was to examine the intelligence side of the decision to go to war rather than the political decision-making process. The Conservatives and Liberal Democrats refused to take part as they regarded its terms of reference as being too limited. It met in secret and reported on 14 July 2004. Its main conclusion was that key intelligence used to justify the war with Iraq had been shown to be unreliable. Blair's refusal to publish the advice of Lord Goldsmith, the Attorney-General, to the Government on the legality of the war also fuelled controversy. A leak of a document written by Goldsmith suggested that he had grave reservations about whether the invasion would be lawful.[6] These events, as well as the war itself, helped to set the scene for the election of 2005.

By 2005 there was no sign that Coalition forces would withdraw from Iraq in the short term. They were helping to restore infrastructure and facilitating the establishment of an elected government, while simultaneously dealing with a growing insurgency. The Coalition Provisional Authority, set up by the Coalition, transferred sovereignty to the Iraqi Interim Government in June 2004. Iraqis voted on 30 January 2005 to elect a 275-member Transitional National Assembly that was given the task of drafting a permanent constitution and pave the way for new national elections at the end of 2005. The violence continued daily. By 26 October 2005, 2,000 US troops had been killed. Soldiers from other nations had also fallen, including 97 British. No WMDs had been found.

BLAIR'S 'LAPDOG COURTIERS IN DOWNING STREET'

One of the most controversial aspects of Blair's premiership was the way he conducted his government, sidelining his Cabinet colleagues and relying too heavily on unelected advisers he had installed in 10 Downing Street. Officially, the Cabinet meets on a regular basis, usually weekly on a Thursday morning, to discuss the most important issues of government policy, and to make decisions. The length of meetings varies according to the style of the Prime Minister and political conditions but, under Blair, meetings tended to get shorter. Traditionally, the Prime Minister was supposed to be the 'first among equals', but this was probably largely a myth. Certainly under Blair it was not, by all accounts, the case. Blair also sidelined top civil servants. In 1997, he obtained orders in council from the Queen to give

Jonathan Powell, Chief of Staff, and Alastair Campbell, Chief Press Secretary, power to direct civil servants, a move that caused alarm among Whitehall officials. They saw it as a politicization of the civil service. Lord Butler, as Cabinet Secretary, was forced to accept these changes in how No. 10 was organized to give Blair's political allies power over civil servants.

Paul Routledge of the *Daily Mirror*, who, by then, 31 October 2003, had observed Labour politicians close up for many years wrote that Blair

> proclaimed his commitment to party democracy, diminishing the power of the unions and 'handing Labour back to its members'. In truth, it has all been a sham . . . he castrated the annual conference, neutered the national executive and concentrated power in a tiny group of lapdog courtiers in Downing Street . . . The situation has been made worse in recent years by the rise of professional politicians, by which I mean men and women who have never done anything but politics. They work for an MP, or a party, or a pressure group and then go into Parliament without ever having done a proper job. These people, of whom Tony Blair is a prize specimen (he was never much of a lawyer) regard democracy as an unnecessary evil, to be controlled from the centre in case the people get ideas above their station.

Routledge thought, 'There is not a great deal that can be done to roll back this insidious trend.'

Robin Cook claimed that the Cabinet reshuffle was settled on polling day, 8 June 2001, in Blair's Sedgefield constituency 'between Tony and his travelling entourage' including Alastair Campbell. 'It was a very tight little cabal in which to decide on the major offices of state.'[7] In the experience of Clare Short, Cabinet meetings were short, colleagues got little on paper before hand and there was no proper discussion. She cites the decision to continue with the Millennium Dome, most of the Cabinet rejected it, but Blair went ahead anyway.[8] Cook backed this up, 'Tony does not regard the Cabinet as a place for decisions. Normally he avoids having discussions in Cabinet until decisions are taken and announced to it.' In the case of military action over Iraq, 'all contributions pointed in one direction'.[9] This was on 7 March 2002 and it was the last Cabinet meeting at which a large number of ministers spoke up against the war. 'I have little sympathy with the criticism of Tony that he sidelined the Cabinet over Iraq.'[10] Over the months that followed it was discussed more than any other topic. As the Hutton and Butler inquiries revealed, Blair preferred intimate, informal chats to the discipline of minuted Cabinet meetings. His Chief of Staff, Jonathan Powell, told Lord Hutton that, out of a possible 17 meetings on an average day in the run-up to the Iraq war, at only three would proper minutes have been taken.[11] Mo Molam claimed that Blair displayed a 'cavalier' attitude to colleagues.

Another charge levelled at Blair was the way he held on to colleagues he liked but who had let down the government. Mandelson and Blunkett are the two obvious examples. The former Trade Secretary Peter Mandelson returned to the Cabinet as the new Northern Ireland Secretary in October 1999. He had resigned from the Cabinet, in December 1998, after it was revealed he took a secret £373,000 home loan from his ministerial colleague, Geoffrey Robinson, whose finances were under investigation by Mandelson's department. Robinson also resigned over the affair. Many were surprised by not only the Prime Minister selecting Mandelson to succeed Mo Mowlam in this sensitive position but also at the speed of his return to the top level of Government. Blunkett was appointed Home Secretary in 2001. In December 2004, he was forced to resign amidst mounting publicity concerning his affair with a married woman, Kimberly Quinn, his attempts to wrest control of Quinn's son and unborn child from her and her husband, abuse of MPs' travel warrants and his abuse of office by speeding up the visa application of Quinn's Filipina nanny. After the 2005 election, Blair called Blunkett back to take over Work and Pensions but, by October, he was in trouble again over a series of bizarre events involving a young woman, an Asian businessman and alleged breaking of the code of conduct for ex-ministers. In her book *A Slight and Delicate Creature*, Dr Margaret Cook portrayed Robin Cook, Foreign Secretary, as cold and unfeeling, saying he abandoned her at London's Heathrow airport on the eve of a holiday when told his affair with his secretary had been discovered by the press. She claimed Cook had a string of affairs during their 28-year marriage, drank heavily and felt he had 'sold his soul to the devil' by abandoning his left-wing principles to support Blair. In this case, Blair probably thought it prudent to keep Cook on board.

BLAIR AND HIS MPS

Blair has been the most successful and the most detested Labour leader since the party was founded in 1906. How do we explain the different positions of Labour MPs, the rebellion of some, the loyalty and conformity of others since 1997? Some were traditional rebels like Dennis Skinner, Tam Dalyell and more recent ones like Jeremy Corbyn, Robert Marshall-Andrews and Alan Simpson, Chairman of the Campaign Group, who did not seek office or other advancement. Some of the rebels were sour and resentful at having been passed over. At the other extreme were those who coveted office to 'make a difference' or just see how far they could go. Some who never expected to get in were naturally grateful to Blair for giving them a new life. A number of older MPs elected in 1997 were among this group. For some, belief in their party meant they did not want to endanger the

Labour government after the long night in opposition. There were those who privately disagreed with several or more policies but who allowed themselves one open rebellion to maintain their dignity. Others feared the wrath of their voters and local party members. Both sides had those who feared being accused of 'betrayal'. Virtually all agreed that even a Blairite government was better than the alternative. The whips could work on these sentiments to get colleagues in line. The parliamentary Labour Party some times appeared more docile than its predecessors, but it was not. Perhaps this was in part because it did not have personalities like Nye Bevan, Barbara Castle, Michael Foot and others. There were 96 back-bench Labour revolts in the 1997–2001 parliament with rebellions on lone-parent benefit, disability benefit, the terrorism laws, Lords reform, trial by jury, freedom of information, and national air traffic services. They involved MPs outside the small circle of 'old Labour' rebels and leftist ideologues. In the second term of 2001–05, back-bench rebellions increased, climaxing with the revolt over Iraq. Apart from the issues themselves this can be explained by the greater experience and self-confidence of MPs elected in 1997, and the growing band of ex-ministers who wanted to whack Blair and perhaps regain their street credibility with their buddies on the back benches.

Michael White, the *Guardian*'s political editor (19 December 2002), was uneasy about the changes to parliamentary hours, with a shorter working day from January 2003.

> For the last few years, the Commons has risen at 7pm on Thursdays and there have been far fewer Friday sittings. When I was a lad it was quite common for the house to sit until 11 or 12 at night, and even stay up all night occasionally . . . The point about old parliamentary procedures was that they allowed backbench MPs to speak – not necessarily the opposition, but members of the awkward squad on their own side: people like Dennis Skinner and Tam Dalyell, Alan Clark and others on the Conservative benches, people who knew parliamentary procedure. It enabled them to call ministers to account in awkward ways . . . I think that many of us are rather afraid that we have created a legislature which is much more amenable to the will of the executive.

In 2005, Simpson promised more in the Parliament elected in May 2005. 'No more privatization in the public services', he demanded. Above all, 'a different style of government' was the first target with much more serious attention to democratic accountability.[12] Outside Parliament, Labour Party membership fell from 1997 onwards. Membership rose from the 265,000 inherited by Blair when he became Labour leader in 1994, to 405,000 when the party won the 1997 election. By May 2005, it had hit a 70-year low of around 200,000.[13] No wonder Blair was relying more on the likes of global steel magnate Lakshmi Mittal, and Lord Sainsbury, the supermarket tycoon turned science minister. Party membership brought few rewards. In exchange for a fee, and helping at elections, and attending often boring monthly meetings in dingy premises, and so forth, you got social contacts, in a few cases met your future wife/husband/partner, the right to vote for members of the National Executive Committee, proximity to power if your candidate became a MP or minister, and perhaps a chance to meet the powerful at the annual party conference at a seaside resort. The annual conferences had become more like those of the German SPD and the US parties. Old-style revolts and denunciations of the leaders were out. Instead, there was a number of well-organized, well-presented sessions on a limited number of issues designed to produce a positive image in the media. Some joined the party to seek office in local government including, nowadays, several thousand pounds extra income or even full-time employment. More than a few Labour MPs had started with a career in local government, which had become more attractive due to remuneration and possibly election to more than one layer of local government.

MPS AND THEIR CONSTITUENTS: LEGISLATORS OR SOCIAL WORKERS?

To a degree, an MP's own profile is bound to influence the sort of mail they receive from their constituents, as is the make-up of the constituency – rural, inner city, suburban, university, military, and so on. In 2005, one high-profile back-bench woman MP got about 170 letters per month, 350 phone calls and 280 emails. In this constituency, two surgeries a month were held at which between 25 and 40 people sought help on immigration law, housing followed by education, environment and crime. Kelvin Hopkins, Luton North, asserts that when he was elected, his stepmother said, 'I thought you were going to be a legislator not a social worker.' He estimated he sent 5,000 letters a year concerning constituency matters, '40 per cent of my casework is immigration and other significant issues include Child Support Agency, tax credits, housing shortages, police matters, neighbour nuisance, school admissions, special needs education cases, social services and children's issues, benefit issues, health/hospital matters, transport and traffic issues and other lesser matters.' It was so different in Wales where Hywell Williams and Alun Ffred Jones received about 1,500 letters each a year or 125 a month from constituents. The three top issues were housing, benefits and pensions. Another high-profile woman MP reported 800 letters or emails a month, mainly about benefits, the Child Support Agency (CSA), planning matters, lobbying issues and during this period of 2005, animal rights and hunting. If urgent, 'I deal *at once* by phone or visit'. Gwyneth Dunwoody's postbag included letters on the Crewe War Memorial, the quality of school meals and the availability of NHS dentistry.

She held surgeries twice a month in three places. Dr Richard Taylor, an Independent, estimated that he received 300 letters from constituents each month. The top concerns were CSA, housing problems, tax credits and health and hospital complaints. In 2004, a south coast MP found at his weekly surgeries more people who 'have serious economic, personal and other problems'.

The Liberal Democrat MP for Bath, Don Foster, wrote (2005),

As Shadow Secretary of State for DCMS I get innumerable letters, phone calls, e-mails and faxes. However, communications directly from or concerning constituents, per month, average around 320 letters; 320 e-mails; 70 visitors (excluding those who attend surgeries); and 110 phone calls. These figures are very approximate and don't truly reflect some of the increasing number of 'round robin' e-mails. [He continued,] My figures certainly do NOT include the 4 or 5 e-mails per day in which apparently wealthy foreigners seek my help in investing £millions (often from their late husbands who were Ministers in some African government)! Casework issues are always dominated by HOUSING which far exceeds any other. High on the list for second place (excluding 'round robins' about some national campaign) would be: Child Support Agency; Tax Credits (particularly high of late); Benefits/pensions; Immigration; Neighbour disputes; Planning; School placements (at the appropriate time). Following those comes almost anything from parking to potholes and from 'interference with my post by the Secret Service' to 'It's too hot for me to sleep, what are you going to do about it?' [These last two were raised within the last 7 days.] The same wide gamut of issues is raised in my surgeries which are held at least once, and often twice, a week. Most of my surgeries are held in my constituency office in the centre of Bath and are by appointment (with 20 minutes allocated to each person). Surgeries elsewhere throughout the constituency are on a first arrive, first seen basis. In the past 13 years I have seen a steady increase in the volume of casework. Most recently, the widespread use of e-mail has led to a further increase.

In truth, it must have been difficult for MPs to keep focused on their constituents given their lives in London. Opening fetes, garden parties, nurseries, drug rehabilitation centres, attending whist drives, youth clubs, working-men's clubs, appearing at churches, chapels and, more recently, mosques, showing enthusiasm for local sports teams, speaking at local trade union, business and branch meetings, always remaining polite even when facing angry critics. Most activities were not about creating the New Jerusalem. For a considerable number of MPs it was also a life of uncertainty. If they failed to get re-elected, many would find it difficult to return to their old jobs.

Members have been required since 1974 to register their sources of paid outside employment, but until 1995 there was no requirement to disclose the amounts of remuneration. There was still no general requirement to register the amounts in 2005. However, the Commons resolved on 6 November 1995 that any Member who had an existing agreement or who proposed to enter into a new agreement involving the provision of services in his or her capacity as a Member of Parliament must deposit it with the Registrar. The agreements, which were and are available for public inspection, must include the fees or benefits of more than £550 (1 per cent of a Member's salary) payable, in bands of up to £5,000, £5,001–£10,000 and thereafter in bands of £5,000. A Member was not required to deposit an agreement where he or she was paid for media work related to his or her parliamentary duties, but was required to register the amount earned, in the same way.

Most MPs elected in 2001 registered no outside financial interests which often meant they were dependent on their parliamentary salaries. Among the 'A's in the alphabetical list of MPs register of interests, 2004–05, were the likes of Graham Allen (Nottingham) who had nothing to declare, and this was true of many his colleagues. Among the other 'A's, however, was Diane Abbott who declared remuneration of 'up to £60,000' for newspaper articles and 'up to £60,000' for her television appearances between January 2004 and March 2005. She also declared, 'Arcadia Lectures in 2004 for School of Oriental and African Studies, London. (Up to £5,000)' and '25 January 2005, fee for Student Lectures. (Up to £5,000) (Registered 8 April 2005)'. Michael Ancram declared, 'Farms on Scottish Borders, from which rental income is received. Houses and miscellaneous property on Scottish Borders, from which rental income is received. Industrial rents (mining) in Lothian, Scotland'. Peter Atkinson declared, 'Parliamentary and public affairs consultant, Countryside Alliance. (£10,001–£15,000)' and 'Sponsorship or financial or material support for research work provided by Countryside Alliance'. As the *Independent* (3 September 2005) reported, the outside business activities of MPs came up during the Conservative leadership campaign. Norman Baker, the Liberal Democrat MP, said: 'The leadership contenders' connections with companies working in questionable fields will remind people of the years of Tory sleaze.' He was referring to David Cameron, Kenneth Clarke and Sir Malcolm Rifkind. 'The three contenders for the leadership are paid for the private directorships on top of their £59,000-a-year MPs' salaries. The directorships are declared in the register of MPs' interests and they are not breaking rules by taking the money. But charities say that working for firms linked to late-night drinking, the cigarette trade and weapons-training raised issues about their judgement.' Of the two other contenders, David Davis, seen as the front-runner for the leadership, had no links with any private firms. His right-wing rival, Dr Liam Fox, declared his shareholding in Arrest Ltd, a medical education agency. David Cameron registered remunerated directorships with Urbium PLC (non-executive), a bar and night clubs business. Former Chancellor Kenneth Clarke registered his remunerated directorships as Deputy Chairman (non-executive) of Alliance Unichem PLC; Director (non-executive) of Foreign and Colonial Investment Trust PLC; Deputy Chairman (non-executive) of British American Tobacco PLC; Chairman (non-executive) of Savoy Asset Management PLC; Director (non-executive) of Independent News and Media (UK). He was also paid for 'Programmes on jazz for BBC Radio 4. (Registered 31 March 2004)'. In addition, five speaking engagements netted many thousands more. Some MPs must have found it difficult to juggle their time schedules because of their wide interests. Most MPs appeared to be dependent on their salaries, a relatively few were able and willing to earn several times their parliamentary salaries by outside work.

IMMIGRANTS: 'SLAVE LABOUR PRACTICES'

Throughout the Blair stewardship there was controversy, at times fierce, over the issues of asylum and immigration. Under its international obligations, 1951 Geneva Convention on Refugees for example, Britain had a duty to give refuge to genuine asylum seekers, and the many dictatorships and armed conflicts produced great numbers seeking a safe haven in the UK. Most of those who arrived, however, were not genuine. They were, nevertheless, able to remain. The same was true of would-be immigrants, both legal and illegal. The majority of British people felt there were too many of them, that they were a burden and transformed parts of towns and cities into foreign ghettos. In fact, in 2004, a poll showed that the majority of the British believed that immigration had damaged their country. The British were more 'xenophobic' than the French, Germans, Spanish and Italians.[14] The trouble was that there seemed to be no coherent policy on who should be let in, and who should be kept out. By 2005, the government secretly calculated there were about 500,000 illegal immigrants in Britain despite repeated claims by ministers that they did not know the scale of the problem. The number did not include spouses, dependants and those not in work. Experts said if these were taken into account, the final figure could have been nearer one million.

Those who favoured immigrants and asylum seekers, for whatever reasons, could cite a wide variety of individuals whose work brought great benefits to Britain. Among foreign-born Nobel prize winners are: Max Born, Ernst Chain, Dennis Gabor, Bernard Katz, Hans Adolf Krebs, Sir Harry Kroto, Peter Brian Medawar, Max Perutz and Joseph Rotblat. Most of them were of Jewish background as were Professor Eric Lunzer, who specialized in child development, Lord Claus Moser, the distinguished statistician, and Professor Samson Abramsky, the computer scientist. Britain's most successful car – the Mini – was designed by a Turkish-born Greek,

(Sir) Alec Issigonis (1906–88). Born in Egypt, the renowned heart surgeon Sir Magdi Yacoub came to Britain, in 1962, and started his pioneering heart surgery in 1967 before beginning work at Harefield Hospital, in 1969. Yacoub returned regularly to his native Egypt to treat sick children free of charge.[15] Many would also include Dr John Sentamu, a former High Court judge who fled Idi Amin's dictatorshop in Uganda and trained for the priesthood, to become the Church of England's first black archbishop in 2005, broadcaster Sir Trevor MacDonald and trade union leader Bill Morris, both of whom came from the West Indies. These are just a few of the better known. Among the 'unknowns' were thousands of overseas nurses, mainly women, doctors, one third of the total, and cleaners who helped to keep the health service going.

Sadly, there were very many cases of individuals whose actions swelled the ranks of those wanting to curtail immigration completely. Kanubhai Patel came to Britain in the 1970s from India. He built up a multi-million-pound London property empire with the proceeds of a complex housing benefit fraud for which he was jailed in 2003.[16] This is not an isolated case. Immigrants were involved in other big fraud cases. A £30 million cheque fraud ring involving Royal Mail workers was smashed on 26 April 2005. Thirty-five addresses were raided under Operation Bangor and 36 arrests made throughout England. The activities of the predominantly Congolese and Angolan gang centred on a postal sorting office in North London, where an insider postman was employed.[17] In another case, Jaswinder Gill, the mastermind of a £1 million sham marriage empire who preyed on vulnerable young Asian women, was jailed in April 2005.[18] Anne O'Brien, a market stall-holder, left Kenya in 1997 and worked briefly as a nurse in Ireland before marrying and moving to London to work as a prostitute and set up her own bordello. Such was the success of her sex empire that she was able to pay more than £1 million in cash for the Mayfair property.[19] Up to 15 girls of different nationalities worked for O'Brien in one of three shifts each day.[20] In 2005, the Metropolitan Police revealed that it had been unable to trace 300 black boys aged four to seven missing from school over a three-month period. Child welfare experts said the number highlighted the scale of the trade in children brought to Britain as domestic servants and covers for benefit fraud.[21] Following this, a Metropolitan Police report into the sacrifice and abuse of children at African churches described how pastors were profiting from the trafficking of black boys into Britain. Uncircumcized boys were being smuggled into the country for human sacrifice by fundamentalist sects whose members believed that their ritual killing would enhance spells.[22] Gun crime among immigrant groups remained high, and Scotland Yard's Operation Trident, the unit that targeted gun crime in the black community, reported that gang members had access to automatic and semi-automatic weapons.[23] And what about the Albanian gangsters? Vice squad officers estimated, in 2004, that, with extreme violence and bribery, Albanians controlled more than 75 per cent of the country's brothels using women from Eastern Europe.[24] Another problem was kidnaps in Britain with rising numbers of abductions mainly by foreign gangs. About half of all victims were foreign.[25] Both legal and illegal immigrants often faced severe exploitation in Britain. The charity Oxfam found, in 2004, that Parveen, in Bolton, was paid £1 an hour, working at home. She belonged to a silent army of more than one million workers exploited for working at home. Some were paid as little as 29p an hour. Their work was seen in leading supermarkets and high street retailers. The study found more than 90 per cent of industrial homeworkers were female and one in two were from other countries, most from Pakistan, Bangladesh and India.[26] The fate of 20 Chinese migrant workers in Morecombe Bay, killed by a rising tide while they were cockle picking on 5 February 2004, exposed the exploitation of illegal migrants in Britain. The local MP, Geraldine Smith, told the Commons, 'The tragedy . . . and the slave labour practices of rogue gangmasters who operate with impunity in 21st century Britain has shamed the nation in the eyes of the world.'[27] Henry Bellington, MP for North West Norfolk, where there had been a large influx of Chinese illegal workers in agriculture, felt that the immigration service was 'woefully understaffed' to deal with the problem. It was up against a powerful opponent, the Snakeheads. These were a group of Chinese criminals, which is one of the most notorious people-smuggling gangs in the world. In an attempt to reassure public opinion, Fiona Mactaggart, Home Office minister and a former director of the Joint Council for the Welfare of Immigrants, reminded the Commons (14 October 2004) that, 'A new offence, trafficking for exploitation, which includes trafficking for forced labour and the removal of organs, is included in the Asylum and Immigration Act 2004 and will also carry a 14-year maximum penalty.' But the trafficking went on. Eight Turkish asylum-seekers who had been granted leave to remain in the UK were arrested in October 2005, for people smuggling. Their ring was estimated to have made tens of millions of pounds from the racket, some of which had been invested in businesses such as property, cafés and snooker halls.[28] Although the NHS was dependent on immigrants at all levels, immigrants also produced extra costs. By the end of 2004, the spread of HIV from immigrants to the resident community had led to a five-fold increase in the number of people catching HIV through heterosexual sex in Britain since Labour was elected in 1997. About half of those infected by HIV-positive immigrants were white Britons, while a quarter were Africans, and a quarter other ethnic minorities. The figures prompted fears among government doctors that HIV cases which were being imported, mainly from southern Africa, could lead to a new type of HIV epidemic in Britain.[29] Across Britain, the number of cases identified each year had risen steadily from 5,000 in 1987.[30] In an effort to curb asylum misuse and illegal immigration, Britain announced an Australian-type points system for those coming to the country for work or study and made it clear that only skilled workers would be allowed to settle long term and employers would be fined for each illegal worker employed. Announcing the new immigration policy in the House of Commons, Home Secretary Charles Clarke said that fast-track processing of all asylum seekers would be adopted, with electronic tagging where necessary.[31] The Home Office seemed to discover, in 2005, that would-be immigrants were posing as students. According to *The Times* (3 September 2005), from China alone there were 60,000 in 2005. The government announced that, unlike the other EU states, Britain would lift restrictions on workers from the new member states immediately they joined. Before the election, the government claimed it expected a few thousand workers from these countries. Between May 2004 and June 2005, more that 232,000 had applied to work in Britain. Most took up unskilled work, most were young and most had not applied for welfare benefits. They represented a pool of cheap labour.[32] Was this what Brown and Blair wanted for the whole of the EU?

IDENTITY: 'OUR PROUD RECORD ON SLAVERY'?

On Thursday, 23 February 2004, the first citizenship ceremony was held in multicultural Brent in north London, when 19 new UK citizens swore the oath of allegiance. This American-style ceremony was to become compulsory in future for all those wishing to become British citizens as part of an initiative to compel every would-be citizen to demonstrate their commitment to their new nationality. The new citizens came from Afghanistan, India, Sri Lanka, New Zealand, Poland, Kenya, Somalia, Nepal and Zimbabwe. All 434 councils in Britain were required to follow Brent with similar ceremonies. The Home Secretary, David Blunkett, who engineered these ceremonies, emphasized that local councils should not water down the British element of the event. Citizens should, in future, 'be able to communicate in the English language (or Welsh or Scottish Gaelic). There are exemptions to this requirement, for example if you are elderly or mentally handicapped.' Would-be Britons would also be required to demonstrate some knowledge of Britain and its culture. Brent was probably chosen because it accepted more immigrants than any other local authority, about 3,000 a year. Each citizen was charged £218 by the Home Office for their ceremony and papers, of which £68 went to the local council. Professor Sir Bernard Crick, who chaired an advisory group on a new citizenship test, criticized the delay in its introduction until at least the end of the year. 'I'm disappointed. The ceremonies are a good thing and to be welcomed but, in terms of helping people make their home here, they are no substitute for the English language classes', he said. David Davis, Shadow Home Secretary, also questioned why the ceremonies were being introduced before the tests. 'Without the tests, this just seems like another headline-grabbing initiative that doesn't amount to much.'[33]

These ceremonies were introduced against a background of fear, alarm and despondency among the 'host' population and quite a few of the newer Britons. Writing in *The Times* (26 July 2005), Libby Purves eloquently summed up what many, especially older people, felt.

> Our public institutions are too shy of our religious heritage to defend Christmas and Easter, the Cross and the Bible, even as cultural symbols . . . Anything that connects us to the past is sneered at as sentimental, naff or cruel, whereas the traditions of incoming communities must be respected (how many of the MPs who ended fox-hunting will condemn halal slaughter? How long has it taken us to condemn forced marriage?). Every hero is hauled down, every poet dismissed as a dead white male. Even sitcoms that glean amusement from humdrum majority life are belittled.

For his part Blunkett urged the English to stop being 'apologetic about our history' and to celebrate 23 April, St George's day. His idea was part of a plan to 'reclaim the patriotic mantle from the right and forge a new English identity for the modern age'. He denied this would stir up racism or bigotry.[34] Not a few English people started to feel a little left out, neglected, by the new multiculturalism including the relative resurgence of Irish, Scottish and Welsh consciousness. This was in part due to the setting up of the parliaments in Scotland and Wales. There was even talk of England being under the 'Scottish Raj' as so many ministers were Scots (and not a few of the others were not natives). Patricia Hewitt, herself an Australian immigrant, backed up Blunkett. Acquiring British citizenship should be more than a bureaucratic process.

> Australia has long expected 'new Australians' to learn English and something of the laws and values of their new country; in return, their new status is publicly celebrated in citizenship ceremonies. Requiring applicants for British citizenship to learn English should hardly be contentious; that it is so is a sign of how muddled we have become about multiculturalism. Particularly after 11 September, we need firmer foundations. Those foundations – essentially, the liberal values of the Enlightenment – include freedom of religious belief and worship. But that does not mean tolerating – and failing to prosecute as criminal offences – the hatred preached by some religious leaders, any more than we should tolerate the racism of right-wing extremists. Nor can it mean compromising on respect for the equal dignity and freedom of women and men.[35]

As the past kept rearing its ugly head, the desire to apologize seemed to gain ground in the 1990s. On 9 August 1993, Pope John Paul II apologized for Catholic involvement with the African slave trade. In May 1995, he asked forgiveness in the Czech Republic for the Church's role in stake burnings and the religious wars that followed the Protestant Reformation. In an open letter, dated 10 July 1995, addressed to 'every woman', John Paul II apologized for the Church's stance against women's rights and for the historical denigration of women. British Prime Minister Tony Blair expressed regret, in June 1997, for English indifference to the plight of the Irish people during the Potato Famine of the 1840s. In January 1998, Japanese Prime Minister, Ryutara Hashiomoto, offered his 'heartfelt apology' to the British government and expressed his 'deep remorse' for Japan's treatment of British POWs in the Second World War. In the same month, Tony Blair apologized for the 1972 'Bloody Sunday' massacre of 19 civilians in Northern Ireland. On 20 February 1998, the Anglican Church of Australia apologized for its participation in the policy of forcibly removing aboriginal children from their mothers. The Vatican apologized, on 16 March 1998, for its silence and inaction during the Holocaust. President Clinton apologized, on 26 March 1998, for inaction during the 1994 Rwanda genocide. In the same month, in Uganda, Clinton said that 'European Americans received the fruits of the slave trade. And we were wrong in that.' Japanese Emperor Akihito apologized to Britain for the Second World War, in May 1998. British Armed Forces Minister, John Reid, apologized, in July 1998, in the House of Commons for the deaths of 306 soldiers executed for cowardice in the First World War. The IRA, in August 1998, apologized for violence and killings in the course of its struggle for liberty and pledged to end its 23-year terror campaign. Pope John Paul II asked, on 12 March 2000, for forgiveness for the sins of Catholics throughout the ages. During a public Mass of Pardon, the Pope said that 'Christians . . . have violated the rights of ethnic groups and peoples, and shown contempt for their cultures and religious traditions.' He issued an apology for sex abuse by priests on 22 November 2001. On 24 April 2002, John Paul II repeated his apology to victims of sexual abuse by priests. The Irish Republican Army apologized, on 17 July 2002, for civilian deaths over its 30-year struggle to unite Northern Ireland with the Republic of Ireland. Dublin Archbishop Cardinal Desmond Connell followed the Pope, apologizing, on 8 October 2002, to people who were sexually abused as children by Church officials.

Britain came heavily under attack for its colonial past and there was no point in denying that not everything Britain had done abroad was simply out of Christian charity. There were calls for Britain to apologize for its part in the slave trade and even for reparations to be paid. As reported by BBC *News World*, on 18 January 2005, Gordon Brown said, while in Africa, that Britain should stop apologizing for colonialism and be proud of its history. While missionaries went to Africa out of a sense of duty, African soldiers died to defend British values of liberty, tolerance and civic virtue. Brown signed a debt relief deal with Tanzania which could cost the UK £1 billion.[36] The *Evening Standard* (6 December 2004) put it boldly,

> Campaigners are demanding that the Queen apologise for Britain's role in the slave trade. She should take no notice. The British state was never involved, nor the vast majority of the British people, nor did slavery itself take root in Britain. It was indeed us who abolished the trade. Previous empires – the Romans, the Ottomans, the Spanish, the United States until 1865 – were sustained by slavery. But in 1807, the famous reformer William Wilberforce pressed through an act of Parliament banning this human traffic, and thereafter British naval ships patrolled the high seas stamping it out. It took a further 50 years for serfdom to be abolished in Russia, and slavery in the US. It continues to be practised in many African countries today. Britain has no need to apologise. We should be proud of our record.

As others have pointed out, in many cases, the nationalist anti-imperialist movements in the non-white colonies took over English political values. Indians, as well as Australians, Afrikaners and French Canadians quoted John Locke and John Stuart Mill, in their struggle for freedom, and got assistance from the British Labour movement. However, many in Britain, especially in its elites, long deluded themselves about the true feelings of resentment felt by many in the former colonies whether they are Afrikaners who still commemorate the British concentration camps, older Cypriots, Egyptians who were bombed in 1956, Jews in Israel who remember the Mandate period, Indians of a certain class and age, Irish Americans who possibly have never set foot in the Emerald Isle, Irish Aussies, Italians interned in the Second World War, Kenyan women ill treated by British troops, Palestinians, the Iranians who still remember the invasion of 1941, Maltese who think the British treated their island paradise as a glorified brothel, Poles who feel Britain let them down in 1939 and again in 1945, Singaporeans who feel they have shown the British how to run an economy, and organize a society, white Rhodesians, Zimbabweans who support Mugabe, and even certain Muslims, and all those who came 'home' and were called chinks, dagos, darkies, micks, paddies, taffies, wops, wogs and, relatively more recently, Pakies or, simply, bloody foreigners. A visit to historical museums in many lands often exposes something of this. The 'home-grown' terrorism of 2005 was, in part, no doubt an expression of such resentment passed down from earlier times and renewed by real and alleged slights and discrimination in the twenty-first century. Of course, there is no country where racism, resentment of the outsider, does not exist.

EDUCATION: 'MIRACLES DON'T HAPPEN OVERNIGHT'

One of the government's 'flagship' schemes for its second term was the city academy programme which was trumpeted as something to give self-respect to inner-city youngsters who had become indifferent to their own education. It was launched in 2000 by the then Education Secretary, David Blunkett, as 'a radical approach to promote greater diversity and break the cycle of failing schools in inner cities'. Under the scheme, in return for £2 million, an individual sponsor could appoint most governors and senior managers and influence the lessons within the national curriculum. The taxpayer was left to pay the rest of the bill and subsequent running costs. In 2005, each academy cost around £25 million to build, more than double the cost of a comprehensive. The government had by then spent £425 million on 17 academies. Another 36 were in the pipeline. The government's programme received a critical report from the Commons Education and Skills Select Committee and threats from teaching unions to fight proposals for new academies. The Labour-dominated committee urged the government, in March 2005, to halt the programme until it could demonstrate that academies represented the best use of public money. It said in a report: 'We fail to understand why the DfES is putting such substantial resources into academies when it has not produced the evidence on which to base the expansion of this programme.' After the election, in June 2005, Jacqui Smith, the Minister for School Standards, confirmed, that the government would press ahead with its plan to open 200 academies by 2010 at a cost of £5 billion.[37] David Cameron, the Shadow Education Secretary, said that he welcomed the initiative. 'City academies follow on from the city technology colleges that the Tories set up', he said. This was, of course, true. Blair was said to be a passionate advocate of the academies and his former chief policy adviser, Lord Adonis, by then an education minister, attracted unpopularity on the Left for his advocacy of them.

The 2004 tables revealed that, of the 11 academies listed, six had improved their results at GCSE. But five failed to show any improvement and one had the second worst results in England. At the Manchester Academy, which chalked up the second worst GCSE results in the country, only 8 per cent of pupils gained five or more A–C passes, compared with 12 per cent before it became an academy. Kathy August, the school's principal, said, 'Miracles don't happen overnight . . . we have improved drastically in terms of attendance, behaviour, attitudes to learning, quality of teaching and quality of learning. This will underpin future improvements in exam performance.'[38] The Unity City Academy in Middlesbrough was failed by Ofsted inspectors. One academy which received much attention was the Kings Academy in Middlesbrough. The Vardy Foundation, set up by car magnate Sir Peter Vardy, ran this academy where students were taught the 'creationist' theory of evolution as well as Darwinian theory. The principal expelled 26 pupils, including 11 in the GCSE year, for bad behaviour – 10 times the national average. But, despite the concerns the Department for Education and Skills continued to insist that academies were an effective way of revitalizing inner city education. In the government's view, the involvement of successful individuals from the private sector would inject enthusiasm and vision into schools which had developed a culture of failure. But opponents claimed the money ploughed into the academies could be invested in schools without handing over a degree of control to private backers.[39]

In another contentious area of education policy, Labour had quietly dropped its earlier policy on grammar schools as it had done on private schools. Under Wilson, from 1964, the then Labour Government instructed all local authorities to prepare plans to create comprehensive schools. Under Blair, Labour has not closed any grammar schools in England. By 2005, there were still 164 grammar schools in England, spread over 36 local education authorities. Since 1995, grammar schools had expanded by 35 per cent, or the equivalent of 46 schools.[40] Public schools and other forms of private education flourished. Although dozens of schools, in 2005, charged fees of more than £20,000 a year, 620,000 children – or 7 per cent of all school pupils – were privately educated in Britain. Just under a third of pupils received some form of assistance with fees, usually in the form of bursaries. Steven King, a spokesman for the Independent Schools Council, acknowledged that fees were still rising at double the rate of inflation'.[41] The UK median spending per 'state' secondary pupil was £3,140 in 2002. Meanwhile, in 2005, parents faced many costs in sending children to a 'state' school. The average cost of a child enrolled in a 'state', local authority maintained, school in England was more than £736 a year, a report for the Department for Education and Skills (DfES) found. Parents were paying for things such as uniforms, food and travel. However, 90 per cent of the parents responding to the survey said school costs were not too expensive. The Child Poverty Action Group called for extra help with expenses for low-income households. Chief Executive Kate Green said,'We know that up to 350,000 children each year are not claiming their free school meals for a number of reasons including fear of stigma and bullying.' A DfES spokesman said the government was investing a record amount in schools, with funding per pupil up 45 per cent, or £1,300, since 1997. Support was available for parents on low income, with free school meals, free transport for pupils and local schemes to assist with the cost of school trips.[42]

Two terms which gained popularity during Blair's second term were 'neets' and 'chavs'. Both represented youth problems. 'Neets' were those not in employment, education or training. Aged between 16 and 24, they numbered 1.1 million and were responsible for a social and economic drag on society that was vastly disproportionate to their numbers. Neets were 22 times more likely to be teenage mothers, 50 per cent more likely to suffer from poor health, 60 per cent more likely to be involved with drugs and more than 20 times more likely to become criminals. Former Director of the Child Poverty Action Group and former Minister for Welfare Reform, Labour MP, Frank Field, believed, 'Single parenthood is the recruiting sergeant for antisocial behaviour . . . Children need a noble male role model to follow.' More than 3 million children were being brought up by single mothers. Influenced by experiments in the US, Labour's answer was establishing new vocational qualifications and specialist vocational schools to give 'neets' practical skills; restructuring the benefit system to reward those in work, education or training; and the introduction of anti-social behaviour orders (Asbos) and curfews to control those who stepped out of line.[43] Chavs overlapped with neets. The term came into widespread use in 2004. It referred to a subculture stereotype 'Council Housed And Violent', a person who was uneducated, uncultured and prone to antisocial or immoral behaviour. Chavs often dressed in baseball cap, track suit and trainers. It was unfair to many respectable council house tenants. Were chavs responsible for the rising number of arson attacks against schools?

London faced greater problems than the rest of the country. It educated around a million pupils in just over 2,250 maintained primary and secondary schools. Around 44 per cent of Inner London maintained secondary school pupils were eligible for free school meals (compared with an average of just 17 per cent throughout England). Around 29 per cent of London pupils in maintained schools spoke English as an additional language, rising to 42 per cent in Inner London. For England, the average figure was 8 per cent. London maintained secondary schools had much higher proportions of children from an ethnic minority: London 41.2 per cent; Inner London average 58.3 per cent; England 12 per cent. In London 3.5 per cent of schools were in danger of failing; in England generally, just 2.4 per cent were in the same position (2000/01).The maintained secondary school teacher vacancy rate was nearly 3 per cent in London, less than 1998/9 but still nearly three times that of the rest of England. Truancy, unauthorized absence, was greater in London maintained secondary schools: London 1.5 per cent, England 1.1 per cent, Inner London 2.2 per cent (2000/01). Authorized absence was around the national average: London 7.9 per cent, England 8 per cent (2000/01). Inner London's maintained schools performed relatively poorly at GCSE/GNVQ by national standards: the percentage of 15-year-olds achieving 5+ A*–C grades in London was 46.1 per cent; Inner London 38 per cent; England generally 47.9 per cent.[44]

Another hotly debated issue was 'faith schools'. Patricia Hewitt told *New Statesman* readers (17 December 2001),

As our state education system already embraces Church of England, Roman Catholic, Jewish and other religious schools, we cannot continue to hold out against other faiths. Nor, I think, is the French route of a secular education system open to us. There is substantial evidence that our existing state faith schools are more effective at providing the strong leadership, ethos and discipline that enable pupils of all abilities to flourish.

She thought the right approach was to 'offer inclusion in the state system to schools of every faith – but we should also be tough in our requirements of those schools'. Despite some reservations of Hewitt and her colleagues, the government went ahead with encouraging more 'faith schools'. Most British people, however, thought 'enough is enough'. In May 2004, more than half of YouGov's sample poll, 53 per cent, believed the Government 'should encourage the parents of all faiths to send their children to the same schools' and another large proportion, 29 per cent, took a broadly similar view but had no objection to continuing state support for schools with a Christian emphasis. In contrast, only a small minority of people, 7 per cent, believed the state should encourage the parents of children of minority faiths, such as Hindus, Muslims and Jews, to send their children to separate religious institutions.[45] Some of Muslim background agreed with the majority, as Yasmin Alibhai-Brown put it in the *Independent* (16 February 2004), 'How bizarre that the Government is boldly pushing integrated education in N. Ireland, while on the mainland, it upholds separatist education. Tony Blair and co are worryingly confused on this.' The Chief Schools Inspector David Bell, head of Ofsted, the education standards watchdog, warned, in January 2005, that there was a danger that the growth in independent faith schools – especially Muslim ones – could undermine the coherence of British society. He chose a Hansard Society lecture on the importance of teaching citizenship in schools to warn of the dangers of a 'significant' growth in the number of independent faith schools in the UK. There were around 300 such schools in the country – including 100 Muslim, 100 evangelical Christian and 50 Jewish schools. He was worried that a traditional Islamic education 'does not entirely fit' Muslim children for life in modern Britain.[46] He repeated such fears in the Ofsted annual report later in the year. In Scotland, the only Muslim boarding school was given a final warning to make substantial improvements within three months or face possible closure. The quality of the management and teaching staff, of pupil learning and the secular curriculum were found to be unsatisfactory at the privately run Imam Muhammad Zakariya School in Dundee, according to HM Inspectors of Education. Pupils aged 16-plus were offered only Arabic, sewing and cookery.[47] Meanwhile, Muslim organizations were campaigning for more Muslim schools in Scotland. Other faith communities, encouraged by Blair's policies, felt encouraged to ask for more. In London, after a 20-year campaign, Yesodey Hatorah girls' school in the heavily Jewish orthodox Stamford Hill finally won state funding. Jewish schools are, of course, a long-standing feature of the British educational patchwork – in 2004 there were 33 of them. None the less, the addition of such a strictly orthodox Jewish school to the state sector raised the kind of questions Bell had mentioned.[48] The debate rumbled on. One particular faith community was badly hit by its record on child abuse. This was the Catholic Church, which had run its own schools for decades. From the early 1990s its priests were exposed in Australia, Ireland, the UK, the US and elsewhere. The Church should not be afraid to acknowledge mistakes and willing to remedy them, according to Cardinal Cormac Murphy-O'Connor, the head of the Catholic Church in England and Wales. Referring directly to the recent child abuse scandals which rocked the Church, the Cardinal told those gathered at St Mary's College, Twickenham, that it was absolutely imperative for the Church to address such issues, and if necessary to follow the Pope's example and offer formal and sincere apologies.[49] This was not just a problem for the Catholic community.

Universities came under mounting pressure to adopt US-style admissions tests to distinguish between the best candidates as record numbers of A-level students gained top grades in 2005. Since 2003, Oxford, Cambridge and other leading universities claimed that they had been forced to set additional entrance exams for subjects such as medicine, law and history, because A-levels alone no longer helped them to identify the very best. The Government ruled out any changes to A-levels until 2008. Ruth Kelly, the Education Secretary, was criticized in 2005 when she rejected radical plans to replace A-levels, GCSEs and vocational qualifications with a four-level diploma.[50] Meanwhile, in 2005, an ONS study based on census statistics revealed social mobility had actually decreased and that parental class and educational level remained the key factors influencing children's success.

A NEW ROYAL WEDDING: 'TRIPE, TRIVIA AND TOSH'?

Writing in the *Guardian* (11 February 2005) about the impending wedding of Prince Charles and Camilla Parker-Bowles, Polly Toynbee seemed near to despair: 'Tripe, tosh and trivia will dominate the press, rising to a climax as the deed is done: if only they'd quietly eloped to Gretna Green.' She continued, 'The glittering emblem of the sovereign infantilises the nation into an unhealthy fascination with the doings of the royal household, children, servants, foibles and every banal saying and doing. It demeans the idea of citizenship and the meaning of the state. Why should these meaningless people be embedded in our national imagination?' She went on,

The tyranny of the monarchy is not in its puny temporal power but in its hold over the national imagination. The monarchy's link with an imperial past – how tight it clings to the commonwealth – encourages all our worst tendencies to strut self-importantly on the global stage: 'punching above our weight' is the Foreign Office's

perpetual forlorn endeavour. It helped to lead us astray on the road
to Baghdad (but not Brussels).

After much public discussion Prince Charles finally married Camilla
Parker Bowles on 8 April 2005. As divorcees, they were unable to have a
church wedding and therefore went through a civil wedding at the historic
Windsor Guildhall. There followed a blessing and service at St George's
Chapel in Windsor Castle conducted by the Archbishop of Canterbury,
Dr Rowan Williams. The service was attended by about 750 guests including
members of the royal family, statesmen and celebrities. The Queen and the
Duke of Edinburgh were at the blessing having decided not to attend the
civil ceremony at the town hall. The run-up to the wedding had been beset
by problems. The pair had to switch venues from St George's Chapel to
the Guildhall and faced legal opposition to their nuptials. The wedding
had to be put back a day because of the funeral of Pope John Paul II,
which the Prince attended. About 15,000 tourists and well wishers turned
out to see them. This compared with about 20,000 who had descended on
the town when Prince Edward married Sophie Rhys-Jones in 1999 and
about 600,000 who had turned out for Charles's first wedding to Lady
Diana Spencer in 1981 in St Paul's Cathedral in London.[51]
    What did people think of the ageing Prince (b. 14 November 1948) and
the monarchy? A Mori opinion poll at the end of 2004 which asked people
to choose between Charles or an elected head of state, found only 55 per
cent opted for Charles. Throughout the 1980s and most of the 1990s, the
monarchy had got more than 70 per cent support. An ICM poll found
only 3 per cent of under-30s identified with Prince Charles. The research
British Social Attitudes, carried out by NatCen in early 2005, found that
only just over a quarter of the population felt that the continuation of the
monarchy was very important for Britain; this had more than halved
between 1983, when 65 per cent thought it was very important, to 2003
when just 28 per cent thought so. Views about the monarchy varied con-
siderably from one group to another. The most pronounced differences
were related to age. Four in ten (41 per cent) of those aged 65 and over
thought the continuation of the monarchy was very important for Britain,
compared with just 14 per cent of 18–24 year olds and 19 per cent of those
aged 25–34.[52]
    Among a more aware minority of people two issues remained contentious.
These were the place of the monarch in the established church, and, more
important to a wider group, the royal finances. The sovereign remained the
Supreme Governor of the Church of England, the officially established
church in England. As such, the monarch, in theory, had the power to
appoint archbishops and bishops. The prime minister, however, chooses
the appointee, though he or she must select from a list of nominees prepared
by the Crown Nominations Commission. The Crown's role in the Church of

England is purely titular; the most senior clergyman, the Archbishop of Canterbury, is seen as the spiritual leader of the Church and of the world-wide Anglican Communion. The monarch is only an ordinary member, and not the leader, of the established Church of Scotland. Because of the changes in Britain with ever fewer people belonging to the Church of England, its establishment was increasingly questioned. The personal lifestyle of Charles also led church members to question his suitability as a future 'Supreme Governor'.

HUNTING BAN: 'MPS ARE BEING INTIMIDATED'

During Blair's premiership much time, and hot air, was expended on the issue of fox hunting. This was an issue on which Blair could give his back-bench MPs some rope to make them feel that not all of their old positions had been abandoned. Blair himself always hoped for a compromise on the issue. The Labour Party manifesto of 1997 pledged 'a free vote in Parliament on whether hunting with hounds should be banned by legislation'. A private member's Bill which would have banned all hunting of wild mammals with dogs was introduced by Michael Foster, Labour MP for Worcester, and won the support of a majority of members of the House of Commons. The Bill later ran out of time. Under continuing pressure from anti-hunt MPs, Jack Straw, as Home Secretary, arranged, in 1999, for a six-month government Committee of Inquiry into Hunting with Dogs in England and Wales. Chaired by Lord Burns, the Committee presented its Final Report to Parliament in June 2000. It was not part of Burns's remit to support or oppose a ban on hunting, but to clear up some of the disputed matters surrounding the issue. Among his other findings, Burns found that banning hunting would have little effect on the number of foxes, and that the number of jobs likely to be lost by a ban was about 700. On animal welfare, Burns reported that hunting 'seriously compromises the welfare of the fox' but that alternative methods of fox control were worse. In its 2001 manifesto, Labour promised to give Parliament the opportunity to reach a conclusion on hunting. In 2003, the government introduced its own Bill, which would have instituted a system of licensing and regulation of hunting. However, anti-hunting MPs passed a series of amendments to introduce a total ban on hunting with exemptions only for rats, rabbits and raptors. Faced with revolts on a number of issues, the government initially accepted them as the will of the House of Commons. This Bill did not complete its stages in the Lords. In 2004, the government reintroduced its Bill in exactly the same form and it passed through the Commons in one day in September, together with a 'suggested amendment' under the Parliament Act procedure that would have delayed the ban for 18 months until 31 July 2006, to give an opportunity for 318 registered hound packs employing several thousand workers to wind down or adapt before the ban came into force. Hunt supporters believed that its primary purpose was to prevent the ban, with its associated protests, from coming into effect a few months before the expected general election in May 2005. Despite many private negotiations among the different factions in the two Houses, no compromise was agreed.

Outside Parliament, Labour MPs and ministers faced a campaign of abuse, threats and intimidation over the decision to ban hunting. In one incident, Lord Whitty, the Agriculture Minister, was surrounded by protesters in Warwickshire and needed a police escort to escape. Later the same day, demonstrators violently forced their way into a Labour Party meeting in Kidderminster, due to have been attended by Michael Foster, MP. His colleague Tony Banks, who was among several to receive threats that their offices would be 'trashed', said, 'MPs are being intimidated because of the way they have exercised their vote. That to me is terrorism directed at the constitution.' During the clashes outside Parliament, Anne Picking, MP, was struck in the face. Alun Michael, the Rural Affairs Minister, was pelted with eggs after leaving a meeting in Exeter. On 15 September 2004, Parliament was suspended after five protesters burst into the Commons chamber while MPs debated the hunting issue. It came as thousands protested outside Parliament. There were some scuffles but it was mostly a peaceful rally. Once the Commons resumed business, MPs voted to back a ban on hunting with dogs – by 356 to 166. The intrusion exposed the poor security at Westminster. Anger appears to have been channelled by organizations such as the Working Hound Defence Campaign and the Countryside Action Network, which favoured direct action. Pro-hunters wanted to force the Government to back down through the sheer weight of protest or unseat MPs through the ballot box. The attacks on MPs mirrored tactics used against animal welfare bodies, which reported several similar incidents. The Countryside Alliance, the main pro-hunting body, dissociated itself from any violent acts.[53] When the Lords and Commons were unable to come to agreement by the end of the parliamentary year on 18 November, the Parliament Act was invoked. On 19 November 2004, Commons Speaker Michael Martin invoked the Act to secure the Bill banning fox hunting, which came into place in February 2005. He told MPs the Act was being used for only the fourth time since 1949 – a move sparked by peers who earlier rejected a ban on hunting with dogs. The Bill was then given Royal Assent, bringing to an end years of wrangling. Legal action and demonstrations ran up to the general election in 2005. In January 2005, Ben Bradshaw, the Minister for Nature Conservation, was injured during a hunting protest in Exeter, and Peter Hain, Leader of the Commons, was besieged in his own home by hunt supporters.[54] As well as fox hunting, deer hunting and hare coursing with dogs were outlawed in England and Wales. The Conservative leader in the Upper House, Lord Strathclyde, said the ban threatened the livelihoods of thousands and 'drew a knife across centuries of tradition in our countryside but will not lead to a single animal being spared a violent death'. RSPCA director of animal welfare, John Rolls, said the Bill was a 'watershed in the development of a more civilised society for people and animals'.

Animal rights protesters celebrated on 23 August 2005 as Christopher and John Hall announced they were closing their family business breeding guinea pigs for scientific research. This followed years of threats, intimidation and harassment including hate mail, malicious phone calls, fireworks, a paedophile smear campaign, paint stripper on cars and arson attacks. The protests appeared to culminate in the gruesome theft in October of the body of Gladys Hammond, mother-in-law of Christopher Hall from the churchyard in Yoxall.[55] The campaign was just part of a much wider protest, attacking research laboratories, suppliers of animals, transporters of animals, importers of animals and firms relying on the research produced for their products. Although there had always been a movement against the use of animals in research experiments, violent actions appeared to be on the increase. This was possibly, in part, due to the disillusionment with party politics, which led some to seek single issues to get involved with. It also grew out of revulsion at factory farming and the use of animals in research for cosmetics.

GAMBLING ACT 2005: 'THIS TACKY BILL'

The Government introduced a Gambling Bill into Parliament on 18 October 2004. It aimed to deregulate the gaming industry in the UK, and proposed the construction of a number of 'mega-casinos' in city centres. It met with much opposition from church bodies and charities. At one point there was talk of as many as 20 regional super-casinos, but the Government was forced to backtrack in the face of a cross-party political backlash. Geraldine Smith (Labour) said (1 November 2004) she was worried about the consequences of problem gambling, 'including financial hardship, debt, exposure to loan sharks, bankruptcy, resorting to theft, imprisonment, neglect of family, the breakdown of relationships, domestic and other violence, poor health, absenteeism, stress, depression, anxiety, suicide, burdens on charities and burdens on the public purse' and children whose parents had a gambling addiction. Gwyneth Dunwoody (Labour) was puzzled because, 'it is not at all clear where this tacky Bill has come from'. John Pugh (Liberal Democrat), MP for the seaside resort of Southport, told the Commons (24 January 2005) his opposition to

the proposal for super-casinos is that there is simply no demand for them. That is an industry-led proposal. There is no necessity to use them as a regeneration tool. My constituency is regenerating itself without any proposal for a casino. The requirement in the Bill for regeneration is more notional than real. It is dependent on very weak planning controls and falls far short of what happens on the continent, where major revenue benefits are secured as part of the package . . . Neither the losses to small businesses nor the threat of ambient gambling to resort communities has been fairly considered.

He thought the proposals 'would aggravate problem gambling and lead to a further redistribution of wealth from the poor to the rich'. His colleague Don Foster commented, during the same debate, 'many parts of the Bill have a great deal of support on both sides of the House, and outside the House – for example, the provisions concerning internet gambling, tougher social responsibility requirements, and a tougher regulator in the shape of the gambling commission, which will replace the Gaming Board – but many people have deep concerns about other aspects. That is particularly true in relation to casinos. The Secretary of State said that the Government should listen . . . but the real question is this: to whom were they listening when they first came up with those proposals?' By granting numerous concessions, the Bill went through in the final moments of the pre-election parliamentary session. It received Royal Assent on 7 April 2005, and became the Gambling Act. The Culture Secretary, Tessa Jowell, had piloted it through the Commons and her office pointed out that the number of super-casinos could be subsequently increased from one up to eight by affirmative resolution in Parliament if the experiment was deemed to have worked. In July 2005 there were 24 casinos in London, 97 in the rest of England, 13 in Scotland and four in Wales. The Salvation Army and the Methodist Church acknowledged numerous changes made to provide more protection for vulnerable people and greater controls to limit the potential increase in problem gambling. However, pointing out that there were 400,000 problem gamblers in the UK and despite the Bill being watered down, the Salvation Army and Methodist Church were still fearful that there would be significant potential for a rise in problem gambling. Tessa Jowell received a 50,000-plus signature petition from these bodies and the children's charity NCH calling on the Government to ban children and young people from gambling on fruit machines. Despite this demonstration of the high level of opposition, the Government remained unwilling to make the necessary changes to the Gambling Bill to protect children. The two churches emphasized that the Gambling Act was not asked for by the public, 93 per cent of whom had said there were already enough opportunities to gamble. We were still the only country in the developed world that allowed children to gamble.[56] Just days after the Gambling Act received Royal Assent it became known that the Gaming Board was investigating Napoleon's Casino one of London's most popular casinos. It was alleged that Chinese gangsters were using the venue to launder vast sums of illicit cash from extortion, vice and people-smuggling operations.[57]

24-HOUR DRINKING: 'PUT CHILLI SAUCE ON THAT'

As controversial as the Government's legislation on gambling were its moves on alcohol and drugs. A report for the Joseph Rowntree Foundation, in 2002, exposed the problem of binge drinking among schoolchildren. Up to a quarter of 13- and 14-year-olds said they had consumed at least five alcoholic drinks in a single session, and 27 per cent of those aged 15 and 16 reported three or more binges in the month before the survey. Alcohol excess hit young people at all levels of society. Euan Blair, the Prime Minister's son, and Prince Harry were both caught binge drinking. But it was not simply youthful excess. Experts believed there were cultural reasons why the British gulped and others merely sipped. The findings echoed earlier reports which suggested that British teens were more likely to get drunk – and more often – than many of their European contemporaries. Researchers said this could be down to the different culture surrounding alcohol. In France, bars generally closed at about 1.30 a.m. and as late as 3.00 a.m. in Paris. In Spain, in many areas, bars were often open 24 hours. In Germany, laws varied from state to state but most city bars stayed open until after midnight. It was thought that, in Britain, 'last orders' engendered almost ritualistic behaviour among pub drinkers, aimed at squeezing a final drink from the landlord. The falling price of alcohol relative to household incomes, and the ability of young people, under age, to buy alcohol from, often struggling, retail outlets were also important parts of the picture. The Government's response was the Licensing Act 2003, which came into force in 2005. This introduced 'flexible hours' on licensed premises. The Government also promised more powers to the police and local authorities and a big educational programme. Rob Marris (Labour) was happy to tell the Commons (12 July 2005) that 'the third largest pub chain in the United Kingdom is headquartered in my constituency and run by the excellent Wolverhampton and Dudley breweries. I spent last Wednesday evening at a dinner in the company of some of its representatives, and although they said that there were some teething problems, they were entirely happy with the Licensing Act 2003.' Much parliamentary opposition to the Bill centred on the complicated forms for bodies seeking a licence to sell alcohol and the problems of extra cost that the legislation would create for village halls, sports clubs and community centres. Theresa May (Conservative) claimed that, 'running such a burdensome, bureaucratic and unnecessarily complex system is introducing additional costs that the industry, let alone voluntary organizations, simply cannot afford to bear'. Jonathan R. Shaw (Labour) challenged, 'As well as 24-hour drinking, on which we have not heard from the right hon. Lady for Maidenhead (Mrs May), she also failed to mention the president of the National Association of Kebab Shops, who thinks that the Bill is top dollar. He has said: "We are happy with this law because the longer opening hours will be available to most take-away shops." There we are. Put chilli sauce on that.' The debate was turning into farce. However, others had more serious concerns. In the run-up to the implementation of the Act, a survey commissioned for ITV1's *Tonight with Trevor McDonald* revealed that almost two thirds of police officers were opposed to 24-hour drinking. They believed it would lead to an increase in alcohol-fuelled violence. The research also found that a majority of the general public, doctors and nurses were opposed to the new licensing laws. Half of the public said they did not support the idea, as did 57 per cent of doctors and 59 per cent of nurses. Publicans were the only group that took part in the survey who did support round the clock drinking. Seventy-five per cent said they favoured longer opening hours, although 29 per cent admitted that they thought it would cause more alcohol-related violence. The Royal College of Physicians added its considerable weight to the argument against the Act. Former Health Secretary Frank Dobson said that reforms of opening times would not stop the British drinking heavily, adding: 'The English – maybe the British – have been binge drinkers since time immemorial. I don't think we'll turn into Tuscany just because the hours have changed.' Conservative Shadow Home Secretary, David Davis, demanded that, 'The Government should immediately delay 24-hour opening until it has got a grip on binge drinking.'[58] As Britain moved towards 24-hour opening, new evidence exposed the dangers to children which already existed.

The survey *Smoking, Drinking and Drug Use among Young People in England in 2004*, issued by the NHS health and social care information centre, revealed that, among 11- to 15-year-olds, little progress was made in 2004 in stemming damaging habits. It also showed that girls were catching up with boys in their drinking habits. They found that 23 per cent of children were drinking regularly, a fall of only two percentage points on 2003. In 1992 only about 17 per cent of children said they had drunk alcohol in the previous week. The survey also found that 10 per cent of girls and seven per cent of boys were regular smokers, about the same as in the previous year. Eleven per cent of schoolchildren had used cannabis in the preious year, down from 13 per cent in 2001 to 2003.

Blunkett, as Home Secretary, reclassified cannabis from a class B to a class C drug in January 2004. The move was intended to enable police forces around the country to focus on the trade in heroin and cocaine. But, by early 2005, senior police at Scotland Yard believed this move had sent out the wrong message to the gangs, who had switched their attention to the softer drug. They reported that demand for cannabis had exploded since the relaxation of the law. A huge increase in cocaine use was cited for the number of people on hard drugs in England and Wales, rising to a record one million. The number of young people using cocaine had more than doubled since 1998. Cocaine use had quadrupled since 1996 and the surge was being blamed on significant increases among people over the age of 24, a Home Office survey said. The charity Drugscope said that the typical price per gram had fallen from £70 to £40 over a decade. The drug was previously the preserve of high-earning show business personalities, but was now being used by young professionals as a recreational drug. The study found, however, that cocaine users were more likely to be semi-skilled or skilled manual workers than members of the professional classes. The results of the British Crime Survey found that 3.85 million people aged from 16 to 59 had used an illegal drug in the past year.[59]

ELECTION 2005

By the time the 5 May 2005 election was announced, many people were already bored with hearing so much about it. It had been on the cards for months with Blair and his ministers neither prepared to confirm the date nor deny it. This gave Blair the advantage of knowing when to launch initiatives and, should the polls reveal declining support, he could always have held on for another year. The death (2 April) and burial (8 April) of Pope John Paul II, the drama of the election of his successor on 18 April, and the marriage of Prince Charles on 9 April gave the media, the government and the public some respite from the election. There was also the build-up to the 60th anniversary celebrations of VE Day.

Although all three main parties displayed large posters at strategic points, there were few of them, and fewer still were displayed in the windows and gardens of their supporters. In fact, one could travel throughout most of England without seeing much sign of political activity. More than ever before, the campaigns were fought by press conferences, photo opportunities, radio and television interviews, party political broadcasts, emails, texting and by delivering set speeches to specially invited audiences of the faithful. Few voters were invited to put their concerns to candidates on the doorstep, and those given this opportunity were mainly in targeted streets of marginal constituencies. Would the lack of direct contact between the parties and the electors prove to be another factor in low turnout? The election was in many respects a rerun of that of 2001. Labour again defended its record on the NHS, the economy, education and law and order. Once again the Conservatives attacked on asylum seekers and immigration and promised 'value for money' in public spending and the restoration of discipline in schools and an early referendum on the European Constitution. The Liberal Democrats' themes were education, council tax and Iraq. All three parties promised help for pensioners, and all three called for 'controlled' immigration. One big difference between 2001 and 2005 was that the Conservatives had Michael Howard leading them, whereas Blair and Kennedy still led Labour and the Liberal Democrats respectively. Kennedy was seen as the most trustworthy by the electorate and the matter of trust was made a key issue in the election. Blair was relentlessly pursued by the Liberal Democrats, the Conservatives, the SNP, PC and by his own party's left wing, over his lack of candour on Iraq. Howard even called him a 'liar'. Howard too faced personal attacks because of his Thatcherite past and because there was 'something of the night' about him. The parties engaged in a great deal of negative campaigning rather than getting their own messages across. As in 2001, the polls consistently showed Labour in the lead, which caused fear of apathy and complacency in Labour's ranks. However, there was much evidence that Labour would have done even better if led by Brown rather than Blair. On the day, Labour strategists were relieved that the weather remained quite dry for most of the day in most places. One other factor which was cause for concern in all the parties was the massive rise in the postal vote since 2001. Traditionally, more Conservatives than Labour supporters had used it. This appeared to have changed. This rise was accompanied by the fear of fraud. On election night it was clear that postal voting had marginally increased turnout from 59.3 per cent to 61.3 per cent. After the polling stations closed at 10 p.m, the BBC/ITN exit poll predicted a Labour majority of 66. Ultimately, domestic policy factors helped Labour achieve a historic third term in office with 356 seats. In this context, the new, reduced Labour majority of 67, with 35.3 per cent of the vote, was viewed by many across the political spectrum as a positive development, a counter to an alleged presidential style of government. The Conservatives increased their Commons tally from 160 to 197 but their share of the vote increased by only 0.6 per cent to 32.3 per cent. They could take some comfort from the local elections held on the same day. Building on their previous gains, they became the largest party in local government, with nearly 8,200 councillors compared with 6,500 for Labour and 4,700 for the Liberal Democrats.[60] They also gained more votes than Labour in England. After the Labour victory became clear, Michael Howard announced that he would be resigning as leader once the internal affairs of his party were stabilized. His party woke up to a £13.5 million hole in its finances. There was shock when it was learned that Lord Saatchi's companies had charged the Conservative Party, of which he was Chairman, £2.5 million for campaigning.[61] Helped again by tactical voting, the Liberal Democrats became the focus for many people who were angry with New Labour. They were constantly described by the media as being against the war in Iraq, they opposed top-up fees for university students, opposed much of the anti-terror legislation, appeared to be more pro-immigrant than the other major parties, and called for a fairer system of funding local government. They had to deny that they were to the left of New Labour. In fact, their treasury spokesman, David Laws, appeared to endorse free-market policies as strongly as both major parties. As it turned out, their advance was very limited. They took around six million votes. That is the same as they received in 1992 and almost two million fewer than they got in 1983. With 22.1 per cent (up 3.8 per cent) of the vote, the Liberal Democrats won 62 seats, having gained 16 seats but lost five.

Led by Simon Woolley, Operation Black Vote (OBV), a non-party campaign of black and faith organizations, aimed to encourage communities in marginal seats to vote, and mounted a strong campaign with a battle bus visiting target constituencies. The term 'black' referred to African, Asian, Caribbean and other ethnic minorities (but not Jews). Overall, 110 'black' candidates were selected compared with the 66 in 2001. The Conservatives fielded 41 ethnic candidates, more than twice as many ethnic candidates as in 2001, compared with the Liberal Democrats' 40 and Labour's 29. Thirteen of the 659 MPs in the 2001–05 Parliament came from an ethnic minority. Twelve of them represented Labour and one was a Liberal Democrat. What were the results in 2005? Amit Roy estimated that the number of constituencies where the Asian vote was important was 'probably between 60 and 70'. The Muslim Association of Britain (MAB) claimed, 'In almost all of the 40 or so constituencies where Muslims form more than 5 per cent of the local population, the effect was clear, positive and undeniable.' However, Asians were said to be disappointed that out of a record number of 73 Asians selected by the three main parties only 10 were elected, including three new recruits Sadiq Khan (Lab Tooting), Shahid Malik (Lab Dewsbury) and Shailesh Vara (Con Cambridgeshire). Among the others was Piara Khabra (Lab Ealing Southall), Britain's oldest MP.[62] Parmjit Singh Gill, Liberal Democrat, who won Leicester South in a 2004 by-election, was defeated and the seat reverted to Labour. Solicitor Yasmin Qureshi (Labour) in Brent East failed to retake this long-time Labour seat captured by the Liberal Democrats' Sarah Teather in a by-election in September 2003. Cardiff Central, Peterborough and Northampton South were other losses sustained by Labour due to Asian desertions. The defeat of Oona King at Bethnal Green and Bow, where there is a large Bangladeshi Muslim community, was lamented in Jewish and black circles. King faced a 'vitriolic and often nasty campaign', said *The Voice* (9 May 2005). The Blair loyalist, whose mother is Jewish and whose father is black, failed to defend a 10,000 majority. She was defeated by the expelled Labour MP, opponent of the Iraq War, Respect candidate George Galloway. 'During the campaign Ms King was pelted with eggs and had her car tyres slashed. Mr Galloway was assaulted by Muslim extremists opposed to the notion of elections.' In Birmingham Sparkbrook and Small Heath, Respect's Muslim candidate Salma Yaqoob was close to pulling off a sensational victory on a turnout of only 51.81 per cent. There 37 per cent of the electorate were Muslim. Labour MP Roger Godsiff, who was defending a huge majority of 16,246, had that slashed to 3,289, a swing of 27.5 per cent. Respect achieved other notable results in London seats with large Muslim populations like East Ham, West Ham, Poplar and Canning Town and at Preston, Lancashire. Predictions that Muslims would effectively cast a 'block' vote against Labour failed to materialize in Blackburn, where Jack Straw was re-elected with support from local Muslim community leaders after savage attacks from a body calling itself the Muslim Public Affairs Committee (MPACUK). Attempts to unseat Mike Gapes (Labour), a former vice-chair of the Labour Friends of Israel, at Ilford by the same body also failed. 'The election results show that no single party can any longer take the Muslim community's votes for granted. The Muslim electorate has become more discerning and that is good news for the health of our democracy', said Iqbal Sacrinie, Secretary-General of the Muslim Council of Britain. New black MPs, that is of African or Afro-Caribbean origin, included Adam Afriyie (Windsor), who had the distinction of being the first black Conservative MP, and Dawn Butler (Labour) who replaced Paul Boateng in Brent South. They joined Diane Abbott and David Lammy, both Labour.

'Israel Lobbyists have given mixed assessment of the prospects for the new Parliament. They say that while most of the fresh intake of MPs are supportive, several pro-Israel figures have lost their seats.' These included Stephen Twigg, Lorna Fitzsimmons, Oona King, Peter Bradley, a victim of pro-hunt campaigners in the Wrekin, and Barbara Roche, ex-minister for immigration, all Labour. The Tories had gained several Friends of Israel and the Liberal Democrats two.[63] Grant Shapps and Lee Scott were among the new Conservative Jewish intake, and Sir Malcolm Rifkind returned to the Commons. On the Labour side, Louise Ellman, Chair of the Israel Group, was returned for Liverpool Riverside, and Gerald Kaufman, Vice-Chair of the All-Party Anti-Semitism Group, but also a critic of Israeli policies, was re-elected in Manchester Gorton, easily seeing off an Asian Liberal Democratic challenger. The Catholic/Irish contingent in the Commons remained strong. Cardinal Cormac Murphy-O'Connor, head of the Catholic Church in England and Wales, had caused controversy by supporting Michael Howard's proposal to lower the legal age of foetus termination from 24 weeks to 20. However, he tried to distance himself from any notion that the Catholic Church was supporting the Conservatives in the election. Nevertheless, some Catholics probably thought this was a hint to look carefully at the candidates' stance on this and similar issues and vote accordingly. Ruth Kelly had faced a keen challenge in Bolton West but, although her majority was slashed, she was returned probably with the aid of some Catholic Conservative and Liberal Democratic voters. At St Albans, Kerry Pollard, who had voted on several occasions against cuts in benefits and taken a conservative view on moral issues, lost to his Conservative challenger. John Battle (Labour), former minister and Chairman of the All-Party Catholic Agency for Overseas Development, was voted back at Leeds West. Its secretary, Helen Jones (Lab Warrington), was also re-elected.

The British National Party slightly increased its share of the vote, but failed to take any seats. The party, which contested 119 seats, took 192,850 votes in total, compared with 47,129 at the 2001 election. It lost its

£500 deposit in 84 seats, leaving it with a bill of about £42,000. Its best result was in Barking, London, where it took 16.89 per cent of the vote. Richard Barnbrook came a close third behind the Tories – the seat was won by Children's Minister, Margaret Hodge, for Labour. BNP leader Nick Griffin polled 4,240 votes in Keighley, West Yorkshire – 9.16 per cent of the total cast. In Dewsbury, David Exley polled 5,066 votes (13.13 per cent). The seat was won by Labour's Shahid Malik. In Dudley North the BNP polled 9.7 per cent; in West Bromwich East, it attracted 6.56 per cent; in West Bromwich West 9.9 per cent; and in Rotherham 7 per cent. The Green Party doubled its share of the votes in two seats, but failed to win its first Commons seat. The Greens' Keith Taylor, a local councillor, came third in their top target Brighton Pavilion with 22 per cent of the votes. The Labour incumbent won. But Taylor, who pushed the Liberal Democrats into fourth place, polled 9,571 – up 13 per cent on 2001's result. In Lewisham, they won 11.5 per cent and doubled their vote in Norwich South. The party got 256,020 votes in total, compared with 166,477 in 2001. The Greens, who contested 200 of the 646 seats, won 1.07 per cent of the vote. Their bill for their lost deposits (£500 deposits in 177 seats across the UK where they failed to win 5 per cent of votes) came to £88,500. The UKIP failed to make an electoral breakthrough, despite its biggest parliamentary campaign. It polled 611,423 votes or 2.35 per cent. Deserted by its high-profile campaigner Robert Kilroy-Silk, it lost its deposits in 451 seats – costing it about £225,500. It was a long way from its 16.1 per cent vote in 2004's European elections, when it took 12 seats. Even its leader, the former Conservative MP Roger Knapman, could only attract 3,914 votes (7.74 per cent) in Totnes, Devon. As leader of his newly formed Veritas, Kilroy-Silk contested Erewash, Derbyshire, coming fourth behind Labour, the Conservatives and the Liberal Democrats. He recorded nearly 3,000 votes (5.85 per cent) but won a victory of sorts, beating the UKIP candidate who got only 941 votes (1.86 per cent). There is some dispute about the extent to which UKIP cost the Conservatives seats. What of the Independents? Remarkably, campaigning on NHS issues, Dr Richard Taylor was re-elected as Independent at Wyre Forest. On a 64.2 per cent turnout he beat Conservatives and Labour and three other candidates. In Wales, at Blaenau Gwent, where Bevan and Foot had sat as Labour MPs, Peter Law defeated Labour, Liberal Democrat, Conservative, PC and UKIP candidates to romp home with 58.17 per cent of the vote. A life-long Labour man, he had opposed his party on all-women shortlists. In his constituency, Blair faced no fewer than 14 opponents. He was re-elected gaining 58.89 per cent of the vote. But his most impressive opponent was Independent Reg Keys, father of a military policeman killed in Iraq. He gained 10.3 per cent of the vote coming fourth. In Scotland the SNP, which presented itself as a left-of-centre party that would 'also commit to a nuclear free future for Scotland

and to save the Scottish regiments', increased its representation from 4 to 6 with 17.7 per cent of the vote. It presented strong competition to Labour, the Liberal Democrats and the Scottish Socialist Party (SSP). It was a disappointing election for the SSP, as its vote dropped across Scotland. Keith Baldassara won one of the SSP's best votes of 1,666 – 5.4 per cent – in Glasgow South West and John Aberdein attracted 5.6 per cent in Orkney & Shetland. In total it attracted 43,514 votes (1.9 per cent). In addition, Socialist Labour gained 6,696 votes.

All three leaders could claim some success and admit disappointment. Blair had delivered the first third victory for a Labour government. However, he had suffered a massive loss of public support, mainly to the Liberal Democrats. Howard had improved the position of the Conservatives but did not even achieve the election of as many MPs as Labour's Michael Foot in 1983. Kennedy had once again increased the Liberal Democrats' Commons strength but failed to meet their minimum expectations of raising their 51 MPs at the 2001 election to 70. Blair returned to 10 Downing Street, but a combination of low turnout and a sharp fall in Labour's share of the vote resulted in his party receiving the support of just 22 per cent of British electors, which undermined the moral authority of the government and fuelled calls for electoral reform.

ELECTORAL FRAUD: 'WOULD DISGRACE A BANANA REPUBLIC'

The head of the West Midlands Fraud Squad, Detective Chief Inspector Dave Churchill, called for a change to the electoral system to stamp out polling fraud. This was after Birmingham City Council admitted, earlier in the year, that fraudulent postal voting probably took place during local elections in May 2002. Churchill said the local authority needed to look at the possibility of introducing ultraviolet stamping or ID cards for voters. 'Where matters are referred to the police to investigate it is clear the Representation of the People Act 1983 and 2000 do not carry adequate powers or penalties that are needed to either investigate or prosecute offenders', he added. There were no definite figures as to how widespread election fraud was in Birmingham but councillors on the Review of Electoral Matters Scrutiny Committee agreed it was getting worse.[64] What part did electoral fraud play in the general election of 2005? In June 2004

> hundreds of people clashed in a fierce street battle as inner city election fever erupted into violence in Birmingham. More than 200 campaigners from rival political parties went toe to toe in the Small Heath brawl, sparked by a row over the controversial use of postal votes. The pitched battle between Labour and [Kashmir]

People's Justice Party supporters was ignited by the appearance of a postman with a bag.[65]

Attempts were made to seize blank postal vote forms he was carrying. In February 2005, Muhammed Hussain, admitted to conspiring to defraud local elections in May 2002. Hussain won a seat on Blackburn With Darwen borough council with 1,728 votes and a majority of 685. However, an investigation found that 233 postal votes were fraudulent.[66] In Bristol, in September 2004, John Astley, an ex-Liberal Democrat councillor, pleaded guilty at Exeter Combined Court to 11 counts of forgery, for ballot-rigging purposes, and was jailed for five months. He was already in prison for downloading child pornography from the Internet. In Birmingham, five Labour councillors were found guilty of an electoral fraud that the judge said 'would disgrace a banana republic'. Richard Mawrey, QC, sitting as an election commissioner, criticized the current postal voting system and gave warning that unless changes were made, electoral fraud would continue unabated.[67] Despite such warnings very little was done before the election of 2005. Postal voting fraud had by then been exposed in Hackney, Guildford,[68] Bethnal Green and Golders Green.[69] Parmjit Singh Gill, who represented Leicester South in the last parliament, accused several elderly Asian constituents of putting pressure on Asian voters to apply for postal votes. Gill alleged that the elders would then tell the hapless Asian voter which way to vote. The allegations brought Britain's rising problem of potential electoral fraud right to the heart of its paragon Indian community. 'We are more influenced by the so-called gatekeepers of the community because of our traditional respect for age', Gill said. He admitted at least two thirds of his constituency's minority voters were people of Indian origin.[70] After the election, police forces across the country began investigations into fraud allegations levelled during the general election. Police investigated an incident in St Albans, where canvassers were allegedly able to read postal votes, enabling them to decide which wards to target.[71] In the past there had been electoral fraud in Northern Ireland and rumours about residents of old people's homes being conned into voting in a particular way, but the general view had been that ballots were properly conducted. However, identity theft for the purposes of electoral fraud was easy in Britain as no ID was required when voting. Seasoned campaigners with local knowledge could easily identify many individuals who had no interest in voting and persuade their confrere to impersonate them. Kidded by their own propaganda, losing candidates would be unlikely to question the result. The British were good losers. A worrying picture of the British voting system emerged from the first mission to a British general election by the Organization for Security and Co-operation in Europe (OSCE). The mission found that the electoral roll had multiple entries impostors turned up unchallenged at ballot stations to vote under false identities; and returning officers made up their own rules. Britain was reminded by the OSCE of its obligations under international covenants to provide everyone with a secret ballot. Women and Muslim communities were seen as particularly defenceless against postal vote riggers in Britain.[72]

NOTES

1 Directgov from 10 Downing Street.
2 *Hansard*, House of Commons, 26 February 2003, Column 295. See also George Jones, *Daily Telegraph*, 27 February 2003.
3 *Hansard*, House of Commons, 18 March 2003, Column 798.
4 ibid., column 821.
5 *Guardian*, 27 January 2004.
6 *Daily Telegraph*, 28 April 2005.
7 Robin Cook, *The Point of Departure* (2003), 7.
8 Clare Short, *An Honourable Deception? New Labour, Iraq and the Misuse of Power* (2004), 69–70.
9 Cook, *The Point of Departure*, op. cit., 115.
10 ibid., 116.
11 Stefan Stern, *New Statesman*, 26 July 2004.
12 See Patrick Wintour and Anne Perkins, *Guardian*, 6 May 2005, for a discussion.
13 *The Times*, 8 September 2005.
14 Fraser Nelson, *Scotsman*, 27 May 2004.
15 *Sunday Times*, 18 June 2001.
16 *The Times*, 1 June 2005.
17 *The Times*, 27 April 2005.
18 *The Times*, 26 April 2005.
19 *The Times*, 28 May 2005.
20 *Edgware & Mill Hill Times*, 2 June 2005; *The Times*, 28 May 2005; *The Nation* (Nairobi), 27 May 2005.
21 Alistair Foster, *Evening Standard*, 13 May 2005.
22 *The Times*, 16 June 2005.
23 *Guardian*, 7 March 2005.
24 *The Times*, 17 July 2004, 28 September 2005.
25 *The Times*, 22 June 2005.
26 *Independent*, 10 May 2004.
27 Geraldine Smith, MP for Morcambe & Lunesdale.
28 *Independent*, 12 October 2005.
29 *The Times*, 16 February 2005.
30 *Birmingham Post*, 31 January 2005.
31 BBC News UK edition, 7 February 2005.
32 *The Times*, 24 August 2005.
33 *Sunday Times*, 22 February 2004.
34 Jackie Ashley and Michael White, *Guardian*, 14 March 2005.
35 Pat Hewitt, *New Statesman*, 17 December 2001.
36 BBC, Gordon Brown in Africa, Tour Diary, BBC News World edition, 18 January 2005.
37 *The Times*, 15 June 2005.
38 *Guardian*, 13 January 2005.
39 *Guardian*, 3 December 2004.
40 *The Times*, 26 July 2005.

41 *The Times*, 15 August 2005.
42 BBC, 25 November 2004.
43 *Sunday Times*, 27 March 2005.
44 All figures published by DfES.
45 Professor Anthony King, *Daily Telegraph*, 26 May 2004.
46 *Independent*, 18 January 2005.
47 *The Times*, 11 May 2005. *The Times*, 28 September 2005, reported that the school had won a reprieve. The Education Minister said that it had made enough progress to avoid being struck off.
48 *Independent*, 12 February 2004.
49 *The Universe*, 24 October 2002. *The Times* reported, 24 September 2005, 'A priest has been jailed for sexually abusing ten boys at Britain's leading Catholic public school, 18 years after his offending first came to light. Gregory Caroll, 66, a monk at Ampleforth Abbey, North Yorkshire, was sentenced to four years in prison after admitting 14 offences of indecent assault against boys aged under 15 between 1980 and 1987.'
50 *The Times*, 15 August 2005.
51 *Daily Telegraph*, 9 April 2005.
52 National Centre for Social Research, April 2005.
53 Terry Kirby, *Independent*, 25 September 2004 .
54 *Observer*, 20 February 2005.
55 *Guardian*, 24 August 2005.
56 *The Salvation Army*, 8 April 2005.
57 *Observer*, 10 April 2005.
58 *Alcohol Alert*.
59 *Observer*, 20 February 2005; *The Times*, 27 July 2005.
60 David Smith, *Observer*, 15 May 2005.
61 *The Times*, 4 August 2005.
62 *Eastern Eye*, 13 May 2005.
63 *Jewish Chronicle*, 13 May 2005.
64 Richard Warburton, *Birmingham Post*, 29 October 2002.
65 *Evening Mail*, 8 June 2004.
66 *Guardian*, 28 February 2005.
67 *The Times*, 8 April 2005.
68 *The Times*, 6 April 2005.
69 *Sunday Times*, 1 May 2005.
70 *Times of India*, 19 April 2005.
71 *Observer*, 8 May 2005.
72 *The Times*, 6 August, 2005.

14

BLAIR'S THIRD TERM

WOMEN IN THE ECONOMY AND POLITICS

By 2005, financial and business services accounted for about one in five jobs in the UK, compared with about one in ten in 1981. This sector saw the largest increase in jobs between 1981 and 2001, part of the postwar growth in the service industries and the decline in manufacturing. In 1985, one in three jobs held by men was in manufacturing. By 2001, this had fallen to about one in five. The proportion of female workers in this sector dropped from nearly one in five to under one in ten. Other changes in Britain's labour force over the two decades to 2005 included a marked increase in the number of jobs performed by women. In 1981, men filled 3.2 million more jobs than women. By 2005, the numbers were almost equal, with men performing 12.8 million jobs and women 12.7 million, although almost half of these were part time. But men and women still followed very different career paths. About a quarter of female employees did administrative or secretarial work, while men were most likely to be managers, senior officials or in skilled trades. Similar proportions of men and women worked in 'associate professional and technical' occupations – computer programmers, technicians and nurses, for example – while one in eight performed low-skilled jobs, such as those in farming, construction, hotels and restaurants. Men were still more likely than women to be self-employed – 73 per cent of the 3 million self-employed people in spring 2001 were male. Around a fifth of all self-employed people worked in construction, with similar proportions in sales and distribution, hotels and restaurants; and in banking, finance and insurance. People from certain ethnic groups were more likely to be self-employed than others, with whites trailing the ethnic minorities.[1] Women still earned less than men. Women earned an average of just over three quarters the salary of their male colleagues.[2] It was women voters who delivered a comfortable majority for Tony Blair. That is the clear message from a detailed analysis of nearly 18,000 MORI interviewees weighted to the final result. Thirty-eight per cent of those women who voted gave their support to Labour, 32 per cent to the Conservatives and 22 per cent to the Liberal Democrats. By comparison, men voted 34 per cent each for Labour and Conservatives and 23 per cent for the Liberal Democrats. What was surprising was that after so many years of having the vote, since 1928 on a par with men, more women were not elected to the Commons. According to the Interparliamentary Union, only 18.1 per cent of the British MPs elected in 2001 were women. Sweden was at the top of its list with 45.3 per cent elected in 2002. But there was Spain, always considered rather conservative, where 36 per cent of the Cortes elected, in 2004, were women. In Argentina, it was 33.7 per cent of the Parliament elected in 2001, and in conservative Switzerland it was 25 per cent. In New Zealand, where women were the first to get the vote in 1893 but were only able to get the first woman elected in 1933, women MPs made up 28 per cent of Parliament in 2002. Many other countries were ahead of Britain. Blair could still claim, however, that he had given more women office than in any previous government in Britain. Undoubtedly, one of his most remarkable, and controversial, appointments was Ruth Kelly. Kelly was born in Northern Ireland and attended the fee-paying Sutton High School, followed by Westminster School for A-levels. She went on to Queen's College, University of Oxford, and then the London School of Economics. She was an economics writer for the *Guardian* from 1990, before joining the Bank of England in 1994. She was married with four children. In the reshuffle following the resignation of David Blunkett (15 December 2004), Kelly entered the Cabinet as Secretary of State for Education and Skills. She became the youngest woman ever to sit in the Cabinet. Her rapid rise was all the more remarkable because she had four babies between 1997 and 2005. This provoked jealousy amongst other so-called 'Blair's Babes', many of whom had put their family life on hold to concentrate on their political careers. She believed that balancing the care of her family with her position in government actually helped her to see the 'bigger picture'. In 2005, three of her four children were old enough to start school and were already in the state system in the London borough of Tower Hamlets.[3] Members of the scientific community expressed concern that Kelly's views, as a practising Catholic, could influence government policy on stem cell research.

Kelly was one of 5 women to 20 men in the Cabinet, in 2005. Margaret Beckett, Secretary of State for the Environment, being the most senior. In the other 'old' EU countries the situation was as follows: Austria, 6 women, 6 men; Belgium, 4 women, 17 men; Denmark, 5 women, 14 men; Finland, 8 women, 11 men; France, 9 women, 34 men; Greece, 2 women, 44 men; Ireland, 3 women, 12 men; Italy, 2 women, 25 men; Germany, 6 women, 9 men; Luxembourg, 3 women, 12 men; Netherlands, 5 women, 11 men; Portugal, 2 women, 15 men; Sweden, 11 women, 11 men; Spain, 8 women, 9 men.

NHS: 'PRIVATIZATION BY STEALTH', BMA

Traditionally, the NHS had been one of Labour's strong points. Many promises were made about its improvement. Indeed, more money was invested under Blair than had been invested for some time. However, controversy raged about Blair's 'reforms' of the NHS. One flagship policy was foundation hospitals, which Alan Milburn, then health minister, described as 'true to our traditions of solidarity, community and fairness'. The Labour Party Chairman, Ian McCartney, even called this policy left-wing. But this did not satisfy Labour stalwarts. One hundred and thirty backbench Labour MPs signed a motion opposing the legislation on foundation hospitals because of fears about privatization, an anxiety echoed by many outside Parliament, including the British Medical Association (BMA) and the Royal College of Nursing. As the *Guardian* (7 May 2003) explained,

> Under the proposed legislation NHS hospital trusts and private sector bodies can apply to become 'public benefit corporations' or foundation trusts – a new form of mutual company that does not have shareholders on the board. However, this is simply a fig leaf for privatization below board level. The bill allows any private sector body – from Bupa to Boots – to apply to be a foundation trust and run NHS services. Furthermore, the board can contract out clinical services directly to the private sector – in which case shareholders of those private companies will make a claim on scarce NHS resources.

Another cause for concern was the privatization of GPs' surgeries. The BMA criticized the growing trend of more GP practices across the UK being run by the private sector, believing the development reflected the determination of the government to privatize the health service. The Deputy Chairman of the BMA's GP committee, Laurence Buckman, commented, 'GPs don't like this. This is privatization by stealth.'[4] In a damning report, the Audit Commission, in October 2005, said the new funding method, where money follows the patient, was destabilizing the NHS and fuelling a financial crisis. Instead of increasing choice, it could have the opposite effect, with services going to the wall unless the payment system was radically reformed. It cautioned that critical services essential to support emergency admissions could close down in some hospitals because of the failure to attract patient referrals. NHS wards, departments and even entire hospitals could be forced to close under these health reforms designed to extend patient choice, the government was warned.

In another blow to the government, fears about hospital hygiene deepened when official figures, published in August 2005, revealed that cases of a potentially lethal infection had soared. According to the Department of

Health, in 2004, in England there were 44,488 cases of *Clostridium difficile*, which causes severe diarrhoea and can prove fatal. In the early 1990s, the total was around 1,000 a year. The previous figures showed that there had been 35,536 cases in England, Wales and Northern Ireland in 2003.[5] UK levels of MRSA bloodstream infections were amongst the highest in Europe, according to the Department of Health.[6] Good news for the NHS was the success in the battle against breast cancer. Improvements in survival meant that almost two thirds of women given a diagnosis of breast cancer, in 2005, were likely to survive for at least 20 years.

LABOUR 'FAILS TO PLUG GAP BETWEEN RICH AND POOR'

Blair's plan to reduce inequality was dealt a blow as research showed that the income gap between rich and poor had widened significantly under Labour. Data from the Office for National Statistics showed that the incomes of the best and worst off had risen by about a fifth between 1995 and 2003. However, that translated into a weekly rise of £119 for the richest 10 per cent, and only £28 for the poorest. The report, *Focus on Social Inequalities*, showed that slow progress had been made to increase the educational achievements of 16-year-olds under Labour. In 2002, 77 per cent of children with parents in higher professional occupations gained five or more top grades at GCSE. This was more than double the 32 per cent achieved by children with parents in 'routine occupations'. While that gap had narrowed to 45 percentage points from 49 in 1998, it was still greater than the 44-point gap achieved by the Conservative Government in 1992. The ONS said: 'People in the United Kingdom are better off than in the past across a range of measures but the benefits are not spread equally. Household income and educational attainment have improved overall but the gaps remain large.'[7] The prosperity, which Gordon Brown was so proud of, was, to a considerable degree, based on high consumer indebtedness, cheap imports especially from China, and government borrowing partly through the public–private partnership schemes. Britain's foreign trade was not looking so good. The current account deficit widened to £5.8 billion (equivalent to 2 per cent of GDP) in the first quarter of 2005. In 2004 as a whole, the UK had a current account deficit of £22.1 billion with EU countries. In contrast, the UK had a deficit of only £0.9 billion with non-EU countries in 2004, although this compared with a £2.1 billion surplus in 2003.[8]

EU: MUST 'RESHAPE AND MODERNIZE'?

On 29 May 2005 a referendum was held in France to decide whether the country should ratify the proposed Constitution of the European Union (EU). Despite the public opinion polls showing a majority against the

Constitution, it was a dramatic campaign with President Jacques Chirac urging his fellow citizens to vote in favour. Earlier, on 20 February 2005, a referendum was held in Spain, where both main parties had campaigned for ratification; the result was a landslide victory for the 'Yes' campaign, with 77 per cent of voters in favour. Turnout, however, was only 42 per cent of the electorate – the lowest in any election since the restoration of democracy in the 1970s. Would the French follow the Spanish and prove the pollsters wrong? They did not. As expected, the result was a victory for the 'No' campaign, with 55 per cent of voters rejecting the treaty on a turnout of 69 per cent. Many French voters were voting against the President rather than against EU, but it was a blow to the pro-Europeans all over the EU as France was a founder member and one of the EU's largest states.

The treaty establishing a constitution for Europe was signed in a ceremony at Rome on 29 October 2004, as an international treaty designed to create a constitution for the EU. Basically, the aim of the treaty was to replace the overlapping set of existing treaties that comprised the EU's current constitutional arrangements, and to streamline decision-making in this expanding organization. However, before it could enter into force, it had to be ratified by all 25 member states of the EU. It was left open to the individual states how they ratified the treaty. By the middle of 2005, Lithuania, Hungary, Slovenia, Italy, Greece, Slovakia, Austria, Latvia, Cyprus and Malta had already completed parliamentary ratification of the treaty with overwhelming majorities. In Germany, parliament had approved ratification, but this was subject to a challenge in the Constitutional Court and the president had not signed off the legislation. In addition, the European Parliament had also approved the treaty (in a symbolic rather than a binding vote). Ten states decided to hold referenda on the treaty and four had taken place. The Netherlands, a founder member, had joined France in rejecting it, while Luxembourg, also a founder member, had joined Spain in voting in favour on 10 July 2005. Dutch voters registered a clear 'No' in a vote on 1 June 2005 with 61.6 per cent rejecting the proposed constitution on a turnout of 62 per cent. It was the Netherlands' first ever referendum. All the main parties were in favour of a 'Yes' vote, as were the trade unions and most newspapers. Opposition to immigration, the proposed entry of Turkey to the EU and a feeling that the euro had fuelled inflation were thought to have caused this upset. Such views were not confined to the Netherlands. In addition, economic liberals complained about bureaucracy, Socialists about its pro-capitalist slant, and Christians about its lack of mention of Christianity. Belgium, Czech Republic, Denmark, Estonia, Finland, Ireland, Poland, Portugal and Sweden had still to decide. After the French 'No' vote, some EU countries confirmed their intention to abandon or postpone referenda on ratification, including the UK, where Foreign Secretary Jack Straw said, on 5 June, there was 'no point' in planning a referendum following the decisions in France and the Netherlands. Straw had a career of Euro-scepticism behind him.

In two strongly worded speeches, the Prime Minister and the Chancellor of the Exchequer both put forward the case for a more economically liberal Europe, with an EU budget targeted towards jobs and growth rather than 'outmoded' agricultural subsidies. Speaking at the Mansion House (22 June 2005) to business leaders, Gordon Brown said the EU must reform inefficient state aids, especially in farming. It must break out of the stand off in trade with the one other advanced global power, North America. With 20 million unemployed, the EU needed to 'reshape and modernize the European social model'. All this was necessary to meet the challenge of globalization. He also concluded that the referendum results in France and the Netherlands suggested 'identities have remained rooted in the nation state – and that familiar national, cultural and political attachments are important'. He called for 'pro-European realism', because 'the old assumptions about feder-alism do not match the realities of our time, now more than ever we need a pro-European realism that starts from the founding case for the European Union, the benefits of co-operation among nation states for peace and pros-perity, but strengthened by the insistence that Europe looks outwards as a Global Europe'. Brown reminded his audience that,

> Two decades ago just 10 per cent of manufacturing exports came from developing countries. Soon it will be 50 per cent. China's wage costs are still just 5 per cent of those of the European Union. But we are not simply competing in low skilled, low wage mass production manufacturing. With 4 million graduates a year from China's and India's universities, we are now competing with Asia on high tech, high skilled, high value added goods too.

Addressing the European Parliament a day later, Tony Blair warned that the EU would fail on a 'grand, strategic scale' unless it embraced the economic reform necessary to face up to the challenges of globalization. Stressing that he remained a 'passionate pro-European', the Prime Minister called for a four-pronged modernization of the EU: an update of its social model to compete with China's and India's emerging economies; a revamp of its budget to reduce the level of agricultural subsidies; an increase of the pace of the Lisbon agenda for labour market reform; and a new 'macro-economic framework' to bolster the performance of the single currency. Although initially greeted with a few heckles, the speech ultimately received healthy applause from MEPs. In a move that chimed with the British case for reform of the agricultural sector, the European Commission unveiled plans for an overhaul of sugar policy within the EU, which had been untouched for 40 years and had led to prices becoming inflated to three times their true level on the world market. The plans would mean EU grants to European sugar farmers being cut back by 40 per cent to cut the link between production and subsidies. Some developing countries that benefited from the artificially high price of sugar when selling their product within the EU were lukewarm on the plans. With several strong Euro-sceptics in his Cabinet, Blair had never made the case for Europe or the euro. The events of 2005 led to demoralization in the pro-EU camp. The cross-party Britain in Europe, founded by Blair, Kenneth Clarke and Charles Kennedy, was 'wound up' at the end of July 2005.

CHINA: THE NEW MECCA, 'EXCITING OPPORTUNITIES'

Early in July 2005, the first Landwind vehicles, manufactured by the Chinese Jiangling car company, which was 30 per cent owned by Ford, were unloaded at Antwerp. In a sign of the competition this presaged for an already crowded market, all 200 vehicles had already been sold at almost half the price of rival models by better known European, American, Japanese and Korean brands. Honda Motor Co., Japan's third largest car manufacturer, started exporting compact cars from a plant in southern China to Europe on 28 June 2005. The Chinese cars came with growing concern about the rising economic power of the country.[9] This seemed to be emphasized when Rover, once the pride and joy of the British motor industry, collapsed and then was bought by a Chinese company, another Chinese company having already bought the design side of the company. Most of Rover's plant looked like being moved to China to take advantage of much lower Chinese wage costs. A decade earlier, China's exports were mostly low-end products including toys, electrical goods and textiles. In the early 1980s, China was one of the world's poorest countries. By 2005, it was overtaking the UK to become the world's fourth biggest money economy. The pace of this transformation was almost entirely because of exports of manufactured goods. In turn, China was becoming a big customer for European and American aircraft and Japanese machine tools. China joined the World Trade Organization to secure access to its fast-growing markets, enabling producers there to invest in new factories and processes with confidence. The West wanted China in the organization to secure reciprocal access to its growing markets for entertainment and insurance and to stop China undermining trade by allowing patents and brands to be pirated.[10] Although the US led the world in R&D spending, in 2003, according to the American Association for the Advance of Science (5 August 2005), China moved to third place: 'China has increased its R&D investments dramatically in recent years and is now the 3rd largest investor in R&D (adjusted for purchasing power), behind only Japan and the U.S.' In 1999, in terms of R&D research staff per 1,000 population, the

US led the way with 42, followed by Japan 52, Germany 31, France 27 and UK 27.[11]

In late 1978 the Chinese leadership began moving the economy from a sluggish, inefficient, Soviet-style centrally planned economy to a more market-oriented system. Whereas the system operated within a political framework of strict Communist control, the economic influence of non-state organizations and individual citizens was steadily increasing. Measured on a purchasing power parity (PPP) basis, China, in 2004, stood as the second largest economy in the world after the US, although in per capita terms it remained poor. China benefited from a huge expansion in computer Internet use, with 94 million users at the end of 2004. Foreign investment remained a strong element in China's remarkable economic growth. Shortages of electric power and raw materials remained a problem. According to the CIA (14 July 2005), 'In its rivalry with India as an economic power, China has a lead in the absorption of technology, the rising prominence in world trade, and the alleviation of poverty; India has one important advantage in its relative mastery of the English language, but the number of competent Chinese English-speakers is growing rapidly.' Exports from China leapt during 2004 as it continued to show breakneck growth. The spurt put China's trade surplus at a six-year high. It led to increased pressure on China to relax the peg joining its currency, the yuan, with the weakening dollar. China's exporting success made the trade deficit of the United States soar even further and made trade with China a sensitive political issue in Washington. The peg keeping the yuan around 8.30 to the dollar was blamed by US lawmakers for job losses at home.[12] However, to most British, European and US consumers low Chinese prices were a blessing. Made-in-China products helped keep inflation at bay for them.[13] There were calls for China to revalue the yuan. The idea was to make China's products more expensive, which in turn would curb exports. But, as one commentator put it,

> If only it were that simple. China's competitiveness is so strong that it could easily compensate for a moderate rise in the currency. The supply of $100-a-month Chinese labor is virtually inexhaustible. And $50 billion in annual foreign investment is pouring into China, much of it going to build state-of-the-art factories for U.S., Japanese, and European multinationals.[14]

The Chinese authorities bowed to years of international pressure on 21 July 2005 and made a modest revaluation of the yuan, raising the currency by 2 per cent from 8.3 to 8.11 against the dollar. This was hailed as a great event in world economic history. Britain's Foreign Office Trade Minister, Ian Pearson, on a visit to China that month talked of the 'exciting opportunities for British businesses'. Earlier, it was revealed that one of these 'exciting opportunities' was arms sales to China. As the controversy continued over the EU's plans to lift its arms embargo on China, the UK Government's quarterly report on arms exports indicated that even with the embargo in place, sales of UK military equipment to China had increased significantly – doubling in two years. The UK authorized the export of rising quantities of military equipment to China. These exports rose from £50 million in 2002, to £76 million in 2003, to £101 million during 2004. This meant that China became the UK's fifth largest arms export market in 2004 (up from eighth position in 2003).[15] Who were the others? Figures released by the government showed that, in 2004, Britain exported arms worth nearly £1.4 billion, compared with £992 million in 2003. Saudi Arabia, the Gulf state of Oman, India and South Africa were among the biggest markets. The government's latest annual report on arms exports also revealed that Iraq was by far the largest market for British small arms and weapons in 2004. The UK provided Iraq with 21,733 weapons, Saudi Arabia with 2,151, and Kenya with 715. Whitehall officials said Iraq was a special case, since Britain was helping to rebuild its security forces. But critics of the arms trade questioned British military exports to Saudi Arabia and Kenya on the grounds that they were used for internal repression.[16]

'VIOLENT CRIME CONTINUING TO SPIRAL OUT OF CONTROL'

Violent assaults quadrupled under Blair between 1997 and 2005 and hit the one-million-a-year mark for the first time, recorded crime figures for England and Wales showed. The continuing increase in violent offences, many of them fuelled by alcohol, marred a fall in overall crime in the year to the end of March 2005. While falls in burglaries and vehicle thefts were helping to drive down overall crime levels, violent crime, particularly on the streets on Friday and Saturday nights, proved as resilient as ever. Rather complacently, Home Office officials claimed that the fall in overall crime was 'historically unprecedented' and that the 20 per cent drop in household burglaries in 2004 was the biggest since 1915. The increase in drink-fuelled violence brought a demand from Mark Oaten, the Liberal Democrats' home affairs spokesman, to halt the introduction of relaxed licensing laws. David Davis, the Shadow Home Secretary, agreed, 'With violent crime continuing to spiral out of control, it beggars belief that the Government's only response is to unleash 24-hour drinking on our town and city centres.' Hazel Blears, the Police Minister, would promise only that the Government would keep the changes to the licensing laws under review. She believed more people were reporting violent crime than in the past thus pushing up the figures. Surely this could not explain the increases in gun crime? Gun crimes rose by 6 per cent to just under 11,000, and

73 people were killed by guns in the year – five more than in the previous year. The annual crime figures revealed that there were 1,035,000 incidents of violence – they did not include sexual offences or robbery – recorded by police in England and Wales in 2004–05. The figure was an 8 per cent increase on the previous year and more than four times the 251,000 when Labour came to power in 1997. When the 60,946 sexual offences are taken into account, there were 1.1 million violent crimes. Sexual offences rose by 17 per cent, although almost all the increase was said to be the result of categorizing indecent exposure as a sex crime. More serious violent crime, including murder, causing death by dangerous driving and serious wounding, rose by 3 per cent to 45,181. Murders in England and Wales increased from 853 to 859, and the number of threats, or conspiracy to murder, rose to 23,600 compared with 9,300 in 1997. The number of harassment offences, which are considered a violent crime, soared by 28 per cent to reach 198,000. Total recorded crime fell 6 per cent to 5.6 million offences, including a 20 per cent fall in household burglaries to 321,000 and a 17 per cent fall in vehicle crime to 738,000. Both falls were due to greater security measures in homes and cars. The crime figures show that the police detection rate rose by three percentage points to 26 per cent. But when fixed penalty notices and formal warnings for possessing cannabis are taken into account, detection rates had not risen. Only 34 per cent of sex offences were detected by police – a fall of five points in a year. White collar crimes did not seem to be diminishing. Fraud of all kinds, sophisticated City fraud, identity fraud, credit card fraud, email fraud, benefit fraud were all in full swing! The separate British Crime Survey (BCS) attempts to measure the amount of crime in England and Wales. This includes crimes which may not have been reported to the police, or recorded by them. It thus provides an important alternative to police recorded crime statistics. The BCS showed overall crime falling by 7 per cent and violent crime by 11 per cent. It estimated there were 10.8 million crimes in the year compared with 5.2 million recorded offences. But the survey did not include crimes against under-16s and businesses. Home Office officials said the fact that the crime survey showed violent crime falling while police recorded it rising was a result of changes to police counting methods and police operations targeting street disorder.[17] Perhaps remarkably, crimes against commercial bodies, including shops, are excluded from the British Crime Survey. An estimate published in July 2005 disclosed that retailers suffered 20.8 million incidents in 2002, the most recent figures available, with manufacturers bearing a further 552,000. They included 11.5 million thefts by customers, 1.8 million assaults or threats, 507,000 vandalism attacks, 294,000 burglaries or attempted burglaries and 133,000 robberies. Adding these to the Home Office's estimate of 12.2 million offences committed against adults and children in 2003–04 gives a grand total of 31,783,000 crimes, after a small overlap is taken into account.[18] Despite many new initiatives from 1997, Blair's team had not brought

crime under control. Glasgow remained the murder capital of Europe but in Greater Manchester resided Britain's most prolific serial killer. This was Nottingham-born Dr Harold Shipman who, addicted to killing, is thought to have murdered hundreds of his patients. Convicted in 2000 of murdering 15, he hanged himself in prison in 2004 still denying any guilt. Previously Peter Sutcliffe, the 'Yorkshire Ripper', convicted in 1981 of the murders of thirteen women and attacks on seven more, was Britain's worst serial killer. Equally horrific were the crimes of the Wests of Gloucester. Fred hanged himself in prison in 1995, awaiting trial for 12 murders. His wife, Rose, was subsequently convicted of 10 murders.

SEN. KENNEDY: 'IRA'S ONGOING CRIMINAL ACTIVITY'

When Sinn Fein and the DUP became the largest parties of the two communities, it was clear (because of the dual majority required by the Good Friday Agreement) that no deal could be made without the support of both parties. They nearly reached a deal in November 2004, but the DUP's insistence on photographic evidence of the decommissioning of weapons, as had been demanded by Revd Dr Ian Paisley, meant the failure of the arrangement. The robbery of £26.5 million from the Northern Bank in Belfast in December 2004, in which two staff members were forced to participate under threat that their families would be killed if they refused, further damaged chances of a deal, as Northern Ireland Chief Constable Hugh Orde blamed the IRA. This assessment was echoed by the Republic's Garda (Police) Commissioner, Noel Conroy. The British and Irish governments, and all political parties except Sinn Fein itself, accepted this assessment. In January 2005, Sinn Fein leader Gerry Adams met separately with Blair and Irish Prime Minister Bertie Aherne. Both told him that the IRA was involved and warned that the IRA's actions could scupper hopes of a re-establishment of the power-sharing government. On 10 February 2005, the Independent Monitoring Commission reported that it firmly supported the Police Service of Northern Ireland and Garda assessments that the (Provisional) IRA was responsible for the Northern Bank robbery and that certain senior members of Sinn Fein were also senior members of the IRA and would have had knowledge of and given approval to the carrying out of the robbery. It recommended further financial sanctions against Sinn Fein Members of the Northern Ireland Assembly. The British Government responded by saying it would ask the Commons to vote to withdraw the parliamentary allowances of the four Sinn Fein MPs elected in 2001. Aherne called Sinn Fein and the IRA 'both sides of the same coin'. The isolation of Sinn Fein was shown in February 2005 when the Republic's parliament passed a motion condemning the party's involvement in illegal activity.

Adams came under heavy fire at home and abroad after the IRA's murder of Robert McCartney, in a bar-room brawl. IRA leaders sparked further outrage with a mafia-like offer to kill those of its members who had fatally beaten McCartney – a cold-blooded offer of vigilante justice. The family of the dead man, though formerly Sinn Fein voters themselves, urged witnesses to the crime to contact the police, even if threatened by the IRA. The IRA's role in McCartney's murder stirred worldwide outrage, threatening Northern Ireland's fragile peace process. In the US, Senator Kennedy decided to decline to meet Adams, 'given the IRA's ongoing criminal activity and contempt for the rule of law', Kennedy's spokeswoman said. The White House, citing IRA violence, cancelled its invitation to Adams and other parties in Northern Ireland to attend its annual St Patrick's Day ceremonies. Kennedy, who lobbied the Clinton administration to grant Adams a visa to jump-start the peace process, decided to take a harder line against Sinn Fein and the IRA.[19] McCartney's sisters were honoured at the White House. Kennedy and congressional leaders also met them. Senators Kennedy and Hillary Clinton introduced a motion into the US Senate calling on Sinn Fein to break off links with the IRA.

In May, the IRA faced fresh questions about its commitment to the peace process after the Independent Monitoring Commission said that it was still involved in paramilitary and criminal activity, including the recruitment and training of new members. The Commission recorded a continuing downward trend in IRA activity but concluded that the organization remained active in a number of areas, including bank robberies, assaults, smuggling and money-laundering. Other illegal organizations continued to pose a threat, on both the republican and loyalist sides. The report was a slap in the face for Gerry Adams, who announced in April that he had appealed to the IRA to use only peaceful and democratic means. Criticizing the IRA's role in the McCartney murder, the Commission said it did not believe the central IRA leadership sanctioned it in advance but added that those concerned 'may have believed they were acting at the direction of a local senior IRA member at the scene'. The IRA had later protected its members and obstructed justice, the report said. The Commission also reported that major loyalist groups, such as the Ulster Defence Association and Loyalist Volunteer Force, remained deeply immersed in the drugs trade. The UDA continued to be involved in other organized crime including robberies.[20] The IRA announced on 28 July 2005 that it was ending its 35-year campaign of violence. IRA units were told to dump their weapons and pursue their objectives through democratic and peaceful means. The move was welcomed in Belfast, London, Dublin and Washington. Ian Paisley, the Democratic Unionist leader, said that the IRA would be judged 'over the next months and years on its behaviour and activity'. Catherine McCartney, a sister of murder victim Robert McCartney, said that it was not enough. 'The IRA has not spelled out where it stands on those within its ranks who indulge in criminal activity. It tells them they have to stop it but it does not say what happens if they don't stop it.'[21] Of course, the criminal activities of the paramilitaries went on, activities which had nothing to do with any political cause. As the *Belfast Telegraph* (24 July 2005) reported, loyalist and republican terrorists were 'raking a fortune selling copies of Hollywood's latest blockbusters – often before their Northern Ireland releases'. The explosion in pirate movie sales in the province was 'costing jobs on the ground, in the distribution and retail sectors of the industry, while fat cat gangsters are living it up on the massive illegal profits'. Northern Ireland Office Minister Ian Pearson said, 'Paramilitary gangs carry out 80 per cent of the intellectual property crime in Northern Ireland, which serves to emphasize the sinister nature of this particular form of criminality.' What was it all worth? Ronan McGreevy, writing in the *Irish Post* (6 August 2005), thought the IRA's campaign was based on a flawed analysis that it could bomb its way to a united Ireland. 'The problem for them is that the very tactic the IRA used in the North has delayed, not hastened, the day of Irish unity. It alienated moderate Nationalists and entrenched the paranoia of Unionists probably for generations . . . The IRA took the pious dream of a united Ireland and turned it into a bloody nightmare. That, ultimately, will be its legacy.' On 26 September, Canadian General John de Chastelain, the head of the arms decommissioning body, announced that the IRA had 'decommissioned' its entire arsenal. Two clergymen who witnessed the work of putting IRA arms 'beyond use' readily endorsed this announcement. The Canadian said, 'We are satisfied that the arms decommissioned represent the totality of the IRA's arsenal.' Unionists remained sceptical.

UGLY COUSINS: TSUNAMI AND KATRINA

On 26 December 2004, when people in Britain and elsewhere were still enjoying Christmas, news came of the deadliest tsunami, the term was largely unkown, in recorded history. The giant wave killed over 310,000 people over an area ranging from the immediate vicinity of the quake in Indonesia, Thailand and the north-western coast of Malaysia to thousands of kilometres away in Bangladesh, India, Sri Lanka, the Maldives and even as far as Somalia, Kenya and Tanzania in eastern Africa. The disaster prompted a huge worldwide effort to help victims of the tragedy, with hundreds of millions of dollars being raised for disaster relief. The help from governments, charities and individuals was influenced by the television footage night after night, and by the fact that thousands of European and Australian tourists died, and many others lived to tell the tale. It once again pricked the conscience of the West, raising awareness of the squalid living conditions of the majority of the world's population. There was perhaps more surprise and less reaction when hurricane Katrina hit just north of Miami, Florida, on 25 August 2005, then again on 29 August along the central Gulf Coast near New Orleans, Louisiana. Its storm surge soon breached the levee system that protected New Orleans from Lake Pontchartrain and the Mississippi River. Most of the city was subsequently flooded mainly by water from the lake. This and other major damage to the coastal regions of Louisiana, Mississippi and Alabama made Katrina the most destructive and costliest natural disaster in the history of the United States covering an area almost as the size of Britain and killing about 1,500 people. As they watched the teaming mass of refugees, mainly black, struggling to survive in filthy conditions, most Europeans, and many Americans, could not understand how this could happen in the world's most powerful nation. There was fear that disease would spread and that the US economy would be injured by the loss of oil-refining facilities. The Bush administration was condemned as, at best, incompetent and, at worst, racist. In between the two disasters another event aimed to touch the peoples of the developed world.

G8: 'WHO IS THIS BEAUTIFUL WOMAN?'

In the greatest comeback gig ever seen, on 2 July 2005, the world once again found a voice for the poor of Africa. In Hyde Park, Sir Elton John, the 58-year-old rocker, and many old and young pop celebrities attempted to entertain and educate their fans in London and those watching around the world about poverty in Africa. Concerts on four continents demanded help from the world's leaders for Africa's destitute masses. They were held on 2 July in Berlin, Chiba (Japan), Johannesburg, Moscow, Paris, Philadelphia, Rome and Barrie (outside Toronto) with TV link-ups. They recalled the Live Aid concerts of 1985 in Wembley Stadium, London, and JFK Stadium, Philadelphia, organized by Bob Geldof, the Irish pop star, Midge Ure, the Scottish rock-and-roll guitarist, singer and songwriter, and Harvey Goldsmith, the music promoter, to raise funds for famine relief in Ethiopia. The event, with some acts performing at other venues such as Sydney and Moscow, was one of the largest satellite link-ups and TV broadcasts of all time – an estimated 1.5 billion viewers in 100 countries watched the live broadcast. In 2005, the concerts were influenced by the terrible famine in parts of Kenya, Malawi, Lesotho, Mozambique, Swaziland, Sudan, Zambia and Zimbabwe. In a break between acts, 'a shaggy-haired prophet emerged from the jungle of giant amplifiers. Dressed all in white with a black cap, Mahatma Geldof shuffled forward. 'Hello,' he said. 'Thanks for coming. It would have been a bit crap if nobody had showed up.'[22] Geldof was there to address not so much the 200,000 fans in the audience, or the 200,000 more who were marching in Scotland. He had in his sights the politicians due to get together at the G8 summit in the plush Gleneagles hotel, near St Andrews. Geldof had Bill Gates, the founder of Microsoft, 'one of the great businessmen of our time and certainly the greatest philanthropist of our age', on hand to support his plea. Kofi Annan, UN Secretary General, joined the likes of Ricky *The Office* Gervais, Mariah Carey, Annie Lennox, Sir Paul McCartney, Madonna, Sting, Robbie Williams, U2 and many others in the call to 'Cancel the debt, Double the aid and Scrap the trade tariffs.' As images of wretched starving children filled the screen Geldof reminded his fans that every three seconds some child died in Africa. Rather dramatically, he then ushered onto the stage a striking black figure. 'Who is this beautiful woman?' he asked. She had 10 minutes to live 20 years ago. 'Because we did a concert, because we did that, last week she did her agricultural exams at her school in the northern Ethiopian highlands. Don't let them tell you this doesn't work.' Birhan Woldu, 24, had survived the famine of 20 years before, thanks to Live Aid. She said simply, 'Hello from Africa, we love you very much.'[23] Critics said the millionaire rock stars would have made greater contributions by donating parts of their personal fortunes. Indeed as some performers had been out of the public eye for some time, their appearances were seen by some as a way of getting back into the limelight. However, Live 8 organizers pointed out that, unlike Live Aid, the 2005 concerts were not intended to raise money, but awareness and political pressure. Another issue was that of getting aid to the people in poverty rather than handing it over to the corrupt governing elites of the countries concerned.

On the same day as the main concerts, 2 July, the 'march against poverty' in Edinburgh started with an estimated 200,000 people involved. It was a mainly peaceful event with participants from a wide range of political, cultural and religious backgrounds under the banner of Make Poverty History. It was believed to have been the largest demonstration in the history of Edinburgh. The final Live 8 concert was held in Edinburgh on 6 July 2005 and went by the name *Edinburgh 50,000 – The Final Push*. It featured performances from some of the artists from the other concerts, and was the closest of the eleven to the actual location of the G8 summit, at Gleneagles, Scotland. On 8 July the G8 leaders agreed a $50bn aid package for Africa. No one thought this was the end of the story. Some, including Geldof, thought it was the end of the beginning. Only weeks after the leaders of the G8 countries – Britain, Canada, France, Germany, Italy, Japan, Russia and the US – met in Scotland pledging to make poverty a thing of the past, the news media began to reveal that a catastrophic famine was unfolding in Niger. On environmental issues, the G8 mouthed platitudes, 'We face serious and linked challenges in tackling climate change, promoting clean energy and achieving sustainable development globally.'

TERRORISM: 'SERIOUS AND SUSTAINED THREAT'

Eliza Manningham-Buller, Director-General of the Security Service (MI5) warned on 8 November 2004 that Britain faced 'a serious and sustained threat of terrorist attacks against UK interests at home and abroad, including against the business community. There might be major attacks like Madrid earlier this year. They might be on a smaller scale. The terrorists are inventive, adaptable and patient; their planning includes a wide range of methods to attack us.' This was probably regarded by many who heard her as an effort to get more funds for her service. No attacks came and the general election, May 2005, went off without incident, and, to some surprise, London's bid for the 2012 Olympic Games was successful, an event which demanded strong assurances of safety. Blair had also persuaded many of the world's top leaders, including US President George W. Bush, Canada's Paul Martin, France's Jacques René Chirac, Germany's Gerhard Schröder, Silvio Berlusconi of Italy, Junichiro Koizumi of Japan and Vladimir Putin of Russia, to come to Britain for their G8 meeting. Anti-capitalist, environmentalist and other protesters had failed to interrupt this gathering held in a fairly remote golf resort, Gleneagles. Suddenly, a storm broke over Blair's jamboree.

On 7 July, British television viewers got a glimpse of the horrors of urban terrorism closer to home than they expected. These were pictures not from New York, Madrid or Baghdad but from London where bomb attacks killed at least 56 people and left 700 injured. Less than 24 hours after the capital had celebrated winning the Olympics, a 56-minute series of explosions blasted through three Underground stations and ripped the roof off a bus in what was thought to be an al-Qaeda-style suicide attack. The attacks began at 8.51 a.m., as the trains were full of commuters on their way to work, in a tunnel near Aldgate station. Five minutes later, at least 21 people died in a blast in a tunnel between King's Cross and Russell Square. At 9.17 a.m., an explosion smashed through a tunnel wall at Edgware Road station, damaging three trains. Exactly 30 minutes later, a fourth bomb went off on a No. 30 bus, packed with commuters forced above ground after the Tube was closed. This was the worst terrorist attack in mainland Britain. The previous highest toll was in the 1974 IRA Birmingham pub bombings, which killed 21. Some were shocked that Britain was rearing its own terrorists. The bombers behind the 7 July attacks were British-born, as were two men who made a suicide attack on a Tel Aviv bar in 2003. Zacarias Moussaoui, the only person in the US charged in connection with the September 11 attacks, had attended mosques in London. So did Richard Reid, the 'shoe bomber', who tried to blow up an aircraft in December 2001. Ahmed Omar Sheikh, sentenced to death for the murder of the journalist Daniel Pearl in 2002, was a British-born Pakistani. These were 'born again Muslims' whose adolescent search for an identity and desire to rebel was comparable to ultra-Left movements such as the Italian Red Brigades, in the 1960s, and the German Baader-Meinhof group in 1970s. Those behind the bombers, four young men, probably calculated that the security forces would be concentrating their main attention on the G8 summit. Blair was forced to leave the meeting and fly back to London. It was surprising that they did not strike again in Birmingham, Manchester or Leeds a day or two later. But, just as things were settling down, terrorists struck again in London on 21 July 2002. Synchronized strikes on three London Tube trains, followed by a blast on a red double-decker bus, evoked memories of the earlier attack. Just like 7 July, the terrorists chose all four points of the compass, or the burning cross as their radical sympathizers preferred to describe it. This time there were no mass casualties, but there was panic. That, say terror experts, was the intention. The following day, the police suffered a serious setback when they killed an innocent man at Stockwell underground station. They described the Brazilian's death as a tragedy and expressed 'regret'.[24] In Egypt, on 23 July, terrorists targeted, again, hotels where foreign tourists were staying and a local market at Sharm el-Sheikh. Among the dead, the majority of whom were Egyptians, were British holidaymakers.

In addition to the widespread sympathy and messages of support Britain got after the bombings, there was some criticism. Prince Turki al-Faisal, the Saudi Arabia Ambassador to London, said that it was too easy for Islamist extremists to stay and preach messages of hate without fear of arrest or deportation. He added: 'Allowing them to go on using the hospitality and the generosity of the British people to emanate from here such calls for killing and such, I think is wrong.' The Ambassador's sentiments echoed those of President Musharraf of Pakistan, angry because two organizations – Hizb'ut Tahrir and Al-Muhajiroun – which had threatened his life continued to operate 'with impunity' in Britain.[25] Most British people agreed with these views. Britain had criticized both these states for tolerating extremists. Germany, France, Italy and Ireland were among the states that had given sanctuary to Muslim fundamentalists and terrorists. Ireland's *Sunday Independent* (10 July 2005) commented, 'Ireland is regarded as a safe haven for international terror groups, including those behind the London bombings, because of failures to implement tough anti-terrorist legislation in the wake of September 11.' A leading Muslim who was called on to present a united front against terror launched a scathing attack on Blair and police tactics in the War on Terror. Mohammed Naseem, the Chairman of the Birmingham Central Mosque, said that there was no proof that the London suicide bombers were Muslims and accused the Prime Minister of being a liar. Dr Naseem claimed that CCTV images of the suspects could have been of innocent passers-by. He said, 'Tony Blair has told lies about going to war with Iraq and in a court of law if a witness has lied he ceases to be a reliable witness. So we can't give our blind trust to this Government.'[26] Professor Anthony King found, 'The group portrait of British Muslims painted by YouGov's survey for the *Daily Telegraph* (23 July 2005) is at once reassuring and disturbing, in some ways even alarming.' Most Muslims

> are evidently moderate and law-abiding but by no means all are . . . However, six per cent insist that the bombings were, on the contrary, fully justified. Six per cent may seem a small proportion but in absolute numbers it amounts to about 100,000 individuals who, if not prepared to carry out terrorist acts, are ready to support those who do. Moreover, the proportion of YouGov's respondents who, while not condoning the London attacks, have some sympathy with the feelings and motives of those who carried them out is considerably larger – 24 per cent.

ALL CHANGE?

By the summer of 2005, British and European politics seemed to be in some kind of interregnum. Blair had agreed that he would go, but not *when* he would go. The forced resignation of Blunkett, his close ally, on 3 November, and the revolt by Labour MPs, on the same day, exposed his declining authority. The revolt, by 33 MPs, which reduced the Government's majority to just one, was against a clause in the Anti-Terrorism Bill which would have extended from 14 to 90 days the maximum period for which police could hold a suspect without charge. The revolt was supported by the opposition parties. Worse came for Blair on 9 November when the same proposal was defeated after 49 Labour MPs, including 10 former ministers, rebelled, others abstained. This was Blair's first defeat. Was this the beginning of the end for Blair? What was happening in the Conservative camp? Howard made the same commitment to go and said farewell at the Conservative annual conference in October. After an attempt to change the election procedure which would have deprived ordinary Conservative members of their votes failed, five contenders threw their hats in the ring. In the end, after Kenneth Clarke, Liam Fox and Malcolm Rifkind had been rejected by fellow MPs, the 300,000 members were faced with a choice between David Cameron (39), old Etonian, Oxford graduate, who was in the bar and night club business, and David Davis (56), ex-minister, ex-director of Tate & Lyle, with a tough council house upbringing and Warwick University and London and Harvard business schools behind him. On 6 December, the verdict was given. Cameron won by 134,446 votes to 64,398. Cameron said that he wanted a modern, compassionate party.

The Liberal Democrats, who had a good year in 2005, looked like having a bad one in 2006. Cameron's lurch to the 'left' prompted fears that he would attract their voters. Worse still, January brought three body blows. First came the news that Kennedy was being forced from office after admitting that he had a drink problem. No doubt he had the admiration and sympathy of the majority of ordinary party members but this did not save him. The plotters against him had not thought out their strategy and a brutal, messy leadership election followed. Mark Oaten quit as Home Affairs Spokesman after his affair with a male prostitute was revealed, and Simon Hughes, Party President, was forced to admit that he had been 'misleading' about his homosexual past. All this raised questions about the honesty and trustworthiness of the party's leadership. It was left to the party's 73,000 activists to sort it out. Opinion polls revealed a slump in support for the Liberal Democrats. The much admired Sir Menzies Campbell (64), a Scottish lawyer and Deputy Leader, took over as caretaker Leader.

Abroad, Germany elected its first woman Chancellor, Angela Merkel. In France, as the President prepared to retire, French ghettos became exploding cauldrons. In Italy, 69-year-old Premier Silvio Berlusconi was under severe pressure and, in the US, the countdown had started for Bush's exit as he encountered increasing difficulties. Kim Jong Il and his clan soldiered on in North Korea, as did the Ayatollahs of Iran as if to remind us that things could get worse. Blair looked like becoming the longest serving Prime Minister, apart from Margaret Thatcher, over the previous century. What had his administration achieved? Under Blair, and his predecessors, Britain had lost most of its manufacturing base and more than one million jobs and was in danger of becoming a largely service, even parasitical, economy. Labour was proud that registered unemployment was lower than in many other EU countries. Yet the number on disability benefit was much higher. 'A crazy set-up', as Margaret Hodge, the Work and Pensions Minister, called it.[27] And how real and secure were the jobs of the many? Call centres, from many of which telephone subscribers were bombarded daily to change their suppliers of electricity, gas, insurance, telephones and water or take out loans, take 'equity release', or get financial advice, employed large numbers of people. And even some of those jobs were going overseas. An advertising sector produced billions of items of junk mail every year, which landed through letter boxes every day. Internet subscribers were harassed by offers of cars, condoms, health pills, loans, imitation Rolex watches, sex, phoney university degrees, phoney jobs and Viagra daily. The culture of litigation was promoted by television advertising. Gambling was encouraged by the government and was gradually becoming a key industry. Blair's crusade to raise education standards was dealt a triple blow in September 2005, with figures showing soaring school truancy levels, a student drop-out rate of nearly 25 per cent and a surprise fall in state school entries to top universities. Truancy jumped by almost 10 per cent, in 2004, to its highest level, despite almost £1 billion in government spending since 1997 to tackle the problem.[28] Brown could smile as he read an analysis of housing statistics showing the number of homes owned outright rose 17 per cent between 1997 and 2003 (following almost two decades of static growth) and represented 29 per cent of all households. Yet many young people found it difficult to get on the property ladder and the number of repossessions reached a high in 2005. The number of people going bankrupt had soared to its highest level since records began in the 1960s, Department of Trade figures showed in November. And, according to the ESRC, the UK was, in 2005, the least 'equal' society in the European Union. Although Brown could claim that Britain had enjoyed a long period of prosperity during his years as Chancellor, the economic future did not look so rosy. He readily admitted that Britain faced immense competition from China and India and other emerging states in the future. Yet spending on R&D by British companies was down for the second year in succession.[29] China was also competing with Britain for political influence. It had taken over from Britain in Burma, Zimbabwe and elsewhere. Would it one day compete nearer home? With Straw, Blunkett and Charles Clarke at the Home Office, crime and the threat of terrorism had increased as had legal and illegal immigration. In 2004 *net legal* immigration hit a new high with 223,000 arriving,[30] roughly equal to a town like Oldham (pop. 217,273 in 2001). Where would they be housed? Worse still, would they, as the Chairman of the Commission for Racial Equality, Trevor Phillips, himself an immigrant, believed, end up in segregated ghettos divided by race and religion? How could they adopt and respect British values in such a situation? Blair's pal, the curry king and multi-millionaire Muslim businessman Sir Gulam Noon, MBE, who employed settled refugees at his frozen food factory, had an answer. He said that immigrants who did not respect British values should 'get out of the country'.[31] Perhaps in a feeble attempt to give pride to newcomers and mollify the silent majority the powers that be held elaborate celebrations marking the 200th anniversary of the Battle of Trafalgar, 'Nelson fever grips the nation', claimed the *Independent* (21 October 2005). Where was Britain going, what were its values, if it survived expected threats from the awaited flu pandemic, environmental pollution, and an extreme winter in 2005–06 and the drinks industry's 'ruthless campaign of economic incentives and psychological tricks to get customers to drink as much as possible when licensing laws are relaxed'?[32] In 2005, 'Jordan', the glamour model Katie Price, had signed a six-figure advance contract with Random House, Britain's largest publisher, to produce an autobiography and two novels before she had written a word. J.G. Ballard, the veteran author of more than 30 books including *Empire of the Sun*, commented, 'I hope she has every success. It might win the Booker Prize. One has to accept that we are living in times when the only things that matter are celebrity and money, and if Jordan writes a novel, that will bring the two together. Whether that's a good thing or a bad thing I'll leave for you to judge.'[33] Jordan's advance rivalled that of Robin Cook for his Cabinet memoirs. A Conservative view was that, we 'have become a soulless nation, obsessed by materialism,

411

pop idols and football stars. We are not a happy people . . .' Author A.A. Gill agreed, 'The English are angry about something.'[34] And did it say something about Britain (or just BBC Radio 4 listeners) that a poll (18 July 2005) named Karl Marx as the greatest philosopher of all time? Marx, revolutionary author of *Capital*, accounted for 27.9 per cent of 34,000 votes cast by the public in a poll for the *In Our Time* discussion programme. Finally, another Conservative MP still thought, in 2004, 'Britain is the best place in the world in which to live', that was why so many wanted to settle here. Who was right?

NOTES

1 *Office for National Statistics*, 31 July 2002; *NS Online*, 2 July 2005.
2 *The Times*, 30 August 2005.
3 *Manchester Evening News*, 7 January 2005.
4 Debbie Andalo, *The Times*, 13 January 2005.
5 Tony Helm, *Daily Telegraph*, 27 August 2005.
6 Figures vary slightly because of differences in research techniques, but the general conclusions are similar. The figures were given by the BBC Action Network Team, 25 October 2004.
7 Rosemary Bennett, Deputy Political Editor, *The Times*, 24 August 2005.
8 *NS Online*, 2 July 2005.
9 *Guardian*, 7 July 2005.
10 *The Times*, 30 July 2005.
11 OECD, 2003.
12 BBC News, World edition, 11 January 2005.
13 *FinancialTimes.com*, 29 July 2005.
14 *Businessweek.online*, 2 December 2002.
15 *Saferworld.org.uk*, 13 April 2005.
16 *Guardian*, 21 July 2005.
17 *The Times*, 21 July 2005.
18 *The Times*, 29 July 2005.
19 *Boston Herald*, 13 March 2005.
20 *Independent*, 25 May 2005.
21 *The Times*, 29 July 2005].
22 *Sunday Times*, 3 July 2005.
23 *Sunday Times*, 3 July 2005.
24 *Sunday Times*, 24 July 2005.
25 *The Times*, 23 July 2005.
26 *The Times*, 28 July 2005.
27 *The Times*, 28 September 2005.
28 *The Times*, 22 September 2005.
29 *Independent*, 23 October 2005.
30 *The Times*, 21 October 2005; BBC News, 20 October 2005; for Trevor Philips, see *Sunday Times*, 18 September 2005; *Independent*, 31 October 2005.
31 *Independent on Sunday*, 23 October 2005.
32 *Observer*, 23 October 2005.
33 *Daily Telegraph*, 27 August 2005..
34 A.A. Gill, 'I Hate England', *Sunday Times*, 30 October 2005, extract from his book, *The Angry Island*.

APPENDIX: TABLES

Table A.1 Principal ministers, 1945–2005

Prime Minister	Foreign Secretary	Chancellor of the Exchequer	Home Secretary
C. Attlee (1945–51)	E. Bevin H. Morrison	Dr H. Dalton Sir S. Cripps H. Gaitskell	Chuter Ede
W. Churchill (1951–55)	Sir A. Eden	R.A. Butler	Sir D. Maxwell-Fyfe G. Lloyd George
Sir A. Eden (1955–57)	H. Macmillan S. Lloyd	R.A. Butler H. Macmillan	G. Lloyd George
H. Macmillan (1957–63)	S. Lloyd Earl Home	P. Thorneycroft D. Heathcote Amory S. Lloyd R. Maudling	R.A. Butler H. Brooke
Sir A. Douglas-Home (1963–64)	R.A. Butler	R. Maudling	H. Brooke
H. Wilson (1964–70)	P. Gordon Walker M. Stewart G. Brown M. Stewart	J. Callaghan R. Jenkins	Sir F. Soskice R. Jenkins J. Callaghan
E. Heath (1970–74)	Sir A. Douglas-Home	I. Macleod A. Barber	R. Maudling R. Carr
H. Wilson (1974–76)	J. Callaghan	D. Healey	R. Jenkins
J. Callaghan (1976–79)	A. Crosland Dr D. Owen	D. Healey	R. Jenkins M. Rees
M. Thatcher (1979–90)	Lord Carrington F. Pym Sir G. Howe J. Major D. Hurd	Sir G. Howe N. Lawson J. Major	W. Whitelaw L. Brittan D. Hurd D. Waddington
J. Major (1990–97)	D. Hurd M. Rifkind	N. Lamont K. Clarke	K. Baker K. Clarke M. Howard
T. Blair (1997–)	R. Cook J. Straw	G. Brown	J. Straw D. Blunkett C. Clarke

Table A.2 British general elections, 1945–2005 (percentage shares of votes and seats)

	Turnout %	Conservative %	Conservative seats	Labour %	Labour seats	Liberal + %	Liberal + seats	SNP seats	PC seats	NI seats	Others seats
1945	73	40	213	48	393	9	12			4	18
1950	84	44	299	46	315	9	9			2	0
1951	83	48	321	49	295	3	6			3	0
1955	77	50	345	46	277	3	6			2	0
1959	79	49	365	44	258	6	6			1	0
1964	77	43	304	44	318	11	9			0	0
1966	76	42	253	48	364	9	12			1	0
1970	72	46	330	43	288	8	6	1	1	6	4
1974 (Feb.)	78	38	297	37	301	19	14	7	2	12	2
1974 (Oct.)	73	36	277	39	319	18	13	11	3	12	0
1979	76	44	339	37	269	14	11	2	2	12	0
1983	73	42	397	28	209	26*	23*	2	2	17	0
1987	75	42	376	31	229	23*	22*	3	3	17	0
1992	78	42	336	34	271	18	20	3	4	17	0
1997	73	31	165	43	419	17	46	6	4	18	1
2001	59	32	166	41	412	18	52	4	4	18	2
2005	61	33	198	37	356	22	62	6	3	18	3

Note: * includes SDP vote; + Liberal Democrats from 1992

Table A.3 Elections to the European Parliament (seats)

	1979	1984	1989	1994	1999	2004*
Labour	17	32	45	62	29	19
Conservatives	60	45	32	18	36	27
Liberal Democrats	0	0	0	2	10	12
Scottish National	1	1	1	2	2	2
Plaid Cymru	0	0	0	0	2	1
Green	0	0	0	0	2	2
UKIP	0	0	0	0	3	12
SDLP	1	1	1	1	1	0
Unionist	1	1	1	1	1	1
Democratic Unionist	1	1	1	1	1	1
Sinn Fein	0	0	0	0	0	1

Source: 1999: *Daily Telegraph*, 15 June 1999; 1994 and 1989: *The Times Guide to the European Parliament June 1994.*

Note: * The total number of UK seats was reduced to 78 from 87 to make room for MEPs from 10 new member states.

Table A.4 Number of women MPs, by party, 1945–2005

	Conservative	Labour	Liberal	Other
1945	1	21	1	1
1950	6	14	1	0
1951	6	11	0	0
1955	10	14	0	0
1959	12	13	0	0
1964	11	17	0	0
1966	7	19	0	0
1970	15	10	0	1
1974 (Feb.)	9	13	0	1
1974 (Oct.)	7	18	0	2
1979	8	11	0	0
1983	13	10	0	0
1987	17	21	2	1
1992	20	37	2	1
1997	13	101	3	3
2001	14	95	5	4
2005	17	98	10	3

Table A.5 Patents registered at the European Patent Office, by country, 1994

USA	16,779
Germany	11,046
Japan	10,442
France	4,384
UK	**3,138**
Netherlands	2,240
Italy	2,046
Switzerland	1,981
Sweden	924
Belgium	695
Austria	573
Spain	338
Denmark	334

Source: Bundestag Report (Bonn), July–August 1996, 9

Table A.6 Personal computers per 100 of the population, by country, 1994

USA	30
Switzerland	22
UK	**13**
Germany	12
France	10
Japan	8

Source: Das Parlament, 9–16 August 1996, 9

Table A.7 University graduates per 100 of the population aged 25–64, by country, 1996

Canada	41
USA	31
Norway	25
Sweden	24
Germany	22
Switzerland	21
Holland	21
UK	**19**
Denmark	19
Finland	18
Ireland	17
France	16
Greece	13
Portugal	7
Italy	6

Source: Bundestag Report (Bonn), July–August 1996

Table A.8 Economic power of the EU states measured by GDP per inhabitant (DM)

Luxembourg	60,200
Denmark	48,400
Germany	42,400
Austria	42,000
France	38,400
Belgium	38,300
Sweden	37,300
Holland	37,000
Finland	35,400
EU average	*32,600*
Italy	27,400
UK	**27,100**
Ireland	27,100
Spain	20,400
Greece	15,400
Portugal	15,100

Note: According to a report of the German Bundesbank, the only states of the EU which were on target to meet the Maastricht conditions for monetary union were Germany, France, Britain and Luxembourg (*Die Welt*, 25 April 1996)

Source: Das Parlament, 2 August 1996, 1

Table A.9 Life expectancy at birth, by sex, Britain, 1931–2001

	1931	1961	1981	1991	2001
males	58.4	67.9	70.8	73.2	75.7
females	62.4	73.8	76.8	78.8	80.4

Source: adapted from *Social Trends* 22 (1992), 123

Table A.10 Defence expenditures as a percentage of GDP (current prices), 1975–98

NATO members	1975–79	1980–84	1985–89	1990–94	1995	1998
Belgium	3.2	3.3	2.8	2.0	1.6	1.5
Czech Republic	n/a	n/a	n/a	n/a	n/a	n/a
Denmark	2.3	2.4	2.0	1.9	1.7	1.6
France	3.8	3.9	3.8	3.4	3.1	2.8
Germany	3.4	3.4	3.0	2.2	1.7	1.6
Greece	5.6	5.4	5.1	4.4	4.4	4.8
Hungary	n/a	n/a	n/a	n/a	n/a	n/a
Italy	2.1	2.1	2.3	2.1	1.8	2.0
Luxembourg	0.9	1.1	1.0	0.9	0.8	0.9
Netherlands	3.1	3.1	2.9	2.4	2.0	1.8
Norway	2.8	2.7	2.9	2.8	2.4	2.3
Poland	n/a	n/a	n/a	n/a	n/a	n/a
Portugal	3.4	3.0	2.7	2.6	2.6	2.2
Spain	n/a	2.2	2.2	1.7	1.5	1.4
Turkey	4.4	4.0	3.3	3.8	3.9	4.4
UK	**4.9**	**5.2**	**4.5**	**3.8**	**3.0**	**2.7**
Canada	1.9	2.0	2.1	1.9	1.5	1.2
USA	5.0	5.6	6.0	4.7	3.8	3.2
NATO total	n/a	4.5	4.5	3.6	3.0	2.7

Source: NATO Review, Spring/Summer 2000

Table A.11 Percentage of full-time
employees working more than 48 hours
per week, by country, 1996

UK	**22**
Ireland	9
Denmark	7
France	7
Greece	7
Portugal	7
Germany	6
Spain	5
Italy	4
Luxembourg	4
Belgium	3
Netherlands	1

Source: Eurostat 1994 data, Observer,
10 November 1996

Table A.12 GDP and employment growth, by country, 1960–95

	% GDP growth		% employment growth	
	1960–73	*1974–95*	*1960–73*	*1974–95*
USA	4.3	2.5	2.0	1.8
Japan	9.4	3.2	1.3	0.9
Canada	5.4	2.9	3.3	1.9
France	5.4	2.2	0.7	0.2
Germany	4.4	2.6	0.3	1.2
UK	**3.2**	**1.8**	**0.3**	**0.1**
Italy	5.3	2.4	−0.4	0.3

Source: Observer, 1 December 1996

Table A.13 Britain's balance of payments current account (£ million), 1984–94

Year	*Amount*	*Year*	*Amount*
1984	1,482	1990	−19,293
1985	2,238	1991	−8,533
1986	−864	1992	−9,468
1987	−4,813	1993	−11,042
1988	−16,475	1994	−1,825
1989	−22,398		

Source: Annual Abstract of Statistics 1996 (Treasury, HMSO), 277

SELECTED BIBLIOGRAPHY

OFFICIAL PUBLICATIONS AND REFERENCE PUBLICATIONS

Annual Abstract of Statistics
Chartered Institute of Public Finance & Accountancy, *Police Statistics 1998–1999 Actuals*, 1999.
Conservative Research Department, *The Campaign Guide*
EP News.
Hansard (Parliamentary Debates)
HM Treasury, *Economic Briefing*
HMSO, *Police Complaints Authority: The First Ten Years*, 1995.
HMSO, *1991 Census Ethnic Group and Country of Birth: Great Britain Volume 1*, 1993.
Keesing's Contemporary Archives
NATO Review.
Office of National Statistics, *International Migration: Migrants Entering or Leaving the UK and England and Wales*, 1997, 1999.
Pears Cyclopaedia
Social Trends
Stefan Reade (ed.), *Inland Revenue Statistics 1999*, 1999.
The Times Guide to the House of Commons (published after each election)

JOURNALS

Contemporary Record
Contemporary Review
Economic History Review
The Economist
History Today
International Affairs
Journal of Contemporary History
Labour Research
Media Culture and Society
National Westminster Bank Review
Parliamentary Affairs
The Political Quarterly
RSA Journal

Talking Politics
Teaching History

Unless otherwise indicated, the place of publication is London.

NEWSPAPERS/MAGAZINES

The Asian
The Asian Times
Das Parlament
Inside Labour: The New Labour Magazine
London Jewish News
West European Politics

ARTICLES

Cowley, Philip, 'The Marginalisation of Parliament?', *Talking Politics*, Winter 2000, Volume 12, No. 2.
Davis, Aeron, 'Public Relations, News Production and Changing Patterns of Source Access in the British National Media', *Media, Culture, Society*, January 2000, Volume 22.
Jones, Alistair, 'UK Relations with the EU, and Did *You* Notice the Elections?', *Talking Politics*, Winter 2000, Volume 12, No. 2.
Margetts, Helen, 'The 1997 British General Election: New Labour, New Britain?', *West European Politics*, October 1997.
Parekh, B., 'Defining British Identity', *The Political Quarterly*, Vol. 71, No. 1, January 2000, pp. 4–14.
Rallings, Colin and Michael Thrasher, 'Assessing the Significance of the Elections of 1999', *Talking Politics*, Winter 2000, Volume 12, No 2.
Windschuttle, Keith, 'Rewriting the History of the British Empire', *The New Criterion* (on line), Vol. 18, No. 9, May 2000.

INTERNET MATERIAL

http://news.bbc.co.uk.

BIOGRAPHY AND AUTOBIOGRAPHY

Adams, Gerry, *Autobiography*, Dublin, 1998.
Anderson, Bruce, *John Major: The Making of a Prime Minister*, 1991.
Ashley, Jack, *Act of Defiance*, 1992.
Baker, Kenneth, *The Turbulent Years: My Life in Politics*, 1993.
Balen, Malcolm, *Kenneth Clarke*, 1994.
Baridge, Trevor, *Clement Attlee: A Political Biography*, 1985.
Beckett, Francis and David Hencke, *The Blairs and Their Court*, 2005.
Bell, Martin, *An Accidental MP*, 2000.
Lord Beveridge, *Power and Influence*, 1953.
J.R. Bevins, *The Greasy Pole*, 1965.
Bower, Tom, *Maxwell: The Final Verdict*, 1995.
Boyle, Andrew, *Montagu Norman*, 1967.

Brandt, Willy, *My Road to Berlin*, 1960.
—— *My Life in Politics*, 1992.
Brown, Colin, *Fighting Talk: The Biography of John Prescott*, 1997.
Lord Butler, *The Art of the Possible: Memoirs of Lord Butler*, 1971.
Callaghan, James, *Time and Chance*, 1987.
Campbell, John, *Nye Bevan and the Mirage of British Socialism*, 1987.
—— *Edward Heath: A Biography*, 1993.
Carlton, David, *Anthony Eden: A Biography*, 1981.
Lord Carrington, *Reflect on Things Past: The Memoirs of Lord Carrington*, 1988.
Carvel, John, *Turn Again Livingstone*, 1999.
Carver, Michael, *Out of Step: The Memoirs of Field Marshal Lord Carver*, 1989.
Castle, Barbara, *The Castle Diaries 1964–70*, 1974.
—— *The Castle Diaries 1974–76*, 1980.
—— *Fighting all the Way*, 1993.
Clark, Alan, *Diaries*, 1993.
Clark, Ronald W., *J.B.S: The Life and Work of J.B.S. Haldane*, 1968.
Cook, Margaret, *A Slight and Delicate Creature: The Memoirs of Margaret Cook*, 1999.
Cook, Robin, *Point of Departure*, 2003.
Cooper, Diana, *Trumpets from the Steep*, 1960.
Cosgrave, Patrick, *Thatcher: The First Term*, 1985.
Crosland, Susan, *Tony Crosland*, 1982.
Crossman, Richard, *The Diaries of a Cabinet Minister, vol. I: Minister of Housing 1964–66*, 1975.
—— *The Diaries of a Cabinet Minister, vol. III: 1968–70*, 1977.
Crozier, Brian, *Free Agent: The Unseen War 1941–1991*, 1993.
Dalton, Hugh, *The Fateful Years: Memoirs 1931–45*, 1957.
—— *Memoirs, 1945–40: High Tide and After*, 1962.
Dalyell, Tam, *Dick Crossman: A Portrait*, 1989.
De La Billière, General Sir Peter, *Storm Command: A Personal Account of the Gulf War*, 1992.
Donoughue, Bernard and G.W. Jones, *Herbert Morrison: Portrait of a Politician*, 1973.
Duberman, Martin, *Paul Robeson: A Biography*, New York, 1989.
Eden, Sir Anthony, *Full Circle*, 1960.
Lord Egremont, *Wyndham and Children First*, 1968.
Ellis, Nesta Wayne, *John Major*, 1991.
Fisher, Nigel, *Iain Macleod*, 1973.
Foot, Michael, *Aneurin Bevan, 1945–1960*, 1975.
Fowler, Norman, *Ministers Decide: A Memoir of the Thatcher Years*, 1991.
Lord George-Brown, *In My Way*, 1971.
Gilbert, Martin, *Winston Spencer Churchill*, 1976.
Godson, Dean, *Himself Alone: David Trimble and the Ordeal of Unionism*, 2004.
Goldsmith, Maurice, *Sage: A Life of J.D. Bernal*, 1980.
Gorbachev, Mikhail, *Memoirs*, 1996.
Gormley, Joe, *Battered Cherub*, 1982.
Grade, Lew, *Still Dancing: My Story*, 1991.
Grant, John, *Blood Brothers: The Division and Decline of Britain's Trade Unions*, 1992.
Griffiths, James, *Pages from Memory*, 1969.
Haines, Joe, *The Power of Politics*, 1977.
Hamilton, Alan, *The Real Charles: The Man Behind the Myth*, 1988.

Hamilton, Willie, *Blood on the Walls*, 1992.
Harris, Kenneth, *Attlee*, 1982.
—— *Mrs Thatcher*, 1988.
—— *The Queen*, 1994.
Harris, Robert, *The Making of Neil Kinnock*, 1984.
Hattersley, Roy, *A Yorkshire Boyhood*, Oxford, 1983.
Healey, Denis, *The Time of My Life*, 1990.
Heath, Edward, *The Course of My Life*, 1998.
Lord Hill, *Both Sides of the Hill*, 1964.
Hogg, Sarah and Jonathan Hill, *Too Close to Call: Power and Politics – John Major in No. 10*, 1995.
Hoggart, Simon and David Leigh, *Michael Foot: A Portrait*, 1981.
Howard, Anthony, *RAB: The Life of R.A. Butler*, 1987.
Howe, Geoffrey, *Conflict of Loyalty*, 1994.
Hull, Cordell, *The Memoirs of Cordell Hull*, 1948.
Hyde, Douglas, *I Believed*, 1950.
Ingham, Bernard, *Kill the Messenger*, 1991.
James, Robert Rhodes, *Anthony Eden*, 1991.
Jay, Douglas, *Change and Fortune: A Political Record*, 1980.
Jenkins, Roy, *A Life at the Centre*, 1991.
Johnson, Lyndon Baines, *The Vantage Point: Perspectives of the Presidency 1963–69*, New York, 1971.
Jones, Jack, *Union Man*, 1986.
Jones, Mervyn, *Michael Foot*, 1994.
Jones, Thomas, *A Diary with Letters 1932–1950*, 1954.
Kellner, Peter and Christopher Hitchens, *Callaghan: The Road to Number Ten*, 1976.
Lord Kilmuir, *Political Adventure: The Memoirs of the Earl of Kilmuir*, 1964.
King, Cecil, *The Cecil King Diary, 1965–1970*, 1972.
Kirkpatrick, Ivone, *The Inner Circle*, 1959.
Lamb, Richard, *The Failure of the Eden Government*, 1987.
Lamont, Norman, *In Office*, 1999.
Lawson, Nigel, *The View from No. 11: Memoirs of a Tory Radical*, 1993.
Lee, Jennie, *This Great Journey*, 1963.
—— *My Life with Nye*, 1980.
Leeson, Nick, *Rogue Trader*, 1996.
Lonsdale, Gordon, *Spy: Twenty Years of Secret Service*, 1965.
Lyttelton, Oliver, *The Memoirs of Lord Chandos*, 1962.
MacIntyre, Donald, *Mandelson: The Biography*, 1999.
Macmillan, Harold, *Memoirs, vol. III: Tides of Fortune, 1945–1955*, 1969.
—— *Memoirs, vol. IV: Riding the Storm, 1956–1959*, 1971.
—— *Memoirs, vol. VI: At the End of the Day, 1959–1961*, 1973.
McSmith, Andy, *John Smith: Playing the Long Game*, 1993.
Major, John, *The Autobiography*, 1999.
Maudling, Reginald, *Memoirs*, 1978.
Mawhinney, Brian, *In the Firing Line*, 1999.
Millis, Walter (ed.), *The Forrestal Diaries*, New York, 1951.
Molam, Mo, *Momentum: The Struggle for Peace, Politics and the People*, 2002.
Lord Moran, *Winston Churchill: The Struggle for Survival, 1940–1965*, 1966.
Morgan, Kenneth O., *Callaghan: A Life*, Oxford, 1997.
Morgan, Kevin, *Harry Pollitt*, Manchester, 1993.
Morrison, Herbert, *Autobiography*, 1960.
Nixon, Richard, *The Memoirs of Richard Nixon*, 1979.

Noel, Gerald Eyre, *Harold Wilson and the New Britain*, 1964.
Osborne, Peter, *Alastair Campbell: New Labour and the Art of Media Management*, 1998.
—— *Alistair Campbell: New Labour and the Rise of the Media Class*, 1999.
Owen, David, *Time to Declare*, 1992.
Page, Bruce, David Leitch and Philip Knightley, *Philby: The Spy who Betrayed a Generation*, 1968.
Parkinson, Cecil, *Right at the Centre*, 1992.
Paterson, Peter, *Tired and Emotional: The Life of Lord George Brown*, 1993.
Pearce, Edward, *The Quiet Rise of John Major*, 1991.
Peston, Robert, *Brown's Britain*, 2005.
Pimlott, Ben, *Hugh Dalton*, 1985.
—— (ed.), *The Political Diary of Hugh Dalton, 1918–40, 1945–60*, 1986.
—— *The Queen: A Biography of Elizabeth II*, 1996.
Pollard, Stephen, *David Blunkett*, 2004.
Ponting, Clive, *Churchill*, 1994.
Prior, James, *A Balance of Power*, 1986.
Prittie, Terence, *Konrad Adenauer 1876–1967*, 1972.
Pym, Hugh and Nick Kochan, *Gordon Brown: The First Year in Power*, 1998.
Radice, Giles, *The Political Diaries of Giles Radice, 1980–2001*, 2005.
Ranfurly, The Countess of, *To War with Whitaker: The Wartime Diaries of the Countess of Ranfurly, 1939–45*, 1995.
Rentoul, John, *Tony Blair*, 1996.
Riddell, Peter, *The Unfulfilled Prime Minister: Tony Blair and the End of Optimism*, 2004.
Ridley, Nicholas, *My Style of Government*, 1991.
Roberts, Frank, *Dealing with Dictators: The Destruction and Revival of Europe, 1939–70*, 1991.
Rose, Norman, *Churchill: An Unruly Life*, New York, 1994.
Roth, Andrew, *Enoch Powell, Tory Tribune*, 1970.
Routledge, Paul, *Scargill: The Unauthorized Biography*, 1993.
Sampson, Anthony, *Macmillan: A Study in Ambiguity*, 1967.
Scammell, Michael, *Solzhenitsyn*, 1985.
Schlesinger, Arthur M. Jr, *A Thousand Days: John F. Kennedy in the White House*, New York, 1965.
Schmidt, Helmut *et al.*, *Kindheit und Jugend unter Hitler*, Berlin, 1994.
Schoen, Douglas E., *Enoch Powell and the Powellites*, 1977.
Scott, Derek, *Off Whitehall: A View from Downing Street by Tony Blair's Adviser*, 2004.
Seldon, Anthony, *Blair*, 2005.
Sergeant, John, *Maggie: Her Fatal Legacy*, 2005.
Shinwell, Emanuel, *Conflict Without Malice*, 1955.
—— *I've Lived Through It All*, 1973.
Short, Edward, *Whip to Wilson*, 1989.
Silver, Eric, *Vic Feather*, 1973.
Steel, David, *Against Goliath: David Steel's Story*, 1989.
Stewart, Margaret, *Frank Cousins: A Study*, 1968.
Stuart, Mark, *John Smith: A Life*, 2005.
Tebbit, Norman, *Upwardly Mobile: An Autobiography*, 1988.
Thatcher, Margaret, *The Downing Street Years*, 1993.
—— *The Path to Power*, 1995.
Thomas, Hugh, *John Strachey*, 1973.

Truman, Margaret, *Harry S Truman*, New York, 1973.
Vernon, Betty D., *Ellen Wilkinson*, 1982.
Walker, Peter, *Staying Power*, 1991.
Whitelaw, William, *The Whitelaw Memoirs*, 1989.
Lord Wigg, *George Wigg*, 1972.
Williams, Francis, *A Prime Minister Remembers*, 1961.
—— *Nothing so Strange: An Autobiography*, 1970.
Williams, Marcia, *Inside Number 10*, 1975.
Williams, Philip, *Hugh Gaitskell: A Political Biography*, 1979.
—— (ed.), *The Diary of Hugh Gaitskell, 1945–56*, 1983.
Wilson, Harold, *The Labour Government, 1964–70*, Harmondsworth, 1971.
—— *Final Term: The Labour Government, 1974–1976*, 1979.
—— *Memoirs 1916–1964: The Making of a Prime Minister*, 1986.
Winstone, Ruth (ed.)/Tony Benn, *The Benn Diaries*, 1995.
Wright, Peter, *Spycatcher*, New York, 1987.
Wyatt, W., *Into the Dangerous World*, 1987.
Lord Young, *The Enterprise Years: A Businessman in the Cabinet*, 1990.
Young, Hugo, *One of Us: A Biography of Margaret Thatcher*, 1991.
Ziegler, Philip, *Wilson: The Authorised Life*, 1993.

BRITAIN

Baston, Lewis, *Sleaze: The State of Britain*, 2000.
Black, Jeremy, *Britain since the Seventies: Politics and Society in the Consumer Age*, 2004.
Blake, Robert, *The Decline of Power 1915–1964*, 1985.
Bogdanor, Vernon and Robert Skidelsky (eds), *The Age of Affluence, 1951–1964*, 1970.
Butler, David and Gareth Butler, *British Political Facts, 1900–1994*, 1994.
Calder, Angus, *The People's War: Britain 1939–45*, 1969.
Calvocoressi, Peter, *The British Experience, 1945–75*, Harmondsworth, 1979.
Cohen, Nick, *Cruel Britannia*, 1999.
Coleman, Terry, *Thatcher's Britain*, 1988.
Dunleavy, Patrick, Andrew Gamble, Ian Holliday and Gillian Peele (eds), *Developments in British Politics*, 1993.
Eatwell, Roger, *The 1945–1951 Labour Governments*, 1979.
Gill, A.A., *The Angry Island: Hunting the English*, 2005.
Gilmour, Ian, *Dancing with Dogma: Britain under Thatcherism*, 1993.
Hennessy, Peter, *Never Again: Britain 1945–51*, 1992.
Hewison, Robert, *Culture and Consensus England: Art and Politics since 1940*, 1995.
Jenkins, Simon, *Accountable to None: The Tory Nationalization of Britain*, 1996.
Kavanagh, Dennis, *Thatcherism and British Politics*, Oxford, 1987.
Kellas, James G., *The Scottish Political System*, Cambridge, 1975.
Lapping, Brian, *The Labour Government, 1964–70*, 1970.
Leventhal, F.M. (ed.), *Twentieth-century Britain: An Encyclopedia*, New York, 1995.
Marr, Andrew, *The Day Britain Died*, 2000.
Marwick, Arthur, *British Society since 1945*, 1996.
Morgan, Kenneth O., *Labour in Power, 1945–51*, Oxford, 1984.
—— *The People's Peace: British History 1945–1990*, Oxford, 1992.
Nairn, Tom, *After Britain: New Labour and the Return of Scotland*, 2000.
Ponting, Clive, *Breach of Promise: Labour in Power, 1964–70*, 1988.
Riddell, Peter, *The Thatcher Era and its Legacy*, Oxford, 1991.

Sampson, Anthony, *The Changing Anatomy of Britain*, 1982.
Shanks, Michael, *The Stagnant Society*, Harmondsworth. 1963.
Sherwood, Roy, *Superpower Britain*, Cambridge, 1989.
Short, Clare, *An Honourable Deception? New Labour: Iraq and the Misuse of Power*, 2004.
Sked, Alan and Chris Cook, *Post-war Britain: A Political History*, 1996.
Zweiniger-Bargielowska, Ina, *Austerity in Britain: Rationing, Controls and Consumption, 1939–1955*, Oxford, 2000.
—— (ed. and contrib.), *Women in Twentieth Century Britain: Economic, Social and Cultural Change*, 2001.

DEFENCE, EMPIRE, FOREIGN POLICY, FOREIGN STATES

Aldrich, Richard J. and Michael F. Hopkins (eds), *Intelligence, Defence and Diplomacy: British Policy in the Post-war World*, 1994.
Ambrose, Stephen E. and Douglas G. Brinkley, *Rise to Globalism: American Foreign Policy since 1938*, 1997.
Barber, Noel, *The War of the Running Dogs*, New York, 1972.
Barker, Elizabeth, *Britain in a Divided Europe 1945–1970*, 1971.
Bartlett, C.J., *The Long Retreat: A Short History of British Defence Policy 1945–1979*, 1979.
—— *'The Special Relationship': A Political History of Anglo-American Relations since 1945*, 1992.
Braddon, Russell, *Suez: Splitting of a Nation*, 1973.
Carr, Gordon, *The Angry Brigade: The Cause and the Case*, 1975.
Central Office of Information, *Britain and the Falklands Crisis: A Documentary Record*, 1982.
Cohen, Sir Andrew, *British Policy in a Changing Africa*, 1959.
Dockrill, Michael, *British Defence since 1945*, Oxford, 1989.
Edmonds, I.G., *The Shah of Iran: The Man and His Land*, New York, 1976.
Epstein, Leon D., *British Politics in the Suez Crisis*, 1964.
Frankel, Joseph, *British Foreign Policy 1945–1973*, 1975.
Frazier, R.L., *Anglo-American Relations with Greece: The Coming of the Cold War*, 1991.
Gimbel, John, *The American Occupation of Germany*, Stanford, 1968.
Gorst, Anthony and Lewis Johnman, *The Suez Crisis*, 1996.
Gowing, Margaret, *Independence and Deterrence: Britain and Atomic Energy 1945–52*, 1974.
Graham, Robert, *Iran: The Illusion of Power*, 1979.
Groom, A.J.R., *British Thinking about Nuclear Weapons*, 1974.
Gullick, J.M., *Malaya*, 1963.
Gupta, P.S., *Imperialism and the British Labour Movement*, 1975.
Gutteridge, W.F., *The Military in African Politics*, 1969.
Hastings, Max and Simon Jenkins, *The Battle for the Falklands*, 1983.
Hendry, Joy, *Understanding Japanese Society*, 1987.
Horsley, William and Roger Buckley, *Nippon, New Superpower: Japan since 1945*, 1990.
Hoyt, Edwin P., *The Bloody Road to Panmunjom*, New York, 1991.
Ignatieff, Michael, *Virtual War: Kosovo and Beyond*, 2000.
Jackson, General Sir William, *Withdrawal from Empire*, 1986.
Johnson, Christopher, *In with the Euro, out with the Pound: The Single Currency for Britain*, 1996.

Judah, Tim, *Kosovo: War and Revenge*, 2000.

Judd, Denis, *Empire: The British Imperial Experience from 1765 to the Present*, 1996.

Kennedy, Paul, *The Realities behind Diplomacy: Background Influences on British External Policy, 1865–1980*, 1981.

King, Gillian, *Imperial Outpost: Aden: its Place in British Strategic Policy*, 1964.

Klein, Herbert S., *The Atlantic Slave Trade*, 1999.

Krisch, Henry, *German Politics Under Soviet Occupation*, New York, 1974.

Laqueur, Walter, *The Israel–Arab Reader: A Documentary History of the Middle East Conflict*, 1969.

Leonard, Mark, *Why Europe will Run the 21st Century*, 2005.

Louis, Wm. Roger, *The British Empire in the Middle East 1945–51*, Oxford, 1985.

Louis, Wm. Roger and Roger Owen (eds), *Suez 1956: The Crisis and its Consequences*, Oxford, 1989.

McAllister, Richard, *From EC to EU: An Historical and Political Survey*, 1997.

Middlebrook, Martin, *Taskforce: The Falklands, 1982*, 1996.

Miller, Davina, *Export or Die: Britain's Defence Trade with Iran and Iraq*, 1996.

Naughtie, James, *The Accidental American: Tony Blair and the Presidency*, 2004.

Nicholas, H.G., *The United States and Britain*, Chicago, 1975.

Northedge, F.S., *Descent from Power; British Foreign Policy 1945–1973*, 1974.

Nunnerley, David, *President Kennedy and Britain*, 1972.

Pierre, Andrew J., *Nuclear Politics: The British Experience with an Independent Strategic Force*, 1972.

Pincher, Chapman, *Their Trade is Treachery*, 1986.

Porter, Bernard, *The Lion's Share: A Short History of British Imperialism 1850–1995*, 1996.

Ramazani, R.K., *Iran's Foreign Policy, 1941–1973*, Charlottesville, VA, 1975.

Ramesh, Randeep, *The War We Could Not Stop*, 2002.

Rees, David, *Korea: The Limited War*, 1964.

Richardson, Louise, *When Allies Differ: Anglo-American Relations during the Suez and Falklands Crises*, 1996.

Rodinson, Maxime, *Israel and the Arabs*, 1968.

Royle, Trevor, *The Best Years of Their Lives: The National Service Experience, 1945–63*, 1988.

Saville, John, *The Politics of Continuity: British Foreign Policy and the Labour Government, 1945–46*, 1993.

Sharp, Paul, *Thatcher's Diplomacy: The Revival of British Foreign Policy*, 1997.

Snowman, Daniel, *USA: The Twenties to Vietnam*, 1968.

Thomas, L.V. and R.N. Frye, *The United States and Turkey and Iran*, Cambridge, MA, 1952.

Thompson, Roger C., *The Pacific Basin since 1945*, 1994.

West, Nigel, *The Secret War for the Falklands: The SAS, MI6, and the War Whitehall Nearly Lost*, 1997.

Yoshino, M., *Japan's Managerial System*, Cambridge, MA, 1968.

Young, John W., *Britain and European Unity, 1945–92*, 1993.

Zabith, Sepher, *The Communist Movement in Iran*, Berkeley, CA, 1966.

Zink, Harold, *The United States in Germany 1944–1955*, Princeton, NJ, 1957.

ECONOMIC, EDUCATIONAL AND SOCIAL POLICY

Alford, B.W.E., *British Economic Performance, 1945–1975*, 1988.

Barnett, Correlli, *The Audit of War: The Illusion and Reality of Britain as a Great Nation*, 1986.

Barry, E. Eldon, *Nationalization and British Politics*, 1965.

Beckerman, Wilfred (ed.), *The Labour Government's Economic Record, 1964–70*, 1972.

Brittan, Samuel, *The Treasury under the Tories 1951–1964*, Harmondsworth, 1964.

Lord Bullock, *Report of the Committee of Inquiry on Industrial Democracy*, Cmnd 6706, January 1977.

Cairncross, Alec, *The British Economy since 1945*, Oxford, 1992.

Church, Roy, *The Rise and Decline of the British Motor Industry*, 1994.

Coates, David and John Hillard (eds), *The Economic Decline of Modern Britain: The Debate between Left and Right*, Brighton, 1986.

Dinterfass, Michael, *The Decline of Industrial Britain, 1870–1980*, 1992.

Douglas J.W.B., *The Home and the School*, 1964.

Galbraith, John Kenneth, *The World Economy since the Wars*, 1994.

Halsey, A.H., *Change in British Society*, Oxford, 1978.

Harrison, Tom, *Britain Revisited*, 1961.

Hutton, Will, *The State We're In*, 1995.

Lipsey, David, *The Secret Treasury: How Britain's Economy is Really Run*, 2000.

Lowe, Rodney, *The Welfare State in Britain since 1945*, 1993.

Marsh, Catherine and Sara Arber (eds), *Families and Households*, 1992.

Marwick, Arthur, *Class Image and Reality in Britain, France and the USA since 1930*, 1981.

Richmond, W. Kenneth, *Education in Britain since 1944*, 1978.

Rubinstein, David and Brian Simon, *The Evolution of the Comprehensive School 1926–1972*, 1973.

Simon, Brian, *Intelligence Testing and the Comprehensive School*, 1953.

Thomas, W.A., *The Finance of British Industry, 1918–1976*, 1978.

Williams, Robin, *Whose Public Schools?*, 1957.

Worswick, G.D.N. and P.H. Ady, *The British Economy 1945–50*, 1952.

ELECTIONS

Butler, David, *The British General Election of 1959*, 1960.

—— *The Electoral System in Britain since 1918*, 1963.

—— *British General Elections since 1945*, Oxford, 1995.

Butler, D.E. and Dennis Kavanagh, *The British General Election of February 1974*, 1974.

—— *The British General Election of October 1974*, 1975.

—— *The British General Election of 1979*, 1980.

—— *The British General Election of 1997*, 1998.

Butler, David and Anthony King, *The British General Election of 1964*, 1965.

—— *The British General Election of 1966*, 1966.

Butler, D.E. and Michael Pinto-Duschinsky, *The British General Election of 1970*, 1971.

Crew, Ivor, B. Gosschalk and J. Bartle (eds), *Political Communications: Why Labour Won the General Election of 1997*, 1997.

Howard, Anthony and Richard West, *The Making of the Prime Minister*, 1965.

King, Anthony, *et al.*, *Britain at the Polls*, Chatham, NJ, 1993.

Kitzinger, Uwe, *The 1975 Referendum*, 1976.

McCallum, R.B. and Alison Readman, *The British General Election of 1945*, 1947.

Nicholas, H.G., *The British General Election of 1950*, 1951.

Smith, Jon, *Election 2005*, 2005.

ETHNIC COMMUNITIES, RACE, IMMIGRATION

Alderman Geoffrey, *The Jewish Community in British Politics*, Oxford, 1983.
Aris, Stephen, *The Jews in Business*, 1970.
Daniels, Roger, *Concentration Camps USA*, New York, 1971.
Department of Defense, *Black Americans in the Defense of Our Nation*, Washington, DC, 1985.
Field, Frank and Patricia Haikin, *Black Britons*, 1971.
Holmes, Colin, *John Bull's Island: Immigration and British Society, 1871–1971*, 1988.
Lewis, Bernard, *The Crisis of Islam*, 2003.
Silberman, Charles E., *A Certain People: American Jews and Their Lives Today*, New York, 1985.
Spencer, Ian R.G., *British Immigration Policy since 1939*, 1997.
Winder, Robert, *Bloody Foreigners*, 2004.

GOVERNMENT, PARLIAMENT AND ADMINISTRATION

Barber, James, *The Prime Minister since 1945*, Oxford, 1991.
Cowley, Philip, *Revolts and Rebellions: Parliamentary Voting Under Blair*, 2002.
—— *The Rebels: When Labour MPs Go Bad*, 2005.
—— *The Rebels: How Blair Mislaid His Majority*, 2005.
Dickie, John, *Inside the Foreign Office*, 1992.
Evans, Peter, *The Police Revolution*, 1974.
Hennessy, Peter, *Whitehall*, 1990.
—— *The Prime Minister: The Office and Its Holders since 1945*, 2001.
Hollingsworth, Mark, *MPs for Hire: The Secret World of Political Lobbying*, 1991.
Kavanagh, Denis, *The Reordering of British Politics After Thatcher*, Oxford, 1997.
Kellner, Peter and Norman Frowther-Hunt, *The Civil Service: An Inquiry into Britain's Ruling Class*, 1980.
Mark, Sir Robert, *Policing a Perplexed Society*, 1977.
Mellors, Colin, *The British MP*, Farnborough, 1978.
Rush, Michael, *Parliament Today*, Manchester, 2005.
Stacey, Frank, *British Government 1966–1975: Years of Reform*, 1975.
Wass, Sir Douglas, *Government and the Governed*, 1984.

MEDIA

Briggs, Asa, *Sound and Vision: The History of Broadcasting in the United Kingdom*, Oxford, 1979.
Cockerell, Michael, *Live from Number 10: The Inside Story of Prime Ministers and Television*, 1988.
Cockerell, Michael, Peter Hennessy and David Walker, *Sources Close to the Prime Minister: Inside the Hidden World of the News Manipulators*, 1984.
Hooper, Alan, *The Military and the Media*, 1982.
Margach, James, *The Abuse of Power*, 1978.
Murphy, Robert, *Realism and Tinsel: Cinema and Society in Britain 1939–49*, 1992.
Pilkington, Sir Harry, *Report of the Committee on Broadcasting 1960*, 1962.
Rosenbaum, Martin, *From Soapbox to Soundbite: Party Political Campaigning in Britain since 1945*, 1997.
Royle, Trevor, *War Report: The War Correspondent's View of Battle from the Crimea to the Falklands*, 1987.

Tunstall, Jeremy, *The Media in Britain*, 1983.
Walker, Alexander, *National Heroes: British Cinema in the Seventies and Eighties*, 1985.
—— *Hollywood England: The British Film Industry in the Sixties*, 1986.
Whale, John, *The Politics of the Media*, 1977.
Wilson, H.H., *Pressure Group*, 1961.
Wybrow, Robert J., *Britain Speaks Out, 1937–87: A Social History as Seen through the Gallup Data*, 1989.

NORTHERN IRELAND

Aughey, Arthur and Duncan Morrow (eds), *Northern Ireland Politics*, 1995.
Bruce, Steve, *God Save Ulster*, Oxford, 1989.
Buckland, Patrick, *A History of Northern Ireland*, Dublin, 1981.
Lord Cameron, *Disturbances in Northern Ireland*, Belfast, 1969.
Compton, Sir Edmund, *Report of the Inquiry into Allegations against the Security Forces of Physical Brutality in Northern Ireland Arising out of Events on 9th August 1971*, Cmnd 4823, 1971.
Coogan, Tim Pat, *The I.R.A.*, 1980.
Devlin, Bernadette, *The Price of My Soul*, 1969.
Dillon, Martin and Denis Lehane, *Political Murder in Northern Ireland*, 1973.
Farrell, Michael, *The Orange State*, 1980.
Holland, Jack, *The American Connection: U.S. Guns, Money and Influence in Northern Ireland*, New York, 1987.
Kennedy-Pipe, Caroline, *The Origins of the Present Troubles in Northern Ireland*, 1997.
McAllister, Ian, *The Northern Ireland Social Democratic and Labour Partry*, 1977.
Rose, Richard, *Governing Without Consensus*, 1971.
Wichert, Sabine, *Northern Ireland since 1945*, 1991.

POLITICAL PARTIES AND MOVEMENTS

Ball, Stuart, *The Conservative Party since 1945*, 1998.
Blake, *A History of the Conservative Party from Peel to Major*, 1997.
Lord Butler, *The Conservatives: A History from their Origins to 1965*, 1977.
Charmley, John, *A History of Conservative Politics, 1900–1996*, 1996.
Clark, Alan, *The Tories, Conservatives and the Nation State 1922–1997*, 1998.
Cook, Chris, *Short History of the Liberal Party, 1900–92*, 1992.
Crew, Ivor and Anthony King, *SDP: The Birth, Life and Death of the Social Democratic Party*, 1995.
De Winter, L. and H. Tursan, *Regionalist Parties in Western Europe*, 1998.
Douglas, Roy, *Liberals: The History of the Liberals and Liberal Democratic Parties*, 2005.
Fairclough, Norman, *New Labour, New Language*, 2000.
Fielding, Steven, *The Labour Party since 1951*, 1997.
Foote, Geoffrey, *The Labour Party's Political Thought: A History*, 1997.
Geddes, Andrew and Jonathan Tonge (eds), *Labour's Landslide*, Manchester, 1997.
Gould, Philip, *The Unfinished Revolution: How the Modernisers Saved the Labour Party*, 1998.
Harris, John, *So Now Who Do We Vote For?*, 2005.
Haseler, Stephen, *The Gaitskellites*, 1969.

Hoffman, J.D., *The Conservative Party in Opposition 1945–51*, 1964.

Jones, Nicholas, *The Control Freaks*, 2002.

Jones, Tudor, *Remaking the Labour Party from Gaitskell to Blair*, 1996.

Kavanagh, Dennis (ed.), *The Politics of the Labour Party*, 1982.

Layton-Henry, Zig (ed.), *Conservative Party Politics*, 1980.

Lindsay, T.E. and Michael Harrington, *The Conservative Party 1918–1979*, 1979.

Ludlam, Steve and Martin J. Smith (eds), *Contemporary British Conservatism*, 1995.

Mitchell, Austin and D. Wiener, *Last Time: Labour's Lessons from the Sixties*, 1997.

Morgan, Kenneth O., *Labour People: Leaders and Lieutenants, Hardie to Kinnock*, Oxford, 1987.

Parkin, Frank, *Middle Class Radicals*, Manchester, 1968.

Pelling, Henry, *The British Communist Party: A Historical Profile*, 1958.

—— *A History of British Trade Unionism*, 1963.

—— *A Short History of the Labour Party*, 1996.

Richter, Irving, *Political Purpose in Trade Unions*, 1973.

Russell, Andrew and Edward Fieldhouse, *Neither Left nor Right? The Liberal Democrats and the Electorate*, 2004.

Shepherd, Robert, *The Power Brokers: The Tory Party and its Leaders*, 1991.

Smith, Martin and Joanna Spear, *The Changing Labour Party*, 1992.

Thompson, Willie, *The Good Old Cause: British Communism 1920–1991*, 1992.

Thorpe, Andrew, *A History of the British Labour Party*, 1997.

Thurlow, Richard, *Fascism in Britain: A History 1918–1985*, 1987.

Watson, Alan, *A Conservative Coup: The Fall of Margaret Thatcher*, 1991.

Weinbren, Daniel, *Generating Socialism: Recollections of Life in the Labour Party*, 1997.

Wrigley, Chris (ed.), *British Trade Unions 1945–1995*, Manchester, 1997.

INDEX